Strategic Planning for Information Systems

Third Edition

JOHN WARD and JOE PEPPARD

Cranfield School of Management,
Cranfield, Bedfordshire, UK

JOHN WILEY & SONS, LTD

Copyright © 2002 by John Wiley & Sons Ltd,
Baffins Lane, Chichester,
West Sussex PO19 1UD, England
National   01243 779777
International (+44) 1243 779777
e-mail (for orders and customer service enquiries):
cs-books@wiley.co.uk
Visit our Home Page on http://www.wiley.co.uk
or http://www.wiley.co.uk

Other Wiley Editorial Offices

John Wiley & Sons, Inc., 605 Third Avenue,
New York, NY 10158-0012, USA

Wiley-VCH Verlag GmbH, Pappelallee 3,
D-69469 Weinheim, Germany

John Wiley Australia Ltd, 33 Park Road, Milton,
Queensland 4064, Australia

John Wiley & Sons (Asia) Pte Ltd, 2 Clementi Loop #02-01.
Jin Xing Distripark, Singapore 129809

John Wiley & Sons (Canada) Ltd, 22 Worcester Road,
Rexdale, Ontario M9W 1L1, Canada

British Library Cataloguing in Publication Data
A catalogue record for this book is available from the British Library

ISBN 0-470-84147-8

Project management by Originator, Gt Yarmouth (typeset in 10/12pt Times)
Printed and bound in Great Britain by Biddles Ltd, Guildford and King's Lynn
This book is printed on acid-free paper responsibly manufactured from sustainable forestry,
in which at least two trees are planted for each one used for paper production.

Wiley Series in Information Systems

CURRENT VOLUMES IN THE SERIES

Currie: *The Global Information Society*

Elliot: *Electronic Commerce—B2C Strategies and Models*

Galliers and Baets: *Information Technology & Organizational Transformation—Innovation for the 21st Century Organization*

Groth: *Future Organizational Design—The Scope for the IT-based Enterprise*

Knights & Murray: *Managers Divided*

Krcmar: *EDI in Europe*

McKeen & Smith: *Management Challenges in IS—Successful Strategies and Appropriate Action*

Remenyi, Sherwood-Smith with White: *Achieving Maximum Value from Information Systems—A Process Approach*

Renkema: *The IT Value Quest—How to Capture the Business Value of IT-Based Infrastructure*

Silver: *Systems that Support Decision Makers—Description and Analysis*

Timmers: *Electronic Commerce—Strategies and Models for Business-to-Business Trading*

Walsham: *Making a World of Dierence—IT in a Global Context*

Wigand: *Information, Organization & Management—Expanding Markets Corporate Boundaries*

Willcocks & Lacity: *Strategic Sourcing of Information Systems— Perspectives and Practices*

Willcocks & Lester: *Beyond the IT Productivity Paradox*

Wiley Series in Information Systems

Editors

Richard Boland	Department of Management Information and Decision Systems, Weatherhead School of Management, Case Western Reserve University, 10900 Euclid Avenue, Cleveland, Ohio 44106-7235, USA
Rudy Hirschheim	Department of Decision and Information Systems, College of Business Administration, University of Houston, Houston, Texas 77202-6283, USA

Advisory Board

Niels Bjørn-Andersen	Copenhagen Business School, Denmark
D. Ross Jeffery	University of New South Wales, Australia
Heinz K. Klein	State University of New York, USA
Rob Kling	Indiana University, USA
Benn R. Konsynski	Emory University, Atlanta, USA
Tim J. Lincoln	IBM UK Limited, UK
Frank F. Land	London School of Economics, UK
Enid Mumford	Manchester Business School, UK
Mike Newman	University of Manchester, UK
Daniel Robey	Georgia State University, USA
E. Burton Swanson	University of California, USA
Robert Tricker	Warwick Business School, UK
Geoff Walsham	University of Cambridge, UK
Robert W. Zmud	University of Oklahoma, USA

Contents

Series Preface   ix

Preface to the Third Edition   x

1 The Evolving Role of Information Systems and Technology in Organizations: A Strategic Perspective 1

Information Systems (IS) and Information Technology (IT)   2
Early Views and Models of IS/IT in Organizations   8
Early Views and Models: up to 1980   14
The DP and MIS Eras: The Lessons Learned   17
The Three-era Model   22
The Strategic Information Systems Era   25
Strategic Uses of IS/IT: classification, factors for success and management
    implications   26
Success Factors in Strategic Information Systems   35
The Management Implications   38
What Is an IS/IT Strategy?   44
The Context for IS/IT Strategy   48
Toward a Fourth Era: An Organizational IS Capability   52

2 An Overview of Business Strategy Concepts and the IS/IT Strategy Implications 64

The Evolving Nature of Strategy and Strategic Planning in Organizations   65
The Strategic Framework   70
Strategy Implementation   85
Strategy Tools and Techniques   86
A Resource-based View of Strategy   111

3   Developing an IS/IT Strategy: Establishing Effective Processes   118

The Evolution of the IS/IT Strategy Process: from Technology Focus to
 Strategic Focus   120
Approaches to IS/IT Strategy Development   122
Problems and Barriers   125
The Environment of the IS/IT Strategy   129
The Challenges of Planning Strategically for IS/IT Today   130
Establishing an IS/IT Strategy Process   135
Purpose and Stimuli Driving IS/IT Strategy Development   141
Scope, Objectives and Expectations   144
An IS/IT Strategy Framework and Approach   151
Deliverables from the IS/IT Strategy Process   162

**4   IS/IT Strategic Analysis: Assessing and Understanding the
Current Situation**   179

Business Re-engineering and IS Strategy   180
Understanding the Current Situation   182
Interpreting the Business Strategy   187
Examining the Current IS/IT Environment   197
Techniques for Interpretation and Analysis   204
Information Requirements to Meet the Current Business Objectives:
the Use of Critical Success Factors and Balanced Scorecards   204
Business Process Analysis   213
Organizational Modelling   226
Evaluating the Gap between Current and Required IS/IT Environments   233

5   IS/IT Strategic Analysis: Determining the Future Potential   237

Aligning the IS/IT Investment Strategy to the Business   239
Value Chain Analysis   244
The External Value Chain (Industry Value Chain or Value System)   245
Information Systems and the Value Chain   248
The Internal Value Chain   262
Alternative Value 'Configuration' Models   265
The Use of Value Chain Analysis   268
'Natural' and 'Contrived' Value Chains   271
Business Re-engineering and the Value Chain   272

6   Determining the Business Information Systems Strategy   276

Strategic Planning Techniques and Their Relationships   277
Framework in which the Tools and Techniques Can Be Used Effectively   279
Identifying How IS/IT Could Impact the Strategy   283
Establishing the Relative Priorities for IS/IT Investments   289
Large Organizations, Multiple SBUs and their Consolidation   295

7   Managing the Applications Portfolio   299

Conclusions from Various Matrices and Models   300
Classifying the Applications in the Portfolio   305
Generic Application Management Strategies   311
Portfolio Management Principles Applied to the Application Portfolio   323
Managing Application Portfolios in Multi-unit Organizations   334

8 Strategic Management of IS/IT: Organizing and Resourcing 339

The Strategic Management Requirement 340
Organizing Strategies for IS/IT Management 345
Framework Guiding Action 354
Provisioning of IS/IT Resources 359
Who Should Manage IS/IT and Where Should It Report? 364
Coordinating Mechanisms for the Strategic Management of IS/IT 370
Managing the IS Function as a Bundle of Resources 384
IS/IT Competency: The Criticality of the Human Resource 391
Managing Relationships 396
Bridging the Gap: Improving the Contribution of the IS Function 405

9 Managing Investments in Information Systems and Technology 420

Introduction 420
Investment and Priority-setting Policies 421
Evaluating IS/IT Investments 422
Setting Priorities for Applications 430
Benefits Management 436
The Benefits Management Process 440
Assessing and Managing Investment Risks 455

10 Strategies for Information Management: Towards Knowledge Management 466

Information as an Asset: The Senior Management Agenda 467
An Information Culture 470
Implementing Business-wide Information Management 472
The Practice of Managing the Information Asset 486
Activities of IAM 492
Policies and Implementation Issues 497
Managing Knowledge Resources 502

11 Managing the Supply of IT Services, Applications and Infrastructure 522

Introduction 522
IT Service Strategies 523
Types of IS/IT Service 524
Application Development and Provisioning Strategies 534
Aligning the Development Approach to the Application Portfolio 536
The Special Case of 'Enterprise Systems' 542
Strategies for Managing the IT Infrastructure 547
Linking the IT Infrastructure with the Business Strategy 549
Justification of Infrastructure Investments 554
Technology Strategies in a Multi-business Unit Organization 559
Outsourcing Strategies 563
Guidelines for outsourcing decisions 566
Applications Service Providers 573

12 Strategic Planning for Information Systems: *Quo Vadis?*   581

Introduction   581
A Brief Resume of Some Key Ideas   583
IS Strategy Formulation and Planning in the 1990s   587
Organization Development Based on IS/IT   589
The Organizational Competencies to Manage IS/IT Strategically   593
A Business Change Perspective of IS/IT   598
A Fourth Era: The IS Capability   603
A Model Linking the IS Capability with IS Competencies and Resources   608

Index   618

Series Preface

The Information Systems community has grown considerably since 1984, when we began publishing the Wiley Series in Information Systems. We are pleased to be a part of the growth of the field, and believe that this series of books is playing an important role in the intellectual development of the the discipline. The primary objective of the series is to publish scholarly works that reflect the best of the research in the Information Systems community. We are also interested in publishing pieces that cannot only help practitioners but also advanced students to understand the myriad issues surrounding IS and, in particular, the management of IS. To this end, the third edition of *Strategic Planning for Information Systems* by John Ward and Joe Peppard is an excellent example. Previous editions have been highly successful, and we believe the third edition will be even more so.

The book adds new material on the latest developments in Information Systems, in particular 'e' (e-business and e-commerce), knowledge management, customer relationship management, enterprise resource planning and outsourcing. But, fundamentally, the book is not simply about technology or techniques but rather the strategic issues of how such technology can be used successfully in organizations. Ward and Peppard focus their attention on why and how to develop a strategy to use IS effectively. Such a treatment is important, and we believe this book will be of interest to practitioners, students and academics alike.

Rudy Hirschheim

Preface to the Third Edition

Since the second edition of this book appeared in 1996, we have seen Information Technology (IT) become an increasingly integral component of everyone's working life and personal environment. IT is now ubiquitous and enables a degree of connectivity that was difficult to envisage even 10 years ago. The technology has evolved rapidly, producing significant advances in its capabilities and hence the business options and opportunities now available. Without doubt, the Internet has evolved into a significant business opportunity—when the second edition was published, Amazon.com, the doyen of the Internet, had only just come into being. Indeed, since the second edition the so-called 'dot.com bubble' has inflated and burst leaving much in its wake. Apart from the spectacular failures, many companies are now downgrading their forays into the world of cyberspace; many online ventures are even dropping their dot.com names. Despite this, there is no doubt that we have still only scratched the surface of the possibilities. Interactive digital television (iDTV) offers great promise in bringing the Internet and new broadcast services directly into the homes of consumers. Wireless technologies are poised to provide further opportunities to organizations as both employees and customers become less dependent on location in carrying out their jobs and conducting business.

In the six years since the last edition, the language of information systems and technology (IS/IT) has also changed. E-commerce and e-business have come into common business parlance and even entered the home via TV advertising! While *e* is largely a relabelling of what was previously known as IS/IT, there are a number of new dimensions in the use of IT implied by *e*. These are considered in this edition. Perhaps, most importantly, the introduction of these new terms attracted increasing senior management interest in IS/IT and its importance to their organizations. Unfortunately, the over-hyped promises have left many senior executives more uncertain than ever before about what can actually be achieved through IT use. One IT director summed up the dramatic changes in sentiment by saying, 'in 2000 you could get any amount of money by putting an *e* in front; but in 2001 anything with an *e* had no chance of funding!'

The late 1990s also witnessed a push to manage corporate knowledge, as organizational success became increasingly dependent on its intellectual rather than its physical assets. Technology is seen as a key enabler of knowledge management (KM), yet many technology-driven KM initiatives have floundered. While managing information has proved difficult, we still have much to learn about how knowledge can be effectively managed before we can begin to understand how best to deploy technology and 'systems' in this context.

Large enterprise-wide systems, such as enterprise resource planning (ERP) and customer relationship management (CRM) applications, are being implemented by organizations to improve the efficiency and effectiveness of their operations, by adopting new business models and through greater integration of processes and information use. The scale and complexity of these systems has proved a challenge to both IS specialists, in terms of implementation, and business management, in terms of identifying and managing the business changes essential to gaining benefits from these very expensive investments.

The greater use of 'outsourcing' for significant aspects of IS/IT supply reflects the increasing sophistication and maturity of the IT industry and provides a challenge to optimize internal and external resourcing options to meet the range of business IS/IT needs. Undoubtedly, the recession of the early 1990s, and the resulting financial pressures, focused management on cost and supply issues, and perhaps increased the rate of outsourcing. Application service providers (ASPs) are now on the horizon poised to have an impact on the provisioning of applications. No longer is it necessary to make a decision either to 'make' or 'buy', but now we must also include 'rent' in the options. Experience has shown that, while outsourcing is a valid part of any strategy, outsourcing the development and management of the strategy itself can lead to serious business problems.

Over the same period, much more has been learned about the practicalities of managing IS/IT strategically and the issues and factors that influence the success of the process in both the short and the long term. This edition considers both the implications of the developments in IS/IT and the most useful of the recent thinking and experiences concerning IS/IT strategic management.

Although some things have moved forward since the second edition, many of the issues that were relevant then remain so today. Managing

IS/IT successfully is perhaps even more difficult in today's environment of faster business change combined with greater choices in IS/IT supply. The turbulence in both business and IS/IT environments may explain why, despite the increasing criticality of IS/IT for business, surveys continue to show that most IS/IT investments still fail to deliver the expected benefits to the organization. Many organizations are still concerned that IS/IT expenditure does not produce demonstrable 'value for money'.

As stated in the preface to the second edition, the following example problems can still result from the lack of a coherent strategy for IS/IT investment:

- Business opportunities are missed; the business may even be disadvantaged by the IS/IT developments of others. Systems and technology investments do not support the business objectives and may even become a constraint to business development.
- Lack of integration of systems and ineffective information management produces duplication of effort, inaccurate and inadequate information for managing the business.
- Priorities are not based on business needs, resource levels are not optimal, project plans are consistently changed. Business performance is not improved, costs are high, solutions are of poor quality and IS/IT productivity is low.
- Technology strategy is incoherent, incompatible options are selected and large sums of money are wasted attempting to fit things together retrospectively.
- Lack of understanding and agreed direction between users, senior management and the IS/IT specialists leads to conflict, inappropriate solutions and a misuse of resources.

Some or all of these can occur when the organization does not have the means to plan and manage IS/IT strategically (i.e. driven by the business needs for the long-term benefit of the organization). Much of the failure of IS/IT to deliver consistent benefits is often due to the short-term business focus and the delegation of IS/IT strategy to IT specialists. Over the long term, any organization will get the information systems it deserves, according to the approach adopted to the use and management of IS/IT.

It is against this background that this book considers how IS/IT strategy development can be brought about and then sustained. The intention is to provide a structured framework and practical approach, expressed primarily in the language of business and management, which can be adopted jointly by senior management, line managers and IS/IT professionals to apply their various knowledge and skills most effectively to identifying *what* needs to be done and *how* best to do it. Developing a strategy is not a one-off exercise; it must be constantly improved and reviewed as achievements are made, options alter or business and IS/IT issues change. Defining a strategy for any organization is a creative and evolving process, which can be assisted by the use of tools, techniques and models to identify and select the most appropriate options.

If there is an overall lesson that can be learned from experience it is that, since new technologies continually come and go, the pursuit of opportunities through IT must be driven, not only by what is technologically feasible but by what is strategically desirable. A key objective of this book is to provide this strategic focus for IS/IT. Clearly, an IS/IT strategy is merely one component of the business strategy and, as such, must be integrated with that strategy. This implies that IS/IT strategy development must become an integral part of the business strategy process. The IS/IT strategy must be understood by the business management and owned by them if it is to be implemented effectively.

In putting together this third edition, we have read a considerable volume of recent research, articles, reports and books. However, some of the seminal work in the IS strategy area is still very relevant today even though it may have been written 10, or even 20, years ago. We have drawn on this, together with the more recent research. On occasions, we have modernized some of the language to reflect the vocabulary of today better. One of us is old enough to remember the first appearance of 'e' with eDP!

In developing the contents of this book, we have also drawn on the work of many others. We recognize the contributions that these researchers and writers have made to the contents at appropriate points in the book. We hope that we have been able to bring it all together in a coherent and readable volume. Over the years, we have worked with hundreds of business and IS/IT executives and managers. Their knowledge, insights and experience and their use of many of the ideas, models and frameworks in this book, has ensured that the approaches described can be applied successfully in practice.

The previous editions of the book have been read by many thousands of students, academics and practitioners. We have attempted to incorporate some of their suggestions for improvement into this current volume. One area, in particular, that we have attempted to improve is navigation through the book. While the overall structure of the book is similar to the previous edition, we have improved the layout of the chapters, incorporated running headings indicating precisely where the reader is and improved the index. We are aware that many readers dip in and out of chapters rather than read the book from cover to cover. In this edition, we have made extensive use of chapter endnotes. Some readers may be interested in following up in more detail some of the points made,

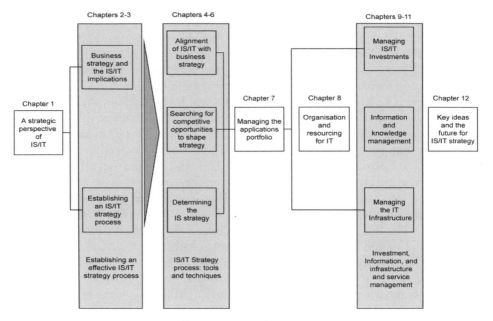

Figure 0.1 *Book overview*

models used or research findings drawn upon—the endnotes will guide them to the original source.

To help the reader navigate through the content of the book, Figure 0.1 illustrates the overall structure.

The book is essentially split into two parts. The first part, Chapters 1–6, is concerned with introducing and describing the context, nature and processes of IS/IT strategy and the associated tools and techniques. Chapters 7–11 address the issues to be managed in delivering the benefits from having the strategy such as managing investments, making resourcing decisions, organizing for IS/IT and the design of the IS function, deciding about insourcing or outsourcing, and managing IT infrastructure.

Any strategy must identify, as far as possible, 'where the organization wants to be' in the future and assess accurately 'where it is now' in order to decide 'how best to get there', given the alternative options and resources available. The first six chapters of the book consider how the organization can assess where it is with regard to IS/IT, in the context of current business environment, and what the business wants to achieve in the future. One key aspect of any strategy is to obtain the maximum value from past investments, which implies achieving an objective, consensus view of the current situation before defining new requirements.

At the same time, the business situation, the environment in which the organization exists, the competitive pressures and the future strategy must be understood to enable the strategic planning process to be focused on areas of criticality for the future. The business objectives and organizational issues must be interpreted, analysed and supplemented by creative thinking, so that the IS/IT strategy not only supports the business strategy but also enhances it where that is possible.

Chapter 1 sets the strategic context for IS/IT. It traces the historical development of IS/IT in organizations, bringing it up to date both in terms of *e*-commerce and *e*-business development and the latest thinking on the strategic role of IS/IT in organizations.

Chapter 2 considers approaches and techniques involved in business strategy formulation and strategic management and their implications for IS/IT strategy development. Chapter 3 considers what is involved in establishing an IS/IT strategy process and presents an approach to IS/IT strategy formulation and planning.

Chapters 4 and 5 describe the tools and techniques that can be used in the process; the focus is on the practical application of these tools. Chapter 6 is a summary chapter and brings together the material introduced in Chapters 2–5 to show how the 'demand side' of the strategy can be coherently addressed.

Chapters 7 to 11 consider how the portfolio of requirements and demands can best be satisfied in terms of 'supply' management strategies—the means by which the strategies are to be achieved. The various ways in which the IS/IT resources can be obtained, developed, deployed and managed most appropriately to satisfy the variety of demands are considered. This must take account of the business and organizational structure, in order to establish the appropriate balance between centralized and devolved roles and responsibilities. The aim is to produce a relevant set of management policies and principles and a partnership between business people and IS/IT specialists cooperating to achieve common goals.

Chapter 7 describes ways in which the current and future applications of IT can be assessed in terms of their business contribution, both individually and as an overall portfolio of IS/IT investments. The appropriate means of managing each element of the portfolio and the overall set of applications can then be selected.

Chapter 8 considers a wide range of aspects related to structuring and organizing IS resources and the governance of IS/IT activities. Chapter 9 presents approaches to managing IS/IT investments, setting priorities to gain the best overall return from those investments and defining and realizing the business benefits that IT-enabled changes can produce. Chapter 10 focuses on information as a strategic asset and the requirements and activities involved in the development of an information management strategy. It also explores the requirements, issues and options associated with the increasingly important role IS/IT needs to play in the management of organizational knowledge. Chapter 11 considers some of the key strategic issues associated with the management of IT infrastructure and the provision of services to satisfy the organization's systems, information and technology requirements. Outsourcing is discussed in detail and the potential role of application service providers (ASPs) is considered.

While the book concentrates on the strategic planning and management mechanisms needed by most organizations today, the last chapter looks to the future of IS/IT strategy development. The effects of IS/IT on any enterprise, its strategy, its operations and even its organization structure have, steadily and inexorably, become more profound and complex over the past 30 years, and this is more likely to increase than abate in the future. Chapter 12 considers the longer-term implications of current trends and emerging issues, which will have a significant influence on organizations' future business and IS/IT strategies and how they are managed.

The overall purpose of the book is to demonstrate why strategic planning for information systems is essential to organizational success and that it is also feasible, even in times of increasingly rapid change. To obtain the whole range of benefits available from IS/IT and avoid the potential pitfalls, every organization must establish the means to manage IS/IT as an integral part of its approach to strategic management. The approaches described in this book are intended to enable greater understanding of both *what* needs to be done and *how* it can be done.

Acknowledgements: This book could not have been written without the help and support of a number of people. Since the last edition was produced, Pat Griffiths has retired and the authors recognize the contribution made by her to the previous editions and therefore to this one.

Colleagues in the Information Systems group at Cranfield School of Management, visiting academics Ed Fitzgerald and John Hoxmeier and the many people who have attended IS Strategy courses and workshops have directly and indirectly contributed a wealth of knowledge and practical experience to the contents. By applying the ideas and techniques, they have not only helped in their development but have also demonstrated the relevance and value of the approaches described. We also acknowledge the contribution of many researchers and writers in the IS field, on whose work we have drawn and referenced throughout the book.

Finally, this book could not have been produced without the expertise and diligence (not to mention hard work!) of Justine Cullen, who prepared the bulk of the text and figures.

1
The Evolving Role of Information Systems and Technology in Organizations: A Strategic Perspective

Today, most organizations in all sectors of industry, commerce and government are fundamentally dependent on their information systems. In the words of Rockart[1] '[i]nformation technology has become inextric- *relationship* ably intertwined with business'. In industries such as telecommunications, media, entertainment and financial services, where the product is already or is being increasingly digitized, the existence of an organization crucially depends on the effective application of information technology (IT). With the emergence of e-commerce, the use of technology is becoming just an accepted, indeed expected, way of conducting business. Consequently, organizations are increasingly looking toward the application of technology not only to underpin existing business operations but also to create new opportunities that provide them with a source of competitive advantage.

In order to manage information systems and information technology (IS/IT) strategically, it is helpful to understand how the role of technology-based information systems has evolved in organizations. While organizations today want to develop a more 'strategic' approach to managing IS/IT, many have probably arrived at their current situation as a result of various short-term 'tactical' decisions regarding IS/IT. Many organizations would no doubt like to rethink their investments, or even begin again with a 'clean sheet', but unfortunately have a 'legacy' resulting from a less than strategic approach to IS/IT in the past. It is rarely possible to start again—many banks and insurance companies still depend on systems first developed over 30 years ago; neither is it necessarily advisable—there is no real reason to expect more success in the future than has been the case in the past, unless ability and knowledge have increased in the meantime. Learning from experience—the successes and failures of the past—is one of the most important aspects of strategic management. Earl has noted that much learning about the capability of IT is experiential, and that organizations tend to learn to manage IS/IT by doing, not appreciating the challenges until they have faced them.[2]

However, no one organization is likely to have been exposed to the whole gamut of IS/IT experiences, and neither is it likely that what has been experienced can always be evaluated objectively. This chapter provides an appraisal of the general evolution of IS/IT in major organizations, against which any organization can chart its progress and from which lessons can be learned for its future management. This evolution of IS/IT in organizations is examined from a number of viewpoints, using a variety of models, some of which are further developed and used later in the book, when considering the particular approaches required in planning strategically for IS/IT investments.

A number of important forces affect the pace and effectiveness of progress in using IS/IT and in delivering business benefits. The relative weighting of each factor varies over time, and will also vary from one organization to another. These factors include:

- the capabilities of the technology;
- the economics of deploying the technology;
- the applications that are feasible;
- the skills and abilities available, either in-house or from external sources, to develop the applications;
- the skills and abilities within the organization to use the applications;
- the pressures on the particular organization or its industry to improve performance.

This list is not meant to be exhaustive and could be expressed in other terms—but it is in a deliberate sequence of increasing 'stress', as the complexity and criticality of the management decision-making process becomes more strategic.

Most assessments of the evolution of IS/IT in organizations tend to focus on one or two aspects of its development—organizational, applications, management of technology, planning, etc.—but, in this chapter, these various perspectives will be brought together, as much as possible.

INFORMATION SYSTEMS (IS) AND INFORMATION TECHNOLOGY (IT)

Before providing any strategic perspective, it is important that there is a clear understanding of the distinction between the terms *information systems* (IS) and *information technology* (IT). While both terms are often used interchangeably, it is important to differentiate between the two if a meaningful dialogue is to take place between business and IS staff and ultimately successful IS/IT strategies are to be developed. It should be remembered that information systems existed in organizations long before the advent of information technology and, even today, there are still many information systems present in organizations with technology nowhere in sight.

IT refers specifically to technology, essentially hardware, software and telecommunications networks. It is thus both tangible (e.g. with servers, PCs, routers and network cables) and intangible (e.g. with software of all types). IT facilitates the acquisition, processing, storing, delivery and sharing of information and other digital content. In the European Union, the term Information and Communication Technologies or ICT is generally used instead of IT to recognize the convergence of traditional information technology and telecommunications, which were once seen as distinct areas.

The UK Academy of Information Systems (UKAIS) defines information systems as *the means by which people and organizations, utilizing technology, gather, process, store, use and disseminate information*. It is thus concerned with the purposeful utilization of information technology. The domain of study of IS, as defined by the UKAIS, involves the study of theories and practices related to the social and technological phenomena, which determine the development, use and effects of information systems in organizations and society. Mingers[3] notes that, although technology is the immediate enabler of IS, 'IS actually is part of the much wider domain of human language and communication, that IS will remain in a state of continual development and change in response both to technological innovation and to its mutual interaction with human society as a whole.'[4]

Some information systems are totally automated by IT. For example, Dell Computers has a system where no human intervention is required, from taking customer orders, to delivery of components to the Dell factory for assembly, to shipment to customers. With this build-to-order model, perfect information and tight linkages match supply and demand in real time. The company can receive an order for a personal computer (PC) directly from a customer via its own website (www.dell.com). Indeed, Dell has built in an element of 'intelligence' into its site to help the customer in making decisions regarding the configuration of components, ensuring that 'non-optimal' configurations or configurations not technically possible are not selected. Customers can also choose from a variety of delivery options. Once a customer order has been confirmed, purchase orders for components are automatically generated and electronically transmitted to suppliers. This has enabled Dell to build exactly what the customer has ordered, resulting in a stock-turn of 56–60 times per year compared with 13.5 for Compaq and 9.8 for IBM's PC business.[5] Dell also feeds real-time data from technical support and manufacturing lines directly through to suppliers on a minute-by-minute basis. They also have links to many of their suppliers' manufacturing lines so that they can see their yields. This information system (or, perhaps more correctly, multiple information systems) is underpinned by a variety of different technologies—servers, storage, software, networks, etc.

Another term that is frequently used along with IS and IT is *application*. Essentially, an application refers to the use of IT to address a business activity or process. There are essentially two types of application:

- general uses of IT hardware and software to carry out particular tasks such as word processing, electronic mail or preparing presentation materials;
- uses of technology to perform specific business activities or processes such as general accounting, production scheduling or order processing.

These applications can be carried out using pre-packaged, pre-written software programs for a particular business activity or be developed to provide particular functionality. Some business-application software packages can be tailored or customized to the specific requirements of an organization. One of the key selling points of large enterprise resource planning (ERP) packages from vendors like SAP, Baan, Oracle or JD Edwards is that they can be configured, to some extent, to meet the specific way in which an organization operates.

Checkland and Holwell[6] have pointed out that many people find difficulty in distinguishing between IS and IT, because technology seems to overwhelm their thinking about the fundamental information system that the technology is to support. Checkland[7] also notes that information systems exist to serve, help or support people taking action in the real world. He asserts that, in order to create a system that effectively supports users, it is first necessary to conceptualize that which *is* to be supported (the IS), since the way it is described will dictate what would be necessary to serve or support it (the IT).

This gives a clue as to why organizations may fail to realize any benefits from their investments in IT—investments are often made in technology without understanding or analysing the nature of the activities the technology is to support—either strategically or operationally—in the organization. For example, over the last few years, many organizations have built websites without sufficient thought to the rationale behind the decision other than because everyone else seems to be getting on the 'Net'. We have heard stories recounted of senior executives returning from business trips abroad demanding that a new technology be purchased or a new application be implemented because they have seen an advertisement in an airline's in-flight magazine. It is important to remember that IT has no inherent value—the mere purchase of IT does not confer any benefits to the organization; these benefits must be unlocked. We shall return to this point throughout the book.

E-business and E-commerce

There are two other concepts that we believe are important to discuss up front, particularly given the prominence both have received: *e-business* and *e-commerce*. Since the mid-1990s, both concepts have entered the everyday vocabulary of managers and, having observed activity in many organizations such as the appointment of 'Directors of e', 'e-managers' and 'e-Czars' and the fact that many have developed 'e-strategies', suggests that e-commerce and e-business are being treated as something new and different from seeking out opportunities to deploy IS/IT. This should not be the case.

Literally, e-commerce refers to the conduct of commerce or business electronically—essentially using Internet technologies. In the 1980s, electronic commerce was already a reality, in this instance referring to inter-company trading, specifically the exchange of business documents, using electronic data interchange (EDI).[8] EDI was a cumbersome technology, requiring the use of a third party (a value-added network supplier or VANS) to facilitate information flow, but it did enable business partners to reduce the costs of exchanging business documents such as orders, invoices and price lists with each other. Indeed, the advent of Financial EDI—the issuing of electronic payment instructions and receiving remittance notices electronically—was seen as closing the loop between purchaser and supplier. Of course, all parties involved had to adhere to particular technical standards in exchanging information and, as has been the case throughout the history of IT, a variety of different EDI standards emerged. Industries such as automotive, banking and retail had their own standards to define message structures. The United Nations did attempt to bring some uniformity to these diverse standards through UN/EDIFACT (United Nations/EDI for Administration, Commerce and Transport), but with mixed success.

With the opening up of the Internet for commercial activity in 1991, a vast new medium was emerging for the conduct of business transactions. This 'network of networks' was based on open standards, facilitating easier connectivity without the need for the use of VANS. More latterly, the emergence of WAP (Wireless Application Protocol) has made it possible for mobile devices (phone, personal digital assistant [PDA], etc.) to connect up to the Internet, thereby permitting everything from 'browsing the Net' to engaging in business transactions while on the move. *M-commerce* has been coined to refer to the use of mobile devices for the conduct of business transactions while *t-commerce* refers to a similar use of television.

E-business, on the other hand, has come to refer to the automation of an organization's internal business processes using Internet and browser technologies. At one extreme, we have the 'pure play' dot.coms, whose business models are often portrayed as being totally web- or Internet-enabled, often reaching out directly to customers. However, unless the product is digitizable, such companies do not exist totally in the virtual world. In industries such as retailing, manufacturing and transportation, the physical aspects overpower the virtual—logistics still wins the day, not glossy websites as many dot.coms have found to their detriment.[9] At the other extreme, we have companies who have 'web-enabled' selected business processes using Internet technologies. Such companies still operate in the physical world and seek to develop a 'bricks and clicks' strategy to integrate the Internet with their mainstream operations.

Unfortunately, the potential benefits and impact of those aspects of IS/IT that have been labelled e-business, e-commerce and latterly m-commerce and t-commerce have been exaggerated, resulting in tremendous hype surrounding these concepts, much of it fuelled by technology vendors and the media. In 1999, just issuing a press release stating the company was embracing the 'net' or announcing an e-commerce strategy was enough to send a company's share price rocketing. Subramani and Walden[10] examined the impact of e-commerce announcements by firms on share price and found that e-commerce initiatives did lead to cumulative abnormal increases in shareholder value. Even changing a company name to incorporate the '.com' label had a significant increase in the share price and trading activity.[11]

Right up until the Nasdaq crash in March 2000, we could not fail to pick up a newspaper or magazine without reading a story about the Internet and its impact. Attention grabbing headlines such as 'The "net" changes everything', 'Log on or log out' or 'The death of the job' and articles spotlighting the 21st century economy with promises of change in the lives of everyone ensured that the Internet became a popular topic of conversation. Acronyms such as B2B (business-to-business), B2C (business-to-consumer), B2E (business-to-employee) and P2P (peer-to-peer) entered the business vocabulary.

Coltman *et al.*[12] have evaluated some of the early predictions about the

Internet and what the reality is some years later. For example, Kalakota and Whinston[13] predicted that brands would die—this has not been the experience. In fact, many 'Internet brands' have themselves become extinct—as many banks have discovered as they attempted to launch 'Internet brands'. The prediction that the middlemen would disappear has again proved false. In fact, a new breed of 'infomediary' has emerged.[14] Evidence also suggests that being first is not the key to success as suggested by Downes and Mui.[15] Yahoo!'s real advantage is not that it was a first mover, but a 'best mover'. If Lycos or some other portal is considered better, it is possible that Yahoo! will decline, as switching costs are low. In many cases, the early follower has the advantage of complementary assets, like brands, that form the real basis of competition for customers. This is what occurred in many industries when the incumbents took on the dot.com upstart. Yet, some predictions have come to pass. The claim that the Internet represents a new nearly 'frictionless market' has some empirical support. In a study of books and CD retailing, Brynjolfsson and Smith[16] found that prices on the Net were 9–16% lower than prices in conventional outlets.

What we are essentially looking at is another technology—in this instance, the Internet, including wireless technologies—to add to the range of technologies that already exist. The fundamental challenge for any organization is still to identify opportunities to deploy this new technology, as with any other. As Porter[17] noted '[w]e need to move away from the rhetoric about "Internet industries", "e-business strategies", and a "new economy" and see the Internet for what it is: an enabling technology—a powerful set of tools that can be used, wisely or unwisely, in almost any industry and as part of almost any strategy'.

It should also be noted that IT is *not* the business strategy. Statements like '[i]n this new age, IT is not *about* the business—it *is* the business'[18] are misleading and unhelpful.[19] Rangan and Adner[20] have dispatched sound advice in this regard. 'The sooner firms stop being distracted by the hype of new technology, the sooner they can focus on the key strategy lessons that business experience of the past couple of decades has taught us: regardless of the industry that a firm operates in, it can achieve and sustain profitable growth to the extent that it grasps and delivers on two strategy fundamentals—product advantage and production advantage.' In a similar vein, Hamel, in his book *Leading the Revolution*,[21] is quite forthright in stating that '[t]he real story of Silicon Valley is not "e", but "i", not electronic commerce but innovation and imagination. ... It is the power of "i," rather than "e," that separates the winners from the losers in the twenty-first century economy'.

Yet, this is not to say that the Internet is not different. Apart from its technical characteristics, three aspects make the Internet distinct from other technologies. First, it is *pervasive*. For example, it directly reaches end consumers, facilitating the conduct of business directly with consumers in new ways—something which has not been possible before, except with dedicated systems like France's Minitel. Interactive Digital TV allows consumers to access Internet services directly from the sitting room of their home. Second, it is *interactive*. This interactive element is of crucial importance since much business activity consists of interactions (human and technical communication, data gathering, collaborative problem solving, negotiation).[22] Third, its virtual nature means that it is a new *medium* that has different characteristics from the physical world—often referred to as the *marketspace* as opposed to the physical *marketplace*.[23] The marketspace denotes the transformation in business activity as moving from the physical marketplace with fixed locations, inventories and products to an information-defined transaction space. This shift ranges from basic business transactions such as ordering and invoicing to utilizing sophisticated business-to-business (B2B) exchanges and electronic marketplaces[24], bringing together industry players in a neutral market setting. This has implications for organizations' brands, for understanding trust, for product and service pricing, for issues of location, for collaborative ventures, for collecting duties and taxes, etc.[25] All of this implies that IS/IT strategy has to be even more tightly aligned to other strategies, especially the external relationships of the enterprise.

EARLY VIEWS AND MODELS OF IS/IT IN ORGANIZATIONS

The use of computers in business began in the early 1950s but really only became significant in the mid- to late 1960s with the development of multi-purpose mainframe computers. Major increases in processing speed, cheaper memory and improved storage capacity afforded by magnetic disk and tape, plus better programming languages, made 'batch' data processing a viable option for many tasks and activities in organizations.

During the 1970s, minicomputers of increasing power and sophistication were used for a variety of business applications that were either not feasible or economic in a mainframe environment. However, the views developed of the role of information systems and their expected evolution were based strongly on a centralized, integrated concept derived from mainframe origins. The most well known of these models, capturing the evolution of IS/IT in an organization, was developed by Gibson and Nolan[26] during the 1970s.[27] This model, in turn, used a hierarchical application portfolio model described by Anthony,[28] who defined a

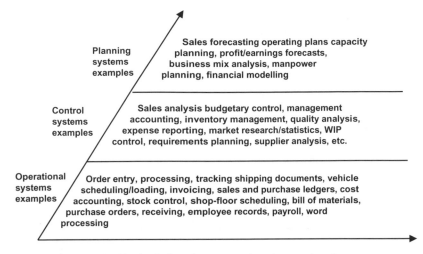

Figure 1.1   *Typical planning, control and operational systems*

structure for information systems in an organization, based on a stratification of management activity into:

- strategic planning;
- management control;
- operational control;

Different applications were built to support the different levels of management activity—hence, it provided an early way of classifying applications. Typical systems developed to support this model are shown in Figure 1.1.

Based on analyses of the use of IS/IT in a number of large US organizations, Nolan and Gibson proposed an evolutionary model containing initially four 'stages of growth'. Later, two further stages were added by Nolan. This six-stage model is summarized in Box 1.1. The analysis involved considered six aspects or benchmarks of IS/IT and its management in the organizations studied. These were (i) the rate of IS/IT expenditure, (ii) the technological configuration (e.g. batch/online/database), (iii) the applications portfolio (as in Anthony's model), (iv) the data processing (DP)/IT organization, (v) DP/IT planning and control approaches and (vi) user-awareness characteristics.

The validity and usefulness of the six-stage model have been explored by a number of researchers since it was published. In a review of past research on Nolan's stage hypothesis, Benbasat *et al.*[29] and King and Kraemer[30] found that empirical support is generally weak and

Box 1.1   Stages of evolution of IS/IT in relation to expenditure

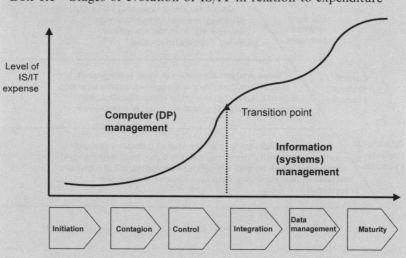

Stages of increasing sophistication and maturity

1. *Initiation*: batch processing to automate clerical operations to achieve cost reduction, purely operational systems focus, lack of management interest.
2. *Contagion*: rapid growth as users demand more applications based on high expectations of benefits, move to online systems, high rate of expense as DP tries to satisfy all user demands. Little control if any, except a drive to centralize in order to control.
3. *Control*: in response to management concern about cost, systems projects are expected to show a return, plans are produced and methodologies/standards enforced. Often produces a backlog of applications and dissatisfied users.
4. *Integration*: considerable expenditure on integrating (via database) existing systems. User accountability for systems established and DP provides a service to users not just solutions to problems.
5. *Data administration*: information requirements rather than processing drive the applications portfolio and information is shared within the organization. Database capability is exploited as users understand the value of the information.
6. *Maturity*: the planning and development of IS/IT in the organization is closely coordinated with business development.

inconclusive. Drury[31] noted that, in practice, the benchmarks did not map consistently on to the stages as suggested by the original model; in particular, in the later stages, the complexity of the real world was not reflected in the simplicity of the model. He concluded that, 'Categorising of DP from initiation to maturity may no longer be feasible with the diffusion of new technologies and functions being introduced.' However, he accepted that individual benchmarks could be usefully adopted in assessing how effectively an organization was coping with the increasing importance of IS/IT.

King and Kraemer[32] believed that the model had several weaknesses. In particular, the empirical evidence for the stages was inconsistent and many of its assumptions were too simplistic to be useful. But they equally pointed out that many aspects of the model ring true to practitioners and researchers and it has had a considerable influence on IS management thinking since the 1970s. Its weakness—its simplicity—may be the key to its popularity! It does suggest an evolutionary approach during which different forces control the destiny of IS/IT in an organization. By the beginning of the 1990s, empirical research concluded that the model provided little help for the CIO or IT director attempting to create a successful IS unit within an organization.[33] But despite its limitations, the model continues to be used by practitioners today.[34]

More significantly perhaps, Wiseman, in his book *Strategy and Computers*,[35] suggested that the influential combination of the Anthony three-tier structural approach to defining organizational systems and the 'Nolan' stage model inhibited the strategic use of IS/IT. He stated that, 'up to 1983 at least, Nolan's general purpose approach to information systems (based in part on the Anthony model) is clearly incomplete, for it offers no guidelines for identifying or explaining strategic information systems opportunities.' Friedman,[36] in analysing critiques of the Nolan model, suggested that, while evolution through the first four stages of the model was generally observable, the arrival in the 1980s of 'strategic systems' introduced a new stage that changed quite fundamentally the concept of how IS/IT evolves to 'maturity' in organizations and industries. Indeed, it is worth highlighting that stages-of-growth models have been applied to other areas of IS; for example, the evolution of the 'information centre', where there is empirical support for their evolution through the stages of growth. It is suggested that the various stages of information centre evolution are necessary in order for the information centre to better serve the changing needs of end-users.[37]

In summary, a model of the evolving role of IS/IT in organizations is of value and, while the Nolan model is a useful starting point, it is not altogether satisfactory—it only really described events up to the 1980s and since then much has changed. Perhaps a more serious problem with

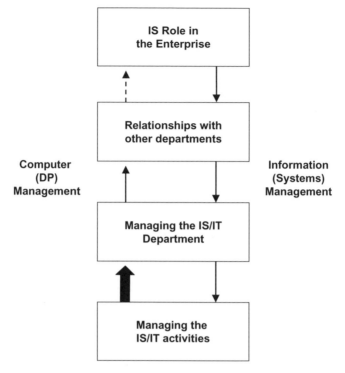

Figure 1.2 Transition between computer and information management: relationships and emphases (source: *partly derived from* EDP Analyser—'*How the management job is changing'*, *June 1984, Vol. 22, No. 6)*

the Nolan model is in the detail of the four or six stages, and the undue emphasis placed by others since on the 'rate of expenditure' associated with each stage: Should it be more or less, increasing or decreasing, and so on? Focusing attention on the trees, one often loses sight of the wood! Viewed from a more distant perspective, the six stages of the model divide into two larger 'eras', separated by a transition point between Stages 3 and 4 (Control and Integration). It can be summarized as a transition from computer (DP) management to information (systems) management, during which major changes occur in who managed what for whom, and how. In essence, it was a fundamental change in how IS/IT resources were managed, and how the role of IS/IT in the organization should be evaluated. The changing relationships involved in the transition are depicted in Figure 1.2.

During the early stages of computerization, the preoccupation was with managing the activities—operations, programming, data collection, etc. Later, a separate organizational unit was established that could cope with a variety of types of application, over an extended life cycle, during which the technology changed significantly. This 'department' was managed as a coordinated set of resources that were planned to meet expected future requirements.

While this was evolving, relationships with users developed, the effectiveness of any relationship being determined by success to date and the users' awareness of the role computers could play in organizational activity—not because of business priorities, but due to the ease with which computers could be applied. Accounting was likely to be far more advanced in computer use than marketing, and if the 'DP department' reported to Finance then that relationship was likely to be very effective—but possibly at the expense of relationships with more business-critical parts of the enterprise. Occasionally, the role of IS/IT in the organization was reviewed but the focus on current issues and problems often prevented an overall picture being seen.

Up to this point, the main driving force had been managing computer resources and activities, with the effort applied, in proportion, to the technical and application difficulties, without much regard for the value to the business of the applications. To achieve effective *Information (Systems) Management*, a new top-down approach was required—a 'strategy' for the management of IS/IT, associated activities and resources throughout the organization. This should be based on a defined role for IS in the enterprise—but that, in turn, depends on the role of IS in relation to the outside world, as will be discussed later.

Research by Hirschheim and colleagues[38] supported the rationale of this transition, based on studying the evolving issues associated with IS/IT management in organizations. They described it in terms of a three-stage model. The stages are described as:

1. *Delivery*: IS issues are mainly internal—improving the ability to deliver and support the systems and technology. Achieving top-management credibility as a valuable function is a prime objective. This means improving delivery performance, not necessarily providing users with what they really need.
2. *Reorientation*: establishing good relationships with the main business functions, supporting business demands through the provision of a variety of services as computing capability spreads through the business. The issues focus is extended outside the 'DP department' and a key objective is to provide a valued service to all business function management. Different areas will benefit differently without regard to business importance.
3. *Reorganization*: the high level of awareness created both 'locally' in the business area and 'centrally' in senior management creates the

need for a reorganization of responsibilities designed to achieve integration of the IS investment with business strategy and across business functions. A key objective becomes the best way of satisfying each of the differing business needs through a coalition of responsibilities for managing information and systems.

The last stage equates to the top-down, strategic view, while the first two describe the 'climb' to the position of considering the 'role [of IS/IT] in the enterprise'.

EARLY VIEWS AND MODELS: UP TO 1980

The evolutionary models used so far have considered the management of IS/IT during the 1960s and 1970s and essentially from the inside—the development of IS/IT management rather than exploitation of IS/IT in the enterprise. During the 1970s, the types of application and how they could be developed changed, thus making the application models used as the basis of evolutionary analysis potentially obsolete.

Starting from the Anthony model of planning, control and operational systems, Nolan and Gibson showed how the applications, developed during the evolution of IS/IT, spread slowly up the hierarchy. Perhaps more importantly, they spread at different rates in different functions of the organization. These differential rates of evolution constrained the potential for integration of control and planning systems, which by their nature are cross-functional. Normally, a firm foundation of operational systems was built first, function by function. On this foundation, control systems were introduced by accumulating operational information and analysing it to improve cross-functional coordination and control. Finally, the portfolio was completed by transforming the information so that planning systems could be developed to help senior management define the future of the business. The control and planning systems forced improvements to be made lower down the portfolio structure, in order to realign information and its processing for planning and control purposes.

By the mid-1970s, approaches to developing successful operational systems, either centrally or on distributed minicomputers, were well established. Control systems, usually centralized, were particularly well understood and, especially in financial areas, could be linked to the required operational data, if only in a 'read only' mode. However, little progress had been made on planning systems beyond crude forecasting.

Traditional, mainly operational and control, systems were essentially of two types:

- monitoring—transaction handling and control;
- exception—triggered reporting and/or action.

Although these provide management with information, they are primarily focused on the processing of data, depending for success on the predefinition and consistency of requirements (i.e. data-processing systems that are primarily operational in nature, but may enable some control and planning).

In the early 1980s, the personal computer (PC) and a new set of software tools such as spreadsheets, word processors, electronic mail and presentation graphics, enabled 'end-user computing' (EUC) to take off. EUC was originally viewed as the direct, hands-on use of computer systems by users whose jobs went beyond entering data or transactions. At about the same time, 'office automation' systems provided new means of processing and communicating information.[39] These advancements permitted two new functions to be added to the repertoire of IS/IT:

- enquiry—flexible access to data and information initiated by user request;
- analysis—decision support, with flexible processing of data and information.

Here, application needs are not predefinable, and often the applications changed rapidly during a short but useful life. They therefore tend to be characteristic of some control and planning systems, rather than operational systems. These applications essentially provide information to managers and professionals who require it and the ability to process/transform it to satisfy their information requirements.

The main differences between these types of application, named *Data Processing* and *Management Information Systems* after their primary objectives, are detailed in Table 1.1. Although these applications have different characteristics, they do to a large extent share a common information base and need to communicate—there is an obvious danger of total separation. Therefore, in addition to managing two different types of application, it became critical that the organization effectively organized its overall information resource.

It can be concluded that, from the 1960s to the early 1980s, IS/IT and its deployment in organizations passed through a major transition, which linked two eras. These two eras can be summarized as:

1. data processing from the 1960s onwards—the DP era;
2. management information systems (MIS) from the 1970s onwards—the MIS era.

Table 1.1   *Differences between DP and MIS*

	Operational and control systems *(data processing)*	Control and planning systems *(management information systems)*
Objectives	Efficient transaction handling and effective resource control	Effective problem resolution and support for decision making
Life cycles	3–12 years, depending on rate of change	From hours to months and occasionally recurring
Information time frame	Recent history, current and short-term future	Consolidated history, current and extended future
Information sources	Internal plus external transactions	Internal plus external 'research' data
Logical processes	Strictly algorithmic	Probabilistic and 'fuzzy'
Users	Operators, clerical staff and first line supervisors	Professionals and middle to senior managers
Technologies	Mainframe/minicomputer-controlled processing at workstations	Local processing linked to information resources

Obviously, from this definition the two eras overlap—DP continuing to mature as MIS emerges and grows. As will be discussed later, the 1980s saw the beginning of a third era, which can be called the 'strategic information systems' (SIS) era. This book will focus considerable attention on the applications and implications of the third era, but it must also be remembered that:

- A considerable part of future investment will be in DP and MIS, and these investments must be part of any strategic plan.
- Much can be learned from the experiences gained in the first two eras to improve the chances of success in the third, when the potential prizes are greater, but the penalties for failure more severe!
- All organizations have to live with the legacy—asset or liability—of the applications previously developed, and often developed for reasons and using methods relevant to the past. Management and user attitudes and understanding of the potential of IS/IT and the IS/IT skills of the organization will in large part be determined by the nature of that legacy.

The implications for the organization are that a complex inheritance must be appropriately managed, improved and replaced, while current opportunities are exploited and future possibilities explored.

THE DP AND MIS ERAS: THE LESSONS LEARNED

There have been essentially three parallel threads of evolution that have enabled more extensive and better information systems to be developed:

- Hardware—reducing cost and size, improving reliability and connectivity, enabling the system to be installed closer to the business problem.
- Software—more comprehensive and flexible operating software and improved languages, enabling business applications to be developed more quickly, with greater accuracy and by staff with less experience. In addition, there was an increased availability of application packages available 'off the shelf'.
- Methodology—ways of organizing and carrying out the multiplicity of tasks, in a more coordinated, synchronized and efficient way to enable ever more complex systems to be implemented and large projects to be managed successfully.

The 'data processing' approach is problem/task/process focused to ensure that the 'automation' through IS/IT of those tasks achieves the required efficiency improvements and thus benefits—the required return on investment. The relationship to business strategy development is similar to that of installing a new widget-making machine, which produces twice as many in half the time, needs fewer operators and produces a better yield from the material (i.e. enabling performance improvements). Similarly, automation of a warehouse improves efficiency and can improve inventory management, but does not fundamentally alter the business process—it is a more effective 'implementation' to support the achievement of strategic aims.

Automation through DP can, however, produce a competitive advantage. For example, the Aalsmeer Flower Auction (Verenigde Bloemenveilingen Aalsmeer) in the Netherlands computerized their auction clocks in the 1970s and linked the auction transactions to the time-critical administration and distribution systems. The speed and integrity of the systems enabled the auction to handle ever-increasing volumes, to the satisfaction of both the flower growers and the buyers—increasing the auction's market and market share.[40] Over the years, the exchange has developed a wider range of buying and selling systems, including

FlowerAccess.com, an information and order system, developed with exporters and wholesalers that enable florists worldwide to order directly. The VBA has also launched a remote system that allows buyers to take part in sales from off-site locations while watching several auctions from computer screens in real time.[41] Computerized reservation systems (CRS) began life as DP systems to enable airlines to manage their inventory of seats but were soon giving them significant competitive advantage as well as becoming more profitable than their owners.[42]

The problems of developing DP systems are generally well known, if not fully resolved, in most organizations. Consequently, they have been addressed most comprehensively. Even in the future, perhaps more than 50% of all IS/IT investments will be about improving efficiency—'data processing' in their philosophy. Wiseman[43] refers to the 'hybrid nature' of many major systems investments. He says that even so-called competitive or strategic systems such as the electronic 'point of sale' (EPOS) systems in retailing include a large data-processing component—data capture, verification, storage, processing, transmission—as well as providing important information that may be employed to improve competitiveness.

As more 'data' became stored in computer systems, managers realized that using the information could increase the effectiveness of decision making in their departments. Database software seemed to provide the means to give the necessary flexible access to information via online enquiry and analysis systems. Coupled with emerging modelling tools, new decision-support systems provided managers with the facility to manipulate data in ways not previously possible. This required managers to think about the information they used and how they used it. However, managers do not use data in predefinable, structured ways. Neither do managers rely solely on 'hard facts' in their decision making.[44] The methods used successfully to construct large volume, structured DP systems did not work given the vagueness of the requirements. Neither could the cost involved be justified easily, given the intangible nature of the benefits and the potentially short life of the systems. Return-on-investment calculations did not look as attractive for MIS as they did for DP, even though both could be based on ever-reducing hardware costs.

The legacy of process-based DP applications, each one optimized in its construction to maximize efficiency, was often at best a fragmented data resource, at worst a chaotic mess of data with little or no integrity. Database disciplines required a heavy user involvement in data definition—a tedious and difficult task. Frustration developed as large restructuring projects were undertaken to reorganize data and applications into integrated data-based systems to enable MIS to be developed. Even when this was complete, the databases often proved inflexible—the users did not get the information in the way they needed it. IS specialists spent inordinate amounts of time on data analysis and design, and then still had to write mundane retrieval systems. The 'response' to the problem by IT suppliers was to introduce new languages—fourth-generation languages (4GLs)—which were easy to use on well-defined data, relational databases to overcome the constraint of rigid structures and personal computers to free the user from the tangled web of IS development. In particular, the personal computer brought with it the 'spreadsheet', which enabled considerable analytical scope without the need for programming.

Most IT departments eventually identified the need for new user-support services. A manifestation of this was the 'information centre'. This was, by whatever name, a new service whose prime purpose was to support and encourage, but minimize the risks of, end-user computing. New relationships were established with users who had previously been on the verge of total rebellion! Many IT departments also adopted the new software tools and used them to improve the responsiveness and productivity of more conventional IS development. Agreement was reached on user and IT roles—which 'systems' aspects were to be entrusted to users and which needed the disciplines already developed. Appropriate organizational policies, rather than DP methodologies, could be established.[45]

In some organizations, however, rifts between users and IT professionals developed, causing active antagonism and consequent failure to resolve the issues of the MIS era. Often, the corporate information resource, instead of being integrated via the database approach, became fragmented as separate users either retained or regained control of their data. Frequently, the MIS applications became divorced from the DP systems—often resulting in, at best, unsynchronized and, at worst, totally different data being used to operate the business and manage it!

Into this arena, in the early 1980s, was thrust the concept of 'office automation'—an unfortunate misnomer, which sent shivers of apprehension through those whose world was apparently about to be automated and offered a new opportunity for conflict between the IT professionals and user management. The net result was that more forms of information—not just data but text and potentially images and voice—could be channelled through the same technology. In some cases, this would enable more efficient information processing and, in others, provide better ways of communicating and presenting information, providing a more comprehensive matching of technology to the tasks of a typical manager.

Unfortunately, two factors served to confuse the progress in evolutionary terms that even the best-managed companies were achieving:

1. How was the large new investment required in hardware and software—many hundreds of workstations, networking costs and multiple licences for software packages—to be justified? This refocused management's attention on technology rather than its use—the much-quoted word 'convergence' distracted management from a need to ensure that their systems and information were appropriate and effective before throwing technology at the problem. Those organizations who succeeded with office automation were those who applied the lessons learned in successful DP and MIS investments to the extension of technology use. The rationale for investment had reverted, in many cases, from 'business pull' to 'technology push' and the management style often regressed accordingly.
2. How should the new applications and supporting technology be managed and, even more critically, who should be responsible? Should the role of the IT unit be extended or should such systems be the responsibility of users? Were the new office systems an extension to a department level of personal computing or an integral part of the organization's information processing ability and resources? How did the management of personal computing and office systems relate?

As the new 'strategic' potential of IS/IT began to be appreciated in the mid-1980s, most organizations were still wrestling with the problems of managing concurrent DP and MIS applications based on rapidly-evolving technology. Policies, planning, organization structures and processes were established to control and coordinate the increasingly diverse and complex requirements. Good practice in the planning and management of DP and MIS was hard won after a long fight. The extended business role, now envisaged, did not undo that requirement—much of the future investment would be of a 'traditional' nature and would produce more benefits if well planned and managed. DP and MIS applications might be less glamorous but management should equally expect them to be more certain of success. Table 1.2 summarizes a number of the key lessons from the first two eras.

Paul Strassman, in his book *The Information Payoff*,[46] assessed the contribution of IS/IT to businesses from a careful examination of the essential premises of the first two eras (i.e. that DP delivers increased efficiency and that MIS improves management effectiveness). From his many observations and conclusions, the following are particularly important:

Table 1.2 *Summary of lessons from DP and MIS eras*

DP lessons:	Need to understand the process of developing complete information systems, not just the programs to process data.
	More thorough requirements and data analysis to improve systems linkages and a more engineered approach to designing system components.
	More appropriate justification of investments by assessing the economics of efficiency gains and converting these to a return on investment.
	Less creative, more structured approaches to programming, testing and documentation to reduce the problems of future amendments. More discipline was introduced with 'change control procedures' and sign-off on specifications and tests.
	Extended project management that recognized the need for co-ordination of both user and DP functions and the particular need to establish user management in a decisive role in the systems development—the user had to live with the consequences.
	The need for planning the interrelated set of systems required by the organization. Better planning produced overall improvements in systems relevance and productivity.
MIS lessons:	Justification of IS investments is not entirely a matter of return on investment/financial analysis.
	Databases require large restructuring projects and heavy user involvement in data definition—data integration had been weak based on the project by project DP approach.
	The IS resource needs to move from a production to a service orientation to enable users to obtain their own information from the data resource—the information centre concept.
	Need for organizational policies, not just DP methodologies.
	Personal computers and office systems enable better MIS to be developed, provided that users and IS specialists both focus on the information needs rather than the technology.

- IS/IT deployment has generally improved the efficiency of information-based functions in organizations when technology is used to automate discrete, structured, repetitive, stable information-intensive tasks (e.g. invoicing, accounting, order handling, word processing, etc.). However, the return on investment is lower than the often-quoted figures such as 25–30%; a net 5–10% return is more likely, although some isolated spectacular gains are possible. Efficiency gains can and should be measured wherever possible, although this can be difficult if tasks are rationalized or integrated when computerized.

- The results with regard to management effectiveness are less consistent. First, measuring effectiveness improvements—'value added' of managers—is difficult. Strassman's measurements considered management's contribution in terms of profitability or those aspects of profit that managers can influence against the costs incurred by management. When IS/IT is added to this cost burden, how does it affect the value-added side of the equation? According to Strassman's research and analysis, the expected happens: good managers get even better; bad managers get worse! This is explained as follows: good management, with a high and improving value/cost ratio, will use new resources to increase their effectiveness further by focusing on adding more value still—getting better at their job—or they will discard the technology. Poor management will focus on improving the value/cost ratio by reducing the cost component and will be looking for IS/IT to produce efficiency savings—implying automation, but of tasks that do not lend themselves to automation. This piecemeal automation approach misses the opportunity to improve personal and collective effectiveness. It could be argued that IS/IT in these circumstances speeds up the mess! It is therefore important to deal with the basic reasons for low management productivity and effectiveness before employing the technology.

More recent surveys and further work by Strassman, using the same approach, have verified these observations, especially where IS/IT is introduced into complex organization structures.[47]

THE THREE-ERA MODEL

Thus far in the evolution of the role of information systems and technology in organizations, two eras have been identified and discussed. There is, in fact, a third era that began in the early 1980s and provides a focal point for this book. This third era can be referred to as the *strategic information systems* era, and it will be discussed at length in the next section.

Although it is tempting to simplify nearly 50 years of often-haphazard, uncertain progress with the benefit of hindsight into three, albeit overlapping, eras, it must be remembered that it is never that simple. A 'three-era model' is proposed from which a number of insights can be drawn that help in planning or developing strategies for the future. While the three-era model is easy to criticize as being oversimplistic, it has proved popular with a number of IS/IT theorists and researchers. Hence, many useful analyses are available from which a pattern of conclusions can be drawn. It is first worth clarifying the fundamental differences and inter-dependencies of the three eras.

The prime objective of using IS/IT in the eras differs:

- *data processing* to improve operational efficiency by automating information-based processes;
- *management information systems* to increase management effectiveness by satisfying their information requirements for decision making;
- *strategic information systems* to improve competitiveness by changing the nature or conduct of business (i.e. IS/IT investments can be a source of competitive advantage).

The objectives of DP and MIS are, strictly speaking, a subset of the SIS objective—to improve competitiveness. But this tends to be achieved indirectly by using IS/IT to improve current business practices. For example, the focus of business process re-engineering (BPR) is often seen as improving competitiveness, but this is achieved through process redesign taking into account the capabilities of IT in providing new and innovative design possibilities. While the SIS objective is more immediately related to the business, success in achieving the DP and MIS objectives can contribute considerably to business success, and further improvements are always possible as IT capabilities are enhanced and the cost reduces.

Galliers and Somogyi, in the book *Towards Strategic Information Systems*,[48] plot the erratic progress of IS/IT, its use and its management through the two eras (note that their Management Services era is what we refer to as MIS) and into the then emerging third era of strategic information systems. They recognized a number of important trends that occurred during that evolution, including the move into the third era. These trends are summarized in Figure 1.3, in the terms used above.

Wiseman[49] has perhaps most succinctly described both the relationship between the three eras and the evolving application portfolio and the application objectives. His key points are:

- Just as good MIS systems rely on good operational DP systems for accurate, timely information, strategic information systems (such as

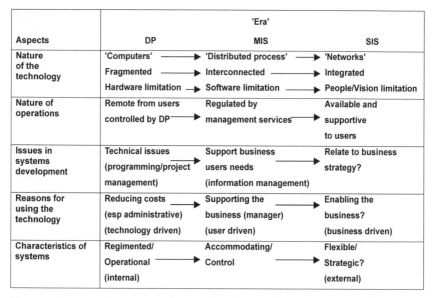

Figure 1.3   *Trends in the evolution of business IS/IT (source: adapted from R.D. Galliers and E. Somogyi, 'From data processing to strategic information systems: A historical perspective', in R.D. Galliers and E. Somogyi, eds,* Towards Strategic Information Systems, *Abacus Press, 1987)*

those linking the company directly to its customers via the Internet) rely on good DP or MIS systems for appropriate information provisioning or dependent processing. Many companies have established websites permitting customers to place orders online, but not yet integrated them with order processing and other back-office systems.

- Strategic information systems are not essentially different applications—the functions are often the same as for DP or MIS applications—it is their impact on the business due to the changes they enable or cause that is different.
- The strategic applications may put considerable stress on the DP and MIS applications that were developed for a less demanding environment—they may need to be redeveloped not because of intrinsic shortcomings but because they inhibit the benefits to be gained from the SIS.

It must be emphasized that 'eras' is not perhaps the ideal word, suggesting as it does a sequential relationship. The DP era is still with us, the ever-improving economics enabling the technology to be applied to extend the automation of processes involving documents, images and voice. So, too, with MIS. A combination of improved economics, more powerful processing capability, sophisticated software and the availability of external data enables the collection, analysis and presentation of information to be made more comprehensive and effective.

THE STRATEGIC INFORMATION SYSTEMS ERA

During the late 1970s, a number of organizations had began to use IS/IT in ways that fundamentally changed how their business was conducted, changing the balance of power in their industry with respect to competitors, customers and/or suppliers. The use of IS/IT was thus directly influencing their competitive position and had become a new weapon to improve their competitiveness, implying a new relationship between IS/IT investment and strategic development.

Among the earliest examples of competitive advantage from IS/IT were the SABRE reservation system of American Airlines and the direct terminal-based ordering system of American Hospital Supplies. Both involved putting technology directly into the customers' sites, and, in the process, precluded similar competitive responses—who wants two or more terminals on their desk?—but also caused fundamental changes in the 'systems' operating in their industries, to their advantage. These two particular cases are extensively documented, along with a number of others—United Airlines, Merrill Lynch, Thomson Holidays, ICI, McKesson, and Dun & Bradstreet.

During the mid-1980s, an endless stream of examples were quoted in many journals and books on SIS under the generic title of 'how IS/IT provides competitive advantages'. These articles often did more than describe what organizations had done: they considered how the advantage had been achieved and proceeded to suggest how any organization might analyse its business and identify similar opportunities. In many cases, a tool or technique was described and substantiated by selected examples.[50] Although these various approaches will be considered in detail later, it is important to note at this stage that they are all fundamentally different from the analysis approaches traditionally employed regarding the deployment of IS/IT. They are therefore additional tools and techniques that need to be included in the IS/IT strategy development and planning toolkit. However, they need to be considered in the overall context of both business strategy and IS/IT strategy, as will be demonstrated later.

It is worth noting at this stage that, although some of the 'classic' competitive advantage examples resulted from a formal approach to strategy development, most were the product of excellent exploitation of situations that arose in the course of business. As a result of his research into strategic information systems, Ciborra[51] asserted that successful applications are often due more to serendipity than any formal approaches to planning. The various tools and techniques that have been developed subsequently should enable organizations to reduce the amount of luck required.

Recently, attention has returned to some of these classic examples. Kettinger *et al.*[52] analysed some 30 of the best known examples, 10–20 years after their initial implementation, to determine whether the advantages achieved by these systems were sustained. Clearly, over such an extended period, many factors can affect a firm's performance, and the results are at best indicative rather than conclusive. In general, they found that, while some 40% of the firms had above-average performance for a few years, only 20% could be said to have sustained the advantage for 10 years or more. However, this is probably to be expected given the advances in technology over the period and, hence, the relative ease of replication (at lower cost) of many of the systems. We shall return to this point again at the end of the chapter, as we believe that the lessons from this and other research studies provide the background to a new fourth era.

STRATEGIC USES OF IS/IT: CLASSIFICATION, FACTORS FOR SUCCESS AND MANAGEMENT IMPLICATIONS

From a research base of over several hundred examples and case studies spanning 20 years of claimed 'strategic systems', the following classification can be shown to be helpful in considering the implications of strategic IS/IT use. In general, the examples can be classified into one of four types, although some of the examples clearly exhibit the characteristics of more than one type.

The four main types of strategic system appear to be:

1. those that share information via technology-based systems with customers/consumers and/or suppliers and change the nature of the relationship;
2. those that produce more effective integration of the use of information in the organization's value-adding processes;
3. those that enable the organization to develop, produce, market and deliver new or enhanced products or services based on information;
4. those that provide executive management with information to support the development and implementation of strategy (in particular, where relevant external and internal information are integrated in analysis).

Other classifications are somewhat similar in their analysis. Benjamin *et al.*[53] divided the types of potential opportunity between those that focus on either the competitive market place or internal operations Within each, IS/IT can be used to improve traditional ways of doing business or to cause 'significant structural changes' in the way the company does business. Notowidigdo[54] divided strategic information systems into:

- internal systems that have direct benefit for the company;
- external systems that have direct benefits for the company's customers.

A similar approach was adopted by Venkatraman[55] in assessing how the strategic benefits from IT resulted from increasing degrees of business change (and risk!). He considered the early 'evolutionary' stages of IT use in much the same way as described earlier in this chapter for DP and MIS. However, he described three types of 'revolutionary' uses of IT, which require considerable transformation in terms of what the organization does or how it does it:

1. *business process redesign*—using IS/IT to realign business activities and their relationships to achieve performance breakthroughs;
2. *business network redesign*—changing the way information is used by the organization and its trading partners, thereby changing how the industry overall carries out the value-adding processes;
3. *business scope redefinition*—extending the market or product set, based on information or changing the role of the organization in the industry.

While not identical, these options are similar to the classification we have developed, with a clear emphasis on the extent of the changes to achieve a strategic advantage from IS/IT. Hence, the four categories suggested above seem to cover many of the possibilities. Each of these types of strategic IS/IT application has different implications in terms of identification, planning and implementation.

Linking to Customers and Suppliers

The key people involved in the consideration of external linkage systems will be sales/marketing and distribution management at the customer end, or purchasing/receiving/quality-control managers at the supplier end. The initiator of American Hospital Supplies' strategic IS developments was a depot manager who provided a disorganized customer with a

Box 1.2 Case examples of IS/IT and competitive advantage through the decades

Merrill Lynch
In the USA, Merrill Lynch launched its cash-management account back in 1978. This combined traditionally separate banking products such as line of credit, cheque, investment and equity accounts into a single monthly statement, with idle funds being swept automatically into a high-interest-bearing account. The new accounts attracted US$1 billion of assets in the first year. Merrill Lynch set out to change the shape of the financial marketplace permanently by taking several existing but separate services and tying them together through information technology to create a new service that shattered the traditional boundaries between the banking and securities industries.

American Hospital Supply
American Hospital Supply competed in the wholesale health-care industry in the 1970s and 1980s. To gain an important edge over its rivals, AHS pioneered an order entry distribution system that linked most of the firm's customers to its computers. AHS-owned terminals were placed directly in the purchasing departments of hospitals, giving them an early mover advantage—hospitals didn't wish to have multiple terminals from different vendors cluttering up their offices. In addition to ordering merchandise, the system allows customers to control their inventories by having direct access to AHS's stock records, increasing the likelihood of their coming to rely upon AHS as a key supplier. The fact that the company's initial move to electronic ordering was spearheaded by a regional manager seeking to meet the needs of a single customer suggests that starting small may be the key to success.

American Airlines
American Airlines gained a lead over the competition as the first US carrier to offer an online reservation system to travel agents. This system, Sabre, captured 10,000 of the 24,000 travel agents in the USA. Sabre listed the flight schedules of over 400 airlines, but, when launched, it gave American a crucial edge by displaying its own flights first. So effective was this tactic that other US carriers persuaded the Government to intervene. American still benefited, however, by charging for every booking made, bringing in significant revenue. In fact, Sabre was more profitable than the airline itself.

Otis Elevators

In the 1980s, Otis Elevators, the US manufacturer of elevators, identified 'customer services' as being a key element of its customer strategy. It decided that one of the aspects of its service that would give its customers most satisfaction was a prompt lift repair service. So, it built an automated system, called Otisline, to dispatch repairmen. Where something started to go wrong with Otis' lifts, they (the lifts!) automatically called in their complaint to a computer—without human intervention. Otis' rivals suddenly had to compete on quality of service as well as the price and quality of lifts themselves.

Schneider National Inc.

Schneider National Inc. is a large truckload carrier based in the USA. 1980 saw the advent of deregulation in this traditional industry and Schneider recognized, earlier than most, the strategic potential of IT. Over the years, the company has developed many applications in order to stay ahead of the competition. The company moved from freight modelling applications, to EDI, to satellite technology with onboard terminals, to incorporating these satellite data into customer communications and load scheduling processes. While each application of technology gave them a significant advantage in the marketplace, their competitors soon developed similar applications and it quickly became standard for the industry. Yet, while the competition was looking to imitate Schneider, they had already moved on to develop a new strategic application. In essence, the competition was continually playing catch-up. Schneider continues to apply its IT capability as it moves into logistics outsourcing. While logistics is an entirely different business from trucking, it similarly depends on fast, cost-effective, strategic implementations of IT. Schneider is not successful because of any particular leading-edge technology, which is also available to its competitors, but because it has developed a capability for applying IT to ever-changing business opportunities.

Amazon.com

Amazon.com is an Internet venture that was launched in July 1995, and has probably become the most famous site in cyberspace. It initially started out with a mission to use the Internet to transform book buying into the fastest, easiest and most enjoyable experience possible. Jeff Bezos, its founder, selected book retailing as it was a fragmented industry, with the two biggest booksellers at the time accounting for less than 12% of total books sales. Unlike traditional bookstores, there are no bookshelves to browse at Amazon.com. From the website, customers can search for a specific book, topic or author, or they can browse their way through the book catalogue. Visitors can also read book reviews from other customers, the *New York Times* and other newspapers and magazines. Customers can browse and then complete the sale by entering their credit card information—in the early days, customers placed their orders online and then phoned in their credit card information. Orders are processed immediately and books in stock, generally best-sellers, are shipped the same day. Customers are contacted by email when their order has been dispatched. Orders for non-best-sellers are immediately placed with the appropriate book publisher by Amazom.com. All contact with the company is done either through their World Wide Web site or by email.

Over the years, the company has also expanded into other areas and now sells CDs, consumer electronics, toys and games, and tools and hardware. It has also branched out into electronic auctions. The company has also pioneered technologies such as customer profiling and '1-click' shopping. The profiling technology has enabled Amazon to recommend books based on previous purchasing history and what other customers who have bought similar books are also reading. In selling CDs, it permits shoppers to listen to excerpts. Even today, the company strives to maintain their founding commitment to customer satisfaction and the delivery of an educational and inspiring shopping experience.

Bootsphoto.com

Boots the Chemist have developed a website Bootsphoto.com to extend the company's existing photo-developing business. The site offers customers the option to have photographs digitized, uploaded and stored on the Bootsphoto.com website. Users can order reprints or enlargements online and create web-based photo albums. By sharing passwords, friends and family can independently view and buy the same photos. While uploading and storage is free, prints are charged for. Boots argue that putting the service online widens the potential number of customers for prints—already a high-margin business.

'Once people have created their online albums, they are not going to want to move them. It's like setting up a bank account and that's an incredible asset for customer loyalty,' say Phil Douty, head of Bootsphoto.com. Although customers can order and pay for prints online, they will also be able to drop off and collect films at any store.

LeatherXchange.com

The worldwide leather industry is highly dispersed, ranging from slaughterhouses and tanneries of developing countries to the manufacturers of luxury leather goods in France and Italy. It is also highly fragmented, with thousands of agents and traders. The biggest company has less than 1% of the market. The absence of common standards in the industry means that the quality of skins and hides varies a great deal. Up to 40% of international consignments are often turned back by dissatisfied buyers, while tanneries are obliged to carry large inventories to make up for the uneven quality of supply.

LeatherXchange.com was established as an online leather exchange to capitalize on the opportunities that the state of this industry offered for an Internet exchange. Hundreds of suppliers are posting their prices and products on the website. Users pay an annual membership fee, plus fees based on their online transactions and use of LeatherXchange's search engines. The site has also developed standards that are now posted on the site to help buyers and suppliers in their negotiations, as are industry contracts to govern agreement between buyers and sellers. The exchange is also planning to launch an inspection service that will provide quality certificates for suppliers.

Ryanair

Ryanair is one of the world's most successful 'low fares' airlines. To support this strategy, the company has looked to the Internet to provide a low-cost distribution channel for its seats. Its online booking facility was launched in 1999, migrating customers away from the more expensive travel agent and call-centre channels. Customers can now search for flights online and book them with a credit or debit card. As a ticketless airline, the customers are supplied with a reference number which is given to staff at check-in. Over 90% of ticket sales are now taken on the website, which is also available in a number of languages including French, German, Swedish and Norwegian. In addition, the site also sells travel insurance, car hire and hotel accommodation. Competitors such as easyJet and Go! have similarly attempted to migrate customers to the Internet.

ATC Bologna
HELLOBUS is the Short Message Service (SMS) created by Omnitel Vodafone in collaboration with ATC, Bologna's public transport company. Travellers can find out the exact time the bus they are waiting for will arrive at any of ATC's 1,300 stops, 24 hours a day. All they have to do is send an SMS with the number of the stop and the chosen line. In a few seconds, the reply arrives on their mobile phone indicating the bus's actual time of arrival.

terminal through which he could place emergency orders. These applications require a strong drive from the sharp-end line management. Also, they are not entirely in the organization's power to control—since suppliers, customers and competitors may take the initiative at any stage—and obviously any such system will require the cooperation of trading partners. e-Procurement and web-based ordering systems have enabled new, but low-cost linkages with customers and suppliers, some systems even permitting customers to track online the progress of orders.

Improved Integration of Internal Processes

To produce effective internal integration of information requires the organization to overcome some of the traditional barriers to successful IS/IT application in the DP/MIS eras: sharing information, reorganization of roles, etc. For instance, telemarketing, for routine selling, can dramatically reduce the cost of generating orders. But, imagine the reaction of a good customer to a telephone call suggesting a reorder when he has just received a final-demand letter from the Accounts Department for payments for goods he did not receive to use on a machine that is idle due to a service engineer calling without the right parts! All of the relevant information about the customer and the organization's ability to deliver is required at the point of selling to make it effective. This is what organizations are seeking to achieve with the implementation of customer relationship management systems (CRM).

Enterprise resource planning (ERP) are configurable information systems packages that integrate information and information-based processes within and across functional areas in an organization.

Senior management need to understand the organizational implications of this new information-based approach to the roles of people and departments, since reorganization will probably be required if significant benefits are to be obtained and any relative advantages sustained.

Information-based Products and Services

The classic example of enhancing the product/service, based on information, is the Merrill Lynch Cash Management Account, a consumer service that combines cheque, credit, savings and investment facilities. Unlike many of the examples, this concept resulted from strategic planning in the corporate planning department, where it was realized that a whole range of financial services were converging. Merrill Lynch realized that providing an information service to customers about what are information-based products could be very lucrative. More recently, online banking has incorporated a similar logic.

To achieve advantages in this type of application requires a thorough knowledge of the products of the industry, their relative merits and, in particular, what the customer uses them for and how the customer obtains value from them. Obviously, an understanding of the organization's own products and services and the economics of providing them is also required.

The ventures into 'direct' selling and servicing of financial-service customers from call centres, pioneered by First Direct and Direct Line, were initially examples of Category 2 above (i.e. improved delivery based on internal integration of processes and systems). The products were essentially the same as those of competitors, but they were delivered directly to consumers via the telephone rather than via agents or branches. However, they could perhaps be considered as new types of product based on the quality of service provided and the focus on the set of banking and insurance needs of individuals. They clearly have made a significant impact on the market, given the development of similar product/service offerings by more traditional organizations such as the Halifax and Canada Life.

In using the Internet, many organizations have looked to add more value to the tangible products they sell by providing additional 'information-based' services. These can include online support, order tracking, order history, etc. Many of these initiatives focus on deepening the relationship with customers and suppliers. Others have moved their trading platform either partially or entirely onto the Internet (e.g. the auction house Christies and the Aalsmeer Flower Auction, mentioned earlier). Using e-procurement, RS Components permits its customers to 'empower' their employees to make purchases from RS's website of non-core, low value (less than €300) items, with RS managing the total process, including establishing purchasing controls. These purchasing control rules cover specific pricing, spending limits, baring the ordering of particular products, cost codes, blanket orders, and order passwords.

Executive Information Systems

The final type of strategic IS/IT application—to provide executive management with information to support strategic decisions—is dependent on other factors for success. For strategic decisions, senior executives need organized information about markets, customers and non-customers; about technology in one's own industry and others; about worldwide finance, and the changing world economy. In addition, the experience of the decision maker is also important. Often, intuition or 'gut feeling' plays a large part in some decisions.

Management information systems, historically at least, rarely satisfy this information requirement and, thus, make little impression on top management in the organization. There are two main reasons for this: (i) the lack of external information included in the systems and (ii) the simplicity of the systems, the rawness of the data, the lack of context (i.e. they require knowledge, not just information).

Recent developments in external business databases, which are readily tapped into using the Internet, plus the potential offered by knowledge-based (or expert-type) systems and scenario planning systems to process and explore options based on information and experience, have made this use of IS/IT more practicable. To date, this type of application provides the smallest number of examples.

Figure 1.4 summarizes the different views of strategic information systems, their context and focus. The dimensions of Figure 1.4 show the changing role of IS/IT—efficiency and effectiveness of existing activities (i.e. improving how things are done, changing what the business does

Purpose / Focus	Operational efficiency	Management effectiveness	Business advantage through change
Internal	1. Data processing—automation of business tasks and processes	2. Management Information Systems (and 'Executive and Information Systems')	3. Internal business integration by process, job and organization redesign
External	4. Electronic links between organizations automating data exchanges	5. Sharing information by direct access from one company to another's information resources	6. External business integration, changing the roles of the firms in the industry

Figure 1.4   *The information systems management environment*

or how the organization functions)—and the changing focus of investment, from internal to external. In the Figure, electronic data interchange (EDI) or e-commerce, at its basic level of automating existing business transactions, is not considered strategic since it merely improves the efficiency of transaction handling. Also, executive information systems (EIS) have been included under MIS since the majority are 'higher-level' versions of MIS; only a few fit the 'strategic' description given above. The other three components of the matrix reflect similar 'transformations' as described by Venkatraman and others.

SUCCESS FACTORS IN STRATEGIC INFORMATION SYSTEMS

A second aspect of the analyses of our research base identifies some of the key factors that seem to recur frequently and underpin success. Few strategic information systems show all of the factors, but many show a number. Again, these factors are often at odds with traditional IS/IT approaches and show more commonality with business innovation.

1. *External, not internal, focus*: looking at customers, competitors, suppliers, even other industries and the business's relationships and similarities with the outside business world. Traditionally IS/IT was focused on internal processes and issues. Toshiba is using wireless technology for remote monitoring of photocopiers, so that technicians can be dispatched as soon as there are signs of a problem. This reduces servicing costs and, since machines are out of action less often, increases usage and revenue.
2. *Adding value, not cost reduction*: although cost reductions may accrue due to business expansion at reduced marginal costs, 'doing it better, not cheaper' seems to be the maxim. This is consistent with the requirements of companies to differentiate themselves from competitors—better products, better services—to succeed. Historically, IS/IT was seen as a way of increasing efficiency—doing it cheaper—and, while this is obviously important in any business environment, it is not the only way to succeed. At Svenska Cellulosa Aktiebolaget, a Swedish pulp and paper company, foremen use a wireless system to send instructions to loggers in the field, specifying which trees to cut and in what order. This enables the company to coordinate harvesting decisions with inventory and transport requirements and match those decisions to market needs.
3. *Sharing the benefits*: within the organization, with suppliers, customers, consumers and even competitors on occasion! In many cases in the past, systems benefits have not been shared even within

an organization, but used instead to give departments or functions leverage over each other. This reduces the benefits and does not allow them to be sustained. Sharing benefits implies a 'buy in', a commitment to success, a switching cost. Almost all of the examples involve sharing the benefits, with suppliers, customers, consumers and competitors, to provide barriers of entry to the industry. For instance, the introduction of debit cards to replace cheque books depended for its success on banks sharing some of the reduced processing costs with the retailers and consumers, since the benefits that the bank could gain depended on the commitment of retailers and consumers. Some would argue that this was achieved by increasing the cost of the alternative (i.e. cheques!).

4. *Understanding customers* and what they do with the product or service: how they obtain value from it, and the problems they may encounter in gaining that value. In the 1980s, McKesson, the pharmaceutical wholesaler, followed this principle very closely in providing a range of information-based services to drugstores, starting from a simple problem of stock control, solved by delivering products in shelf-sized batches. Black and Decker, a low-cost producer, supplied a value-added service to retailers to enable them to 'swap' goods they had over or understocked for the season. They did not want returns, but the retailer could not be expected to predict precisely how many lawnmowers, for instance, would be sold. It helped to solve a customer's problem. Federal Express has built on its original customer-service system, which tracks every movement of every package, and extended access direct to customers.

5. *Business-driven innovation, not technology-driven*: the pressures of the marketplace drove developments in most cases. This tends to cast doubt on the idea of competitive advantage from IT, but, in practice, it means that new or existing IT provides or enables a business opportunity or idea to be converted into reality. The lead or the driving force is from the business, not necessarily a traditional route to using IS/IT, which has often been driven by technology, pushed by the IT suppliers and professionals, not pulled through by the users. It is only relatively recently that the latest technology has become of interest to business managers. But the business issue does not change: why take two risks at the same time—that is, a new business process based on new technology? It is a recipe for failure! Keen[56] summed it up well by saying, 'Major failures in using IT are often based on much better technology and bad business vision. Successes come from good enough technology and a clear understanding of the customer.' An early prediction of the demise of many dot.com ventures?

6. *Incremental development*, not the total application vision turned into reality. Many examples show a stepped approach—doing one thing and building on and extending the success by a further development. To some extent, this is developing applications by experimentation but also not stopping when a success is achieved but considering what could be done next. This, again, is against the traditional notion of clarifying all requirements, defining all boundaries and agreeing the total deliverables of the system before embarking on the expensive, structured process of design and construction, freezing the requirements at each stage. Prototyping of systems obviously has a key role to play here.

7. *Using the information gained* from the systems to develop the business. Many mail order and retailing firms have segmented their customers according to the purchasing patterns shown by transactions and then providing different, focused catalogues or special offers. Product and market analyses plus external market research information can be merged and then recut in any number of ways to identify more appropriate marketing segmentation and product mix. This aspect has been exploited particularly well by the 'direct' insurers, who are able to target the lower risk, more profitable customers very accurately. Through using the information gleaned from customer transactions, the Britannia Building Society in the UK has developed a sophisticated segmentation strategy based on creating customer propensity models, which have helped the Society increase the average number of products per customer from 1.3 to over 2.0.[57] Before Safeway introduced its loyalty card scheme, they knew virtually nothing about customers. They didn't know who they were, what they bought or even if they were the same customers who shopped at the store the previous week. By introducing a loyalty card scheme, it persuaded customers to tell them what they bought, and yielded significant information such as: most customers aren't profitable; average shopping range is 250 lines; women are 50% impulsive, men 90%; customers shop for concepts not commodities (e.g. Sunday lunch, kids treat, Italian meal); Feta cheese is the 298th most popular cheese on units sold, but leaps to 25th in terms of basket size.[58]

As discussed above, these factors, in general, imply different attitudes to the use of IS/IT than have prevailed in the past, implying that we need new ways of thinking about IS/IT techniques to uncover such opportunities, and then new approaches to managing these applications to ensure success.

Another general observation can be made from these examples, by considering what actually produces the success—information technology, information systems or information. Technology itself is the 'enabler', which provides short-term advantage and the opportunity to develop new systems and to capture and use potentially valuable information. But, normally, competitors will be able to purchase the same technology, and any advantages could soon be negated. However, the new information systems that developed, utilizing the technology, could provide advantages that may be less vulnerable to erosion by competitive copying. The potential gain will depend on how conclusively and exclusively the systems alter business processes and relationships.

In time, however, the existing competition or new entrants enticed into the profitable parts of industry could redefine the relationships by introducing alternative information systems. If the firm wishes to sustain its competitive advantage, it must use the information gleaned from its systems to improve its products or services—to match the requirements of the marketplace or influence its development.

THE MANAGEMENT IMPLICATIONS

By viewing IS/IT evolution another way, we can portray the management implications ascending from the basement of the business to the penthouse executive suite, from where strategic vision is possible and, more importantly, IS/IT can be incorporated into senior management's 'theory of the business'.[59] Figure 1.5 attempts to summarize the changing focus.

The focus of data processing was, and still is, on the effective application of systems and technology to automating operations and thereby increasing efficiency. The planning focus is therefore on the business tasks involved in the project—the application and its successful design and implementation. The main prerequisite for success is a design for the system that carries out the operation to improve efficiency.

Management information systems involved user management in considering the information they used and how they used it. The IS professionals had to find new techniques of information analysis (such as data modelling and entity analysis) to devise ways of organizing and delivering information for effective use by management. Since managers rarely rely on a single source for information, the focus of planning has moved to the integration of individual systems into coherent sources of management information.

Before the SIS era, the view of IS/IT in the business was an internal resource, over which management had total discretion as to its use. The portfolio models mentioned earlier described the overall structure and logic of the process of IS/IT application to the business. It was very

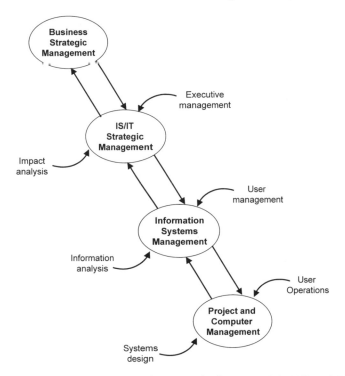

Figure 1.5   *The relationship between the business, SIS, MIS and DP*

much an internally-driven choice as to whether, and how much, to invest in IS/IT. IS/IT strategic management in the SIS era is different for two main reasons. First, the outside world (i.e. competitors, customers and suppliers) may be the instigators of IS/IT uses that affect the organization's own need for new types of applications—external as much as internal factors drive the needs. Second, executive management have to make judgements about such investments in terms of how they will affect the business strategy of the organization and, in some cases, how IS/IT can be used to shape that strategy. Management need some way of assessing the importance of IS/IT in business terms, and the opportunities need to be elicited via business-based techniques to enable that management judgement to be applied. These two needs have been grouped together under the terms *competitive impact analysis*—ways of understanding the potential of IS/IT from a business strategic perspective—and *strategic alignment* of investment in IS/IT with the overall objectives and direction of the organization.

In summary, the contribution and performance of IS/IT in the business has become more significant, hence the level of management involvement required has been elevated to executive level—no longer is their task to sign the cheque; they now have to understand and often decide what is being purchased. However, a note of caution is needed to avoid overstating the importance of IS/IT. As early as 1987, King[60] expressed concern that he saw 'evidence that the competitive advantage argument is beginning to be used excessively—primarily to rationalise projects that cannot otherwise be justified.' This causes the idea to lose management credibility. He noted that we must manage IS/IT and its various applications in accord with the type of contribution it is making—improving efficiency, effectiveness and/or competitiveness through business change—not elevate all aspects to a new and artificial plane of importance. But, of course, an organization cannot afford to ignore the strategic opportunities that IS/IT may offer, and, therefore, 'the potential of information as a strategic resource should be incorporated as a routine element of the business planning process, so that all managers become used to thinking in these new terms.'

Earl[61] supports the argument that focusing on the technology itself does not lead to its successful strategic application. He suggests that the most effective route to achieving strategic benefit from IS/IT is to 'concentrate on rethinking business by analysing current business problems and environmental change—and considering IT as just one ingredient of the solution.' He called for the distinction to be made between IS strategy and IT strategy.[62] This he did as he found that most of the IT strategies, at that time, were strong on technology issues and technical terminology and weak on identifying application needs and business thinking. He suggested that IS strategy be concerned with the organization's required information systems or application set, in essence addressing the 'what' question; and the IT strategy be concerned with the technology, infrastructure and associated specialist skills, or the 'how' question. This relationship is depicted in Figure 1.6.

What can be concluded is that we should treat IS/IT like any other part of the business, which—like marketing, production or purchasing, for example—must be carried out efficiently and effectively for the business to survive but which can also provide competitive/strategic leverage for the organization if it is managed astutely. This implies an approach to developing strategies for information systems and technology that are derived from and integrated with other components of the strategy of the business.

If the organization were developing the marketing part of its business strategy, then it would first analyse its position in the marketplace (i.e. have a marketing input to the process). After evaluating marketing requirements and options in conjunction with other needs, opportunities and constraints, a marketing strategy would result that would be aimed at

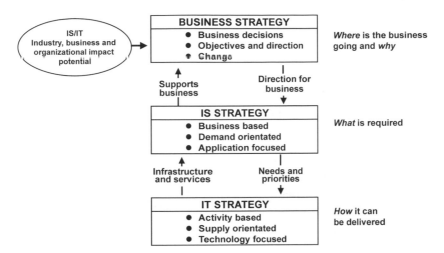

Figure 1.6   *The relationship between business, IS and IT strategies*

achieving the appropriate effects in the marketplace. That is all the diagram shows—that we should do the same with IS/IT: identify the potential impact first, then evaluate what information and systems are needed to enable delivery of the strategy and, then, determine how best to achieve those information systems via the technology.

However, an additional complexity is the fact that information permeates all organizational activity and is used by all organizational employees—from senior management to front-line staff to back-room operatives—in the performance of their job. For example, although marketing and production are business functions, they both demand the processing of information from internal activity as well as from customers, suppliers, regulatory authorities, financial institutions, etc. In addition, the internal information network binds the organization together. Whereas organizations tend to plan other resources, little effort is generally devoted to planning the type of information needed, when used, where it is to be collected and stored, how it will be used or who is responsible for it.

This model is perhaps too simple to deal with complex businesses in rapidly-changing environments and, in later chapters, it will be refined and further developed, but it serves as a good starting point to clarify key relationships and issues.

An Applications Portfolio for the 'Combined Era'

The applications in the overall DP, MIS and SIS portfolio need to be planned and managed according to their existing and future contribution

STRATEGIC	HIGH POTENTIAL
- **Applications that** *are critical to* **sustaining future business strategy**	- **Applications that** *may be important* **in achieving future success**
- **Applications on which the organization** *currently depends* **for success**	- **Applications that are** *valuable but not critical* **to success**
KEY OPERATIONAL	SUPPORT

Figure 1.7   *Applications portfolio*

to the business. Traditional portfolio models considered the relationship of systems to each other and the tasks being performed, rather than the relationship with business success. A portfolio model for the combined era can be derived from a matrix concept developed by McFarlan,[63] which considered the contribution of IS/IT to the business now and in the future, based on its industry impact. This variation on the matrix is represented in Figure 1.7.

The model proposes an analysis of all existing, planned and potential applications into four categories based on an assessment of the current and future business importance of applications. An application can be defined as strategic, high potential, key operational or support, depending on its current or expected contribution to business success.

The original McFarlan Strategic Grid was devised as a way of plotting the overall expected contribution of IS/IT to the business success. This is of limited value, since every enterprise is likely to have some strategic, some key operational, some support and some high-potential applications. Over time, the contents of the portfolio will change, and, for any organization, the contents of segments of the portfolio will be influenced by a variety of internal and external factors, as described later. The usefulness of this derivative matrix is borne out by the ease with which management is willing to and can categorize applications according to their perceived business contribution and potential. The limitations of the original Strategic Grid are also described by the research of Hirschheim *et al.*,[64] who found, when surveying the views of IS management, that 'it was an unhelpful way of categorising (the whole) IS function since virtually every company had systems in all four categories.'

This derivative model has, however, proved effective in providing a framework by which agreement on the portfolio of business applications available and required can be reached from the often divergent views of senior management, functional line managers and the IS/IT professionals. Once that agreement has been reached, the organization can move forward along mutually agreed paths toward delivery of the required portfolio. It is a simple concept, which enables consensus to be achieved both as a strategy is developed and later, as the business and its requirements evolve.

The four quadrants categorize information systems based on their business contribution. While this portfolio will be discussed in detail later in the book, briefly these application categories are:

- *Strategic* applications that are critical to future business success. They create or support change in how the organization conducts its business, with the aim of providing competitive advantage. Note that whether the technology used is 'leading edge' does not indicate that the application is strategic—assessment must be based on business contribution.
- *Key operational* applications that sustain the existing business operations, helping to avoid any disadvantage. It can be argued that, in many industries, substantial numbers of applications (e.g. EPOS [electronic point of sale], ATMs [automated teller machines] and ERP) have become so pervasive that they have become 'mandatory' for survival in the industry.
- *Support* applications which improve business efficiency and management effectiveness but, in themselves, do not sustain the business or provide any competitive advantage.
- *High potential* innovative applications which *may* create opportunities to gain a future advantage, but are as yet unproven.

The portfolio, as described here, shows some obvious similarities to other portfolio matrices used in other management disciplines, such as the Boston Consulting Group's 'Boston Matrix' for product portfolios. Those similarities, concerning balancing the portfolio, life cycles, management approaches, etc., will be examined in detail in Chapter 7, when the value of the matrix in IS/IT strategic management is explored. At this stage, it is sufficient to point out that the four segments will require quite different strategies to achieve successful planning, development, implementation and operation of the applications—because they fulfil different roles in the business.

WHAT IS AN IS/IT STRATEGY?

We have alluded to the concept of an IS/IT strategy, without actually defining exactly what is meant by the concept. Figure 1.6 provided a glimpse of its fundamental components. Essentially, an IS/IT strategy is composed of two parts: an IS component and an IT component. The IS strategy defines the organization's requirement or 'demand' for information and systems to support the overall strategy of the business. It is firmly grounded in the business, taking into consideration both the competitive impact and alignment requirements of IS/IT. Essentially, it defines and prioritizes the investments required to achieve the 'ideal' applications portfolio, the nature of the benefits expected and the changes required to deliver those benefits, within the constraints of resources and systems interdependencies. The specific components of an IS strategy are addressed in Chapter 3. The focus of this book is on presenting an approach for the development of an IS strategy.

The IT strategy is concerned with outlining the vision of how the organization's demand for information and systems will be supported by technology—essentially, it is concerned with 'IT supply'. It addresses the provision of IT capabilities and resources (including hardware, software and telecommunications) and services such as IT operations, systems development and user support.

Throughout this book, we will often use the term *IS demand* to refer to the IS strategy. Similarly, when we use the term *IT supply*, we are referring to the IT strategy.

Strategic Alignment

There is a difference between having an IS/IT strategy and having an IS/IT strategy that is making a contribution to the creation of business value. In the late 1980s, a number of models were developed to assess the extent of alignment of business strategies and IS/IT strategies.

While the concept of strategic alignment has been in use for many years, the Massachusetts Institute of Technology (MIT) *Management in the 1990s* research project attached a particular meaning to the concept in the context of IS/IT management.[65] Their interpretation is based on the premise that the inability of organizations to realize value from IS/IT investments is, in part, due to lack of alignment between business and IS/IT strategies. They developed a model that represented the dynamic alignment between the business strategic context and the IT strategic context. This model is based on the building blocks of strategic integration and functional integration. Henderson and Venkatraman[66] argue that the alignment perspective should—at minimum—involve four

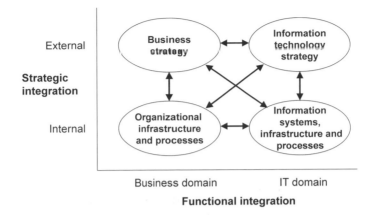

Figure 1.8 *The strategic alignment model*

domains of strategic choice: business strategy, organizational infrastructure and processes, IT strategy and IT infrastructure and processes (see Figure 1.8). Each domain has its own underlying dimensions. Box 1.3 presents the 12 components of alignment. The strategic alignment model (SAM) assesses the range of strategic choices facing managers and explores how they interrelate.

In an empirical study that explored business and IS/IT strategic alignment in the Australian banking industry, Broadbent and Weill[67] reported that central to alignment is the nature of the firm-wide strategy formulation processes of the banks. They noted that a key factor for the banks in developing a realized IS/IT strategy, consistent with business needs, is a flexible and issue-oriented strategy formulation process, with concurrent processes taking place at different organizational levels. In addition, their data indicated that those banks with the most effective management of IS/IT occurred when those resources were managed by those closest to business needs.

Another conclusion from the application of the alignment model is that management should not simply seek to identify and adopt the best available technologies to restructure the organization or streamline the business processes, without due consideration of the two relevant alignments that have IS/IT strategy as the driver: competitive potential and service level.[68] The former identifies the potential impact of IS/IT on business strategy with consequent implications for organizational infrastructure. The latter seeks to provide the best possible supply of IT resources—the IT strategy.

Luftman[69] has developed a Strategic Alignment Maturity Assessment instrument to assess the maturity of an organization's strategic

Box 1.3 The 12 components of alignment (*source:* J. Luftman, 'Assessing business-IT alignment maturity', *Communications of AIS*, Vol. 4, reproduced with permission)

I. Business strategy

1. *Business scope.* Includes the markets, products, services, groups of customers/clients and locations where an enterprise competes as well as the competitors and potential competitors that affect the business environment.

2. *Distinctive competencies.* The critical success factors and core competencies that provide a firm with a potential competitive edge. This includes brand, research, manufacturing and product development, cost and pricing structure, and sales and distribution channels.

3. *Business governance.* How companies set the relationship between management, stockholders and the board of directors. Also included are how the company is affected by government regulations, and how the firm manages its relationships and alliances with strategic partners.

II. Organizational infrastructure and processes

1. *Administrative structure.* The way the firm organizes its businesses. Examples include centralization, decentralization, matrix, horizontal, vertical, geographic, federal and functional.

2. *Processes.* How the firm's business activities (the work performed by employees) operate or flow. Major issues include value-added activities and process improvement.

3. *Skills.* HR considerations such as how to hire/fire, motivate, train/educate and culture.

III. IT strategy

1. *Technology scope.* The important information applications and technologies.

2. *Systemic competencies.* Those capabilities (e.g. access to information that is important to the creation/achievement of a company's strategies) that distinguishes the IT services.

3. *IT governance.* How the authority for resources, risk, conflict resolution and responsibility for IT is shared among business partners, IT management and service providers. Project selection and prioritization issues are included here.

IV. IS infrastructure and processes
1. *Architecture*. The technology priorities, policies and choices that allow applications, software, network, hardware and data management to be integrated into a cohesive platform.
2. *Processes*. Those practices and activities carried out to develop and maintain applications and manage IT infrastructure.
3. *Skills*. IT human-resource considerations such as how to hire/ fire, motivate, train/educate and culture.

alignment. He rates maturity along five levels, beginning with an *ad hoc* process rising to Level 5 where there is an optimized alignment process. He notes that achieving alignment is evolutionary and dynamic, requiring strong support from senior management, good working relationships, strong leadership, appropriate prioritization, trust and effective communication, as well as a thorough understanding of the business and technical environments. These aspects will be addressed throughout this book.

Why Have an IS/IT Strategy?

We have been making a strong argument for organizations to have an IS/ IT strategy. Although we shall explore in depth how an organization can go about developing this strategy, it is worth highlighting that there is a considerable amount of research and practical evidence illustrating that the consequences of *not* having an IS/IT strategy are severe. These implications include:

- Systems investments are made that do not support business objectives.
- Loss of control of IS/IT, leading to individuals often striving to achieve incompatible objectives through IS/IT.
- Systems are not integrated. This can also lead to duplication of effort and data leading to inaccuracy and no coherent information resource.
- No means of setting priorities for IS projects/resources and constantly changing plans leading to lower productivity, etc.
- No mechanisms for deciding optimum resource levels or the best means of supplying systems.
- Poor management information; it is either not available, inconsistent, inaccurate or too slow.

- Misunderstanding between users and IT specialists leading to conflict and dissatisfaction.
- Technology strategy is incoherent and constrains options.
- Inadequate infrastructure investments made.
- All projects evaluated on financial basis only.
- Problems caused by IS/IT investments can become a source of conflict between parts of the organization.
- Localized justification of investments can produce benefits that are actually counterproductive in the overall business context.
- Systems, on average, have a shorter than expected business life and require, overall, considerably greater IS/IT spending to redevelop more frequently than should be necessary.

THE CONTEXT FOR IS/IT STRATEGY

Before embarking on developing an IS strategy, it is important to understand the context within which this strategy is being developed. This context is likely to be different in different organizations. In this section, two perspectives are presented. The first is largely an internal perspective focusing on the role of IS/IT in the organization. The second is an external perspective exploring the overall dynamics of IS/IT.

The Internal Context

Sullivan[70] has suggested a simple matrix to explain how the IS/IT strategic environment is being affected by forces outside the control of any individual organization. He describes two axes within which an organization can consider the implications of these forces:

- *infusion*—the degree to which an organization becomes dependent on IS/IT to carry out its core operations and manage the business;
- *diffusion*—the degree to which IT has become dispersed throughout the organization and decisions concerning its use are devolved.

These axes not only reflect the increasingly strategic nature of IS/IT but also the changing economics of the technology and the ability to use it without the need for highly-skilled technical staff. Sullivan's framework is shown in Figure 1.9. By plotting high and low degrees of infusion and diffusion, four essentially different environments are established. Considering each one in turn:

- *Low diffusion/low infusion*—highly-centralized control of IT resources, and IS is not critical to the business. This, Sullivan describes

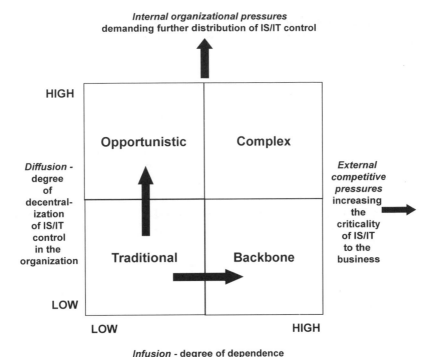

Figure 1.9 *Environments of IS/IT strategy*

as a 'traditional' environment typical of companies using IT solely to improve efficiency on a system-by-system basis.

- *Low diffusion/high infusion*—highly-centralized control, and IS is critical to business operations and control. The business could be seriously disadvantaged if systems fail. Therefore, high-quality systems are needed with, normally, a high degree of integration. The systems have become part of the 'backbone' of the organization, in Sullivan's terms.
- *High diffusion/low infusion*—largely-decentralized control, giving business managers the ability to satisfy their local priorities. Any integration of systems occurs due to user–user cooperation (a 'federation' of interests), not by overall business or IT design. The management approach is essentially 'opportunistic', driven by short-term priorities that may create business advantage in some areas.
- *High diffusion/high infusion*—largely-decentralized control but the business depends on the systems for success, both in avoiding dis-

advantage and in achieving its overall business objectives. Sullivan describes this as a 'complex' environment that is difficult to manage. Too much central control to avoid poor investments will limit innovation, hence new strategic opportunities may be missed; too little control and the core systems may disintegrate.

As organizations evolved through the DP and MIS eras, they tended to move from the low–low quadrant into one or other of the high–low quadrants. This often depended on the timing of their particular evolution and the availability of centralized (mainframe) or decentralized (distributed or PC) technology solutions to the DP and MIS needs. The arrival of the SIS era forced organizations to enter the high–high quadrant, and, depending on the direction taken in the previous eras, the changes to be made will be different. In both cases, however, senior business management will need to make some key decisions about IS/IT in concert, rather than allow local business managers total discretion or the IT department to control the types of investment.

The overall implications are that, as the organization becomes more dependent on IS/IT, essentially to avoid being disadvantaged, the more centralized and structured the approach to planning and control should become. But, to facilitate the innovative uses of IS/IT to create future advantages, technology control needs to be close to the business user to enable appropriate connections between business need *and* technology solution to be made. Gaining advantage and avoiding disadvantage implies both high diffusion and high infusion, and, hence, a complex, balanced set of management approaches (described by Sullivan as 'eclectic'). Most organizations are facing this situation, and both internal and external pressures will increase, as indicated in Figure 1.9. Probably the best interpretation of the word 'eclectic' is to say that every organization needs approaches to IS/IT strategy formulation and planning tailored to its individual circumstances, as determined by the industry and business situation and the organization culture.

The External Context

The dynamics of IT and, hence, the consequences for both business and IS/IT strategy development, are complex. Figure 1.10, however, attempts to shed light on this complexity and capture these dynamics. The Figure first illustrates the duality of technology in that it not only *supports* the strategy of an organization (arrow *a*—strategic alignment) but can also *define* the business, as strategic moves may not be possible without technology (arrow *b*—competitive impact). For example, organizations such as ebay, eSteel and Covisint all deploy business models that are

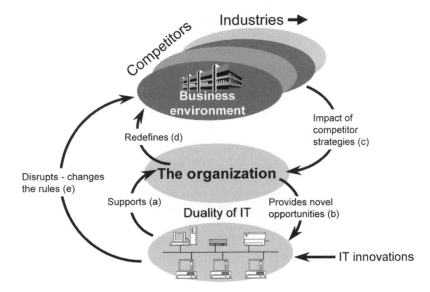

Figure 1.10   *The influence and impact*

fundamentally defined by technology. Technology also facilitates new ways of organizing, new process innovations and can enable the creation of innovative 'network-based businesses'. The Lotus Development Corporation, for example, have a development strategy that 'follows the sun', where a virtual team work 24 hours a day on a project: the day begins in Dublin, eight hours later the work is handed over to Los Angeles and after a further eight hours the work is moved to Singapore, eventually returning back to Dublin 24 hours after it first began. This way of organizing work is critically dependent on technology.

However, an organization does not exist in isolation (unless it occupies a monopoly position), but has competitors and is part of a wider industry system and business environment. Competitors' moves, including new entrants, affect the dynamics of an industry and, consequently, the organization itself and its strategies (arrow *c*); at the same time, strategic plays made by the organization effect competitor moves (arrow *d*). Technological innovations can have disruptive effects on an industry (arrow *e*), rewriting the rules of competition and even challenging traditional notions of industry structure. For example, many retailers and utilities have entered the financial services industry as they argue that they know more about the customers of banks than the banks know about their own customers. Consequently, we may define an industry not by the Standard Industrial Classification (SIC) code, as has traditionally been the case, but by the amount of customer information an organization has.[71]

While this dynamic is driven by new technological innovations, it is less of a technology revolution than a revolution in the economics of information and how information is captured, processed, stored, planned and used in an organization. This point has been eloquently made by Microsoft founder Bill Gates who noted, 'I have a simple but strong belief. The most meaningful way to differentiate your company from your competition, the best way to put distance between you and the crowd, is to do an outstanding job with information. *How you gather, manage, and use information will determine whether you win or lose.*'[72]

It is within this context that management must determine how the organization can best utilize technology to leverage information discontinuities, asymmetries and imperfections for business advantage.[73] For example, recent research has presented evidence suggesting that the control, dissemination and manipulation of CRS information by the owning airlines continued to allow them, despite legislative restrictions, to capitalize on their investment at the expense of competitors during the 1990s.[74]

TOWARD A FOURTH ERA: AN ORGANIZATIONAL IS CAPABILITY

Both the IS research literature pre-1990 and media reports reflected a general optimism concerning IS/IT's potential for creating advantage. More recently, there has been interest in exploring the essence of 'sustainability' from IS, as few organizations continuously achieve advantage from their IS/IT investments and the exemplars often quoted tend to be from different organizations. Although organizations may gain some 'first mover advantage' with an innovative application, it can be quickly copied and does not produce an advantage that is sustainable,[75] particularly when patent protection for IS applications is almost non-existent and where keeping an IS innovation secret is difficult, especially for systems used by customers or suppliers. Indeed, there is a strong argument that the use of standard applications packages such as those developed by vendors (e.g. SAP, BaaN or JD Edwards), a common strategy today, can limit an organization's ability to innovate.[76] At the same time, investments made in technology infrastructure are becoming increasingly significant and inappropriate decisions in this area can severely affect an organization's ability to respond swiftly and flexibly to changing market conditions and can, in fact, become a significant competitive liability.[77]

The strategic management discipline has long sought to elicit the sources of sustainable competitive advantage[78] and there is a significant body of research that has focused on this objective, some of which will be discussed in the next chapter. Yet, what is often not made obvious when reading this literature is that a clear distinction between *sustainability* and *competitive advantage* must be drawn. Competitive advantage is an outcome; sustainability is an ongoing state existing 'after efforts to duplicate that advantage have ceased'.[79] As an outcome, a particular competitive advantage may be short-lived, and is increasingly likely to be so in today's technological world. When competitive advantage is enduring,[80] it is not that a particular outcome is enduring, but that there is 'something' in the very fabric of the organization contributing toward creating ongoing and continuous advantage.

Sustainability, from an IS perspective, can be defined as an organization's ability to continually deliver explicit business value through IS/IT, thus leading to advantage. The challenge that both practitioners and researchers face today is to understand what contributes toward the development of this sustainability. Some insights have been provided by recent research literature. Box 1.4 highlights some relevant extracts from these studies. Box 1.5 describes how Bankinter, a mid-sized Spanish Bank, has deployed IS/IT over the years to achieve continuous advantage through combining innovative business thinking with IT-based opportunities and an ability to deliver new applications and business changes.

In an analysis of some of the early examples of IS/IT and competitive advantage, Kettinger and colleagues[81] concluded that the attainment of sustained IS/IT-based competitive advantage may be more a process of building organizational infrastructure in order to enable what they referred to as 'innovative action strategies'. More recently, Powell and Dent-Micallef[82] investigated the linkages between IT and the performance of firms in the retail industry, asserting that 'IT alone is not enough'. From their study, they concluded that some firms have gained advantage by using IT to leverage intangibles, complementary human and business resources such as organizational flexibility, integrating business-strategy planning and IS/IT strategy, and supplier relationships.

In a conceptual analysis of IS/IT and competitive advantage, Mata *et al.*[83] concluded that only IS management skills are likely to be a source of sustained advantage. They described these skills as the ability of IS managers to understand and appreciate business needs, their ability to work with functional managers, their ability to coordinate IS activities in ways that support other functional managers and their ability to anticipate future needs. They suggest that, in the search for IS/IT-based

Box 1.4   Extracts of findings from recent research studies on IT and competitive advantage (listed in chronological order).

- When every leading firm in an industry has access to the same technology resource, the management difference determines competitive advantage or disadvantage (Keen, 1993).
- The attainment of sustained IT-based competitive advantage may be more a process of building organisational infrastructure in order to enable innovative action strategies as opposed to 'being first on the scene' (Kettinger *et al.*, 1994).
- Successful application of IT are often due more to serendipity rather than any formal planning (Ciborra, 1994).
- Only IT management skills are likely to be a source of sustainable competitive advantage (SCA) (Mata *et al.*, 1995).
- Some firms have gained advantage by using IT to leverage intangibles, complementary human and business resources, such as flexible culture, strategic planning–IT integration, and supplier relationships (Powell and Dent-Micallef, 1997).
- What distinguishes companies deriving significant value from IT is not technical wizardry but the way they handle their IT activities (Dvorak *et al.*, 1997).
- Companies must do more than excel at investing in and deploying IT. They must combine those capabilities with excellence in collecting, organising and maintaining information, and with getting their people to embrace the right behaviours and values for working with information (Marchand *et al.*, 2000).
- Results from this study ... suggest that inconsistent statistical findings about the relationship between IT and firm performance may be attributed to our incomplete understanding of the nature of a firm's resources and skills and to the fact that IT investment dollar serves as a poor surrogate for assessing a firm's IT intensiveness. IT-capability is not so much a specific set of sophisticated technological functionalities as it is an enterprise-wide capability to leverage technology to differentiate from competition (Bharadwaj, 2000).

P.G.W. Keen, 'Information technology and the management difference: A fusion map', *IBM Systems Journal*, Vol. 32, No. 1, 1993, 17–39; W. Kettinger, V. Grover, S. Guha and A.H. Segars, 'Strategic information systems revisited: A study in sustainability and performance', *MIS Quarterly*, Vol. 18, No. 1, 1994, 31–55; C. Ciborra, 'The grassroots of IT and strategy', in C. Ciborra and T. Jelessi, eds, *Strategic Information Systems: A European Perspective*, John Wiley & Sons, Chichester, UK 1994, pp. 3–24; F.J. Mata, W.L. Fuerst and J. Barney, 'Information technology and sustained competitive advantage: A resource-based analysis', *MIS Quarterly*, Vol. 19, 1995, 487–505; T.C. Powell and A. Dent-Micallef, 'Information technology as competitive advantage: The role of human, business and technology resources', *Strategic Management Journal*, Vol. 18, No. 5, 1997, 375–405; R.E. Dvorak, E. Holen, D. Mark and W.F. Meehan, 'Six principles of high-performance IT', *The McKinsey Quarterly*, No. 3, 1997, 164–177; D.A. Marchand, W. Kettinger and J.D. Rollins, 'Information orientation: People, technology and bottom line', *Sloan Management Review*, Summer, 2000, 69–80; A. Bharadwaj, 'A resource-based perspective on information technology and firm performance: An empirical investigation', *MIS Quarterly*, Vol. 24, No. 1, 2000, 169–196.

Box 1.5 Evolution of IS/IT leadership at Bankinter

Although the Spanish banking system ranks as one of the most efficient in the world, Spain is not a technologically-advanced country; Internet penetration is low and the telecommunication system still lags behind its European counterparts. Yet, it is in this environment that Bankinter, a medium-sized bank, has flourished as one of the best Internet banks in Europe. In 2000, *Euromoney* ranked Bankinter, as 'Best European Internet Bank'. Similarly, Salomon Smith Barney included Bankinter as one of the leading Internet banks, ready to take advantages of the opportunities that the Internet offered.

Bankinter was founded in 1965 as a wholesale bank, a joint venture between Bank of America and Banco Santander. Supported by sophisticated information systems and a flexible commercial approach, it has entered into a series of new businesses, thereby changing the bank's business profile throughout the years for middle-market banking to private banking and finally to retail banking. It has been a pioneer in the Spanish banking market in offering competitive conditions to customers not only in terms of price but also in terms of speed, quality and flexibility of services.

The bank has one of the most sophisticated customer bases. It addresses the high end of the retail market by attracting financially-sophisticated clients wishing to receive a different customer service and a more intelligent product offering.

Bankinter is the most developed example of a multi-channel bank in Spain, and possibly in Europe, operating through the following channels:

- branches located in urban areas across Spain;
- virtual branches located in large corporations;
- telephone banking;
- a network of independent agents;
- Internet.

The changing distribution of transactions by channel since 1995 is clearly visible in the table below:

Distribution by channel (%)	1995	2000
Branches	69	39
Electronic banking	14	13
Telephone banking	13	16
Internet	0	27
Cards	3	5

(*Source:* Annual Report, 2000)

Bankinter has always maintained a high level of investments in technology. Nonetheless, in 2000, as a result of its strategic focus on Internet-enabling the entire bank, Bankinter made significant additional investments in this area (24% of total operating cost). The objective of this focus was to migrate all banking products and services to the Internet. According to the Chairman, '*2000 was ... a transition from the traditional banking model to a new multi-channel structure focused on customer service quality and on the great opportunities opened by the new technologies to the banking business ... an enormous transformation effort at the bank to consolidate ... our leadership in Internet banking in Spain and Europe*' (Jaime Botin, Chairman of the Bank, Chairman's letter, Annual Report, 2000).

Bankinter's main competitive strengths are its light and flexible operating structure, superior information and technology systems, and proven ability to adapt to changing market conditions by offering new banking services. It has illustrated how it is possible to compete with limited resources through innovation, intelligent marketing and superior customer service.

Bankinter has always invested heavily in technology—10% of operating costs during the 1990s. These investments, significantly higher than its competitors, have allowed the bank to become the market benchmark in innovation and technology. The implementation of a multi-channel approach has also relied heavily on technology. As CEO Juan Arena repeatedly states, 'This [Bankinter] is not a bank. This is a technology company that happened to do banking.'

With its objective of achieving technology leadership, the following initiatives show how it doggedly approaches this objective:

- Launched first full service telephone-banking operations in 1992, rated as the best and most successful operating model in Spain.
- Opened its Internet-free access service to customers in 1996—its ISP is ranked seventh in Spain with 180,000 customers. This movement revolutionized the ISP market in Spain from a monthly-fee business model to a free-access business model.
- Launched the first Spanish online broker in 1997. Currently, more than 95% of securities transactions pass through this service.
- Full range of online banking completed in 1999. The first bank to support a full online mortgage offering, achieving a market share of 6%.
- Between 1999 and 2000, it created an Internet-enabled organization and migrated all products and services to the Internet.
- Opened virtual branches in the most visited portals and financial portals in 2000 (Lycos Spain and Invertia.com).

Through a combination of innovative business thinking and an IS capability, Bankinter has managed to pave the way in Spanish banking and consistently holds an advantage over its rivals.

sources of sustainable advantage, organizations must focus less on IT, *per se*, and more on the process of organizing and managing IT. Further support for this position is provided by Dvorak *et al.*[84] who concluded that what distinguishes organizations with high-performance IT is not technical wizardry but the way they manage their IS/IT activities. Keen[85] noted that the 'wide difference in competitive organisational and economic benefits that companies gain from this information technology rests in a management difference and not a technical difference. Some business leaders are somehow able to fit the pieces together better than others.' Ross *et al.*[86] and Bharadwaj[87] have argued that, for an organization to apply IT to enhance competitiveness, it must develop an effective 'IS capability'.

However, to date, no one has clearly defined 'IS capability' beyond an expression of its core objective of enabling an organization continuously to derive and leverage value through IS/IT. This presents a serious challenge for organizations who seek to understand and develop an ongoing IS capability, as there is little guidance about how organizational resources contribute toward both its development and deployment. Remember that Dell, Cisco, Bankinter, Amazon.com and the many other companies mentioned in this chapter have gained advantage by using technologies that are non-proprietary and widely available to all. In the final chapter, this concept of IS capability is further explored and developed, and we suggest that it does represent the emergence of a new era.

SUMMARY

The evolution of information systems and technology in a business and organizational context has been erratic, but, without doubt, IS/IT has inexorably increased its importance as the economics and capability have enabled more to be achieved. Increasingly, competitive business environments have provided a motivation to invest in more efficient and effective ways of carrying out business processes and managing the business. Although the progress has been fitful and unsynchronized, patterns can be observed.

The two major 'eras' of DP and MIS are well established and much can be learnt from them—in particular, that the best ways of planning for applications, given the contribution they can make to the business, were only discovered well into the eras, from painful experience in many cases. Often the secret of better IS/IT planning was only discovered after initial enthusiasm had turned to frustration—just before disillusion was about to occur; necessity perhaps being the mother of invention of better approaches!

We are now well into the third era, with bigger prizes and, reciprocally, greater risks, when the business can become critically dependent on its investment in systems not just for its success but for its very survival—planning for information systems has become strategic for many companies. That does not mean that previously-developed, good IS/IT strategy formulation and planning practice is obsolete, merely inadequate for the new era. Can companies afford to wait to find the appropriate strategy approaches until the enthusiasm has faded into frustration? It may then be too late. The SIS era implies winners and losers with IS/IT, not just relative success and failure, which may not reflect directly in the overall business performance.

In this new millennium, increasing business pressures and the improving capabilities and price/performance of IT have led to the consideration of more radical strategies than previously. These can require the transformation of business processes, organizational structures and relationships to achieve major improvements in business performance. Clearly, changes to the organization's information systems will be an integral component of this 'industry re-engineering'—in creating and implementing the new processes and enabling new organization structures to function. But, also, innovations in the use of information and new technologies are essential ingredients in creating the options for change. Hence, strategies for IS will have to be more radical and more adaptable in the future than they have been in the past.

The last obvious conclusion about the evolution of strategic planning for IS/IT is that it is now clearly a process that depends on users and senior management involvement for success. It has become difficult to separate aspects of IS/IT strategy from business strategy. Hence, it is important to use the tools and techniques of business strategic analysis and planning to ensure that approaches to IS/IT strategy formulation and planning are knitted into the pattern of business strategic management. Indeed, the emerging fourth era seeks to embed an IS capability in the very fabric of the organization. Chapter 2 starts this integration process by considering the processes and tools of business strategic management.

ENDNOTES

1. J. Rockart, 'The line takes leadership—IS management in a wired society', *Sloan Management Review*, Summer, 1988, 57–64.
2. M.J. Earl, 'The risks of outsourcing IT', *Sloan Management Review*, Spring, 1996, 26–32.
3. J.C. Mingers, 'What is the distinctive nature and value of IS as a discipline?', *Systemist*, Vol. 17, No. 1, 1995, 18–22.
4. Orlikowski and Iacono have questioned whether we have now gone too far by not devoting enough attention to the artefact of technology. See W.J. Orlikowski and C.S. Iacono, 'Research commentary: Desperately seeking the "IT" in IT research—a call to theorizing the IT artefact', *Information Systems Research*, Vol. 12, No. 2, 2001, 121–134.
5. Figures taken from D. Tapscott, D. Ticoll and A. Lowy, *Digital Capital: Harnessing the Power of Business Webs*, Harvard Business School Press, Boston, Massachusetts, 2000.
6. P. Checkland and S. Holwell, *Information, Systems and Information Systems: Making Sense of the Field*, John Wiley & Sons, Chichester, UK, 1998.
7. P. Checkland, *Systems Thinking Systems Practice*, John Wiley & Sons, Chichester, UK, 1981.
8. See, for example, H.R. Johnston and M. Vitale, 'Creating competitive advantage with interorganisational information systems', *MIS Quarterly*, Vol. 12, No. 2, 1988, 153–165; G.K. Janssens and L. Cuyvers, 'EDI—a strategic weapon in international trade', *Long Range Planning*, Vol. 24, No. 2, 1991, 46–53; B. Konsynski and F.W. McFarlan, 'Information partnerships—shared data, shared scale', *Harvard Business Review*, September–October, 1990, 114–220.
9. Both incumbents and new entrants have learnt expensive lessons in their Net forays. See, for example, A. Edgecliffe-Johnson, 'A billion-dollar mistake', *Financial Times*, 10 July 2001; J. Willman, 'Merrill to scale back online role', *Financial Times*, 7 December 2001;

M. Trombly, 'Bank One's Wingspan fails to take off online', *Computerworld*, 25 September 2000; T. Barker, 'Boo.com on brink as push for funds looks likely to fail', *Financial Times*, 17 May 2000; J. Harding, 'Reed falls 10% after unveiling internet strategy', *Financial Times*, 25 February 2000.

10. M. Subramani and E. Walden, 'The impact of e-commerce announcements on the market value of firms', *Information Systems Research*, Vol. 12, No. 2, 2001, 135–154.

11. P.M. Lee, 'What's in a name.com?: The effects of ".com" name changes on stock prices and trading activity', *Strategic Management Journal*, Vol. 22, No. 8, 2001, 793–804.

12. T. Coltman, T.M. Devinney, A. Latukefu and D.F. Midgley, *E-business: Revolution, Evolution or Hype?* Working Paper 2000/08/Mkt, 2000, INSEAD, Fontainebleau, France.

13. R. Kalakota and A.B. Whinston, *Frontiers of Electronic Commerce*, Addison-Wesley, Boston, 1996.

14. J. Hagel III and M. Singer, *Net Worth: Shaping Markets When Customers Make the Rules*, Harvard Business School Press, Boston, 1999; J. Hagel and J. Rayport, 'The new infomediaries', *McKinsey Quarterly*, No. 4, 1997, 54–70; S. Vandermerwe, 'The electronic "go-between service provider": A new "middle" role taking centre stage', *European Management Journal*, Vol. 17, No. 6, 1999, 598–608.

15. L. Downes and C. Mui, *Unleashing the Killer App: Digital Strategies for Market Dominance*, Harvard Business School Press, Boston, 1999.

16. E.B. Brynjolfsson and M.D. Smith, 'Frictionless commerce? A comparison of Internet and conventional retailers', *Management Science*, Vol. 46, No. 4, 2000, 563–585.

17. M. Porter, 'Strategy and the Internet', *Harvard Business Review*, March, 2001, 63–78.

18. Quoted from G. Moore, *Living on the Fault Line*, Harper, New York, 2000.

19. See also 'Starting up in higher gear: An interview with venture capitalist Vinod Khosla', *Harvard Business Review*, July–August 2000, 92–100; and M.J. Earl and D. Feeny, 'How to be a CEO for the information age', *Sloan Management Review*, Winter, 2000, 11–23.

20. S. Rangan and R. Adner, *Profitable Growth in Internet-Related Business: Strategy Tales and Truths*, Working Paper, 2001/11/SM, February 2001, INSEAD, Fontainebleau, France.

21. G. Hamel, *Leading the Revolution*, Harvard Business School Press, Boston, 2000.

22. Recent research has suggested that 51% of US and 46% of German labour costs are accounted for by interactive events. See P. Butler, T.W. Hall, A.M. Hanna, L. Mendonca, B. Auguste, J. Manyika and B. Sahy, 'A revolution in interaction', *The McKinsey Quarterly*, No. 1, 1997, 5–23.

23. J.F. Rayport and J.J. Sviokla, 'Managing in the marketspace', *Harvard Business Review*, November–December 1994, 141–150.

24. Also called e-hubs, see S. Kaplan and M. Sawhney, 'E-hubs: The new B2B marketplaces', *Harvard Business Review*, May–June 2000, 97–103.

25. See, for example, B. Friedman, P.H. Kahn Jr and D.C. Howe, 'Trust online', *Communications of the ACM*, Vol. 43, No. 12, 2000, 34–40; L.P. Pitt, P. Berthon, R.T. Watson and M. Erving, 'Pricing strategy and the Net', *Business Horizons*, March–April 2001, 45–54; C. Shapiro and H.R. Varian, *Information Rules: A Strategic Guide to the Network Economy*, Harvard Business School Press, Boston, 1999.

26. R.L. Nolan, 'Managing the computing resource: A stag hypothesis', *Communications of the ACM*, Vol. 16, No. 7, 1973, 399–405; C.F. Gibson and R.L. Nolan, 'Managing the four stages of EDP growth', *Harvard Business Review*, January/February 1974, 76–88; R.L. Nolan, 'Managing the crises in data processing', *Harvard Business Review*, March–April, 1979, 115–126.

27. Multistage evolutionary models are widely used to describe a wide variety of phenomena such as the evolution of organizations over time, product life cycle, biological growth, etc.

28. R.N. Anthony, *Planning and Control: A Framework for Analysis*, Harvard University Press, Cambridge, MA, 1965.

29. I. Benbasat, A.S. Dexter, D.H. Drury and R.C. Goldstein, 'A critique of stage hypothesis: theory and empirical evidence', *Communications of the ACM*, Vol. 27, No. 5, 1984, 476–485.

30. J.L. King and K.L. Kraemer, 'Evolution and organisational information systems: An assessment of Nolan's stage model', *Communications of the ACM*, Vol. 27, No. 5, 1984, 466–475.

31. D.H. Drury, 'An empirical assessment of the stages of DP growth', *MIS Quarterly*, Vol. 7, No. 2, 1983, 59–70.

32. J.L. King and K.L. Kraemer, 'Evolution and organisational information systems: An assessment of Nolan's stage model', *Communications of the ACM*, Vol. 27, No. 5, 1984, 466–485.

33. R. Galliers and A. Sutherland, 'Information systems management and strategy formulation: The "stages of growth" model revisited', *Information Systems Journal*, Vol. 1, 1991, 89–114.

34. I. Benbasat and R.W. Zmud, 'Empirical research in information systems: The practice of relevance,' *MIS Quarterly*, Vol. 23, No. 1, 1999, 3–16.
35. C. Wiseman, *Strategy and Computers*, Dow Jones-Irwin, Homewood, Illinois, 1985.
36. A. Friedman, 'The stages model and the phases of the IS field', *Journal of Information Technology*, Vol. 9, 1994, 137–148.
37. Today, the 'information centre' concept is usually referred to as a 'helpdesk' or 'service centre'. S.R. Magal, H.H. Carr and H.J. Watson, 'Critical success factors for information centre managers', *MIS Quarterly*, Vol. 12, No. 4, 1988, 423–425.
38. R. Hirschheim, M.J. Earl, D. Feeny and M. Lockett, 'An exploration into the management of the IS function: Key issues and an evolving model', in *Proceedings of the Joint International Symposium on IS: Information Technology Management for Productivity and Strategic Advantage*, IFIP TC-8, Open Conference, Singapore, March 1988.
39. While Office Automation was a popular concept in the early 1980s, due primarily to the arrival of the PC, in fact researchers were writing about OA back in the 1960s. See, for example, D.R. Hoos, 'The impact of office automation on workers', *International Labour Review*, Vol. 32, No. 4, 1960, 363–388; and D.R. Hoos, 'When the computer takes over the office', *Harvard Business Review*, November–December 1960, 102–112.
40. For more information on VBA, see A. Kambil and E. van Heck, 'Reengineering the Dutch Flower Auctions: A framework for analyzing exchange organizations', *Information Systems Research*, Vol. 9, No. 1, 1998, 1–19; and J. Heezen and W. Baets, 'The impact of electronic markets: The case of the Dutch Flower Auctions', *Journal of Strategic Information Systems*, Vol. 5, 1996, 317–333.
41. See E. Muller, 'Dutch flower auction blooms', *Financial Times*, 11 October 2001.
42. J.D. Pemberton, G.H. Stonehouse and C.E. Barber, 'Competing with CRS-generated information in the airline industry', *Journal of Strategic Information Systems*, Vol. 10, No. 1, 2001, 59–76.
43. C. Wiseman, *Strategy and Computers*, Dow Jones-Irwin, Homewood, Illinois, 1985.
44. D.J. Isenberg, 'How senior managers think', *Harvard Business Review*, November–December 1984, 81–90; W.H Agor, 'How top executives use their intuition to make important decisions', *Business Horizons*, January–February 1986, 49–53.
45. There is a body of research that has explored the success factor of end-user computing. See, for example, M. Alavi, R.R. Nelson and I. Weiss, 'Strategies for end-user computing: An integrative framework', *Journal of Management Information Systems*, Vol. 4, No. 3, Winter, 1987–1988; S. Rivard and S. Huff, 'Factors of success for end-user computing', *Communications of the ACM*, Vol. 31, No. 5, 1988, 552–561; E.M. Trauth and E. Cole, 'The organizational interface: A method for supporting end users of packaged software', *MIS Quarterly*, Vol. 16, No. 1, 1992, 35–53.
46. P.A. Strassman, *The Information Payoff*, Free Press, New York, 1985.
47. P.A. Strassman, *The Squandered Computer: Evaluating the Business Alignment of Information Technology*, The Economics Press, New Canaan, Connecticut, 1997 and *Information Productivity: Accessing the Information Management Costs of US Industrial Companies*, The Economics Press, New Canaan, Connecticut, 1997; A. von Nievelt, 'Managing with IT: A decade of wasted money?' *Information Strategy: The Executive's Journal*, Vol. 9, No. 4, 1993, 5–17; *Productivity in the United States, 1995–2000*, McKinsey Global Institute, October 2001.
48. R.D. Galliers and E. K. Somogyi, 'From data processing to strategic information systems: A historical perspective', in R.D. Galliers and E.K. Somogyi, eds, *Towards Strategic Information Systems*, Abacus Press, 1987, 5–25.
49. C. Wiseman, *Strategy and Computers*, Dow Jones-Irwin, Homewood, Illinois, 1985.
50. For example, see F.W. McFarlan, 'Information technology changes the way you compete', *Harvard Business Review*, May–June 1984, 93–103; B. Ives and G.P. Learmonth, 'The information system as a competitive weapon', *Communications of the ACM*, Vol. 27, No. 12, 1984, 1193–1201.
51. C. Ciborra, 'The grassroots of IT and strategy', in C. Ciborra and T. Jelessi, eds, *Strategic Information Systems: A European Perspective*, John Wiley & Sons, Chichester, UK, 1994, 3–24.
52. W. Kettinger, V. Grover, S. Guha and A.H. Segars, 'Strategic information systems revisited: A study in sustainability and performance', *MIS Quarterly*, Vol. 18, 1994, 31–55.
53. R.I. Benjamin, J.F. Rockart, M.S. Scott Morton and J. Wyman, 'Information technology: A strategic opportunity', *Sloan Management Review*, Spring 1984, 3–10.
54. M.H. Notowidigdo, 'Information systems: Weapons to gain the competitive edge', *Financial Executive*, Vol. 52, No. 3, 1984, 20–25.
55. N. Venkatraman, 'IT induced business re-configuration', in M.S. Scott Morton, ed., *The*

Corporation of the 1990s: Information Technology and Organizational Transformation, Oxford University Press, New York, 1991, 122–158.

56. P.G.W. Keen, *Shaping the Future*, Harvard Business School Press, Cambridge, Massachusetts, 1991.

57. Interview by Joe Peppard with Gerald Gregory, Director of Marketing Britannia Building Society, September 2001.

58. Presentation by B.R. Keeting, *Transforming the Business with Information*, Cranfield School of Management, 25 July 1995.

59. A phrase coined by Peter Drucker referring to the assumptions upon which the organization has been built. See P.F. Drucker, 'The theory of the business', *Harvard Business Review*, September–October, 1994, 95–104.

60. W.R. King, 'It's time to get out of the dark', *Datamation*, July, 1987.

61. M.J. Earl, 'Putting IT in its place: A polemic for the nineties', *Journal of Information Technology*, Vol. 7, 1992, 100–108.

62. M.J. Earl, 'Information systems strategy formulation', in R.J. Boland and R.A. Hirschheim, eds, *Critical Issues in Information Systems Research*, John Wiley & Sons, Chichester, UK, 1987.

63. F.W. McFarlan, 'Information technology changes the way you compete', *Harvard Business Review*, May–June 1984, 93–103.

64. R. Hirschheim, M.J. Earl, D. Feeny and M. Lockett, 'An exploration into the management of the IS function: Key issues and an evolving model', in *Proceedings of the Joint International Symposium on IS: Information Technology Management for Productivity and Strategic Advantage*, IFIP TC-8, Open Conference, Singapore, March 1988.

65. M.S. Scott Morton, ed., *The Corporation of the 1990s: Information Technology and Organizational Transformation*, Oxford University Press, New York, 1991.

66. J.C. Henderson and N. Venkatraman, 'Strategic alignment: Leveraging information technology for transforming organisations', *IBM Systems Journal*, Vol. 32, No. 1, 4–16. See also N. Venkatraman, J.C Henderson and S. Oldach, 'Continuous strategic alignment: Exploiting information technology capabilities for competitive success', *European Management Journal*, Vol. 11, No. 2, 1993, 139–149; and J.N. Luftman, P.R. Lewis and S.H. Oldach, 'Transforming the enterprise: The alignment of business and information technology strategies', *IBM Systems Journal*, Vol. 32, No. 1, 1993, 198–221.

67. M. Broadbent and P. Weill, 'Improving business and information strategy alignment: learning from the banking industry', *IBM Systems Journal*, Vol. 32, No. 1, 1993, 162–179.

68. N. Venkatraman, J.C Henderson and S. Oldach, 'Continuous strategic alignment: Exploiting information technology capabilities for competitive success', *European Management Journal*, Vol. 11, No. 2, 1993, 139–149.

69. J. Luftman, 'Assessing business-IT alignment maturity', *Communications of the AIS*, Vol. 4, December 2000.

70. C. H. Sullivan, 'Systems planning in the information age', *Sloan Management Review*, Winter, 1985, 3–11.

71. J. Sampler, 'Redefining industry structure for the information age', *Strategic Management Journal*, Vol. 19, 1998, 343–355.

72. B. Gates, *Business @ the Speed of Thought: Using a Digital Nervous System*, Penguin Books, London, 1999.

73. In the strategic management literature, Chakravarthy recently noted that most of the existing frameworks assume a benign environment that is simple and not very dynamic. See B. Chakravarthy, 'A new strategic framework for coping with turbulence', *Sloan Management Review*, Winter, 1997, 69–82. See also H.G. Courtney, J. Kirkland and S.P. Viguerie, 'Strategy under uncertainty', *Harvard Business Review*, November–December, 1997,
66–97; and G. Hamel, 'Strategy, innovation and the quest for value', *Sloan Management Review*, Winter, 1998, pp. 7–14.

74. J.D. Pemberton, G.H. Stonehouse and C.E. Barber, 'Competing with CRS-generated information in the airline industry', *Journal of Strategic Information Systems*, Vol. 10, No. 1, 2001, 59–76.

75. E.K. Clemons and M.C. Row, 'Sustaining IT advantage: The role of structural difference', *MIS Quarterly*, Vol. 15, No. 3, 1991, 275–292; F.J. Mata, W.L. Fuerst and J. Barney, 'Information technology and sustained competitive advantage: A resource-based analysis', *MIS Quarterly*, Vol. 19, No. 4, 1995, 487–505.

76. T.H. Davenport, 'Putting the enterprise back into enterprise systems', *Harvard Business Review*, July–August, 1998, 121–131; C.K. Prahalad and M.S. Krishnan, 'The new meaning of quality in the information age', *Harvard Business Review*, September–October 1999, 109–118.

77. M. Broadbent and P. Weill, 'Management by maxim: How business and IT managers can create IT infrastructures', *Sloan Management Review*, Spring, 1997, 77–92; P.G.W. Keen, *Shaping the Future: Business Design Through Information Technology*, Harvard Business School Press, Boston, 1991.

78. Hamel and Heene have written that '[s]ustaining a profitable existence and thus creating welfare and reduced poverty in society is the basic mission of any company. Academics (as well as consultants) should develop concepts, techniques, approaches and frameworks to assist business people in fulfilling this basic mission. Based on this general mission, a theory of strategic management should primarily focus on the dynamics of "sustainable competitive advantage" as one of the most prominent driving forces for long-term profitability and survival' (p. 315). See G. Hamel and A. Heene, eds, *Competence-Based Competition*, John Wiley & Sons, Chichester, UK, 1994.

79. Barney writes that an organization is said to 'have a competitive advantage when it implements a value creating strategy not simultaneously being implemented by any current or potential competitors' (p. 102). See J.B. Barney, 'Firm resources and sustained competitive advantage', *Journal of Management*, Vol. 17, 1991, 99–120.

80. Barney notes that it is not the 'period of calendar time that defines the existence of a sustained competitive advantage, but the inability of current and potential competitors to duplicate that strategy that makes a competitive advantage sustained' (p. 103). See J.B. Barney 'Firm resources and sustained competitive advantage', *Journal of Management*, Vol. 17, 1991, 99–120.

81. W. Kettinger, V. Grover, S. Guha and A.H. Segars, 'Strategic information systems revisited: A study in sustainability and performance', *MIS Quarterly*, Vol. 18, No. 1, 1994, 31–55.

82. T.C. Powell and A. Dent-Micallef, 'Information technology as competitive advantage: The role of human, business and technology resources', *Strategic Management Journal*, Vol. 18, No. 5, 1997, 375–405.

83. F.J. Mata, W.L. Fuerst and J. Barney, 'Information technology and sustained competitive advantage: A resource-based analysis', *MIS Quarterly*, Vol. 19, 1995, 487–505.

84. R.E. Dvorak, E. Holen, D. Mark and W.F. Meehan, 'Six principles of high-performance IT', *The McKinsey Quarterly*, No. 3, 1997, 164–177.

85. P.G.W. Keen, 'Information technology and the management difference: A fusion map', *IBM Systems Journal*, Vol. 32, No. 1, 1993, 17–39.

86. J.W. Ross, C. Mathis Beath and D. Goodhue, 'Develop long-term competitiveness through IT assets', *Sloan Management Review*, Fall, 1996, 31–42.

87. A. Bharadwaj, 'A resource-based perspective on information technology and firm performance: An empirical investigation', *MIS Quarterly*, Vol. 24, No. 1, 2000, 169–196.

2
An Overview of Business Strategy Concepts and the IS/IT Strategy Implications

As discussed in Chapter 1, most organizations are today aware that information systems strategies must be developed within the wider context of the corporate and business strategy formulation and implementation processes. Further, it has become increasingly important, in the last decade, that investments made in information systems and technology throughout an organization are directed toward the achievement of business objectives and plans. This does not imply that IS/IT is only a means of implementing chosen strategies; IS/IT can also be an enabler of new business strategies, strategies that are not possible without the application of IT. However, in the past, a significant proportion of the money spent on information systems and technology has had little relationship to those objectives, which is one of the many reasons why the potential benefits from investments made in IT have frequently not been realized. Success in managing IS/IT involves both maximizing the return on the money invested in acquiring, processing and using information within an organization, and enabling the strategic use of information either to gain competitive advantage or to repel competitive threats.

Consequently, it is vital that business managers are involved in the process of developing information and systems strategies, which means that this process must be clearly understood by those managers.[1] It must be related to their business issues and be conducted using tools and techniques that are familiar to them, in a language that they understand, completely avoiding the jargon that surrounds IT.

Formal approaches to business planning began in the 1950s and, since then, a wide range of approaches and planning tools and techniques have been developed. These continue to evolve in response to the increasingly complex and rapidly changing business environment. In this chapter some of these well-established business strategy and planning concepts and techniques are briefly outlined. As each of the concepts or techniques is discussed, implications that can immediately be derived for the development of IS strategies are considered. The approaches adopted by organizations for the strategic planning IS/IT are discussed in more detail in the next chapter.

THE EVOLVING NATURE OF STRATEGY AND STRATEGIC PLANNING IN ORGANIZATIONS

All organizations have some form of strategy, whether implicit or explicit, and the essence of business strategy lies in creating future competitive advantages faster than competitors. Yet, formal strategic planning, as we know it today, is a relatively recent phenomenon and arose as a result of developments in program planning and budgeting developed during World War II. During the 1950s, a second stream of thought, pioneered at the Harvard Business School, highlighted the importance of having an overall corporate strategy to integrate the various functional areas.

Yet, as early as 1976, Ansoff *et al.*[2] recognized the failure of strategic planning, at that time, to resolve the problems of the firm in the post-industrial era. They suggested *strategic management*, within which formal planning would be but one component of a much more complex sociodynamic process that brings about strategic change in an organization.

Exploring the evolution of strategy and strategy planning in organizations, Gluck *et al.*[3] developed a model to describe its increasing maturity. Although there have been many changes in the business world, particularly since 1980, the model describes how the core issues have evolved, along with the need for new approaches to developing and implementing strategies. The basic model is depicted in Figure 2.1.

In Phase 1, the focus is on cash flow and annual financial planning, and involves relatively simple techniques to develop medium-term budgets. These exercises are usually carried out internally, department by department, and consolidated. The focus of planning is to reduce everything to a single financial issue—meeting the budget.

At Phase 2, the focus is on trying to predict, or forecast, what is likely to happen within, say, a three to five-year planning horizon, usually by reference to historical performance, analysed and projected into the future using internal trends and external parameters such as economic and market research data. It forecasts sales and market growth and predicts the effect on income and expenses and changes to the balance

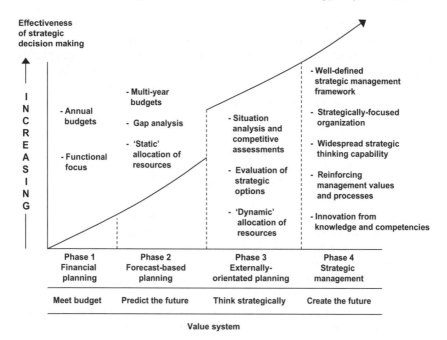

Figure 2.1   *Evolution of strategic management maturity*

sheet. Plans, though, are still quantitative and internally orientated, focusing on the gap between what is targeted and the resources that are available.

Within Phase 3, the organization, for the first time, considers the external environment to gain a thorough understanding of the nature of competition in its industry, in order to assess and consider potential threats and position itself to gain advantage. The organization might need to revise its product portfolio to match demands in more attractive market sectors, or increase the value-added features of existing products and services, or significantly reduce its unit costs. Each of these situations implies the identification of new product development, sourcing or marketing options and their evaluation to find those that not only suit the organization, but also best satisfy the pressures and demands of the competitive marketplace.

By Phase 4, the organization is driven by innovation and becomes capable of creating its own business environment, at least to some extent. This phase implies that, while products and competitive positioning are clearly important, they are only so at a given point in time. In today's dynamic business environment, products quickly become obsolete and the only real source of competitive advantage is the ability to respond consistently to changing markets with new products and ever-improved competitiveness. The organization's values, culture and structure will reinforce the processes and competencies required to develop and sustain a leading role in the industry thus enabling it to have significant control over its own destiny. Obviously, sustaining this leadership will require continuing innovation.

While some organizations are capable of a truly creative strategy, at least for significant parts of the business, they also have to monitor the competitive environment, forecast effectively and deliver an annual profit. Progressing to Stages 3 and 4 implies that 1 and 2 are handled effectively, so that strategic thinking can be converted to the required financial results. The major step change depicted in the move from Stage 2 to 3 reflects the reorientation to adopt an external perspective and obtain the new knowledge required by the organization, to assess realistically what it does and how well it does it in the context of its competitive environment. The model is not time dependent; unfortunately, some organizations still remain in Phase 1.

It is worth making a few observations about the evolving nature of strategic management issues based on this maturity model:

- The approach to IS/IT strategy development is often, despite the best of intentions, 'behind' the approach adopted for business strategy formulation. While the organization may well be managing overall in Phase 3 or even 4, the approach to IS/IT strategy may, in reality, still be in Phase 1 (the current project plan and annual IT budget driving the plans) or perhaps Phase 2 (IT management planning future resource requirements based on a forecast of likely needs). Where this occurs, the IT unit is often seen by the business as 'living in a world of its own' and unable to react to the rapidly changing environment. In many ways, the purpose of this book is to realign the processes and thinking of IS/IT strategic planning with the real-world pressures and requirements in Phases 3 and 4.
- During the early 1990s, many organizations actually regressed down this maturity curve as recession deepened and they were forced to focus on short-term financial survival. In the UK, government policies saw the introduction of privatization, devolvement to agencies and market trading (e.g. in the National Health Service [NHS]), forcing many organizations to plan on a much shorter time horizon, often based on one-year financial measures. As a result, many public and private sector organizations that had perhaps been planning for the long term now had to produce improvement in financial performance year on year. This seriously affected those investment plans, including IS/IT, that cannot often

easily deliver demonstrable improvements within a 12-month time horizon.

- During the 1990s, the business environment changed at a faster pace than ever before, creating increased uncertainty and making forecasting more difficult. Except in a few, relatively stable industries, it was no longer possible to interpret the past as a reliable indicator of future trends. Even though the period saw the longest sustained period of economic growth in history, increasing globalization, rapid technological advances and increasingly sophisticated customers meant that firms not adept in Phases 3 and 4 of the model suffered badly. Even household names such as Marks & Spencer in the UK and Sears in the US found the retail clothing market increasingly difficult to understand and predict. Since the 1980s, shareholders have been demanding more certain and higher returns, making strategic planning more difficult, given the increasing uncertainty about future forecasts. This has also, therefore, shortened the planning horizon causing management to focus on shorter-term, financial performance but also change strategies more frequently.

- It is not coincidental that the focus on creating distinctive brands and brand strategies has increased over the last 20 years. *Brand management* is aimed at achieving success in Phase 4—external recognition of real or perceived uniqueness, plus the clarity of strategy required to marshal and align all the internal resources and capabilities 'behind the brand'.

- In the late 1990s, the commercialization of the Internet and the reduced cost of information technologies offered many opportunities to create 'new' strategies—to reach new markets and offer new products and services. As is usual in such circumstances, it was difficult for many large incumbent companies to adjust their strategies to become more creative and less risk averse. Most of the 'new economy' developments were initiated by start-ups, the 'dot.coms', who had no legacy of business structure or existing IS/IT environment to inhibit them. But, as rapidly became clear, neither did most of them have the full set of organizational competencies, those acquired in Stages 1–3, to succeed in highly competitive markets and industries. However, the speed with which new competitors could emerge through innovative applications of IT has forced many, more conservative organizations to realize that astute investment in IS/IT can enhance a business strategy, or at least that a lack of investment could leave the organization at a serious disadvantage. While it is oversimplistic to state that the arrival of 'e-business' at last made senior management realize the importance of IT, it was only in the year 2000 that companies' share prices were affected by whether or not they had an e-business strategy![4]

Strategy versus Planning

Recent debates around strategy and planning have highlighted a misconception and confusion that exists in many organizations regarding the two terms.[5] Mintzberg[6] asserts that 'strategic planning' is not 'strategic thinking'. He writes, 'when companies understand the difference between *planning* and *strategic thinking*, they can get back to what the strategy-making process should be: capturing what the manager learns from all sources (both the soft insights from his or her personal experiences and the experiences of others throughout the organisation and the hard data from market research and the like) and then synthesising that learning into a vision of the direction that the business should pursue.'

Similarly, Hamel[7] asserts that planning is about programming not discovering, that strategy making must be democratic and is not the sole preserve of senior managers. He wryly poses the question of how often has the monarch led the uprising? Given the creative nature of the strategy process, he notes that you 'cannot see the end from the beginning', a situation that is similar when embarking on developing an IS/IT strategy.

Porter suggests many organizations have confused operational effectiveness with strategy. While not rejecting the need for operational effectiveness, he argues that it is a necessary but not a sufficient condition. Operational effectiveness means performing similar activities better than rivals perform them. In contrast, strategic positioning means performing different activities from rivals' or performing similar activities in different ways.

This implies that 'strategy' is not the result of strategic planning but the product of a number of processes. Strategy can therefore be defined as: *an integrated set of actions aimed at increasing the long-term well-being and strength of the enterprise relative to competitors.*[8]

There are essentially three interrelated processes that can contribute to the establishment of such a strategy:

- *strategic thinking*—creative, entrepreneurial insight into the ways the enterprise could develop;
- *strategic planning*—systematic, comprehensive analysis to develop a plan of action;
- *opportunistic decision making*—effective reaction to unexpected threats and opportunities.

To achieve any or all of these, a thorough understanding of the business environment, pressure groups, stakeholders and the enterprise's capability is required. Having an effective combination of coherent planning, incisive thinking and astute opportunism is probably best described as *strategic management*, which includes not only setting the strategy but also implementing and adapting it.

Notwithstanding these arguments, organizations require a framework to guide strategizing and strategic decision making. Indeed, tools and techniques can be useful in provoking the thinking necessary to develop insights, visions and innovative strategies.

THE STRATEGIC FRAMEWORK

Many of the analysis techniques of strategy formulation are used to focus on a particular strategic issue such as the analysis of competitors, the strength of the existing portfolio of products or the relative merits of different courses of action. However, there exists a far broader context within which the techniques and tools are applied, described here as the 'strategic framework'. Any organization in Stages 3 and 4 of the above model will need to consider most aspects of this framework to succeed.

The framework considers the factors involved in business strategic management in three layers (see Figure 2.2):

- the external environment;
- pressure groups and stakeholders;
- internal business strategizing and planning.

Each of these is considered briefly below, before some of the approaches and tools that can be used to analyse their impact and formulate appropriate strategies are outlined.

External Environment

Businesses or enterprises operate within a broadly-defined external environment, many aspects of which need to be thoroughly analysed, understood and interpreted early in the business strategy process. The six factors that are of enduring importance and relevant to most industries and organizations are considered here.

These environmental factors are normally considered together, in the early stages of strategic thinking, using a PEST (Political, Economic, Social and Technological) analysis approach (legal factors are normally included with political factors and ecology with social factors in a

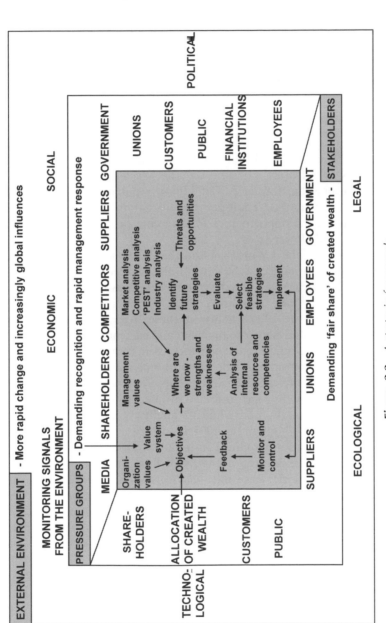

Figure 2.2 A strategic framework

standard PEST analysis). These are important because of the speed with which they are changing and the effect they have on an increasingly 'global' business marketplace. Careful monitoring of these factors may lead to significant business opportunities or identification of potential threats in time to take action to mitigate the effects. Some examples will serve to illustrate the need for analysis.

Economic

The swing in emphasis to monetarism and the economics of free market could not have been predicted before the end of the 1970s. However, today, this is a feature not only of the Western world but also of Eastern Europe, the former Soviet Union republics, China and other ex-communist countries. The opportunities for increased trade are undeniable, as are the opportunities for sourcing products from countries with significantly lower costs.

The impacts of Third World debt on the Western financial system and the vigorous performance of the newly-industrialized countries with their strong trading surpluses had led Western countries to focus their attention on the Far East and away from Africa and South America. However, during the 1990s, many of those 'tiger' economies suffered severe recessions, due mainly to financial and currency problems resulting from an inability to adapt to the demands of an increasingly 'free market' for trade. Protectionism in many of their home markets had concealed a lack of real competitiveness in earlier years. As a result, companies have looked to Eastern Europe and at an increasingly attractive Latin America, due primarily to political stability, for both markets and sources of supply—although the 2001 monetary crisis in Argentina highlights that the situation requires continual appraisal.

The effects of the relative strengths of different currencies, inflation rates, money market rates and tax legislation impose increasingly complex challenges on global business. They affect decisions on where to invest and develop new markets and where to take profits.

It was argued (by some!) during 2000 that, due to the commercialization of the Internet and the restructuring of industries that was predicted, the 'old economy' logic no longer prevailed and that the economic 'rules' had been changed.[9] It seems this was due to 'new millennium euphoria', and not based on substantive evidence or analysis, given the rapid return to the old economy in 2001. However, investment in new economy stocks created a short-lived boom for high-tech companies, many of which invested too much in high-risk options. The licence fees paid by telecom companies for '3rd generation' mobile operations (so-called 3G) have left them with high levels of debt as income streams from existing operations reduced. Others, like Marconi, reconfigured their business from 'old' to 'new' economy activities, with devastating results when the predicted explosive growth did not materialize.

Social

The social environment can exert a major impact on strategies and strategic options. For example, within the social environment, there is a growing awareness of the problems and opportunities afforded to organizations by the increasing numbers of retired people and their relative affluence. As the general population is living longer, there is a consequent demand on pensions and geriatric health-care services. On the other hand, this part of the population has a high level of disposable income, with few commitments. It is anticipated that a large proportion of children born in Western Europe in 1988 will live to be 100. The impact of this is going to be enormous. Governments will have to contend with supporting a large number of retired people from a shrinking taxable labour force. On the other hand, there is ample scope for changing the face of the leisure and consumer retailing industries to cater for the tastes of the older population. IT itself has now become a 'social factor', in terms of social inclusion or exclusion being affected by individuals' access to the Internet as both an information source and channel of communication. Management philosopher Charles Handy[10] talks about the 'information haves' and the 'information have-nots' and the social implications of a group that are becoming increasingly marginalized. Many companies now have strategies for social responsibility. Vodafone Group's CEO has noted that, by extending the company's customer base, expanding geographically and developing innovative services, the company has achieved a global reach that brings worldwide responsibilities. 'Fulfilling our passion for excellence involves reaching the highest standard of social responsibility, just as much as providing outstanding service to our customers.'[11]

Political

Although the European Economic Community had existed for 30 years before 1992, the Maastricht Treaty forming the European Union was one of the most significant changes to take place in Europe for many years, with the dismantling of trade barriers between member states and the removal of restrictive legislation. This has been followed by a synchronization of taxes on purchases, elimination of tariffs and, from 1 January 2002, a common currency across the majority of member states. Combined with the legislation that provides for free movement of labour within the Union, the EU will soon be a market of sufficient buying power and size to be able to offer a real competitive threat to the US domestic market.

On the wider front, there is also a similar strengthening of economic ties between the USA and its North and South American and Pacific Rim trading customers. It is very important, clearly, that enterprises should take note of these developments in their strategizing.

The 1990s were a period of (relatively) political stability across the world, following the dramatic changes at the end of the previous decade. The future may not prove as conducive to global trade development if major 'new' economies become politically unstable, as is currently the case in Indonesia. The 11 September 2001 terrorist attacks in the USA have also resulted in further destabilization of the geopolitical environment and heightened levels of uncertainty.

Legal

In direct response to the impact of IT, many countries have introduced some form of Data Protection or Privacy Act, in an attempt to protect the interests of individuals from inappropriate use by corporations and governments of information about them (see Box 2.1 for an overview of UK legislation). However, the extent of coverage varies across countries.

The Internet has raised issues related to privacy as it provides unprecedented opportunities to profile the browsing and consumption habits of website visitors.[12] In the USA, privacy advocates led an outcry over disclosures that DoubleClick, the biggest Internet advertising company, was quietly accumulating masses of personalized information on people's surfing and purchasing habits. Many companies do not realize that there are legal limits to what they can do with the data they collect.

The status and validity of 'paperless trading', via e-commerce, is an area where the laws of different countries have to cope with new situations and also need to be more consistent. Internet-based trading has created new legal problems regarding the point of transfer of ownership and where tax on purchases is to be paid and by whom. The music industry is the first to 'go to court' to resolve the increasingly sensitive issues of intellectual property and royalties for material sold (or otherwise) across the Internet. It is suggested that computer-based fraud is now frequent and is costing organizations billions of pounds—but detection is difficult, and successful prosecution has proved nearly impossible.

Ecological

The ecological lobby has become increasingly vocal throughout the world. The emergence of the Green movement and Green political

Box 2.1   Data Protection Act

The European Union's Directive on Personal Data, implemented in the UK as the Data Protection Act 1998, restricts the use of personal information and, in some cases, makes it illegal. The act limits the use of personal data by requiring 'data controllers' to process such information in accordance with eight data-protection principles. These principles provide that data must be:

- fairly and lawfully processed;
- processed for limited purposes;
- adequate, relevant and not excessive;
- accurate;
- not kept longer than necessary;
- processed in accordance with the data subject's rights;
- secure;
- not transferred to countries without adequate protection.

Personal data are any data relating to individuals, not only UK citizens. Such data include basic details such as names and addresses, perhaps collected when gaining access to a website or in a purchase transaction. E-mails can also be included as they may have registered domains and Internet protocol addresses identifying users' terminals, regarded as personal identifiers and, therefore, within the scope of the Act.

parties in Western Europe are clear signs of an increasing awareness of the need to protect the environment. This has had substantial effects on such diverse activities as commercial whaling and the generation of power, with a swing away from nuclear power generation back to hydrocarbons (with the consequent problems of carbon dioxide and acid rain emissions) and an increasing emphasis on the search for alternative sources of power.

The more radical environmentalists or 'eco-warriors' extended their scope, in the late 1990s, to address social and economic issues. The *Reclaim of the Streets* movement brought the protest into urban areas to highlight both government and corporate neglect of the environment and people in the pursuit of economic goals. Tens of thousands of protestors lobbied the World Trade Organization summits and meetings of the Global Forum to demand action to stop environmental damage and exploitation of the people and resources of developing countries by global corporations. The Internet was used to mobilize the protestors and organize the demonstrations. Technology has enabled protest movements to orchestrate campaigns around the world and become 'global' themselves in order to lobby against the adverse consequences of economic globalization. In the Philippines, the country where text messaging is most popular, the use of the technology by protesters is credited with helping to overthrow the country's former president, Joseph Estrada.

As well as trying to impose limitations on companies, these pressures can lead to increasing activity in research and development, and new business opportunities. Environmental groups argue that a more environmentally-conscious view of the world would create many millions of new jobs as well as 'save the planet'.

Technological

The technological environment, in general, is changing faster than ever before, creating innovative products and services and facilitating new ways of doing business and, in the process, making 'old' products obsolete more quickly. Consider the major changes in the information technologies in the past 15 years. These have included:

- Changes in telecommunications, including fibre optics, satellites and wireless networks, now enable companies and people to communicate far more quickly and extensively, particularly as bandwidth has increased. This has no doubt increased the intensity and speed of business activity as well as enabling more effective interchange and use of information.
- The unceasing improvements in price/performance of computers and software has meant that, for a few hundred pounds, anyone can have access to an immense variety of information resources and the ability to 'process' that information. This effectively 'empowers' the individual, who is able to carry out a greater range of tasks and communicate with far more people. Harnessed properly, this power can enhance an organization's strategic ability, creating agility in the workforce; mismanaged, it can lead to organizational chaos, and the misuse of time and resources.
- As computers become ever more portable, individuals are less deskbound, and some organizations are questioning the need for offices at all. For many companies, the traditional concept of the office has been redefined as merely places to plug-in to a network or meet other people.

- The ability of individuals, as customers, to search for alternative product sources and the emergence of online buying groups, who aggregate the purchasing requirements of many customers, has undoubtedly increased the power of buyers in many consumer industries.
- The advent of digital television offers even further options; not only for commercial organizations but also for provision of services by public sector organizations to members of the communities they serve.
- Further major advances have occurred in the areas of document and image processing, new standards like XML (eXtendable Mark-up Language) will facilitate exchange of all forms of digital images and documents among all types of access devices including the videophones that will arrive in the next decade.

Signals from the external environment must be monitored constantly and interpreted quickly in order to be able to position the enterprise both offensively and defensively for the future. To assist management in obtaining and understanding the implications of such signals, many public databases and other online information sources are now available, providing hard data and commentary on many of the factors described. A key problem is often finding the appropriate sources for relevant, up to date, reliable information.

With very few exceptions, an individual enterprise can only react to its environment, and cannot, by itself, control or change the environment. However, by grouping together with others in the same industry or with a common interest, it is possible for the group to exert influence over its external environment either by direct action (e.g. the establishment of standards and protocols), or indirectly via trade associations that, through effective lobbying, can change or influence laws and regulations. In some cases, a large enterprise can shape the external environment to its particular requirements (e.g. by establishing *de facto* standards), thus creating significant, sustainable, long-term competitive advantage.

Pressure Groups and Stakeholders

The enterprise functions within the context of the external environment and also under the direct influence of two sets of forces. These two groups are represented in Figure 2.2 and are categorized as *pressure groups* and *stakeholders*. Examples of the two categories are considered in Box 2.2.

Pressure groups are characterized by making demands of the organization. They require that the enterprise acknowledges their existence and the effect they can have, and they expect appropriate responses from

Box 2.2   Examples of the influence of pressure groups and stakeholders

Pressure groups

1. *Shareholders:* can exert considerable pressure on companies in terms of how they conduct the business as well as what they do with shareholders' funds. Annual general meetings are more frequently an opportunity for individual shareholders and shareholder groups to demonstrate their power by voting down proposals, rejecting nominated directors and strong questioning of company policies and objectives. Recently, small investors have questioned the justification for large pay rises and valuable share options for senior executives—who were 'saved' from censure by institutional shareholders. A bank had to change its policy on communicating account changes following an orchestrated campaign by discontented members. Some shareholder groups such as pension funds control significant votes and will only invest if they are assured of long-term prospects, based on properly developed long-term plans.

2. *Competitors:* the most obvious pressure group, whose activities are designed to reduce each other's success, but also in combination determine the overall economics and development of the industry in the short and long term.

3. *Customers/suppliers:* are obvious pressure groups, each exerting direct business pressure in its own particular way due to their mutual interdependence; each of them being part of the 'value chain' involved in bringing a product or service into the market. These are dealt with in more detail later in this chapter.

Stakeholders

1. *Shareholders:* who expect increased dividends year on year and an increased stock market valuation (i.e. income and capital growth, the former having become more important over the past few years to meet the cash-flow needs of pensions). There has also been a change in the type of shareholder. Institutional investors and pension funds still control significant blocks of shares, but, with privatization of nationalized industries taking place on a worldwide basis, there are now millions of private individuals who are shareholders. During the dot.com boom and bust of 2000, it was often small shareholders, trading online, who created or amplified market price fluctuations.

2. *Competitors:* are stakeholders to the extent they share an interest in the success of the industry overall, and the successs or failure of an organization can influence the view of investors of the whole industry. In reality, successful industries need strong constituent firms.

3(a). *Customers:* who are constantly requiring higher-quality products or services from the enterprise at the same or lower cost, in order to improve their own financial performance.

3(b). *Suppliers:* who are always looking for an increase in the volume and price of the goods that they sell to or via the enterprise.

4. *Government:* exerts pressure in a number of different ways by framing legislation and then monitoring conformance. This includes monopolies and mergers, health and safety legislation, taxation levels and laws, product liability, and both industry regulation and deregulation. Pressure may also be exerted by other groupings such as the United Nations or the European Parliament and Commission, particularly in respect of international standards, trade embargoes and tariffs.

4. *Government:* would expect to benefit from the success of the enterprise by way of increased taxation, overall economic growth, provision of more jobs, training for employees, etc. Equally, much of a country's infrastructure is now provided directly or indirectly by private enterprises and government depends on firms making sufficient profits to make those investments.

5. *Employees:* the pressure that employees can exert can take many forms, including the needs for comparability across job functions, job enrichment, personnel appraisals and evaluations, and less directly in terms of their overall attitude to work.

5. *Employees:* who expect to share in the success of the organization through improved financial reward but also via other demonstrations of success of the company such as pensions, additional holidays and other benefits. Their personal future depends on the success of the company.

6. *Unions:* these exert pressure, particularly when it comes to grievances and working practices. This type of pressure was historically very high during the 1970s but has diminished, in the UK particularly, with the advent of much higher unemployment in the 1980s; and changes in the law. In other countries, unions are seen as more constructive and are often represented on firms' boards.

6. *Unions:* who negotiate for better conditions of service, a better quality of working environment, including investments for safety of employees, more sick pay, more holidays and, of course, higher wages.

7. *The public:* can exert pressure, for example, through the boycotting of certain consumer items, and through the unpredictable nature of fashion. The impact of fashion goes beyond clothes to many other products, including foods, as was shown in the move to more organic food products in the 1990s. Consumer pressure inspired by Greenpeace caused Shell to change its plans to dispose of an obsolete oil rig.

7. *The public:* the general public would expect to see benefits from the success of an enterprise. For example, a successful company in a small town might feel obliged to donate a community centre to the town for the benefit of the people living there. Many communities are dependent on the success of large firms for both economic viability and their social and recreational infrastructure. It is not just employees who gain but also the

many small retailers and service companies in the area. This can be seen from the rapid economic decline of many towns when large factories close. In reverse, when firms are attracted to an area, the value of property rises and new amenities are created.

8. *Financial institutions:* exert pressure by demanding increasing amounts of information to enable the increased level of analytical ability within the institutions. It is important for enterprises to meet the needs of these financial analysts in order to keep a reasonable stock market valuation and debt rating. This can be self-defeating: enterprises must perform to financial analysts' expectations, or risk reducing their valuation and rating, putting more strain on them for ever-increasing performance.

8. *Financial institutions:* who are individually funding an organization and collectively setting the expected rate of return to be delivered by the enterprise. The institutions in the UK are often criticized in terms of their short-term focus, lack of commitment and risk aversion, in comparison to institutions in other countries, especially Germany and Japan.

9. *The media:* where business planning is concerned, the influence of the financial press is very strong indeed. This is possibly strongest in the UK, where the standard of investigative and analytical journalism within the financial media is probably the highest in the world. It is common for companies to report substantial increases in turnover and profit, but media-reported issues about the company's long-term prospects can still cause negative effects on the company's share price.

management to satisfy their particular interest. The interfaces with each of the pressure groups must be constantly monitored not only because they pose a potential threat if mishandled, but also because they offer opportunities that can be exploited to the advantage of the organization.

The stakeholders have a direct financial interest in the organization, and demand a fair share of the wealth created. All stakeholders expect some form of material and financial benefit from the success of the organization. It is a characteristic of those companies that have been most successful in the past that the rewards of their endeavours have indeed been passed on, not just to the shareholders by way of increased dividends, but also through to the community at large and especially their customers, suppliers and employees. Increasingly, legislation has been introduced to protect the interests of some stakeholders, to ensure their fair treatment[13] (e.g. investment customers in financial services).

It is important to note that some groups can be both pressure groups and stakeholders (e.g. shareholders, customers and employees). The most sophisticated planning mechanisms take account of each group and recognize that the signals can be those of divergent and often conflicting needs, depending on the environmental circumstances prevailing at the time. In a competitive environment, the company that understands the needs of external parties and reacts to or, better still, anticipates them most effectively will succeed in the longer term. All these external parties increasingly require businesses to provide more information to address their interests and hence become more accountable. Equally, following 'privatization', many public sector organizations now have to accommodate these external pressure group and stakeholder perspectives, as well as internal preferences, in their strategies.

Business Strategy Formulation and Planning Processes

Having considered the signals coming from the external environment and the threats and opportunities posed by the pressure groups, the organization has to identify, evaluate and decide the strategies it is going to pursue. It then has to establish how to achieve these strategies by planning for the required actions and by effective development and use of resources. The key components of a business planning process are considered below and their relationships are depicted at the core of the framework in Figure 2.2. The process as described here is highly structured and procedural, to aid understanding of what needs to be done. The limitations of this approach and the need for alternative, more 'flexible' versions have been outlined earlier, and how this can be achieved for IS/IT strategies is discussed in Chapter 3.

A key issue of any strategy process is to determine the scope. Should it cover the organization as a whole, or should the organization be considered in smaller, discrete parts where it may be more appropriate and easier to develop coherent strategies and plans? These organizational components are often called 'strategic business units' (SBUs). A business unit can be defined as: *a unit that sells a distinct set of products or services, serves a specific set of customers and competes with a well-defined set of competitors.*

Most major organizations have moved more toward business units and away from functional structures over the past 20 years. An advantage of the SBU approach, as far as developing strategies is concerned, is that it encourages creativity and innovation, both of which are important aspects of Phase 4 in the maturity model described earlier. This usually results in better responsiveness to markets, greater operational flexibility and clear accountability for results.

Clearly, in the derivation and development of strategies, it is important to consider both the enterprise, as a whole, and the individual business units. This can be reconciled by considering the enterprise strategy as the combination of achievement of corporate objectives via the contribution of the SBUs. The strategy processes used also have to reflect the corporate/SBU relationships and the possible inter-SBU relationships.

Objectives

A key element in any business planning process is to set business or organization objectives. These are usually described by reference to profitability, growth, market share, customer satisfaction, new product development, employment, social responsibility, etc.

Objectives are not simply plucked out of the air, but reflect the values held by the organization, by management and by major stakeholders. These values are often expressed in terms of the 'mission' of the organization, which is usually a statement of its long-term aims and purpose. Examples of mission statements and objectives are considered in more detail in Chapter 4, as part of the process of identifying how IS/IT investment can be aligned to the business strategy.

The mission or vision statement may be relevant for many years, until stakeholder interests change. Objectives will change from year to year, and may evolve quite significantly over a period of time. The objectives will set specific measurable targets to be achieved in a given time period. It would seem more logical to set objectives following the 'situation analysis' stage described below, but, in most organizations, the objectives are set first, then the situation is reviewed in the light of those objectives. Later, the objectives may be amended if they appear unattainable or are insufficiently challenging. Often, however, the objectives are left unchanged in spite of evidence to suggest that they are inappropriate.

Situation Analysis

'Where we are now' consists of two essential elements, one looking inside the organization and one looking outside. The first concerns the current strategy and an understanding of the enterprise's strengths and weaknesses. This involves a thorough analysis of:

- the resources available within the organization in terms of their capability to make and deliver the products and services, both existing and those being developed;
- the financial health of the organization in respect of its debt, liquidity, assets;
- the employees, their skills, training, experience, motivation and the resulting business competencies possessed by the organization;
- the physical assets, their age, the technology employed, its usefulness;
- research and development, the proportion of turnover reinvested into researching new products and markets, the number of new products awaiting development, the quality of the past history of research and development (R&D) activity;
- the organization, its structure and relationships, attitudes and culture, and the effectiveness of the operational and management processes, and its ability to adapt to changing circumstances.

The second element involves analysis of the competitive environment so that the enterprise can quite clearly identify its position in the market-place and possible future strategic options. This will involve looking at:

- market segments and market shares within those segments, to identify options for increasing the share of the market, increasing the total size of the market or targeting different segments;
- the organization's position in the product life cycles by considering products that are maturing or declining toward obsolescence, products where demand is still growing and those of future importance coming from research and development, and whether the product life cycles themselves need to be shortened or can be extended;
- an examination of all current and potential competitors to understand their current and potential strategies, their strengths and weaknesses in the various markets in terms of products, services, marketing, finance, people and processes;
- future competitive actions that may take place to introduce potential substitute products or whether the current environment enables new entrants access to the enterprise's chosen markets.

This type of analysis is often called SWOT (Strengths, Weaknesses, Opportunities and Threats). Then, using more creative thinking (e.g. brainstorming sessions) the enterprise searches for ways in which it can use its strengths to exploit opportunities, while addressing its weaknesses and defending against threats.

Future Strategies

Once the organization has a good understanding of what it is trying to achieve by way of objectives, and exactly where it is by reference to its current strengths, weaknesses and analyses of the competition, then it still has to identify future strategies, both to avoid being at a disadvantage and to create advantages wherever possible. While, historically, these could mainly be derived from the knowledge of people within the organization, based on past experience, this has become increasingly limiting in recent years. Many organizations now seek to discover future options by undertaking scenario planning to identify 'discontinuities' and predict the potential implications or bring in outside experts to facilitate 'breakthrough thinking'.

These future possible strategies should be evaluated against a number of criteria, to enable both the most beneficial and most feasible to be selected. For example:

- the risks, both financial and managerial, and the likely responses of the main competitors;
- the degree to which the organization needs to create new capabilities to be offensive or improve control in order to be more defensive;
- whether the current organization structure is appropriate for achieving the intended strategies or if major reorganization is a prerequisite;
- the ability of the organization to implement the strategy in terms of competencies, resources, processes and culture;
- the implications for customers and other trading partners, since more aspects of strategy rely heavily on the intentions and capabilities of others;
- whether the organization requires or should create alliances or joint ventures to enable or secure the strategy.

It may sound obvious, but, in any evaluation of options, it is important to determine priorities and also decide which are not going to be pursued! Many strategies fail to explicitly prevent undesirable courses of action. And many others are too ambitious and create 'initiative overload' in the organization leading to poor implementation of many of the important components of the strategy.

Summary

In an ideal world, this strategy framework would be sufficient for the organization to use to address the planning needs at all levels and across all functions in the organization. However, it is evident that such frameworks are not widely used, perhaps due to the high degree of formality implied in this approach. It need not be bureaucratic or prescriptive, but each of the elements should be addressed. Instead, it would appear that many organizations use a number of different strategy tools, but often without an overall framework, resulting in inadequate synthesis of the outputs from the various analyses and processes.

STRATEGY IMPLEMENTATION

Strategies are only a means to an end, to achieve anything they need to be implemented! This requires that adequate resources are obtained, and allocated effectively; that the appropriate organization and responsibilities are in place and that people are motivated to contribute to the achievement of the strategies.

As these strategies are being implemented, it is obviously important both to monitor performance and to control activities to ensure actions taken are producing the specific results that will lead to achievement of the overall set of objectives. The results of this performance measurement will be used in a feedback loop to refine the objectives of the organization, whether the strategies are being realized or not.

Other models of strategic management reflect this real world, in which strategy 'formation', based on an evolving situation, prevails over a strategy 'formulation' approach as described on page 81. A model developed by Johnson and Scholes[14] perhaps describes these processes and how they relate most clearly (see Figure 2.3).

While, at any one time, an organization can use all its knowledge and experience to devise its intended strategy and plan for its implementation, things will not turn out as predicted.[15] Unexpected constraints or new options will occur, changes will be enforced by the actions of others, new opportunities will arise that could not have been predicted and some parts of the strategy will fail to be implemented successfully. By having the combination of processes, the organization will be more able to 'craft' its strategy,[16] such that a different but realizable strategy can emerge. The organization must also consciously accept that when aspects of the original strategy become unrealizable, it must stop pursuing them. This is often easier said than done in large organizations! Having a strategic management process that can adapt in this way to changing circumstances is not a substitute for initial strategic analysis and planning, it is a way of making it work! This approach also, perhaps, enables the talent of the people in the organization to become involved in its strategic

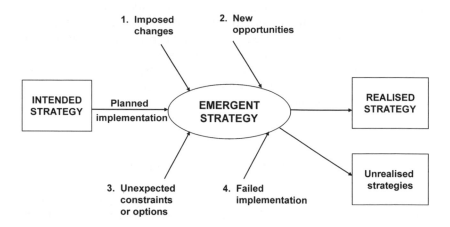

Figure 2.3   *The realities of strategy development* (source: *G. Johnson and K. Scholes,* Exploring Corporate Strategy, *Prentice-Hall, Englewood Cliffs, New Jersey, 2002)*

development, rather than merely used to implement a strategy devised by a small group of senior management.

STRATEGY TOOLS AND TECHNIQUES

In formulating strategy, there are many tools and techniques used in practice. In this section, some of those most commonly used in Phases 3 and 4 of the strategic management evolution (described in Figure 2.1) are introduced. Most of these techniques have been developed since the 1960s in response to the uncertainties and complexities of commercial and industrial environments. In reality, most of the techniques apply to Phase 3, since Phase 4 requires not just analysis and synthesis but also creativity, which few tools or techniques can produce. However, inspiration or creativity with no relation to the organization's real situation will probably create problems, not opportunities!

As the various techniques are considered, the implications for IS/IT strategy formulation that can immediately be derived are discussed. Achieving effective alignment of IS/IT and business strategies will happen more easily if the thinking processes are intimately linked as early as possible in the derivation of the intended business strategy.

Portfolio and Planning Matrices

The Boston Consulting Group Business Matrix

The Boston Matrix (or Boston Square) is one of the earliest examples of the use of portfolio matrix techniques. It is essentially based on two precepts—a product life cycle and the relationship between market share and profitability. It also reflects the rationale of the 'experience curve', whereby the more times something is made the lower the cost will become due to continuing improvements in the process and the achievement of economies of scale. The experience curve is more relevant to manufacturing than service industries.

While the model applies to many types of product and many industries, it does not work in certain circumstances. For instance, in some commodity markets, there is a high degree of government intervention, which distorts the market by artificial control.

The product life cycle (shown in Figure 2.4) explains how the market for a product evolves over time from 'testing' the market acceptance through growth to saturation (maturity) and eventual decline according to customer demand. In a similar way, the types of customer who buy the products at different stages of the life cycle can be used to identify market segment strategies for products through time. Not all products follow the same cycle: some never get off the drawing board; others never gain market acceptance. Life cycles can be very different in duration. Some products, like whisky, are still successful, if declining, after more than 100 years. Mobile phones emerged in the early 1990s, were high growth for nearly 10 years, but the market (in the USA and Western Europe) is now maturing—most of the major manufacturers have announced plans to cease production, in the near future, of the current generation of mobile phones. Others, including many toys, go through the whole cycle in a few months. The model does not work well in cases where the industry is dominated by consumer fashions or fads, producing very short life cycles. Whole industries also go through life cycles of emergence, growth, maturity and decline, although, with improving economic conditions, new markets have opened up for products in decline in more advanced economies (e.g. cigarettes and electrical goods).

Relating the product life cycle to the market position produces the 2×2 matrix that plots market growth against relative market share (see Figure 2.5). The four cells in the matrix reflect two of the stages (growth and maturity) in the life cycle and the relative success of the product *vis-à-vis* competitive products. It is important to remember that the matrix considers *relative*, not absolute market share. In high-growth markets, demand exceeds supply and a price premium can be obtained. High-growth markets attract many competitors and, hence, it

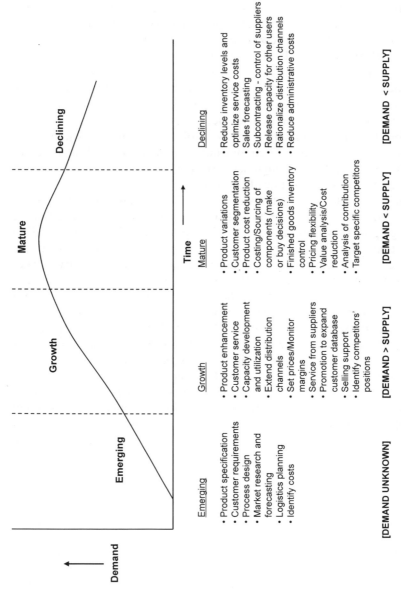

Figure 2.4 *Industry and product life cycles—information and systems focus (source: derived from an analysis in J.M. Higgins, Strategy Formulation, Implementation and Control, Dryden Press, New York, 1985, pp. 130–135)*

Demand

Emerging | Growth | Mature | Declining

Time

Emerging

- Product specification
- Customer requirements
- Process design
- Market research and forecasting
- Logistics planning
- Identify costs

[DEMAND UNKNOWN]

Growth

- Product enhancement
- Customer service
- Capacity development and utilization
- Extend distribution channels
- Set prices/Monitor margins
- Service from suppliers
- Promotion to expand customer database
- Selling support
- Identify competitors' positions

[DEMAND > SUPPLY]

Mature

- Product variations
- Customer segmentation
- Product cost reduction
- Costing/Sourcing of components (make or buy decisions)
- Finished goods inventory control
- Pricing flexibility
- Value analysis/Cost reduction
- Analysis of contribution
- Target specific competitors

[DEMAND < SUPPLY]

Declining

- Reduce inventory levels and optimize service costs
- Sales forecasting
- Subcontracting - control of suppliers
- Release capacity for other users
- Rationalize distribution channels
- Reduce administrative costs

[DEMAND < SUPPLY]

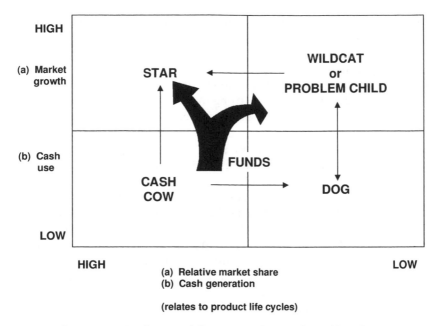

Figure 2.5   *Product portfolio (source: Boston Consulting Group)*

is possible for many players to have profitable products with a relatively low market share due to the high prices obtainable. As markets mature, prices are depressed since supply exceeds demand and the less successful companies leave the market. Only those products able to compete on price, due to low costs of production or by providing features valued by customers, will still succeed. Maintaining a high relative share, by increasing actual share, is essential to both customers' perception of the product and achieving necessary economies of scale. The position of a product, or a whole business, on the matrix gives indications as to appropriate future strategies.

The 'stars' are products with high growth in demand and the best profit potential, provided a high market share is achieved. Star products generate significant revenue, but also require substantial investment in order to establish themselves in the markets and provide the production capacity or service delivery.

Products in the quadrant where market growth is high, but current market share is low, are called 'problem children' or 'wildcats'. These products require a significant investment but generate little cash in return. The cash is sourced from the cash cows and is used to develop and promote some of these wildcats, in the hope that they will achieve higher market share and become tomorrow's stars and future cash cows. Other wildcats should be disinvested, because they will never turn into stars and may even become 'dogs' straightaway!

When the demand slows down as the market matures, the product is well established and, although fewer new customers buy it, it generates repeat sales. At this point, the previous star products require less cash to be injected and should, given a strong market share, generate significant positive cash flow. These are called 'cash cows'. During this period, the firm endeavours to maintain a level of product and service quality and sufficient marketing to preserve its share of the market, but seeks lower costs of supply, production and distribution to maintain the net cash generation for as long as possible.

If a profitable market share is never achieved or market share is eroded as the product is superseded by new, better or cheaper products or by the effects of fashion, the product is becoming obsolescent and the company must be wary of putting more money into the product with a consequent reduced rate of return. These products are called 'dogs' and, ideally, should be disinvested or targeted more precisely at those sectors of the market where demand still exists.

The model emphasizes a few key issues in strategy:

- the need to manage products according to market opportunities and pressures, not internal factors;
- the need to reinvest net cash inflows into future products to ensure continuing sources of revenue;
- the need to have a complete and balanced portfolio if the business is to thrive in the long term.

Increasing pressure from shareholders to dispense a greater share of the profits (from the cash cows) in dividends has created problems for even successful companies, by reducing their ability to reinvest in the development of future products and services.

Although the Boston Matrix is a useful analysis and planning model, because it provides focus for key issues such as cash flow, market share and industry growth, it may oversimplify many of the factors involved in achieving business success. Its underpinning rationale, derived from manufacturing of products, is less valid in the service industries that now form the majority of US and European organizations. Growth rate and market shares are only two aspects of industry attractiveness and competitive position, respectively, and more variables need to be considered. A number of such matrices, their pros and cons and the detailed business and management issues implied by the various segmentations are described in detail by Higgins.[17] Some are summarized here to give an overview of the different variables accommodated.

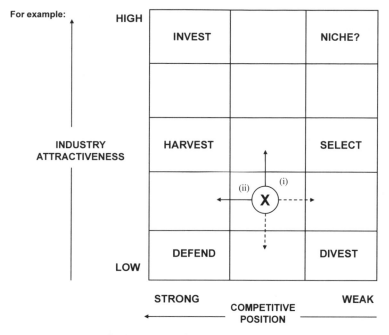

Figure 2.6   *Policy/portfolio matrices*

Other Planning/Policy Matrices

These all extend the number of variables considered and hence the options available, resulting in a 3×3 or 3×5 matrix, as shown in Figure 2.6. Some matrices consider more of the stages in the product and industry life cycles. As mentioned earlier, the Boston Matrix is only really useful in the *growth* and *mature* stages in the full four-stage cycle of emergence, growth, maturity and decline during which strategies must change. High-growth markets are inherently more attractive but other factors that make industries more or less attractive are: size, market diversity, existing competitive structure, prices, profitability, technology development effects, and legal, social and environmental factors. Market share obviously is a reflection of a company's strength, but other factors are important such as technology position, people, brand image, financial structure, capacity and strengths in related markets.

The first stage in using any of the matrices is to understand the current position of the business unit or product—*x* in Figure 2.6. Then, two options exist for growth, by (i) developing the industry, perhaps also to the benefit of others, by product or service innovation or by attracting new types of customer, or (ii) gaining market share from competitors. Equally, strategies need to be considered to defend the existing position against industry decline or competitive pressure. In general, any strategy must enable manageable moves through the matrix—then, new options will open up as the business migrates over time. But, it is not realistic to jump dramatically across the matrix unless some major innovation is achieved that others cannot copy.

All of the matrices are useful in describing the current position of a business and its products in relation to the market and the position of competitors, and the consequent issues the strategy needs to address. They help management to select feasible options from those potentially available, both to improve the position and to counter threats from competitors. They also enable changing positions to be monitored, the causes and implications to be understood and the organization's resources to be allocated or reallocated to achieve the maximum overall benefits to its stakeholders.

Implications for IS/IT Strategy

Figure 2.4 shows typical aspects of the stages of a product life cycle, especially those key business activities that could be enhanced by more effective IS/IT deployment. Industries can also be considered as having a life cycle and most industries can be described as being in one of the four stages at any particular time (e.g. the car industry is 'mature', whereas mobile telephony is in 'growth', biotechnology is 'emerging' and agriculture in Western countries is in 'decline'). As strategies for a business will be different in emerging, growing, mature and declining industries, IS/IT investments should be targeted differently, as with other investments. For a particular product, investments in its promotion, distribution channels and production capacity would be for different purposes, at different stages of the life cycle and will vary in accordance with its market position:

- For a *wildcat* product (low market share in a high-growth market), the route to eventual success is likely to be through innovation in the general marketplace or selecting a clearly-focused niche in the market—a size of market segment that can be addressed effectively. Thus, the IS/IT strategy is likely to focus on product and/or process development or, alternatively, be used to identify potential customers, segment customer types and, then, ensure that effective information exchanges occur about the product/service with the chosen segment of customers, to enable exact specification of service and product requirements.

- *Star* products and businesses (strong market position in an attractive or high-growth market) imply a leading role for the company. Keeping ahead of, or at least in pace with, developing customer requirements and competing product offerings is vital to success, as is matching sales growth with market growth. Systems and information focus will be toward the customer—identifying customers and their requirements to achieve a better understanding of demand than actual or potential competitors. The systems might also be aimed at allowing growth in business, handling greater order volumes or variety of product mixtures, or types of customer service. The main emphasis will be on business innovation—to satisfy market requirements and differentiate the firm in that marketplace. Systems investment focus should therefore be to add value and cope with growth.
- *Cash cow* products and businesses (strong market position in mature, lower-growth markets) are to be 'milked', by defending the current position, ensuring that costs are lower than, or at least as low as, those of competitors and that demand is satisfied in the optimum way. Matching the details of supply and demand volumes is important to keep customers satisfied, as is organizing resources and processes to obtain maximum capacity utilization. Business productivity and control of customers and suppliers to defend a market position is the main aim—not to allow competitors to gain advantage—and systems will tend to focus on control of the business relationships and activities rather than innovation.
- *Dog* products and businesses (weak position in a low-growth or declining market) are unlikely to attract much corporate investment funding, unless it can clearly be seen to increase market share and/or improve deliverable profits. Divestment may be the eventual aim and, so, it is often undesirable to consider integration of IS strategy with the rest of the business. Alternatively, a niche market may be carved out by segmenting the products/markets. In general, IS/IT investment should follow the business direction—selective, strongly financially-justified investments to improve profit performance by reducing costs or securing customers. Very little innovative IS/IT use can be expected.

These suggestions may seem rather generalized, if only because the matrices themselves make no claim to precise investment guidelines— they are ways of helping understand situations, enabling the assessment of different options. If nothing else, they can help sharpen the debate between managers. During the industry evolution cycle, a firm will change its business focus from customers to products to customers, etc. as the cycle evolves, in order to achieve market growth and improved

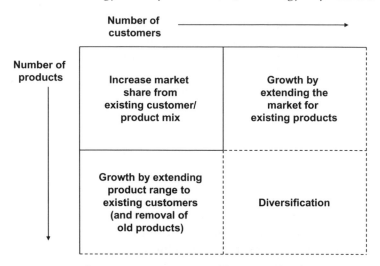

Figure 2.7   Dimensions of business growth

market share (see Figure 2.7). Growth is more manageable if, at any particular time, either the product or customer base is relatively stable. Either existing products are marketed to a wider customer base or new products are developed for a known set of customer needs. Information systems focus can be expected to follow this pattern, being used to attract, and establish channels to, potential new customers and support the logistics of servicing those customers, or to enable the development and delivery of new, better or lower-cost products or services to achieve growth through existing market links. At no stage will the other parameter be ignored, but, at any one time, the emphasis is likely to be on product *or* customer 'development'.

Figure 2.7 only shows products and customers, whereas the model can have a third dimension—distribution channels. The Internet has opened up electronic channels to all types of customer, including directly to end-consumers. Selecting the appropriate channel to serve target customer groups or for delivery of the product or service is a key strategic decision. The newer channels, call centres and the Internet are IS/IT based and the development and operation of these customer links is an integral part of both the business and IS/IT strategies. Managing the channel mix (e.g. in a bank with branches, call centre and online banking) is not just a matter of matching delivery to customers' needs in each channel, but also requires decisions on the extent of cross-channel service integration to be provided.

Obviously, once a product or customer base has been extended, the scope of the firm's coverage has moved. Once a wider range of products have been developed for a known market, it probably means that a broader market is now available. Equally, given that a broader market for a restricted product range has been established, a wider variety of needs are known and can be economically satisfied, justifying further product investments.

Historically, diversification—new products to new customers—has usually proved unsuccessful, unless achieved in the steps above or by acquisition. More recently, two approaches have proved more successful. First, the establishment of 'superbrands', such as Virgin and Nike, has enabled organizations to develop both new products and target new market segments under the brand 'umbrella'. Second, organizations such as HSBC and the Prudential have set up separate new businesses to sell, exclusively, telephone or Internet-based banking products to customer segments where they are traditionally weak. In these cases, the IS/IT strategy is very specific to that business unit and would not, at this 'wildcat' stage at least, be linked to strategies elsewhere in the business.

Competitive Forces and Competitive Strategies

The portfolio models described on pages 87–91 were the main tools of strategic analysis in use in the 1960s and 1970s. They are still proving useful today, but other approaches developed during the 1980s, mainly by Porter,[18] have had significant influence in strategy formulation over the last 20 years.

An enterprise exists within an industry, and, to succeed, it must effectively deal with the *competitive forces* that exist within the particular industry. For example, the forces in an emerging industry such as biotechnology or genetic engineering are considerably different from those of a growth industry, say leisure or financial services, or the more mature or declining industries such as automobiles or coal mining. In addition, the pressures of operating globally, as in the software industry, are very different from those in localized industries, like DIY retailing, where international competition is very limited at present.

The enterprise interacts with its customers, suppliers and competitors, but, in addition to these interactions, there are potential new entrants into the particular competitive marketplace and potential substitute products and services. To survive and thrive in this environment, it is obviously vital to understand these interactions and the implications, in terms of how to avoid being disadvantaged and to understand the opportunities to gain competitive advantage. Figure 2.8 outlines these five forces—buyers, suppliers, competitors, new entrants and substitute

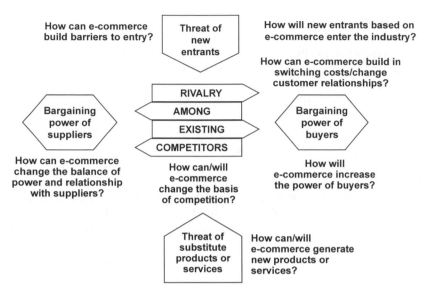

Figure 2.8   *E-commerce in relation to industry competitive forces*

products—and overlays some typical questions about the potential impact of e-commerce on these forces.

At any one time, one or more of the forces may be exerting particular pressure on the competing firms. The existing rivals may be competing viciously via a price war and/or aggressive in new products and services or advertising campaigns. Alternatively, competitors may be 'cooperating' to ward off an external threat. The buyers or suppliers may be powerful enough to bargain away much of the profitability available to the firm and its immediate competitors. Increasing buyer and supplier switching costs, making a change of relationship expensive, can reduce that power. New companies may be a threat in terms of new entrants to the industry because of low entry barriers or weak competitive rivals. Substitute products are always possible, not just in terms of replacement products or services but also as alternative ways for buyers to spend their money (e.g. holidays versus luxury goods).

If all the forces are exerting intense pressure at the same time, the company faces serious problems! But, if it addresses the competitive forces according to their potential impact now and in the future, it can establish a better business position than its rivals. Figure 2.8 suggests some ways in which IS/IT can affect these forces and this is considered in more detail on page 103. Table 2.1 briefly outlines the types of factor that determine whether the forces will have a major influence on a business.

Table 2.1   *Factors affecting the impact of competitive forces*

New entrants will be inhibited by:
- capital requirements;
- patents and specialist skills required;
- distribution channels available;
- achieved/required economies of scale and resultant cost advantages;
- number and size of existing rivals and intensity of competition;
- differentiation and brand establishment/loyalty;
- access to raw materials/critical resources, etc.

Substitute products/services (implies achieving a higher priority for customer spend):
- customer awareness of needs and means of satisfaction;
- customer sensitivity to value for money and ability to compare;
- existing loyalty of customers—impact of 'industry' promotion;
- ability to differentiate products, etc.

Competitive rivalry will be intensified by:
- market growth slow (or in decline);
- small number of similar sized competitors dominate;
- high fixed costs and/or high exit barriers for all rivals;
- overcapacity, and/or capacity increments are large units;
- commodity-like, undifferentiated products, etc.

Buyers' power will be increased by:
- concentrated/few buyers making high volume and/or high value of purchases;
- low switching costs across suppliers;
- price sensitive and many alternative sources of supply;
- weak brand identities, products not differentiated;
- buyers capable of backward integration due to low 'entry' costs, etc.

Suppliers' power will be increased by:
- few suppliers—high switching costs for rivals and suppliers deal with many small customers;
- potential substitute supplier/resources not easily available;
- supplied goods make up large part of firms' costs;
- suppliers capable of forward integration or bypass to customers, etc.

Achieving long-term success in any competitive environment, according to Porter's rationale, results from being the lowest-cost producer of the product or service or by differentiating it from those of competitors in terms of its value, as perceived by the customers. Lowest cost is normally associated with volume production (i.e. high market share), or by flexible manufacturing or distribution systems. These two strategies can either be followed overall or by focusing on particular segments of the market—'niches'.

An example of these generic strategies can be seen by reference to Mercedes. The Mercedes limousine is regarded in most parts of the world as being the type of car that a successful businessman should be driving. The company has consistently advertised its cars in that way, with the emphasis always on high quality, high reliability and high price—Mercedes is differentiating itself from its competitors in the executive car market. However, within Europe, the Mercedes is probably the most common car to be seen in taxi fleets. Taxi operators are not known for their profligate expenditure on executive cars, but are usually very careful to assess the long-term costs of running their taxi fleet. In this regard, Mercedes comes out extremely well due to the emphasis of the company on high reliability, low maintenance costs and high resale value, thereby making their cars the most attractive, on average, for a taxi fleet operator. In this way, Mercedes is operating in the niche market of the taxi fleet operator by being the market leader using a low-cost strategy.

More recently, Mercedes has developed models to compete in the small car market, where price competition is fierce. It remains to be seen whether it can achieve success in differentiating its product in a price-sensitive mass market.

Some of the major requirements for an enterprise to be able to adopt the two basic generic strategies are shown in Table 2.2. The key aspects of each are quite different and would imply different organizational structures, types of people employed and management styles, resulting in quite different corporate cultures. The most common error that organizations make is to get stuck between strategies by not deciding on their market scope and basic source of advantage—low cost or differentiation. Consequently, costs are too high and prices cannot be sustained, leading to low margins.

Implications for IS/IT Strategy

These basic concepts of analysing competitive opportunities, threats and strategies have been used by a number of people as a basis for considering IS/IT and its potential impact. In the 1980s, Parsons,[19] McFarlan,[20] Cash[21] and others used Porter's models to examine how IS/IT had and could impact certain industries and affect any particular firm in that industry, depending on its business position in the industry and its adopted business strategy. More recently, Porter[22] himself has applied these models to explore the impact of the Internet on firms and industries. This implies that the opportunities and threats that IS/IT can offer and pose will vary over time in an industry, partly due to the role IS/IT can

Table 2.2 *Characteristics of generic strategies*

Generic strategy	Commonly required skills and resources	Common organizational requirements
Overall cost leadership	Sustained capital investment and access to capital	Tight cost control, frequent, detailed control reports
	Process engineering skills	Structured organization and responsibilities
	Intense supervision of labour	Incentives based on meeting strict quantitative targets
Differentiation	Strong marketing abilities and creative flair	Strong coordination among functions in R&D, product development, and marketing
	Product-engineering skills	Subjective measurement and incentives instead of quantitative measures (market-based incentives)
	Strong capability in basic research	Amenities to attract highly-skilled labour or creative people
	Corporate reputation for quality or technological leadership	Looser, more trusting organizational relationships
	Strong cooperation from distribution channels	

play and partly due to the economic and competitive situation of the industry. But, as with product innovation, IS/IT innovation can stimulate new industry growth or, in some cases, hasten the decline of certain industries. While the arrival of Amazon.com has had a serious impact on traditional book retailers, the total sales of books have increased significantly. In some cases, IS/IT impact can be immediate and obvious but, in others, the effects are secondary and require other changes in business economics and social behaviour or parallel developments in other fields before they become fully effective. This is the case with e-retailing in 2002, the predicted effects being dependent more on costs of distribution and changes in shopping preferences and habits, than on the ability to browse and purchase online—the demise of online grocer Webvan being indicative of this.

Industry Analysis

Both Parsons and McFarlan address this area by posing questions: 'Can IS/IT …?', suggesting that management should ask questions regarding how IS/IT could affect the essential industry ingredients:

- the products and services;
- markets, distribution channels and customer behaviour;
- economics of production, distribution or servicing.

Obviously, if IS/IT can have a major effect on any of these, the implications for all the competing firms are significant, and management must consider, in more depth, how those effects will or could manifest themselves.

1. *How can/could IS/IT affect the nature and value of the product or service and its life cycle?*
    - Financial and business information services such as Dun & Bradstreet and Reuters have developed new services for commercial organizations to interrogate directly, as have brokers and banks, enabling new ways of trading shares and securities and making new types of bank account available to consumers.
    - Online journals are rapidly replacing printed versions. The new products can be customized to meet the needs of particular groups and provide links to topic coverage across editions. Search engines, based on new sophisticated algorithms, can greatly speed up inquiries. Consequently, many university libraries are now mainly network access points to electronically-published papers.
    - Life insurance companies can develop new insurance and pension policy types, providing complex investment combinations from concept to the target market in weeks rather than months. This can render older products uncompetitive very quickly, creating problems of long-term commitments to supporting obsolete products.
    - Many recruitment services now operate exclusively via the Internet. Job applications can only be submitted electronically

in many cases, even if the job advertisement is posted in the traditional media. The initial response and filter of applications is often done via computer systems, rather than people—an essential feature given the global reach of online job adverts and the potentially high volume of interest!

In general terms, the questions to be asked are: can IS/IT generate a new product or a new line of business, or enable, or be used to add additional features or services to increase the product's value—as perceived by the consumer/customer—to change the basis for purchasing? This is generally more feasible if the product has a very high information content.

2. *How can/could IS/IT affect the demand for products and services, segment markets more effectively, extend them geographically, or provide new distribution channels to reach the market?*

- Well-known examples are the new 'direct' financial service companies such as First Direct and Direct Line insurance; and, more recently, the online-only banks such as Egg, Cahoot and IF are able to offer consumers financial products by telephone and the Internet, removing the need for branches and intermediaries. By doing so, they have a significant cost advantage over traditional rivals and are also able to gather information from customers to understand their needs better. In particular, younger customers are attracted to these 'modern' products and services, whereas they would probably not consider the traditional services offered by the same companies.
- Feeny[23] cites a number of examples of successful online marketing, including Amazon's prompting customers about new books, based on their profile of previous purchases. Dell not only offer a product configuration service online, plus product purchasing, but also configurable support services for corporate customers.
- Most auction-based markets had been revolutionized over the past 20 years by IS/IT, even before the arrival of the Internet. The effects on share dealing, securities and currency markets are well known—parochial markets are now global and the firms dealing in those markets are no longer dependent upon the services of specialist or 'licensed' traders. Much of the trading is actually done by the computer systems, implying that the systems are causing market behaviour!

The use of the Internet has produced new kinds of auction, both consumer and commercial, thereby changing the buying and selling processes for many products and services, not just 'information' products. Euronext, the result of the merger of the Amsterdam, Brussels and Paris stock exchanges, has launched exchange-traded wine futures while BordeauxIndex.com and WorldwineXchange.com have developed derivative products.[24] Electronic marketplaces or trading hubs now exist in most industries and are forecast to handle a large proportion of trading transactions over the next 10 years.[25]

Again, the typical questions to be asked are: Can IS/IT enable us to reach more, or more appropriate, customers or to match our different products/services to customers more appropriately or enable the product or service to be distributed in new ways? Or can we use IS/IT to get closer to the marketplace rather than deal through intermediaries? These questions are considered again, in more detail, in the context of the industry value chain and the role of information in Chapter 5.

3. *How can IS/IT affect the cost base of the key processes in the industry or change the balance in the trade-off between flexibility and standardization?*

- An obvious example is the publishing industry, where the use of IS/IT from the basic preparation of material by authors to the final printing process has dramatically changed the basic economics of producing newspapers, journals, magazines and books. The revolution in newspaper production is well documented. Journalists can produce stories remotely and transmit them electronically, the edition of the paper can be set on 'desktop' publishing systems and transmitted for printing to as many locations as necessary. Not only has the production cost base been dramatically altered, so have the economics of distributing the newspapers. The revolution in book production may not be so obvious but, given the reduced set-up time per book, the economic batch runs become much smaller, enabling:
  - lower-selling books to become profitable;
  - more books to be available on the market due to lower launch costs;
  - the ability to respond to demand changes more quickly and accurately.

- Automated warehouses, linking physical goods access to logistics and inventory systems, enable some wholesaling companies to stock much wider ranges of goods and respond to customers' orders more quickly and anticipate changing demand earlier. Delivery routes and order profitability can also be optimized. Tracking systems enable carriers to identify the exact location of any consignment at any time and provide more accurate delivery information to the customer. Much of this can be made directly accessible by customers over the Internet

* Digitization of documents and images has enabled the automation of many back-office processes in information-intensive industries, such as insurance. When combined with workflow technology, both productivity and customer service can be improved in handling both new business applications and approvals and claims. This has kept costs down and allowed the organizations to deal with business volumes barely foreseen 10 years ago.

Once more, these are only examples, but they should prompt the following types of question: Can IS/IT enable the product/service to be produced more economically or enable production and associated logistics to be integrated to produce greater flexibility of resource use? Or can improved logistics and control change the basic working capital structure of the industry? Or can IS/IT enable a higher quality of product or service to be offered at a much lower cost than traditionally?

This first level of 'interrogation' of IS/IT potential in the industry focuses on products, markets and economics and considers options available to all the firms in the industry and, importantly, to potential new entrants, including start-up companies, who can exploit new technology to develop and sell new products or services, or create new channels that address the needs of some or all the industry customer base, or both. Gaining an advantage at this level is difficult for others to counter except by copying or by risking even more dramatic and effective innovation. Consequently, many of the anecdotes of sustained success derive from companies who have fundamentally changed one of these aspects. These changes are irreversible in that, if the factors for success in the industry and the relevant capabilities required by companies wishing to succeed in the industry are fundamentally altered, the competitive game will have a new set of rules!

Analysis of Competitive Forces to Identify IS/IT Opportunity and Threats

Each of the five forces described on page 96 should be examined by questioning whether IS/IT can affect the nature and degree of impact that force has on determining the future of the industry or the balance of power of the firms in the industry. These factors were outlined in Table 2.1.

In the airline industry, all competitive forces have been and are still being affected by the use of IS/IT, as described in Table 2.3. IS/IT has

Table 2.3   *The airline industry: how IS/IT has affected competitive forces*

1. *How can IS/IT build barriers to entry?*	By increasing IT entry cost for reservation systems (£20m+)
	By tying in distribution channels (travel agencies)
	By sharing capacity and ticketing costs via alliances and integrated systems
2. *How can IS/IT build in switching costs for customers?*	By linking purchasing and remittance systems to reduce overheads of customer
	Discount/volume packages to discourage piecemeal purchase
3. *How can IS/IT change the basis of competition?*	Lower costs: optimize yield per aircraft
	Differentiate service: reconfiguring aircraft due to demand
	Niche/focus service into high yield sectors (e.g. business travel)
	Low-cost/low-price 'no frills' service with online direct booking, bypassing agents
4. *How can IS/IT change the balance of power in supplier/ customer relationship?*	Agent is constantly aware of seat availability of competing airlines
	Airline can readily promote unsold capacity via chosen agents or direct to customers via online booking with variable pricing based on sales patterns
5. *How can IS/IT generate new products/services?*	Integrated travel package to high mileage business customers, bypassing agencies
	New routes/schedules to cater for demand

had a considerable impact on all forces in the industry because of the nature of the 'product', how it is purchased and the information needed to be exchanged in order to complete a transaction. Other industries, such as financial services and publishing, are even more information intensive in that the product itself is information. Even in other industries, where the bases of competition are not as dependent on information as airlines, travel, financial services and publishing, one or more of the forces has been significantly impacted by an enterprise using IS/IT quite deliberately to achieve a competitive advantage.

Over the last 20 years, food supermarkets have built barriers to entry through Electronic Point of Sale (EPOS) systems linked to purchasing and logistics—the size of the investment and control of the supply chains reducing the potential for new entrants. More recently, via loyalty cards, Tesco and other retailers have increased consumer switching costs as well as obtained valuable information on buying patterns, enabling both higher leverage over suppliers and the tailoring of store layout and product mix to the local market. In addition, by building basic financial products through the loyalty cards they have become new entrants in the financial service industry. Finally, the same infrastructure has facilitated a move into online e-tailing, extending the range of options to the customer, and limiting the scope for new entrants or substitute services to gain a foothold.

The Internet has changed the competitive landscape in many industries and new business and industry models are beginning to emerge. In general, three effects seem to happen across most industries. Buyer power increases as more choice becomes available online, through portals and search engines; buying groups, normally based on a common interest, have emerged to produce collective rather than individual buying power. Both disintermediation (cutting out existing intermediaries by selling direct via the Net) and reintermediation (new firms providing information-based services connecting buyers and a range of sellers) can occur through the industry supply or value chain. As mentioned earlier, trading hubs, auctions and e-market places are expected to have a major influence over both selling and procurement processes in the next decade and may lead to restructuring in some industries. Combined with the inherent global reach of online trading, actual and potential competitors are no longer restricted by geography; these changes imply a wider view of the competitive issues has to be taken. The response in most cases is to tighten the links, especially information sharing, between the sellers and their customers to increase switching costs and prevent 'gaps' appearing that new entrants can exploit.

For any firm in any industry, the questioning process, according to Porter and Millar[26] and others, should proceed in two stages. First, what forces are determining the future of the industry and our potential success? Who dominates the industry and by what strategy? For example:

- Who might enter the industry, why and what would the effect be?
- What substitute products might affect the market for existing products?

- On what basis are we currently competing and how might that change?
- What leverage do suppliers exert and how could the control of key resources affect success?
- How much power and discretion do buyers (customers) have and how will this change market/product possibilities?

As indicated in Figure 2.8, the potential of IS/IT to cause these changes is increasingly important in the analysis. However, these are all *business* questions, the result of which may be that only one or two of the forces are critical at any particular time. Once that has been established, more specific IS/IT questions should focus on these areas of concern—both opportunities and threats—to identify the available options. A final stage should then be to reverse the thinking process by looking at the other, less critical, forces to identify whether IS/IT could change their importance in the future. Cash[27] takes this view and suggests a general set of actual or potential implications. A modified version of his analysis is presented in Table 2.4. While this analysis dates from the 1980s, the options and issues it suggests have become even more relevant today.

Generic Business Strategies

Companies that succeed in an industry in the long term need to outperform the competitors, either by achieving lower costs or by differentiating themselves in the view of the customer, enabling them to obtain a price premium. Some companies, for a period of time at least, can achieve both. For instance, Kodak in the 1960s and early 1970s achieved this in the colour film market and IBM in the 1970s with mainframe computers. Most companies, however, have to strive for one advantage or the other, at least in the short to medium term.

The other critical decision is to define the extent of the market within which the company wishes to gain that advantage. The scope can be defined as 'industry wide', implying that the company must have a range of products to meet the requirements of the majority of potential customers. Ford and General Motors in the car industry are good examples, as are the big four UK banks in the financial services industry. Other companies choose a segment of the marketplace, focus on a particular niche to obtain an advantage by matching their products and services to the needs of a subset of the potential customers. BMW, Volvo, Jaguar and Mercedes are all examples of companies focusing in the motor industry. The UK's Giro Bank, while offering similar services to the major banks, has tended to focus its services on the lower-income end of the consumer market.

Table 2.4 *Impact of competitive forces and potential IS/IT opportunities* (source: adapted from J. Cash, 'Interorganizational systems: An information society opportunity or threat?', The Information Society, Vol. 3, No. 3, 1988, 98–110)

Key force impacting the industry	*Business implications*	*Potential IS/IT effects*

Threat of new entrants	Additional capacity
	Reduced prices
	New basis for competition
		Provide entry barriers/
		reduce access by:
		– exploiting existing
		  economies of scale
		– differentiate
		  products/services
		– control distribution
		  channels
		– segment markets

Buyer power high	Forces prices down Demand higher quality Require service flexibility Encourage competition	Differentiate products/ services and improve price/performance Increase switching costs, of buyers Facilitate buyer product selection
Supplier power high	Raises prices/costs Reduced quality of supply Reduced availability	Supplier sourcing systems Extended quality control into suppliers Forward planning with supplier
Substitute products threatened	Limits potential market and profit Price ceilings	Improve price/ performance Redefine products and services to increase value Redefine market segments
Intense competition from rivals	Price competition Product development Distribution and service critical Customer loyalty required	Improve price/ performance Differentiate products and services in distribution channel and to consumer Get closer to the end-consumer— understand the requirements

The role of IS/IT in enabling and supporting each of the fundamental generic strategies—low cost and differentiation—will be considered first. The essential business characteristics of these two strategies were described in Table 2.2.

Low-cost Strategy

Cost leadership strategies require the organization to identify the lowest-cost approaches to the direct activities of the business, minimize the indirect/overhead expenses and provide management with detailed reporting on all aspects of fixed and variable costs incurred and their recovery. Low cost is achieved through structure and conformity and 'value engineering' the processes of the business, plus accuracy in control and measurement of performance, and early identification and action when variances occur from expected results—a 'systems' environment. Traditionally, IS/IT has been employed process by process, often causing inefficiency between processes. If that inefficiency is moved into the customer and passed back to the supplier, then the low cost may be offset by other problems. But, again, IS/IT offers potential solutions. Black and Decker, for instance, achieves low costs by moving stock into dealers early in the product season (e.g. lawnmowers) and does not want returns! Dealers, however, may well misjudge demand and either end up with too many or not enough to satisfy their customers. Black and Decker did not want dissatisfied customers and provided a network for dealers to exchange shortage/surplus stock information, which the company would then help in redistributing—anything to avoid returns! Ryanair, the no-frills airline, uses the Internet to support its low-cost strategy. It sells over 90% of seats over the Internet, bypassing more expensive channels such as call centres and travel agents.

In such an environment, systems will be required to deal with basic business information processes efficiently and link them together effectively, not necessarily to produce a highly-integrated information resource. Flexibility in systems increases their cost of development and operation; simple systems, often standard packages implemented without change, are more cost-effective and force user adherence and conformity. Integration can reduce the opportunities to improve the efficiency of any particular process as technology offers further, specific cost savings. Information is not seen as a key resource for exploitation, but as an overhead cost to be processed efficiently with minimum additional IS/IT overhead! Integration produces added-value potential but incurs overheads. Electronic commerce, for example, will probably provide cost advantages if it is used to avoid processing paper—orders, invoices, statements—(i.e. more efficient transaction handling). It also enables invoices to be rendered unnecessary by triggering funds transfer at a certain period after goods receipt (to be reconciled later). The relative costs to both customer and supplier of paperwork processing and debtor funding can be optimized. This is linking two systems together to produce greater efficiency in both. Similar relationships can also be continually improved by better systems within the organization.

Differentiation Strategy

The majority of organizations have to follow a differentiation strategy, since, theoretically at least, only one company can have cost leadership of a product or service at any one time. The essential emphases are innovation and creativity, market orientation and people-driven rather than systems-driven management controls. For instance, incentive schemes will be market or sales based, not production based. Often, key components of differentiation will be the creation of strong brand and corporate images and close, mutually beneficial links with distribution channel firms. The strategic use of IS/IT will focus on enabling new things to be achieved or existing things to be done better. That is not to say that opportunities to use IS/IT to reduce cost will be ignored.

In the 1980s, pharmaceutical distributor McKesson differentiated itself in serving drugstores by taking over many of the systems aspects of running a small business—stock control, ordering, sales analysis, prescription insurance processing, etc. These systems became most effective when the drugstore dealt with only one supplier! Other distributors took the matter to court, crying foul over 'one supplier agreement'. The drugstores supported McKesson, denying that they were under any obligation to buy only from McKesson—they just preferred to!

While basic business process systems will need to operate efficiently in dealing with the bulk of transactions and basic calculation and reporting requirements, the value of having flexibility to extract information from an integrated database or comprehensive data warehouse will drive the systems toward sophistication and user tailoring rather than standard solutions. Even where major packages such as ERP or CRM software are implemented for core processes, it is likely that additional functionality will be needed to address the organizational subtleties that lead to differentiation. If mismanaged this can, of course, lead to unnecessary spending on IS/IT.

The opportunities for strategic advantages will derive from asking such questions as how can IS/IT help:

- find out more about customer requirements?
- monitor customer perceptions of service?

- enable rapid and accurate response to customer queries?
- provide a range of delivery options to meet customer needs?
- reduce new product introduction lead times?
- enable knowledge sharing across the organization to facilitate innovation?

Companies that achieve greatest success realize that costs must be controlled *and* value must be added. For IS/IT this means that, in any organization, cost-reduction and value-adding opportunities will exist— but the driving forces will be different depending on the prevailing generic strategy.

Niche/Focus Strategy

Within a market niche, an organization will need to adopt a differentiation or low-cost strategy to achieve long-term success in that niche. All that has been said in the previous two sections will then apply. However, in addition, IS/IT may be a competitive weapon in identifying and then establishing a strong hold on a particular niche.

An example quoted by Meyer and Boone[28] is of a relocation service firm that developed systems to enable them to provide comprehensive services to people who were moving house due to company relocation in New England (i.e. a market sector of 'enforced moves'). The service not only located suitable housing but could satisfy other specific requirements such as schooling, leisure facilities and mortgage arrangements. Not only was it a service to buyers, but also to sellers where houses on offer could be channelled towards 'enforced movers', who would be likely to be more reliable purchasers. The total service advantage to an individual both buying and selling was significant. Companies were keen that employees used such a service to minimize the delays and stress involved in moving employees around locations. The service would not have been possible, at an economic service cost, but for a comprehensive system linked throughout the office network. On the Internet, many estate agents now provide similar services.

In general terms, the uses of IS/IT to achieve success in a limited subset of a general market will be in:

- identifying the target market, and developing a unique base of information about the selected market and its needs; and/or
- establishing a specialist process via systems to produce a clear cost advantage or distinctive customer value proposition *vis-à-vis* general market servers; and/or

- linking the organization via systems into the business processes of customers to increase switching costs and establish potential barriers to re-entry from general market servers.

A RESOURCE-BASED VIEW OF STRATEGY

It was stated earlier in the chapter that these planning tools have evolved since the 1950s and are continuing to evolve. Until the 1990s, the approach to defining strategies was based on establishing objectives and then defining how to achieve them—the traditional 'ends–ways–means' approach. In the 1990s, many strategic thinkers, building on the work of Wernerfelt,[29] Barney[30] and others, started to develop new ways of considering strategies. Is there value in the concept of looking at means, then ways, then ends; that is, defining what resources are available to the enterprise as a basis for defining what can be achieved by the enterprise? Or, equally, consideration of the ways the organization does things uniquely or exceptionally well—its abilities or competencies—may lead to defining more appropriate ends or the procurement and development of improved, more valuable resources.

Over the past few years, the approach to strategic management has evolved toward a balance or reconciliation between competitive positioning and resource or competence-based strategic development. While many of the tools and models described earlier in this chapter enable organizations to understand their competitive environment and strategic options, the resulting strategy is essentially reactive. As 'strategic thinking', as opposed to strategic analysis or planning, began to emerge, the suggestion was that longer-term success would result from a realignment of the organization's resources and capabilities to match the demands of the environment. This implies a closer examination of an organization's assets, skills, knowledge processes, culture, etc. and how each of those attributes needs to be realigned. In some cases, the mismatch was considerable and radical readjustment was necessary and, in the early 1990s, 're-engineering the business' became a hot topic. Business re-engineering is not a strategy, it is the means of changing strategies in response to a changing environment, where continuous or incremental change is insufficient. Unfortunately, many organizations only require changing radically because they have not been adjusting continuously over time. It is clearly difficult to achieve radical change successfully in an enterprise that has not changed for a considerable time. Either by incremental, continuous realignment or radical change, organizations are essentially trying to establish a set of competencies that will deliver future success. To be successful in Stage 4 of the maturity model by sustaining advantages, can create (see Figure 2.1) an organizational need to develop a unique set of resources or competencies that others cannot easily acquire or replicate. Inherent in this argument is that the knowledge an organization possesses is both a resource and a source of competence. The term 'knowledge management' emerged in the last decade and, while it is not a 'technical' issue, it implies an extended role for IS/IT in creating organization capabilities.

Creating a sustainable advantage in that environment, through some unique business capability, requires a further form of assessment. Porter's generic strategies are a starting point, since he argues that 'low cost' or 'differentiation' provide that sustainable advantage. However, these concepts do not seem to address all the options available and also leave many questions about *how* lowest cost or differentiation can be achieved.

Competencies and Competitive Advantage

Based on the concept of resource-based strategies, Treacy and Wiersma[31] suggest that there are 'three paths to market leadership', each of which require different sets of competencies and in each of which IS/IT has a critical role to play. That is not to say that there are only three routes, although the three—'Operational (or Process) Excellence', 'Customer Intimacy' and 'Product Leadership'—probably cover a significant range of the possibilities. They are simple yet useful concepts in enabling business managers to define medium-term business strategy and establish an appropriate IS/IT strategy. They are a way of expressing quite succinctly a necessary alignment between internal capabilities and ambitions and the requisites for success in a particular environment, at a certain time (see Figure 2.9):

1. *Operational Excellence*—enabling products and services to be obtained reliably, easily and cost-effectively by customers. This implies a focus on business processes to outperform others and can deliver both low costs and consistent quality of customer satisfaction. Treacy and Wiersma quote examples such as Dell Computers, Wal-Mart and Federal Express as leaders in operational excellence in their industries. In all cases, the companies' information systems investments are a critical component enabling business simplification and efficient processes that are highly integrated throughout the core activities of the business. An example of such a strategy is General Electric (GE), which effectively reinvented the supply chain for white goods with new information systems. Instead of encouraging dealers to hold stock of GE's products by offering discounts for bulk

BUS!NESS STRATEGY

Figure 2.9 *Forces that shape strategy*

purchase, GE refuses dealers purchases for stock, but provides demonstration models, against which customers can order for next day direct delivery through GE's 'Direct Connect' system. GE holds all the stock and dealers can order any model online, on behalf of the customer. Dealers are now effectively paid commission on sales made rather than items purchased. This enables GE to encourage customers to buy the latest models rather than the often older models stocked in large quantities by dealers. The system has helped smaller dealers to compete more effectively with large discount warehouses, enabling them to meet more of the customers' needs, and has reduced stock holdings in the supply chain by about 12%. Also, since GE has to arrange delivery, it gathers useful consumer data. The direct insurers, led by Direct Line, have had a dramatic impact on the general insurance industry by simplifying the processes for selling policies and handling claims. By carrying out most transactions by telephone (and now online) and having integrated systems, it has both reduced costs and hence premiums and improved customer satisfaction with the responsiveness and efficiency of the service.

2. *Customer Intimacy*—targeting markets very precisely and tailoring products and services to the needs of particular customer groups. The purpose here is not just to 'satisfy' but to 'please' customers by understanding their needs and meeting them on every occasion. This can obviously be expensive but it can build long-term customer loyalty. Examples quoted include Home Depot, a DIY retailer whose purpose is to 'solve the consumer's home-repair problems' rather than merely sell products, and Kraft and Frito Lay in consumer

packaged goods, who both offer an extensive range of products to match the preferences of many different types of consumer. Their information systems enable a retail outlet to tailor the 'product offer' to the locality through 'micro-merchandising' programs affecting product range, promotion, pricing and store layout. Within such a strategy, information systems will focus on collecting and analysing customer information, covering not merely purchases but also other relevant attributes and feedback on products and services. This enables careful segmentation of the marketplace and targeting of the desired segments. In almost all the examples quoted, deciding who not to sell to, especially those who buy merely on price, is as important as targeting desired customers. In the UK, an example of customer intimacy is RS Components, who sell by mail order electrical and other components to engineers. The 'customers' are the engineers, not the organizations they work for, and RS effectively provide a problem-solving and rapid delivery service, for which the engineer, and consequently his organization, is happy to pay a premium. The extra cost is easily offset by the time the engineer saves in determining what he or she needs to buy and where to get it.

3. *Product Leadership*—continuing product innovation meeting customers' needs. This implies not only creativity in developing new products and enhancing existing ones, but also astute market knowledge to ensure that they sell. The strategy involves delivering a continuous stream of new products and/or services, where what is new is valued by the customers. Johnson & Johnson are quoted as a good example of a 'product leader', and a particular instance quoted is its contact lens business, where it pioneered the introduction of disposable lenses. The rapid gain of market acceptance and market share were due not only to the innovative product itself but to new systems to control the manufacturing and distribution of the product, which is more akin to fast-moving consumables than traditional eye-care products. 3M has traditionally followed a product leadership strategy in the adhesives and coating market, and the story of Post-it notepads is now legendary—how a 'failed' new adhesive became the basis for a best-selling product—what would we do without it?

Although these three competence-based strategies are not the only routes to success, they can be used to:

● Understand and agree the main direction, rationale and focus of the business's strategy. Although Treacy and Wiersma quote examples of

Figure 2.10 *Advantage and disadvantage—dimensions of competency* (source: M. Treacy and F. Wiersma, The Discipline of Market Leaders: Choose Your Customers, Narrow Your Focus, Dominate Your Market, *HarperCollins, London, 1995)*

companies succeeding in more than one dimension, most organizations can be successful by excelling in one of them. Most strategies imply 'majoring' on one of these areas for the next stage of development—probably one to two years ahead. At the same time, the business must not become uncompetitive in the other two. Action may well be needed to (say) ensure that its processes do not become markedly less effective than those of its competitors while it develops its new products, or costs will increase too quickly. Alternatively, it must not dissatisfy its customers while making major improvements in operational effectiveness. Figure 2.10 attempts to show this in terms of the relative degree of competence required to achieve advantage (prosper), sustain its position (succeed) or avoid merely fighting for survival.

- Gain consensus and agreement among the business management about what has to improve and why, which can be critical in establishing the 'themes' behind both the business and IS strategy, as described in Chapter 3. The set of planned investments on IS/IT should relate to overcoming deficiencies in existing capabilities and to developing the organization's future competencies. Otherwise, the organization will be unable to link the priorities for IS/IT investment to other business-development initiatives and change programs that are essential to achieving the strategy.

These aspects of strategic management have significant implications for the overall role of IS/IT, which can be a differentiating competency or may be an essential ingredient to support, enable or enhance other competencies. As mentioned in Chapter 1, the development of an 'IS capability'—a combination of competencies and resources—that can be instrumental in creating, delivering and sustaining advantage is discussed in later chapters.

SUMMARY

It is vital that the IS/IT strategies and plans be linked directly to the objectives and strategies of the business unit and of the corporation as a whole. There are now a number of examples where IS/IT strategy formulation and planning takes place within the same process as corporate strategy formulation and planning, and, indeed, the entire strategy process is now fully integrated. However, the evidence, as quoted in Chapter 1, is that this applies to a minority of organizations, as yet.

Each of the tools and techniques described above has been shown to have value in the various strategy development and planning processes. If there are going to be close links between IS/IT and business strategies, then these same tools and techniques should have direct relevance in IS/IT strategy formulation and planning, if only because they enable business managers to become positively and actively involved.

Traditionally, IS/IT was seen as an instrument of implementation of strategy. In many of its uses, it is still exactly that; however, as described in Chapter 1 and shown in Figure 1.5, IS/IT now has to be considered as an input to business strategy, in terms of its potential to change this strategy or create new strategies. It must be remembered that the same IS/IT-based opportunities may also exist for competitors and, therefore, IS/IT can constitute a threat, just like a new competitive product.

The next task is to establish that context for IS/IT strategy more coherently. Chapter 3 will develop models and approaches to IS/IT strategy development—but all those models and approaches recognize the need to link effectively to the business strategy, its determination and management, both to achieve alignment of the strategies and to take advantage of the strategic opportunities IS/IT can create.

ENDNOTES

1. There is much research and commentary to support this position. See, for example, T.S.H. Teo and J.S.K. Ang, 'An examination of major IS planning problems', *International Journal of Information Management*, Vol. 21, 2001, 457–470; C.P. Armstrong and V. Sambamurthy, 'Information technology assimilation in firms: The influence of senior leadership and IT infrastructures', *Information Systems Research*, Vol. 10, No. 4, 1999, 304–327; S. Dutta, 'Linking IT and business strategy: The role and responsibility of senior management', *European Management Journal*, Vol. 14, No. 3, 1996, 255–268; 'The end of delegation? Information technology and the CEO', *Harvard Business Review*, September–October, 1995, 161–172.

2. H.I. Ansoff, R.P. Declerck and R.L. Hayes, eds, *From Strategic Planning to Strategic Management*, John Wiley & Sons, New York, 1976.
3. F.W. Gluck, S.P. Kaufmann and A.S. Walleck, 'Strategic management for competitive advantage', *Harvard Business Review*, July–August 1980, 154–161.
4. M. Subramani and E. Walden, 'The impact of e-commerce announcements on the market value of firms', *Information Systems Research*, Vol. 12, No. 2, 2001, 135–154; P.M. Lee, 'What's in a name.com?: The effects of ".com" name changes on stock prices and trading activity', *Strategic Management Journal*, Vol. 22, No. 8, 2001, 793–804.
5. A. Campbell and M. Alexander, 'What's wrong with strategy?', *Harvard Business Review*, November–December, 1997, 42–51.
6. H. Mintzberg, *The Rise and Fall of Strategic Planning*, Free Press, New York, 1994.
7. G. Hamel, 'Strategy as revolution', *Harvard Business Review*, July–August 1996, 69–82.
8. M.E. Porter, *Competitive Strategy: Techniques for Analysing Industries and Competitors*, Free Press, New York, 1980.
9. See, for example, K. Kelly, *New Rules for the New Economy*, Viking Press, New York, 1998.
10. C. Handy, *The Empty Raincoat*, Hutchinson, London, 1994.
11. *Vodafone Future: Corporate Social Responsibility Report 2000–2001*.
12. See L.F. Cranor, 'Internet privacy', *Communications of the ACM*, Vol. 42, No. 2, 1999, 28–38; and H. Wang, H.K.O. Lee and C. Wang, 'Consumer privacy concerns about Internet marketing', *Communications of the ACM*, Vol. 41, No. 3, March 1998, 63–70.
13. Campbell and Alexander note that companies that don't win the loyalty of stakeholders will go out of business. See A. Campbell and M. Alexander, 'What's wrong with strategy', *Harvard Business Review*, November–December 1997, 42–51.
14. G. Johnson and K. Scholes, *Exploring Corporate Strategy*, Prentice Hall, Englewood Cliffs, New Jersey, 2002.
15. H. Mintzberg, 'Patterns in strategy formulation', *Management Science*, Vol. 24, No. 9, 1978, 934–948; H. Mintzberg and J.A. Waters, 'Of strategies, deliberate and emergent', *Strategic Management Journal*, Vol. 6, 1985, 257–272; and J.B. Quinn, *Strategies for Change: Logical Incrementalism*, Irwin, Homewood Illinois, 1980.
16. H. Mintzberg, 'Crafting strategy', *Harvard Business Review*, July–August 1987, 66–75.
17. J.M. Higgins, *Strategy Formulation, Implementation and Control*, Dryden Press, New York, 1985.
18. M.E. Porter, *Competitive Strategy: Techniques for Analysing Industries and Competitors*, Free Press, New York, 1980 and *Competitive Advantage: Creating and Sustaining Superior Performance*, Free Press, New York, 1985.
19. G.L. Parsons, 'Information technology: A new competitive weapon', *Sloan Management Review*, Fall, 1983, 3–15.
20. F.W. McFarlan, 'Information technology changes the way you compete', *Harvard Business Review*, May–June 1984, 98–110.
21. J.I. Cash, 'Interorganizational systems: An information society opportunity or threat?', *The Information Society*, Vol. 3, No. 3, 1988, 199–228.
22. M. Porter, 'Strategy and the Internet', *Harvard Business Review*, March 2001, 64–78.
23. D. Feeny, 'Making business sense of the e-opportunity', *MIT Sloan Management Review*, Winter, 2001, 41–51.
24. A. Roberts, 'Online wine exchanges plan derivatives', *Financial Times*, 14 June 2001.
25. Y. Bakos, 'Reducing buyers' search costs: Implications for electronic marketplaces', *Management Science*, Vol. 43, No. 12, 1997, 1676–1692; Y. Bakos, 'The emergence of electronic marketplaces on the Internet', *Communications of the ACM*, Vol. 41, No. 8, 1998, 35–42.
26. M.E. Porter and V.E. Millar, 'How information gives you competitive advantage', *Harvard Business Review*, July–August 1985, 149–160.
27. J.I. Cash, 'Interorganizational systems: An information society opportunity or threat?', *The Information Society*, Vol. 3, No. 3, 1988, 199–228.
28. N.D. Meyer and M.E. Boone, *The Information Edge*, McGraw-Hill, New York, 1986.
29. B. Wernerfelt, 'A resource-based view of the firm', *Strategic Management Journal*, Vol. 5, 1984, 171–180.
30. J.B. Barney, 'Firm resources and sustained competitive advantage', *Journal of Management*, Vol. 17, 1991, 99–120; 'Looking inside for competitive advantage', *Academy of Management Executive*, Vol. 9, 1995, 49–61; *Gaining and Sustaining Competitive Advantage*, Addison-Wesley, Reading, Massachusetts, 1997.
31. M. Treacy and F. Wiersma, 'Customer intimacy and other value disciplines', *Harvard Business Review*, January–February 1993, 84–93; *The Discipline of Market Leaders: Choose Your Customers, Narrow Your Focus, Dominate Your Market*, HarperCollins, London, 1995.

3
Developing an IS/IT Strategy: Establishing Effective Processes

Developing an IS/IT strategy is taken to mean thinking strategically and planning for the effective long-term management and optimal impact of information in all its forms: information systems (IS) and information technology (IT) incorporating manual and computer systems, computer technology and telecommunications. It also includes organizational aspects of the management of IS/IT.

A concise but somewhat narrower definition offered by Lederer and Sethi[1] is 'the process of deciding the objectives for organizational computing and identifying potential computer applications which the organization should implement.' A further perspective, underpinning the close relationship between business and IS strategies is: 'An IS strategy brings together the business aims of the company, an understanding of the information needed to support those aims, and the implementation of computer systems to provide that information. It is a plan for the development of systems towards some future vision of the role of IS in the organization.'[2] A more recent definition, which fits with the approach of this book, is 'the process of identifying a portfolio of computer-based applications to be implemented, which is both highly aligned with corporate strategy and has the ability to create an advantage over competitors.'[3]

The most common aims for organizations adopting an IS/IT strategy process are:

- alignment of IS/IT with the business to identify where IS/IT contributes most, and the determination of priorities for investment;
- gaining competitive advantage from business opportunities created by using IS/IT;

- building a cost-effective, yet flexible technology infrastructure for the future;
- developing the appropriate resources and competencies to deploy IS/IT successfully across the organization.

This chapter is concerned with establishing a framework and process for developing IS/IT strategies. It assumes that it must be closely integrated with business strategy, and that, to be effective, it must be a continuous process, with a flow of deliverables that dovetail with the outcomes of business strategic thinking and planning.

Where an IS/IT strategy-formulation process has not become established, it may be necessary to undertake initiatives in one or more areas of the business, to foster awareness of the importance of delivering real benefits to the business through the deliberate application of IS/IT in support of its critical business needs, and to achieve the transition in an acceptable timescale. This will also offer the opportunity to ensure that old, inappropriate planning methods are stopped, and better, more comprehensive approaches are adopted. The process should introduce the required disciplines, controls and new techniques, establish good relationships, and identify tasks and responsibilities and thus define planning resource requirements. However, as soon as possible, the IS/IT strategy process needs to become an integral part of the development of business strategy, business plans and their subsequent implementation.

One of the most compelling arguments for integrating business and IS strategy formulation and planning is so that the finite resources of the business can be allocated in a coherent manner to achievable strategies and plans that collectively will deliver benefits to the business.

The IS/IT Strategy Process: Some Definitional Clarity

The writings in the area of IS/IT strategy can be a little confusing, not least because of the variety of terms encountered and the inconsistent usage of language for seemingly similar concepts. In the research literature, 'strategic information systems planning' (SISP), 'information systems planning' (ISP), 'information systems strategy planning' (ISSP) and 'business systems planning' are just some of the terms frequently encountered. Examining the meanings of these concepts as they are used reveals that they are essentially similar. Indeed, the emphasis on 'planning' probably originates as a consequence of portraying IS/IT as part of the implementation of the business strategy—IS/IT investments were planned once the business strategy had been formulated. With IS/IT increasingly shaping the strategy of a business, the strategizing aspect must be emphasized.

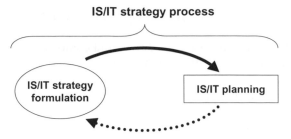

Figure 3.1   *IS/IT strategy process*

In this book, a distinction is made between IS/IT strategy formulation and IS/IT planning—this difference between 'strategy' and 'planning' was addressed in Chapter 2. Formulation is concerned with developing the IS/IT strategy and is addressed in this book through a process of alignment and competitive impact. Once that strategy has been formulated, an implementation plan can then be constructed—IS/IT planning. The IS/IT strategy process refers to *both* formulation and planning (see Figure 3.1). While the IS/IT strategy drives IS/IT planning, constructing the IS/IT plan may reveal aspects that cause the IS/IT strategy to be reconsidered.

THE EVOLUTION OF THE IS/IT STRATEGY PROCESS: FROM TECHNOLOGY FOCUS TO STRATEGIC FOCUS

Research has highlighted that, in many organizations, approaches to IS strategy formulation have tended to follow an evolutionary process. In Stage 1, the focus is on planning to deliver technology. At Stage 5, the organization has reached a stage of maturity where the emphasis is on assessing the competitive impact of IS/IT and in ensuring the alignment between business strategies and IS/IT investments. This evolution can be explained as follows:

- *Stage 1*—typical early data processing (DP) planning—the IT department need to plan the interfaces between applications developed separately, project by project, in order to make them work effectively and efficiently, both in business operations and the utilization of technology. Obtaining management understanding of the increasing dependence of the business on its systems is the key objective, to enable a more coherent, less piecemeal, approach to be adopted. Essentially, support applications are being built and management

perceives IS/IT in that limited role, but the dependence is steadily
increasing.

- *Stage 2*—management, now aware (often because of some crisis or
  key system failure), initiate a top-down review of IS/IT applications
  in the light of business dependence—priorities are agreed based on
  the relative importance of business needs. For example, should the
  order processing redevelopment take precedence over the new sales
  analysis system? The approaches used are very methodological,
  normally based on derivatives of IBM's 'Business Systems Planning'[4]
  or similar methodologies, and involve gaining a management consensus of criticalities and priorities. An extended, prioritized
  'shopping list' of key operational type applications for both operational and management information requirements will generally
  result.
- *Stage 3*—the next stage is centred around detailed IS/IT planning, to
  determine the best way of implementing the applications and
  supporting technologies or, in some cases, reimplementing existing
  systems in more appropriate, integrated and perhaps less costly ways.
  The portfolio needs to be better balanced—greater attention is paid
  to the now (perceived to be critical) key operational systems and less
  resource is dedicated to support applications, each having been
  'prioritized' in Stage 2. An 'Application Support Centre' or 'Help
  desk'[5] concept may be implemented for support-type systems, and
  application packages will probably be introduced to rationalize and
  replace internally-developed systems. Stage 3 can take considerable
  time to implement effectively and, while this is going on, nothing else
  can really happen, since all IT resources are budgeted against a
  known detailed 2–3-year plan.

Through Stages 1 to 3, the evolution from isolated 'efficiency'-driven
applications to integrated 'effectiveness' systems has been occurring—
but the objective has not yet been overt use of IS/IT for competitive
advantage; the main purpose is to stop IS/IT being problematic and to
ensure that it is causing no disadvantages.

- *Stage 4*—the users take the reins, not necessarily encouraged by
  senior management, but not discouraged either, because they do
  not wish to prevent business-led, entrepreneurial use of IS/IT by
  users seeing new opportunities, using information in new ways to
  provide business leverage/competitive advantage. This may start
  during Stage 3 as frustration builds up in the 'jam tomorrow' stage
  of detailed planning and implementation. It is important that users,
  unfettered in any way by IS/IT procedure or control, exercise this

freedom to innovate, even if 90% of the ideas are of little strategic potential. It is the source of tested ideas that, with later IS/IT support, can be turned to advantage—literally, high potential opportunities driven by the business. Many strategic applications originate this way.[6]

- *Stage 5*—this is the difficult stage to reach, particularly if Stage 3 is delayed and Stage 4 is more user-rebellion than business stimulated innovation. It requires bringing it all back together—not just IS/IT-based strategy formulation as in Stage 2, but also the formulation of business strategy. In essence, the innovation ideas of Stage 4 require evaluation in the business context along with the opportunities now made available from the key operational infrastructure (i.e. the knowledge of what to do and the ability to deliver it effectively). Linking IS/IT potential to the business strategy is the main task, and this requires the simultaneous attention of senior executives, line management and IT specialists—the first time in this process that they have all acted as a coalition together. There is no 'methodology' available—multiple methods implies business strategizing and planning methods plus IS/IT top-down and bottom-up approaches. Strategic applications can be identified and agreed upon in the context of the business strategy.

The 'process' does not always occur sequentially in an organization, and there will always be overlap across the stages. In large organizations, different businesses or functions may be at different stages in their evolution. What is surprising, in some ways, is how often the stages are followed quite sequentially as an organization gets more sophisticated in its application and deployment of IS/IT. All these variations on the IS/IT strategy process will be discussed in more detail later in the book, with special focus on the latter stages, which most organizations now have to address successfully.

APPROACHES TO IS/IT STRATEGY DEVELOPMENT

There is a difference between having an IS/IT strategy and having an IS/IT strategy that is closely aligned and integrated with the business strategy. Over the years, organizations have adopted a variety of approaches in planning IS/IT investments; unfortunately, these have not always resulted in the organization deploying IS/IT strategically. Earl[7] has studied the changing focus and increasing maturity of the IS/IT strategy process in a number of organizations and has identified five main types of approach. The chief characteristics of these five types are summarized in Table 3.1, adapted from Earl's more detailed assessment. The analysis considers the main task that is carried out, the main objectives, who drives the planning forward and the approaches adopted. By looking at each of these aspects, the effectiveness of the linkage between IS/IT strategy and business strategy can be determined, and consequently how likely the organization is to gain competitive advantage from IS/IT. This implies that, although an organization should develop more 'mature' approaches to IS/IT strategy formulation and planning in order to achieve a full and relevant portfolio, some earlier approaches need to be maintained in order to manage the total matrix of applications. Not every application of IT needs all the complexity implied in Stage 5. However, one thing is certain, if the organization is poor at formulating business strategy, it will have considerable difficulty developing an IS/IT strategy.

An organization can identify from the types of planning approaches in place (i) where it is in relation to the eventual need for integration of IS/IT and business planning, and (ii) which approaches it needs to adopt in the short term to move it toward that eventual goal.

The names given by Earl to the dominant rationale at each stage (see the summary description in Table 3.1) imply the following:

1. *Business led*—carried out mainly by IT specialists who define an IS/IT investment plan based on the current business strategy. While acknowledging IS as a strategic resource, with this approach the organization is taking the view that business strategy should lead IS/IT strategy and not the other way around. The business strategy is not challenged and the approach does not explore competitive opportunities through IS/IT unless incorporated in the business strategy.

2. *Method driven*—the use of techniques (often a consultant's methodology) to identify IS needs by analysing business processes—an 'engineering' philosophy based on top-down analysis of information needs and relationships.

3. *Technological*—IS/IT planning is seen as an exercise in process and information modelling. Here, IS professionals use analytical modelling and tools (e.g. Computer Aided Software Engineering [CASE]) to produce IS plans in the form of blueprints—perhaps one each for applications, data, communications and computing. Earl noted that the word 'architecture' may replace 'plans' or 'strategies'.[8]

4. *Administrative*—the main objective is to establish IT capital and expense budgets and resource plans to achieve approved IS applications, usually based on a prioritized wish list from users. Business

Table 3.1 Increasing organizational maturity with respect to IS planning (source: M.J. Earl, 'Experiences in strategic information systems planning', MIS Quarterly, Vol. 17, No. 1, 1993, 1–24)

	Stage 1	Stage 2	Stage 3	Stage 4	Stage 5
Main task	IS/IT application mapping	Defining business needs	Detailed IS planning	Strategic/Competitive advantage	Linkage to business strategy
Key objective	Management understanding	Agreeing priorities	Balancing the portfolio	Pursuing opportunities	Integrating IS and business strategies
Direction from	IT led	Senior management initiative	User and IT together	Executives/Senior management and users	Coalition of users/management and IT
Main approach	Bottom-up development	Top-down analysis	Balanced top-down and bottom-up	Entrepreneurial (user innovation)	Multiple method at same time
Summary	'Technology led'	'Method driven'	'Administrative'	'Business led'	'Organization led'

plans, usually at a functional level, are analysed to identify where IS/
IT is most critical in meeting short to medium-term needs.

5. *Organizational*—the development of key themes for IS/IT investment
derived from a business consensus view of how IS/IT can help
meet overall business objectives, agreed by the senior management
team.

It is not too difficult to align these approaches to the characteristics of the
planning environments described by Sullivan (see Figure 1.9). The fit is
not exact but the Technology led, Method driven and Administrative
approaches are more appropriate and practical where diffusion is low
(i.e. low decentralization of IS/IT control) and fit the needs of the traditional and backbone environments best. Business led and Organizational
appear more relevant to high degrees of diffusion, the former being most
appropriate for creating new opportunities and the latter for providing
the eclectic type of planning for the 'complex' part of the matrix.

In an empirical study using Earl's descriptions, Doherty et al.[9] found
that the Organizational, Business-led and Administrative approaches
could be identified and clearly distinguished in the sample of 267 companies. The study also showed that the organizations believed they were
more successful in IS planning if they followed the Organizational
approach; of the three, Business-led came second and Administrative
was third. They argued that the Organizational approach had, based
on the survey evidence, very similar characteristics to the 'rational adaptation' mode of planning that Segars et al.[10] had observed as the most
successful approach in their study.

Doherty and colleagues, however, could not clearly distinguish
between Method led and Technology led, even in their large sample,
and suggested that the two, together, formed an intrinsically IT-led
approach they called 'systematic'. This is a reasonable conclusion,
given that, over the last decade, many large application and utility
software packages have effectively become part of the infrastructure.
Application software and technology plans cannot always be separated,
but require highly integrated, detailed planning (i.e. *systematic*). In the
survey, the *systematic* approach had a similar level of perceived success as
Business led.

PROBLEMS AND BARRIERS

Despite an understanding of the importance of strategic planning for IS,
in the past decade many organizations have developed perfectly sensible
IS strategies that have been left to gather dust, or have been implemented

in a half-hearted manner, because they did not have enough management commitment invested in them. These were not merely uplifted user 'wish lists' that had been renamed 'strategies', nor IT-inspired total systems—information and technology architectures—that never deserved to gain business backing. Rather, they were derived from a thorough investigation of business needs and priorities, driven from business strategy and objectives, and constructed by business teams. They may have even obtained the sought-after sign-off from the board, but were then left with the IS function to implement them, while management got on with its 'real' job of running the business.

A number of surveys have attempted to identify criteria for successful IS/IT strategy development. Lederer and Mendelow[11] surveyed 20 US companies to determine the senior management problems preventing effective development of IS/IT strategic plans. An earlier survey had shown that obtaining top-management commitment was a prerequisite for success, but that it was often difficult to obtain. Their research identified the following reasons for this, in order of frequency of occurrence:

1. Top management lacked awareness of the impact IS/IT is having generally and did not understand how IS/IT offered strategic advantages. They tended to see 'computers' in purely an operational context—still essentially a DP era view.
2. They perceived a credibility gap between the 'hype' of the IT industry as to what IT can actually do and how easy it is to do it, given the difficulties their organization had had in delivering the claimed benefits.
3. Top managers did not view information as a business resource to be managed for long-term benefit. They only appreciated its criticality when they could not get what they needed.
4. Despite the difficulty in expressing all IS benefits in economic terms, top management still demand to see a financial justification for investments.
5. Finally, and an increasingly apparent problem today, is that top managers have become action orientated with a short-term focus that militates against putting much effort into long-term planning, especially of IS/IT, given the other issues above.

In a similar UK survey, Wilson[12] identified a number of barriers that prevented an effective IS/IT strategy being developed and then implemented. Organizations claiming to have an IS/IT strategy (73 of the total of 186 surveyed) were asked to identify barriers inhibiting, first, the development of the strategy and, second, implementing it. In this survey, top-management commitment was less critical than the ability to measure benefits from the overall plan, to deal with major business issues such as diversification or growth and to provide appropriately-skilled user and IT resources. The factors cited seem to reflect views based on the past evolution of IS/IT, rather than its future implications. The survey also highlights one or two of the 'softer' issues—politics and middle management's insecurity in the face of change. Ninety per cent of respondents claimed that the IS/IT strategy was either a formal, documented part of the business strategy, or that the strategy was aligned to strategic aims.

In a more recent survey of senior IS executives, Teo and Ang[13] identified the major problems associated with the IS/IT strategy process. Dividing the process into three phases (the launch phase, the plan development phase and the implementation phase), they reported that, in all three phases, failing to secure top management support is the most serious problem. Not having free communication flow and not being able to obtain sufficiently-qualified personnel are the other two major problems in the first phase. In the second phase, respondents reported ignoring business goals and failing to translate these goals/strategies into action plans as major problems as well. Table 3.2 summarizes the top problems in the first two phases.

Earl's survey of 21 UK companies, referred to earlier, ranked the unsuccessful features of strategic IS planning as: resource constraints, the strategy not implemented fully, lack of top management acceptance, length of time involved, and poor user–IS relationships. In research exploring the enablers and inhibitors of alignment between IS and business strategies, Luftman and Brier[14] identified the six most important enablers and the six main inhibitors (see Table 3.3). What is striking about these is that the same topics (executive support, understand the business, IT–business relations and leadership) show up as both enablers and inhibitors. Our research supports these conclusions.[15]

All these surveys indicate that several of the prime requirements for the effective formulation of IS/IT strategy revolve around people. Undoubtedly, it is essential for knowledgeable, experienced, highly skilled and well-motivated staff to be involved and for them to be committed to the work. This was borne out by the findings of Lederer and Sethi[16] in their survey of 80 companies. The pitfalls in establishing an effective IS/IT strategy process relating to people, which were among the most frequently cited, are listed in Table 3.4.

While all the foregoing problems and barriers focus on IS strategy, a number of them originate in the business strategy, and many of the same problems could be cited for business strategy development and planning. This is partly because the strategic developments required for organizations to meet the challenges facing them are often poorly served by traditional, functionally orientated business plans. For example, many

Table 3.2   *Problems encountered in the IS strategy process* (source: *adapted from T.S.H. Teo and J.S.K. Ang, 'An examination of major IS planning problems', International Journal of Information Management, Vol. 21, 2001, 461)*

Problems in launching the IS strategy process	*Problems with the IS strategy process*
1. Failing to get top management support	1. Failing to involve top management sufficiently
2. Not having free communication and commitment to change throughout the organization	2. Ignoring business objectives
3. Being unable to obtain sufficiently qualified personnel to do a proper job	3. Failing to translate business objectives and strategies into action plans
4. Delegating responsibility to an individual without sufficient experience, influence or time to do a thorough job	4. Failing to involve users sufficiently
5. Not investing sufficient 'front-end' time to ensure that all strategy and planning tasks and individual responsibilities are well understood	5. Relying exclusively on user 'wish lists' for application ideas
6. Not having a steering committee that is highly committed	6. Neglecting to assess realistically internal weaknesses of the IS function in determining capabilities to implement the recommended strategy
7. Not having a clear-cut business strategy to guide the IS strategy effort	7. Not performing a top-down analysis to identify critical functional areas that the IS strategy has to support
8. Failing to anticipate new developments in IT that might affect the strategy	8. Failure to consider and explicitly evaluate alternative IS strategies in order to give top management a meaningful choice.
9. Ignoring the people and politics side of strategy formulation and planning	9. Failing to review the IS strategy with all managers so as to obtain support and cooperation for its implementation.

organizations have an impressive array of mission statements, objectives, values, critical success factors and performance targets, but when the task of translating the strategy into effective and coordinated action plans has been left to the functional directorates, it has all too rarely been consolidated and managed as an integrated business-wide program. The functions have been, on the whole, too focused on current problems to be able to put a satisfactory strategic perspective into their plans.

Table 3.3   *Enablers and inhibitors of strategic alignment (source: J. Luftman and T. Brier, 'Achieving and sustaining business–IT alignment', California Management Review, Fall, 1999, 109–122)*

Enablers	Inhibitors
• Senior executive support for IT	• IT/business lacks close relationships
• IT involved in strategy development	• IT does not prioritize well
• IT understands the business	• IT fails to meet commitments
• Business–IT partnership	• IT does not understand business
• Well-prioritized IT projects	• Senior executives do not support IT
• IT demonstrates leadership	• IT management lacks leadership

Table 3.4   *Pitfalls to planning, in relation to people (source: adapted from A.L. Lederer and V. Sethi, 'The implementation of strategic information systems planning methodologies', MIS Quarterly, Vol. 12, No. 3, 1988, 445–461)*

Problems, listed in order of severity

1. Difficulty in obtaining top management commitment for implementing the plan
2. Success of the approach is greatly dependent on the planning team leader
3. Difficulty in finding a team leader who meets the criteria specified for the role
4. Difficulty in convincing top management to fund the planning exercise
5. Difficulty in finding team members who meet the specified criteria
6. The exorbitant number of hours demanded from top management
7. Failure to establish a permanent planning group as a result of the planning exercise
8. Time and expense involved in finding planning support staff

THE ENVIRONMENT OF THE IS/IT STRATEGY

The requirement to determine the information systems strategy over an extended period demands that a consolidated approach should retain the flexibility to respond to changing business and organizational needs and incorporate new IS/IT options. In order to do that, the processes used to analyse situations and assess opportunities must be capable of being revisited in part, at any time, to assess the implications without a major rethink of the whole strategy.

In Chapter 1, a simple model relating business, IS and IT strategies was described (see Figure 1.6). In Chapter 2, a view of the business strategic process that considered the realities of attempting to plan in an ever-changing environment was also described (see Figure 2.3). Combining this view from Johnson and Scholes[17] with the earlier, simpler model, a more comprehensive and pragmatic model can be defined, which describes the environment within which IS/IT strategy formulation and planning takes place.

Figure 3.2 shows that, while, at any one time, a comprehensive analysis of the business and IS/IT internal and external environments can be carried out to define an intended set of strategies, it is unlikely that all aspects of these strategies will be realized. Changes will occur in both the business and IT environments, and these will cause changes to be made to the IS strategy. The 'intended' IS strategy may also fail to be implemented successfully and hence will have to be revised either in timescale or content.

In addition, changes in the business or IT environments may impose constraints on the IS strategy or open up new IS opportunities. These factors, which force changes from the intended strategies, will not always occur at convenient moments in the planning cycle! All three strategies, business, IS and IT, must be realigned whenever new opportunities or constraints emerge. Equally importantly (and this is often overlooked), these changes to the strategy will make parts of the old strategy redundant. In many organizations, considerable IS/IT effort and resource can be consumed pursuing effectively obsolete requirements because the plans, derived perhaps a year earlier, have been overtaken by events—events that have not been interpreted in terms of their effects on the IS/IT developments already under way. This problem can be compounded where large IS/IT projects are involved and the majority of the money has been spent—'we've started, so we'll finish' seems to be the rule, even if by finishing the system development no actual benefits will now occur! Even in such circumstances it is best to stop work and redirect the resources to the new emerging needs.

The need to be able to revisit and revise any aspect of the strategies implies that, as far as possible, all facets of the internal and external environments that can affect the strategies are included in the initial derivation. Then, if any of them change, the implications of the changes can more easily be identified and understood in order to revise the strategies appropriately.

THE CHALLENGES OF PLANNING STRATEGICALLY FOR IS/IT TODAY

The necessity to improve return on investments, coupled with the high risk potential of investing very substantial sums unwisely, have long been

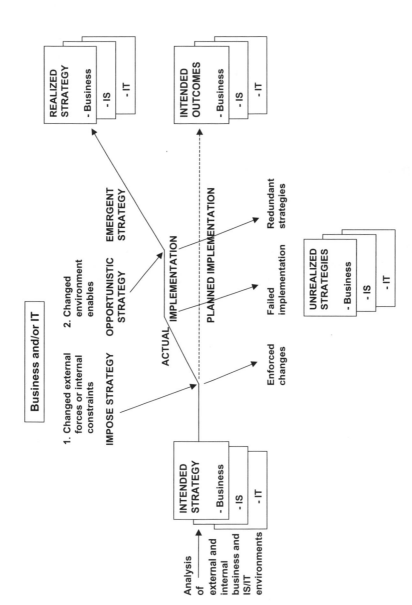

Figure 3.2 A revised model for IS strategy (source: after Johnson and Scholes, 2002)

key objectives for developing a strategy for IS/IT. Prominent among them are the vast sums of money that organizations have spent on 'e-commerce' or 'Internet' strategies that have, on average, delivered little business value to date. In addition, an ever-increasing number of examples, cited as demonstrating improved competitive success resulting from implementing computer and telecommunications systems, has also boosted awareness and interest. American Airlines, Merrill Lynch, American Hospital Supplies, Thomson's Holidays and several others were reported so extensively, in the 1980s and 1990s, that they have been elevated almost to legend status. More recently, the exploits of some organizations on the Internet such as Amazon.com, Lastminute.com, eBay.com and Betdaq.com, coupled with the media hype, has also raised awareness. There are many other examples that have so far received less widespread coverage but are equally significant as sources of ideas for other organizations. Many of these are referred to throughout this book.

As the focus on delivering customer value and improving customer service becomes ever more critical for so many enterprises, and competitive, economic and regulatory pressures mount, there is a recognition by enlightened businesses that incremental and disconnected improvements will not be good enough. There is also the growing recognition that delivering satisfactory performance is dependent on robust business processes. This is the environment in which gaining control of key processes has become a popular focus of attention, and many major change programs revolve around improving the performance of core business processes. In this environment, business process redesign gained a strong foothold, which continues today. Hammer[18] cautioned against 'paving the cow paths' with IT, and called on managers to look for opportunities to redesign processes to take account of the opportunities provided by IT.

In this context, a fully-integrated business strategy framework is needed that can encompass the development and implementation of major change programs, a series of supporting strategies in response to key business drivers, and the management of a coordinated program of strategic and tactical projects (see Figure 3.3).

Developing an IS/IT strategy in today's competitive environment is not easy to achieve. By definition, it must be deeply embedded in business issues, since it promotes IS/IT as direct tools of competitive strategy. At the same time, it must continue to meet information processing and managerial information needs, but its primary orientation has turned from merely cost reduction to direct value adding; from mainly administrative efficiency and organizational fluency to delivering competitive impact, both to gain advantage or avoid being disadvantaged. A key point is that its objectives and priorities are derived from business

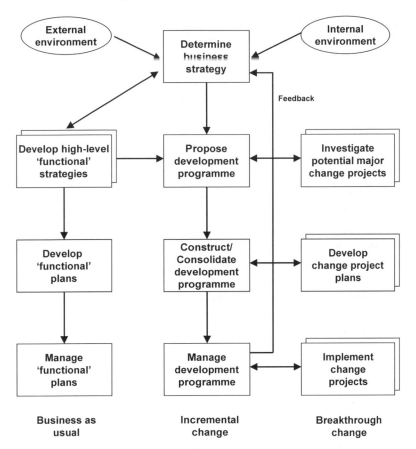

Figure 3.3   *Integrated business strategy framework*

imperatives. Long-term benefits are sought from the strategic exploitation of information and it has a formulative part to play in advancing business strategy.

The business environment and approaches to strategy formulation and planning were examined in Chapter 2, which laid out in some detail the elements that make up the wider business environment and the more specific aspects of strategy. If the contribution from IS/IT is to be maximized, it is necessary not only for IS specialists to understand business issues but also for business people to have an awareness of the potential offered by technology. Unfortunately, this close working relationship does not always exist in organizations. In Chapter 8, we explore how an organization can begin to improve this relationship: failure to do so will severely impact any attempt to develop a more strategic perspective of IS/IT.

There is no standard approach that can guarantee success, and this book is not attempting to put forward a prescriptive methodology for conducting IS/IT strategy formulation and planning. It would be fool-hardy to attempt to do so, since each situation is unique, warranting careful consideration, and requiring its own tailored approach. Rather, a framework and 'tool box' of techniques for IS/IT strategy formulation and planning are proposed that can be adapted to fit a wide spectrum of environments from the most to the least sophisticated, and which responds to the many external and internal, business and technical drivers.

Similar views about the need for flexible and evolutionary approaches to the IS/IT strategy process were expressed almost two decades ago by Sullivan.[19] He proposed a number of key elements within effective planning approaches that were needed to enable the realization of the competitive potential of IS/IT. Even today, they are still valid, and are embedded in the approach advanced in this book. He proposed:

- The search for competitive advantage through the application of IS/IT.
- A broader scope for planning, which incorporates a wider spectrum of technologies, rather than just traditional uses of IT for processing data and information.
- The need to unite technologies, as they emerge, as well as with the installed base.
- The development of information, systems and technology architectures to guide the introduction and integration of new and existing systems and technologies.
- A shift away from traditional, formal structured plans toward much more flexible approaches, whose aims are to find and implement the most important initiatives for the benefit of the business, and epitomized by their:

    - responsiveness in being able to shift resources to where they are needed;
    - increasingly creative use of IT by users;
    - ability to evaluate options;
    - use of benchmarking to establish standards of performance of external and competitive organizations.

Similar conclusions have been reached by Earl, Segars, Lederer, Doherty and others.

The framework and outline of the process for developing IS/IT strategies are described in this chapter, and the techniques for assessing the environment and identifying information needs and future opportunities are covered in Chapters 4 and 5.

ESTABLISHING AN IS/IT STRATEGY PROCESS

A Continuous Process

Once a strategic perspective on IS/IT is established and a strategy process is instituted, it should become a continuously evolving process, where the strategies and plans are refreshed regularly and even frequently, according to external forces, business needs and opportunities, the planning timetable, culture of the organization, and the benefits delivered by implementation of the strategy. Depending on the scope of the strategy process, the main deliverables, hard or soft, may be virtually unchanged or may be completely revised. For example:

- plans arising from the IS/IT strategy need to be updated as required, the frequency determined by the underlying pace of change;
- development or acquisition of applications takes place in response to prioritized demands, tightly linked to broader business initiatives;
- the supporting IT infrastructure, once defined to meet a business strategy, should have a relatively long lifespan;
- mechanisms for monitoring internal and external business and IS/IT perspectives are essential elements of the strategic management process and, once put into place, are likely to stay in place, although the parameters monitored will vary.

A Learning Process

As well as being a continuous process, strategic IS planning is also a learning process. Both IS specialists and business people are becoming more aware of business and technology issues, and learning to identify and exploit opportunities within a cooperative environment. At best, the culture of partnership between the IS function and the rest of the organization reorientates itself to treat information, systems and technology as core resources in the day-to-day life of the business and its continuing development. This also takes place alongside a continuing evolution in the maturity of the IS function.

For the organization that does not have a strategic perspective on IS/IT and has not begun to develop an IS/IT strategy, there is an understandable problem in not knowing how to go about it. It is a far from trivial change to go from the tactical planning used to develop information systems based on catalogued users' demands—usually referred to as 'wish lists'—or from IT technical infrastructure planning, to developing an IS/IT strategy closely aligned with the business strategy, especially since the outcome of such an approach is very likely to have far-reaching impacts on the future role of the IS/IT in the business and the role of the IS function.

When the move is from traditional developmental planning, focusing on technology delivery, to IS/IT strategy development, where the target applications portfolio is more balanced and where the emphasis is on future strategic importance, then several characteristics need to change. Typically, timescales for the planning horizon move out from one to two or more years, and development and provisioning plans are driven by current and future business needs rather than being incremental extensions from earlier developments or recorded backlog lists. Alternatively, the shift may not entail an extension of the planning horizon, but a radical change to achieve rapid strategic moves, where the focus is on flexibility, responsiveness and fast delivery.

Initiating the Strategy Cycle

Before embarking on the development of an IS/IT strategy, whether for the first time or as part of a continuous strategic management process, there are many aspects to be considered, so that a clear brief and Terms of Reference (TOR) can be agreed for the planning activity. These will not be set in stone, but should give a sound foundation to build on.

It is crucial that an adequate amount of time and effort is spent in the process of planning for planning, since the effort spent here can determine whether 'success' is achievable. How to go forward depends on the maturity of the process, particularly experiences to date, the starting point, the purpose of planning and the targets being sought, if they can be defined. It is also markedly affected by the issues and stimuli prompting the activity. Box 3.1 contains a list of questions that require answering before embarking on an IS/IT strategy process. The key questions are examined in the following sections, although, clearly, the answers will vary widely within different organizational contexts.

It should be re-emphasized that there is no one 'best' way to tackle strategy formulation and planning for IS/IT. It is essential to assess the situation and the needs carefully, and then to deploy the most appropriate people, methods and techniques to suit this context. Each organization merits a different approach, which will vary according to its current circumstances, and the stimuli prompting the need for strategy

Box 3.1 Questions that need to be answered before embarking on IS/IT strategy formulation and planning

- What are the purpose and the main stimuli prompting the need for planning, and what are the key business drivers to be addressed?
- What aspects of the current business and technical environment, and what issues, constraints, underlying problems and risks are likely to affect the conduct and outcome of the process?
- What should be the scope of planning, and where should planning be focused—on the corporate organization as a whole, at strategic business unit level or on specific core business processes?
- How can the IS/IT strategy process be effectively integrated with business strategy?
- What are the expectations and objectives to be met, and what deliverables are required?
- How should the IS strategy be 'marketed' and consolidated with the other elements of the business strategy to ensure that optimal support and cooperation are obtained from the organization?
- Should the approach employed be totally prescriptive, tailored or a mixture of both, and how can the organization build on its previous experience of IS/IT strategy formulation and planning?
- What are the most effective approaches, and which techniques achieve the best results (e.g. determining the critical success factors associated with top-level business functions or employing business analysis down to a very detailed level)?
- What resources, from which areas of the business, fulfilling which roles and responsibilities, and with which skills, should ideally be involved in the process and are they available? What training will be required?
- What other resources are required (automated tools, administrative support, physical facilities)?
- How long will the strategy process take and what will it cost?
- How should the process be steered and managed?

development. Once the questions are answered, the TOR can be created and senior management's role in the process established—their active involvement is essential from the start, as it signals that 'strategy and planning' is actually going to happen.

Establishing Success Criteria

What is a good approach to IS/IT strategy development and how can success be ensured and measured? Assuredly, the impact of an IS/IT strategy is not instantaneous, and it may, in fact, take some time—often two or more years—between embarking on an IS/IT strategy formulation and planning process, for the first time, and demonstrating any significant impact on business practices and results.[20] The outcome of strategizing and planning varies widely with:

- the starting point (how comprehensive or how constraining is the current application portfolio and how appropriate are IT supply services);
- the opportunities (whether to search for some 'early winners'—easily-achieved, high-impact applications—or to build or acquire a portfolio of applications that meet the current and future business requirements);
- the degree to which top management is involved in and committed to the process;
- the history of IT, particularly 'IS/IT success' in the organization.

These and other issues such as defining and implementing an appropriate relationship between the IS function and the business, and establishing objectives for IS/IT, have to be addressed.

At the outset, it is important to distinguish between IS/IT objectives and implementation issues. The objectives for an IS/IT strategy should not be concerned with object orientation, relational database technology, the Internet, HTML, hardware specification, or with end-user or central IT development. These are prominent implementation issues. Any objectives set for IS/IT must be similar to those for the business, focusing on, for example, improving customer service, enhancing productivity or providing the means for product differentiation.

At the same time as defining objectives for the strategy process, it is helpful to sharpen the perspective on these by establishing criteria for how success will be measured. Clearly, it is impossible to give a general set of success factors for any strategy process, as these will be dictated by a number of factors including objectives, stimuli and perception of the business community. Establishing success criteria is likely to reveal any 'hidden agenda' behind the stated TOR and objectives (e.g. understanding and meeting the expectations of executives, or 'achieving and maintaining credibility of the IS function in the business environment'). They may also include one or two reminders to the strategy team (e.g. to avoid delving into too much detail at any point, or to keep the final product in mind). Once success criteria and measures are agreed, they can be reviewed regularly; at least, at every progress meeting, to ensure that they are being satisfied.

The primary objective of developing an IS strategy is to identify a value-added portfolio of applications that will have a strategic impact on the organization and increase its performance. Yet, a key challenge is how to define and measure strategic impact and how to relate the approach to IS strategy formulation to organizational performance. There are a number of reasons that this is difficult, including the long lead time before benefits are realized, the intangible nature of certain benefits and different purposes for engaging in an IS/IT strategy process.

There are a number of ways in which IS strategy success can potentially be operationalized and measured.[21] In a conceptual treatise, King[22] suggested a framework to measure success, arguing that the measurement of success should be multidimensional, and based on both judgemental and objective assessments. Dimensions proposed by King include the effectiveness of the strategy approach, its relative worth, the role and impact of IS strategy, the performance of IS/IT plans, and the relative efficiency of the strategy process, the adequacy of resources made available and strategic congruence.

Ramanujam and Venkatraman[23] conducted an empirical study involving 207 organizations in the USA, aimed at examining the relationship between the IS strategy process and success dimensions. The IS strategy process dimensions include contextual dimensions (resources and resistance levels) and systems design dimensions (internal, external, functions and techniques). IS strategy effectiveness dimensions include system capability, objective fulfilment and relative competitive performance. The study found evidence of a strong relationship between the strategy process dimensions and strategy effectiveness dimensions. The findings also indicated that the most important influence on the effectiveness of the IS/IT strategy process is the extent of stakeholders' resistance, followed by the resources committed to the exercise.

More recently, Segars and Grover[24] conducted an empirical study involving 253 senior IS executives in the USA, aimed at exploring and examining success dimensions and measurements. Using the earlier work of Ramanujam and Venkatraman, they described four common approaches to measuring IS/IT strategy success: goal-oriented judgement, comparative judgement, normative judgement and improvement judgement. *Goal-oriented judgement* refers to the assessment of the degree of attainment in relation to the goals of the strategy process. *Comparative judgement* refers to the comparison between a particular system of planning and other similar systems. *Normative judgement* refers to the comparison between a particular system of planning and

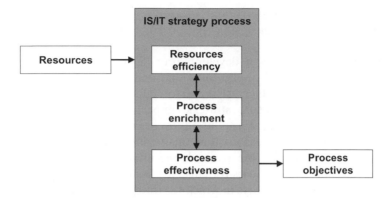

Figure 3.4   *Success criteria*

an ideal system. *Improvement judgement* refers to the assessment of how the strategy process has evolved or adapted in supporting organizational strategic planning needs. Segars and Grover note that comparative judgement and normative judgement have a narrow focus and, therefore, are more relevant to assess a specific approach to strategy formulation, whereas goal-oriented judgement and improvement judgement have a wider focus and, therefore, are more relevant to assess the broader processes involved in developing this IS/IT strategy.

From analysis of the research literature,[25] the following success dimensions can be gleaned:

- improving the contribution of IS/IT to the performance of the organization;
- extent of alignment of IT investment with the business strategy;
- gaining competitive advantage through deployment of IS/IT;
- identifying new and higher payback applications;
- identifying strategic applications;
- increasing top-management commitment;
- improving communications with users;
- better forecasting of IT resource requirements;
- improved allocation of IT resources;
- development of an information architecture;
- increased visibility for IS/IT in the organization.

Figure 3.4 illustrates a model that relates resource inputs to the IS/IT strategy process and the objectives of the process. IS strategy process dimensions can be summarized in three aspects: resource efficiency, process enrichment and process effectiveness. This multidimensional perspective of the IS strategy process provides a more comprehensive method of assessing success.

Resource efficiency refers to the efficient use and management of input to the process or resources required for the process. This dimension, in some respects, is similar to 'the relative efficiency of IS planning system' and 'the adequacy of IS planning resources', as described by King. It deals with the ability of the strategy process to manage the input resources in order to maximize their use. Resources involved in the IS/IT strategy process include financial resources and time and effort of IS staff, users and management.

Enrichment is process-oriented and refers to the improvement, enhancement and adaptability of the IS/IT strategy process, enabling it to be responsive to continuous changes in the environment and to produce incremental learning. It focuses on communications, interaction, innovation, learning, commitment, motivation, control, change and improvements, advanced by conducting a strategy exercise.

Effectiveness is output-oriented and refers to the effectiveness of the IS/IT strategy process in meeting the intended goals. Goals of the process include predicting future trends, evaluating alternatives, avoiding problem areas, enhancing management understanding and knowledge, improving short-term and long-term performance, IS–business alignment, agreement concerning development priorities, viable implementation schedules and clarifying managerial responsibilities.

PURPOSE AND STIMULI DRIVING IS/IT STRATEGY DEVELOPMENT

The purpose in developing an IS/IT strategy is to ensure that the best possible value can be delivered from IS/IT investments. This can be achieved by tightly aligning the IS demand to the business strategy— strategic alignment—and by exploring opportunities for IS/IT to shape the business strategy where it is possible to improve the overall competitiveness, productivity and fitness of the organization to meet the forces acting upon it—competitive impact.

The arrival of threats and opportunities cannot be forced into a convenient timetable to suit the business strategy cycle. An organization that is setting out to be flexible and responsive needs to be prepared to respond to fast-moving stimuli and to change its plans accordingly, and the IS strategy needs to be able to respond in the same way. Figure 3.5 shows how the pace of change in the external environment can prompt business responses. The effect can mean activity in all four quadrants, with IS/IT following the business lead. There is always the

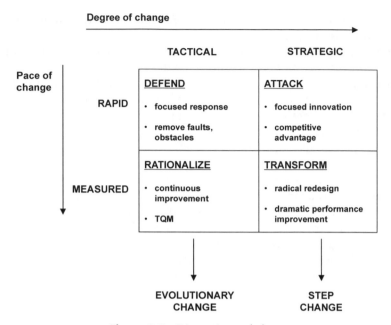

Figure 3.5   *Dimensions of change*

danger that all of the activity falls into the 'Defend' box, but IS/IT can help to strengthen the ability to respond by building up strategic capability.

There are a number of sources of stimuli for IS/IT strategy development, or revising the existing strategy, any of which may have an effect on the aims and objectives of planning.

External Business Factors. These factors drive the development and revision of business strategy. They were discussed at some length in Chapter 2, and were mentioned above.

External Technology Factors. These sometimes pose threats or opportunities that directly stimulate IS/IT strategy activity. For example:

- competitive opportunities and threats (real or potential) based on new IS/IT developments (e.g. the Internet and wireless technologies);
- new products or markets created by IS/IT;
- major cost-factor changes giving real or potential competitive advantage, producing an urgent need to improve productivity via technology or risk losing business.

If the emphasis in the strategy is on exploitative and entrepreneurial use of technology, it probably implies new attitudes to the use of IS/IT are required, as well as for new skills and for different people to become involved with new types of technology. It is important that the IS function keeps abreast of technology trends, innovative use of technology and how competing or similar organizations are applying IS/IT, so that they recognize when significant and achievable opportunities emerge, or when to respond to technology threats.

Internal Business Factors. Changes in the nature of the business or the structure and organization of the enterprise may result in the need to revisit or reconsider the IS/IT strategy. The stimuli may be as diverse as:

- response to the regular business-planning cycle or budgeting cycle;
- takeover by a new owner(s) or the appointment of a new CEO or management team—this may simply mean a new attitude to technology, or it may herald more drastic change if it occurs as a result of a merger or takeover;
- major rationalization caused by, for example, downturn in the economy, necessitating a severe trimming of IS/IT budgets;
- restructuring—often resulting from corporate strategic planning (e.g. changing a business from a production-led to a marketing-led orientation, and leading to radical business re-engineering);
- new products or markets or channels-to-market—where there is a recognition that the present infrastructure is incapable of adapting to new requirements;
- recognition of the importance of strategy formulation and planning for IS/IT, based on the need to increase its direct contribution to the business.

Internal Technical Factors. These factors may arise from the need to deliver increased value for money, to cut costs, to improve the working relationship between the IS function and the business, the recognition that the current environment and legacy systems are starting to 'creak' and numerous other factors. They may all prompt IS management or business management to recognize the need to reassess the role of IS/IT and its current strategy. For example, the inability of many legacy systems to handle the new millennium dates absorbed the greater part of many IT budgets for up to two years to solve the so-called Y2K problem.

Assessment of the Current Organizational Environment

During the initiation stage of strategy formulation, the current organizational environment and any pertinent issues will need to be understood, so that the planning activity is set up to deal with these factors. While the precise issues will be specific to the organization at the time of planning, there are common factors worth assessing so that the IS strategy process is properly positioned and set up to be successful such as:

- A broad overview of the business perspective, as far as it is available—its long-term mission, goals, vision for the future, strategy, drivers for change, proposed change initiatives, structure, values, culture, management style, performance monitoring and any short-term critical demands. Detailed analysis and interpretation of all these will take place later on in the planning process.
- How effective IS has been in supporting business strategy in the past, and the composition and strengths and weaknesses of the current application portfolio.
- The current role of IS/IT in the organization, its effectiveness, coverage, structure, skills and maturity, and the role IS/IT is playing in comparable external organizations in the same industry or similar businesses.
- The views held by business managers regarding IS/IT.
- How IS/IT strategies have been developed in the past, their deliverables and the benefits derived.

SCOPE, OBJECTIVES AND EXPECTATIONS

Having confirmed the purpose of the IS/IT strategy process and assessed the current organizational environment, it is then necessary to determine clearly the scope and objectives of the planning activities, and to ensure that the business has clear expectations of what will emerge as a result. In establishing the scope, it is important to reiterate a point made in Chapter 1. While most IS/IT practitioners understand that their objectives have shifted, there is still a tendency to consider technology issues alongside business needs in such a way that confuses the supply (technology as a means of delivery) and demand (business needs expressed as information systems requirements). This is why it is critical to make the distinction between IS strategy and IT strategy.

IS strategy deals with *what* to do with information, systems and technology, and how to manage the applications from a business point of view. It thus focuses on the close alignment of information and systems in support of business needs and on identifying and exploiting competitive opportunities for IS/IT. IT strategy designates *how* technology is to be applied in delivering information and how the technology resources are managed to meet the range of business needs.

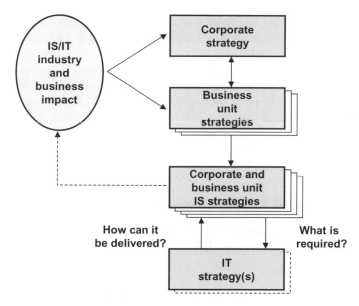

Figure 3.6 *IS/IT strategy in context*

The Strategic Business Unit (SBU)

In a large organization, where there are likely to be a number of distinct business units, it is probable that each should have its own IS strategy, tightly coupled to its business strategy. The available evidence suggests that organizations that have done this achieve and recognize a more direct contribution from IS/IT to business performance. It does not necessarily follow that there should be IT strategies one for one with IS strategies in that organization. A single IT strategy may be appropriate for the whole organization, especially if there is centralization of other corporate functions. On the other hand, it may be more effective to focus IT support at divisional, regional or even unit level in a diverse and highly-distributed enterprise (see Figure 3.6).

A PIMS/MPIT study[26] showed that IS/IT is, generally, more effectively deployed in organizations where vertical integration is between 50 and 75% (i.e. 50–75% of total business costs are under the control of the business unit), enabling management to control the degree of systems integration across functions. Second, the study showed it is more feasible to develop a coherent IS/IT strategy for a strategic business unit than for any other organizational grouping. Given the arguments above, this would seem to follow.

In practice, information flows through the business, along its primary business processes, to and from customers, across logistics and product processes, and to and from suppliers, to enable supply and demand and the use of resources to be reconciled. The primary systems requirements depend on effective linkages through these processes. The secondary/supportive control and planning systems can be overlaid on that structure, although, in the past, these types of system have often driven the primary systems requirements. This aspect will be considered in more detail when the value chain analysis techniques are discussed later in Chapter 5, and also when business process redesign and business re-engineering approaches are discussed.

Implications of Focusing IS Strategy Formulation on the SBU

Considering the implications of focusing strategic planning activities at the business unit level, as reflected in Figure 3.6, some conclusions can be drawn:

- Historically, 'strategies' were essentially the cumulative total of functional and/or departmental systems 'strategies', which often lacked integration with the business and each other. Personal computing, in the 1980s, often caused an even lower set of 'individual' strategies to develop, as discussed in Chapter 1. The senior management and IS management reaction was often to attempt to develop a 'corporate IS/IT strategy'. There is little evidence that this can be achieved. Most case histories of the attempts of large companies to develop an overall, comprehensive 'corporate IS/IT' strategy from the centre show that lengthy planning blights descend on the units and then nothing results! It can work where all the units are replicas of one another, operating in different locations. Unless the corporation is essentially a single business-unit company, or the units are nearly identical, the task is almost impossible.
- Developing IS/IT strategies at 'group level' is equally unlikely to be successful, unless it is a group of very similar businesses. There are potential dangers associated with attempting to develop common systems across group companies. Unless the whole organization is very similar in terms of its products, operational strategies and markets, then each unit is likely to have very different business needs. In this case, an IS strategy that meets one unit's needs is not likely to be optimal for another's. Even when the individual business units are very similar, they are still likely to have different IS priorities. For example, their market penetrations may be different, or their customer base has a different profile or, because of scale factors, their unit costs are very different. Even where organizations

have 'imposed' common strategies for ERP or CRM applications, the implementation in each unit may vary considerably, producing little commonality in terms of systems, although the software package is the same. Often, group reorganization can occur such as the refocusing and restructuring of many organizations in the 1990s from a manufacturing- or product-based structure to more market-based, making a nonsense of any previous group systems synergy.

- In conglomerates, where the buying and selling of businesses is a key part of the corporate strategy, it obviously makes most sense to align the strategy to each business unit, and it is probably impossible, in reality, to do much else.

IS Strategy for the 'Corporate' SBU

The 'corporation', in many cases, is best seen as a business unit in its own right—it will have information system needs based on the way it chooses to manage the component businesses, whatever at any one time they are. At one end of the scale, a holding company may only be concerned with a very limited number of objectives and, as such, may only need a few elementary enquiry and modelling systems, to access, say, profit and revenue figures. Alternatively, there may be a need for an IS strategy to meet corporate information requirements, which are entirely different from those of the business units, whose interests are in supporting their own particular business strategies. Corporate information needs support long-term planning and allocation of resources, and draw on consolidated information from the business units. Frequently, common policies for IT across the whole organization are implemented to achieve economy of supply and consistency across internal interfaces. The focus of strategies at the corporate, business and IS/IT levels and the relationships between these levels are illustrated in Figure 3.7.

Selecting a Starting Point

While the scope may be obvious when there is only one SBU under consideration, it may be more difficult when there are several. A few pointers that are worth considering in making the choice of starting point, for example, when choosing an SBU where:

- strong management commitment and involvement are assured;
- clear business plans and direction are known and available;
- the role of IS/IT is already respected;
- strategic business planning is well established.

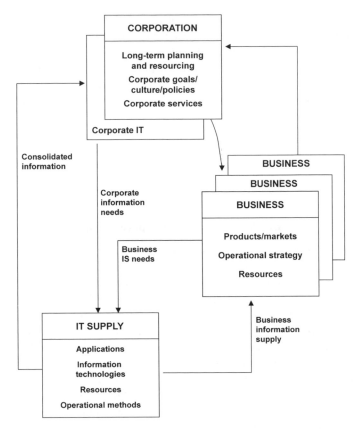

Figure 3.7 *Relationships and information demand/supply*

In cases where an IS/IT strategy process is not well established, it might be more appropriate to scale down the scope of the exercise so that the learning curve can be contained and the new techniques and processes of IS strategy formulation and planning can be exercised on a small scale to demonstrate their validity, before being applied to a larger organizational unit.

Consolidation across Business Units

If more than one unit is engaging in an IS/IT strategy process, and especially if the units are similar in their business profile, then cross-referencing during the strategy process is a good idea. Alternatively, planning activities can be staggered to take advantage of common elements. There may well be common factors emerging from the outputs for each unit. Opportunities for mutual support can be as diverse as:

- Acting as sounding boards during analysis, perhaps holding some joint-opportunity identification workshop sessions.
- Sharing tools or, at least, using common tools for capturing planning output.
- Sharing application portfolios or individual applications. Similar portfolios do not necessarily emerge from what, at first sight, are similar businesses. Synergy is most likely to occur when the product/industry profiles are in comparable stages of maturity, when their generic strategies are similar and when there are sufficient common features in their business competitive strategies.
- Sharing software developments, if appropriate. When environments and implementation policies differ, this may only be for requirements analysis.
- Building common conceptual models for selected parts of the business. This may occur even when the application portfolios differ considerably. There may still be substantial overlap in the information architecture, and benefits from transferring 'best practice', as well as saving in cost and time from sharing high-level models, common naming standards and data dictionary definitions. This is covered further in Chapter 10, which considers information management. Some rationalization may be needed between models for different units.
- Allowing for effective intercommunications, by using consistent information definitions. This could facilitate sharing databases, or pave the way for sharing systems, implemented in different environments, or to make them available to other businesses in the organization.

Some large businesses have well-defined, comprehensive corporate IS/IT management strategies, which impact all the business units. Such strategies can include policies for consolidation (e.g. to combine business data models across the corporation). However, if corporate headquarters are only interested in, say, financial considerations, then the potentially-massive task of rationalizing models across a large enterprise would not be sensible or justifiable, except for the finance functions.

Objectives

The objectives for IS strategy development and planning are primarily derived from the business objectives and drivers for change. It is necessary to ensure that these objectives are sensible and achievable given the current situation and available resources. A very general set of objectives may be set as in Table 3.5. They could form a blueprint set of objectives for introducing a strategy process for IS/IT into an organization, but they

Table 3.5   *General set of objectives for IS/IT strategy formulation and planning*

To build a robust framework for the long-term management of information, information systems and information technology and to:

- Identify current and future information needs for the organization that reflect close alignment of business and IS/IT strategies, objectives and functions. Recognize that the needs of the business will evolve, and that long-term needs are likely to change.
- Equip the IS function to be responsive to fast-changing business needs, and to be able to meet urgent requirements.
- Determine policies for the management, creation, maintenance, control and accessibility of the corporate information resource.
- Reposition IS function more centrally in the business, with representation at top management level.
- Ensure that a sound information systems architecture is created so that high-quality systems can be built and maintained.
- Identify a portfolio of skills that will be required over the lifetime of the plans, and develop migration plans to overcome weaknesses and exploit the skills in the IS function.
- Determine an effective and achievable organization structure for the IS function.
- Ensure that the IS function is outward looking and not focused internally on technology issues, and that the aims of the function are not only clearly linked to business needs but also widely communicated.
- Ensure that there is an acceptance of shared responsibility between IS/IT and business people for the successful exploitation of information and technology.

hardly meet the real-world conditions normally encountered. Usually, there are pressing stimuli and obvious problems to be resolved. These, in turn, predetermine the focus and critical requirements. Clearly, every case is different and must be examined on its merits, balancing needs, starting position, resources, etc.

Even when the primary objectives are the alignment of business and IS/IT, and the pursuit of competitive advantage, it is likely that the recommendations will include the creation of an integrated architecture, coupled with the stabilizing of the information resource and minimizing maintenance, among other things.

Expectations

It has been stated several times that no two strategy formulation and planning initiatives will have the same objectives. The variations arise because of factors such as:

- the size of the business unit under consideration;
- the sophistication of the current application portfolio and current IS/IT operation;
- the stage of development of the organization's strategic processes—as discussed in Chapter 2;
- the immediate problems facing the management team.

Depending on the reasons that prompt IS/IT strategizing in the organization, different emphasis may be placed on certain activities and deliverables. For example, a set of common scenarios that reflect varied expectations are given in Box 3.2. They illustrate how the focus of strategy and planning may vary from business to business. There are others that are rather more 'tactical' in nature—for instance:

- Justification of the IT budget—it is quite common for IT management to be under attack from senior management for the seemingly endless rapid increases in IT budgets. If the budget can be directly related to the business strategy, these attacks can be avoided.
- How to select new technological environments for the future.
- How to distribute data and systems development capabilities to end-users.

It is also often wise to state clearly the reverse of objectives and scope (i.e. what the strategy process will not do), for example:

- no recommendations will be made concerning specific hardware and software products;
- overseas and branch companies are outside the scope.

AN IS/IT STRATEGY FRAMEWORK AND APPROACH

The process of strategy formulation for effective exploitation of IS/IT is complex, if tackled comprehensively. It needs to address several dimensions within its overall scope, and, thus, a combination of approaches and tools are required. It seeks to satisfy efficiency, effectiveness and competitive or value-adding objectives. Its implementation timescales encompass the immediate future and a time horizon in keeping with the horizon for the business strategy. While the critical future applications are probably 'strategic' systems, it is likely that the planned development portfolio will include entries in all quadrants. In addition, there is a high probability that improved integration of information and systems is needed. Because of the legacy of current information and systems

Box 3.2 Common scenarios indicating expectations from IS/IT strategy process

- *Gradual evolution of IS/IT strategy:* where alignment with business strategy is relatively new, or being pursued for the first time, one focus of IS strategy may be to effect a gradual reorientation from a technology-based to a business-based focus.

- *Gaining management understanding:* in an environment where there is a low level of awareness of the potential of IS/IT among the business community and a history of disappointed expectations from the business viewpoint, the focus may be to determine objectively the value of the contribution made by existing systems to the current and future needs (where known) of the business.

- *Determining priorities for allocation of budget and resources:* frequently, one of the main objectives of strategy is to develop prioritized plans for provision of information and systems. These could stem from new systems, enhanced existing systems and more accessible integrated information. Invariably, this is coupled with the need to budget and resource from an insufficient supply of funds and skills.

- *Gaining a competitive edge:* seeking out opportunities for using IS/IT as a competitive weapon, directly or indirectly, in offensive or defensive competitive activity is often quoted as an objective. It would appear that few organizations, including it for the first time in their planning, know how to go about finding the most promising opportunities.

- *Finding an early winner:* a high-risk objective for strategic planning may be taken up by the IS/IT group to find one or two 'prizewinner' ideas that can be implemented quickly, bringing significant benefit to the enterprise. The underlying reason may be to win over reluctant supporters within the executive controlling body to commit to IS/IT taking a more central role in the business.

- *Defining a global information architecture:* the focus here is the creation of a global architecture for each business unit, where the purpose is to instil consistency and integrity throughout the information resource and to provide a springboard for comprehensive and flexible provision of information from an integrated resource.

infrastructure, this could be a very complex and costly operation, and requires careful justification.

As far as recommending an approach to IS/IT strategy formulation, this book supports a mixture of the formal and informal. Formal techniques are used if the requirements demand that all appropriate elements of the business are explored in a structured manner, and the business drivers are applied to achieve effective prioritization within a consolidated program of business IS initiatives. But, informal techniques are also included to capture innovative ideas where they arise in the business, both during the initial strategy process and thereafter. The overall approach put forward in the book consists of a composite model in which business planning, business analysis, information analysis and innovative thinking all have a part to play.

While giving guidance and structure to the process, the emphasis is on suggesting a wide variety of techniques, and providing an adaptable framework that can meet most eventualities for delivering a good strategy and plan. The most important ingredients are a well-balanced high-quality team, endowed with a good balance of knowledge, strategy and planning skills, experience and more than a pinch of common sense.

The IS/IT Strategy Formulation and Planning Framework: Overview Model

An overview model, shown in Figure 3.8, illustrates the building blocks of the strategy formulation and planning framework—the inputs, outputs and essential activities. Briefly, these are:

Inputs

1. *The internal business environment:* current business strategy, objectives, resources, processes, and the culture and values of the business.
2. *The external business environment:* the economic, industrial and competitive climate in which the organization operates.
3. *The internal IS/IT environment:* the current IS/IT perspective in the business, its maturity, business coverage and contribution, skills, resources and the technological infrastructure. The current application portfolio of existing systems and systems under development, or budgeted but not yet under way is also part of the internal IS/IT environment.
4. *The external IS/IT environment:* technology trends and opportunities and the use made of IS/IT by others, especially customers, competitors and suppliers.

They are described in some detail in Chapter 4.

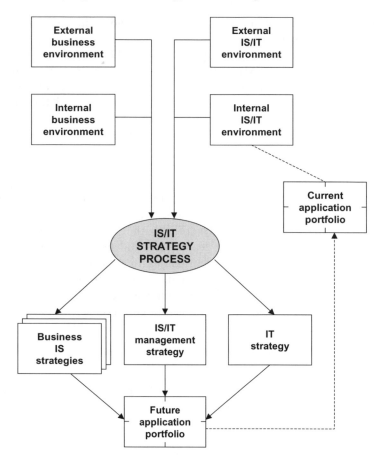

Figure 3.8   *The IS/IT strategic model*

Outputs

1. *IS/IT management strategy:* the common elements of the strategy that apply throughout the organization, ensuring consistent policies where needed.
2. *Business IS strategies:* how each unit or function will deploy IS/IT in achieving its business objectives. Alongside each of them are application portfolios to be developed for the business unit and business models, describing the information architectures of each unit. The portfolios may include how IS/IT will be used at some future date to help the units achieve their objectives.
3. *IT strategy:* policies and strategies for the management of technology and specialist resources.

These and other 'soft' outputs are described under the heading 'Deliver-ables from the IS/IT Strategy Process', later in the chapter.

Selecting, Defining and Implementing a Strategy Approach

Having confirmed the scope, the objectives and the deliverables, the next step is to ensure the IS/IT strategy process is linked effectively to business strategy formulation activities and existing business strategies and plans. This will in part depend on the comprehensiveness of the existing IS/IT strategy, how long since it was updated, how much change is needed and how well that strategy was integrated with the business strategy.

The process needs to be understandable and acceptable to all con-cerned, and it must not be too complex or constrained by unnecessary bureaucracy. No approach will, by itself, guarantee success. Responsi-bility for a successful outcome rests heavily on the leader of the strategy process and the people involved. It is their responsibility to understand why each step in the process is being done and why each document or diagram is being produced. Failure to do this could result in the endless 'diagram production' syndrome. This commonly arises because the team is using a generalized method and diligently produces the diagrams men-tioned, simply because 'the method says to do it'.

In any strategic process, some sort of structure to the approach and clear principles are obviously necessary. Box 3.3 contains a set of char-acteristics that are recommended in any approach adopted. Whichever approach is chosen, it will have to be suitable for the explicit needs, and the environment, culture, organizational maturity and skills available. In summary, the approach chosen should have the following characteristics:

- flexible, modular and able to pick up deliverables from earlier or parallel activities;
- emphasis on deliverables;
- clear checkpoints;
- recognition of the interactive and cyclic nature of the process;
- recognition of the importance of the human side of the process;
- simple diagramming tools.

Without attempting to constrain the process, it is nevertheless helpful to propose a framework that enables all the essential elements to be incor-porated. Once IS/IT strategizing and planning is established in an organ-ization, several of the deliverables will be available from the previous cycle, and in need of review and update only, rather than building

Box 3.3   Characteristics recommended to be included in any IS/IT strategy approach

1. *Overview:* the approach chosen should include a way of obtaining an overview, or top-down view, of the whole area to be studied, although one may be available from an earlier activity. One of the biggest dangers in IS strategy development is the attraction of using a detailed tool (e.g. normalization for data analysis) that is a very good tool in itself but completely inappropriate for the top-down view needed in strategic planning.

2. *Consistency:* the philosophy of the approach and the techniques used need to be consistent between the various stages of the process and any earlier strategy deliverables. It would be inadvisable, for example, to be obliged to redraw diagrams containing essentially the same information simply because a particular approach advocates using one schematic diagram and another advocates a different one in two separate stages. Furthermore, the outputs from the various stages in the process should be consistent with other company methods (e.g. the process may need to take output from a parallel business process redesign project) and the outputs should be in a form that can be used as direct input to any encyclopaedia of information and process objects, used in application development.

3. *Communication:* one of the major reasons for using a standard approach is to facilitate communication between team members and the business community. This means that the approach and techniques advocated should be relatively easy to learn and use. In particular, they should not be so complex as to dominate the whole process.

4. *Documentation:* the hard deliverables of the process are reports and business and portfolio models. This implies that any approach should give clear guidance as to the contents and form of these 'deliverables' and their supporting appendices.

5. *Rationalize decisions:* any strategic planning approach should provide management with a vehicle to make rational decisions. These decisions should be made at logical and clearly-defined checkpoints, which break the whole process up into easily-comprehended units of work and prevent wasting time on unwanted deliverables.

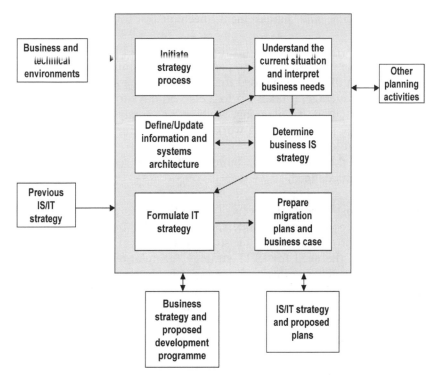

Figure 3.9 *Framework for IS/IT strategy formulation and planning process*

from scratch. For example, the business model could be unchanged, except in minor details, unless the business is undergoing major revision of core processes. On other occasions, the requirement may be to focus on one short-term need and to adapt the existing strategy to accommodate this. Figure 3.9 illustrates the main components of the framework, briefly described below.

Initiate Strategy Process

This is the set-up stage of the process, in which:

- The purpose, objectives, scope and deliverables are confirmed.
- The approach is determined and resources acquired, such as automated tools.
- Business participants are identified and the team assembled and, if necessary, trained.

- The steering and management mechanisms for the process are created.
- How the work will interface with and feed into business planning.
- The people who are needed to participate are identified. This gives an indication of the time needed for the fact-finding and analysis stage, since, on average, it takes 1.5 to 2 elapsed days to conduct an interview, including its planning, writing up, analysis and feedback. Organizing and conducting workshops and documenting the results takes even longer.
- Plan for the work, tasks, timing, roles and responsibilities, and checkpoints defined.

One of the most important aspects of the initiation stage is that it enables the sponsor to develop an understanding of the business needs and drivers that prompted the IS/IT strategy process. This is required in order to 'sell' the need for IS/IT strategy formulation and planning to take place, not only to other senior management, but also to operational management and professional staff whose knowledge is vital to the process, but who all have a full-time 'day job' to do. Some may see 'planning' as a threat to their current independence of action concerning IS/IT. In the case of the strategy process, it must be shown that its conduct and the resulting strategy will assist all levels of management in achieving their objectives and resolving key problems.

It is also important that management accept that the costs involved are merited. In the case of the strategy, the cost should be repaid by focusing future investment in IS and IT more precisely on the achievement of corporate objectives, by undertaking projects with clearer, deliverable benefits. It also ensures that management avoid doing 'the wrong projects'—which have no chance of success or are not of any strategic value. The costs of undertaking the process are relatively easy to derive—they are people costs for the team, consultants (if they are used) and the time of participants in workshops and interviews.

A checkpoint at the end of this stage is to ensure that the TOR are clear and acceptable to the senior management and key participants, that adequate resources are allocated, and that interdependencies and consolidation plans with the rest of the business strategy and plans are achievable.

Team education is essential to ensure that everyone has a common basis and adequate understanding to proceed. Some time is probably required in order for the team to:

- understand the principles behind the IS/IT strategy process;
- understand the approach being adopted and learn how to use the

techniques of IS/IT strategy formulation such as determining critical success factors, information analysis, value chain analysis, organizational modelling and interviewing;
- agree on individual tasks and review the analytical tools and techniques available;
- understand deliverables and take responsibility for specific report activities and outputs.

Given the mix of people involved, some of the team members will have absolutely no knowledge of any information analysis methods or procedures. Conversely, some of the more technical people will have little or no knowledge of the business world of the organization. This means that education will be a continuous on-the-job process for all team members.

Understand the Current Situation and Interpret Business Needs

This step can take various forms including studying existing documents, interviewing users, holding workshops and brainstorming sessions with groups of users. Its purpose is to develop an extensive understanding of the business in its environment, and to interpret its current, planned and future potential needs. These fall into three categories:

1. Analysis of the business strategy, objectives, critical success factors, critical problems and processes, in order to determine the current situation, its strengths and weaknesses, and the information needs and thus the focus for investment in systems to meet these needs. This is covered in Chapter 4.
2. Evaluation of the current IS/IT operation, its systems, information provision, resources, organization, skills and services, to determine coverage and contribution and where improvements would be beneficial. This aspect is also addressed in Chapter 4.
3. Analysis of the external and internal business environment to identify business-based innovations that depend on potential applications of IS/IT. This is considered in Chapter 5.

Tools such as high-level information analysis, critical success factor and balanced scorecard analysis, value chain analysis and creative techniques for identifying opportunities are put to use here. They are described in subsequent chapters.

Determine the Business IS Strategy

The accumulated business IS demand is turned into recommendations for the deployment of IS/IT at SBU level and throughout the organization. These are documented in the management and business IS strategies. Conceptual information systems are consolidated and mapped onto an applications portfolio, representing the current, required and future potential position, for each SBU considered.

They are described briefly in this chapter in the section headed 'Deliverables from the IS/IT Strategy Process', and are considered in some detail in Chapter 6.

Define Information and Systems Architecture

This step takes the results of the analysis of processes and information needs in order to build a proposed business model for the business. It represents the future 'ideal' in terms of process, information and systems, and is necessary in order to plot a direction when developing migration plans. The work can commence once analysis of the environment begins, and continues up until the end of the formulation of the business IS strategy. The development of the architecture is described in Chapter 4.

Formulate IT Supply Proposals

The remaining tasks are to define the elements of the IT supply proposals. They are listed in this chapter under 'Deliverables from the IS/IT Strategy Process', and are addressed in detail in Chapters 7–11.

In practice, at this point the IS strategy and the IT supply proposals can be fed back into the business strategy process for consideration, and ultimately for consolidation. Senior business management can then decide on the most beneficial and feasible investment program for the business. Outline plans can then be constructed to plot a route map and milestones for the main initiatives established. This is likely to entail close cooperation with the business areas to pull together the IS/IT and business aspects of the 'approved' developments to produce an outline migration plan and a high-level business case for each. Detailed business cases will still need to be prepared for each element of the program when development funding is actually requested.

Analytical and Creative Techniques

While the strategy framework and its essential components have been described, it is important to understand the use of both analytical and creative techniques in order to ensure that the necessary dimensions are explored adequately, and the deliverables are achieved. The former takes a structured route through the upper levels of the organization, systematically analysing and decomposing the business requirements into their constituent parts, and delivering a structured view of the business objectives, strategy, activities and information needs. The latter, enabled by techniques that facilitate more lateral thinking, focuses on areas of likely high potential and relies more on sharing knowledge and creative thinking. There is a good deal of crossing over since, in the initial analysis of the business environment, it is likely that embryonic ideas for future winners may emerge. Figure 3.10 illustrates the approaches and their common roots:

- Top-down techniques are used to examine and decompose the business requirements into their constituent parts and to extract information needs, from which the required applications portfolio is derived.
- Top-down information and process modelling to assess current business models. These continue the top-down analysis of the business, with the emphasis on core processes and the information needs and activities that are already in place, or need to be implemented to support objectives and strategy.
- Bottom-up examination of the information and processes reflected in the existing application systems portfolio fleshes out the systems and information requirements.
- Creative techniques are used to identify business opportunities that can be sustained, strengthened or created by application of IS/IT. Increasingly, innovative proposals are based on the systems and technology themselves where the product or service has an intrinsic IS/IT element or is delivered via the technology.

The creative element provides additions to the portfolio, since it looks for opportunities (or threats) within the business, and especially at the boundaries with the external environment, where innovative information systems or use of technology may be possible. Searches for such opportunities are not appropriate in all circumstances and probably not at all if the culture of the organization is risk-averse or not sympathetic to innovation, preferring to copy others in its use of IS/IT. It may be that one or more creative ideas can be brought to fruition very quickly, and it is often one of the aims of the strategic process to find and implement such ideas in order to demonstrate the potential contribution of IS/IT. In Chapter 1, the main types of strategic systems and commonly-observed characteristics of such systems were described.

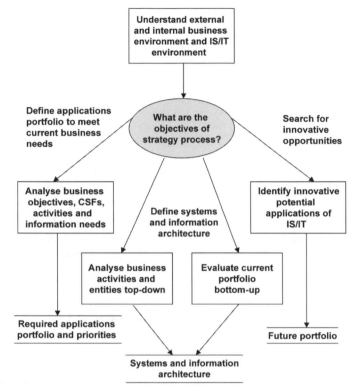

Figure 3.10   *Analytical and creative approaches to interpret business strategy*

DELIVERABLES FROM THE IS/IT STRATEGY PROCESS

The outputs stemming from the IS/IT strategy process are a mixture of hard and soft deliverables. The hard outputs are documents defining strategies and plans, and frequently include computer-based material in the form of dictionaries, matrices and information analysis models. Soft outputs relate to human factors such as skills, awareness and motivation. The main purpose of the hard outputs is to document:

- the current situation;
- the vision and rationale for what is being put into place—information, systems, technology, people and so on;
- the plans for how it is going to be achieved, with the milestones along the implementation route.

The timescale for the vision and plans has to be consistent with the business vision and its plans, and similarly will be reviewed in line with business strategy and planning reviews.

Structure for the Deliverables

Every organization will decide on the best structure to use for its purposes, depending on house style and how 'strategy' is communicated in the organization. However, whatever structure and format an organisation may choose to document its strategy, the objective is to ensure that users, management and IS professionals all understand the key elements of the strategy and each thoroughly appreciate those parts of the strategy they have to carry through. The structure described below is consistent with the model for the strategy process shown in Figure 3.8.

The following are a few general points relating to the deliverables:

1. The statements of demand, in terms of requirements for information, systems and technology, are contained in the business IS strategy and the accompanying application portfolio. The supply elements are contained in the IT strategy, while the IS/IT management strategy contains the overall policies for satisfying and balancing the demand and supply.
2. There should be one IS/IT management strategy for any organization where consistent policies for IS/IT are applied throughout the corporate body. However, there may be several business IS strategies, one for each SBU, or even separate strategies for defined functional or geographic units. There may only be one IT strategy for the whole organization, although there could be separate hardware and IT services dedicated to certain business units (see Figure 3.6).
3. The executive summary is a short paper comprising summaries of conclusions and recommendations, drawn from all the elements of the strategy. This may be the only paper to be read by the executive management team, and needs to be succinct and underpinned by effective presentations and discussions. (If possible, an executive summary should be avoided to encourage a more detailed understanding of the strategy by senior management.)
4. The strategy needs to record the current business and IS perspective, and their respective issues, as a record of the starting point in any planning cycle. The 'library' of deliverables is also valuable in providing supporting evidence of the rationale for choices made.
5. The IS perspective is important due to the pace of change in the industry in general. This pace of change may be in stark contrast

with the innate conservatism of many an IS function, which is often resistant to change while expecting user departments to accept change willingly!

IS Strategy: Management of Demand

The business IS strategy states how the business will deploy IS/IT in achieving its objectives, and the responsibility for its relevance and comprehensiveness lies with the executive management of the business unit. Its purpose is to link IS/IT clearly and firmly to the business strategy. The strategy, defined by the business management and users, states the applications and service requirements, with reference to the business plans and activities, and any associated priorities for development of infrastructure or application systems. Not all the requirements will be for new application developments. Some will demand extensions to existing operational systems to improve their effectiveness. Box 3.4 shows the contents of a typical business IS strategy.

If the organization is contemplating or undertaking business process redesign, then it is very likely that its information needs and information systems requirements will display a much higher degree of integration than formerly. It is also likely that freer flows and access to information along end-to-end processes and across external boundaries will become priority IS requirements.

'Soft' Factors

These consist of the unit's management style, corporate values and cultural factors, as well as its skills, resources and competencies. Such information may already be documented in the corporate or business unit strategies; if not, this is an appropriate time to determine these details. In the context of defining IS and IT strategies that have considerable impacts on the business, organizational dynamics play a significant role, since it is necessary to be able to assess the effect of a strategy that runs counter to the culture of the business. In this case, it is necessary to assess with great care whether to implement the recommendations or whether it may be better first to focus on changing the underlying contrary behaviours. If they cannot be changed, then it is unlikely recommendations will deliver their potential benefits, and it may be better to revise the strategy, taking a more incremental approach to change.

One engineering business, managed jointly by two managing directors, embarked on developing an IS/IT strategy using external consultants. The sponsor—one of the two managing directors—was taken ill during the course of the planning process and was forced to retire. Having lost

Box 3.4 Basic structure/contents of IS strategy documents

1. *Purpose of IS strategy*—reasons for new/updated strategy—key changes in business and IT context since last strategy: it is feasible for the IS strategy to be an annual update of the previous one.

2. *Overview/summary of business strategy*—to provide context for IS strategy: objectives and Critical Success Factors (CSFs), if known, plus analysis of competitive forces and/or similar analyses (e.g. strengths, weaknesses, opportunities, and threats [SWOT], competencies) and resulting issues affecting the IS strategy. *These tools will be described later in Chapters 4 and 5.*

3. *Argument* for:

   - new IS opportunities (to gain advantage);
   - critical improvement areas (to avoid disadvantage).

   These should be based on Item 2 above but with further detailed analysis of competency issues, value chains (external and internal) and CSFs/balanced score card to determine the opportunity/problem areas and reasons for investment in them. Details of methods (e.g. value chains) should be included in Appendices.

4. *Summary of opportunities/problem issues*—'1 page' for each—explaining the application/opportunity/issue: outline description, the rationale, potential benefits from investment, any critical dependencies and initial action to be taken in the context of an overall estimated time frame for the investment (more detailed plans can be included if known). These opportunities/issues should be separated into:

   - strategic, high potential, key operational (and possibly support); and
   - prioritized high/medium/low based on business timescales (e.g. H = within 6 months, M = 12 months, L = 2 years).

   For each application, the business managers responsible should be identified.

5. *Review of current application*—portfolio and status of current projects (i.e. other investments currently in hand) and the overall resource implications of:

   - completing outstanding work and ongoing commitments (major components should be described in Appendices);
   - resources available to address new work from Item 4 above;

> - any critical issues requiring resolution within the existing strategy.
> 6. *Future application portfolio*—incorporating the output from Item 4 above to show the intended/potential investments, with priorities, and the implications for the rest of the portfolio (e.g. replaced systems, etc.).
>   Initial resource estimates (and costs) of the investments should be appended to the portfolio, with an initial plan (including a simple Gant chart).
>   (It is often useful to show how the balance, in using resources, is changing as the portfolio evolves.)
> 7. *Issues arising from the IS strategy*—these are things that require senior management attention (e.g. the establishment of a steering group) to enable decisions affecting the strategy (priorities, resources, organization, other initiatives, etc.) to be made in the required time frame. These may also include issues to be addressed by the IT strategy in order to provide the infrastructure to support the future applications portfolio.
>
> How the document is used/ratified will depend on the organizational management processes, but it is likely that a 'draft for discussion' will be needed, probably its key aspects presented to senior management and subsequently an agreed version produced as the basis for detailed planning (and budgeting) and progress review.
>
> *(N.B.* No executive summary is suggested here—if one is deemed necessary, it should be at the end, not the beginning, since it discourages busy managers from understanding the real content! The strategy *is* the summary of a lot of work/discussion, etc. and further summary often loses the important details.)

his very vigorous commitment, the positive attitude hitherto displayed by the directors and senior managers collapsed, prompted by the second MD, who had not shared his former colleague's optimism and active leadership.

Application Portfolio

Brief details of application systems requirements are recorded within the business IS strategy. The portfolio is categorized in terms of the applications and their role in supporting current and future business strategy in the four categories already described—strategic, high potential, key operational and support.

The portfolio not only contains stated requirements but may also include potential applications and propositions for enhancing the business strategy in the future. These proposals are most likely to address customer-related and competitive activities, and may well be described in outline only at this point, since significant further work may need to be undertaken before they are introduced within a competitive initiative. It may turn out that the way to proceed is to develop one or more small pilot ideas, with the intention of adding increments as the ideas prove themselves.

IT Strategy: Management of Supply

The IT strategy should not only cover the responsibilities of the 'central' IS function but also the responsibilities of users, where appropriate. Its prime purpose is to define how resources and technologies will be acquired, managed and developed to satisfy business IS strategies within the management strategy framework. In addition, it should reflect current trends and developments in IT that could cause future opportunities or constraints.

Many of the elements of the required IT infrastructure may have already been defined separately, in which case there are also likely to be procedures for reviewing and updating the strategy. Nevertheless, a review of the IT policies, methods and standards in place, and adherence to them is needed. The IT strategy will then focus on the areas where change is necessary due to business requirements, or where new options are available due to changes in technology, experience or capability, which may not have been previously recognized and pursued.

Whether defined during the IS/IT strategy process or separately, the IT strategy will normally address the following supply factors:

- application portfolio management;
- organization of IS/IT, the management of its resources and administrative matters;
- managing the information resources and provision of information services;
- managing application development;
- managing technology.

These are considered in detail in Chapters 7–11.

IS/IT Management Strategy

The management strategy covers the common elements of the strategy that apply throughout the organization, ensuring consistent policies where needed. It is particularly necessary where several SBUs develop their own business IS strategy and may or may not operate their own IT supply function.

Where there is a high degree of centralization in the organization, then the number of issues addressed in the management strategy and the degree to which common policies are imposed will be considerably higher than in an organization where the central corporate body is small and each unit operates virtually autonomously. Even then, it is quite likely that the autonomous units will share centralized support functions, of which IT services are quite likely to be one. It may cover technology directives that state mandatory factors concerning the IS/IT infrastructure and other principles that should be followed (e.g. portability of applications around the group).

Any information systems needs of the corporate body can be addressed in a business IS strategy treating the corporate body as if it were an SBU. Clearly, some of its information needs will be closely linked to the other SBUs and frequently derived by consolidation of output from applications run in the SBUs. Aside from its information needs, the management strategy should state known corporate objectives and critical success factors (CSFs) relating to corporate activities and needs. The strategy should also contain a concise summary of the individual business IS strategies and any IT strategies derived for the organization. It should also relate them to its own stated corporate aims and CSFs.

In a single SBU organization, or one with complete autonomy, the IS management strategy can be amalgamated with the business IS strategy. A minimum number of common issues may also be addressed in the management strategy, namely:

1. *Scope and rationale*—it will need to lay out the business background, scope and rationale for the directives it is stating, and preferably describe a vision of the corporate IS/IT environment and its expected impact on the business community. If major changes are in the offing, it will need to describe them and give a timetable for their introduction.
2. *IS function*—organization, resourcing and the allocation of responsibility and authority for IS/IT decisions. This includes both formal and informal structures and any steering group or management committee overlay structures to provide coherence. The allocation of

authority and responsibility indicates how much control is retained in the corporate body and how much is devolved into the business and functional units.

3. *Investment and prioritization policies*—implementation of the strategies will require many separate decisions on investments to be made. Management cannot consider each one in detail and certainly not continuously allocate and reallocate priorities. Rules must be defined—pertinent to each of the elements of the portfolio (strategic, key operational, etc.)—stating how investments should be appraised, the need for financial evaluation and acceptance of business judgement of line and IS managers and the balance and discretion expected. They should state how the budgeting for expense and capital items and later project or capital expenditure allocation processes tie together. They also need to define a mechanism that reflects the investment decision-making process, for day-to-day priority setting for resource allocation to ensure that the best return on investments is obtained from the actual resources available. Some measurement of results and any control and audit procedures should be incorporated here. This is covered in detail in Chapter 9.

4. *Vendor policies*—these may state specific vendors, or the parameters that must guide choice of vendors, such as interconnectability, financial soundness, service provision, etc. They should also cover differences in policies where central approval is needed or where local decisions can be taken.

5. *Human impact policies, including education*—it is only too easy to jeopardize IS/IT strategies due to mismanagement of the people issues—new job content, reorganization, even redundancy. Some organizations have 'technology agreements' with unions or staff groups. Where organizational issues are seen as critical to success, this must be adequately addressed at a corporate level. A common set of policies and guidelines must be laid down to avoid evolution by precedent and a negative, reactive stance by those affected. Each project, in each area, with each new technology should not need separate negotiation—progress will be slow and inconsistent, the strategy will undoubtedly be continually disrupted.

6. *IS accounting policies*—in many organizations, strategies can fail due to insensitive or inappropriate accounting policies for the charging of IS/IT resources. The objectives of such policies should be clearly stated and understood. While they initially appear to be management accounting systems for cost allocation, once implemented they become 'transfer pricing' systems on which users will make decisions. The policies will depend on, among other things:

- other cost accounting/transfer pricing policies for other services;
- profit/cost centre management of organizational units (including IS unit);
- the cost of administering the charging system itself, which, when the budgeting complexity is added, may prove very expensive to carry out.

For each of these, and any other elements of the IS management strategy considered at a corporate level, there should be a clear statement of rationale, objectives, policy and procedures for review and exception handling.

It is quite likely that the IS/IT management strategy has been determined in a separate phase before any individual SBU conducts its own IS/IT strategy process. In this case, it has to ensure that the policies laid down in the management strategy are consistent with the business needs being addressed and that there is a mechanism for feeding back into the IS strategy management process any anomalies or troublesome constraints uncovered during the strategy process.

'Marketing' the IS/IT Strategy

As well as the hard deliverables, there are a number of other benefits to be gained from a well-conducted and well-received strategy process. The people who have been heavily involved are likely to be well motivated and well versed, not only in the planning process, but also with a very broad understanding of the business, its people, direction and environment. They should continue to motivate the organization toward maximum exploitation of IS/IT from wherever they are based, be it managing the IS/IT strategy, in business planning or in their management or professional role. The other 'soft' output should be an enthusiastic and committed senior management. This is most likely to be gained if the enthusiasm and commitment was earned before the process began and has been courted throughout.

The Audience for the Strategy

It is not possible to generalize about who should be informed and kept informed, and at what stage or to what depth, since this depends on so many factors in each situation. But, it is likely that the audience should include:

- senior management;
- IS/IT management and staff;

- all participants in the planning activities;
- line and functional management and user area representatives;
- individuals in existing project teams;
- other interested parties within the organization (e.g. corporate strategy and planning groups, human resources, etc.);
- in some cases, major shareholders and non-executive directors may also be part of the audience;
- in the public sector, the audience could also include elected representatives and other government departments, etc.

It may also be useful to include certain external bodies such as suppliers of systems and technology, or selected suppliers or customers of the business, particularly if proposed systems emphasize communication between them and the firm.

There are substantial benefits to be derived from effectively communicating the strategy. First and foremost is the need to obtain demonstrable and actual commitment across the organization to implementing the recommendations and to providing the resources to do so. It is also important to obtain agreement from all concerned on how the impacts on the organization will be absorbed. Other benefits from communication can be obtained by asking for feedback from people who did not participate directly in the planning process (usually for straightforward practical reasons). They may be able to identify problems that were not exposed during the process and perhaps introduce potentially better options than those proposed.

The strategy needs to be communicated in a consistent fashion so that the right items are emphasized and so that misunderstanding and false impressions are avoided. It should reach audiences at different levels, with different interests and over an extended period, possibly several months. It is therefore worthwhile developing high-quality 'marketing' presentation material and collateral that can be tailored to each type of audience.

Managing the Process and Resources

A suggested structure for managing and steering the process is shown in Figure 3.11.

Management Sponsor

This person, who is preferably a director or senior executive of the organization, should fulfil the following functions:

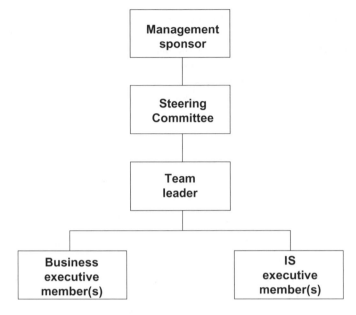

Figure 3.11   *Strategy process management structure*

- chairing the steering committee and approving the budget and plan for any IS/IT proposals;
- assuring management participation and commitment, through active backing and allocation of the right resources;
- representing the interests and priorities of the planning process in the business;
- heading the 'marketing' effort (which should not be underestimated);
- acting as the focal point for decisions about the scope, TOR and conduct of the work.

Steering Committee

Depending on the scope of the planning process, it may be necessary for this group to meet once every month, or simply to be present at the appropriate checkpoints. A minimum requirement is that the management sponsor should function as a one-man steering committee and report to the board of directors where necessary. Typical steering committee functions are:

- providing strategic direction and guidance on business requirements, and priorities to the planning team;

- reviewing and approving plans, and taking up risk management issues;
- conducting checkpoint reviews;
- authorizing continuation of work on the next planning activity;
- reviewing and contributing to final strategic plans, before submission to the business executive team.

Other roles are shown in Box 3.5.

Team composition and *modus operandi*

- The enterprise, as a whole, needs to be convinced that the strategy and planning exercise is important. If the most senior executives work on the planning activities, then this message will come across.
- The participants in discussions will be from very senior levels. They must know and respect the team or they will not have confidence in the resulting strategy.
- During discussions or workshops, the strategy team must recognize if they are being deliberately or unconsciously misled or the resultant strategy will be rejected.
- A large part of the information requested and given will be sensitive and confidential. This will be more readily given to peer group members than to subordinate group members.
- During analysis and strategy formulation, team members have to be capable of taking decisions that will ultimately affect the whole organization, so the organizational level of these team members has to be high, for both the user and IT team members. These people, with the qualities mentioned above, are precisely those executives who do not have time to spend on such work!

In addition to the senior end-users and IT staff, it is often beneficial to include one or two IT staff who are experienced in documenting interviews and workshop outputs using diagramming tools and in undertaking the subsequent information analysis. Also, if the strategy process is new to the organization, it may be appropriate to retain a consultant who specializes in this area.

Usually, if the management committee has agreed to finance the strategy process, they will recognize the importance of the type of person on the team and provide the requisite managerial backing. The acid test of involvement is the decision physically to relocate the prospective team member for a significant portion of his working time. This avoids the syndrome where a manager will say that he is available any time, but in practice is impossible to contact in his native habitat.

Box 3.5   IS/IT strategy team composition and roles

Strategy team leader
- Plan, manage and do much of the day-to-day work. As such, this role involves a major time commitment on his or her part.

Strategy team members, drawn from both the user and the IS communities
- At least two full-time members are needed, in general. They may require the assistance of other part-time members like technical specialists. The number of people required will vary with the size of the project and the desired completion date. A critical factor is the number of people to be interviewed, if this is a major requirement of the process, as this is a most time-consuming process.
- There is a further factor to consider in team selection. Acceptance and commitment from the members of the 'formal' management team is obviously needed. What is not so obvious is the need to involve people who, although they do not have formal titles, are the effective powers behind the throne. Such a person could, for example, be the bright young economics graduate in the finance department who has set up an elementary, but much admired, budgetary system for the directors on his semi-legal PC. These people are sometimes known as 'gatekeepers' because they effectively control the gate of acceptance or rejection of any information systems proposals. Whether or not they are included in the team is a matter of judgement, but the team must be aware of their existence and importance.
- Another point to consider is that, although it is possible and perhaps necessary to use external personnel in the team, it is essential that the organization itself provides at least one full-time team member, if not from the user community then from the IS function. This is because the strategy process should result in the specification of a number of subsequent projects, and someone from the organization, who has participated in the process, is needed to guide these projects during implementation.

Business participation
- It is necessary to identify, right at the start of the strategy process, those members of the organization who will participate

in discussions, interviews or workshops. They can be briefed about what is involved, sold to, if necessary, and appointments may be set up in their diaries.

- Other participants may be identified later, but the great majority should be prepared at the start. A few of them may be included purely for political reasons, rather than for any positive contribution they can make.

Strategy team composition and skills
The quality of the products depends on the quality of the team selected. The team leader and members should come from different parts of the organization and have:

- Broad knowledge of the business and its organizational objectives, management styles, culture, processes and people.
- Good communication skills.
- Ability and authority to make and implement plans and decisions that may affect the whole organization.
- Respect of management and staff.
- An interest in areas other than their own and an ability to analyse objectively.
- Experience of IS/IT strategy formulation and planning in at least some of the team.

Another catch here is the person who is only available for, say, 30% of the time. This occurred during one strategy exercise where, right up to the start, all of the planning had been done assuming that the person in question would be a full-time team member. His explanation, and his manager's explanation, was that, as he thought he knew only about one-third of the business, he would only be needed for one-third of his time! It should be impressed on all concerned that a substantial commitment is needed from all team members, with the exception of the sponsoring management and steering committee members, who are required to read reports, attend review meetings and be available for *ad hoc* discussions when required.

Automated Support Facilities

The conduct of an IS/IT strategy will require the use of basic automated tools such as word processing, spreadsheet and drawing tools. In particular, the graphical ability of drawing tools to construct any necessary diagrams (e.g. matrices, flow diagrams and data models) should be assessed. In addition, the provision of a suitable data dictionary structure for the recording of such things as descriptions of data and activities, interview results and definition of business objectives is a general requirement for any drawing tool selected.

Before deciding on the use of any automated tool, the team must decide on what information it wishes to record and how this information is to be structured (i.e. connected). For example, it is important to know such things as: How much detail is to be recorded from each interview? Is a standard interview record format required (normally, the answer is yes)? What is to be recorded about each major business activity and data group?

Physical Facilities

At the very least, there needs to be one room dedicated to the team. It is usual to keep lists, tables and diagrams of general interest (e.g. company structure charts and process models) permanently on the walls of this room for easy reference. The information collected, both from desk research and from discussions, is usually highly confidential and sensitive. Therefore, the strategy process room must be secure at night or facilities provided for the locking away of such sensitive material.

It is preferable to have rooms set aside for discussions, equipped with manual and printing whiteboards, flip charts, etc. and arranged so as to be conducive to good interviews and workshops. It is infinitely preferable if meetings and workshops, especially with senior executives, can be held physically away from their own offices, reducing the likelihood of any interruptions and getting the executive away from 'today's' problems.

SUMMARY

Devising a strategy for the role of IS/IT in the SIS era is accepted as a major issue, and despite a plethora of methodologies, automated planning tools and brigades of consultants willing to propel organizations into strategic systems developments, is still more of an art than a science.

This chapter has focused on an overall approach to strategizing and planning for IS/IT and emphasized the continuous nature of that process, involving the combined knowledge of key business and IS/IT staff, thus facilitating genuine, lasting and productive partnerships between business and IT.

Experience has shown that the most effective strategy process takes place at the strategic business unit level, with appropriate rationalization and consolidation across the whole organization. In addition, there is no 'ideal' approach to IS/IT strategy formulation and planning, but there are a number of factors that could be considered critical for its success:

- Using the 'best' people available from the business, IS function, external advisers—they provide the invaluable knowledge of the industry and the business, the IS/IT relevance and, above all, the creativity, none of which can be derived from a methodology.
- Gaining the enthusiasm, commitment and involvement of top management.
- Getting a thorough understanding of the internal and external business and IS/IT environments, the business imperatives and culture and the real stimuli driving strategy and planning.
- Setting objectives consistent with experience and maturity, and tailoring the approach to meet them, employing a mixture of analytical and creative techniques.

However, it should be remembered that having a good strategy is only a means to an end—its implementation is when the value of the strategy is actually realized. A key aspect of the formulation process is ensuring the organization is both willing and able to implement its chosen strategy. This will depend as much on how the strategy was derived, and who was involved, as it will on the actual content of the strategy.

ENDNOTES

1. A.L. Lederer and V. Sethi, 'The implementation of strategic information systems planning methodologies', *MIS Quarterly*, Vol. 12, No. 3, 1988, 445–461.
2. T.D. Wilson, 'The implementation of information systems strategies in UK companies: Aims and barriers to success', *International Journal of Information Management*, Vol. 9, 1989.
3. N.F. Doherty, C.G. Marples and A. Suhaimi, 'The relative success of alternative approaches to strategic information systems planning: An empirical analysis', *Journal of Strategic Information Systems*, Vol. 8, 1999, 262–283.
4. *Business Systems Planning, Planning Guide*, GE20-0527, IBM Corporation, White Plains, New York, 1981.
5. The unit providing direct support to end-users has evolved over the years from an *information centre* concept to more latterly a *help desk* or *service centre*. The original concept of the information centre referred to the facility and dedicated staff, generally within an IS function, devoted to helping users develop and maintain their own applications.
6. C. Ciborra, 'The grassroots of IT and strategy', in C. Ciborra and T. Jelessi, eds, *Strategic Information Systems: A European Perspective*, John Wiley & Sons, Chichester, UK, 1994, pp. 3–24.
7. M.J. Earl, *Management Strategies for Information Technology*, Prentice-Hall, Englewood Cliffs, New Jersey, 1989; M.J. Earl, 'Experiences in strategic information systems planning', *MIS Quarterly*, Vol. 17, No. 1, 1993, 1–24; M.J. Earl, 'Information systems strategy ... why planning techniques are not the answer', *Business Strategy Review*, Vol. 7, No. 1, 1996, 54–67.
8. The work of Zackman is influential here. See J.A. Zackman, 'A framework for information

systems architecture', *IBM Systems Journal*, Vol. 26, No. 3, 1987, 276–292; J.F. Sowa and J.A. Zackman, 'Extending and formalizing the framework for information systems architecture', *IBM Systems Journal*, Vol. 31, No. 3, 1992, 590–617.

9.   N.F. Doherty, C.G. Marples and A. Suhaimi, 'The relative success of alternative approaches to strategic information systems planning: An empirical analysis', *Journal of Strategic Information Systems*, Vol. 8, 1999, 262–283.

10.   A. Segars, V. Grover and J. Teng, 'SISP: Planning system dimension, internal coalignment and implementations for planning effectiveness', *Decision Sciences*, Vol. 29, No. 2, 1998, 303–341.

11.   A.L. Lederer and A.L. Mendelow, 'Information resource planning: Overcoming difficulties in identifying top management's objectives', *MIS Quarterly*, Vol. 11, No. 3, 1987, 389–399.

12.   T.D. Wilson, 'The implementation of information systems strategies in UK companies: Aims and barriers to success', *International Journal of Information Management*, Vol. 9, 1989.

13.   T.S.H. Teo and J.S.K. Ang, 'An examination of major IS planning problems', *International Journal of Information Management*, Vol. 21, 2001, 457–470.

14.   J. Luftman and T. Brier, 'Achieving and sustaining business-IT alignment', *California Management Review*, Fall, 1999, 109–122.

15.   J.W. Peppard and J.M. Ward, 'Mind the gap: Diagnosing the relationship between the IT organization and the rest of the business', *The Journal of Strategic Information Systems*, Vol. 8, 1999, 29–60.

16.   A.L. Lederer and V. Sethi, 'The implementation of strategic information systems planning methodologies', *MIS Quarterly*, Vol. 12, No. 3, 1988, 445–461; 'Critical dimensions of strategic information systems planning', *Decision Science*, Vol. 22, No. 1, 1991, 104–119.

17.   G. Johnson and K. Scholes, *Exploring Corporate Strategy*, Prentice-Hall, Englewood Cliffs, New Jersey, 2002.

18.   M. Hammer, 'Reengineering work: Don't automate—obliterate', *Harvard Business Review*, July–August, 1991, 104–112.

19.   C.H Sullivan, 'An evolutionary new logic redefines strategic systems planning', *Information Strategy: The Executive's Journal*, 1986.

20.   It is worth pointing out that research exploring the relationship between IT investment and organizational performance has highlighted one that of the major problems in assessing performance improvements is due to the time lag between making the investment and the actual realization of benefits. See E. Brynjolfsson, 'The productivity paradox of information technology: Review and assessment', *Communications of the ACM*, Vol. 36, No. 12, 1993, 67–77; E. Brynjolfsson and L. Hitt, 'Paradox lost? Firm level evidence on the returns to information systems spending', *Management Science*, Vol. 42, No. 4, 1996, 541–558; S. Devaraj and R. Kohli, 'Information technology payoff in the health-care industry: A longitudinal study', *Journal of Management Information Systems*, Vol. 16, No. 4, 2000, 41–67.

21.   This section draws on work undertaken by Mohdzaher Mohdzain at Cranfield School of Management, UK.

22.   W.R. King, 'How effective is your information systems planning', *Long Range Planning*, Vol. 21, No. 5, 1988, 103–112.

23.   V. Ramanujam and N. Venkatraman, 'Planning system characteristics and planning effectiveness', *Strategic Management Journal*, Vol. 8, 1987, 453–468.

24.   A.H. Segars and V. Grover, 'Strategic information systems planning: An investigation of the construct and its measurement', *MIS Quarterly*, Vol. 22, No. 2, 139–163.

25.   N.F. Doherty, C.G. Marples and A. Suhaimi, 'The relative success of alternative approaches to strategic information systems planning: An empirical analysis', *Journal of Strategic Information Systems*, Vol. 8, 1999, 262–283; A.L. Lederer and V. Sethi, 'Key prescriptions for strategic information systems planning', *Journal of Management Information Systems*, Vol. 13, No. 1, 35–62; A.H. Segars, V. Grover and J.T-C. Teng, 'Strategic information systems planning: Planning system dimensions, internal coalignment, and implications for planning effectiveness', *Decision Science*, Vol. 29, No. 2, 1998, 303–345; R. Sabherwal, 'The relationship between information systems planning sophistication and information systems success: An empirical assessment', *Decision Science*, Vol. 30, No. 1, 1999, 137–167; B.H. Reich and I. Benbasat, 'Measuring the linkage between business and information technology objectives', *MIS Quarterly*, Vol. 20, No. 1, 1996, 55–81.

26.   *Management Productivity and Information Technology*, Overview report, Strategic Planning Institute, 1984.

4
IS/IT Strategic Analysis: Assessing and Understanding the Current Situation

The first three chapters have considered the evolution of IS/IT in organizations from a strategic perspective and outlined approaches to developing business and IS/IT strategies that can enable the required improvement in the integration of both. More specifically, in Chapter 3, 'what is involved' in establishing an IS/IT strategy process and its deliverables were examined against a background of the various issues affecting the process. This and the following chapter concentrate on determining the content and main deliverables of the IS strategy, comprising:

- analysis of the existing and expected future business and IS/IT environments and strategies;
- the organization's IS requirements arising out of the current business strategy, by aligning these requirements with stated business needs and initiatives;
- the future potential from IS/IT through identifying opportunities to impact the business strategy and significantly raise its competitive performance.

If both *strategic alignment* and *competitive impact* are being pursued, then, in practice, there will be considerable overlapping of the two threads of analysis. However, for ease of exposition, they are treated separately in this book. The derivation of the IS strategy by alignment with the business strategy is covered in this chapter. This is established through a combination of analytical and evaluative methods, although it should be remembered that creative ideas can arise at any time in the strategic analysis. Chapter 5 will introduce concepts for the more creative dimension, by exploring external IS/IT opportunities, the competitive environment and the industry 'value system'. The techniques used in these analyses may in turn provide new insight into results from the more internally-focused analysis presented in this chapter.

In pursuing both alignment and impact, a thorough understanding of the business and technology environments, and of the apparent and expected opportunities and threats, is required, as well as a sound knowledge of how IS/IT may be applied innovatively to change the business along any one of a number of dimensions—strategy, structure, processes, culture, etc. It is also essential to build up a picture of the expected outcome, both in terms of the changes to be brought about through business and IS/IT initiatives, and the required changes to the IS/IT environment, both the application portfolio and the supporting IT infrastructure. An objective assessment of the strengths and weaknesses of the business overall and its IS/IT capability is also required.

Based on a clear understanding of the starting position, the future business perspective and the IS strategy, the gap in terms of IS/IT requirements can be analysed and an achievable migration plan constructed. This point is picked up in Chapter 6, where we bring together the various approaches considered in both this chapter and the next into an overall framework to determine the prioritized information systems requirements for the organization. It must be remembered that the focus at this stage is primarily on the business IS strategy (i.e. *what* is required—the needs and priorities from a business perspective). Later, the IT strategy (i.e. how to deliver it) will be addressed. Nevertheless, as the requirements are identified, the current ability of the organization to 'supply' or satisfy those requirements will inevitably be assessed. Hence, this part of the analysis will also focus on the capability of IT resources as reflected in the existing organization and practices, and in the current applications and information resources of the organization. The result of the IS strategy formulation is a target application portfolio that meets corporate and business needs and can be sustained in terms of technologies and resources. Various techniques can be used to achieve the mixture of fact finding and analysis that goes into determining the IS demand, and several of them are described in this chapter.

BUSINESS RE-ENGINEERING AND IS STRATEGY

One of the hottest concepts to arrive on the management agenda in recent years is that which has been labelled *business process re-engineering* or

BPR for short.[1] First articulated in the late 1980s as a result of research at the Massachusetts Institute of Technology,[2] it has become the means by which many organizations are seeking to emulate the transformations achieved by the early pioneers. Companies such as Ford, Hewlett Packard, First Mutual, Taco Bell, Hallmark Cards were shown to have achieved significant improvement in the performance of selected areas of their business by redesigning the processes through which work in organizations is performed.[3]

The redesign of business processes continues to be a popular approach taken by organizations to improve performance. While the concept has attracted negative press over the years, some of it warranted,[4] we find today that it often appears under a number of guises such as customer service initiative, e-procurement project or major cost reduction—all demanding significant redesign of business processes. While this book is not setting out to cover re-engineering approaches in any depth,[5] it is nevertheless pertinent to consider the subject alongside the development of an IS strategy, for a number of reasons:

- In developing the IS strategy, a thorough understanding of the business strategy is essential. Most re-engineering initiatives will spring from, and be part of, the business strategy.
- In many instances, the early work in developing an IS strategy is first to flesh out the details behind the headlines in the business strategy, and this means working with the business areas to help determine what those business initiatives will be and their expected contribution to business objectives. These could include re-engineering initiatives.
- Most, if not all, re-engineering initiatives have a significant IS/IT element, which will be accommodated in the IS strategy, and need to be allocated the same priority that the business places on the change program.
- There is a common need in both IS strategy development and business re-engineering to build up a model of the business as it currently exists and other potential models of how it will look following transformation or evolutionary change.
- Success in re-engineering, as with the development and implementation of an IS/IT strategy, demands a strong business–IS function partnership.[6]
- Designing or redesigning business processes to take advantage of IS/IT capabilities is essential if the traditional problems of automating poorly-designed processes or inefficient work practices through IT are to be avoided.

Much has been written about the role of IS/IT in business re-engineering. In particular, there are conflicting views as to whether IT is the driver for re-engineering, or an enabler or one of the means of implementation. Davenport and Short[7] argued for the first of these, although they recognize its role in the other two, insisting that two key questions must be asked:

- How can business processes be transformed using IT (based on a full understanding of the capabilities of IT)?
- How can IT support business processes?

Many organizations have not adequately or systematically addressed the first question, such that IT has barely been exploited at all in such situations. Teng and colleagues[8] suggest that IT is an enabler, but that its potential role should be overtly recognized and incorporated in an 'integrated business process redesign planning model'. This they describe as a 'policy loop', which combines business strategy and IS/IT strategy. Within this overall process are two subsidiary 'loops', one concerning business innovation (with little IS/IT involvement), the other dealing with implementation, where IS/IT becomes critical for achieving the benefits of change.

The relationship between IS/IT and BPR can be summed up as shown in Figure 4.1, whereby IS/IT has to be considered in different ways at the different stages of identifying, evaluating and implementing 'radical' process change. This enables a reconciliation of the fundamental questions of impact and alignment of IS/IT strategy development with the rationale for 're-engineering' initiatives. Table 4.1 summarizes these questions.

In the past, the most effective IS strategies have assiduously sought to be developed in line with the business strategy, so that change initiatives could be worked out on as broad a basis as possible, and certainly not confined to IT development work. The main difference between these and current business re-engineering schemes is often in the name applied to the program.

UNDERSTANDING THE CURRENT SITUATION

Understanding the current situation involves obtaining an in-depth understanding of the business strategy, the business and technology environments and the current status of IS/IT in the business. This makes it possible to determine the opportunities, threats and requirements inherent in the business strategy, and to recognize the strengths and

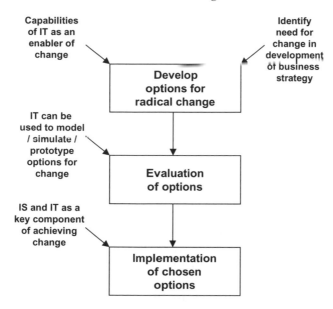

Figure 4.1   *The role of IS/IT in business process re-engineering*

Table 4.1   *Reconciling IS/IT and BPR*

Questions	*Business process re-engineering*	*IS/IT strategy formulation and planning*
Formulation	1. How can we re-engineer our business to provide advantage?	1. How can IS/IT be exploited to provide business advantage? (impact)
Implementation	2. How can we improve our processes to ensure success of the strategy?	2. How can IS/IT ensure the success of the business strategy? (alignment)

weaknesses of the business and its IS/IT operations. This is vital, because the current situation represents the starting point from which any change programs begin.

Determining the IS/IT Requirements: The IS Demand

One way of determining the IS strategy is to ask each area of the business what their requirements are. This is likely to deliver a comprehensive 'wish list', but would result in no insight into the relevance, or genuine priorities, and little knowledge of the inherent IS/IT requirement in the strategy of the business.

Another way is for a group, charged with defining or updating the IS/IT strategy, to absorb every written strategy statement and interpret them into relevant IS/IT principles and critical success factors (CSFs), application requirements associated with major planned initiatives, and a set of supply criteria to deliver the service demanded by the business. This would be possible if the strategy were documented in sufficient detail and the business strategy documents contained comprehensive descriptions of the current and planned business activities and environments. Its main defect would be in the inability to feed into the development of the strategy and initiatives the opportunities for exploiting IS/IT to its fullest potential. In practice, this level of documentation rarely exists, unless it was built up in an earlier business or IS strategy cycle and has been updated to reflect the current situation and requirements.

Undoubtedly, the best course is for the IS strategy to be developed in parallel with the business strategy, feeding trends, opportunities and ideas into the business strategy process, and then working closely with all areas of the business in building up a set of achievable business and associated IS/IT initiatives that will deliver the targeted performance. The IT strategy—supply—can follow directly from this analysis.

To achieve the desired results, it is necessary to obtain a complete understanding of the drivers for change and the current situation ('where we are') and then to articulate the situation being sought ('where we want to be') and start to propose how the gaps might be closed ('how to get there'). This will include both business and IS/IT initiatives. These are identified through a mixture of fact finding and analysis focused on the elements of the business and technical environments. This is illustrated in Figure 4.2. Table 4.2 contains an extensive list of fact-finding and analysis tasks that could be undertaken, and the purpose or deliverables associated with each of these.

Gathering the Relevant Data

The quality and value of any IS/IT strategy that is ultimately developed is dependent upon the depth of understanding of the business and its needs, and the constructive interpretation of these needs into appropriate information, systems and IT services. To this end, if the information is not readily available and accessible to address the areas in Table 4.2, some or all the tasks in this table should be undertaken. Whatever techniques and approaches are used, the results are more useful if they are recorded in a

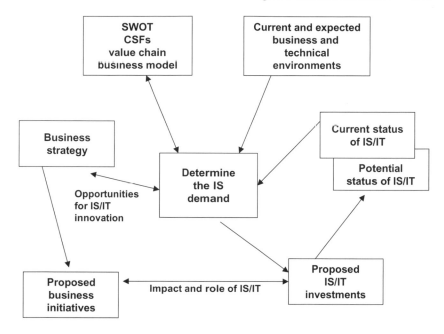

Figure 4.2   *Determine the IS demand*

manner that facilitates analysis. The approach described here relies on constructing a clear, structured set of information, and, where appropriate, constructing models showing the organizational, business and information requirements. A potentially significant problem with IS strategy development is of being engulfed by a surfeit of data. What is required is sufficient understanding of the business and information environments to be able to develop sensible and realistic strategies—but not the type of exhaustive analysis associated with detailed design and development of systems.

Much of the key information required is often in the heads of employees at all levels in the organization and needs to be elicited through discussion. However, discussions and workshops will be wasted effort and frustrating for business people if used to establish facts that can be obtained from available documentation. Not only does it waste time but it also means that important opinions expressed will not be seen in a factual context. Such problems can be avoided by reviewing as much available documentation as can be found ahead of any discussions. These may include business strategy documents, or at least formal statements of objectives and key performance indicators (KPIs). Other useful documents are likely to include annual plans, budgets and forecasts.

Table 4.2   Fact finding and analysis tasks and deliverables

Task	Purpose or deliverable
Analysis of the business strategy	Identify its components and the associated information needs derived from it
Analysis of the current and expected future external business environment, and analysis of the current and future portfolio of the business, and its competitive strategy	Determine how IS/IT can contribute to strengthening the business's competitive positioning
Analysis of the internal business environment	Understand the relevant organizational characteristics, SWOTs and other factors
Identification of the critical success factors of the business. These are frequently the drivers for change	Crystallize the essential characteristics of success in meeting the objectives stated in the strategy
Information analysis	Model the logical activities and inherent information elements of the business
Evaluation of the effectiveness of the current processes	Identify where changes need to occur, and how IS/IT can improve the performance of the processes
Identification and analysis of the internal and external value chain	Identify the most important information flows through the business and across its value chain partners
Further value chain analysis	Bring into focus potential opportunities for improving the value delivered by information, or identify potential hazards, where success may be jeopardized by poor interfaces
Creation of a conceptual architecture showing how the enterprise's information and processes might be restructured	Ensure maximum contribution to performance targets. Modelling future processes is a key element in business process redesign if it is being undertaken as part of re-engineering the business
Compilation of a catalogue of all the hardware and software being used by the organization, and the principal functions performed by each of the systems	An input into migration planning
Evaluation of the current application portfolio	Determine the inventory of information systems in use and in development, and assess their contribution and potential
Evaluation of current IS/IT policies, organization, processes, services, capabilities, etc.	Assess their applicability to meet current and future business needs

INTERPRETING THE BUSINESS STRATEGY

A framework for developing an IS/IT strategy was described in Chapter 3 and illustrated in Figure 3.8. Two of the inputs relate to the business perspective—internal and external. The elements of both these perspectives should be identified and analysed, so that the demands they place on IS can be derived and that ways of exploiting opportunities or countering the threats they contain can be determined. The majority of information needs are internal, generated in the operational activities, in pursuit of ever-improving performance and the measures that are needed to monitor it, and in the communications passing between activities. Others relate to external factors and are of particular significance in areas concerned with customer and supplier relationships and competitive activity.

Internal Business Environment

The elements of the internal environment that need to be identified, analysed and understood are:

- the business strategy, not just the objectives but the intended means of achieving them;
- the current business processes, activities and the main information entities (e.g. customer, stock item, account) and how they relate to other entities;
- the organizational environment, covering its structure, assets and skills, and the less tangible factors such as knowledge, competencies, values, style, culture and relationships.

From these, the information, systems and technology needs arising from the business strategy and the current activities of the business can be assessed and prioritized. This can be illustrated by considering two types of activity driven by the business strategy, and how they determine information needs:

- Activities that must be performed in order to contribute directly to the achievement of the business objectives, and their supporting information needs, have to be identified. For example, the business objectives may include ones to increase market share and improve customer satisfaction. One of the initiatives proposed to achieve this may be to launch a new product or service. Associated information requirements include market size, competitor products and services, and customer requirements.

- Secondary activities that have to be performed in order to measure performance toward achieving those objectives must be identified. For example, once a new product has been launched, it is necessary to monitor the take-up of the product or service to see if additional funding is required for advertising and to plan the resourcing levels required to sustain the sale of the product in its particular market and meet customer demand.

The Business Strategy

In analysing the business strategy, the main requirements are:

- To identify the current strategy and, in particular, any emergent new elements since the previous strategy development cycle.
- If necessary, to interpret and analyse the strategy, and describe it in a structured manner. This is best tackled by a mixed group with both business and IS disciplines and skills represented.
- To compile and confirm the consequent IS requirements.

The business strategy may exist in a variety of forms: as formally recorded corporate, business unit or functional area strategy documents or less formally in other documents and/or in the heads of individuals. In the latter case, it can usually be understood and confirmed through discussions with senior management. The main constituents are defined and described in Box 4.1.

The best context for IS strategy development and implementation is:

- Deriving the IS strategy alongside all other component strategies such as marketing or product development, or within a business re-engineering program or redesign of business processes.
- Implementing a program of initiatives to deliver the business strategy that includes the critical IS/IT developments alongside and within other business initiatives. Business re-engineering is again a good example.

However, in many instances, business strategies and objectives are not recorded formally, are not well constructed or not well communicated. Then, they can only be identified through questioning, analysis and creative prompting. In such cases, it may be necessary to work back from current actions and derive an implied business strategy. Indeed,

Box 4.1   Core constituents of a business strategy

Mission

An unambiguous statement of what the organization does and its long-term, overall purpose. Its primary role is to set a direction for everyone to follow. It may be short, succinct and inspirational, or contain broad philosophical statements that tie an organization to certain activities and to economic, social, ethical or political ends. Often called 'strategic intent'. Values are also frequently stated alongside the mission. Three widely-differing examples of missions are:

- 'To be the world's mobile communications leader, enriching the lives of individuals and business customers in the networked society' (large global telecommunication company).
- 'To eradicate all communicable diseases worldwide' (World Health Organization).
- 'The company engages in the retail marketing on a national basis of petroleum products and the equitable distribution of the fruits of continuously increasing productivity of management, capital and labour amongst stock holders, employees and the public' (a large public company).

Vision

Increasingly found in business strategy deliverables, this gives a picture frequently covering many aspects that everyone can identify with, of what the business will be in the future and how it will operate. It exists to bring the strategy to life and to give the whole organization a destination that it can visualize, so that every stakeholder has a shared picture of the future aim.

Business Drivers

These are a set of critical forces for change that the business must respond to. They may represent short, medium and long-term factors on which the business must focus in order to meet the objectives and satisfy the CSFs. They are frequently weighted and can be used in prioritizing improvement proposals. For example, the main short-term driver may be reduction of the cost base, the main medium-term driver may be increased market share and the main long-term driver may be zero-defect quality.

Objectives
The targets that the organization is setting to take it toward achieving its vision. They are usually small in number, but embody the most important aspects of the vision such as financial returns, customer service, manufacturing excellence, staff morale, social and environmental obligations. They are statements of future results or steady states that an organization wishes to achieve at its global or strategic business unit level. They are normally quantified with associated values and deadlines. Ideally, they should display the following characteristics:

- unambiguous and results orientated;
- measurable, verifiable and not too numerous;
- established by those involved in their achievement;
- relevant, achievable and encouraging high performance;
- consistent with any higher-level objectives.

Examples are:
- 'Reduce manufacturing costs by 10% each year for the next five years'
- 'Achieve zero overdue orders within 12 months'
- 'Reduce staff turnover to less than 15% per annum within 2 years'
- 'To lead in each local market by customer and brand loyalty, lowest-cost position, share of profit pool and employee satisfaction'

Usually, the mission and the organization's strategic objectives are cascaded down through the business, and each business function or core process is given the opportunity to develop its own objectives in response to the high-level ones. They are frequently tactical in nature and give rise to short-term IS requirements.

Strategies
They define the way in which objectives will be met. They may reinforce existing policies (e.g. the steering committee structure for approving capital expenditure) or initiatives that will continue to be pursued, perhaps with expanded resources (like a customer care programme). They may also state a new set of policies and new initiatives that will be put into practice like the redesign of the production processes of the business.

Frequently, they do not exist, and one of the ways in which the IS strategic process can help is in facilitating the identification and documentation of candidate schemes for achieving the objectives.

Critical Success Factors (CSFs)
CSFs are the few key areas where 'things must go right' for the business to flourish. It is very important to identify them when aiming to obtain a profound understanding of the business. The very act of determining CSFs may help to crystallize objectives and strategies, and certainly to emphasize priority activities. CSF analysis is considered in more depth later in this chapter.

Business Area Plans
They are the plans of the various areas of the business, which document their response to the business strategy. In many cases, this may reflect a continuance of business as usual, with a focus on the key targets being introduced or reaffirmed. Though not part of the strategy, they contain pointers to information needs and need to be investigated.

the main achievement of the IS strategy process may be to focus attention (subtly, if necessary!) on the inadequacies and, at best, assist in formulating a business strategy that considers technological opportunities as significant elements.

There may be no business strategy at all and objectives that only point at the 'bottom line'. In this case, probably the best that can be achieved is to analyse and record current activities, tactics and operational needs, from a top-down viewpoint. Analysis of the business and of its critical components will provide invaluable input into any future formulation of business strategy. In the interim, short-term IS planning can focus on supporting current high-priority business needs and on identifying and alleviating critical problems that threaten the business with competitive disadvantage. The main techniques, in this case, revolve around undertaking a detailed analysis of implications of current critical success (or failure) factors (CSFs, CFFs).

Information needs may arise from all the elements in the business strategy and they are a significant source of requirements in the compilation of the IS strategy. For example:

- The mission, vision, strategic and tactical objectives and key performance indicators set the targets for defining or assessing current initiatives; the external business drivers supply the basis for new or potential initiatives.

- The strategies or initiatives, if they have been articulated, are increasingly likely to have an IS/IT content that is often essential to achieving the desired result. These usually represent medium-term requirements that may be application-specific or may point to required improvements in IT services and the infrastructure. Longer-term requirements emerge, once IS/IT opportunities are identified, for impacting the business and its competitive strategy through innovative application of IS/IT.
- The business area plans usually have short-term IS/IT requirements, often carried forward from earlier cycles, but perhaps with different priorities, based on the current objectives.
- The CSFs (often used in conjunction with a 'Balanced Scorecard'— see later in this chapter) lead to two different types of IS/IT requirements: those that will enable success and those that monitor progress.

Business Processes, Activities and Key Entities

Another set of deliverables, derived from analysis of the current situation, are models that depict the processes, activities and main information elements, and how they relate to one another. These models make up the business model and, together with supporting IS models, comprise an IS architecture for the business (see Figure 4.3). These models offer a number of benefits. They provide:

- A valuable aid to understanding what is happening in the organization and for clearly visualizing the business processes and information flows, independent of organizational structures.
- A communications vehicle for explaining and illustrating them to a business audience in a manner that is easy to comprehend.
- A means of reviewing the merits or otherwise of the organizational structure, when viewed against the business model. This is a very valuable feature, especially when evolutionary development has created anomalies in the structure of the business, as, for example, when a particular executive has 'carried' a part of the organization with him when he moved to a different area of the business or assumed another responsibility.
- A basis for highlighting particular messages. These might be:
  - the disjointed nature of the processes, which inhibits effective operations and interrupts information flows;

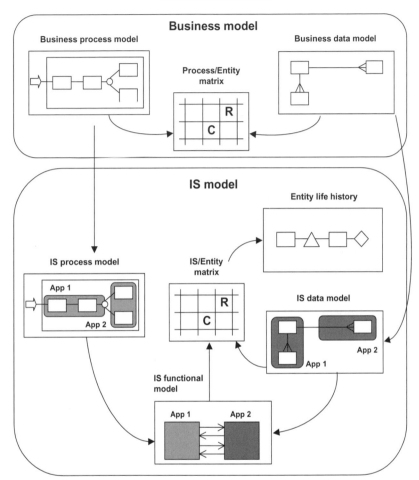

Figure 4.3 *An example of an architecture model, comprising a business and an IS model (source: M. Cook, 'Architecture models', working papers, Glaxo Wellcome Operations, 1995)*

  – where CSFs are focused;
  – high-cost and other problem areas;

- A basis for conceptually defining activities and for designing and illustrating improvement opportunities.
- A basis for indicating the scope of application areas and for defining the future systems architecture.

- A mechanism for mapping current applications against the processes they support.
- A basis for explaining the importance of having a common set of terms in a business. It is quite common for organizations to have different understandings of a particular term used within the same organization. For example, one particular managing director commented that, at a board meeting, he had four different parts of the organization giving him four different answers to a question about sales. The production department said that they had produced for sale a certain quantity of goods, and that was their 'sales figure'. The marketing department had another set of figures for 'sales', which was independently derived from their forward-marketing projections. The sales department had a figure based on customer orders, while the finance department had a figure based on actual invoiced sales. Each of those directors was talking about what he thought was the same information, but clearly there were four entirely different sets of figures involved.
- A means of identifying high-level redundancies. As an example, an analysis was conducted at a financial institution using the techniques of data-flow diagramming and entity modelling. One particular area of the organization was reviewed, and it was found that, while considerable activity was taking place within the department and information was coming into it, nothing, in fact, was leaving it! This had arisen because, some years before, exchange controls had been introduced by the government of the country concerned and this department was then established to monitor exchange control. However, when the exchange controls were relaxed the department carried on, but there was then no purpose to it!

An example of a business model and its associated IS model is given in Figure 4.3. The IS model indicates applications and their relationships. The individual models are created to depict:

- *Business processes*—the sets of interlinked activities or roles that deliver specific outputs to identified customers inside or outside the organization. In many cases, a functional organization inhibits the effective operation of the business processes, by placing barriers at the functional boundaries, and, in effect, preventing the timely and smooth flow of information. Nevertheless, the underlying processes may be identified and modelled. Value chain analysis, a technique covered extensively in Chapter 5, is invaluable in identifying and confirming the key processes in the business, and across its external boundaries. It ensures that the process ends at a point when a satisfactory business outcome is delivered (i.e. when value has been delivered to the next partner in the chain). Later in this chapter, we consider how business processes are analysed.

- *Activities*—the elements of the business processes that the organization undertakes to produce, promote and distribute its products or services, to develop, support and administer its infrastructure, and to measure performance against objectives.
- *Key entities*—within an activity, those 'things' that are of fundamental importance to the business processes, and for which there will be associated information, although not necessarily held as computer information. They may include people (customers, suppliers, employees), objects (products, invoices), places (workshop, laboratory) or abstractions such as events (sale, order). The models also indicate relationships between the entities (optional or mandatory, one-to-one, etc.).

These models are obtained from top-down analysis of the business. They are all high level and tend to be somewhat imprecise, since so much of the detail is absent, but are capable of successive decomposition so that they can become increasingly more precise, when later undertaking feasibility studies and systems development activities. They are frequently called 'fuzzy' models at the high level. The entities themselves are likely to become the focus of the subject databases subsequently developed and maintained. The IS models are likely to include:

- *Process flow models* or *process dependency charts*, which show the end-to-end series of information dependencies and actions that deliver satisfactory business outcomes to external or internal customers. An example might be 'develop a new product'.
- *Hierarchical activity models* or *functional decomposition diagrams*, describing the business units' activities. They are produced by activity analysis and show how the high-level functions of the business are broken down into broad activity categories defining what it does or wants to do (sell and produce products, etc.) and then into more detailed subordinate activities.
- *Entity relationship models*, showing the relationships of the key entities or entity groups relevant to the organization. Their main purpose is to define the underlying information architecture, independent of any functional considerations. They also provide a means of clarifying company-wide business language and are the source of the initial entries into the business unit's data dictionary.
- *Data flow diagrams* (DFDs), indicating the movement of information around, into and out of the business. A DFD is a network

representation of business information systems and shows the logical dependency of one activity upon another for its data. The most significant characteristics of DFDs are that the situation is represented from the viewpoint of data, not a person or organization. The diagrams are graphic and can be partitioned and layered so that rather complex flows can be easily shown. They can be structured so that functions can be decomposed into more detailed self-contained models.

- *Activity/Entity matrices*, providing a tabular representation of the business and illustrating the relationship between information entities, conceptual business activities and conceptual application areas. They plot the usage of information entities against the business activities and also record whether the particular activities create, use or modify the entities. This enables a first-pass attempt at matching application areas to important business needs and showing how information will be shared across applications.

More details regarding IS modelling tools can be found in Avison and Fitzgerald,[9] Avison and Wood-Harper,[10] and Checkland.[11]

The creation of models, and the accompanying fact finding and analysis, is frequently performed within the IS strategy development process by information analysts in the team, working with people from the business side to obtain the relevant information. They are often initiated at workshop sessions with business people, held to discuss the business strategy and IS requirements. Alternatively, the models may have been built by the IS function independently of the IS/IT strategy development process, or they could be built as part of a business re-engineering initiative. If the models already exist, they may just need verifying and updating. Many of the large enterprise systems vendors also supply generic industry process models. Some modelling tools such as ARIS[12] also have a library of models for different industries.

Once process models have been developed, the processes can be evaluated for their effectiveness in meeting business needs. An approach for assessing the effectiveness of processes is presented later in the chapter.

Information models may be created for the whole corporate body or at strategic business unit (SBU) level or even major business function level. In the latter case, there may need to be a rationalization process to identify common entities, cross-functional entity relationships and common logical activities. Policy and implementation issues relating to rationalization would then follow in the management of corporate information and development of application systems. There may also be organizational implications if there is merit in rationalizing operational activities.

In a large organization with several business units, it is most probable that separate models will be created for each unit, but that there will be no attempt to create a global model for the whole organization. However where there is a good deal of similarity between the units, or business synergy, then reconciliation between common entities becomes important, when the business relationships are explored. Similarly, when consolidation of information from various units up to corporate level is considered, reconciliation may also be desirable.

Organizational Environment

When considering the process and information needs of an organization, it is also essential to have a clear understanding of the organization's current structure, relationships and the people of which it is composed. These organizational dynamics form an important input into the planning process. It is necessary to understand the environment and its skills, resources, values, culture and social interactions, as well as its management style and its relationship with the external environment. These become increasingly important when the magnitude and pace of change has implications for all aspects of a business. There are a number of organizational development and organizational modelling techniques that can be used to prompt the analysis, one of which is covered later in the chapter.

External Business Environment

This external environment was described in Chapter 2. For the purposes of IS strategy formulation, it is essential to understand and analyse the environment, so that opportunities for IS/IT to impact the business and contributing to the shaping of the business strategy can be identified and explored. The analysis of the external environment and the development of IS/IT initiatives to exploit its opportunities and counter its threats is further covered in Chapter 5.

EXAMINING THE CURRENT IS/IT ENVIRONMENT

In order to assess and prioritize IS actions, it is also necessary to examine the current IS/IT environment to establish the gap between current and future targeted provisions, so as to determine whether the environment can sustain the changes required or itself needs changing. Gaps may relate to the provision of the target portfolio, either by enhancement of existing applications or by developing new ones. The remainder may affect any of the other aspects in the IS/IT environment, including the organization, its competencies, the technical infrastructure or supplier relationships.

While most of the analysis of the current IS/IT environment relates to factual matters, a further important aspect is to ascertain a business manager's perception of the role and current effectiveness of IS/IT. This will enable IS/IT management to determine whether they have to address issues creating the perceptions held and will also give a good indication as to the level of commitment the business is likely to give to any proposals. Chapter 8 addresses issues regarding the relationship between the IS function and the business.

Examination of the external IT environment enables the strategists to take account of trends and opportunities from emerging technologies and to investigate how competitive or complementary organizations are applying IT. This will lead to a more objective appraisal of current effectiveness, as well as to new ideas for potential application of IT.

Assessment of the *internal IS/IT environment* comprises:

- an evaluation of the current application portfolio and the applications under development to determine their content, coverage and contribution;
- a similar evaluation of current information resources;
- an evaluation of the current infrastructure and IT services and resources, accomplished through a technology assessment.

The results are the basis of the assessment of the gap between current and required provisions. While this work can be conducted independently from the analysis of the business environment, there are obvious advantages in maintaining frequent contact between the two activities to ensure that the assessment of IS/IT is conducted in the context of what the business wants to achieve. The most significant aspect is the current application portfolio, since it represents the starting point from which future development will begin. It is also a key determinant of how the business community in the organization perceives the value and contribution of IS/IT.

Current Portfolio Evaluation

The current suite of applications includes centralized, distributed, web-enabled and end-user systems and databases that support various aspects of the business—administrative, operational, control, planning and strat-

Table 4.3   *Deliverables from a current portfolio assessment*

- Categorization in terms of application portfolio segments—strategic, high potential, key operational and support
- Assessment of coverage and contribution of systems to business needs, and any major opportunities to increase business value
- The extent to which the systems integrate or interoperate
- Assessment of the effectiveness and robustness, and the unrealized potential in current systems, and of the enhancement required to increase contribution
- Common elements and differences between current portfolio and required information and systems architecture
- Supporting information to enable estimates of potential improvement projects
- Supporting information to allow prioritization of enhancement and support work on current systems
- Opportunities that exist to improve quality of information
- Strengths and weaknesses assessed against the business CSFs
- Assessment of the risks of failure from the current portfolio

egic. Gaining a thorough and agreed understanding of the portfolio enables measurement of its value to the business and the contribution that systems make towards satisfying business objectives. This will include a description of the functions performed by each of the systems and an assessment of their technical and functional effectiveness, as well as the opinion of the users in terms of utility and value to them. The analysis includes not only existing systems and databases but also those under development and those planned but not yet under way. Clearly, any of these could be revised as a result of the strategy process.

Typical deliverables from a systematic assessment are listed in Table 4.3. The likelihood is that key operational and support quadrants will be well populated, and that a few systems will indicate some strategic use of IT. Often, there are a number of high-potential systems created by end-users experimenting independently with innovative ideas.

The analysis involves gathering and collating a substantial amount of factual and subjective information, both technical and user orientated, for each system from two main sources:

- The users of the information systems and databases—to gain information about how the system supports business objectives and processes; the functionality and business information in its scope; users' views on system quality and the usability of the application; dependence on the application; documentation, training and systems support quality; users' views on its future potential.

Table 4.4 *Sample questions for evaluating the current portfolio (source: adapted from a questionnaire developed by T. Osborne, 'Current portfolio questionnaire', working papers, Glaxo Wellcome Operations, 1994)*

1. What business activities are 'contained' within the system?
2. What information (automated and manual) flows through the system and how is the information accessed and transferred?
3. Does the system support a critical business process, with reference to objectives, critical success factors, drivers, value chain? Does the system inhibit the effectiveness of the core process?
4. How does the system map on to process maps, entity charts and the conceptual architecture? How does it map on to the future applications architecture, if one has been developed?
5. What problems—gaps, poor links, duplications, etc.—are revealed?
6. How does the system contribute to meeting the IS demand determined in business strategy analysis?
7. How effective is user support in terms of responding to and clearing up problems, and how effective is training, documentation and usability?
8. How useful, accurate and timely is the information put into and taken out of the system?
9. Are there any better ways of using the system?
10. How flexible is the system for making changes?

- The IT development and technical staff—to gain information about the structure and interfaces of information systems and databases: their technical characteristics, quality, age and technical robustness, ease of maintenance and extent of data duplication.

This part of the strategy process can be very extensive and time consuming, and care must be taken not to spend too much effort here, which may not be repaid. A relatively short evaluation may be quite adequate to obtain a broad picture, then, later, when the intended initiatives are becoming clearer, further investigation can be made of targeted areas of the portfolio.

The information may be collected by discussion or questionnaire, or by a mixture of both. A questionnaire may be the only practical method, because there are often multiple users for major business systems and databases. A selection of the type of questions that might be asked is given in Table 4.4.

Current/Previous Strategy and Policies

If IS/IT strategic formulation and planning is a continuous process, it is very likely that a previous IS/IT strategy exists, which documents the previous 'current situation', the policies that were to be adopted and plans for accomplishing the changes. This would have included the investment in capital expected and the expenditure expected in relation to turnover or organizational budget. It would also have documented pertinent policies (e.g. information management policies or policies governing the selection of technology products, services and vendors). Careful scrutiny of the previous strategy and its business rationale will guard against making critical policy decisions that may be difficult, if not impossible, to implement. Chapters 8–11 address many of the factors in the IS/IT environment, which are briefly described in the following subsections.

IS Organization and Processes

This covers a number of aspects that will be more or less relevant, according to how effective the current services are and whether the role of IS/IT in the organization needs to change drastically. It is likely that the following factors will need assessing for their suitability:

- the IS function, its size, structure and relationship with the business at organizational, functional, departmental and individual levels;
- the organization for the provision of IT resources and services;
- sourcing strategy for IT resources and services;
- how the IS function is managed and the level at which it reports into the corporate level and individual businesses;
- the IS/IT governance structure, including decision-making processes and any steering committee structure in place;
- how business cases and budgets for IS/IT investments and expenditure are prepared and by whom, and how they are authorized.

These topics are covered in detail in Chapter 8.

Current Assets, Resources and Skills

These are the assets of the organization in terms of hardware, software, communications capability and any other technology employed, together with the information resources, human assets and skills of IS/IT people and users. This inventory must be reviewed for its relevance and ability in meeting future requirements.

Methods and Training Provisions

This refers to the methods in use for business and systems analysis, business process re-engineering, systems design and development, data management, project management and control, quality assurance and control, and estimating. It includes any systems development methodologies, object-oriented methods, technical standards, use of rapid application development (RAD) methods, decision support, expert systems or any other specialized tools. It also covers training and education methods employed, and any particular awareness programs directed at the business to raise understanding of IS/IT. Similarly, any awareness or other training available for technical people on business matters is also covered.

Much of the assessment of the IS function and its processes can be accomplished by focusing the organization modelling technique, described later in the chapter, on the IS function itself. This provides a framework of questions and a structure for assessing the answers.

What Does the Business Think of IS?

It is advantageous to have an objective view of the current role and contribution of IS/IT in the business, the role and contribution of the IS function itself, and of the perception of this from the rest of the business. This is not an exact science, but an objective and largely qualitative perspective can be drawn by considering a number of different aspects:

- Analysis of the current application portfolio can provide a great deal of information. By categorizing the portfolio into strategic, high potential, key operational or support systems, it can indicate how well current and future business strategy is supported. This is also a key indicator in assessing how IS/IT is perceived by business people. If, for example, there are no strategic or high-potential applications, this suggests that management consider IS/IT of little strategic value to the business. Chapter 7 describes in detail how to assess the applications and the resulting management options and issues.
- Consideration of how many of the business functions and processes are underpinned by systems, and of the size of the applications development backlog, gives an indication of the level of support given to the operational and management needs of the enterprise.
- Assessment of levels of user satisfaction across the range of IS/IT services gives a preliminary view of the effectiveness of the relationship achieved between IS/IT and the business. User roles in managing projects and in developing business cases, together with the IS function, gives a measure of the cooperation existing between the business and IS function.

- The level of integration achieved between systems and across different technologies, and the status of information management in the business, gives a good measure of the degree to which information is considered a key corporate resource.
- Analysis of the role and the structure of the IS function, in relation to the structure of the organization, indicates whether IS/IT is already well integrated with the business.
- An indicator of the current role and value of IS/IT comes from the level in the management hierarchy where overall responsibility for IS/IT resides. This is increasingly a board-level appointment in businesses where IS/IT is considered strategic.

Peppard and Ward's[13] research has indicated that, where IS function is perceived as making a value-added contribution to the business and where there is a close relationship between the IS function and the rest of the business, IS/IT has a significant positive impact on business performance. If the relationship is poor, the organization is probably faced with a long struggle, first of all, to, improve the perception of IS/IT and, second, to get business managers involved in IS/IT decision making. Implementing an IS/IT strategy process, as outlined in this book, will be challenging, particularly when exploring the impact of IS/IT and seeking opportunities for innovative application (as opposed to alignment). In Chapter 8, the relationship between the IS function and other areas of the business is explored in more detail.

External IS/IT Environment

This final input into the strategy process relates to the external IS/IT environment, where the purpose is to gain a perspective on technology trends and opportunities for using IS/IT in new and innovative ways. It does not necessarily mean seeking ideas for implementing leading-edge technology, although these are not precluded. The aim may be to find ways of using existing technology at lower cost or in previously unconsidered ways.

Part of this involves looking at what competitors or other comparable organizations are doing. This outward view is useful not only to pick up ideas but also to obtain a measure of the relative maturity of the business's own IS/IT contribution. It may be a deliberate policy of the company not to be a pioneer of any new technology in its own business sector or a leader in innovative use of IT at all, but to follow at a measured pace behind the recognized leaders.

Another aspect of this external survey may be to categorize elements of technology that may be worth evaluating in more detail later, when implementation issues are addressed. Clearly, any organization that makes a point of following external trends and opportunities through an established mechanism will have the required information available as input to the planning process.

IT research establishments such as Gartner, IDC and Forrester Research can be another good source of technology trends and information. However, organizations should exercise caution when reading many of their reports, particularly regarding vendors, as they may not be as independent in their assessment as it might seem. Not only do many of the research organizations charge for providing information but they also charge vendors a fee; failing to pay usually means a vendor is not included in any of their assessments or analysis despite the fact that they may be providing a superior solution.

TECHNIQUES FOR INTERPRETATION AND ANALYSIS

There are many techniques that can be used in analysing the current situation and business strategy. Some of them are included in Table 4.5, which also indicates the main deliverables derived from the techniques. Those marked with a single asterisk have already been described or will be described in this chapter; those marked with two asterisks are essentially 'impact'-seeking techniques and are described and their use explained in Chapter 5. The remainder includes standard techniques such as SWOT (Strengths, Weaknesses, Opportunities, Threats) analysis and business strategy analysis. Business process redesign is also referenced and, although it is described in overview several times in this book, as already noted it is too large a topic to cover in detail here.[14]

The aim of the rest of this chapter is to briefly describe these techniques and to suggest why and how they are used.

INFORMATION REQUIREMENTS TO MEET THE CURRENT BUSINESS OBJECTIVES: THE USE OF CRITICAL SUCCESS FACTORS AND BALANCED SCORECARDS

In order to position critical success factor (CSF) analysis and the Balanced Scorecard, it is useful to develop the link between data, information and business results. Figure 4.4 illustrates such a model, the DIKAR model (Data, Information, Knowledge, Action, Results), derived from the work of Venkatraman.[15] Viewing the model from left

Table 4.5 *Techniques used in creating the IS demand statement*

Technique	Deliverables
Business strategy analysis	Business strategy—mission, objectives, etc. Global business initiatives Business area initiatives Business priorities IS requirements leading to IS demand
Critical Success Factor (CSF) analysis*	Areas of business activity 'where things must go right' Potential IS/IT thrusts Performance measures
SWOT analysis	Analysis of Strengths, Weaknesses, Opportunities and Threats of internal and external business and IS/IT environments
Balanced Scorecard analysis*	Business objectives and key information requirements Performance measures
Business portfolio and competitive strategy analysis**	Options for long term IS investment to strengthen competitive position
Value chain analysis (internal and external)**	Internal information flows High-level 'industry' information flow model Potential impact of IS/IT
Process analysis*/Business process re-engineering*	Identification of core business processes Effectiveness of processes in meeting drivers Process improvement options Process redesign blueprints (that deliver significant performance improvement regarding drivers) Resultant IS/IT options
Organizational modelling*	Comprehensive assessment of the business and IS/IT environments Filtering mechanism in assessing options for change
Business modelling—information analysis techniques*	Enterprise model: —entity models —object models —process dependency charts —data flow diagrams —functional decomposition diagrams —conceptual architecture

continued

Table 4.5 *(Continued)*

Technique	Deliverables
Current portfolio evaluation*	Profile of current applications Coverage and contribution to business user and technical satisfaction Contribution of applications to business strategy
Technology assessment and IS/IT infrastructure review	Inventory of current hardware and software Assessment of IS organization, procedures, skills and methods

* Covered in this chapter
** Covered in the next chapter

to right represents an IT perspective where the focus is on data processing and the provision of information to the business. Viewing it from right to left, the focus is on business results and the actions and knowledge required to achieve those results. (This model is used again in Chapter 10 when the concept of knowledge and its management is explored in detail.)

The Balanced Scorecard identifies the information required to measure performance against the business objectives. CSF analysis, on the other hand, identifies what has to be done, or changed, in order to achieve the objectives, including new information and/or systems needed. In combination, they provide a way of obtaining agreement as to the priority of IS investments relevant to achieving the explicit business objectives for the next 6–12 months.

Balanced Scorecard

The Balanced Scorecard has become a popular tool for managing the performance of organizations and, laterally, for the development of strategy itself. Developed by Harvard Business School academics Kaplan and Norton,[16] it is based on the premise that financial measures only report the results of past decisions and that, if performance measurement is to have any real meaningful impact, a more balanced set of objectives and measures is required. The Balanced Scorecard promotes the examination of performance from four interrelated perspectives, each seeking to address specific questions (see Figure 4.5):

- *Financial:* How do we look to our shareholders and those with a financial interest in the organization?

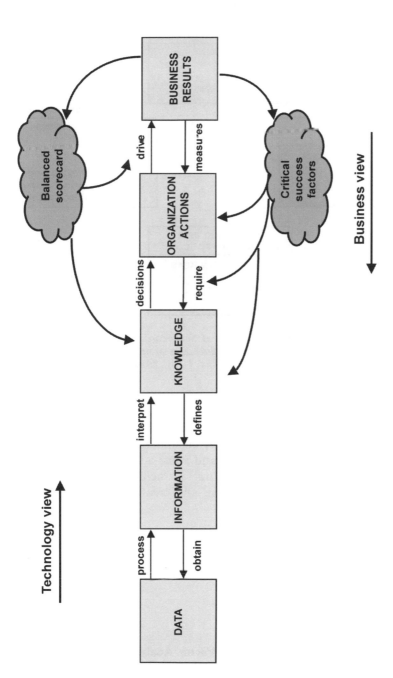

Figure 4.4 *Information in context (source: based on the work of N. Venkatraman presented at Cranfield School of Management, February 1996)*

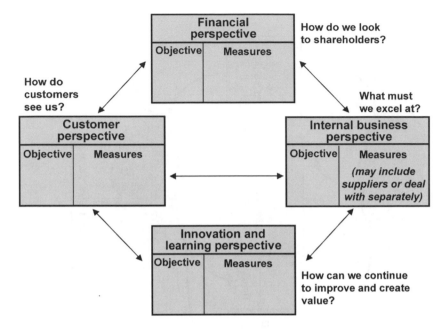

Figure 4.5 *Information and the Balanced Scorecard* (source: R.S. Kaplan and D.P. Norton, 'Using the Balanced Scorecard as a strategic management system', Harvard Business Review, January–February 1996, 76. Used with permission)

- *Internal business perspective:* What do we have to excel at if we are to meet the expectations of our employees and trading partners?
- *Customer perspective:* How do our customers perceive us in term of products, services, relationships and value-added?
- *Innovation and learning perspective:* To achieve our future vision, how will we continue to improve and create future value for our stakeholders?

For each of the four perspectives, objectives can be established and relevant measures, often called key performance indicators (KPIs), assigned against each objective, leading to the information needed to measure performance.

Critical Success Factor Analysis

CSF analysis is a powerful and deservedly popular technique not only in developing an IS/IT strategy but also for business strategy development.

Table 4.6 *Uses of critical success factor (CSF) analysis*

- It is a most effective technique in involving senior management in developing the IS strategy, because it is wholly rooted in business issues and in gaining their commitment to proposed IS actions that contribute to achievement in critical areas
- It enables linking of candidate IS projects through CSFs to objectives, and thus clearly demonstrates alignment with the business strategy, and provides a compelling basis for gaining wholesale agreement by the top-management team
- In individual interviews with senior management, it is a good catalyst in unearthing their own individual information needs
- By providing a link between objectives and information requirements, the CSFs play an important role in prioritizing potential investments
- It is particularly useful in IS planning when the business strategy has not progressed beyond objectives by focusing attention on the most critical aspects of the business that need action taken to improve their performance
- It is extremely powerful when used alongside value chain analysis in identifying the most critical processes, and enabling ownership of the CSF and its associated actions to be accurately pinpointed

The technique often appears under many guises (e.g. 'key issue analysis' and 'do wells') and is probably the most commonly used tool in the IS strategies toolkit. It can be used in a number of different ways and for different purposes, as indicated in Table 4.6. As described here, it is used for the purpose of interpreting the business objectives in terms of actions required to achieve them, the key information and application needs of the organization and its managers, and for assessing the strengths and weaknesses of existing systems, in that context.

The technique can be used at the macro-level to examine the overall industry (i.e. define industry CSFs), the company as a whole or a particular business unit. It can also be used at individual executive level to determine which of those activities that he or she performs are the most important for achievement of success against a particular objective. In this way, the CSF process can assist in prioritizing activities and information requirements, both at individual manager and at business unit levels. In both cases, the CSF technique helps to focus attention on the key issues.

What Are Critical Success Factors?

Rockart[17] defines CSFs as being 'the limited number of areas in which results, if they are satisfactory, will ensure successful competitive

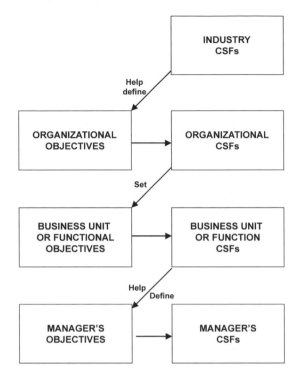

Figure 4.6   *Objectives and CSFs*

performance for the organization.' They are the few key areas where 'things must go right' for the business to flourish. As a result, the CSFs are areas of activity that should receive constant and careful attention from management. The current status of performance in each area should be continually measured, and that information should be made widely available.

Every firm in an industry may have some common CSFs such as access to raw materials or timely delivery, due to pressures on or in the industry. The overall organization, which could have units in many industries, will have CSFs relative to its objectives of diversification, return on investment and portfolio mix. The key area for determining CSFs as part of IS strategy development is the business unit, since—as stated in Chapter 3—this is the practical level to determine strategy. The agreement of the business unit managers as to what these CSFs are is important in obtaining consensus on the major IS/IT investments. There will also tend to be a structured, cascading relationship in a large organization between objectives and CSFs, as illustrated in Figure 4.6.

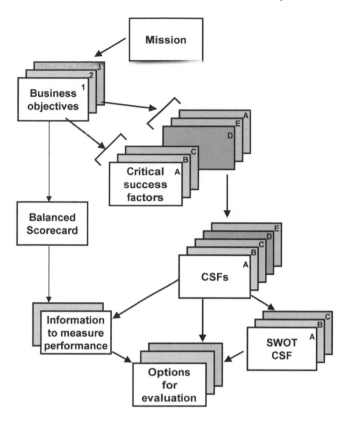

Figure 4.7 *Critical success factors basic processes*

The determination of CSFs should only be started when objectives have already been identified. The first stage is to identify CSFs against each objective, then, second, to consolidate them across objectives, since many CSFs will recur (see Figure 4.7). Ranking of objectives and the number sharing the same CSF will give a relative priority to the achievement of CSFs. Only then should the importance of information or systems in achieving those CSFs be considered. 'How can IS/IT help achieve the CSFs?' and 'How do existing systems inhibit achievement of CSFs?' are both important questions to consider, and this implies a SWOT analysis of existing systems against the CSFs. By implication, if the CSF is achieved, the probability of achieving objectives is increased. That assumes that there are a reasonable number of CSFs per objective— between five and eight per objective is a useful rule of thumb. Too many suggest that the objective is unachievable; too few and it is not ambitious enough!

From the above description, it may appear that the CSF is the universal management tool. This is not the case, for the following main reasons:

- To be of value, the CSF should be easily and directly related back to the objectives of the business unit. From experience in the technique, it generally loses its value when used below the third level in an organizational hierarchy.
- CSFs focus primarily on management control and tend to be internally focused and analytical, rather than creative.
- The nature of CSFs and KPIs reflect a particular executive's management style. The chief executive of one airline judged performance by load factors. His predecessor judged performance on the number of letters of complaint. Both are valid, but reflect different approaches.

When used effectively, it achieves a number of requirements, all of which are vitally important to the strategic process. They are:

- involving top management in the IS/IT strategy process and gaining their commitment;
- developing a consensus view of IS applications in the business;
- linking IS activity to business strategy;
- providing guidance for defining executive information needs.

When used ineptly, the approach can cause frustration, even despondency, and may even turn management against the strategy process. The most common cause of such problems is that 'critical' is not differentiated from 'important', resulting in long lists of factors that effectively describe everything the organization does! The strengths and weaknesses of the CSF approach are well documented. Shank et al.[18] list practical guidelines as to their use. They highlight the need:

- to use them in a formal, structured way;
- to educate people in advance regarding the process;
- not to link them solely and explicitly to the derivation of information needs.

In addition, the eliciting of CSFs works best (and is certainly done more quickly) in a group-working process rather than by conducting interviews with numerous individuals and then trying to collate the results. The value of a group approach is demonstrated by Hardaker and Ward[19] who report the use of CSF analysis as part of a concept called Process Quality Management in IBM. The CSF process must produce agreement to move in a coherent direction, which is very difficult to achieve by later consolidation, rather than achieving consensus as the analysis proceeds. This also enables the CSFs to remain focused on the management 'business agenda' rather than the personal agenda of an individual and avoids ambiguity being left unchallenged.

It can be summarized by saying that the process is as important as the product, since it achieves commitment to the outcome. If well prepared for the process, senior managers find little difficulty in articulating CSFs, since they are often merely overt statements of issues that they are aware of or are already addressing anyway. Guidance in establishing an effective process, based on real organization use, is provided in the articles already mentioned in addition to Rockart and Crescenzi.[20] It is important to remember that consensus of the senior managers must be achieved in order to get eventual agreement on IS/IT strategies. It forces analysis of the strengths, weaknesses, opportunities and threats, and ensures a proper understanding of the mission and objectives, often for the first time!

Consolidating the Balanced Scorecard and CSF Analysis

The outputs from the construction of the Balanced Scorecard and the CSF analysis can be combined to provide a more comprehensive set of IS requirements. The Balanced Scorecard links measures to business objectives, while CSF analysis identifies what is critical to achieving results. Together, both techniques provide a rigorous assessment of prioritized IS opportunities, given the current business strategy.

Box 4.2 describes an example application of the combined use of Balanced Scorecard and CSF analysis. It illustrates how the combination can lead to the derivation of improvements to operational activities and the identification of both the internal and external information required by those operational activities, and for performance measurement in relation to business goals or objectives. It is always better to have a crude measure of something important rather than a refined measure of something that does not matter! CSFs help to differentiate the two.

BUSINESS PROCESS ANALYSIS

Business process analysis is a technique for assessing the effectiveness of core business processes in support of business objectives and drivers from one or a number of SBUs, or from specific business areas within an SBU.

Box 4.2   The application of Balanced Scorecard and CSF analysis

This example relates to a manufacturing company providing a product and parts service primarily to SMEs. This company produces a wide range of electrical products that are assembled mainly from imported components. Orders tend to be for unique products configured to customer specification. As far as possible, the company attempts to meet all customer orders direct from component stock. However, this has implications for stockholding costs, both of components and finished products. The time between order placement and fulfilment can be severely impacted by the availability of component parts.

Using the Balanced Scorecard, the company constructed a scorecard of objectives and associated measures for each of the four perspectives. A partial view of the scorecard is illustrated below. So, for example, from a customer perspective, one objective is to increase responsiveness for both firm orders and inquiries. Associated measures to indicate the extent to which this objective is being achieved include:

- order to delivery lead time;
- enquiry response times.

Objectives	Financial	Measures
- To reduce stock costs		(a) Stock turn (b) write-offs (c) Stockhandling costs
- To increase product profitability		(a) Product margins (b) Gross profit

Objectives	Customer	Measures
- To increase responsiveness		(a) Order to delivery lead time (b) Enquiry response time
- To be more price competitive		(a) Benchmarks versus competitor prices (b) Customer value/price perception

Objectives	Internal	Measures
- To provide fast-track service to best customers		(a) Reduced lead time to specific customers (b) Customer satisfaction
- To remove interface costs/delays with agents		(a) Cost of rework (b) Number of referrals

Objectives	Innovation	Measures
- To reduce new product lead times by 30%		(a) Design to sale time (b No slack in elapsed time
- To find new channel to reach SME customers		(a) New channel exists (b) Number of options reviewed/tested

Using CSF analysis, the focus shifts to identifying the actions necessary to support each objective. So, for example, one of the objectives is to reduce stockholding costs. The CSFs with respect to this objective are:

- earlier identification of obsolete items;
- improved forecasting to reduce safety stock.

As illustrated in the figure below, working from the CSFs, we can determine both the information and systems requirements in order to support these CSFs:

- new analysis of stock-vturn to separate fast-moving/slow-moving items (A, B, C-based praeto analysis);
- improved stock forecasting based on more accurate sales forecasts/actuals;
- new stock replacement algorithms for different types of stock.

Deciding which systems to ultimately develop depends on business priorities.

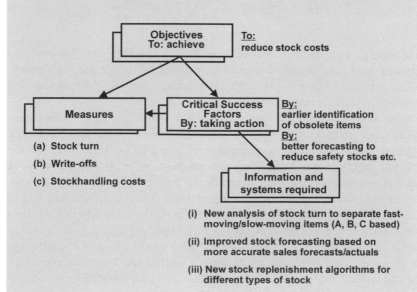

The outputs from Balanced Scorecard work and the CSF analysis can then be consolidated, as illustrated below.

Financial perspective			
Objectives	**Measure(s)**	**Action (CSF)**	**IS Needs**
- To reduce stock costs	a) Stock turn b) Write offs c) Stockhandling costs	- By earlier identification of obsolete items - By better forecasting to reduce safety stocks	i) New stock turn analysis (ABC) ii) Improved sales and stock forecasting iii) New stock replenishment algorithms

Customer perspective			
Objectives	**Measure(s)**	**Action (CSF)**	**IS Needs**
- To increase responsiveness	a) Order to delivery lead time b) Enquiry response time	- By identifying causes of all late deliveries - By informing customers in advance of problems - By tracking all enquiries/progress daily	i) New accurate measure of all order/delivery times ii) Analysis of all types of delivery failure iii) New/dynamic customer/order monitoring system to instigate action iv) New enquiry recording/tracking process and system

Ultimately, as a result of process analysis, a decision may be made to embark upon major redesign of one or a number of business processes. Whatever the outcomes, the IS/IT elements can be determined and assessed and built into the IS demand.

The assessment of business processes is aimed at defining the areas where the greatest opportunities exist to improve performance. At the highest level, an initial assessment can be made of how effective the current processes are in meeting the business objectives and drivers. A second assessment can then be made to predict how effective the processes could and should be in making their fullest contribution to the drivers. For example, if the driver relates to increased market share, then the customer acquisition processes would expect to play a greater role in achieving this than the process for servicing existing contracts, although both would have potential for making a worthwhile contribution. Comparing current and potential performance gives an indication of the gap that could be made up by improving the process.

Adopting a Process Perspective

Over a decade after the concept of business process re-engineering emerged, the majority of organizations are still structured along functional (or departmental) lines, with each having their own hierarchy. The 'chain' of linked departments allows for specialization where the overall task is broken down and people with specific expertise can be applied as required. Such specialization of labour, whether on the manufacturing shop floor or within offices, has been a normal way of working for a long time. 'Levels' of seniority evolve within these functions to form the organizational hierarchy. This model is so widely established that it has rarely been questioned. BPR is a concept that questions this 'functional' way of thinking and makes 'processes' a central focus for organization design.[21] In short, processes are becoming the building blocks of organizations and seek to capture natural workflows (see Figure 4.8).

A process focus means examining the way a customer order is fulfilled, a new product developed or a customer account established without concern for functional boundaries or specialization. For example, when requesting repair of a telephone fault, the customer is not generally interested in which department the engineer works for, whether he travels by public transport or buys spare parts in the local hardware shop, as long as the service is restored.

The *Oxford English Dictionary* defines process as *a continuous and regular action or succession of actions, taking place or carried out in a definite manner, and leading to the accomplishment of some result; a continuous operation or series of operations.* In its simplest form, a process has an input and an output and is made up of a sequence of individual activities through which this input passes to become an output. With this traditional view, the process itself can be anything that transforms, transfers or merely looks after the input and delivers it as output. Organizations adopting a process approach find that, for example, many of the steps in their order cycles have nothing to do with delivering the required outcomes.[22] Indeed, it is sometimes difficult to identify why some steps exist at all! Often, it is for no better reason than because they always have! Getting rid of all these unnecessary steps can result in faster throughput or quicker customer service and at considerably lower cost.

However, the traditional view of a process being composed of activities can be problematic, particularly in information and knowledge industries. In such contexts, it is perhaps more appropriate to view the process in terms of *roles*, with a process portrayed as a number of roles collaborating and interacting to achieve a goal. This perspective can be extended to make explicit reference to behaviours: a process is an organized collection of behaviours that satisfies a defined business purpose,

Traditional functional structure

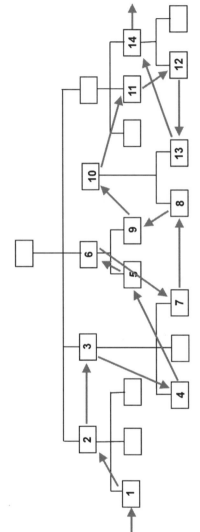

Process flow

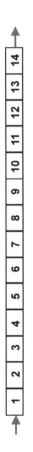

Figure 4.8 *Adopting a process orientation*

performed according to specific targets. This view is of relevance in knowledge work or in areas where there is a high degree of interaction between people. For example, specifying the precise activities in customer service processes is difficult, if not impossible. Guidelines as to the behaviour to be exhibited can be given, however attitude is often the crucial ingredient in determining whether or not a customer is satisfied.

Many IT implementations have focused on automating traditional ways of working that existed at that time— existing work practices remain. However, an order-to-fulfilment process could be further enhanced by examining the fundamental assumptions that underlie the design of this process with a view toward radically redesigning how work is performed. For example, the assumption that salespeople take orders, or the assumption that accounting staff perform credit checks, or the assumption that payment is made on receipt of an invoice, guide the design of the process. Why can't the customer phone, fax or electronically send (via the Internet) the order directly to the factory, where, using expert system technology, the order can be verified, a credit check performed, availability of stock determined and shipment to customer arranged? Purchase orders could also be sent electronically to suppliers. The company could also consider the introduction of 'invoiceless processing', where customers submit payment based on receipt of goods rather than on receipt of an invoice, subject to the usual credit terms and conditions. This is how Dell and Cisco operate.

This, in essence, represents the fundamental message of business process re-engineering. It is not merely automating existing work practices but seeking opportunities where existing ways of working can be totally transformed. The power of information technology, in particular, provides the opportunity for new and innovative ways of organizing and enabling organizational work to be performed in ways that are not possible manually. Box 4.3 provides a summary description of approaches to redesign.

Identifying Processes

Despite the intuitive appeal of processes, identifying and understanding processes is not as simple as it might at first seem. For example, in the delivery of most products and services, companies operate a highly complex set of processes. A key challenge, however, is to identify processes and define them at an appropriate level. Evidence suggests that many organizations are redesigning processes that make little contribution to business success as a whole, even if the processes selected are successfully redesigned. Performance improvements reported are very often expressed relative to the process being redesigned rather than the business unit as a whole. Although such results may look impressive in

Box 4.3   Approaches to redesigning processes

Once an organization has identified a process to be redesigned, how does it proceed in determining the new design? Having examined many BPR initiatives, two broad approaches to redesign can be identified: the *systemic approach* and the *clean sheet approach.** In reality, however, organizations usually adopt a combination of both.

In adopting a systematic redesign approach, an organization maps out and attempts to understand an existing process and then work through it systematically to create new processes to deliver the desired outcomes. The clean sheet approach, on the other hand, demands a fundamental rethink of the way that the product or service is delivered and designs new processes from scratch.

Redesigning an already existing process or, for that matter, refining a newly-designed one, is usually about making it better, cheaper and/or faster. *Better*, in that it delivers higher levels of satisfaction to its stakeholders, particularly for customers. *Faster*, in that it does so as quickly as possible thereby also increasing responsiveness. *Cheaper*, in that it does the above to the highest levels of efficiency.

When redesigning existing processes, the emphasis is on the elimination of non-value-adding activities and the streamlining of the core value-adding ones. The rules for doing this can best be summarized using the acronym ESIA: *eliminate* all non-value-adding activities; *simplify* aspects of work where possible; *integrate* elements of the process and *automate* where appropriate. The table below highlights the main areas of attention within these four domains.

Areas of attention for systematic redesign (source: J. Peppard and P. Rowland, The Essence of Business Process Reengineering, Prentice-Hall International, Hemel Hempstead, UK, 1995, p. 181)

Eliminate	Simplify	Integrate	Automate
Overproduction	Forms	Jobs	Dirty activities
Waiting time	Procedures	Teams	Difficult activities
Transport	Communication	Customers	Dangerous activities
Processing	Technology	Suppliers	Boring activities
Inventory	Problem areas		Data capture
Defects/Failures	Flows		Data transfer
Duplication			Data analysis
Reformatting			
Inspection			
Reconciling			

With the clean sheet approach, assumptions implicit in the existing process are discarded and a fundamental rethink of the way the process is undertaken ensues. It is built on the premise that, to achieve significant performance improvement, work within the process must be done differently. The clean sheet approach is about working back from that target to a design that will make it happen.

Organizations adopt a 'clean sheet' approach either because in their opinion they have reached a 'breakpoint', or simply that previous attempts to re-engineer the existing processes through a systemic strategy have failed to result in any significant performance improvement. This is not to suggest that systematic redesign is any less creative or innovative. The main disadvantage of the clean sheet approach is that the required organizational changes can be difficult, though not impossible, to implement incrementally. Overall, with this approach the risk is higher and the pain and disruption greater. During implementation, a crucial problem, faced by many organizations who have used this method, is that the new processes differ so fundamentally from the existing ones that workers have great difficulty in relating to them. Unless great care is taken and management commitment is solid, workers may refuse to switch to the new methods of working.

Sometimes, organizations decide a new division or operation is necessary rather than try and change the existing organization. Midland Bank's decision to set up a separate telephone banking company, First Direct, and even General Motors' Saturn business unit are examples of this strategy. This 'greenfield site' approach has a number of distinct advantages; not least, the chance to design the facilities from scratch taking into account the latest thinking in organization and management and exploiting the latest technological innovations without having to deal with legacy systems. Creating the desired culture with a new workforce is also much easier than where significant to an existing one are required.

In reality, there is a great deal of middle ground between both methods with many organizations choosing a combination of the two. The choice between the two approaches will depend on what the organization is most comfortable with, and also on the time-scales involved. Whichever alternative is selected, it is important to ensure that the analysis of existing processes is not overdone, though the danger of this is higher in the systematic redesign approach. Always remember that the objective, regardless of the approach chosen, is to obtain significant improvement in performance. More attention should therefore be paid to the new process rather than the old, which is merely a starting point.

The redesign of any process is a creative activity and there are many techniques that can be used to get those involved in the redesign to engage in 'out of the box thinking'. There are also many software packages on the market specifically designed for process mapping. However, many companies simply choose to use large sheets of paper and Post-It notes with the same effect. It should be noted that any map is only to aid in understanding although the simulation facility provided by some packages can be used to good effect in modelling different redesign options. There are also a number of different process mapping techniques including simple flow charting, IDEF(0) and Role Activity Diagrams.

* A detailed description of both these approaches can be found in J. Peppard and P. Rowland, *The Essence of Business Process Reengineering*, Prentice-Hall International, Hemel Hempstead, UK, 1995.

the context of the process prior to design, in reality they have little impact on the organization's overall competitiveness or profitability.

Hammer,[23] whose work has helped promote the concept of business re-engineering, acknowledges that process identification is almost certainly the most intellectually-challenging component of redesign. Identification is complicated because, as we have seen above, business processes cross departmental and hierarchical boundaries. In a factory, one can at least follow the flow of incoming material through to the point of departure of the finished product. This may be complicated, with many materials being combined into one; however, the physical flows are visible and can be identified and understood relatively easily. In services and office environments, it is much more difficult to understand a process that includes paperwork, and other forms of communications such as telephone calls, electronic messages and information, which must be followed.[24] In addition, many employees working in the process often have little idea of how the whole process works, how the output they create is used or even why it is produced. They often only understand their particular role and set of tasks. The nature of business processes is such that they can be construed as almost any activity that goes on in the organization—everything can be considered as a process—and consequently processes can exist at any level. An approach to identifying business processes based on their strategic importance and, hence, potential beneficial redesign is described in Box 4.4.

Box 4.4 Identifying processes (for more information on this method, see C. Edward and J.W. Peppard, 'Organizationalizing strategy through process', *Long Range Planning*, Vol. 30, No. 5, 1997, 753–767).

One approach to identifying processes is to examine the expectations of stakeholders and then determine the processes required to deliver these expectations. In Chapter 2, the influence and impact of stakeholders on business strategy was highlighted. Stakeholders hold a variety of expectations; through its marketing activities, the organization seeks to understand and often influence these expectations, particularly those of external constituents.

The figure below illustrates a view of the relationship between strategy, stakeholders, expectations and processes. In this model, the interplay between strategy and stakeholders is critical: the strategy of the business defines who the stakeholders are, and stakeholders themselves shape the strategy. These expectations, when consolidated in the context of the business strategy, define the requirements placed upon the organization and the processes that will deliver them. It is these processes, when executed, that deliver these expectations that in turn satisfy stakeholders. In effect, the strategy is defining the required processes but indirectly via stakeholders and expectations.

The technique works by first listing out the expectations of each stakeholder, placing some level of priority against each expectation. Then, for each stakeholder expectation, determine whether an already identified process exists to satisfy that expectation. For example, with a new expectation, a process will need to be created (as by definition no process can yet have been created); an example of this may be 'to educate visitors', which results from an expectation on the part of visitors to a zoo to be educated. For another expectation, management need to decide if it is to be met by the existing process or if a new process needs to be originated. This decision involves considering if an existing process fully matches the expectation described and the degree of importance of that stakeholder and that expectation to the organization. If no existing process is able to deliver the expectation, then a new process is originated. If an existing process only partly meets the expectation and if satisfying the expectation is critical to the strategy, then a further process will need to be created; or an existing process needs redesigning to include meeting the expectation. Each time an expectation is subsumed into a process, or a new process is originated, the list of performance measures for that process must be updated to reflect the enlarged scope of the process or the amended process focus. The link between expectation and process should be documented for later consideration.

To reiterate, processes are seen as consolidations of stakeholder expectations and reflect *what* the organization must do. It does not include an indication of *how* it will be undertaken or *who* is to do it; this is determined in the design of the process. Processes themselves do not actually do anything: they exist to provide focus for achieving a desired outcome (i.e. an expectation). They are a device to enable a grouping of the activities and/or roles that will be required to be performed if the outcome is to be achieved. In other words, a collection of activities are the physical manifestations of a process. For example, the process 'to educate customers' visiting a zoo could be satisfied in a multitude of ways (e.g. installing a multimedia computer beside each cage, providing human guides or issuing a leaflet for later reading). It is a management decision to evaluate and select the particular set of activities that are appropriate to achieve the process.

Processes defined at an organizational level can be broken down into more detailed sets of subprocesses. These subprocesses, in turn, can also be decomposed into further levels of detail and so on until we reach the level of the individual task or role.[25] It is important in re-engineering that the processes selected for redesign or benchmarking are meaningful to the organization, if significant benefits are to be achieved.

Process redesign has wider implications than merely redesigning how a process operates and implementing new technology. Job descriptions will probably need to be rewritten, multifunctional job skills and the ability to work in teams becomes a priority, performance measurement and reward systems fostering individuality or functional priorities and internal competitiveness must be revised, new information systems must be designed and implemented. This can entail behavioural and cultural changes within the organization. Invoiceless payment, for example, demands a much closer and trusting relationship with customers and suppliers that may require a mindset change by management in their attitude toward suppliers, and even customers!

Process Importance–Performance Assessment

To identify potential candidates for redesign, it is useful to examine the importance of the processes to achieving business objectives and addressing the business drivers and plot this against the organization's performance in this process *vis-à-vis* competitors (see Figure 4.9). This importance–performance matrix[26] helps focus attention on those areas that are in most need of improvement. The matrix can also be used to obtain stakeholder feedback, and it is often interesting to contrast the views obtained from internal stakeholders with those from external stakeholders. Benchmarking may also be necessary to assess actual and relative performance.

American Express adopted a variant of this approach when selecting processes suitable for redesign. The primary criteria was on the gap

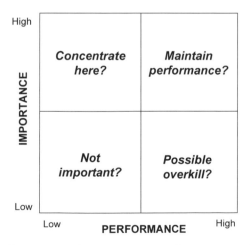

Figure 4.9   *The importance–performance matrix*

between their stakeholders expectations and their current performance and the potential impact this gap could have on their continued growth.[27] On the basis of these criteria, they decided to focus on two processes: travel service delivery (travel reservations and ticketing) and customer relationship management. The travel service delivery process was falling short of the expectations of both customer and shareholders as measured by the company's service performance monitor—the monthly tracking of customer satisfaction—and margins, and this underperformance was limiting growth prospects. The process underlying the management of customer relationships had become so complex that they hindered employees in meeting customers' needs, as measured by the company's annual survey of key contacts at client corporations.

ORGANIZATIONAL MODELLING

Organizational modelling is a structured technique used to ensure comprehensive examination and documentation of a business and its IS/IT environment. It is a valuable technique in IS/IT strategy development, and, if the business is also conducting any business re-engineering exercises, this or a similar means of obtaining a very broadly-based understanding of the organization is essential.

There are a number of different techniques that can be used. The organizational model at the heart of this technique, which is described here, is based on original work by Kotter.[28] This model of the organization is made up of seven elements: a central 'process' element labelled core business processes and six 'structural' elements—the external environment, employees and other tangible assets, formal organizational arrangements, the internal social system, the organization's technology and the dominant coalition. In his book, Kotter[29] developed a set of questions to understand the nature of the organization, although it is not expected that definitive answers can be obtained for all the questions. What is needed is a sensitivity to the potential relevance of each element or variable in the model, combined with an understanding of the activities within the organization and the information required to support these activities.

The original work by Kotter has been substantially modified and enhanced for the particular purpose of IS strategy formulation. Generally, the questioning approach is conducted on a macro-basis for the organization as a whole and in micro-form for the IS function itself. The questioning is tackled as part of the overall assessment process, where the main focus is on determining objectives, activities and information flows, in relation to the model, so that an appropriate representation

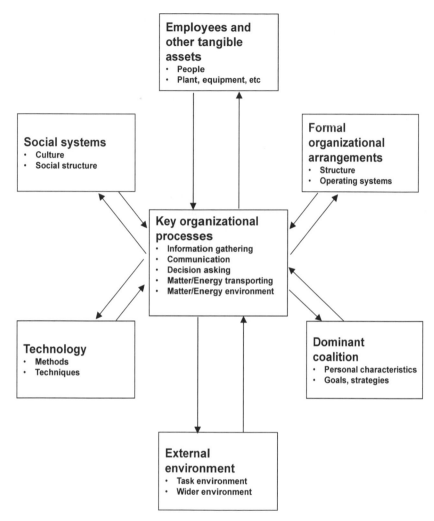

Figure 4.10 *The organizational model: environment and culture* (source: *adapted from J.P. Kotter,* Organizational Dynamics: Diagnosis and Intervention, *Addison-Wesley, Reading, Massachusetts, 1978)*

of the organization and how it functions is developed and understood by the senior management. Figure 4.10 shows the components of an organizational model, which can be built up in the following way:

- *The external environment*—questions are asked concerning the impact of legislative and fiscal policy, industry and economic trends, the basis of competition in the particular industry, industry standards, competitor practices and products, as described in Chapters 2 and 5.

- *The dominant coalition*—these are the key internal influencers who constitute the driving force behind the organization: What are their values? What are their aims? How do they work together as a team? What is the source of their power and influence, and how do they see the future of the organization? It is essential to identify this group because they will need to be convinced of the need for changes in information systems for competitive advantage; without their commitment, there is little likelihood of success. This topic is considered again in Chapter 8.
- *Formal organizational arrangements*—the plans, budgets, organization charts, job definitions, performance measurement and control systems are reviewed in order to develop an understanding of how the organization records the way in which it operates.
- *Employees and other tangible assets*—the quality and quantity of people, their skills and training and the level of turnover, and the physical, intellectual property and financial assets of the organization.
- *Social structure*—the formal arrangements within the company are reviewed along with employee and trade practices and relationships with trade unions, if applicable. The informal arrangements and customs and practices, staff attitudes to management and other workers, and to employee policies are also reviewed.
- *Technology employed*—the level of use of technology within the enterprise itself, in relation to the available technology and that used industry-wide, is also determined. This is not just concerned with IT but includes a 'catalogue' of the main hardware and software within the enterprise.
- *The core processes*—these are the processes and activities within the organization that convert the raw material into the finished products or bring resources together to deliver services.

Extracts from the questionnaire to help in constructing the model, developed from Kotter's original, are included in Box 4.5. Sample questions only have been included from a complete set of over 100. They are intended to give an indication of the depth and breadth of detail that may be elicited. Without this kind of model, it is very difficult to develop strategies for information systems that are consistent with the values and culture of the organization. In his book, Kotter described how to use the model to bring about organizational change. This is often a feature of implementation of strategy and, in its subsequent management, provides further justification for adopting this type of technique.

Box 4.5　Organizational modelling: extracts from a sample questionnaire to elicit required facts and options　(*source:* adapted from J.P. Kotter, *Organizational Dynamics: Diagnosis and Intervention*, Addison-Wesley, Reading, Massachusetts, 1978)

A　The External Environment

1. What are the key external groups that the organization has to take notice of?
2. Who dominates/determines the development of the industry?
3. What is the industry growth, maturity, size, etc.?
4. What makes for success in that particular industry?
5. How dependent is the organization on the external groups and what influence does it have over them?
6. What is the basis of its own power?
7. What is the industry value chain? How intense is the information value-added?
8. Could IT be used to increase customers' switching costs?
9. How are competitors/suppliers/customers using IS/IT?
10. Is there potential for pre-emptive use of IT with customers/suppliers?

B　The Dominant Coalition

1. Describe individually, for the key power holders, their personal skills, attitudes and motives and how they think the organization should be run.
2. How do they work as a group?
3. How do they seem to look at the future of the organization?
4. How powerful are they really in the organization, and where does such power come from?

C　The Formal Organization Arrangements

What formal procedures exist for:

1. Corporate strategy and planning?
2. The financial control of unit performance? The measurement of individual or unit performance?
3. Controlling information (i.e. is information being managed as a resource)?
4. Deciding directives for information systems users or IS/IT?
5. Determining policy with respect to distributed processing, use of personal workstations, etc.?
6. Determining corporate or SBU strategy?

7. Reporting of IS/IT? Is its top manager part of the senior management team?
8. IS strategy and does this relate to corporate strategy?

D   Employees and Other Tangible Assets
1. What are the organization's main physical and financial assets?
2. How many employees are there and of what general types?
3. Are the physical assets in good condition and up to date?
4. Are there strict financial limits imposed on the IS function or can projects proceed on the basis of justifications?
5. Comment on the existing application portfolio. How adaptable is it; how integrated, how cohesive?
6. Comment on the relative maturity of the IS organization.

E   The Internal Social System
1. What are the attitudes of the employee groups to company loyalty, hard work, cooperation with management and cooperation among themselves?
2. Are there any special cultural values that employees hold that affect the organization?
3. Are IS/IT personnel formally organized into groups or unions?
4. What is staff turnover? What are the recruitment and career development policies?

F   The Organization's Technology
1. What main techniques are used to produce the most important product of the organization?
2. What are the products and potential substitutes?
3. What is the information content of the products/services?
4. Can IT change the products/product life cycles/production economics?

With particular reference to company-based information systems:

5. Is the installation relatively large or small?
6. Is computer power centralized or distributed?
7. What is the degree of flexibility within the IS/IT environment?
8. Does the technology have a high or low impact on the enterprise itself?
9. How much is there by way of telecommunications, office automation, new technology, etc.?
10. How are the costs of IT passed on to the users?
11. How are IS investments evaluated and prioritized?

G   The Key Organizational Processes
1. What does the organization require so that it can operate (e.g. raw materials, energy, information, special skills, etc.)?
2. Are any of these especially costly or difficult to obtain?
3. How are these resources converted into goods or services?
4. How are the goods or services disposed of?
5. How does change come to be considered?
6. In IS/IT, are there any steering committees or groups giving guidance and direction?
7. How are key decisions made in IS/IT? Are there any user consultative groups? Are consultants used for second opinion? How much authority does management have?
8. How is IS/IT performance measured/objectives set?
9. How is any R&D funded?
10. What formal systems are used for development (methodologies)?
11. Is there an information centre and does it include PCs?
12. How does use of resources compare with strategic importance of applications?
13. Is maintenance separate from development and does it include enhancements?

There are three main reasons for developing the organizational model:

1. When embarking on an IS strategy process, there are a multitude of options available to the organization. It may want to develop new management information systems, or there may be a focus on obtaining competitive advantage. However, the strategy development and planning activities need to be completed quickly so that the enthusiasm and commitment that develop during the process can be sustained and so that work can start toward achieving the benefits of these improved systems. It is necessary, therefore, to have an effective filtering system so that the most relevant, realistic and implementable applications are considered for the future. The organizational model provides an effective filtering mechanism, since it contains substantial information about the resources that could be made available to implement systems, the culture of the organization, and its values and priorities. It helps prevent proposals for new information systems that would be unable to be resourced or that would be totally foreign to the culture.

2. However, it may be essential to implement new systems and strategies that require changes in behaviour and run counter to the current culture of the organization. If that is so, then the behaviours, and perhaps even the culture itself, needs to be modified. Here, the model is of considerable benefit because the required cultural changes can be compared against the model to determine their impacts and how to effect them. It is for this reason that it is suggested that two models be developed: the macro-version for the organization as a whole and the micro-version for the IS function, since almost inevitably there will be changes required to both.

3. The third, important use of the organizational model is to provide a comprehensive collective understanding of the environment, both external to the organization and internally, precisely when strategic decisions are taken. This is important because, when the strategy is revisited, questions may be asked why certain options were discarded or why certain choices were made. Without this historical perspective, it would be difficult to answer those questions, which could result in work being performed again or, worse, a decision being reversed, to the detriment of the organization. It also provides the perspective against which changes can be monitored. There will be a finite elapsed time before revisiting the strategy, and, during that time, changes will take place in the external environment concerning competitors, the legal environment and the economic situation, and, internally, concerning the way in which employees work, new salary structures and so on. It is important to know the impact that all these may have on future strategy. The model provides a way of examining these changes to determine their possible impacts. It will enable systems to be developed and implemented that are sensitive to the influences of the various pressure groups and stakeholders.

As mentioned above, it is worth considering developing a second organizational model for the IS function itself. This is often necessary because the IS function has its own particular culture, values and methods of working, which may be quite different from those of the rest of the organization. It may be possible to develop a good IS strategy that fulfils all the criteria of supporting the business and being accepted by senior management, but which is unimplementable due to its not being accepted by the IS function or beyond its existing capability. The relationship between the IS function and the rest of the business is explored in Chapter 8.

EVALUATING THE GAP BETWEEN CURRENT AND REQUIRED IS/IT ENVIRONMENTS

The IS/IT requirements that result from this process form the basis of a framework within which we can critically assess the IS strategy itself. It consists of candidate developments to build or enhance applications and schemes to upgrade the provision of IT resources. Unless the strategy process has focused on a very small number of critical initiatives that will be certain to go ahead, the IS demand and IT supply proposals will need to be prioritized against the business objectives, either on their own merits or in conjunction with the business plans that they support. This stage, resulting in an application portfolio development plan, is discussed in Chapters 6 and 7.

The IS demand is the main deliverable to come out of the analysis of the current situation and the business needs, stemming from its strategy and the collection of demands from the current business operations. It will also contain the needs arising out of analysis of the external business environment. This chapter has concentrated on the current business needs that usually produce short-term IS requirements and medium-term requirements that arise from the business strategy. Chapter 5 will move the analysis out to a longer-term horizon, in seeking new ways of impacting the business through IS/IT.

The assessment of the current IS/IT environment indicates the capabilities of existing IS/IT resources in relation to the *known* business strategy. There will almost certainly be a gap between the current resources and competencies and those needed to satisfy the future IS demand. The gap identifies the requirements for change:

- Processes in need of recognition, simplification, streamlining or redesign—all with significant IS/IT requirements.
- New or upgraded information resources. The list of information needs can be compared with current systems and databases to determine where the new information will come from or whether new sources must be found. Quite often, new information needs can be fulfilled by relatively minor modifications to existing systems or databases. Obviously, these could be tackled in the short term. Other information needs may only be satisfied by developing new applications, and will take longer to be implemented.
- Changes in IT supply resources and competencies to support the role IS/IT needs to play.

By analysing the coverage of systems across the core business processes, it is possible to consider and compare a disparate set of information systems requirements across the whole organization and put them into proper context related to the benefit to the business. For example, the production engineering department may wish to invest heavily in systems that will enable the factory to respond quickly to customer orders, the marketing department may want to spend money on developing analytical CRM systems to segment markets and develop propensity models, and the sales department may want to spend money on developing a system to increase salesforce productivity in managing contacts and generating repeat orders. It would be very difficult for anybody to say which of those three systems should be developed first without reference to the overall strategy and priorities of the organization.

SUMMARY

This chapter has introduced one part of the process of determining the IS strategy, by getting a good understanding of the current situation in the business and by eliciting IS requirements that are inherent in the existing business strategy to achieve a high degree of alignment between the two. The main stages involved in establishing the current situation and logical requirements are fact finding, analysis and interpretation. The processes occur iteratively and rely heavily on each other. The purpose is to identify the activities and business processes that support the objectives and strategy of the business, and the associated information requirements. The 'fact finding' can result in a large volume of information, which needs to be recorded in a way that facilitates analysis and interpretation. Whether the data are text, lists, tables or graphical models, they can be recorded in a number of ways, but need to be structured. The various modelling and analysis tools described here help with structuring and comparison of information derived from different sources. Some of the information will be associated with the business strategy, where the strategy components afford a natural structure; some may result from organizational modelling, which offers a further structure for recording much of the 'soft' information.

The key points to draw from this chapter are:

- there is a process for fact finding, which needs to be followed if the relevant information for defining the IS strategy is to be obtained;
- the techniques for analysis must provide sufficient insight and interpretation for developing the IS/IT strategy, but no more;
- the analysis task is not trivial and a variety of modelling and assessment techniques will need to be used and the outputs reconciled;

- while the techniques discussed in this chapter are essentially analytical and logical, rather than creative, going through the processes will almost certainly generate a number of original and creative ideas. These need to be captured and developed.

But, this is only one side of the picture of determining the IS strategy; in order to enrich this strategy by looking for new ways to *impact* the business and strengthen its competitive performance, more creative techniques have to be brought to bear. This is the subject of the next chapter.

ENDNOTES

1. Business process re-engineering was initially referred to as business process *redesign*.
2. The report of this project can be found in M. Scott Morton, ed., *The Corporation of the 1990s: Information Technology and Organizational Transformation*, Oxford University Press, New York, 1991. See also T.H. Davenport and J. Short, 'The new industrial engineering: Information technology and business process redesign', *Sloan Management Review*, Summer, 1990, 11–27.
3. These examples are elaborated on in M. Hammer, 'Re-engineering work: Don't automate, obliterate', *Harvard Business Review*, July–August, 1990, 104–112 and M. Hammer and J. Champy, *Re-engineering the Corporation: A Manifesto for Business Revolution*, Nicholas Brealey, London, 1993.
4. Research highlights that many re-engineering initiatives fail. See CSC Index, *The State of Reengineering*, CSC Index, London, 1994; K. Grint, P. Case and L. Willcocks, 'Business process reengineering reappraised: The politics and technology of forgetting', in W.J. Orlikowski, G. Walsham, M.R. Jones and J.I. DeGross, eds, *Information Technology and Changes in Organisational Work*, Chapman & Hall, London, 1996, pp. 39–61; G. Hall, J. Rosenthal and J. Wade, 'How to make reengineering really work', *Harvard Business Review*, November–December, 1993, 119–131.
5. See Hammer and Champy and others.
6. E.V. Martinez, 'Successful reengineering demands IS/business partnership', *Sloan Management Review*, Summer, 1995, 51–60.
7. T.H. Davenport and J.E. Short, 'The new industrial engineering: IT and business process redesign', *Sloan Management Review*, Summer, 1990, 11–27.
8. J.T.C. Teng, V. Grover and K.D. Fielder, 'Redesigning business processes using IT', *Long Range Planning*, Vol. 27, No. 1, 1994, 95–106.
9. D.E. Avison and G. Fitzgerald, *Information Systems Development: Methodologies, Tools and Techniques*, second edition, McGraw-Hill, London, 1995.
10. D.E. Avison and A.T. Wood-Harper, *Multiview: An Exploration of Information Systems Development*, Blackwell Scientific, Oxford, 1990.
11. P. Checkland, *Systems Thinking Systems Practice*, John Wiley & Sons, Chichester, UK, 1981; and P. Checkland and S. Holwell, *Information, Systems and Information Systems: Making Sense of the Field*, John Wiley & Sons, Chichester, UK, 1998.
12. A.-W. Scheer, *ARIS— Business Process Frameworks*, second edition, Springer Verlag, Berlin, 1998; A.W. Scheer and F. Habermann, 'Making ERP a success', *Communications of the ACM*, Vol. 43, No. 4, 2000, 57–61; T.W. Malone, K. Crowston, J. Lee, B. Pentland, C. Dellarocas, G. Wyner, J. Quimby, C.S. Osborn, A. Bernstein, G. Herman, M. Klein and E. O'Donnell, 'Tools for inventing organizations: Towards a handbook of organizational processes', *Management Science*, Vol. 45, No. 3, 1999, 425–443.
13. J.W. Peppard and J.M. Ward, '"Mind the gap": diagnosing the relationship between the IT organization and the rest of the business', *The Journal of Strategic Information Systems*, Vol. 8, 1999, 29–60.
14. D.K. Carr and H.J. Johansson, *Best Practices in Reengineering: What Works and What Doesn't in the Reengineering Process*, McGraw-Hill, New York, 1995; M. Hammer, *Beyond Reengineering: How the Process-Centred Organization is Changing Our Work and Our Lives*, HarperCollins, London, 1996; M. Hammer and S.A. Stanton, *The Reengineering*

Revolution: A Handbook, HarperBusiness, Sydney, Australia, 1995; G.A. Pall, *The Process-Centered Enterprise: The Power of Commitments*, St Lucie Press, Boca Raton, Florida, 2000; J.W. Peppard and P. Rowland, *The Essence of Business Process Reengineering*, Prentice-Hall, Hemel Hempstead, UK, 1995.

15. N. Venkatraman, *The Value Centre*, presentation made at Cranfield School of Management, February 1996.

16. R.S. Kaplan and D.P. Norton, *The Balanced Scorecard: Translating Strategy into Action*, Harvard Business School Press, Boston, Massachusetts, 1996; *The Strategy-Focused Organization: How Balanced-Scorecard Companies Thrive in the New Business Environment*, Harvard Business School Press, Boston, Massachusetts 2001.

17. J. F. Rockart, 'Chief executives define their own information needs', *Harvard Business Review*, March–April 1979, 81–92.

18. M.E. Shank, A.C. Boynton and R.W. Zmud, 'Critical success factor analysis as a methodology for MIS planning', *MIS Quarterly*, Vol. 9, No. 2, 1985, 121–129.

19. M. Hardaker and B.K. Ward, 'Getting things done: How to make a team work', *Harvard Business Review*, November–December, 1987, 112–120.

20. J.F. Rockart and A.D. Crescenzi, 'Engaging top management in information technology', *Sloan Management Review*, Summer, 1984, 3–16.

21. It should be noted that manufacturing has always taken a strong process perspective. Different product types, depending on volume and variety, require differing process configurations.

22. For more on the order-to-fulfilment process see W.E. Hoover Jr, M. Tyreman, J. Westh and L. Woolung, 'Order to payment', *McKinsey Quarterly*, No. 1, 1996, 37–49; and B.P. Shapiro, V.K. Rangan and J. Sviokla, 'Staple yourself to an order', *Harvard Business Review*, July–August 1992, 113–122.

23. See M. Hammer and S.A. Stanton, *The Reengineering Revolution: A Handbook*, Harper-Collins, London, 1995.

24. For an interesting example of a hospital that was redesigned around patient flows, see J. Teboul and J. Tabet, *Karolinska Sjukhust*, INSEAD Case, Fontainebleau, Paris, 1995 (European Case Clearing House reference 695-008-1).

25. Even a task or activity can be considered a process (or subprocess) in its own right; however, it is not the objective of this chapter to enter into this debate.

26. The intellectual basis for this matrix is drawn from J.A. Martilla and J.C. James, 'Importance-performance analysis', *Journal of Marketing*, January, 1977. For an excellent extension of this work and its application to operations management, see N. Slack, 'The importance–performance matrix as a strategic improvement priority tool in service operations', *Warwick Operations Papers*, Warwick Business School, University of Warwick, UK, 1993.

27. R. Ballou, 'Reengineering at American Express: The Travel Services Group's work in process', *Interfaces*, Vol. 25, No. 3, 1995, 22–29.

28. J.P. Kotter, *Organizational Dynamics: Diagnosis and Intervention*, Addison-Wesley, Reading, Massachusetts, 1978.

29. J.P. Kotter, *Organizational Dynamics: Diagnosis and Intervention*, Addison-Wesley, Reading, Massachusetts, 1978.

5
IS/IT Strategic Analysis: Determining the Future Potential

The techniques of assessment discussed so far enable the current role that IS/IT is—or should be—playing in the business to be analysed, both critically and constructively. It is always important to understand where you are—a situation appraisal of the systems that exist and how well they support and enhance operational performance, management control and the ongoing development of the business. A key aspect of this assessment is to what extent these systems enable the separate activities and functions of the business to perform harmoniously. This implies an understanding of the information-based relationships of the business, both internal and external, as well as information processing requirements. Often, this analysis reveals areas of systems deficiency, obsolescence, ineffective linkages and poor utilization of existing information. Dealing with the critical inadequacies—ensuring IS/IT is not hindering current business performance and is not a potential or real source of competitive disadvantage—is a key part of the strategy development process.

Directing resources and actions toward areas that will affect the achievement of future, known business objectives is then the next step in developing the strategy. The use of a combination of 'Balanced Score-cards' (BSCs) and 'critical success factors' (CSFs) are an effective way of achieving the appropriate focus of management attention. They are designed to put IS/IT onto the management agenda, to ensure IS/IT strategy and plans are in alignment with organizational intentions and management's priorities for a given period. This probably implies within the objective setting horizon of one to two years.

Therefore, these are analytical techniques that enable the effective support of the current or intended strategy from IS/IT developments.

However, as described in Chapters 1 and 2, adept investment and deployment of IS/IT can enable new strategic options to be developed, thus shaping the strategy of the business. Equally, changes elsewhere in the industry, caused by IS/IT investments by customers, competitors and suppliers may affect the organization's intended strategy. Hence, the potential opportunities and threats from IS/IT and its ability to change industry dynamics and relationships must be addressed. This assessment of new IS/IT application areas requires a degree of creative thinking as well as analysis of business options, to determine the potential impact of IS/IT on the business.

The analytical techniques that have been described so far are not sufficient to carry out such an 'impact analysis', neither do they easily express the options and issues in terms familiar to line managers. The tools and techniques of strategic thinking and analysis frequently used in business strategy formulation offer another approach, which will be more easily adopted by business line managers, whose commitment is critical to converting good ideas to actual strategic uses of IS/IT. Many of these were described in Chapter 2, where the IS/IT strategy implications were also discussed. The techniques described in this chapter offer a more focused brainstorming or creative analysis approach, and help to forge a coherent link between the business strategic issues and options and the rationale for the nature and purpose of future IS/IT investments. They are undoubtedly not an exhaustive coverage of all that could be used, but they are those that have often been successfully adopted in assessing the potential future impact of IS/IT on many industries and on many businesses.

One problem with a 'tool kit' approach is deciding which tool to use and when. It is always convenient to have a methodology that clearly indicates which tool to apply when, what result to expect and what to do next if you get (i) the right result or (ii) the wrong result! Unfortunately, such a clear definition of an IS/IT strategy development process is not, and probably never will be, possible. Many writers over the last 20 years have described the application of many of the techniques introduced in this chapter, and most agree that a prescribed methodology is not appropriate, concluding that what is required is a tool kit. Neumann[1] describes essentially the same set of techniques, but refers to them as 'frameworks for strategic information systems'. He recognizes that they are a means of helping the thinking process, not a recipe for ensuring the identification of strategic systems. More recently, in the context of 'e' opportunities, Feeny[2] and Timmers[3] suggest a similar set of techniques within an overall logic for their application.

Although no methodology can be proposed, in Chapter 6 each of the tools will be considered as part of a process that can be adopted for

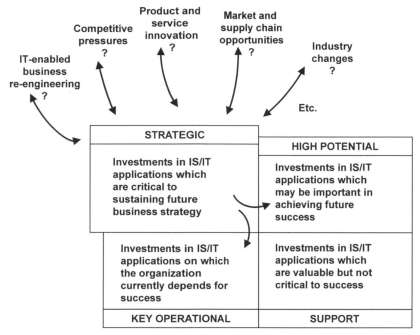

Figure 5.1 *Developing the application portfolio from a strategic perspective*

developing IS/IT strategies, within the overall context described in Chapter 3. In terms of the application portfolio, the focus of this part of the assessment is primarily to identify strategic investments (see Figure 5.1). However, the approaches may also suggest high-potential possibilities that need further investigation, before their contribution can be decided. They may also identify whether existing or planned key operational systems either provide a good basis for exploitation or could be a constraint to future business options provided through IS/IT.

ALIGNING THE IS/IT INVESTMENT STRATEGY TO THE BUSINESS

Development of business strategies can be carried out in a variety of ways, but, as discussed in Chapters 2 and 3, this is probably most effective if the organization is considered as a group of (strategic) business units. This enables the market/product relationship to determine strategic thinking and functional/organizational aspects become secondary, ensuring that external strategy drives internal strategy rather than vice versa. Within a business unit, the portfolio of products and/or customers can be analysed to identify how each grouping contributes to or makes demands on resources available.

The business unit is also the level at which the analysis of competitive forces provides the sharpest focus and for which the generic strategy concepts best apply—low cost, differentiation, niche—since it is both possible and essential to develop and operate a coherent set of consistent behaviours for a business unit. Low-cost versus differentiation conflicts within a business unit will cause confusion and suboptimal or even contrary decisions to be reached. But, within a corporation, two business units operating in two different environments might adopt low-cost and differentiation strategies, yet still trade internally with each other.

For these reasons alone, it is important that IS/IT strategic analysis should align itself to the business unit approach. Quite different business attitudes to investment, including investment in IS/IT, are likely to prevail in units following differentiation or low-cost strategies, and the opportunities for strategic IS investments are unlikely to be the same. Applications for similar business functions like order processing could well be very different in practice due to the different relationships with customers that the two generic strategies imply. Units operating in niche markets will have different opportunities for exploiting IS/IT options from those serving a wide range of market sections, especially with customers and suppliers.

As discussed in Chapter 1, the most significant difference in the SIS era is the external focus of systems. Organizations have adopted the strategic business unit (SBU) approach to business planning, in part to achieve the more effective strategic decision making implied in Phase 3 of approaches to strategic management discussed in Chapter 2 (see Figure 2.1) (i.e. more effective, externally orientated, planning), based on:

- situation analysis and competitive assessments;
- evaluation of strategic options;
- dynamic allocation of resources.

This would include an assessment of the role of IS/IT in terms of its use in the industry, by competitors, suppliers and customers, as well as the effectiveness of its use within the business unit.

Chapter 2 described how, using these techniques, it is possible to interpret the results in terms of high-level implications and priorities for IS/IT investment for a business unit, or enable pertinent questions about IS/IT opportunities or threats to be included in the business

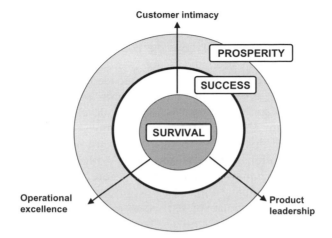

Figure 5.2 *Advantage and disadvantage—dimensions of competency* (source: *after M. Treacy and F. Wiersma,* The Discipline of Market Leaders: Choose Your Customers, Narrow Your Focus, Dominate Your Market, *HarperCollins, London, 1995)*

strategic analysis (see, e.g. Figure 2.8 and the discussion on pages 95–100).

Determination of priority IS/IT investments also depends on the chosen 'value discipline', as per Treacy and Wiersma,[4] for achieving advantage *and* the relative strength of the organization in the other disciplines (i.e. Operational Excellence, Customer Intimacy and Product Leadership). Figure 5.2 portrays levels of relative competence of the organization along each of the axes—survival, success and prosperity. The last of these implies that, if the organization is beyond the 'success' line in at least one competency and equal to competitors in the other(s), it should deliver above-average profits in the industry. However, if any of the competencies are within the 'success' circle, any potential advantage is likely to be offset by poor performance elsewhere.

For example, a bank that had developed a new and excellent mortgage product for younger people (as defined by independent benchmarks) and had as good customer relationships as any other bank (again via independent surveys), could not understand why sales were so poor. The reason was the slowness and unreliability of the mortgage application process, which used a much older system designed for an earlier generation of products. The process could not deliver the 'service promise' inherent in the product and, given the target customer group, many customers went elsewhere to obtain an inferior product, faster.

This is just one example of how the competency analysis can help identify how priority IS investments are essential to avoid competitive disadvantages. Where the organization is outside the success line (i.e. is outperforming most others in one dimension), more creative thinking is needed to identify how IS/IT can be used to develop the competency further and sustain the advantage. For example, having established 'personal' relationships with its book-buying customers, Amazon.com is able to analyse purchase patterns and identify other books of potential interest to an individual customer—a far more valued service than sending a general catalogue, either by post or electronically.

Some suggested questions, of particular relevance to the electronic commerce dimensions of the strategy, have been overlaid on the basic model in Figure 5.3. They attempt to show how generic e-commerce options—improving the value proposition, mass customization, performance improvements and cost reductions—require combinations to be addressed.

As stated in Chapter 2, this technique proves very valuable in gaining agreement among managers about what has to improve and why, and, especially, whether the purpose is to gain advantage or avoid disadvantage. It helps integrate the 'themes' inherent in the business and IS strategies and focus resources on medium-term IS priorities.

Although the relationship will not always be perfect, the changing content of the application portfolio should reflect the evolving strategic themes. Applying these ideas in a number of organizational situations, they have proved very useful in clarifying the business rationale for IS/IT investment plans. Generally speaking:

- Strategic applications should relate readily to the dimension in which the organization seeks to excel in the next one to three years (i.e. product leadership, customer intimacy or operational excellence), with the objectives of gaining advantage in the marketplace.
- Key operational application improvements are essential in any dimension if the systems are causing performance levels to fall below those essential to success (i.e. are causing disadvantage).
- High-potential projects would normally be 'prototypes' related to specific strategic developments or evaluations of ideas relevant to the other dimensions (i.e. early, tentative steps in finding out how IS/IT might provide future opportunities once the current focus of the strategy changes).

Over a period of time, an organization might pursue all three of these

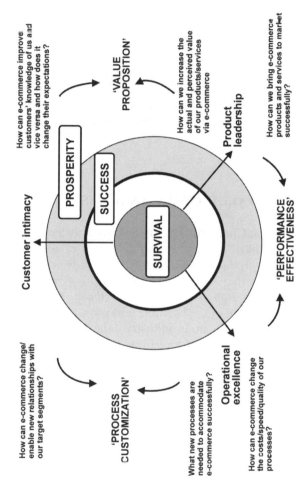

Figure 5.3 E-commerce and the dimensions of competence

directions. It will probably have to change if it is to maintain a leadership position in response to the actions of competitors. But, it is extremely difficult to 'major' in more than one at once, and any indecision will cause ever-changing priorities, inconsistency and even confusion within the business—a recipe for failure with IS/IT investments.

Analysis of the business situation, from both external and internal perspectives, is essential to establish the context within which opportunities can be identified and assessed. The techniques described below need to be used following an assessment of the business environment and with an agreed purpose, based on the priority 'themes' for improving performance through IS/IT. Otherwise, the assessment can become an unfocused exercise in which interesting options are identified, but without a natural and coherent link to the overall future intentions and direction of the business. As such, they will not be seen and treated as priority or strategic business investments.

VALUE CHAIN ANALYSIS

The concept of Value Chain Analysis is described at length by Michael Porter[5] who notes that: '*Every firm is a collection of activities that are performed to design, produce, market, deliver and support its products or services. All these activities can be represented using a value chain. Value chains can only be understood in the context of the business unit.*'

Equally, the value chain of the business unit is only one part of a larger set of value-adding activities in an industry—the *industry value chain* or *value system*. The value chain of any firm therefore needs to be understood as part of the larger 'system' of related value chains—those of its suppliers, customers and competitors, before it can be optimized. The actions of those other parties will have a significant impact on what the firm does and how it does it. This is especially true in the area of information systems. For example, the considerable investment made by food retailers in Point-of-Sale (POS) systems has changed the way information is passed to food manufacturers and has dramatically changed the delivery service required from those manufacturers. This has implications for the information systems within the food-processing companies and, in turn, the systems that relate to their suppliers. For an organization to identify the overall implications of e-commerce for its business in terms of opportunities and threats, the information flowing through the industry—the *external value chain*—needs to be analysed before the information processes can be optimized inside the business—by considering the *internal value chain*.

THE EXTERNAL VALUE CHAIN (INDUSTRY VALUE CHAIN OR VALUE SYSTEM)

Figure 5.4 gives a schematic view of an industry value system. In particular, it emphasizes the key roles information plays throughout the chain. The overall performance of the industry, in terms of its ability to maximize its value-added and minimize its costs, is primarily dependent on how well demand and supply information are matched at all stages of the industry. To achieve the highest possible income and profit from the consumption of goods or services produced by the industry, the resources of the industry need to be focused on the value-adding activities involved, by producing those goods and services as efficiently as possible to the satisfaction of the consumers. If poor information means that those resources are wasted or used inefficiently, costs rise without increases in revenue, and overall profitability falls. In such situations, all that firms can do to improve profit is compete with their suppliers and customers to share out the limited available net profit. This almost inevitably leads to some firms going 'bust', the equilibrium is destroyed and the industry has to be reorganized in some way. It is not always the least efficient that suffer, it is often those with the poorest information about what is happening in the industry who go to the wall.

While the above discussion is primarily about 'profit', the value chain approach can be used in any industry, since every industry uses funds, incurs cost and uses resources to deliver services of some sort to consumers. In 'non-profit' industries such as government, health care and charities, there is always a matching of supply and demand to achieve a break-even, if not a profit.

The type of industry value chain model depicted above is appropriate for 'traditional' manufactured goods. Alternative models are considered on pages 265–268 that represent service-based industries. However, the following general issues apply to all the models.

Obviously, if an organization can match the demand for its products and services very closely to the supply of resources at all times, performance can be optimized and efficiencies maximized. Equally obviously, if the firm, 'the business unit' in Figure 5.4, is operating at some distance from the ultimate consumer and primary suppliers, it is difficult to obtain precise demand and supply information. Interestingly, we would expect organizations that have component businesses in different parts of the same industry value chain to be able to exploit their combined information to outperform others who cover less of the chain. In fact, that is often not the case, especially when the businesses operate as profit centres—the 'internal competition' that produces often means they actually cooperate less well than independent firms in sharing information!

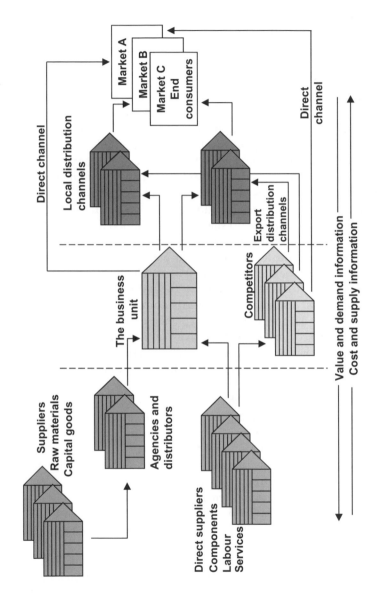

Figure 5.4   The external value chain

When starting to understand how industry information flows affect the firm itself, the firm should be treated as a 'black box' (i.e. how things are done inside the firm should be ignored—that will be considered later when looking at the internal value chain). The consideration should start at the end-consumers in terms of what information is available about the consumers' needs, who they are, etc. and how they can be influenced.[6] Then, the needs for information exchange with more immediate customers can be examined in terms of how effective it is for both parties. Eventually, all the flows of information to and from the firm downstream in relation to the consumers and intermediaries can be understood, in terms of critical information the firm needs and the current and potential sources of that information. The same process can be repeated in terms of immediate suppliers and their suppliers of key resources, raw materials and services.

Then, each of the key information flows can be examined to see how the process could possibly be improved in terms of accuracy, speed, cost or timeliness and how that might benefit the business. It might be, for instance, beneficial if a distributor could provide raw sales data directly, rather than consolidate their sales in order to place larger orders. This may enable the firm to give that distributor a more reactive service, allowing the distributor to hold lower stocks, yet satisfy more of its customers. At the other end of the chain, it may be possible to do similar things with suppliers and, while these are simple examples, they form the basis of 're-engineering' the way the industry operates to everyone's benefit.

It may be, of course, that many of the information exchanges cannot easily be improved, or cannot be improved without the willing cooperation of trading partners. Cooperation may only be forthcoming if there is some mutual benefit in changing that particular information flow or by changing another flow to provide the partner with a balancing benefit. It could be that, to produce the improvement, existing trading partners have to be bypassed and information exchanged with other parties further upstream or downstream in the chain. This may eventually lead to significant realignment of business relationships.

It is important to understand the type of 'value' and 'cost' added by each firm or process in the chain (i.e. what is different between the outputs and inputs); for example, a financial broker provides more choice to a customer than one insurer, but takes a % commission from the insurers on sales. Each key process in the chain should be assessed from two viewpoints:

(a) How does it add value to the (next) customer in the chain?
(b) How does it add value to those providing the input?

A retailer adds value to the customer mainly through the range of goods offered and local access to them, and adds value to the supplier by providing consumer availability, sharing stock costs and administration of low-value transactions, etc. When assessing changes to the chain, it implies that new value can be added, or existing value-adding and costs will be redistributed, or costs of adding the same value can be reduced, enabling price reduction or increased profit. In Internet shopping, the consumer's (invisible) costs are reduced, but costs are switched to home delivery. Unless this is offset by another cost reduction (e.g. lower stock holdings), the increased cost of supply will require an equivalent increase in price (payment for delivery)—or the profit in the chain will be reduced. These are relatively simple and obvious examples, but it is necessary to understand the overall chain economics and utility if changes are to be successful.

Many options will usually present themselves from the analysis, only some of which will prove feasible and beneficial to implement, at least in the short term. However, an understanding of the complete picture may lead to further options emerging in the longer term. It will certainly enable the organization to understand the implications of potential actions by others and then determine a more strategic response.

INFORMATION SYSTEMS AND THE VALUE CHAIN

Obviously, business performance is dependent on the processes that gather and disseminate information. Links can be developed to various levels of sophistication and mutual dependence. Figure 5.5 shows three types of relationship. Normal business transactions (invoices, orders, payments, etc.) could be addressed by a company with most of its customers and suppliers who have computers, simply by connection via the Internet. This has indeed already happened in some industries, especially those dominated by large retailers, where the majority of basic business transactions with suppliers are now electronic. This basic use of e-commerce is spreading through different industries at varying rates. It not only improves the economics of transaction processing but also enables the whole chain to respond more effectively to real-time demand and supply changes—provided transaction information is shared.

Figure 5.5, based on work by Rayport and Sviokla,[7] considers two further types of value chain information flow that are being challenged by e-commerce. First, the implications of the promotional flow of information, which informs customers further down the chain of the products and services available, have to be understood. E-commerce offers an

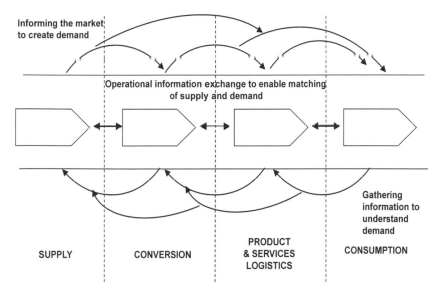

Figure 5.5 *Understanding the information issues in the value chain* (source: *after Rayport and Sviokla*)

additional channel for this flow, but also provides customers with the ability to search the whole chain for information directly or via inter-mediaries, on whom firms become increasingly dependent to provide an electronic shop window/shelf space for their products and services. Demand from the end-consumer may well change more rapidly than in the past, given the combined e-commerce attributes of effective 'promo-tion' linked to the immediate ability to transact business.

Second, e-commerce offers huge potential to gather information and intelligence about consumer and customer preferences and attitudes online, rather than through traditional market research. More impor-tantly, customer behaviour can be tracked with greater accuracy than before via e-transactions and hence correlated with both the promotional stream and the intelligence gathering stream. Unless each organization and the chain as a whole can assess this information coherently, it is likely that major misinterpretations of changing demand patterns will create potential chaos in the supply chain. The issue is therefore that, in the e-commerce environment, three information streams that could previously have been reconciled off-line now have to be integrated if the value chain is to function economically.

A firm will not be able to determine its own destiny with regard to its information systems. It is not just a matter of company size, but clearly the larger players have more to gain and hence tend to force the smaller companies to comply with their demands. As most industries develop standards for electronic trading and information exchange, the potential risks for the small company diminish since it will not have the cost of satisfying a variety of requirements for different suppliers or customers. The arrival of XML (Extended Mark-up Language) will produce a general standard for the majority of organizations to utilize and reduce the need for industry-specific standards for many types of information transfer.

According to Porter,[8] we are entering a new stage of evolution in terms of how IT is affecting industry value chains. Previously, each firm has achieved improved performance by integrating its activities and processes as well as *its* supplier and customer interactions through IS, most recently via Enterprise Resource Planning (ERP) and Customer Relationship Management (CRM) software packages. He believes this new stage, 'which is just beginning, enables the integration of the (. . .) set of value chains in an entire industry, . . . as end-to-end applications involving customers, channels and suppliers . . .'. It is difficult to predict whether the emergence of 'e-marketplaces' (or trading hubs) or the ability to integrate throughout the value chain will have the more significant effects on industry economics and customer/supplier relationships. Could trading hubs become the centres though which IRP ('Industry Requirements Planning') systems operate, linking everyone's ERP systems together to provide seamless, integrated information flows?[9] However, even in sophisticated and mature industries, there is often a huge gap between what is possible and the current reality. Box 5.1 gives examples of the problems in the motor industry value chain that needs major information systems and process changes if the benefits, potentially available from information integration, are to be realized.

By whatever means information systems are used to enable better information exchanges through the industry value chain, significant benefits can be obtained from the improved links. These benefits should enable a firm to spend more of its business energy in outperforming its real competitors rather than competing with its trading partners for the available profit. The essence of the argument is:

(a) At any one time, an industry generates a certain amount of net profit (total sales – total costs). That profit is shared among the organizations contributing to the value chain for the industry. Clearly, intermediation increases the number of firms among whom the profit is shared, and the attraction of disintermediation is that the opposite occurs.

(b) If, in the version of the value chain that includes our firm, the overall net profit can be increased, we can take a share of that increased

Box 5.1   Information problems affecting the performance of the automotive industry value chain (*source:* M. Howard, R. Vidgen, P. Powell and A. Graves, 'Planning for IS related industry transformation: The case of the 3DayCar', in *Proceedings of the 9th European Conference on Information Systems, Bled, Slovenia, June 2001*, pp. 433–442, used with permission of the authors)

The automotive industry operates a sophisticated but complex IS/IT throughout the supply chain. However, current systems act as a major inhibitor both to time compression in the order-fulfilment process and to organizational change. For example, a customer order entered into a system at a car dealership must complete five overnight updates on existing IS, involving batch processing and code conversions, before it is released into vehicle production.

The European automotive industry is facing a period of significant change, driven by poor profitability, excess finished stock and overcapacity. Customers are more price conscious and less patient, demanding vehicles built to individual specifications and delivered in short lead times. Vehicle manufacturers can no longer rely on selling cars from existing stock and are shifting their business models away from mass production toward mass customization and build to order. This increases the importance of existing systems for efficient order execution and integrated information flow. Yet, many IS reflect the functional departments for which they were originally conceived.

The key objective of the 3DayCar project is to develop a framework in which a vehicle can be built and delivered to customer specification in minimal lead times, with three days order-to-delivery (OTD) time as the ultimate goal. The current average OTD lead time is 45 days. The diagram on the following page illustrates the current IT barriers among the key players in the automotive industry.

Problems and issues include:

- The lack of integration between Dealer Management Systems (DMS) and Dealer Communication Systems (DCS) causes high levels of typing and information duplication. For example, when an order is placed, significant levels of duplication of information occur, with identical data such as vehicle description and owner details typed into both systems.
- Many DCSs do not give a delivery date or have significant time delays in confirming them—a particular problem for

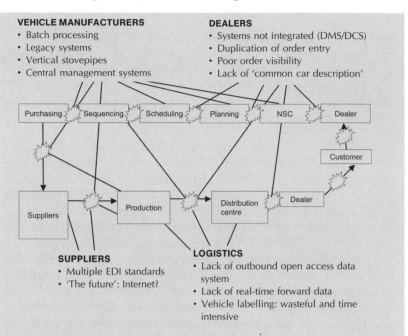

VEHICLE MANUFACTURERS
- Batch processing
- Legacy systems
- Vertical stovepipes
- Central management systems

DEALERS
- Systems not integrated (DMS/DCS)
- Duplication of order entry
- Poor order visibility
- Lack of 'common car description'

SUPPLIERS
- Multiple EDI standards
- 'The future': Internet?

LOGISTICS
- Lack of outbound open access data system
- Lack of real-time forward data
- Vehicle labelling: wasteful and time intensive

custom-built orders. When dealers are given delivery dates on the system, these often change and are not guaranteed. Dealers have poor visibility of orders throughout the network.

- There is an unwillingness among dealerships to share information.
- The current configuration of vehicle manufacturers systems typically results in individual mainframe systems updating overnight, processing batches or buckets of orders in time-intensive cycles that add four to five days to the order lead time. As information flow through the batch-processing systems is largely unsequenced, it is possible for the output of one process to miss the start of the next window, adding further time into the process.
- Poor business process integration. Within vehicle manufacturers, systems were developed within separate functions and not driven by a true customer order fulfilment philosophy and inhibit smooth order flow—production push rather than customer pull.
- Suppliers perceive the major IT barrier as a lack of adherence to EDI standards by vehicle manufacturers, in terms of protocol (language used during transmission) and format (the label

layout or visual interface). Suppliers already receive messages in about a dozen different formats, all of which must be converted to a common standard before they can be processed internally. This causes delay and disruption to the system, particularly in the event of a system malfunction.

profit and hence outperform our direct competitors, who are not part of that version of the chain.

(c) If we initiate the changes but also share the benefit with our customers and suppliers (i.e. they too become more profitable), they will prefer to trade in our more efficient version of the industry. It is very likely that rival firms will be competing for those suppliers and/or customers—but they should give us preference because they are more profitable when they do. This brings about long-term advantages and in due course affects the whole industry structure.

To achieve (b), only three things can be done:

 (i) create more demand;
 (ii) satisfy more of the available demand (gain market share);
(iii) reduce the cost of satisfying the demand.

By better information exchange through the value chain, all or any combination of the three can be done at the same time. For example, by sharing consumer market-research information obtained by retailers, a manufacturer may be able to enhance a product to open up and develop a new market segment. Or, earlier feedback on changing tastes may enable the production plan to be rescheduled to meet the new consumer preference. This is particularly important in fashion goods and in very seasonal products like toys. Benetton, the clothing company, has developed highly-integrated systems that link the franchised shops right through to the subcontractors who make the clothes. This enables them to respond faster than their competitors to changes in fashion and they are far more profitable than the average clothing company.

There are many ways in which better information exchange can reduce costs that occur at the boundaries between companies. Table 5.1 provides a number of examples, all of which can be seen in a number of industries, with the effect of reducing interorganizational costs very significantly.

Table 5.1 *Reduction of intercompany costs due to better information exchange along the value chain—examples*

Cost	Potential e-commerce impact
1. *Administration*	Electronic transmission of orders and invoices, etc. directly between customers and suppliers
2. *Inventory*	Sharing information on stocks and demand to avoid both companies carrying unnecessary stock
3. *Transport/storage*	Optimizing delivery to ensure transport or storage space is utilized effectively to meet agreed service levels
4. *Design*	Sharing product design data interactively to enable faster development of a better product and less 'rework'
5. *Financing*	Electronic payments to improve cash flow and reduce the need for working capital and reduce Accounts Receivable and Payable costs
6. *Capacity*	Matching the use of resources across firms to avoid idle resources in one part of the chain and/or overload in another
7. *Services*	Linking third-party service suppliers to service requests to reduce delays in delivering and costs of administration

One final example may serve to illustrate the long-term effects of integrating information flows through a value chain. In 1982, UK tour operator Thomson Holidays introduced the TOP system, which enabled travel agents to book holidays via a Viewdata system directly on the Thomson computer. This immediately reduced some of the double-handling costs of bookings (in the travel agency and at Thomson) and speeded up the process of booking, hence saving agency time and cost. As a result, agents 'directed' consumers toward the Thomson brochure, since they earned more commission per man-hour spent booking the holiday. Later, Thomson developed similar links to their suppliers (airlines, hotels and other service providers). In effect, this enabled Thomson to respond better to changing demand than others, which for a number of years gave them an advantage, but other tour operators were still profitable since demand for holidays was increasing. The 'system', however, gave Thomson a major advantage when demand dropped suddenly as it did in 1987 (USA bombed Libya) and 1991 (Gulf War). In 1987, Horizon Holidays (No. 3 in the industry) failed and, in

1991, International Leisure Group (No. 2 in the industry) went bust. Neither of them were able to respond to the rapid changes in demand as effectively as Thomson, and both had lower margins due to higher cost structures. Thomson were able to adapt more quickly and were more efficient in the context of the overall industry value chain.

In summary, an understanding of the industry value chain, and the key information flows in the industry, can enable an organization to intercept and influence those information flows to its advantage, to the benefit of its trading partners and at the expense of its competitors. Box 5.2 is another example of a real value chain—for the ethical pharmaceutical industry (i.e. prescription drugs)—showing where information systems applications have had and/or are having a significant effect on the performance of the industry.

Customer Relationship Management and the Value Chain

While the concept of Customer Relationship Management (CRM) emerged in the mid-1990s, key tenets underpinning the concept such as relationship marketing, customer value analysis and mass customization have been around much longer. However, they remained essentially theoretical concepts; aspirational rather than a practical reality. Technology has changed this, making CRM a feasible option for organizations by providing the tools to operationalize these concepts.

'Customer resource life-cycle analysis', described in detail by Ives and Learmonth,[10] is a powerful tool to analyse relationships with customers. By examining its customer relationships via the model, companies can determine not only when opportunities (and threats) exist for improved or new information exchanges but also which specific applications should be developed. Ives and Learmonth suggest that the Resource Life Cycle (RLC) model should be viewed from one end only (i.e. toward the customer), but the same possible options will apply in reverse in relationships with suppliers. Hence, the RLC model could be a customer or supplier resource life-cycle model, depending on point of view!

The RLC model relies on the fact that an organization's products/services go through a typical life cycle, when viewed as a *resource* by the customer. The four main stages of this life cycle are:

- requirements determination;
- acquisition;
- stewardship;
- retirement or disposal.

These are expanded in more detail in Table 5.2.

Box 5.2   Value chain for pharmaceutical company

N.B. This is for an 'ethical' drug company where the whole strategy is based on differentiation of the product and its treatment efficacy. Key areas where information flows/relationships are critical to success and provide opportunity to gain advantage or achieve significant performance improvements:

1. Provision of drug information to clinicians/doctors who will prescribe the treatment and the influencers—either eminent people in the field and/or 'panels' of experts who advise hospitals, etc. Traditionally, these were medical people, but now they include health economists and insurers who decide on the financial aspects of the treatment's effectiveness in relation to alternative uses of funds. The same influencers also determine whether pharmacists will 'stock' the drug and dispense it. In return, the prescribers and dispensers feed back information on the use of the drug and, particularly importantly, any side-effects or adverse reactions encountered. Unless this 'loop' is well managed, a drug can fail, especially a new drug.

2. The pharmaceutical company relies on forecasts of requirements and then orders from third parties (wholesalers may be the distribution channel for 80%+ of drugs to dispensers) in order to set schedules, etc. for manufacturing. This is a particular problem with new drugs where forecasts rather than orders drive the production scaling/economics. Underestimates lead to lost sales, overestimates to significant waste and cost. The quality of forecasts and, then, consistency with order patterns are key, making online demand and supply information exchange crucial to both parties.

3. The skill in pharmaceutical market research is to establish both the nature and size of the market from a variety of particular and statistical data and to determine a development opportunity in a therapeutic area where the company has distinctive skills/competency. Often, today, the opportunities arise from gaps in current treatments, which are known to influencers mentioned in Item 1 above. Collecting data from diverse sources and interpreting them can be greatly assisted by electronic data input.

4. Testing of a drug during development can take many years, and reducing the development time from, say, 8–12 years to maybe 5–6 means more of the patent life is unexpired for production, and this affects drug profitability dramatically over its patented

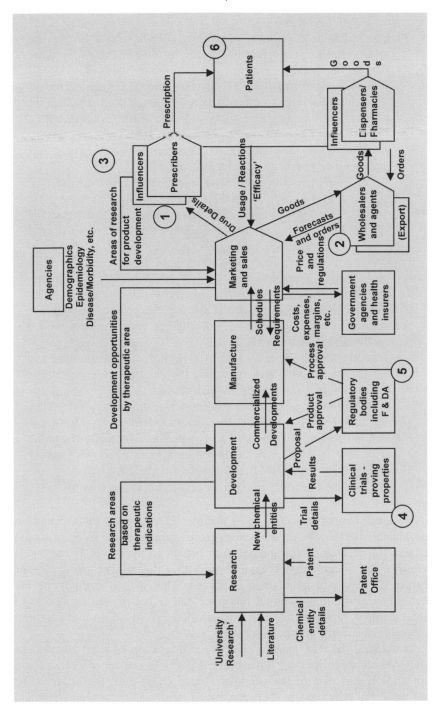

life (hundreds of millions of pounds). Much testing is in-house and controllable, but clinical trials by doctors must be done outside the organization and can take many years. The key to success is organizing the trial—getting the right clinicians to test it on the right population, which requires good information on the test population, etc. to avoid delay and wasted effort. Equally, getting the results in is a major data collection/logistics exercise where 'e-commerce' is essential both for speed and gathering comprehensive/valid trial data.

5.   To be able to produce the drug, regulatory approval must be obtained by submitting all the evidence about the drug—this can run to 120,000 pages! The most demanding agency is the US FDA (Food and Drug Administration). Once the proposal is submitted, endless questions will be asked and if the information is not well organized the queries can take months to resolve. Most drug companies use IT to develop/store/submit the package of information and enable the regulatory authority to enquire into it electronically. This again can save considerable time and reworking of data to satisfy the regulators and speed up the time to market the drug.

6.   With the increasing access consumers have to information via the Internet, many 'patients' now inform their doctors of the treatment they think they require! In the USA, 'self-prescription' is now an option for some drugs, although, in the UK, the doctor still has to prescribe the drug. However, as information is increasingly available to the public, it is likely the value chain will have to include the patients more effectively, rather than leave them isolated as suggested in this model.

Each of these stages involves a number of processes of information exchange—between buyer and seller—to enable the stage to be managed effectively, thereby ensuring maximum benefit to the buyer and seller. If at any stage the exchange breaks down, either the current transaction or future business will be adversely affected. The further through the life cycle the information exchange has gone, the higher the switching cost to the customer, who will have to retrace the steps at additional cost and inconvenience with another supplier.

In essence, the RLC analysis forces consideration of what happens to the product or service once it has become part of a customer's value chain or while it was part of the supplier's value chain and, thence, leads to information relationships between buyer and seller over an extended

Table 5.2 *Resource life-cycle analysis* (source: *after Ives and Learmonth*)

Requirements	
Establish requirements	To determine how much of a resource is required
Specify	To determine a resource's attributes
Acquisition	
Select source	To determine where customers will buy a resource
Order	To order a quantity of a resource from the supplier
Authorize and pay for	To transfer funds or extend credit
Acquire	To take possession of a resource
Test and accept	To ensure that a resource meets specifications
Stewardship	
Integrate	To add an existing inventory
Monitor	To control access and use of a resource
Upgrade	To upgrade a resource if conditions change
Maintain	To repair a resource, if necessary
Retirement	
Transfer or dispose	To move, return or dispose of inventory as necessary
Account for	To monitor where and how much is spent on a resource

timescale while the product/service is being consumed or, in reverse, while it is being developed and made available. Most of the steps in the four stages can be improved by direct electronic links and by asking 'how can e-commerce (or IT) improve our ability to help the customer to ...?' can identify quite specific opportunities to enhance the relationship.

The RLC model suggests that the information relationship is an extended one, eventually resulting in a replacement sale or purchase. The life cycle may be very short (days) for consumable items, but many years for capital items.

A slightly extended and updated version of the basic model is described by Feeny[11] to address the increased ability of online service provision to meet a wider range of customers' requirements at lower costs via the Internet. Gathering information about the customer throughout the relationship life cycle becomes much easier, and more economic, as more information exchanges become electronic. Information gleaned 'post-purchase' from customers is the most valuable in terms of understanding what they actually value regarding service and product requirements and preferences.

An example of the use of a 'technical service' system in adding customer value to what is essentially a catalogue can perhaps help demonstrate the ideas. RS Components, a business-to-business distributor, offering a large range of electronic and mechanical components and tools through catalogues, has achieved major advantages in dealing with its customers (engineers) by paying particular attention to Stage 1 as well as developing very responsive and efficient systems to deal with Stage 2. Often, a customer will phone, or enquire via the Internet, not knowing what he or she wants, merely able to describe the symptoms of a problem with a piece of equipment. By putting technical data about the majority of its products online, about 80% of such 'problems' can be converted to appropriate component orders for delivery within 24 hours by the engineers themselves or by staff with little or no technical knowledge. The remaining 20% need to be considered by the company's technical staff. The system is to help the customer specify his or her requirements and to ensure that the parts dispatched are those most likely to solve the customer's problem.

Already, e-commerce has been used by many firms to help customers establish and specify their needs by providing more extensive information than ever before with easy access. Many new entrants provide 'sourcing' systems via e-commerce to enable buyers to find the best deal. New means of trading, to enable customers to obtain the product/service, have been introduced, including customer pricing against which the supplier can choose to sell. Home delivery has grown dramatically to balance the new remote buying. The challenge is how to gain and maintain customer loyalty in the new environment through 'stewardship' services that encourage further purchases. This depends on establishing an electronic dialogue with the customer to learn more about them and tailoring the relationship as individually as possible to their needs. Customer Relationship Management (CRM) systems are designed to cover the whole life cycle, providing a comprehensive view of the customers' pattern of interactions and relationships with the firm, enabling tailored and proactive rather than reactive approaches to meeting their needs.

A similar technique for generating information systems ideas during value chain analysis—the 'strategic option generator'—has also found renewed favour with the rapid developments in e-commerce. The approach was described by Rackoff et al.[12] and is explored in great detail by Wiseman.[13] It considers the impact of IS/IT in relation to:

- *Suppliers*—anyone supplying essential resources. It may be necessary to subset them either by the nature of what they supply or their strength, or their ability to exert pressure on you and other customers.
- *Customers*—this could include the consumers as well as direct customers if the latter are essentially distributors. The customers should

be segmented in terms of what (and what else) they buy or how much leverage they exert.

- *Competitors*—obvious competitors who sell very similar products or services should be supplemented by actual or potential new entrants into the market and 'threatening' substitute products and services should be included as competition. Consideration should also be given to the threat of new intermediaries or options for disintermediation by others.

For each of them, alternative 'strategic thrusts'—offensive or defensive moves—can be made by the firm:

- *Differentiation*—ensuring that superior quality is delivered and perceived, leading to obtaining a premium price. It could also imply being a 'preferred customer' to obtain preferential service.
- *Cost*—being cheaper or enabling suppliers or customers to reduce their costs (sharing the benefit) and thereby preferring to conduct business with the firm (ways may also be found to increase competitors' costs!).
- *Innovation*—introduce a new product, service, process or way of doing business that transforms the relationships and competitive forces in the industry. This may require the active involvement and cooperation of suppliers and/or customers.
- *Growth*—enable volume or expansion in geography or increased flexibility of production and distribution to meet different segments needs.
- *Alliance*—forging agreements, joint ventures or joint investments in systems to prevent new entrants or competitors achieving advantage.

It may be that each of the above are appropriate with different groups of suppliers or customers or even competitors, implying that a great variety and range of options could be identified, many of which may prove infeasible!

To identify what benefits are potentially available, a questionnaire approach is suggested. Table 5.3 shows some sample suggested questions that might lead to the identification of options. Some of the questions imply a degree of lateral thought. For instance, 'reduce suppliers' costs' tends to go against the grain! The full question should be perhaps 'reduce the suppliers' cost, when he does business with us' (in order to create more profit in the chain and share the benefit).

The strategic option generator approach relies on a thorough understanding of the state of the industry, the firm's competitive position, the determining factors for success in the industry value chain, plus a clear

Table 5.3   IS/IT opportunity analysis—questions

---

1.   *Suppliers*—Can we use IS/IT to:
     Gain leverage over our suppliers (improving our bargaining power or reducing theirs)?
     Reduce buying costs?
     Reduce the suppliers' costs?
     Be a better customer and obtain a better service?
     Identify alternative sources of supply?
     Improve the quality of products/services purchased?
     etc.

2.   *Customers*—Can we use IS/IT to:
     Reduce customers' costs and/or increase their revenue?
     Increase our customers' switching costs (to alternative suppliers)?
     Increase our customers' knowledge of our products/services?
     Improve support/service to customers and their needs?
     Identify new potential customers?

3.   *Competitors*—Can we use IS/IT to:
     Raise the entry cost of potential competitors?
     Differentiate (or create new) products/services?
     Reduce our costs/Increase competitors' costs?
     Alter the channels of distribution?
     Identify/Establish a new market niche?
     Form joint ventures to enter new markets?
     etc.

---

business strategy. It is most helpful in being specific about who will benefit and how from the options for change in relationships through the value chain.

THE INTERNAL VALUE CHAIN

Much of what has been said about the external value chain above applies to the firm's internal value chain—the contribution of these activities to the creation of value in the organization as well as the relationships between its value-adding activities. Before trying to improve the organization's internal use of information, its wider role in the industry needs to be understood, since those external interfaces should be a major influence on the way information is gathered, organized and used in the organization. In many cases, the actions of trading partners and competitors will have a direct impact or constrain what the company would ideally like to do.

The purpose of Internal Value Chain analysis, like many other techniques for assessing and improving how a company operates, is to divorce *what* the company does from *how* it does it (i.e. look at the activities it performs, to contribute to the value-adding processes of the industry, rather than its organization structure). Historically, the information systems a company has will have usually resulted from the organizational needs at functional and departmental level. Only subsequently will these systems and information resources have been aligned to the processes that the firm carries out to satisfy its customers and govern the business. This means that the systems tend to fit the functional structure well, but are less effective in ensuring an appropriate flow of key information through the business to optimize its overall performance. As external trading relationships change, the internal processes and systems will also have to change to enable the new business model to operate efficiently.

The value chain approach first distinguishes between two types of business activity.

(a) *Primary activities*—those that enable it to fulfil its role in the industry value chain and hence satisfy its customers, who see the direct effects of how well those activities are carried out. Not only must each activity be performed well, they must also link together effectively if the overall business performance is to be optimized.

(b) *Support activities*—those which are necessary to control and develop the business over time and thereby add value indirectly—the value being realized through the success of the primary activities.

Each activity adds value in terms of creating a product or service that generates revenue from customers or enables value-adding activities to be coordinated or ensures that value has been added, at an acceptable cost. Some activities only add value if they are effectively integrated across primary and support parts of the chain. These are often information intensive activities such as forecasting—estimating demand, planning capacity and scheduling resources and activities—and pricing, which requires input from many components in the chain and will have effects on many others.

In a multi-unit business, each operating unit will have a set of primary activities it must perform successfully to satisfy its set of customers. The support activities, or some of them, may be shared by the operating units because it is more cost-effective to do so, or because there are synergistic benefits by providing a central service to each of the units (e.g. Human Resource Management, Finance or IT).

The Traditional Value Chain Model

Porter[14] classifies the primary activities into five groupings, which can be considered in sequence starting with suppliers and ending with customers:

1. *Inbound logistics*—obtaining, receiving, storing and provisioning the key inputs and resources in the right quality and quantity to the business. This may include recruiting staff as well as buying materials, components and services and dealing with subcontractors and acquiring equipment.
2. *Operations*—transforming the inputs into the products or services required by the customers. This involves bringing the resources and materials together to make the 'product' (e.g. a car) or provide the service (e.g. a banking current account).
3. *Outbound logistics*—distributing the products to the customers either direct to the consumer or to the appropriate channel of distribution, so that the customer can obtain the product or service and pay for it appropriately (e.g. a car could go via a dealer to the customer, although it is possible for the customer to buy direct from the manufacturer and have the car delivered from the factory; or the delivery of cash to a bank customer via an Automatic Telling Machine (ATM) installed in a grocery retailer).
4. *Sales and marketing*—providing ways in which the customers and consumers are aware of the product or service and how they can obtain it, including how to induce them to buy or use the product or service. This would apply to a new car model, or a bank account, but also to cancer screening in the Health Service, for instance.
5. *Services*—adding further value by ensuring the customer gets full benefit or value from the product once purchased (e.g. car warranty, or information on how to use a bank account to avoid unnecessary charges).

Porter's structuring of the activities fits most easily to a manufacturing company, but, using the same logic of obtaining resources, transforming them, delivery, getting the customer to 'buy' and then get maximum value from the product or service, value chains can be drawn for any business.

Figure 5.6 shows sets of activities grouped in the structure described above and also some of the associated support activities we would expect to find in a manufacturing company. The nature of the primary activities a firm performs will to an extent be predetermined by the industry, its products, customers and suppliers—its success is determined by how well it performs the range of primary activities in concert. That will decide

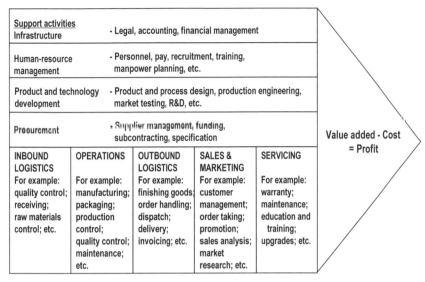

Primary activities

Many activities cross the boundaries - especially, information-based activities such as:
sales forecasting, capacity planning, resource scheduling, pricing, etc.

Figure 5.6 *Firm's value chain—manufacturing example*

how much value is derived and how much the activities cost and, hence, the primary profit margin.

ALTERNATIVE VALUE 'CONFIGURATION' MODELS

The traditional value chain model was based essentially on a manufacturing/retail view of industry and works well for 'physical goods'. However, while it can be applied quite successfully to some service businesses, in many others it does not really represent what the business does or its relationships with customers and suppliers. For example, most aspects of insurance and investment businesses involve no physical product (except paper and money), nor does the model represent businesses where suppliers can also be customers (e.g. banking) and it is especially weak in describing many newer service businesses like those based primarily on electronic commerce.

Stabell and Fjeldstad[15] describe two alternative 'value configuration' models that attempt to address these problems. The focus is on the primary value chain activities since the support activities are often very

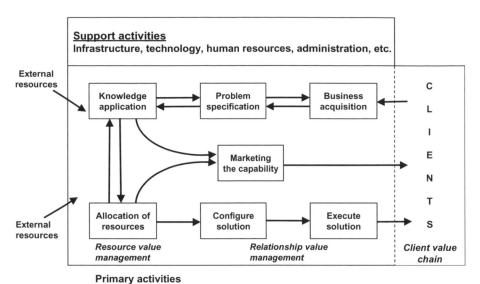

Figure 5.7   *Value chain: service businesses ('Value Shop') (client is actively involved in and affected by the processes) (source: after Stabell and Fjeldstad)*

similar to the Porter model. They call these two alternatives: 'Value Shops' and 'Value Networks'.

Value Shops are businesses that essentially are 'problem solving', delivering value by providing solutions for clients. They are characterized by intense and extensive information exchanges both in setting up the business transaction and delivery of the solution. Examples are as widespread as oil exploration companies, design engineering, management consultancy, insurance, advertising, etc. They are characterized as non-flowline, since each problem is, for the client, unique and the client is normally involved in both the design and implementation of the solution.[16]

Figure 5.7 shows an example of such a value chain, which better reflects a service business, where the objective is to satisfy the client or customer requirements, by bringing together the appropriate knowledge and resources from inside the firm or by using other external resources.

The chain involves two flows, to determine the client needs and (assuming they can be met) designing and implementing a solution that satisfies the client requirement. This can be relatively simple (e.g. a new hairstyle) or very complex (a new oil refinery). Considerable information exchange is often required (in the more complex situations!) and IS/IT offers opportunities to increase the efficiency of such exchanges, reduce elapsed time and improve the accuracy of the exchange.

Value Networks are businesses that provide exchanges and mediation between buyers and sellers, enabling relationships to be established. They earn revenue from either or both in their use of the firm's network 'everyone's a customer'. The UK's Post Office is an example both in its mail and parcel delivery and its counter services where it is acting as an agency for government service delivery (DVLC, Social Security, etc.). The services may extend beyond connection to revenue collection, contract management, systems integration, information source, etc., in terms of adding additional value for a customer or customer segment. Many new Internet Service Providers (ISPs), cable and media companies as well as more established telecoms providers are in this group as well as a range of financial service and investment businesses (e.g. share trading). Many of the new online trading models (auctions, clubs, etc.) are Value Networks. No doubt many more will emerge in the future.

The primary activities of such firms include infrastructure development and maintenance to provide capacity and access, service provision to cater for the needs of different buyer/seller relationships and promotion to both buyer and seller groups to recover the capacity costs via transaction-based revenues. Figure 5.8 suggests how this model differs from the other two.

In all types of model, information about what customers want and how that demand can be satisfied should flow freely through the organization, enabling the management of each activity to determine how best to deploy its resources to maximize customer satisfaction in the most effective way. Any action taken would be immediately visible to other activities in the chain, who can then take further action accordingly or inform the other activities of problems in meeting the requirement. The chain can be continuously rebalanced across all the activities. In addition to the flow through the organization, each activity (e.g. warehousing, sales force management) will need information systems to carry out and manage its part of the business. In themselves they may be very extensive but should link in to the flow as required. For instance, the warehouse management system must know where every item is in the warehouse, but the rest of the business only needs to know what is in it, and, while the manufacturing department needs to schedule each machine in detail, the rest of the business only needs to know that products will be ready to meet orders from customers. Equally, in a consultancy-type business, resource management activities do not need to know the detail of each assignment, but need to know who is committed and for how long.

One engineering company, producing electrical switching systems, studied how information flowed through the primary activities involved and were able to simplify the flows from the customer enquiry through to

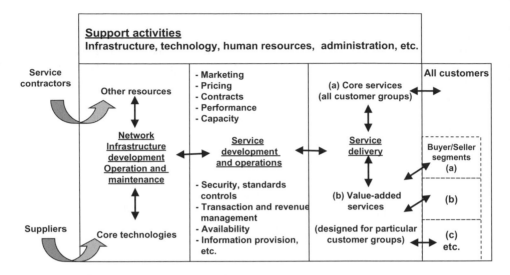

Figure 5.8 *Value chain: service businesses ('Value Network') (source: after Stabell and Fjeldstad)*

the component suppliers, and back again, to reduce delivery lead times from 27 to 5 days. The result was a 37% increase in sales—sales they were losing because their delivery times were too slow and unreliable. That was only for one product, but, when the same logic was applied across the whole product range and associated processes, dramatic performance improvements were made, often at very little cost and with the result that the systems became much simpler. Once these improvements have been made, e-commerce investments to enable online enquiry and ordering were able to deliver further benefits rather than cause even more operational problems.

THE USE OF VALUE CHAIN ANALYSIS

Value chain analysis is essentially a form of high-level industry, and business process/activity analysis—a way of describing an industry as a network of key components and their interrelationships. The basic, rather structured, concept of the value chain—the 'big arrow'—is sometimes difficult to apply to non-manufacturing industries where the product is not tangible and there are no obvious raw materials. A bus company, the police, car hire, building societies, estate agencies, the Inland Revenue and education are all examples where the five linear components of the internal value chain are difficult to identify. The two more recently developed value models—'shops' and 'networks'—are more helpful in describing how activities interrelate to provide the customer with value. And all activities cost money! The process of analysis should be relatively flexible, describing 'freehand' the relationships among the customers, the service/product and the resources consumed. The main objective in all cases is to represent the main activities in the business and their relationships in terms of how they add value so as to satisfy the customer and to obtain resources from suppliers—not in terms of how the organization currently is structured—(i.e. to focus on core business requirements). By considering that value chain as a component of an industry value system, a broader view of systems implications and opportunities can be determined. It is equally important to separate those primary activities from support activities that are there for organizational or institutional purposes and only indirectly contribute to adding value! Organizations have greater discretion over how they carry out support than primary activities, since the latter have to fit successfully into the processes of industry.

However the value chains are drawn, they can enable further analysis of any or all the following:

- The information that flows throughout the industry and how critical that information is to the functioning of the industry and the success of the firms in it, by determining where and when that information is available, who has it and how it could be obtained and turned to advantage or used against the firm.

    For instance, in some industries like fashion goods, 'demand' information is the critical factor, but, in others such as confectionery (the price and availability of cocoa) and timber (the price and availability of wood), 'supply' data can be critical to success. Manufacturers who have good information and can respond to changing demand/supply fastest can outcompete those who lack the relevant information. In the UK timber industry, the price of softwoods is affected over a six-month cycle by the US building industry, 'housing starts' in the USA determining availability and price elsewhere. As the world's largest purchaser of wool, Benetton would find huge stocks on its hands if it failed to anticipate and satisfy demand—hence, the importance of its point-of-sale system in its franchised shops to obtain daily sales data in a volatile market.

- The information that is or could be exchanged with customers and suppliers throughout the chain to improve the performance of the business or lead to mutually-improved performance by sharing the benefits (e.g. the information that is required for the customer to sell on the product/service or the supplier to acquire input resources).

Suppliers of particular components or resources may have longer lead times than appropriate, given the volatility of the company's business. Providing plans for forward requirements, even buying on its behalf to spread both companies' risks, might help. The information links between companies are far more complex than often appreciated and the value chain approach allows them to be analysed. Obviously, the use of electronic commerce is becoming the main basis for such information sharing across various companies' information systems.

In the 1980s and early 1990s, EDI-based systems were seen as a major strategic option for most organizations. The reality has been that major players in certain industries, usually retailers, generally determined the strategic impact of EDI by their action or inaction. A study by Benjamin et al.[17] concluded that, for the majority of organizations, 'EDI applications will be built out of competitive necessity ... and will become a cost of doing business.' The evidence of the study showed that EDI for basic business transactions will provide, at best, short-lived advantages, since they are easily copied. Sustained advantage comes from changing the relationships with trading partners and using the information exchange to conduct business in new, mutually-beneficial ways, as explained earlier. This is almost certainly true of the Internet and e-commerce applications. Once the available cost savings have been 'shared out' equitably between buyers and sellers, advantage will only accrue to those who innovate in business processes, provide new value to customers and/or can find significant numbers of new customers to satisfy.

• How effectively the information flows through the primary processes and is used by them:

  – within each activity to optimize performance;
  – to link the activities together and avoid unnecessary costs and missed opportunities; and
  – to enable support activities to contribute to the value-adding processes, not hinder them.

Historically, systems were first developed to meet functional needs, and the links between them from marketing to outbound logistics, for instance, were added later. This often resulted in armies of people with the generic job title of 'professional reconciler', working to overcome the weaknesses at the system interfaces. Many business re-engineering initiatives often accompanied by implementing integrated software packages have been focused on eliminating such inefficiencies. One insurance company reduced the number of 'handlings' of new policy details from 14 to 3 without any loss of control. Porter suggests that the companies who succeed with IS are those who link their systems together along the value chain most effectively. For instance, it may be most effective to supply daily sales data in its raw form direct to the procurement and inbound logistics activities to determine ordering requirements much earlier. Otherwise, they could effectively hinder the marketing effort in the long term.

'NATURAL' AND 'CONTRIVED' VALUE CHAINS

O'Sullivan and Geringer[18] explain how, by understanding the role of information in both 'internal' and 'external' value chains, major business performance improvements can be made by changing how the chain works. They introduce the concept of 'natural' and 'contrived' value chains. The natural value chain describes the (unattainable) optimum structure for the industry's value-adding processes and information flows, based on *what* needs to be done. The contrived value chain shows *how* (in far from optimal ways) things are currently done. They identify characteristic differences in natural and contrived value chains. These are shown in Table 5.4. The first purpose in analysing the value

Table 5.4 *Natural versus contrived value chains*

Contrived value chain represents *how* things are done by resources in the industry/ organization:

- driven by organization structures, historical evolution and compromise
- is often very complex, confused and 'messy', and poorly understood
- contains many reconciliation activities and reacts slowly
- can take many forms, is continuously being modified to meet business changes

Natural value chain represents *what* has to be done to succeed in market requirements:

- based on value-adding activities and the resources needed to carry them out
- defines essential interrelationships and dependencies and the ideal way to achieve business purposes
- contains few reconciliation activities and responds quickly
- usually only one ideal exists, and it does not change significantly or frequently

chain in information terms is to reduce the existing complexity either inherent in the current information relationships or caused by them. The second purpose is to identify new, often faster, options for information to flow to where it enables the value-adding processes to be performed more effectively and at the ideal time. In doing so, the way the chain works should change from whatever 'contrived' state it has reached through evolution to something more like the 'natural' view of the chain.

In order to achieve this and to ensure that the more beneficial IS/IT investments are identified, it is important to start with an understanding of the overall external value chain and how it affects the internal value-adding processes. Otherwise, even significant IS investments may deliver no noticeable overall benefit and they may even result in business disadvantages due to the actions of others in the chain.

BUSINESS RE-ENGINEERING AND THE VALUE CHAIN

The upper three levels of impact of IS/IT on business described in Chapter 1, from the MIT's *Management in the 1990s* Research Programme, requiring revolutionary change or transformation include two—process redesign and network redesign—that imply changing the internal or external value chain components and relationships. Business re-engineering, as a mechanism for strategic change, normally includes a significant process dimension, which will lead inevitably to implications for IS/IT. Most of the successful business re-engineering initiatives have also had an external drive or focus, ensuring that internal changes deliver perceived improvements to the customers. Almost by definition, the starting point for determining what to change, why and how to change it, is an understanding of the value-adding processes in the industry and/ or the firm.

Much of the information systems and business re-engineering literature uses the same words for defining the actions to take to improve business performance: eliminate unnecessary processes, then rationalize the rest to ensure the value-adding processes are optimized, integrate to improve responsiveness and reduce unnecessary effort and error; finally, automate where technology can deliver further improvements. By the 1990s, in many companies, IT had become a constraint to redesign, because, in the past, IT used to automate badly-designed processes that had become expensively petrified in silicon! In many ways, business re-engineering is a restatement of the aims of IS investment over the past 30 years, but those aims were often subverted in the drive to employ IT. In many organizations, the need for rapid, relatively radical change is now imperative and IT provides a wide range of capabilities to assist in implementation. Rather than devise their own business models and hence core systems, many organizations have implemented enterprise systems software packages (e.g. ERP and CRM) to obtain those new business processes and modern, upgradeable software. These solutions involve adopting a value-chain-driven approach to understanding 'how the business works' and hence can be improved via a combination of business re-engineering and new IS.

SUMMARY

Information systems have always been part of the value-adding processes that comprise any enterprise, whether it be a commercial company, a public service or a charitable body. Historically, though, IS/IT has been mainly deployed to improve individual component processes or activities of the enterprise. Initially, this improvement was targeted at reducing the costs of the supporting activities rather than improving the performance of the primary activities of the business. Even when systems became focused on primary activities, they tended to be aimed at optimizing the performance of the main operational activity of the business, and only then on activities that directly interact with suppliers and customers, but with a view to not compromising or jeopardizing the effectiveness of internal operations. Historically, the emphasis has been on:

- internal operations and control;
- key processes in the organization;
- internal critical success factors;
- the firm not the industry.

The value chain analysis techniques suggest that the firm's information systems should be considered in an extended context—that of the industry value chain—in order to achieve maximum leverage from IS/IT investments and benefits from industry and internal developments. The value chain represents the flow of goods and services and use of resources through the industry, and there are simultaneous, parallel flows of information running through the industry. The value chain analysis tools make the organization consider how those industry information flows affect the firm, and, potentially, how they can influence it and where it is worth investing to achieve superiority with respect to others by exploiting the information and its flow or avoid being disadvantaged by the actions of others. This form of analysis also enables the assessment of existing systems and known requirements to be considered in a broader and longer-term context.

In planning future information systems and technology for an organization, it is important to identify the business opportunities and threats presented by the increasing and developing use of IS/IT in the firm's industry. The objective is to identify strategically-important applications, those applications that directly support chosen business strategies or enable new business strategies to be developed and implemented. If the organization is not in a strictly-competitive environment, strategic applications will be those focusing on meeting organizational objectives. These strategic applications are only a part of the organization's IS application portfolio, but a very important part.

This chapter has described a number of approaches that can be taken to understand an organization's information and systems possibilities and the potential business benefits. The use of each technique has been exemplified by what others have done. The various techniques have been described from the 'top down', from the industry down to particular aspects of information exchange with customers or suppliers. Beneficial options can arise at any stage of the analysis or equally by inspiration. The various models used also offer a basis for testing the value of 'good ideas' resulting from *ad hoc* inspiration.

There are undoubtedly other techniques that could have been considered here—the most widely-accepted ones have been included. All these techniques have a common theme—they must be used by people with knowledge of the business and its environment, and therefore cannot be tools for IS/IT specialists alone to use. Senior management and line managers must become familiar with the basic approaches to this type of analysis. All the tools and techniques described are really IS/IT subsets of business strategic analysis tools, which should enable such managers to become actively involved in determining the future potential, both potential opportunities and potential threats, that IS/IT has to offer the organization.

In the next chapter, the ideas of this and the preceding two chapters will be brought together—in terms of how they can be integrated into the process of IS strategy development.

ENDNOTES

1. S. Neumann, *Strategic Information Systems*, Macmillan, London, 1994.
2. D. Feeny, 'Making business sense of the e-opportunity,' *MIT Sloan Management Review*, Winter, 2001, 41–51.
3. P. Timmers, *Electronic Commerce: Strategies and Models for Business to Business Trading*, John Wiley & Sons, Chichester, UK, 1999.

4. M. Treacy and F. Wiersma, 'Customer intimacy and other value disciplines', *Harvard Business Review*, January–February 1993, 84–93.
5. M.E. Porter, *Competitive Advantage: Creating and Sustaining Superior Performance*, Free Press, New York, 1985.
6. For an exploration of the linkages between activities, see P.C. Ensign, 'Value chain analysis and competitive advantage', *Journal of General Management*, Vol. 27, No. 1, 2001, 18–42.
7. J.F. Rayport and J.J. Sviokla, 'Exploiting the virtual value chain', *Harvard Business Review*, November–December, 1995, 75–85.
8. M. Porter, 'Strategy and the Internet', *Harvard Business Review*, March 2001, 63–78.
9. J.M. Ward and E.M. Daniel, *Watch this Space, 2001: A Market Odyssey*, GartnerGroup, London, 2001, pp. 16–17.
10. B. Ives and G.P. Learmonth, 'The information systems as a competitive weapon', *Communications of the ACM*, Vol. 27, No. 12, 1984, 1193–1201.
11. D. Feeny, 'Making business sense of the e-opportunity,' *MIT Sloan Management Review*, Winter, 2001, 41–51.
12. N. Rackoff, C. Wiseman and W.A. Ullrich, 'Information systems for competitive advantage: Implementation of a planning process', *MIS Quarterly*, Vol. 9, No. 4, 1985, 285–294.
13. C. Wiseman, *Strategy and Computers*, Dow Jones-Irwin, Homewood, Illinois, 1985.
14. M.E. Porter, *Competitive Advantage: Creating and Sustaining Superior Performance*, Free Press, New York, 1985.
15. C.B. Stabell and O.D. Fjeldstad, 'Configuring value for competitive advantage: On chains, shops and networks', *Strategic Management Journal*, Vol. 19, 1998, 413–437.
16. Analysis taken from D. Tapscott, D. Ticoll and A. Lowy, *Digital Capital: Harnessing the Power of Business Webs*, Harvard Business School Press, Boston, 2000.
17. R.I. Benjamin, D.W. de Long and M.S. Scott Morton, 'Electronic data interchange: How much competitive advantage?', *Long Range Planning*, Vol. 23, No. 1, 1990, 29–40.
18. L. O'Sullivan, and J.M. Geringer, 'Harnessing the power of your value chain', *Long Range Planning*, Vol. 26, No. 2, 1993, 59–68.

6
Determining the Business Information Systems Strategy

Through in-depth analyses of the business environment and the strategy of the business as well as an examination of the role that information and systems can and could fulfil in the business, a set of known requirements and potential opportunities can be identified. These needs and options will result from business pressures, the strategy of the business and the organization of the various activities, resources and people in the organization. Information needs and relationships can then be converted into systems requirements and an appropriate organization of data and information resources.

To enable these 'ideal' applications to be developed and managed successfully, resources and technologies will have to be acquired and deployed effectively. In all cases, systems and information will already exist, and, normally, IS resources and technology will already be deployed. Any strategy, therefore, must not only identify what is eventually required and must also understand accurately how much has already been achieved. The IS/IT strategic plan must therefore define a migration path that overcomes existing weaknesses, exploits strengths and enables the new requirements to be achieved in such a way that it can be resourced and managed appropriately.

A strategy has been defined (on page 69) as 'an integrated set of actions aimed at increasing the long-term well-being and strength of the enterprise.' The IS/IT strategy must be integrated not only in terms of information, systems and technology via a coherent set of actions but also in terms of a process of adaptation to meet the changing needs of the business as they evolve. 'Long term' suggests uncertainty, both in terms of the business requirements and the potential benefits that the various applications and technologies will offer. Change is the only thing that is certain! These changing circumstances will mean that the organization will have to be capable of effective responses to unexpected opportunities and problems.

This chapter considers how the models and processes of IS/IT strategic planning from Chapter 3 and the tools and techniques of analysis from Chapters 2, 4 and 5 can be consolidated into an IS/IT strategic management approach for the organization: an approach that enables it continuously to identify the appropriate application systems and information resources it requires and, at the same time, to take advantage of new opportunities as they arise.

As discussed in Chapter 3, an organization's IS strategy is a result of its own decisions—the choices it makes in the context of evolving business and information technology environments (see Figure 3.8). However, it must adapt to events, changing priorities and emerging options as well as adjust its plans according to how well and how quickly the intended IS strategy is actually realized. Business objectives are now often updated and even radically revised within months of their establishment, and this can cause frequent reassessment of investment opportunities and priorities. To avoid wasted IS/IT investments and misuse of resources, some aspects of the IS strategy will have to be adjusted quickly and decisively, but, equally important, much of the strategy will not need to change. Frequent, unnecessary reassessment can waste resources and often causes implementation failures. The approach described in this chapter describes how this can be allowed for, as well as illustrating how the various tools and techniques can be successfully blended together into a practical and adaptable process.

STRATEGIC PLANNING TECHNIQUES AND THEIR RELATIONSHIPS

In Chapter 1, a simple model for describing the IS application portfolio of a business was developed. This model suggested that IS/IT applications could be described in terms of 'strategic', 'high potential', 'key operational' or 'support' (see Figure 1.7). The main factors that influence the balance of that portfolio for any business (i.e. which applications reside in which sectors and the relative strategic importance and criticality of each) can be classified as (see Chapter 3 for more detail):

(1) *External long term*—external business environment

- the state of the industry in terms of profitability, growth and structure;

- the degree to which IS/IT is, or is capable of, changing the products, markets and interrelationships of the industry.

(2) *External short term*—external IS/IT environment

- the actual use of IS/IT by competitors and others in the industry to gain a relative advantage;
- the opportunities created by IS/IT to change the balance of competitive forces and influences on the industry, both in the existing value chain and by new entrants or product/service substitution.

(3) *Internal long term*—internal business environment

- how new IS/IT applications could more effectively support or enhance the business strategy of the enterprise;
- how new IS/IT applications could enable the business to adopt a more appropriate strategy to suit the future business environment.

(4) *Internal short term*—internal IS/IT environment and current application portfolio

- the degree to which existing systems support the chosen strategy and the criticality of those systems to avoiding business disadvantages and/or sustaining existing advantages;
- the existing approach to IS/IT management and its appropriateness to the business strategy;
- the IS/IT resources and competencies the organization has or can easily acquire.

Chapter 4 primarily dealt with the internal factors, both short and long term, that determine the overall structure of the portfolio, and Chapters 2 and 5 focused mainly on external factors. At this stage, these factors are considered in terms of their influence in determining *what* could and should be done rather than *how* to do it—the demand-management part of the basic demand/supply rationale of IS/IT strategic management depicted in Figure 1.6. The models in Chapter 3 considered in greater depth the issues of both demand and supply management. There is obviously an iterative relationship; supply can constrain the demand, and any modification of demand will require different strategies for supply. How to achieve the appropriate supply will be considered in depth in Chapters 8–11, as will the detailed issues of the management of the portfolio (in Chapter 7).

The processes for formulating the IS/IT strategy described in Chapter 3 emphasize the need to determine requirements before deciding how to satisfy them, but the ability to conceive the requirements will be coloured by a historical predisposition based on a knowledge of the organization's ability to deliver. Despite these convolutions, which can potentially result in an inability to do anything, the determination of future demand is the most critical, and often most difficult, aspect of strategy formulation. Consequently, approaches and methods used need to be brought together to ensure that a comprehensive and coherent set of demands is identified and agreed.

Demand for IS/IT in a particular business unit can be most easily described as a 'business information systems strategy' using the portfolio concept above. The previous two chapters have described techniques for trying to 'fill' the portfolio with applications. Figure 6.1 summarizes the inputs to the approach to IS/IT strategy formulation and the techniques used to populate the portfolio. (The numbers on the diagram refer to the chapters in which the tools are described.) Although it might appear from previous discussion that the strategic quadrant is all-important, appropriate investments in applications in the others will produce significant contributions to improved performance. An inability to manage support or key operational systems successfully will both reduce the ability to realize available benefits and absorb resources on applications of lesser importance. The objective at this stage of strategy formulation is to determine what future applications would be appropriate for the business. So far, a model has been developed that has inputs, tools and techniques and a conceptual product! The next stage is to consider how the various techniques and approaches can be brought together to ensure that the products of analysis are consistent and can be reconciled during more detailed planning.

FRAMEWORK IN WHICH THE TOOLS AND TECHNIQUES CAN BE USED EFFECTIVELY

It would be convenient if a 'methodology' or structured, repeatable process could be proposed, but this is not realistic given the need simultaneously to relate existing situations to requirements to ideas. However, a framework within which the various concepts can be used more effectively, rather than as isolated techniques, is essential if the determination of the business systems strategy is to be a manageable task. Also, as circumstances alter and progress is made, the strategy will require updating, without the necessity to reappraise all the analysis and resulting conclusions.

The main objective of determining the IS strategy is to identify the required applications and their priorities, and be able to deploy resources to achieve them successfully. The outline framework depicted in

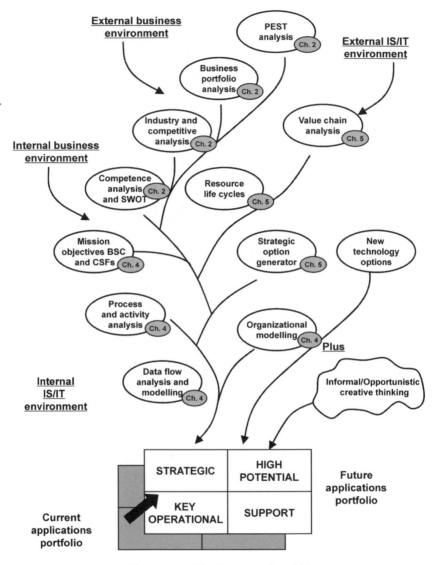

Figure 6.1   *The inputs and tool kit*

Figure 6.2 illustrates, as the end product, the portfolio divided into three components:

(1) *The existing applications*—those currently in place and being developed to be installed in the near future, usually 6–12 months. They

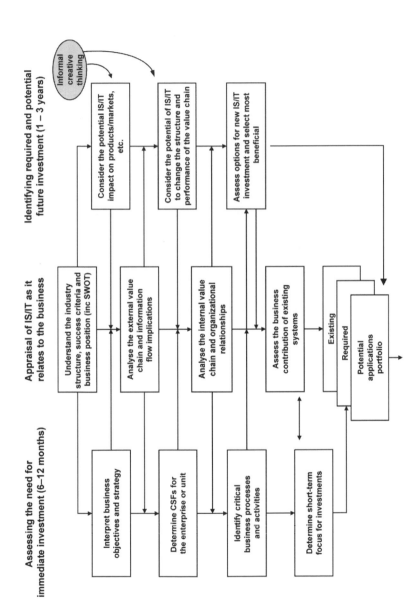

Figure 6.2 *Overall framework for determination of the business IS strategy*

Assessing the need for
immediate investment (6–12 months)

Appraisal of IS/IT as it
relates to the business

Identifying required and potential
future investment (1 – 3 years)

Informal creative thinking

Interpret business objectives and strategy

Determine CSFs for the enterprise or unit

Identify critical business processes and activities

Determine short-term focus for investments

Understand the industry structure, success criteria and business position (inc SWOT)

Analyse the external value chain and information flow implications

Analyse the internal value chain and organizational relationships

Assess the business contribution of existing systems

Consider the potential IS/IT impact on products/markets, etc.

Consider the potential of IS/IT to change the structure and performance of the value chain

Assess options for new IS/IT investment and select most beneficial

Existing

Required

Potential applications portfolio

should be assessed in terms of their contribution to existing business processes and performance and how well they support the achievement of known future requirements. The strengths and weaknesses of each need to be understood, but in a future as well as a current context.

(2) *The required applications*—those that will be necessary to achieve the business objectives and strategy within the business planning horizon and can be shown to have specific contributions to make.

(3) *The potential applications*—those that might prove valuable in the future, provided they prove feasible to deliver and can be shown to produce relevant benefits, either to the strategy directly or by significant indirect effects through improved business performance.

The different types of application and their implications are likely to result from (respectively) a thorough situation appraisal of the business and its information requirements, an analysis of the business strategy and objectives, and a creative assessment of possibilities for IS/IT in the business environment. The products of each of these processes needs to be interrelated and consolidated, which implies that the process will be somewhat iterative. Ideas, as they crystallize, will have to be reconsidered in relation to each other and the overall business options. The three columns of Figure 6.2 refer to:

(a) the need continually to reappraise how both the external and internal environments are changing and the role that IS/IT is or should be fulfilling in the business and its relationships—*central column*;

(b) the need to identify and monitor new or emerging IS/IT-based opportunities to create potential advantages for the organization (or that might result in disadvantages if ignored)—*right-hand column*;

(c) the need to make decisions on how best to deploy available business and IS/IT resources in the immediate future—*left-hand column*.

The horizontal arrows on Figure 6.2 suggest the most effective route through the 'map' when the strategy is first formulated, but also indicate what also needs to be considered if any changing variable causes the strategy to be reappraised.

In the following sections, the overall framework described in Figure 6.2 will be considered in more detail, in terms of the processes, the products of each process and their interrelationships. All the various tools and techniques have been described in previous chapters, and this framework is a more detailed description of the overall processes and deliverables described in Chapter 3.

IDENTIFYING HOW IS/IT COULD IMPACT THE STRATEGY

The first part of the discussion considers the steps that address the range of opportunities and threats that IS/IT offers and poses for the business. This primarily involves addressing the top six boxes of the framework, as shown in Figure 6.3: assessing the IS strategy implications of the industry environment, exploring competitive forces, assessing external value chain relationships and the analysis of the current business strategy. Any innovative ideas for exploiting IS/IT, identified separately from the main strategy development process by informal, creative thinking, should be incorporated and assessed during this part of the framework.

Understanding the Industry and the Potential Impact of IS/IT on Products and Markets

Understanding the industry and the potential impact of IS/IT on products and markets is a prerequisite to any development of an IS/IT strategy. The first step is the assessment of the overall business situation in relation to the external environment, and this should be done by the business management as an integral part of the business strategy. The key issues to be considered are:

- the business units and their relationships to each other and to the corporate body;
- the stage of maturity of the industry or industries within which the businesses compete;
- the product and customer portfolios of the business units and the contributions to revenues and profits, and demands on resources that each group of products/markets makes;
- the competitive forces affecting the business units and the corporation, and their impact on the business—this in turn leads to a SWOT (Strengths, Weaknesses, Opportunities and Threats) analysis of the companies' positions regarding each of the forces to identify areas of greatest concern and need for action;
- the key competencies required to succeed in the industry and the relative status of the organization's competencies in each dimension—customer, product and operations.

This stage is essentially the business strategic analysis process described in Chapter 2, and it leads immediately in two directions:

(1) to consideration of the business strategy and objectives in the established business environment (see Chapter 4); and

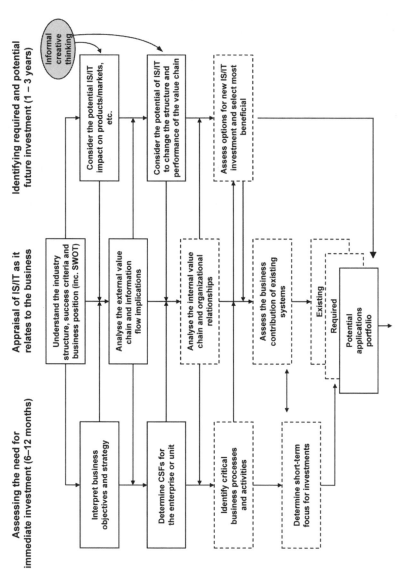

Figure 6.3 *The steps which define the strategic IS potential and options*

(2) to identification of ways in which IS/IT could impact the industry in terms of products/services/economics and be used to affect the relative strengths of the competitive forces (see Chapter 2).

Perhaps the main product of this stage of analysis is the understanding of the organization in terms of business units, their relationships and the similarities and differences among them and the environments in which they operate. For each unit, the strategic competency assessment can identify in which dimensions (product, customer or operations) the organization could expect IS/IT to sustain its advantages or create new ones, and in which the immediate IS/IT investment focus should be to redress existing or emerging disadvantages. This enables a basic investment stance on IS/IT to be adopted—innovative, aggressive, defensive or survival—and this will act as guidance to the types of opportunity to be sought.

In the discussion below, it is assumed that a business unit is being considered; the additional implications across business units and for corporate information will be considered at the end of the chapter.

Interpreting Business Objectives and Strategy

Business objectives and strategies are the products of a number of considerations:

- what the organization *might do*, based on the environment within which it operates or by moving into new environments;
- what the organization *wants to do*, based on the values and views of, chiefly, the senior executives and stakeholders;
- what the organization *must do* if it is to survive in its environment, depending on the pressure groups and their influence;
- what the organization *can do*, based on its resources and capabilities.

Overall business objectives can be classified in a number of ways for further analysis and formulation of strategies—the Balanced Scorecard being one of the best known and most frequently used. The overall strategy will define specific objectives for the whole organization, which will then need to be analysed and interpreted to develop functional and/ or initiative-based strategies to achieve them, to reflect how each part of the organization will contribute to meeting the overall objectives. The scorecard process can be extended and formalized into a strict 'management by objectives' (MBO) scheme, which allocates responsibility to individuals for achieving their contribution to the objectives. The objectives need to be prioritized—if only into high, medium and low—and measurement criteria established to complete the scorecard.

Another way of structuring objectives, adopted by a major retailer, for use in determining IS/IT requirements considers objectives at three levels:

- *permanent objectives*, which reflect the mission and overall goals of the company and its long-term intentions;
- *strategic objectives*, which the company wants to achieve in the medium term;
- *tactical objectives*, which the company and its divisions can and must achieve in the short term to make strategic and permanent objectives attainable.

In terms of 'usable objectives' in IS/IT strategy formulation, the last two are the most relevant and can be assessed in terms of critical success factors (CSFs). The permanent objectives essentially provide the background to 'why' the company needs or intends to do things.

Although objectives should be driven by business requirements and be set primarily in relation to external demands, often they reflect the way in which the current organization and its managers interpret that external world in terms of what they see as necessary to do. They may not, therefore, consider enough options or may address only some of the issues. IS/IT may change objectives due to its potential impact on the business environment. Therefore, at this point, we need to bring together the potential impact of IS/IT on the industry and the objectives of the organization either to develop new objectives or qualify the priority given to existing objectives based on IS/IT threats and opportunities.

Before looking at CSFs, it is worth considering both the objectives and potential impact of IS/IT on the business in more detail in terms of industry relationships.

Analysing the Industry (External) Value Chain and the Information Flows

The industry value chain is effectively a high-level information flow model, which can demonstrate the role that information plays in determining the overall performance of the industry and how it can be used by suppliers, customers and competitors to effect the potential achievement of the enterprise's strategy. The product of such analysis is an understanding of the information relationships and 'entities' that all players in the industry need to manage well to achieve success. This, in turn, can lead to an extension of the IS requirements and potentially new or modified objectives.

Appraising these possibilities in the light of business objectives and strategies, and overlaying them on the overall industry value chain, enables consideration of what the organization wishes to do to take advantage or otherwise of the options. The result will possibly lead to refinement of objectives and should produce a more focused consideration of the potential opportunities or threats. It will also identify the external organizations required to become involved in any changes in relationships and processes required or resulting from IS/IT options.

The external value chain and high-level information models then form a framework for more detailed considerations of the internal implications (see page 289). More specific analysis techniques such as data flow analysis and entity modelling can then be used to define the detailed information involved, its potential sources and uses. Process analysis and modelling techniques can produce a first view of how the options might be developed and implemented.

Determining Critical Success Factors

As discussed in Chapter 4, Critical Success Factor (CSF) analysis has been the most commonly-used tool in the IS strategies toolkit and its value is increased if used in conjunction with the Balanced Scorecard.

The establishment of a set of CSFs against a set of business objectives and measures, within a Balanced Scorecard framework, requires consolidation into a matrix of objectives and relevant CSFs, as described in Chapter 4. This is reasonably straightforward, provided there are not too many of either! The priority for dealing with the CSFs is not determined by the CSF ('critical' implies that no priority can be set), but by the priority of the objective that caused the success factor to be identified and by the number of objectives that will be affected by its satisfactory achievement. The next stage in the process is not, however, as straightforward. Interpreting CSFs in terms of information and information systems cannot easily be done without reference to the activities of the business and its organizational structure, which is considered below.

Determining the Strategic Potential

The next stage is to consider in more detail how the key business processes (in information and systems terms) relate to and are affected by other organizations' 'systems' in the industry value chain. The strategic potential of IS/IT and its effects on the overall value chain can then be identified.

The refinements of the value chain analysis described in Chapter 5— resource life-cycle analysis and strategic option generators—enable consideration of which other parties in the industry, to what extent and for what purposes, the organization can and should extend information systems through the external value chain, and to exert appropriate influence and accommodate external changes in industry structures and processes. The CSFs define how important it is for the organization to do so (if at all) in order to meet its objectives. This analysis should lead to the definition of new information needs and potential systems options. How feasible it is actually to develop or change processes and systems to take advantage of such opportunities will depend on:

(a) the effectiveness of existing internal systems in linking the chain together;
(b) the possibility and economics of obtaining additional information; and
(c) the willingness of suppliers and customers to cooperate, based on the benefits they perceive.

To summarize the process so far, Figure 6.3 shows how far the analysis has progressed through the framework of tools and techniques. The overall products are effectively a view of the opportunities and threats of IS/IT for the business, based on its relationship to the business environment and its overall strategy. No consideration has been made of its ability to deal with them, to take advantage or avoid being disadvantaged. The remaining steps in the process are essentially to assess the strengths and weaknesses of the existing IS/IT applications and information within the context of the broader business issues and to identify priorities for action and needs for enhancing the capability. So far, the analysis and thinking has taken an external ('outside-in') and top-down view of the business. This needs to be counterbalanced by an internal, bottom-up analysis, before selecting which application areas are to be addressed and over what timescale.

Before proceeding, however, it is worth considering how long this first 'half' of the analysis should or can take and the resulting implications for the rest of the strategy formulation process. It must not take too long, because it is important to obtain a senior management buy-in to the potential of IS/IT in terms of business opportunities and threats. If management interest and involvement cannot be obtained at this stage, sufficient to commit the organization to the second, more internally-focused stage of the process, then there is little chance of later success. Given the knowledge and types of analysis involved, a group of senior managers need to come together for a number of sessions to enable their knowledge and views to be shared effectively. Their available time will be limited and the work must be done over a short period, since continuity needs to be maintained and to avoid repeated reworking of the analyses and ideas. It is realistic, from experience of companies that have undertaken this, to expect one to two months to elapse at the most, with the main working done in a series of workshops, led by a business manager. The role of IS/IT staff is to facilitate the process and perhaps document and consolidate the rationale and conclusions, without attempting to initiate action unilaterally on ideas arising, unless it is apparent that resources are currently being seriously misused or that decisions currently being taken are obviously inappropriate.

During the next stage of the process, the IS role is significantly increased, in providing management with input to help strategic decision making and identify the specific implications of available options. That does not mean, however, that this second stage should take too long. From identifying the opportunities and threats to eventually describing an outline business systems strategy for the unit should again take no more than one to two months. If it takes much longer, earlier work may have to be repeated or management will have lost interest, since nothing appeared to result from the time they spent. The second half of the process will now be considered in more detail (see Figure 6.4).

ESTABLISHING THE RELATIVE PRIORITIES FOR IS/IT INVESTMENTS

Analysing the Internal Value Chain and Organizational Relationships

One thing is almost certain at this stage: the analysis of the internal value chain to identify what the business does and how it could be better carried out, and the analysis of the organization to show how it is structured to do it, will produce a degree of mismatch. When the dynamics of how the organization actually works are considered, this will probably confuse the picture even more! Equally inevitably, existing systems and information resources will have been established more from an organizational than a value chain perspective. In addition, the situation is not static. The business will be changing, developing or retrenching, and reorganization of functions, people and structure will be a continuing process.

The value chain offers a firmer foundation than the current organizational structure or relationships, in terms of understanding and analysing the key business processes and activities and identifying appropriate information and systems requirements. It is, therefore, important to identify the primary activities of the business—those essential to the value-adding processes and to describe the key information requirements of each and the links among them. These can then be considered as part

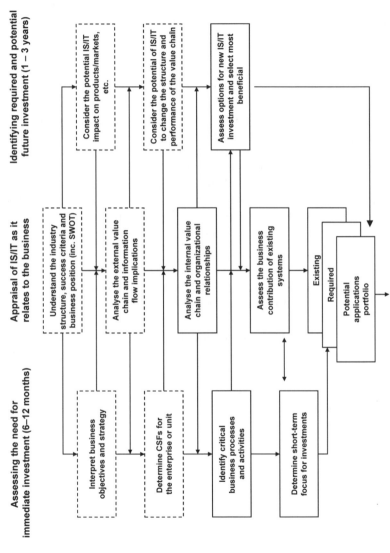

Assessing the need for immediate investment (6–12 months)

Appraisal of IS/IT as it relates to the business

Identifying required and potential future investment (1 – 3 years)

Understand the industry structure, success criteria and business position (inc. SWOT)

Consider the potential IS/IT impact on products/markets, etc.

Analyse the external value chain and information flow implications

Consider the potential of IS/IT to change the structure and performance of the value chain

Analyse the internal value chain and organizational relationships

Assess options for new IS/IT investment and select most beneficial

Assess the business contribution of existing systems

Interpret business objectives and strategy

Determine CSFs for the enterprise or unit

Identify critical business processes and activities

Determine short-term focus for investments

Existing

Required

Potential applications portfolio

Figure 6.4 The steps which establish the relative priorities within the overall demand

of the information flow through the industry in relation to suppliers and customers, and, if necessary, the existing value chain can be 'extended' or redefined in terms of those external relationships. Which processes need most improvement through IS/IT should be identified from an analysis of competency. For example, if customer intimacy is a potential source of advantage, IS/IT should be targeted on innovation or extension of customer-facing activities. If operational performance is far from excellent and is in fact a cause of disadvantages, the particular processes that are problematic need to be targeted with IS/IT investments to bring performance back to the required levels. Each of the dimensions should be considered in terms of the value chain activities and processes that have the greatest impact on overall performance in that dimension.

The internal primary chain essentially describes how the business operates, not how it is controlled or developed. Control and development involve both primary and support activities, and information to enhance these processes will be derived from and be overlaid onto the information and systems in the primary activities. Control and development activities are more dependent on the organization structure and functional responsibilities than the core business value-adding processes. The value chain model is less useful in analysing the support activities and defining the consequent information and systems needs.

Opportunities for gaining advantage from IS/IT exist in both primary and support activities, as do 'opportunities' to incur a disadvantage, although the disadvantage incurred will be more immediately obvious due to failure in the primary activities. This reinforces the need to establish a clearly understood internal primary value chain within which to evaluate the strengths and weaknesses of existing applications—a high-level information flow model that accurately reflects how and how effectively the business operates and relates to its trading partners. Different types of internal value chain model were described in Chapter 5. It is important to understand which type of model reflects the nature of the business most accurately.

Having established the model, the organization structure can be examined to identify how the activities of each function contribute to or fulfil a primary role in the model. Many organizational units will contain primary and support functions, and they need to be separated. Some support activities will exist merely because of poor linkages with other functions, their existence being the result of 'failure' in another part of the organization. Many will have evolved due to systems or information management weaknesses elsewhere, and the problems that resulted in 'unnecessary' reconciliation or recovery activities need to be cured at source. The value chain is likely to expose such problems—organizational analysis may obscure them.

As has been noted, support activities are more organizationally dependent: they either assist in planning or controlling the primary activities, where integrated and/or consistent planning processes or controls are needed, or are instrumental in the development of the business by co-ordination of the acquisition and deployment of resources and organizational knowledge across primary and secondary functions. They require analysis in terms of the information they need from primary functions, plus any additional information, and in terms of how primary functions can obtain information from them in order to manage their activities successfully.

Information and systems can be used to improve efficiency, enhance management's effectiveness or add value to the business in terms of external relationships and perceptions. To focus attention appropriately, therefore, it is important to identify why and where costs are incurred, where success depends specifically on management effectiveness and how and where value is actually added.

Accounting systems offer a basis for cost allocation, although they will inevitably reflect organizational rather than value chain groupings of cost. It should be possible, via even a rudimentary activity-based costing process, to reallocate the costs of the business to the value chain processes to identify areas of most potential benefit. This, again, will separate 'primary' and 'secondary' costs. Business objectives, Balanced Scorecards and CSFs offer a basis for assessing management effectiveness, through measured achievement or otherwise. A very useful step in the analysis is to position each of the CSFs in the value chain to identify which activities, or sets of related activities, need most attention to sustain or improve overall business success. CSFs that cannot be allocated need to be questioned, since organizational ownership of a CSF is important if it is to be dealt with effectively. The external view of the business, developed earlier in the process, offers guidance as to how and where the company adds value in relation to suppliers/customers and in comparison with competitors. This can be transposed into the value chain to highlight areas for enhancing the value-adding aspects of the business.

Identify Critical Business Processes and Activities

From this stage, it is now possible to identify the critical business processes and activities, based on CSFs and the way in which the company adds value/incurs cost and is managed. The overlay of CSFs will also show up the interdependence of activities. The nature of the potential for business improvement will vary depending on the relationship between the value adding, cost and the CSFs associated with activities and processes:

- a high-cost, low-value-adding activity with few CSFs clearly only offers cost-reduction possibilities from IS/IT investment;
- a high-value-adding activity could be made more effective through IS/IT investment, but this will only be worthwhile if its improvement relates directly to agreed business CSFs. If, however, it is a high cost as well as a high-value-adding activity, then IS/IT may still help to reduce the cost;
- where a number of activities are associated with a CSF, then they need to be assessed collectively in terms of options for enhancing the value or reducing the cost of each, via IS/IT developments;
- however, if an activity adds little value and is not associated with any of the CSFs, it is more important to question whether it is needed at all than to consider how to improve it through IS/IT! Every organization carries out some activities that actually add no value, and some organizations have even computerized them!

The information and systems implications can now be categorized into those that are critical to current business success, those that are likely to affect future success and those that merely support the business processes (i.e. strategic, key operational or support). Again, the data flow and data entity models (as described in Chapter 4) will show the dependence of processes on sources of data across the organization, and the need for integration or otherwise of systems and information resources.

Assessment of New Options for Investment

Having understood the relationship between the value chain, the organization structure and the criticality of processes and activities, it is now possible to assess the value of the various IS/IT opportunities developed earlier through the 'creative' thinking route, in terms of whether they could have an immediate impact or are of longer-term potential. The ideas and options need to be reassessed in terms of *whether* and *how* they could provide the organization with specific advantages or reduce foreseeable threats, and whether and how, in the shorter term, they can contribute to the existing business strategy by improving the current operational and developmental processes. This will depend on how closely they align with the objectives/CSFs and, hence, address known critical business activities. Because of the rationale of the overall process, the options and their current relevance should not be at odds with the prevailing business issues or strategies. Some, however, may be beyond the current objective horizon, but should be kept within the portfolio as high-potential ideas, which may become more valuable as the business moves forward and the environment changes. It may well be worth some investment to test the ideas, determine the possible benefits and examine the feasibility of achieving them. That is especially true of ideas that would apply equally well to competitors. The selection process is essentially a decision on each idea in terms of why it should be pursued or not, in the next few months or year (i.e. is it currently strategic to the business?).

The overall route through the 'creative' chain can be summarized as:

- What could IS/IT do for all the firms in the industry, in terms of changing business parameters and relationships?
- What could IS/IT do for the organization, based on its particular position within the industry?
- Which options offer most immediate benefit in terms of the business objectives/strategy and the way the company operates and is managed?

Determining the Future Applications Portfolio

Each of these last steps in the process is focused on defining the future portfolio of applications. The creative route will produce ideas that will be generally categorized as:

- high potential: worth evaluating further; and
- strategic: the idea relates directly to the business strategy.

The current situation analysis will probably highlight the need for new applications in each quadrant, although they are more likely to be key operational and support rather than the other two. From this will come a need to consolidate strategic and high-potential applications derived from various routes, plus a need to address the weaknesses of existing key operational and support systems. Determining which weakness to address first will depend not only on current impact but on whether it will be increasingly or decreasingly important in the future. That, in turn, depends on how critical the activity it supports will be or whether it can affect any of the CSFs. Will, for instance, not integrating a system make a further strategic application impossible? CSFs determine what is of strategic importance, what offers the highest potential and which key operational weaknesses must be overcome. They have little, if anything, to do with support applications, where decisions are based on the net economic benefits of investment. An approach to assessing the contribution (and strengths and weaknesses) of the existing applications is described in detail in Chapter 7. At this stage, it is worth emphasizing that it is perhaps more important to deal with serious weaknesses first, especially if they could soon result in a real threat to the business or are precluding opportunities being taken. In addition, some opportunities that are not dependent on anything else should be pursued, in particular where they build on existing strengths, giving more chance of success.

It must be stressed again that this approach to using the models and techniques is not a methodology, but a way of bringing them together to ensure that the overall results are more complete and of greatest overall value to the organization. No one technique provides a comprehensive view of the business options for IS/IT investment and no one technique can produce certainty of conclusions. Figure 6.2 has one additional arrow showing the need for the next stage—managing the resulting portfolio. Before considering that in detail, one further aspect needs to be discussed: How can this process be used in a multi-SBU company and what are the implications?

LARGE ORGANIZATIONS, MULTIPLE SBUs AND THEIR CONSOLIDATION

Most multi-business-unit organizations will have some scope to benefit from examining not just one business unit but also looking across business units, before deciding on how best to meet information and system requirements. Figure 3.7 demonstrates the basic relationships.

Both synergistic and economic opportunities will be affected by a number of factors, not least of which is corporate management's desire to gain such benefits across business units. It is possible that each business unit is seen merely as part of a 'portfolio' that is continually being changed by buying and selling businesses for primarily financial reasons. In such a case, synergistic and economic benefits will at best be short-lived, if achievable at all. In most other circumstances, however, the overall corporate benefits from IS/IT opportunities will often exceed the sum of the parts.

The factors that can affect the corporate as opposed to purely business unit 'value added' of IS/IT can be outlined as follows:

- whether the units compete in the same or different industries and the similarity or otherwise of their products and services;
- whether the units are in similar competitive positions in their industries, whether the industries have similar rates of growth (or decline) and whether the types and mix of competitors are different;

- whether they have similar levels of strategic competency in each of the three key dimensions—customer, operations and product;
- whether they have the same (or similar) customers, distribution channels, and/or suppliers, with whom information can be shared and value chain links can be mutually developed;
- whether they trade with one another (i.e. are related in a value chain, where IS/IT links could give the company an overall advantage);
- whether they carry out similar processes (i.e. are the internal value chains of the same type and/or are some or all of the primary value chain components similar?);
- whether they are of similar sizes and scale of operation (e.g. numbers of customers or suppliers);
- whether they have similar objectives and are adopting similar strategies, and, as a consequence, have similar CSFs (units with different CSFs will have significantly different IS/IT priorities);
- whether the parent company requires a consistent, even standard, structure of information from all the units;
- whether support activities are broadly similar and (can be) organized in the same basic structure.

These imply that opportunities for further benefits exist in each of the inputs to the IS/IT strategy process (i.e. external and internal, business and IS/IT environments) for the corporation overall to gain from synergy and economies. A threat or weakness for one business unit may be able to be overcome by transferring knowledge or even applications from another business unit. It is, therefore, important to compare the results of the analyses and to share ideas. Any of the techniques, at any stage of the process outlined above, could reveal such cross-unit opportunities, so all results should be 'pooled' and made available for others to adapt, adopt or join in the development, if appropriate. An idea from one part of the business, adapted by another, may even offer more benefits.

SUMMARY

Chapters 2 to 5 described approaches to IS strategy formulation, providing an overall organizational process with associated tools and techniques of analysis. This chapter has attempted to bring these key components together in summary form, in order to describe a framework within which the business information systems strategy can be developed and then represented in terms of what information and systems the business *must*, *should* and *might* have to achieve maximum benefit in its business environment.

The IS/IT strategy consists of much more than this, but, without business needs and opportunities so identified and defined, the rest of the strategy is worth very little. Although not every threat can be anticipated, every opportunity spotted, each strength exploited or every weakness overcome, the framework for using the tools and techniques should enable fewer threats and opportunities to be missed, and IS/IT strengths and weaknesses to be understood better in terms of their business implications.

The framework may seem rather conceptual, even theoretical, and it may be that various steps can be short-circuited and appropriate conclusions drawn much earlier in the process. There is no point in exhaustive examination when ideas obviously make sense, but many ideas cannot be properly evaluated without consideration and testing from a number of viewpoints.

The framework attempts to bring together analytical processes and focused, creative thinking approaches to enable the products of both to be considered as they arise. This is more realistic than waiting for all the analysis and all the ideas to be generated, and then examining them all together, to distil all the resulting conclusions. That is not how the best ideas and strategies evolve and develop. Good ideas and insights will occur throughout the process, and they need to be capitalized on there and then, as far as possible, not put on the shelf for later consideration when their rationale and 'value' may have been forgotten.

Although the framework is therefore somewhat 'ideal', it does include most of the tools and techniques that are generally found to be useful, in a logically linked process. It also ensures that all types of strategic input, both external and internal, are assessed in relation to one another. It does enable an outline business IS strategy to be identified and a consensus of agreement and management endorsement to be achieved in a matter of a few weeks or, at worst, a very few months.

It must also be remembered that planning is a continuous and continuing process, and the formulative framework described above will have to be repeatedly revisited to ensure that the portfolio as foreseen is still relevant. As factors inside or outside the business change, in the business or IS/IT environment, the conclusions to be drawn from each step in the framework may change, therefore some paths through the process will have to be revisited to identify the implications of changes and reflect these quickly in the form of a revised portfolio. However, it is equally important not to need to repeat the whole process if any particular factor changes.

The management of such application portfolios is considered in depth in Chapter 7, in terms of ensuring that demand for applications based on needs and ideas generated, as above, can be successfully supplied. Later chapters then consider in more detail the strategies for managing key aspects of the delivery of that supply to satisfy the variety of requirements inherent in the applications.

ENDNOTES

There are no endnotes for this chapter—all the relevant references, etc. are covered in preceding chapters.

7
Managing the Applications Portfolio

The applications portfolio concept, introduced in Chapter 1 (see Figure 1.7), is a means of bringing together existing, planned and potential information systems and assessing their business contribution. It has been referred to in previous chapters, which have been concerned primarily with how to populate the portfolio with required applications. Gaining business management understanding and agreement on the contribution expected from the variety of current and future systems is the cornerstone of any strategy.

The usefulness of the matrix is borne out by the ease with which management is willing and able to categorize systems in this way. A survey of some 300 organizations that had become aware of the concept showed that 70% were using it within their approach to managing IS/IT. One reason is probably the familiarity of business managers with similar portfolio models like the Boston Consulting Group's 'Boston Matrix', described in Chapter 2. As will be seen in this chapter, these similarities are more than superficial—many proven attributes of other portfolio models can be adapted to address key issues in IS/IT management. Another reason for its usefulness is its simplicity, which also implies that it has limitations and cannot deal with every conceivable situation. But, it can provide valuable insight and guidance in addressing the issues associated with the majority of business applications of IS/IT.

The application portfolio, as described so far, owes much to the 'McFarlan Grid'[1] used to assess the overall contribution of IS/IT to business success. The limitations of this perspective were discussed in Chapter 1. In this chapter, we develop this basic model into a management tool.

Two-by-two matrices are very popular ways of describing the implications of unrelated, but interacting variables, and a number of other such matrices related to the management of IS/IT have been developed. The first part of this chapter briefly reviews some of them in order to synthesize a set of relevant issues, attributes and options associated with the portfolio segments. The main purpose in classifying applications is to ensure that they are managed successfully and that the expected contribution is delivered. Based on the issues relevant to each segment, appropriate implementation strategies can be adopted. These, in turn, can be related to the strategy formulation and planning approaches, as described in Chapter 3 (based on work by Earl[2]) to provide consistency of management from strategy formulation to implementation.

As noted above, any simplification of a complex situation has its limitations. Precision should not be expected; merely relevant guidance to enlighten and support management decision making in what is often an area fraught with uncertainty and even conflict. It is a valuable 'framework', which helps to link together and reconcile the complexities involved in managing the demand and supply components of the IS/IT strategy, in particular to achieve ownership by business managers of their IS/IT applications and the issues that have to be addressed in achieving success. The application portfolio will evolve over time, and how the effects of that evolution can be managed successfully will be considered.

CONCLUSIONS FROM VARIOUS MATRICES AND MODELS

A number of matrices have been produced to help management decision making with respect to IS/IT planning, utilization and resourcing. The early versions were analysed in detail by Ward.[3] Some of the conclusions from that analysis are useful to show how the ideas and concepts are generally complementary, even convergent. More recent versions, devised to address developments in the 1990s, are also, in essence, very similar, even if the terminology used is different. A composite matrix, including some key ideas, is shown in Figure 7.1. The main models on which the composite matrix is based include the following:

1. The Sullivan[4] matrix, which has already been described (see Figure 1.9), considered the range of IS/IT management issues that depend on the combination of infusion and diffusion of IS/IT in the organization. Infusion is 'the degree to which IS/IT has penetrated a company in terms of importance, impact or significance', and diffusion is 'the degree to which IS/IT has been disseminated or scattered throughout the company'. Sullivan identified the need for new, demand-driven and decentralized planning approaches to improve

| H | STRATEGIC (Attack) | HIGH POTENTIAL (Beware) |

Degree of dependence of the business on IS/IT application in achieving overall business performance

Figure 7.1 *A composite matrix*

the management of the strategic and high potential quadrants, in addition to the better understood strategy formulation and planning approaches required for 'backbone' (key operational) and 'traditional' (support) systems. He expressed the need for an 'eclectic' planning method to deal with the strategic developments when IS/IT is considered in establishing the business objectives or is being used to transform business processes (i.e. when there is an interdependent relationship between IS/IT and business strategies, which is increasingly becoming the case).

2. The Information Technology Assessment and Adoption (ITAA) matrix developed by Munro and Huff,[5] based on work by Benjamin *et al.*,[6] considered how organizations have adopted IS/IT as a competitive weapon. Most companies, according to Munro and Huff, are either 'technology driven'—looking for ways of deploying new technology to advantage—or 'issues driven'—looking for new business opportunities within the known possibilities of existing

technology. These relate mainly to high potential and key operational-type environments, and few companies achieve 'normative' planning where business issues, opportunities and technology are effectively matched—an 'ideal' planning relationship as they describe it (i.e. that required for strategic applications to be developed).

Galliers[7] developed a matrix for a similar purpose that, like the Sullivan matrix, considers factors affecting planning methods, but this time in relation to:

- long-term and short-term thinking, strategy or issue driven; and
- business issues versus technology-driven planning.

Galliers separates the need for IS/IT to react to current business issues (key operational) from the need to react to changing future objectives (strategic), and compares them to the proactive IS/IT stance required for high potential opportunities. Like most others, he identifies an efficient, problem-solving basis for managing support-type systems.

3. Two matrices, developed by Ives and Learmonth[8] and Galliers,[9] both considered how the 'value adding potential' of IS/IT in the business and the 'quality of IS resources' (i.e. the capability of the organization) affect how IS/IT is deployed and how it is managed. They showed how a vision of what is possible *plus* strength of resources are essential if IS/IT is to be used as an offensive (i.e. strategic) weapon, and how the two are often interrelated. In many organizations, the lack of vision reduces the ability of even good resources to do more than 'explore' opportunities as issues arise. Low quality of resource implies a 'safe' support systems-only approach, and the organization will become very vulnerable, due to its inability to respond to new, high potential or strategic applications developed by competitors. In such a case, 'vision' is not enough—the resource must be improved at the same time and the organization must 'beware' of IS/IT investments by competitors.

4. An example of more recent matrices, which were devised to help management address 'e-business' options, is the 'e-business value matrix' described by Hartman and Sifonis.[10] The axes of the core matrix are (a) business criticality and (b) practice innovation, and the four resulting segments equate closely with those of the application portfolio. Low criticality and low innovation are defined as the *new fundamentals*, and the characteristics are close to support. Key operational is a direct equivalent of *operational excellence*—high criticality, low innovation. High innovation but low criticality is called *rational experimental* and the parallels with the high potential segment are obvious. Finally, the strategic part of the matrix equates reasonably

well with the high criticality, high innovation combination called *breakthrough strategies* by Hartman and Sifonis. The implications they describe in terms of the best approaches to identifying, justifying and managing e-Investments in an organization are similar to the guidance that can be obtained from combining the attributes of previous matrices.

In most of the models, all of which address similar issues from different directions, clear differences can be seen in the ways in which applications in each of the four quadrants need to be planned and managed. Not all ideas map precisely onto the application portfolio, and there is not always full agreement on the specific needs of the strategic and high potential segments, perhaps due to their more uncertain and changing nature. However, there is general agreement in the key operational and support areas. The composite matrix in Figure 7.1 attempts to reflect the key ideas from the various matrices in terms of the issues or options for managing the portfolio segments. These are examined in more detail later in the chapter. The axes are derived primarily from McFarlan's work. The horizontal axis attempts to reflect the ability of an organization to control its destiny, whereas the vertical axis reflects the uncertainty due to external forces of future IS/IT impact.

Matrix analysis approaches are attractive because they reduce an apparently infinite continuum of alternatives to a manageable, pertinent number of discrete options from which high-level directions can be determined. They demonstrate relationships that evolve over time, but that will normally have to be managed to success simultaneously in the organization. Like many such models developed to assist management, they are often overly simple, and more complex models would be needed to reflect the diversity of reality. As complexity is added, however, clarity of perception often dims. Without intending to introduce confusion by complexity, it is worth considering a few further aspects of the models.

In relation to the Sullivan model, which considered the impact of IS/IT on a business (infusion) in relation to the ability to devolve IS/IT decisions (diffusion), an organization in the complex quadrant will have, almost by definition, a comprehensive application portfolio. Diffusion equates to 'informality' in that each part of the business can decide what it wishes to do, but some formality is needed if applications spanning different parts of the business are to be identified and the benefits delivered—and most strategic systems cross organizational or functional boundaries and/or require business processes or organizational relationships to change.

Figure 7.2 suggests a number of cause-and-effect relationships, which are generally borne out by observation in many organizations:

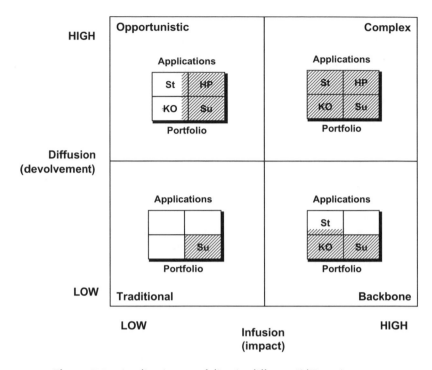

Figure 7.2   *Application portfolios in different IS/IT environments*

- Organizations that have a traditional, low impact view of the role of IS/IT with highly centralized IT decision making will tend to have a predominance of support applications.
- Those with devolved IT decision making, because it is not seen as particularly critical to overall business success, will also produce a profusion of support systems, solving local problems. A number of high potential ideas will probably also be developed, but it will be difficult to bring them to strategic fruition because of the localized view of their value and the limited IT capability available in each area. Decision making is localized and, so, although some key operational systems will be implemented, integration across the business will be poor because system interrelationships are not considered when satisfying the local needs.
- Where the impact of IS/IT has increased, probably due to external pressures, but IT is kept highly centralized, both key operational and support systems will be developed and continually improved, but more innovative uses of IS/IT will not be instigated, because of the limited knowledge in the business of what is possible.

There are reasons for these cause-and-effect relationships, based on the way in which IS/IT evolves in organizations and the way in which the IS/IT strategy has to respond and become more sophisticated and better balanced over time. This also implies that a number of different methods need to be in place at any one time to develop a relevant and complete portfolio.

Most of the models address the need to accommodate both centralized and decentralized management approaches, the balance of which will depend on the degree of integration required in the business and organizational processes. Particular competitive opportunities and new uses of IT will tend to address singular or few applications and, initially at least, can be exploited most advantageously close to the business opportunity. Applications that produce benefits by business integration or sharing of assets require strong business coordination, competent IS/IT management and sustained investment in resources. The Sullivan model helps understanding of how the application portfolio will evolve by the effects of these forces within an organization.

CLASSIFYING THE APPLICATIONS IN THE PORTFOLIO

How to populate the portfolio with future IS/IT investments is described in the preceding chapters, and the basic rationale for a portfolio approach was discussed in Chapter 1. Describing the existing and future applications in this way helps the task of obtaining a consensus among executive management, line managers and the IT management on the content of the IS strategy. Once the portfolio is understood and agreed, decisions on how best to manage each application, both existing and future, can be made, along with overall decisions on the use of resources across the portfolio and the selection of the most effective sources for supply—which aspects should be managed in-house and which can and should be outsourced.

While agreeing the contribution and, hence, portfolio positioning of future investments is important, so is understanding the role of and value to the organization of the existing application set. Some applications may be obsolete and no longer required, others may need significant investment to avoid future business problems, some may be underexploited and others may be consuming undue amounts of resource in relation to their business value. Table 7.1 suggests a set of criteria that can be used as a basis for a strength, weaknesses, opportunities and threats (SWOT) analysis of the current applications, to determine the need for action, either to improve their contribution or enable other, related applications to be developed or used better.

Table 7.1   *SWOT analysis of existing portfolio*

Analysing the applications in the portfolio (SWOT)

EXPLOIT STRENGTHS:

- high future potential, currently underexploited;
- can be extended, enhanced to be of more value;
- could be more valuable if integrated more effectively or used more extensively;
- critical to the business, but data quality is poor;
- needs to be developed to meet current and future business needs;
- must be enhanced to meet changed business requirements for future;
- system required, but needs to be reimplemented to absorb less resources or overcome technology obsolescence;
- system will be less important in future—needs to be simplified/reduced to real needs;
- system is no longer of value—should be discontinued.

OVERCOME WEAKNESSES

Merely classifying current and future applications into a 2 × 2 matrix is of no great value, unless it causes each application and the overall portfolio to be managed more effectively. The process of classifying the applications is as important as the end result, since the discussion involved will enable different perspectives to be understood (and hopefully reconciled!) and the implications of the decisions made to be appreciated by all parties. If a particular application is considered by one group of users as strategic, due to their uses of the output, and as support by another that provides the input, it is unlikely that the maximum benefits available will be delivered, due to the differing operational priorities and quality of information management in each group. A realistic and agreed assessment must be made.

Each organization will have slightly different interpretations of the terms used for each segment. Hence, a decision-support tool that would fit every organization's criteria for classification cannot be defined, but Box 7.1 contains a simple starting point for the process, by posing questions that can help the analysis. It should only be used to guide the assessment, not as a 'rule book'. Normally, it is relatively easy to agree and classify most of the applications into the quadrants, although there are always some where discussion, based on different perceptions of their role and contribution is necessary.

If agreement cannot be reached, it often means that the 'system' needs to be considered at a lower level, in terms of the main functions it performs. For example, an Accounts Receivable system may consist of

Box 7.1 Classifying the applications in the portfolio

Questions
If the development* succeeds, will it:

(a) Result in a clear competitive advantage for the business?   Yes/No

(b) Enable the achievement of specific business objectives and/or critical success factors?   Yes/No

(c) Overcome known business disadvantages in relation to competitors?   Yes/No

(d) Avoid foreseeable business risks becoming major problems in the near future?   Yes/No

(e) Improve the productivity of the business and, hence, reduce long-term costs?   Yes/No

(f) Enable the organization to meet statutory requirements?   Yes/No

(g) Provide benefits not yet known, but may result in (a) or (b) above?   Yes/No

* For existing applications the question is, is the application delivering benefits that ...'

Interpretation
In answering the questions above, the reasons for the judgement should be stated. The table below shows how the answers can be interpreted and the application classified, based on whether or not any Yes answers appear in a column.

If more questions produce a Yes answer in any one column (i.e. the application appears to be in more than one category), then it should be reassessed by splitting it into its major components and considering each of them in the same way (i.e. the application should be broken down into subprojects). If this is not done, the risks of failure will increase dramatically due to the mixed objectives and the confusion that it can cause once the project proceeds.

	High potential	*Strategic*	*Key operational*	*Support*
(a)		Yes (i)		
(b)		Yes (i)		
(c)			Yes	
(d)			Yes	
(e)				Yes
(f)			Yes (ii)	Yes (ii)
(g)	Yes			

> (i) If either applies, the supplementary question is   Yes/No
> then, 'Is it clear what the business benefits are and
> how they can be obtained?' If Yes it is *Strategic*, if
> No it is *High potential*.
> (ii) To clarify which it is, the following question should   Yes/No
> be asked, 'Will failure to comply lead to significant
> business risks (be specific about the risk)?' If Yes it
> is *Key operational*, if No it is *Support*.

several business processes or subprocesses, some of which may be more business critical than others—bad-debt control may be key operational, whereas statement production is support. Although many applications are often provided via large packages (e.g. ERP and CRM software), the purpose of the analysis is still to classify the business activities that the package covers (e.g. order processing, purchasing), rather than the package itself. An ERP package can deliver applications in all quadrants, depending on the competitive positioning, the business strategy and the maturity of IS/IT development in the organization.

It also follows that the portfolio is not a way of classifying technologies—email, groupware, intranets, the Internet and a data warehouse can all be used for a variety of applications, making different contributions to different business activities. And to reiterate a point made in Chapter 1, an application utilizing cutting-edge technology does not imply that it is automatically classified as strategic—classification must be based on business contribution.

An example portfolio for a manufacturing company, produced using the question set in Box 7.1 and showing a simplified version of the SWOT analysis described above, is shown in Figure 7.3.

Reconciling Demand and Supply Issues in the Applications Portfolio

Before considering the best approaches to managing the applications in the different segments, it is important to understand the key differences in the rationale for the types of application and the resulting issues to be addressed in implementation. Discussion in Chapters 4–6 considered what might be described as the driving forces for applications in each segment of the portfolio (i.e. *why* they are being developed and *how* eventual success or failure will be determined). They can be translated into some critical requirements to be satisfied in the delivery of the application. These key issues are described in Table 7.2.

STRATEGIC	HIGH POTENTIAL
* Direct Marketing and Telesales system ** Advertising and Promotion-Campaign Management ** Sales forecasting/Market analysis ? Customer Relationship Management	** e-Procurement (general items) ? On-line customer specification system ** Product tracking/traceability ? Product profitability analysis ** Data warehouse-customer analysis
* Product database/Inventory Management, Manufacturing Requirements Planning[1] * Order processing, Dispatch, Invoicing, etc.[1] * Production control * Purchasing-materials ( ) Costing systems (activity and product) ( ) Sales analysis[1] * Warehouse Management * Wholesaler EDI (ordering, etc.), etc.	* Payroll and Personnel systems * Ledgers - Receivables[1] - Payables[1] * General Ledger and Budgeting[1] * Office systems ( ) Purchasing-general[1] * Samples Management etc.
KEY OPERATIONAL	SUPPORT

Key   *   Existing system is satisfactory   (Note [1] - applications carried out
       ( ) Existing system needs improvement   by SAP or planned to be)
       ** Planned system
       ?   Potential system

Figure 7.3 *Example portfolio for a manufacturing company*

To ensure overall success, it is important that decisions about *how* to implement the system (e.g. package or bespoke development) are directly related to decisions about *what* is required. Both of them have to derive as clearly as possible from the initial decision making on *why* the investment is being made, in terms of the contribution required. Albeit somewhat simplistically, Figure 7.4 attempts to pose simple questions that the chosen implementation strategy should address. Understanding the management implications of these questions offers guidance on how best to manage each application through its life cycle.

Figure 7.4 shows how the questions become more complex as we move around the matrix. For support applications, the general objective is clear (*why* = efficiency) and *what* needs to be improved is determined by existing tasks and activities. The main question is *how* to do that successfully, in terms of the most cost-effective use of IT. For key operational applications, the *how* question still has to be addressed, but in addition

Table 7.2 *Some key issues in the segments of the portfolio*

	Driving forces	*Critical requirements*
High potential	New business ideas or technological opportunity Individual initiative—owned by a 'product champion' Need to demonstrate the value or otherwise of the idea	Rapid evaluation of prototypes and avoid wasting effort/resources on failures Understand the potential benefits (and the economics) in relation to business strategy Identify the best way to proceed—the next step
Strategic	Market requirements, competitive pressures or other external forces Business objectives, success factors and vision of how to achieve them Obtaining an advantage and then sustaining it	Rapid development to meet the business objective and realize benefits within the window of opportunity Flexible system that can be adapted in the future as the business evolves Link to an associated business initiative to sustain commitment
Key operational	Improving the performance of existing activities (speed, accuracy, economics) Integration of data and systems to avoid duplication, inconsistency, and misinformation Avoiding a business disadvantage or allowing a business risk to become critical/comply with industry legislation	High-quality, long-life solutions and effective data management Balancing costs with benefits and business risks—identify the best solution Evaluation of options available by objective feasibility study
Support	Improved productivity/ efficiency of specific (often localized) business tasks General legislation Most cost-effective use of IS/IT funds and resources available	Low-cost, long-term solutions—often packaged software to satisfy most needs Compromise the needs to the software available Objective cost/benefit analysis to reduce financial risk and then control costs carefully

STRATEGIC		HIGH POTENTIAL	
WHY	do we want to do it in strategic terms?	WHY?	- not clear
			and/or
WHAT	does the system need to do to gain the advantage?	WHAT?	- not certain
			and/or
HOW	best to do it?	HOW?	- not yet known
Why	to improve performance and avoid disadvantage	Why	to reduce costs by improving efficiency
WHAT	actually has to improve and by how much?	What	of existing necessary tasks
HOW	best to do it?	HOW	best to do it?
KEY OPERATIONAL		SUPPORT	

Figure 7.4   *Key questions on the applications portfolio*

considerable thought may be needed to define specifically *what* has to be done, and to which systems, to avoid potential disadvantage (*why* we need to do it). Again, both *what* and *how* questions need to be resolved in strategic applications, but in addition we need to clearly understand *why* we wish to do it in terms of the business strategy. Strategic applications require creative thinking and will cause change, probably externally as well as internally, and the reasons for and intended benefits of such changes must be agreed on. By definition, the strategic systems cannot be copied from others (since we will already be potentially disadvantaged!), hence their rationale has to derive explicitly and coherently from the strategy of the organization. If one or two of the *why*, *what* or *how* questions is unanswered, it implies that the application is high potential, and appropriate evaluation is needed to answer the remaining questions before making a large-scale investment.

GENERIC APPLICATION MANAGEMENT STRATEGIES

Given the variety of factors affecting success in the different segments and the business consequences of success or failure, no single implementation approach is likely to deal effectively with the range of issues involved. Equally, adopting a unique approach to each and every new development will lead to a degree of chaos and probably result in as many failures as successes. A limited set that meets the majority of requirements and is well understood throughout the organization is more likely to enable the best approach to be selected in each instance and increase the chances of success.

Based on extensive observation of the realities of IS/IT management processes in many organizations, Parsons[11] described five strategies that are prevalent as the means by which organizations link the management of IS/IT to the corporate or business management processes. These 'linking strategies' are 'general frameworks which guide the opportunities for IT which are identified, the IT resources which are developed, the rate at which new technologies are adopted, the level of impact for IT within the firm, etc.'

They are 'the central tendencies which firms use to guide IT within the business'. As they are 'general frameworks,' the term 'generic strategies' is used in the discussion below. They are essentially alternative strategies for the implementation of IS/IT, ensuring that the nature of the demand is matched by the appropriate means of supply. How these implementation strategies can be aligned and reconciled with Earl's planning approaches will be considered on pages 321–323.

Parsons described the characteristics and implications of each strategy in detail, and they are summarized in Table 7.3. As can be seen from the table, the strategies define different roles and responsibilities for the three key parties involved in enabling successful implementation:

- executive management;
- line management: functional or process managers and users of the systems;
- IS/IT specialists: whether or not they are internal to the organization (centrally located or in business areas) or external.

As such, the strategies are behavioural and each set of behaviours will cause certain effects. The effects required are determined by the nature of the contribution of applications in the portfolio—the generic strategies, therefore, are ways of causing the right effects to occur.

Parson's strategies are: centrally planned, leading edge, free market, monopoly and scarce resource. They are well titled, since the very names evoke a basic understanding of the attitudes and behaviour that each is likely to produce. The key points of each, and their pros and cons, will be outlined at the same time as considering how they relate to the applications portfolio.

Table 7.3 Rationale and requirements for generic strategies (source: after Parsons)

	Centrally planned	Leading edge	Free market	Monopoly	Scarce resource
Management rationale	Central coordination of all requirements will produce better decision making	Technology can create business advantages and risks are worth taking	Market makes the best decisions and users are responsible for business results Integration is not critical	Information is a corporate good and an integrated resource for users to employ	Information is a limited resource and its development must be clearly justified
Organizational requirements	Knowledgeable and involved senior management Integrated planning of IS/IT within the business planning process	Commitment of funds and resources Innovative IS/IT management Strong technical skills	Knowledgeable users Accountability for IS/IT at business or functional level Willingness to duplicate effort Loose IT budget control	User acceptance of the philosophy Policies to force through single sourcing Good forecasting of resource usage	Tight budgetary control control of all IS/IT expenses Policies for controlling IS/IT and users
IT role	Provide services to match the business demands by working closely with business managers	Push forward boundaries of technology use on all fronts	Competitive and probably profit centre—intended to achieve a return on its resources	To satisfy users' requirements as they arise, but non-directive in terms of the uses of IS/IT	Make best use of a limited resource by tight cost control of expenses and projects. Justify capital investment projects
Line managers and users role	Identify the potential of IS/IT to meet business needs at all levels of the organization	Use the technology and identify the advantages it offers	Identify, source and control IS/IT developments	Understand needs and present them to central utility to obtain resources	Identify and cost-justify projects Passive unless benefits are identified

Centrally Planned

This generic strategy implies that senior and executive management need to be fully aware of the development, due to its potential impact on the future business strategy. It is therefore most appropriate for *strategic* systems. Ensuring success in such circumstances demands the attention of senior management, to ensure that the objectives are met and that the necessary resources are applied to deliver the solution in the time required. Most strategic developments are likely to span a number of business areas, and, while the nature of the system can often be easily defined in outline, it will be its uniqueness and its close fit to the business strategy that will deliver the business advantages. To gain those advantages, it is almost inevitable that changes to business practices and even organization structure will be necessary.

To meet all these requirements, a 'task force' approach is best suited. Led by a senior business manager, the team will need dedicated, preferably full-time, high-quality business resources, which have excellent knowledge of the areas affected and the authority to agree to business changes. Equally, it will need good IS/IT skills and knowledge in the team to design the system and manage the technical aspects of its implementation. This dedicated team require direct access to top management to resolve issues that will undoubtedly arise during the development. Subject to this senior management agreement, the team has the authority to decide both what the system will do and how, in business and IT terms, that will be achieved. It is likely that the design and development will be iterative, comparing possible solutions with emerging or changing requirements. This requires very close working relationships among the members of the team, individuals' contributions depending more on their knowledge than formally designated roles.

Although the idea of a dedicated team is attractive, it is often difficult to achieve successfully in many organizations. The people it requires are often the most valuable in their existing jobs and are not readily given up by their functional management for the duration of the project. Even though it may not be the most efficient use of skilled and knowledgeable people, it is a very effective way of achieving clear objectives in a tight timescale. The need for key people dedicated to such teams may also limit the number of strategic developments that can be undertaken at any one time, since such key people are often in short supply. It is better to reschedule the projects based on the availability of key resources than to spread the resource too thinly or substitute lower-calibre or less experienced people. This centrally planned strategy addresses the needs of strategic applications most effectively, but it could be used in certain circumstances to carry out a short, sharp evaluation of a high potential opportunity or even attack a key operational development where the business faces the prospect of serious short-term disadvantage (e.g. Y2K compliance or Euro conversion).

Leading Edge

With this strategy, the senior management of the organization believes that, by adopting information technology that is 'leading edge' in the context of its industry, it should be able to gain some business advantage. It follows that they must be willing to fund some experimentation to evaluate technologies and ideas *and* accept that not all of the evaluations will succeed. While the new technologies may be identified by IT specialists, the evaluation should be in relation to some potential business idea or need and carried out in conjunction with the business. The objective is not to understand the technology for its own sake. Alternatively, the lead may come from the business, through seeing a technology in use elsewhere that may be potentially applicable for the organization. While that business 'vision' may be appropriate, IT specialists need to be involved in the evaluation, to provide an objective assessment of the capabilities of the technology and determine the longer-term implications to the organization of adopting a particular technology. This is essential, to counterbalance the often enthusiastic business user who has fallen prey to the persuasive pitch of a professional IT salesperson!

While the technology is 'brand new' to the organization, it should be confined to the *high potential* box for evaluation. It is very high risk to apply untried technology in any other segment of the matrix. Once evaluated, it may well be that the technology has significant potential for the business and becomes part of a strategic application. Alternatively, it may not, and it would be prudent if the technology is only relevant to key operational or support needs to proceed more carefully in line with the pace of adoption of technology in the industry. If there is no advantage to be gained, it is perhaps best to let others take the risks.

Free Market

The strategy that follows is 'monopoly' and, before considering the free market strategy in more detail, it is worth clarifying the key differences between the two in terms of the decision-making roles of the three parties involved. Table 7.4 attempts to do this.

The philosophy behind the free market approach is that line managers are accountable for the performance of the business activities within their area of responsibility. As part of that responsibility, subject to their normal degree of authority, they should be able to make beneficial

Table 7.4 *Free market versus monopoly strategies—key differences (N.B. In some cases, the Monopoly may be a combination of IT specialists and a particular function [e.g. for accounting systems])*

		Free market	*Monopoly*
Demand	Who decides *what* is done and whether it is done—the IS decision	Line or functional management	Senior management based on needs agreed by line management
Supply	Who decides *how* it will be done in terms of the IT approach	Line or functional management with or without advice from IT specialists	IT specialists with endorsement of senior management (IT can veto 'unacceptable' solutions)

decisions about IS and IT and not be hindered in any way by another group in achieving their performance targets. The alternative view, expressed by the monopoly philosophy, is that, while line management decide what is needed subject to senior management agreement to resource those needs, it is best if there is central coordination and control of how those needs are met. These two apparently opposing views can be reconciled by understanding how each satisfies the issues in different parts of the portfolio.

The benefits of the free market strategy are that business problems are resolved by IS/IT solutions close to the problem. This leads to strong motivation to make the system work, design solutions that fit the problem better in terms of need, cost and time, and, in some cases, a degree of business-driven innovation in the use of IT. This is very attractive to strong line managers with clear targets and objectives for their function, although the longer-term issues and costs of supporting the resulting systems are often overlooked in the drive to deliver short-term results. The downside is clearly that, if everyone pursues such a strategy, integration of data and systems is extremely difficult and the organization will acquire a wide range of often incompatible hardware and software. The long-term costs of such a situation can become unacceptable, but— possibly even more critically—the business overall may be prevented from gaining strategic benefits from IS/IT, which largely arise from the integration of systems and information resources.

Against that background, the free market strategy, operated within some limits to the types of technology 'permitted' in the organization, is most effective in producing many of the *support* systems needed by the various functions in the organization. It is also an appropriate strategy for some *high potential* evaluations—those driven by a business idea and that can be tested with limited IT help, to the point where the potential benefits can be understood. Beyond these two segments of the portfolio, it can be a dangerous and expensive strategy in the long term.

Monopoly

In many ways, monopoly is the opposite of free market, whereby the influence of the centralized IT management of supply options will standardize on solutions, to provide integration of data and systems and also to control the cost of technology to the organization. This may well mean that the most expedient and perhaps ideal solution in each case has to be compromised to enable the long-term best set of solutions for the organization to be achieved, at an acceptable overall cost. Each functional manager will not necessarily achieve the most cost-effective or timely satisfaction of his or her needs. This may cause resentment, unless there is a general understanding of how the various systems of the organizations interrelate across the functional areas. Often, this is because the IT monopoly has exceeded its brief and is setting priorities for what is done (probably because no one else will!), rather than optimizing how best to achieve all that needs to be done. Senior management must set the priorities to make best business use of the IT resource available or, if that is unsatisfactory to line managers, increase the size of the resource.

The positive attributes of the monopoly strategy are that, if it is well directed in terms of business priorities and if users are competent in specifying their needs, high quality, integrated, maintainable systems are procured or developed and then supported in an overall cost-effective way. This is what is required for *key operational* systems, where a low-risk, controlled approach to the development process is essential to avoid systems failure and consequent disadvantage. The monopoly strategy can be adopted for support systems, but may produce relatively high-cost solutions where cheaper, less comprehensive options would have sufficed.

Scarce Resource

This is essentially a financial strategy that controls the spend on IT through a budget limitation, within which those investments that provide the greatest return for the spend will get priority. Each investment should be financially justified and the most cost-effective solution to deliver economic benefits should be selected. Expenses are then tightly controlled against the agreed budget to ensure that the maximum net financial benefit is delivered. This approach tends to promote local specific solutions to meet local needs, and militates against flexible or integrated solutions, which will always be more expensive. The emphasis on purely economically-justified use of IT is very appropriate for *support* applications, and may produce effective key operational systems in the short term but at the expense of longer-term opportunities derived from integration. It does not encourage innovative or speculative (i.e. high potential) uses of IT, and precludes many strategic investments due to the demand for quantified financial benefits to be detailed in advance. However, a limited budget for research and development (R&D) or *high potential* activities, allocated from the centre to innovative ideas, is a version of scarce resourcing to reduce overall R&D risks.

On the other hand, setting priorities on the basis of financial 'return on investment' criteria forces both users and IT to find the lowest-cost solution, based on long-term economics, and hence encourages the buying of packaged software that is normally available for most support applications. It is more cost-effective to modify business practice to use available software than to develop new software to satisfy non-critical tasks. The strategy does focus for good reason on the IT costs, and it should be complemented by an equally strong drive to ensure that all the claimed efficiency and economic benefits are realized. Often, this is not the case, and a full audit of many apparently financially-justified investments would reveal a very poor actual return.

The above outlines are meant to describe the key attributes of each strategy sufficiently to differentiate them and allow understanding of why each is more appropriate in a particular segment of the portfolio. In each case, the strategies can be seen to correlate closely with the application driving forces and requirements described in Table 7.2. Figure 7.5 summarizes that relationship. These strategies offer considerable guidance to management about options available and choices to be made if IS/IT investments are to be managed successfully—they are important 'principles' to be understood and employed.

There are many similarities between these generic strategies and the styles of management proposed by Simon[12] to address the nature and degree of change involved in projects. Most IS/IT developments now involve business change, of increasing extent and significance and uncertain outcome as investments become more strategic. Simon considered two particular dimensions—the balance of prescription versus discretion that the project team has in determining what to do and how, against the level of explicit knowledge in the organization of how to achieve success. This resulted in four management styles:

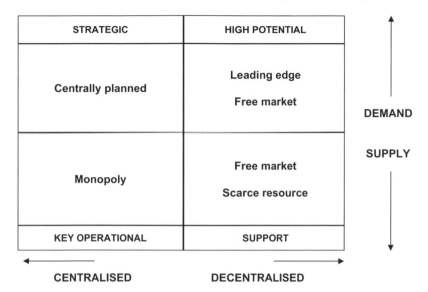

Figure 7.5   *Relationship of applications portfolio and generic IS strategies*

- *boundary control*, appropriate when the objectives and constraints are clear, but allows the project team discretion about how best to achieve the required outcome, which matches the change requirements of the support segment and correlates with aspects of *free market* and *scarce resourcing*;
- *diagnostic control*, implying a clear, prescriptive control based on sound knowledge of what has to be done to achieve performance targets, which is appropriate for key operational projects and implies similar levels of prescription as *monopoly*;
- a combination of Simon's *interactive control*, which is appropriate when there is a vision of the potential 'end point', but much to learn in order to define, scope and develop an appropriate solution and *belief system*, where the project team is expected to create a new and innovative application that will be closely congruent with the business strategy, relate to needs of the strategic investments—the uncertainties, change issues and learning required—and together are very similar to the concept of *central planning*;
- none of his styles is directly related to the R&D nature of the high potential segment, given that knowledge is the product rather than any implemented change.

In total, the strategies address the range of IS demand and IT supply issues in all segments and offer the balance of centralization and decentralization needed. *Central planning* is a demand management strategy, whereas monopoly is essentially a supply management approach; both obviously mean strong centralization of control. *Free market* and *leading edge* are demand management approaches, letting users decide and/or new technology initiate demand. *Free market* can also be used to determine supply and is obviously decentralized, and *leading edge* is dependent mainly on external supplies of technology. *Scarce resource* is a supply management strategy and is decentralized in that, once the justification rules are set, the ability of any user function to satisfy them will determine what is done. Clearly, an organization with a comprehensive portfolio will use most of the strategies simultaneously.

Using Generic Strategies in Developing the IS/IT Strategy

The generic strategies have primarily two uses in the process of developing the IS/IT strategy:

1. *Diagnostic*—they are a way of assessing the current strategies being used—a clear way of expressing how IS/IT applications and investments are actually being managed. There is a strong correlation between the successful applications developed and the strategies adopted. Equally, the failure of many investments can be simply explained—the wrong generic strategy was adopted! The generic strategies can encapsulate the apparent complexity of the existing situation and, by describing it succinctly, explain it.

2. *Formulative*—once a future portfolio of applications can be identified using the various techniques described in earlier chapters and the strengths and weaknesses of the existing applications assessed, the generic strategies can be used to identify a migration path toward the mix of approaches required in future. It is superficially attractive to say that *central planning* is needed, but it might be an overkill and it is impossible to centrally plan everything. Allowing more freedom, using new technology or tighter, monopolistic control may be more appropriate in the short term. More rigorous scarce resourcing of support systems might release resources to be deployed on strategic systems. No definitive mixture can be prescribed for every situation, but the generic strategies provide a limited number of basic options from which to select the set that matches best the application portfolio requirements. This avoids the requirement to 'invent' the strategy entirely from the 'ground up'—it is easier to define the approach by modification from proven approaches to suit the particular need and then to identify the action necessary to achieve the migration path.

In a single business-unit company, these concepts are reasonably easy to apply and, as is discussed on pages 334–337, comparisons of portfolios and strategies can be made across business units to gain further benefits.

Relating Approaches to IS Strategy Formulation and the Generic Implementation Strategies

It would appear that there should be a logical relationship between how an organization plans for its IS investments, as described in Chapter 3 (based on Earl's work), and the approach it adopts for the implementation of the resulting applications. Although the two concepts of 'planning approaches' and 'generic strategies' are derived from different sources, there are some clear connections that can be drawn, and the evolution of the generic strategies used in many organizations can be reconciled with the development of IS/IT planning described by Earl. The correlation is not perfect and there are some anomalies:

- *Organization led* planning implies cross-functional views of IS to ensure that investments are targeted on the business objectives and key themes implied by these objectives. It follows that the *centrally planned* strategy for implementation would best maintain that strategic view.
- *Business led* with IS investments, driven by the plans for the particular business areas, should lead to uncovering high potential opportunities and, in due course, perhaps to strategic investments, but will also often lead to a plethora of applications that, in the overall business context, are actually support. This aligns closely with the *free market* strategy, which is good for enabling innovation but also appropriate for support systems. In many cases, because of the purely functional view taken of the systems, the organization fails to realize the full benefits and in practice only localized, support-type benefits materialize.
- The *administrative* approach to planning implies that the main objective is budgetary control of IS/IT, which can result in a *scarce resource* approach to implementation, whereby each investment is asked to justify a budget allocation via a financial case. Alternatively, one way of ensuring overall effective administration is to bring all the resources and costs together in one place, to plan and control the whole investment program through one budget centre, normally the IS function. This effectively creates a *monopoly* channel through which all investments are vetted. This does not imply financial constraints, merely centralized budgeting and monitoring of expenditure.

- *Method driven* planning involves a highly analytical and structured approach to determining the needs and priorities for investment, and it would seem prudent to follow through with the consistent, quality-based, highly-structured implementation process that *monopoly* brings. Both the planning approach and the implementation strategy are risk averse and work well where a long-term plan to improve the performance of relatively stable business activities is needed and feasible (i.e. key operational applications).

- *Technology led* planning and *leading edge* implementation approaches appear very similar, but also seem anomalous when placed in the portfolio context. Reconciliation is not obvious, given that Earl's work suggests that technology led is most relevant to identifying only support applications, whereas *leading edge* is best applied to high potential opportunities. The difference is one of perception and time. The technology led approach implies an incremental adoption of technology as it is available and proven, to enable technology efficiency to substitute for people's inefficiency (i.e. automation through technology). *Leading edge* implies using a relatively new, possibly unproven, technology to discover whether it has strategic benefit to the business. For example, technology led planning would lead to replacement of older, inefficient environments (such as mainframes and client server) with newer, more user-efficient environments (such as Web-enabled and browser-based systems). But *leading edge* would involve a completely new type of IT being evaluated (e.g. third generation mobile phones). This difficulty in reconciliation in some ways reflects a traditional dilemma in terms of how far 'technology-push' should be allowed to influence an organization's IS/IT strategy.

In terms of the evolution of IS strategic management, described in Chapter 3, many organizations develop or evolve their mix of planning and implementation strategies in the following way (see Figure 7.6):

- *Stage 1*—no coherent strategy—a mix of *free market, monopoly* and *scarce resource*—which is likely given the 'bottom-up' process, and the only planning is of technology supply.
- *Stage 2*—a monopolistic strategy tends to prevail, linked to the need for structure and integration related to the method driven planning used to avoid systems ineffectiveness.
- *Stage 3*—a combination of *monopoly* and *scarce resourcing* is common to provide the necessary controls of implementation processes and costs in line with the emphasis on the budget (administrative led).

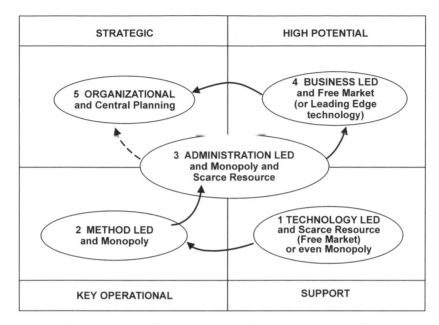

Figure 7.6   *Portfolios, planning and generic strategies evolution*

- *Stage 4*—users pursuing localized opportunities opens up *free market* activities in addition—which should be based on business led planning, in terms of local functional priorities. Alternatively, emerging new technologies provide the opportunity to innovate in creating new business processes or radically change existing ways of working. Linking the technology to a genuine business need is the first step in determining the benefits of adopting the technology.
- *Stage 5*—the use of the *centrally planned* strategy occurs for the implementation of strategic applications, as the organization identifies the links between its strategic themes and the role of IS/IT.

Those who succeed in the longer term are those who can understand, accommodate and use the required mixture of planning approaches and implementation strategies most effectively.

PORTFOLIO MANAGEMENT PRINCIPLES APPLIED TO THE APPLICATIONS PORTFOLIO

The obvious resemblance of the applications portfolio to the better known 'product portfolio' of the Boston Consulting Group and customer/channel management portfolios has already been mentioned. The similarities are important, since products and IS/IT applications must be managed according to their contribution to the business over an extended life cycle. That contribution is determined by both internal and external factors—in the case of IS/IT, the external market-driven factors are becoming increasingly important. The lessons from 'other portfolios' have become more pertinent still as IS/IT becomes integral to products, services and relationships with customers and suppliers. Comparisons will be drawn directly with portfolios of products/services, though similar parallels exist with customer portfolios.

First, both applications and products have life cycles, and move around the matrix over time. High potential applications and wildcat products are both risk investments that need to be carefully assessed as to whether or not they are of strategic importance or can become star products. As the competitive balance is restored and the application is commonly in place across the industry, it becomes key operational, as a star product should become a cash cow when the market matures. Finally, as the industry moves on to a new competitive basis, applications may be of support value only, and, similarly, products move from cash cows to dogs eventually. It is important in both cases to avoid high potential or wildcat investments from drifting straight down into the support or dog quadrant, as a result of indecisive management or an inability to capitalize on any knowledge gained.

Second, both applications and products require investment funding. This is easily seen with products, where the cash generated by today's profitable products is reinvested in cash-hungry future products. For applications, this implies reinvesting the benefits derived from today's systems into new applications. What are these benefits? They are:

- skills, knowledge and experienced resources;
- the capability to develop and manage complex business systems and the evolving 'IT supply chain';
- management commitment to the use of IS/IT in the business, based on successes achieved and a perception of the value of IS/IT investments;
- data (or information) held in the existing applications, if well organized, is a potential source of advantage if exploited through its use in strategic applications.

Lack of reinvestment will in all cases cause the value of previous investments to depreciate, steadily but surely, over time.

Third, both applications and products need to be managed and have resources allocated in accordance with their business importance, not their technical or operational peculiarities. Management capability and resources are normally in short supply, and need to be continuously reallocated to obtain the best business results and maximum benefits from the overall portfolio. Balancing the available resources and expertise to match the evolving portfolio needs is essential to sustain success.

Overall, the main reason the product portfolio model offers useful input to the application portfolio is that it reflects the competitive business environment. The model was developed to assist in managing and planning in an uncertain, market-driven environment, where management decisions are made within a total environment that can only be influenced, not determined. IS/IT is also subject to the forces of the marketplace—external parameters now define the effectiveness of an organization's IS/IT management. Of the various analyses and conclusions that can be drawn from business portfolio models, some have particular relevance to the application portfolio and, hence, provide valuable insights for managing IS/IT. In their book, Hartman and Sifonis[13] draw very similar parallels in describing the issues and approaches in their 'e-business value matrix'.

Figure 7.7 superimposes the product and applications portfolio matrices. Maximizing the long-term contribution of products depends on successful management in the relevant quadrant and successful transition management across quadrants, as determined by prevailing market

STRATEGIC (STARS)	HIGH POTENTIAL (WILDCATS)
- Continuous innovation - Vertical integration - High value-added	- Process research and design - Minimal integration - Cost control
- Defensive innovation - Effective resource utilization - High quality	- Disinvest/Rationalize - Efficiency - Sustained quality
KEY OPERATIONAL (CASH COWS)	SUPPORT (DOGS)

Figure 7.7   *The business/systems portfolio matrix*

forces. IS application management depends on the same two factors. The particular parallels will be drawn by following the evolution of an application around the matrix.

High Potential (Wildcats)

IS/IT high potential applications resemble wildcat products due to the degree of uncertainty of success—the amount of risk they involve. Many will fail. Identifying and then transforming the successes into the next phase of the life cycle is the objective. This implies dealing effectively with the failures and not pouring good money and resources after bad. Three particular approaches to management are appropriate to achieving this:

- *Process R&D—not 'product'*. From the business lessons: how to make, market, distribute, resource the new product, not just achieve the ultimate in product design. A common weakness in many firms is 'over-engineering' products—satisfying the designer, not the customer! A similar problem exists in IS—satisfying the technical professional, not the user. Any prototyping or pilot implementation of an application should be undertaken to find out how the organization, and/or its trading partners, can benefit most from a new use of IT, not to discover all that the technology can do. Many prototypes of electronic commerce, knowledge management and CRM systems have failed—not because there were no benefits to be gained from the technology, but because the organization failed to discover how to implement it in the way that would deliver those benefits.
- *Minimal integration*. While being evaluated, risky ventures should be separated from mainline activities. Should they fail, aspects of the business should not have become dependent on them and, at low cost, the prototype can be aborted. Neither will the evaluation be clouded by issues not directly relevant to it. A key part of the evaluation is to decide how the integration can best be achieved— therefore, any initial integration could preclude the most effective options. Often, new IT applications produce disappointing results due to evaluations that are prejudiced by existing activities to which they are attached. Non-separation of new products has caused similar problems—contribution to the business being impossible to assess, and commitments having been undertaken that make decisions to pull out expensive.
- *Cost control*. The only common factor that applies across prototypes is money. A budget is the only consistent link with normal management processes, where the unknown is being explored. This need for

strict budget control reinforces the need for non-integration to ensure that the specific financial implications can be assessed. To improve the cost control further, it is usually worth restricting the time allowed for evaluation, even though it is difficult to predict how long it will take when it is a unique R&D project. Most evaluations can be made in three to six months: sufficient to determine whether further investment is worthwhile. Even if the work is not 'finished' (it never will be!), it is better to review the progress formally after, say, three months and decide whether further work is still needed or whether the evaluation has provided sufficient evidence to proceed. Strong cost-based management is the only effective control available, and it must be understood that the 'investment' may have to be written off. It is better if these evaluations are funded from an R&D budget—either specific to IS/IT or a business R&D fund— and not compete with funds required for the rest of the portfolio.

As new technology options are now emerging faster than ever, even relatively conservative organizations will need to 'experiment' more in the high potential segment to avoid falling behind their competitors in IT use. Successful management of IS/IT 'R&D' is becoming an increasingly important aspect of most firms' strategies, but one with which many are unfamiliar.

Strategic (Stars)

A star product or strategic application is one that the company is dependent upon for future success in a competitive, changing marketplace, where any advantage gained can be expected to be eroded quickly. The value of the application can only be judged by its effectiveness *vis-à-vis* competitors. Using the Internet to link customers directly into an organization's order-taking systems will only work if it is of value to the customer—a judgement that the firm can influence, but the customer will make!

Again, particular approaches should be adopted:

* *Continuous innovation*—this applies to what the system does and how it does it, to increase its value-added as an integral part of the business. These improvements will be business driven, based on the need to sustain or increase the perceived advantages. Whether to spend more money will be a business manager's decision, based not simply on return-on-investment calculations, but on the risk to the business if the system fails to stay ahead of the competition. A website offering access for buying products may become obsolete

very quickly if a competitor offers advice and other service features that the customer finds more valuable or easier to use.

- *High value-added and vertical integration*—in order to achieve appropriate innovation, the business manager has to understand how the system can enhance the business process and then have the capability to make further changes to increase the value created, or improve process performance, as and when required. This implies business control of IS/IT resources and the right to satisfy the unique needs of the particular situation without prevarication or accepting lower value-added compromises. The processes of systems management should be vertically integrated with the business unit management to obtain maximum strategic leverage from the system or the information it delivers. Most applications in the strategic box are normally associated with a highly information-intensive part of the business, and the business manager will not be able to take full advantage if he or she has insufficient discretion over IS/IT deployment.

This process of value-adding is expensive and resource intensive and is only justified where IS/IT can change the business performance to gain a specific, sustainable advantage. As the rest of the industry catches up, diminishing returns will result from adding further value and greater returns can be obtained by reducing the cost of matching performance to industry norms.

Key Operational (Cash Cows)

As with its cash cows, an organization expects its key operational systems to make a significant and lasting contribution to the business. This depends on keeping the product or system in line with current market and business demands in the most cost-effective way. The particular business lessons in this case are:

- *Defensive innovation*—the system should only be enhanced or re-developed in response to changes in the business that threaten to put the business at risk through a reduction of competitive capability (i.e. avoiding disadvantage). This risk should be quantified as far as possible to ensure that the expenditure involved gives a net benefit over time. Deciding on further investment now requires a joint evaluation—users deciding the benefit or risk of action or inaction and IT professionals identifying the costs and consequences of any action.
- *High quality*—key operational systems are expected to have an extended life over which they make a significant business contribu-

tion. Compromises on system quality will reduce that effective economic life due to increased user costs for 'workarounds' to overcome system deficiencies or increased IT 'maintenance' costs due to increasing numbers of systems problems. In the long term, the low cost of support depends on professional quality management—data and processing integrity and accurate integration of the system with other key operational systems and databases as well as related processes and procedures.

- *Effective resource utilization*—key operational systems cannot be afforded the dedication of resources given to strategic systems—it is not justified. This implies the integration of the support for the system with other systems—sharing resources and expertise to reduce the costs. This is a familiar lesson from systems development—transferring the management of a system from a dedicated development team to a general support group after implementation. This reduces the cost, improves development quality control and discourages continuing poorly-justified 'enhancements'. There is another important reason: integrating the system's support activities will allow opportunities to reduce costs further from general improvements in IT infrastructure capacity and capability, whose justification is based on the number and range of applications that use it.

The overall approach to managing key operational systems is to reduce costs while sustaining the business value derived from the use of the system. Integration of systems and resources with other applications will provide this net gain.

Support (Dogs)

Support systems, like dog products, are not critical to an organization's future, unless they waste valuable resources or the marketplace changes unexpectedly. The business lessons are therefore:

- *Disinvest/rationalize*—reducing the organization's commitments to systems can be achieved in a number of ways: by using software packages and/or outsourcing their operation and support. Each involves the substitution of resources—money for scarce skills— and the decision is essentially a financial one, which often gives very good returns. Alternative solutions are available for these applications, because they offer no competitive advantage and service/ package providers can make a profit from the range and volume of similar applications in many companies.

- *Sustained quality and efficiency*—the quality of the system should be maintained in proportion to the costs of failure and, if necessary, calculated risks should be taken, based on the efficiency of resource use involved. In general, the system should not be enhanced unless there is a very demonstrable economic case—to ensure that resources are only consumed where a return is certain. The disinvestment process discussed above will automatically reduce the pace of enhancement to that of the generally-available service or package. The general rule here is to adjust the business activity to fit the package, not the other way round—or costs will increase dramatically, not reduce!

A number of immediate observations can be made from the above analysis:

- The rate of enhancement to any application should reduce as it progresses around the life cycle.
- The justification for application investment becomes more quantifiable over the evolution, and financial evaluation becomes both more meaningful and more decisive in the key operational and support quadrants. This is dealt with in more depth in Chapter 9.
- To achieve the appropriate balance of resource use to business contribution, different management approaches are required in the different quadrants—which implies that the system may have to be rebuilt or at least reimplemented when it crosses the boundaries to optimize the net organizational benefits. For instance, the degree of enhancement and probable expediency of change control in the strategic quadrant can militate against effective resource utilization when it becomes key operational, unless some consolidation or rationalization is undertaken during the transfer.

Some of the key issues described above that have to be considered as an application migrates around the portfolio are summarized in Figure 7.8.

While the migration from high potential via strategic to key operational is the most common sequence and delivers the maximum contribution over time, mismanagement in the early stages can reverse the logic and outcome. This occurs most frequently when applications using a new technology are allowed to evolve without effective management. Based on studies of Intranet applications,[14] a number of examples showed a different evolution:

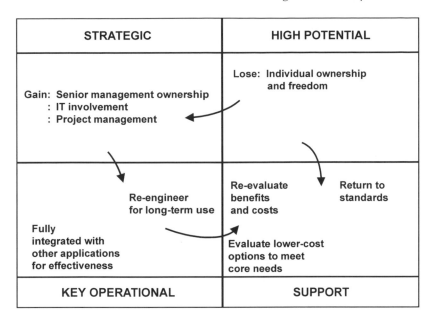

Figure 7.8 Key issues in managing the evolution of an application over time

- Initial experimentation (high potential) enabled knowledge-sharing applications to be developed, saving time, etc., but the benefits were not 'strategic'. Therefore, they soon became support applications; they were still used, but the costs of support were minimized.
- Over time, due to their ease of use, the applications were relied upon as a source of operational information, even though the 'content' was not managed in a disciplined way—there were no procedures for maintenance or clear ownership of the components of the information base. Eventually, a major operational problem or failure occurred due to incorrect or out-of-date information content. Only then was the key role that the 'informal' information system was now fulfilling realized and appropriate disciplines, procedures and support resources put in place.

In one example, salespeople were selling services to customers based on information from the (informal) Intranet catalogue. The company no longer offered some of those services, but no procedure or control existed to remove the out-of-date information. Only when contracts were about to be signed did the customer (and salesperson) discover the problem. Several valuable contracts were lost! This is not an issue of Intranet-based applications, it can happen when informal, free market management of applications appears in the key operational segment, due to a change in the business role of the system.

Application Management Styles

Another important concept developed from the product portfolio is how the management style should change during a product's life cycle in response to the evolving issues to be addressed. Since managers cannot be totally adaptive in style, this often implies changing the manager! Equally, different styles of management are required to success-fully develop and deliver the different types of application in the portfo-lio. The lessons of product portfolio management offer significant guidance.

High potential applications require a similar style to wildcat products, namely entrepreneurial, to champion the application through phases of doubt or decide to stop if the potential is not realizable. 'Entrepreneurs' are highly motivated, expecting personal recognition of their success. At the same time, they recognize that they must not be judged to have failed by others and will either be adept at avoiding failure or be the first to decide it is not worth proceeding. Also, they do not obey 'the rules' and will cause change and innovation, which implies challenging preconceived ideas or ignoring or bypassing accepted custom and practice. This mode of operation is very appropriate for the high potential situation, but would be wholly inappropriate elsewhere in the matrix.

Strategic systems require more nurturing, to gain organizational accep-tance through demonstrated contribution to future strategy. A style of 'developer' best describes the type of manager required: someone who will build a team and develop the resources necessary to achieve the task objectives. Other terms to describe this are 'organizational climber'—someone whose career ambitions will be met by being related to the achievement of organizational success—or 'empire builder'—a much maligned term! A developer is a planner who achieves results through others, a team manager who moulds the resource to match the needs of achieving the objective and who can be flexible to changing circum-stances—adapting the means to achieve the end result.

Key operational systems require a different style of management entirely: that of a 'controller' who is risk-averse, wanting everything to be done correctly and failure never to occur. Assurance of success implies reducing risk to a minimum via strict adherence to procedure and standards, and building an organizational structure and mentality that is self-checking and control conscious. The best way of achieving quality control is to build it into the organization structure through job respon-sibilities and procedures. The controller approach is essentially inflexible and resistant to change, since change causes confusion and error! Within clearly defined parameters, the status quo will be defended and requirements carefully scrutinized and evaluated, before changes will be allowed, in order to prevent business problems and even serious disadvantages due to systems failure.

Support applications are ideally best managed by 'caretakers', who get their satisfaction from achieving 'the impossible, with no resources, repeatedly' and have to be congratulated for it! It is a reactive, problem-solving approach, where planning and resource management are less important than getting the job done expediently and efficiently to the satisfaction of the client. This implies a multitasking, flexible approach to achieving results that are not of any strategic impact, but will cause a major distraction from more strategic matters if not dealt with in a timely and adept manner. Support systems have no great future potential impact, but can be a constant source of irritation if mismanaged.

An entrepreneur is impatient to achieve results to demonstrate his or her personal capability, whereas a developer has longer-term career aims of achieving success through the organization. A controller wants to prevent the failure of the organization and a caretaker wants to be recognized as an effective user of limited resources in solving problems. The nature of these management styles reflects the generic strategies required to manage the various components of the portfolio:

- an entrepreneur is a free marketeer, who pays little attention to established procedure;
- a developer is a central planner, close to the organizational goals, who builds resources to achieve results;
- a controller is a monopolist, uncomfortable with anything outside his or her control;
- a caretaker is a scarce resourcer, proving that he or she can achieve as much with less!

If the strategy is to be achieved overall, then the appropriate management styles must be adopted; the strategy will not be achieved by managers who are 'square pegs in round holes'—a developer managing in the support segment will produce ever larger, more significant versions of relatively inconsequential systems; a controller expected to evaluate a high potential opportunity will never take the first risk, and so on. It must be remembered that all these roles are important and each has a major part to play in managing a complex portfolio over time. The basic attributes are summarized in Figure 7.9.

STRATEGIC	HIGH POTENTIAL
DEVELOPER - Organization goal seeker - Risk accommodating - 'Central planner'	ENTREPRENEUR - Personal achiever - Risk taker - 'Free marketeer'
CONTROLLER - Long term/quality solutions, stability - Risk reducing - 'Monopolist'	CARETAKER - Immediate/Efficient solutions - Risk avoiding - 'Scarce resourcer'
KEY OPERATIONAL	SUPPORT

Figure 7.9   *Management styles*

MANAGING APPLICATION PORTFOLIOS IN MULTI-UNIT ORGANIZATIONS

Once IS strategies for each business unit can be expressed in terms of the application portfolio, it becomes easier to identify possible mutual benefits across the organization, by taking advantage of successful innovations as well as meeting similar needs more economically. Figure 7.10 depicts the minimum gains to be made by a coordinated approach across the organization, when the applications portfolios are compared across business units.

In the support segment, even if the businesses are diverse, the applications are likely to address similar administrative requirements, and packages are a common choice. At worst, a limited number of packages should be used; at best, a single, common suite of applications could be used. This will obviously depend on the diversity of the types of business. For example, manufacturing and financial services organizations will require different systems, but several types of retail companies in different market sectors could easily use common accounting systems.

The same logic applies throughout the matrix, but the benefits of commonality of actual applications are likely to decrease as we move from support to key operational to strategic, although in the strategic

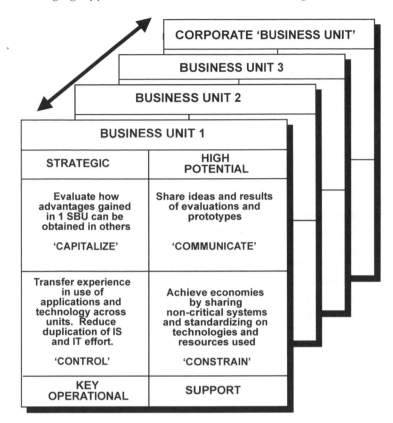

Figure 7.10   *Portfolio management in a multi-business-unit organization*

quadrant benefits may be realizable through different implementations of the same idea. Transferring the knowledge gained from one organization to another may accelerate the development of strategic applications. This implies business-based sharing of how to achieve the benefits available, even if the details of the applications vary. Links to suppliers, for instance, are likely to achieve similar benefits to manufacturing and retail companies.

It could well be that, due to the different state of development of the different industries in which the units operate, a key operational system in one business could provide a competitive advantage in another. One company was able to transfer a system that was well established for managing consumer goods inventories and distribution to a chemical industry business. The approach was new to the chemical industry and enabled that unit to gain an advantage through better customer service levels and lower stock holdings.

This kind of opportunity can only be identified if the existing and required future portfolios of the different businesses are compared, within the context of the competitive environments and strategies of those businesses. However, there is an inherent danger in this approach, if business units are 'forced' to accept systems from other units for largely economic reasons, without due recognition of their differing business situations, competitive priorities and organizational competencies.

The real objectives are to ensure that opportunities are not missed or that time, resources and funds are not needlessly wasted. This can only be achieved if a similar rationale has been used to define the portfolios. If the effort of the IS/IT strategy process is worthwhile, then additional work to build on or share ideas could yield significantly greater benefits and avoid considerable duplication of effort across the overall business.

There is consistency between the rationale for the degree of coordination advised for each segment with the planning and implementation approaches described on pages 311–318. The generic strategies can be used to summarize the actual or required relationship between the corporate body and the business units, and among those units. In a diversified conglomerate, evolving through acquisition and divestment of businesses, the corporate IS/IT generic strategy is likely to consist of a minimal centralized (monopolistic) component—perhaps financial control systems—with an otherwise free-market philosophy. This is appropriate to the business.

However, if the company is predominantly in one industry where synergy is a potential source of advantage, the business unit strategies are likely to be supplemented at a corporate level by some central planning of IS/IT applications and a monopolistic control over the ways of meeting key operational needs to avoid proliferation and incompatibility of solutions. Where the organization cannot benefit from vertical synergy, but consists of like types of company (e.g. manufacturing, retail or financial services), similarity of functional requirements might be more effectively or economically satisfied from a central utility (monopoly) or by 'monopolistic' management of outsourced supply, for those systems that are needed by many companies.

In Figure 7.10, the term *constrain* in the support segment implies corporate scarce resourcing for applications that are not unique in any of the units. Monopolistic *control* is suggested for key operational applications to reduce unnecessary diversity over time to enable both reduction in costs through effective resource use and to develop and sustain expertise in application operation and use. *Capitalizing* on strategic application success requires some (business) central planning across the units to determine whether and how the same benefits can accrue across the organization. Finally, while any corporate 'interference', however well intended, can stifle innovation in the units, sharing knowledge of new technology, its capabilities and limitations—by ensuring the results of R&D work is made available to others—could increase the speed of exploitation and reduce wasted effort. The *communication* facilitation is probably best established at the corporate IT centre, via a 'bulletin board' or similar knowledge-sharing mechanism.

SUMMARY

This chapter has tried to demonstrate the rationale behind adopting an applications portfolio management concept as a core framework within the IS/IT strategies. The basic 2×2 matrix model has been explored from a variety of directions to identify the potential advice and guidance it can offer organizational and IS/IT management in defining, selecting and implementing the variety of applications required. While not all the advice is identical—after all, it has been derived from many diverse sources—it is never contradictory, and the patterns that emerge are generally consistent. It must be reasserted that the simple model does not reflect the full complexity of the IS/IT strategic management environment, but it does allow much of the complexity to be analysed to enable the issues and alternative solutions to be understood better.

From what has been said in this chapter, it follows that different approaches will be needed to deal with the detailed aspects of resourcing and technology development and deployment in the segments of the matrix:

- different development methodologies, processes and application development tools will be more or less appropriate;
- different degrees and types of involvement of executive and line management in IS/IT governance and projects;
- different IS organizational structures, services competencies and resourcing policies including procuring and supporting the required technologies;
- how IS/IT investments are justified/evaluated, prioritized and costs allocated—a singular approach will tend to produce one type of application to the exclusion of others.

These and other aspects of the issues of business and IS/IT management that enable the successful evolution of the portfolio will be considered in more depth in later chapters. The objective of the IS/IT strategy process is not to have a strategy document *per se*, but to develop and sustain the organization's ability to implement the ideal set of business applications in the most effective way. This requires appropriate demand and supply management approaches in each segment and coherent means of migrating systems around the matrix in relation to their evolving business contribution.

ENDNOTES

1. F.W. McFarlan, 'Information technology changes the way you compete', *Harvard Business Review*, May–June 1984, 93–103.
2. M.J. Earl, *Management Strategies for Information Technology*, Prentice-Hall, Englewood Cliffs, New Jersey, 1989; M.J. Earl, 'Experiences in strategic information systems planning', *MIS Quarterly*, Vol. 17, No. 1, 1993, 1–24; M.J. Earl, 'Information systems strategy ... why planning techniques are not the answer', *Business Strategy Review*, Vol. 7, No. 1, 1996, 54–67.
3. J.M. Ward, 'Information systems and technology: Application portfolio management—an assessment of matrix-based analysis', *Journal of Information Technology*, Vol. 3, No. 3, 1988, 205–215.
4. C.H. Sullivan, 'Systems planning in the information age', *Sloan Management Review*, Winter, 1985, 3–11.
5. M.C. Munro and S.L. Huff, 'Information technology and corporate strategy', *Business Quarterly*, Summer, 1985.
6. R.I. Benjamin, J.F. Rockart, M.S. Scott Morton and J. Wyman, 'Information technology: A strategic opportunity', *Sloan Management Review*, Spring, 1984, 3–10.
7. R.D. Galliers, 'Information technology planning within the corporate planning process', in A. Duling and D. Berry, eds, *Controlling Projects within an Integrated Management Framework*, Pergamon Infotech State of the Art Report, Maidenhead, UK, 1987.
8. B. Ives and G.P. Learmonth, 'The information system as a competitive weapon', *Communications of the ACM*, December, 1984, 1193–1201.
9. R.D. Galliers, 'Information systems and technology planning within a competitive strategy framework', in P. Griffiths, ed., *The Role of Information Management in Competitive Success*, Pergamon Infotech State of the Art Report, Maidenhead, UK, 1987.
10. A. Hartman and J. Sifonis, *Net Ready—Strategies for Success in the e-Economy*, McGraw-Hill, New York, 2000.
11. G.L. Parsons, *Fitting Information Systems Technology to the Corporate Needs: The Linking Strategy*, Harvard Business School Press, Boston, 1983, Teaching Note 9-183-176.
12. R. Simon, 'Control in an age of empowerment', *Harvard Business Review*, March–April 1995, 80–88.
13. A. Hartman and J. Sifonis, *Net Ready—Strategies for Success in the e-Economy*, McGraw-Hill, New York, 2000.
14. J.M. Ward, K. Breu and P.N. Murray, 'Success factors in leveraging the corporate information and knowledge resource through Intranets', *Knowledge Management and Virtual Organizations*, Idea Group Publishing, Hershey, Pennsylvania, 2000, pp. 306–320.

8
Strategic Management of IS/IT: Organizing and Resourcing

So far, the book has demonstrated how the potential that IS/IT offers a business or organization can be assessed in relation to its environment, objectives and strategy. The focus so far has been on the inputs to the strategy development process and the tools and techniques of analysis and formulation. Chapter 7 used the application portfolio matrix to show how the approaches taken to managing IS/IT in an organization are inextricably linked in a cause-and-effect relationship with the portfolio. High-level (generic) management strategies were reviewed, from which organizations can derive a mix that is appropriate to their needs, leading to a set of management approaches to achieving success in managing applications across the portfolio. In order to develop an overall organizational capability to exploit IS/IT effectively over an extended period, further aspects of IS/IT require coherent and consistent strategic management. These key strategy areas are:

- for managing *investments* in IS/IT, to deliver the maximum value in terms of benefits to the business;
- for managing the data, *information* and knowledge resources of the organization to ensure that its business value is fully exploited and protected;
- for managing the acquisition, deployment and utilization of information *technologies*, through IS/IT services, to the benefit of the organization and relationships with technology and service suppliers;
- for organizational management of the range of IS/IT-related *resources*, the activities they perform and the governance and administration of IS/IT, both in its unique features and in relationships with other parts of the business.

This chapter deals with the last of these in order to establish an organizational context for the more specific strategies for the management of investments, information and infrastructure and the associated IT services. Earl[1] notes that it is the 'organisational issues in the strategic management of IT that matter most', and research highlights that what distinguishes organizations that are successful with IT is not technical sophistication, but how they manage IS/IT.[2] This chapter presents models and frameworks for guiding management action to address the organization dimensions of the IS/IT strategy. The 'organizational' strategy for IS/IT resources cannot be prescriptive. It must evolve over time as the organization becomes more dependent upon, and demands more from, IS/IT. More freedom of action in terms of greater discretion or tighter control of resource use will be appropriate at different stages of that evolution. With the increased use of outsourcing, the selection of different sourcing options for services and resources will depend both on the economics of IT supply and the evolving mix of business applications over time. The organizational context also exerts both enabling and constraining influences that shape the ultimate strategy.

THE STRATEGIC MANAGEMENT REQUIREMENT

The formulation of strategy is only the first step on the road to successful IS/IT management. The strategy must be implemented, and delivering the results and updating the strategy to reflect changing business and IS/IT environments are obviously critical to eventual success. Failure to achieve the intended strategy is often the result of organizational, political and cultural issues being inadequately addressed.

The basic IS/IT strategy development model (reproduced in Figure 8.1) ignores explicit reference to the inevitable 'refinement' of strategy during planning and implementation, and its continuing adaptation as achievements (or otherwise) occur or any environmental input changes. As noted in Chapter 2, strategic management is a combination of formal planning, creativity, innovation, informal thinking and opportunism, all of which must be effectively exploited and integrated. From establishing the strategic direction, through defining specific strategies to eventual achievement of results, the balance moves from formality to relative informality and opportunism. This set of activities also requires some feedback or control mechanism to ensure that plans and their implementation are appropriate for the strategic direction or to enable changes of direction should achievement prove impossible. Sometimes, the strategy as originally formulated has to be revisited as a new strategic context emerges; at other times, the implementation processes have to be

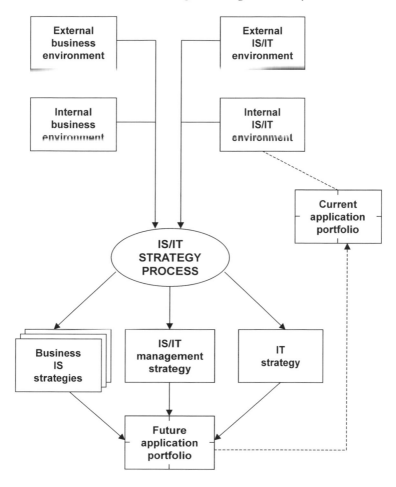

Figure 8.1   *The IS/IT strategic model*

reconsidered in the light of the strategy itself. Figure 8.2 depicts these relationships.

In order that the formal strategy process does not inhibit the realization of each step in the implementation of strategy and changes to the strategy, policies and practices must be established to avoid slowing up business progress. At the same time, many organizations have suffered the consequences of lack of coordination in IS/IT management, which can cause the existing (and potential) application portfolios effectively to disintegrate. Figure 8.3 considers how this might happen: the strategic direction is disregarded as localized opportunistic developments and/or

FORMAL STRATEGIC PLANNING

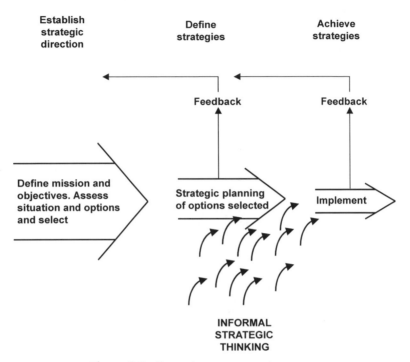

Figure 8.2   *Strategic management processes*

uncoordinated business initiatives effectively disable the overall IS/IT strategy.

In the longer term, this failure can have three major effects:

1. the systems that are developed and implemented do not meet overall business needs;
2. resources are misused;
3. strategy formulation is essentially a retrofitting process, producing enormous rework.

Any or all three can occur. The cause can usually be attributed to three main reasons:

1. lack of alignment between the business and IS strategies;
2. uncoordinated management of IS demand and IT supply;
3. over-centralization or decentralization of responsibility regarding

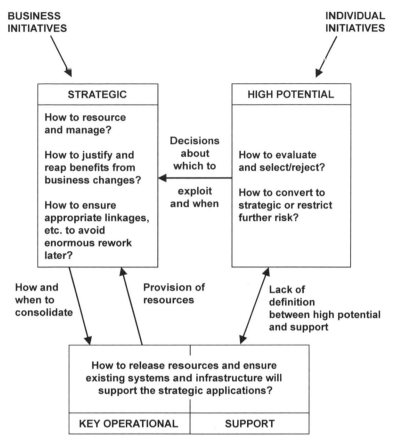

Figure 8.3   *Avoiding the disintegration of the applications portfolio*

IS/IT investments with lack of mechanisms to ensure coherence across centralized and devolved IS/IT decisions and activities.

It is the effectiveness of the overall IS/IT management strategy and resulting policies and practices that determines whether all other aspects of strategy development and implementation succeed. This IS/IT management strategy must not only deal with the 'rational' aspects of strategy like investment appraisal but also with behavioural and cultural considerations. While defining such strategies is predominantly an intellectual process, implementing them requires appropriate behaviours throughout the organization.

The central objectives of the IS/IT management strategy are listed in Table 8.1. These are requirements that senior management must ensure

Table 8.1   *Requirements of strategic management*

- To ensure IS/IT strategies, policies and plans reflect business objectives and strategies.
- To ensure potential business advantages from IS/IT are identified and exploited.
- To ensure strategies, etc. are viable in terms of business risks.
- To establish appropriate resource levels and reconcile contention/set priorities.
- To create a 'culture' for the management of IS/IT that reflects the corporate culture.
- To monitor the progress of business-critical IS/IT activities.
- To achieve the best balance between centralization and devolvement of IS/IT decision making.

---

are dealt with by clear delegation of responsibility and/or appropriate organizational processes. The rest of this chapter will consider how these can be addressed, in practical terms and in conjunction with the need to manage the development of the application portfolio and supporting technologies and resources.

It might be tempting to include 'corporate information systems'—the set of applications required by the corporate body—in this overall management strategy, but they are essentially an IS strategy to satisfy corporate requirements, not issues of management policy. Equally, potential synergy between systems or benefits from rationalization of systems across the business are obviously of interest to corporate management, but, again, they are application or technology strategy issues. A 'management edict' to use common systems or software from a particular vendor (such as SAP, Baan, PeopleSoft or JD Edwards for ERP applications) across a number of business units will only work if the businesses concerned can see the benefits in their applications. The investment and organizational policies should encourage these approaches, but, in many cases, the policies, like accounting practices, can mitigate against the intended strategy.

Hayward,[3] in an article on developing IS strategies, argues for a similar structure for the IS/IT strategy in terms of the model in Figure 8.1. He identifies a 'management strategy', an 'applications strategy' and a 'technology strategy' as the components, as in the model used in this book. Earl[4] made a similar distinction, using the terms 'information management strategy', 'information systems strategy' and 'information technology strategy', respectively. He considers the information management strategy as 'putting the management into IT' or outlining the way IT is to be managed in the organization.[5] He portrays it as addressing questions such as the mission and organization of the IS function, control and accounting for IT, and the design of the management processes required across all the IT activities of an organization.

ORGANIZING STRATEGIES FOR IS/IT MANAGEMENT

This section will consider not only aspects of overall organizational alternatives and the position of IS functions in the organization but also organizing options (structure and resource configuration), allocation of decision rights (centralization versus devolution) and resourcing strategies (both insourcing and outsourcing). While these depend on the approaches adopted for information, application and technology management, it is most critical that the IS function is organized to satisfy its 'customers' requirements as well as to manage itself effectively. And customers today are not necessarily located in the business, but can be actual customers (e.g. as with e-banking) and suppliers (e.g. as with e-supply chains).

In addition to defining organizational responsibilities concerning IS/IT management, corporate management also has to decide *if* and *how* that structure should be overlaid by other 'governing' processes such as committees or steering groups for coordination and control. Most large private sector and public bodies have realized that no one organizational alternative can achieve appropriate management of all aspects of IS/IT. To overcome this, upward of 80% of major US and UK organizations have constituted some form of IS/IT management steering group.

However, in many of these organizations, the 'steering group' is seen as a failure, or at best an irrelevance, by both line management and IS managers, and even by some senior executives. Others, however, are very effective as mechanisms for developing a more concerted approach to the strategic management of IS/IT. The reasons for these differing realities will also be explored and an overall 'ideal' model for effective governance will be outlined.

Beyond Centralization versus Decentralization

The positioning of the main IT resource of the organization in the organizational structure has been problematic since 'computing' began, but the problems have become compounded as IS/IT has pervaded and affected many parts of business. Over the years, a 'tug of war' has often developed between centralized and decentralized control of IS/IT resources. Much has been written about the positioning, structuring and organization of the IS function, or indeed whether or not one should even exist, and the findings from these studies will be drawn upon in this section.[6] Getting it wrong can be very costly, but how can an organization know when it is right?

For example, in a decentralized engineering group, a very centralized monopolistic IS function was failing to provide a satisfactory service. Rather than evaluate why, the management bowed to political pressure from the operating company managers and rapidly devolved IS/IT resources to the business units. Systems development virtually ceased and support for existing systems was adversely affected. Many of the best people left, and at no site was there sufficient resource to achieve major developments, while local management had no experience of running an IS group. Gradually, it was realized that some aspects of IS/IT should be recentralized to avoid duplicated expertise, avail of synergies, etc. and that some aspects, reinforced by user resource investments, should remain in the units. There are many similar instances of swings between extreme centralization and decentralization, neither of which proves successful, for the rather obvious reason that—as seen in Chapter 7—some things are best centralized and others devolved!

Undoubtedly, much application expertise is devolving into the user organization, although, in the process, the quality of many systems and the integrity of data can decline. At the same time, the need to develop technical infrastructures and information architectures is forcing more centralization of certain responsibilities. Discussion regarding the organization of IS/IT and the role of the IS function often re-emerged as a consequence of the proliferation of 'e'-related activities, which have often resulted in even more disparate systems that are not integrated—a situation referred to as 'islands of automation' in the 1970s and 1980s! Also of significance is the fact that these activities have often failed to make any real contribution to the overall business. For example, Citigroup, parent company of Citibank, Soloman Smith Barney and Travelers Insurance, launched e-Citi in 1997 as an incubator for Web-businesses. The task of e-Citi was to keep the rest of the group on its toes and was free to cannibalize business from other group companies. However, the only thing it managed to do was gobble up money—between 1998 and 2000 it lost over US$1 billion. From being seen as separate from the business, the Internet is now seen as an integral part of corporate strategy and a Corporate Internet Operating Group has been established to oversee the complete Net strategy across all businesses.[7]

It is not easy to produce a general statement of the ideal organizational arrangement for IS/IT resources. A number of factors will always have to be weighed for any organization:

● the organization's dependence on IT;

- its stage of maturity in terms of its application portfolio;
- the geography of the enterprise, especially for organizations with a global presence;
- its business diversity and rate of change of the types of business and competitive pressures in each business;
- the potential benefits of synergy between businesses in both trading goods and services and information exchange;
- the economics of resourcing, obtaining and deploying skills.

Nearly 20 years ago, *EDP Analyser*,[8] in an edition entitled 'Organising for the 1990s', focused on how the role of IS/IT was changing at that time. It observed the trend away from 'production' to 'service' orientation, and to providing the architectural support for the applications, and concluded that the data or information architecture will become a critical component of strategy, which 'someone' in the organization must tackle. However, despite the passage of time, this aspect still remains so.

'Whither the IT organization?' was the question posed by La Belle and Nyce,[9] who discussed how the IS/IT resource was reorganized in Manufacturers Trust Co.[10] to respond to a major company reorganization. The company considered many alternatives before arriving at the need to 'recentralize' (as they put it) some aspects of IS/IT in order to support a decentralization of the business into five units to match the customers each served. Previously, IS/IT had been steadily decentralizing, but in support of a different business structure. They concluded that, while the business units should be responsible for applications—architecture, development and operation—certain areas should be centralized. These included: telecommunications, hardware and software architecture, information architecture, risk management and security, shared services and utilities, and human resources.

In each of these areas, the central IT group would be able to assist, advise and, if necessary, control the activities of the business units where they could provide improved economies or supply-related options and/or demonstrate added value from corporate synergy. To do this, the activities of the units had to be coordinated with the central architectural development via a 'steering group' structure, which is similar to that described later in this chapter. This brief description does scant justice to the detail of the restructuring involved and the careful planning and implementation required to change not only the organization but also the culture to accept the implied changes in responsibility. Table 8.2 summarizes the divisions of responsibility for one aspect—'IT architecture management'.

If the overall application strategy is to fit the business strategy, the business unit management must be accountable and responsible for

Table 8.2 *Division of responsibility: IT architecture management (source: after La Belle and Nyce)*

Function	Central IT group	Business unit operations
Develop and maintain information architecture	● Monitor process; provide assistance if requested	● Complete business architectures defining business (within sectors) by location ● Complete translation of strategy into technology requirements ● Define information architecture
Develop and maintain application architecture	● Set standards, monitor process ● Review architectures and report on adequacy to Technology Committee ● Ensure appropriate commonality	● Define requirements and develop architecture ● Coordinate between units for common businesses
Develop and maintain data architectures	● Coordinate development/ establishment of common database management process ● Create/maintain corporate databases	● Define requirements ● Develop in accordance with standards
Develop and maintain hardware/operating system architectures	● Monitor development/ implementation within sectors ● Develop and maintain architecture for corporate users-support operations	● Develop in accordance with corporate standards and business requirements ● Request variances as appropriate; make change recommendations
Develop and maintain telecommunications architectures	● Develop in accordance with standards and business requirements	● Define requirements ● Report performance/ responsiveness problems

the deployment of the unit's resources in developing and maintaining the applications. This applies whether they are employed as part of the business unit or contracted from a central IS function or third-party vendors for the duration of a project, or the life of the application.

This responsibility includes the application architecture for the unit, even if some applications are also part of the corporate portfolio and/or shared with other units. Where there are significant potential gains from synergy, sharing experience or resources, or from economic optimization, an additional corporately-sponsored 'central planning and control' of the application architecture and delivery will be beneficial. The more geographically dispersed the organization, the less attractive the concept of coordinated planning becomes in the short term, but perhaps the more attractive are the long-term benefits of not resourcing very similar applications separately in multiple places.[11]

The degree to which information is a shared business resource will determine how centralized the information architecture and data control processes will become. Similarly, how closely technologies need to be coordinated will depend on the relationships among applications and data utilization as much as on the economies of supply or technical simplicity or flexibility achieved.

Undoubtedly, in every major organization other than the most diversified conglomerate, there are potential gains from the centralization of some resources. But, as described in all the models, these centralized functions are primarily required to service the various needs of the business units—their *raison d'être* is that, if the resource were distributed, it would be less effective. In addition, where there are potential benefits to the organization as a whole that are greater than the sum of the parts (of the business units), then some planning and coordination at the centre can add value to ensure that these additional benefits are achieved.

Balancing IS Demand and IT Supply

The management of 'demand' and 'supply' and achieving balance between both is complex. The previous section illustrated that the debate is generally portrayed as alternating between centralization and decentralization. However, the 'middle ground' has become an appealing alternative.[12] Von Simson,[13] for example, subscribes to an IS functional design with IS/IT roles played by both a central IS function and the business units and prescribes a 'centrally decentralized' IS function with strong dotted-line reporting relationships. He argues that clear structures and distinct roles and responsibilities must be defined with a mix of centralized and decentralized resources. Otherwise, confusion, conflict, duplication of effort and/or inadequate systems integrity will occur. In a similar vein, the *federal structure* is often seen as capturing the benefits of both centralization and decentralization.[14] With such a structure, business units receive a responsive service from decentralized IS functions, while at the same time a corporate IS function provides group-wide IT services and exerts some degree of central leadership and control of IT activities (see Figure 8.4). While intellectually appealing, little guidance can be found as to what these decision areas are and how to make it work.

The key questions are what aspects of IS/IT are best managed centrally and which are best devolved—degree of diffusion in Sullivan's[15] terms—and whether IS/IT activities are managed by a specialist IS function at all or should they be managed by business management themselves. Table 8.3 summarizes the dominant structural arrangements for IS activities, highlighting the advantages of each type and identifies the critical management issues.

Imperatives for the Management of IS/IT

Rockart *et al.*[16] have suggested a number of imperatives for the 'new' IS function to take account of the changing business and technical environments. They are:

1. achieve two-way alignment between the business and IS/IT strategy;
2. develop effective relationships with line management;
3. deliver and implement new systems;
4. build and manage IT infrastructure;
5. reskill the IS function with new competencies and knowledge;
6. manage vendor partnerships;
7. redesign and manage the federal IS organization.

Venkatraman[17] argued the need for a different approach to managing IT resources that considers the sources of value to be derived from IT resources and proposed that resources should be managed as a *value centre*. The value centre is an organizing concept that recognizes four interdependent sources of value from IT resources: cost centre, service centre, investment and profit centre. He argues that the very act of adopting these perspectives permits companies to differentiate the management approaches needed to realize these distinct sources of value. The relative mix among the four components reflects the strategic role for IT within a particular business and will undoubtedly change over time:

- The *cost centre* has an operational focus that minimizes risks with an emphasis on operational efficiency. Cost-centre activities are good candidates for outsourcing.
- The *service centre*, although still minimizing risk, aims to create an IT-enabled business capability to support current strategies.

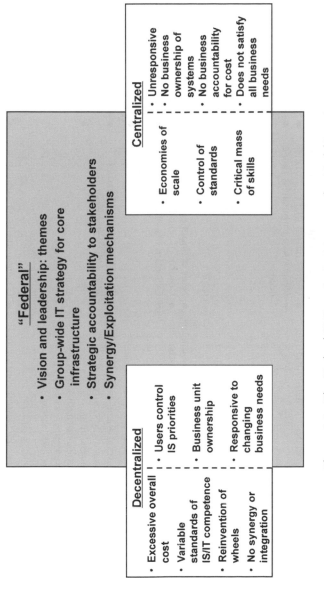

"Federal"

- Vision and leadership: themes
- Group-wide IT strategy for core infrastructure
- Strategic accountability to stakeholders
- Synergy/Exploitation mechanisms

Centralized

- Economies of scale
- Control of standards
- Critical mass of skills

- Unresponsive
- No business ownership of systems
- No business accountability for cost
- Does not satisfy all business needs

Decentralized

- Users control IS priorities
- Business unit ownership
- Responsive to changing business needs

- Excessive overall cost
- Variable standards of IS/IT competence
- Reinvention of wheels
- No synergy or integration

Figure 8.4 The 'Federal IT Organisation' (source: after Hodgkinson)

Table 8.3 Summary of structural arrangements for IS function in multiple business units

Structural arrangements for the IS Function	Strategies for managing IS/IT activities	Advantages	Critical management issues
Independent IS/IT activities in business units	• Business units pursue independent system initiatives	• Business units have ownership • Users control IS/IT priorities • Responsive to business unit's needs	• Integration • Lack of quality control of data • Variable standards of IS/IT competency • 'Reinvention of wheels' and duplication of effort • Little synergy across business units • Managing cost
Centrally-driven IS/IT activities	• Corporate wide IS/IT solutions imposed on business units	• Scale economies • Control of standards • Critical mass of skill	• Politics • Unresponsive • Does not meet every business unit's needs • Effect on customer
Informal cooperation in IS/IT activities across business units	• Informal social networking between the centre and business units • Usually brought about by movement of key IS/IT personnel across business units	• Awareness of IS/IT issues across the enterprise	• Coordination and direction setting • Leaving too much to chance
'Federalism' (integrated IS/IT)	• Balancing central control and business unit autonomy without losing the advantage of global coordination and integration	• Group-wide IS/IT strategy and architecture with devolution where appropriate	• Complexity • Execution • Timing • Defining 'where appropriate'

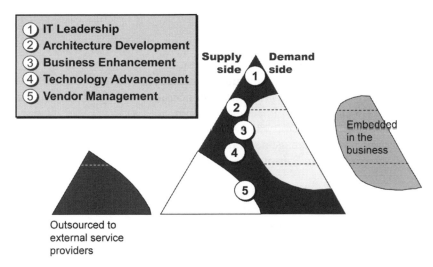

Figure 8.5   *IS Lite (source: IS Lite: The Future, Research Report, GartnerGroup, Egham, UK, 1999, also Stamford, Connecticut)*

- The *investment centre* has a long-term focus and aims to create new IT-based business capabilities. It seeks to maximize business opportunity from IT resources.
- The *profit centre* is designed to deliver IT services to the external marketplace for incremental revenue and for gaining valuable experience in becoming a world-class IS function.

The clear message is that the organization and management of IS/IT resources are going to get more complex. GartnerGroup[18] contends that sharper demarcation between centralized and decentralized IS activities, specialization in centres of excellence, process-based work and outsourcing will lead to what they refer to as *IS Lite* (see Figure 8.5). With this structure for the management of IS/IT, much conventional IS/IT work is either outsourced or embedded in the business, with the IS function remaining as an intermediary to perform an important value-adding service between suppliers, on the one hand, and users, on the other. In addition, the IS function concentrates on driving IS/IT-based innovation in the business. Similarly, Earl and Khan[19] note that the key change in the role of the IS function in the so-called 'digital economy' is that it has become a key contributer and builder of the business, particularly as business processes become even more dependent on IT, distribution channels become electronic and products become digital.

Gartner have identified the five key competencies of this cut-down IS function, IS Lite, as:[20]

1. *IT leadership*, which includes IT envisioning, fusing IT strategy with business strategy, and managing IS resources.
2. *Architecture development*, which is concerned with developing a blueprint for the overall IT technical design.
3. *Business enhancement*, which includes business process analysis and design, project management and managing relationships with users.
4. *Technology advancement*, which is application design and development.
5. *Vendor management*, which includes managing and developing relationships with vendors and suppliers, negotiating and monitoring contracts and purchasing.

This changing role of the IS function not only involves developing new organizational alternatives to meet new demands but also to reduce the resource commitment to old demands. The emotive picture of the disintegrating portfolio, as illustrated in Figure 8.3, is as much the result of the organization failing to manage its legacy from the past, as the development of new demands. It is often this legacy that prevents organizations moving away from old structures, based on IT supply issues, to newer ones, based on balancing demand and supply issues. Swanson and Beath[21] consider the conflicts in the IS function between the demand for new developments and the need to 'maintain' the legacy. They suggest that most IS functions are designed for development because the importance of the repair and enhancement of existing systems is 'undervalued'. While they recognize the need for 'service-driven' organizations, they argue that a key part of that service should deal efficiently with maintenance and minor enhancement—a service that has particular attributes and requires different skills (especially operational application knowledge) from development or other services.

A FRAMEWORK GUIDING ACTION

What Needs to Be Managed?

Before presenting a framework guiding action, it is first useful to consider the nature and content of IS/IT activities. The activities that are traditionally seen as necessary for 'IT', and consequently considered as taking place within the IS function, can be portrayed as delivering a range of services to the business. They range from the planning of the investment

Table 8.4   *Examples of IS activities*

Strategy and planning services
- IS strategy development
- IT strategy development
- IT planning and resource development
- New technology options 'evaluation' (technology road map)
- 'Account' management
- Consultancy/business analysis
- Contingency planning
- Capacity planning
- New service development

Application development services
- Systems analysis
- Systems design
- Package evaluation
- Systems implementation
- Programming and software development
- Software acquisition
- Project management
- Information management

Application and technical services
- Training
- Application maintenance and change control
- First line user-support/problem resolution
- Advice centre
- Security/Access control
- Information 'procurement' (from external sources, etc.)

Technology delivery and maintenance services
- Installing, PC, servers, cables
- Keeping network running
- Maintenance of hardware
- Upgrading software/version control
- Supplier and contracts management

in IT to building applications, to installing and maintaining servers, software and networks, to providing end-user support. These services can be categorized under four headings: strategy and planning, application development, application and technical services, and technology delivery and maintenance. Examples within each of these service categories are outlined in Table 8.4.

In deciding on the organization of IS/IT resources, two key issues must be considered. First, the *location of IS/IT decision rights* regarding IS/IT

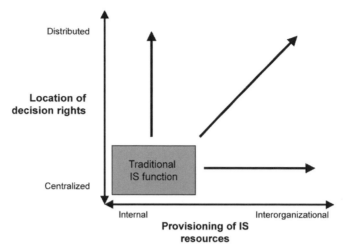

Figure 8.6 *Trade-offs in the organization and resourcing of IS/IT (source: based on an idea from N. Venkatraman and L. Loh, 'The shifting logic of the IS organization: From technical portfolio to relationship portfolio',* Information Strategy: The Executive's Journal, *Winter 1994, 5–11)*

activity in the organization. What decisions, for example, should be centralized and what aspects of IS/IT management should be devolved into the business and out of the IS function? In addressing this question, the organization needs to define authority, responsibilities, policies, co-ordinating mechanisms and control procedures. The second aspect to consider is concerned with the *sourcing of IS/IT resources.* Traditionally, most IS/IT resources were provided from an in-house function under its direct control. However, today, there are a range of sourcing options open to the organization, and it is not necessary to provide all IS/IT resources from within the IS function. Even if an IT activity is deemed business critical, it does not mean that all its elements have to be kept in-house. This interorganizational arrangement places new stresses in the management of IS/IT resources, demanding additional coordination and vendor relationship management.

Figure 8.6 depicts a framework that maps 'location of decision rights' against 'sourcing' options. Most organizations operate in all areas of this framework, with decision-making responsibility spread throughout the organization and making greater use of the external market for the supply of IS/IT resources. Organizations engaging in outsourcing at some stage identify the need to realign, change and/or develop different parts of their IS/IT structures, competencies and skills to enable them to maintain the link between IS/IT and business prerequisites. This only serves to increase the complexity in managing IS/IT.

Location of IS/IT Decision Making

It has already been noted that some IS/IT decisions can be centralized while others are better devolved out into the business. IT does raise certain questions concerning scale, infrastructure planning and risk.[22] Most people can quickly recognize the need for technology components to interoperate easily and hence accept the need for certain technical standards to be adhered to throughout the organization. The problems that technical incompatibility pose for integrating systems becomes all too apparent when attempts are made to link disparate technologies. Yet, for IS/IT services and IS demand decisions, there is generally less awareness of the need for coherence. For example, who decides project priorities and how? Should applications be common across all operating units? If business units can develop their own applications, how much freedom should they have? In implementing an ERP system across a number of business units, will a certain amount of leeway be given to these units in customizing the application or is it a case of 'one size fits all?' Should a common methodology be used for systems development or project management? We often find that responsibility for technology supply may well be more centralized than responsibility for managing and coordinating IS demand.

Devolving IS/IT decision making into the business requires outlining authority and responsibilities, defining the set of rules guiding information, systems and technology decision-making areas, and managing the interdependencies across the range of decisions. In short, the organization must put in place guidelines for decision making and define mechanisms to achieve coherence across the range of decision areas. These aspects require defining:

- *Content*—the decision areas that are being managed. Included here are decision areas about the whole realm of IS demand and IT supply—areas outlined in Table 8.4. Examples include resource allocation, systems development and maintenance, personnel, establishing project priorities, project management methods, disaster recovery, documentation, privacy and purchasing.
- *Authority*—the individuals or groups that have the power actually to make decisions in the various areas. They are ultimately answerable for the outcomes of the decision made. For example, some decisions may be made directly by the IT director, others by business managers; there may be other decisions that require ratification by a 'committee' or forum of some sort.
- *Responsibilities*—the individuals or bodies responsible for day-to-day execution in decision areas. The definition of responsibility needs to

be integral to each person's job role and function, whether technical or non-technical. The degree of importance attached to any responsibility will be reflected in the seniority of the role and will vary across the organization. Roles that carry responsibility do not necessarily carry authority.

- *Coordination*—essentially, the mechanisms and processes for ensuring coherence across all decision areas. It is concerned with defining the mechanisms (steering committees, management groups, etc.) for ensuring a coordinated approach to IS/IT decision making, including the roles to be played by both individuals and groupings. This aspect will be addressed toward the end of this chapter.
- *Policies*—statements of principles or actions defining acceptable behaviour. They provide a basis for consistent decision making and resource allocation. Policies may exist for security, development methodologies and the approach to IS/IT strategy development. Policies may define the extent to which common systems will be used across all business units; they may even specify that software be purchased from a particular vendor.
- *Control*—outlining the approaches to policing decisions, ensuring conformance across the organization. This might include the implications and procedures for non-conformance to policies or decisions. Also included are financial control and charge-out mechanisms.

Some decisions are one-off; for example, deciding on a project management method to use across the whole organization. Indeed, such a decision may be enshrined in a policy statement. Other decisions are more ongoing like dealing with changing business priorities, and a key task is defining how these situations are to be dealt with.

IS/IT Policies

In a devolved environment, there is a need for defining policies that frame the decision-making rules and options. Policies determine the amount of discretion that IS and business managers have in decisions regarding IS/IT. For example, charge-out policies were once seen as one way of introducing more accountability into a centralized mainframe environment, promoting particular behaviours regarding usage of computing resources.

The key to defining a workable set of policies is to recognize that there are two categories of policy: *restraining* policies and *enabling* policies.[23] Restraining policies are seen as describing the rules of federation. They define the parameters within which decisions are made. Enabling policies

Table 8.5 *Enabling and restraining policies*

Restraining policies	Enabling policies
1 Technical compatibility standards	1 Making group-resourced services available to divisions
2 Standards for buying equipment and services	2 Negotiating volume discounts
3 Common systems mandate, if any	3 Managing supplier relationships
4 Disaster recovery, security and quality policies	4 Influencing behaviour through charge-out rules
5 Group systems standards (are purchasable and integratable components preferred over custom built or extensively modified products?)	5 Setting criteria for selecting common systems
	6 Funding shared assets
	7 Establishing tendering procedures
	8 Developing common systems
6 Group job specifications	9 Using consultants
7 Any conformance to industry standards	10 Carrying out post-audit reviews
8 Outside revenue-earning ability of IS function	11 Negotiating groupwide technology agreement
9 Charge-out mechanisms and benefit reclaim	12 Vendor selection procedures
10 Ergonomic standards	
11 Staffing levels	

essentially relate to the dissemination of best practice. Table 8.5 presents examples of each.

Information management, especially concerning its quality, confidentiality and security, also require corporate policies to be established. This area of strategy is considered in Chapter 10, not because it does not deserve management attention, but information management strategies[24] need to be seen as an integrated set of approaches in user, senior management and IS/IT terms.

PROVISIONING OF IS/IT RESOURCES

Deciding from where IS/IT resources should be sourced has become a critical issue for organizations. While most IS/IT resources have traditionally been provided in-house by a central IS function (commonly referred to today as *insourcing*), a wide range of sourcing options are now available. For a variety of reasons, many organizations have looked to the market to provide them with the IS/IT resources that the business requires, a practice generally referred to as *outsourcing*. Clark *et al.*[25] define outsourcing as 'the delegation, through a contractual arrangement, of all or part of the technical resources, the human resources and the management responsibilities associated with providing IT services, to an external vendor.'

The outsourcing of IT is not new and can be traced back to the 1960s when computers were expensive and physically large. During that period, computers required considerable space and controlled environmental conditions so as to operate them successfully. This situation demanded that companies had to make substantial capital investments in order to have their own computing facilities. In order to avoid such expenditure, many organizations contracted out their routine data processing, particularly payroll and accounting, to large data-processing service bureaux. This arrangement was referred to at that time as facilities management. While a major problem in the 1960s was the cost of hardware, the 1970s saw a huge increase in software development costs. Due to rapidly increasingly demand for IT applications and the inadequate supply of IT personnel, managers sought a solution through contract programming, a form of outsourcing.

Outsourcing during this period was important, but largely peripheral to the main IT activities that took place in medium and large organizations. Loh and Venkatraman[26] suggest that the Eastman Kodak–IBM outsourcing deal of 1989 marks the beginning of the current outsourcing revolution. This deal saw Kodak outsource the bulk of its IT operations. Never before had such a well-known organization, where IT was considered to be a strategic asset, contracted out for IS services.

The arrival of the Internet and the rush to e-commerce has seen many companies look to outside vendors to supply necessary skills and competencies, as these are often not available in-house. Developing e-commerce applications can place great demands on companies, and managers often conclude that the only way to meet short deadlines for new technology projects is to contract for specialist services. In addition, engaging in e-commerce means that external parties will inevitably be involved, including telecommunication operators and providers, Internet service providers (ISPs), etc.

Outsourcing Rationales

The decision to outsource IT is not an easy one to make. Experience highlights that it demands considerable managerial attention and should not be made without rigorous analysis and discussion. The outsourcing decision is further complicated by the fact that some variables in the decision can be viewed as an advantage by the proponents of outsourcing and a disadvantage by others.

Financial and Economic Reasons

The difficult economic conditions in which many national economies found themselves during the early 1990s, combined with intense competition in turbulent global markets, exerted a lot of new pressures on companies and the public sector leading many to assess outsourcing as a way of cutting costs. Surveys during this time confirmed this, and, as IT spend accounted for an increasing percentage of budgets, it was an obvious candidate for outsourcing.

Cost savings were generally assumed to occur from vendor economies of scale. When an organization contracts with professional IS service providers, reduced costs can also be realized in the area of technology acquisition. The outsourcing vendor is able to distribute fixed costs of computer hardware over a broad base of customers. In addition, the vendor is seen as having the relevant technology and experience and many hardware vendors offer products with decreasing incremental costs per unit of power.

Outsourcing can provide an opportunity to liquefy the client organization's capital assets, thus strengthening its balance sheet and avoiding capital investment in the future. One viewpoint is that outsourcing shifts expenditure from the capital budget to operating budget, which can provide some flexibility. However, this shift may have an adverse effect on the tax liability of the organization. For instance, if there are any purchased computers in the client organization, their value will be depreciated. In addition, outsourcing the total IT operation is reported to increase an organization's return on equity. Complete outsourcing reduces equity because computer hardware is transferred to the vendor. Therefore, the return on equity is expected to increase. A number of outsourcing arrangements involve upfront payments from the vendor to a client organization. In effect, this is the selling of the IT assets of the client to the vendor, which in turn generates cash.

Technical Reasons

We have seen that IT is increasingly becoming an integral part of many businesses. The marketplace offers a wide range of choices regarding specialist information technology products and services. Technical reasons why organizations choose to outsource include: improving technical expertise, gaining access to technical talent and technical expertise not available in-house, gaining access to new technologies. Third-party contractors may also deliver applications more quickly because the existence of a contract puts pressure on the supplier, compared with internal development, to deliver a quality product on time and within budget.

Business Reasons

There are a number of business reasons why an organization may decide to outsource some or all of its IT activities. Occasionally, it may be to eliminate an ineffective and 'burdensome' IS function or as a catalyst to restructure the IS function and how it is organized and resourced (the topic of this chapter). It can also be used to reduce the applications backlog, particularly when strategic applications are slow 'going live'. Fluctuating demands for IS services can place a significant burden on the IS function, and through outsourcing some of this demand can often be met more economically and efficiently.

A number of companies have used outsourcing to facilitate mergers and acquisitions (M&A). The rationale being that outsourcing should solve the technical incompatibilities, absorb the excessive IS assets like data centres and assimilate the additional IS employees generated by M&A activity.

Classifying Sourcing Options

There are a number of sourcing options available to the firm, and Figure 8.7 illustrates a framework that can be useful in classifying them.[27] This framework maps purchasing style and purchasing focus. A *Transaction* style refers to one-time or short-term contracts with enough detail to be the original reference document. A *Relationship* style refers to less detailed, often incentive-based contracts, centred

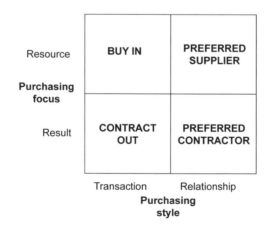

Figure 8.7 *Clarify sourcing options (sources: adapted from M.C. Lacity, L.P. Willcocks and D.F. Feeny, 'The value of selective IT sourcing', Sloan Management Review, Spring, 1996, 13–25; and M.C. Lacity, L.P. Willcocks and D.F. Feeny, 'IT outsourcing: Maximizing flexibility and control', Harvard Business Review, May–June 1995, 84–93)*

around the expectation that the customer and vendor will do business for many years. With a *Resource* option, organizations buy vendor resources such as hardware, software or expertise, but manage the use of the resources in-house. With a *Result* option, vendors manage the delivery of the IT activity, using whatever resources are necessary, to provide the customer with specified results. This analysis leads to four distinct contract types or sourcing strategy. Only two of them—contract out and preferred contractor—are strictly outsourcing contracts:

- *Contract out strategy*—with this strategy the vendor is responsible for delivering the results of IT activity.
- *Buy-in strategy*—this strategy sees the organization buying in resources from the external market, often to meet a temporary requirement. Contracts often specify the skills required and cost, with the resources then managed in-house.
- *Preferred contractor strategy*—with this approach, organizations contract long term with a vendor to reduce risk, with the vendor responsible for the management and delivery of an IT activity or service. To ensure vendor performance, an incentive-based contract is generally constructed.
- *Preferred supplier strategy*—this strategy takes the buy-in approach further, with an organization seeking to develop a long-term close relationship with a vendor in order to access its resources for ongoing IT activities. The organization, not the vendor, takes responsibility for managing these resources.

Even with 'complete outsourcing', there are vital competencies that need to be maintained in-house in order to mitigate risks inherent in IS outsourcing. These have been identified by Willcocks and Lacity[28] as:

- the ability to track, assess and interpret changing IS/IT capability and relate them to organizational needs;
- the ability to work with business management to define the IT requirements over time;
- the ability to identify appropriate ways to use the market, specify and manage IS/IT sourcing;
- the ability to monitor and manage contractual relations.

These are similar to the five key roles of 'IS Lite', highlighted earlier in the chapter.

IS demand decision areas are never outsourced and should always be retained in the organization. The challenge is to decide where in the organization these decisions are best made—in a central IS function or devolved into the business and made by a local IS group or perhaps business management themselves. Approaches to outsourcing and the key management issues to be addressed are considered in more detail in Chapter 11.

WHO SHOULD MANAGE IS/IT AND WHERE SHOULD IT REPORT?

While aspects of IS/IT will be managed by the IS function and aspects devolved into the business, there is generally someone in the organization who has overall authority for IS/IT. Ultimately, someone at board level (represented at the highest executive level of the company, not necessarily with director status as defined by legislation), even the chief executive officer (CEO) by default, is accountable for IS and/or IT. In practice, many board members are actually responsible for IS, given the diffusion of systems throughout the whole organization. Even then, someone will probably be primarily responsible for IT, although often that will not be his or her main responsibility at board level. But, should that be the case? Should not someone be charged at board level with responsibility for all (or most, or some?) aspects of IS/IT management within the organization, and have that status primarily based on the IS/IT management tasks? This question has no doubt been discussed in the boardrooms of most major organizations. A variety of answers have resulted.

Griffiths[29] considered the implications of locating responsibility for IT with the IT director (or chief information officer [CIO]), finance director, business unit heads and the board. She identified the plusses and minuses of each, and this assessment is summarized in Table 8.6.

At some level in the organization, an individual (or in a devolved business, several individuals) will be responsible solely for IS/IT activities and services and for a significant resource and budget. For simplicity, he or she will be referred to as the IT Director or chief information officer (CIO), although in reality other labels are encountered. In a multi-business unit company, there are likely to be 'IS (biased) managers' in each unit with an 'IT (biased) manager' at the centre, and this seems sensible given the earlier organizational arguments. The split of responsibilities discussed earlier would give application responsibility to the units, leaving some areas of IS/IT at the centre for economic and strategic reasons. The IT manager at the centre is the more problematic because his or her reporting position will affect his or her ability to do the job. Given any autonomy in the units, they will easily be able to overrule or ignore the central role, if it is too junior. The IS managers in the units will be considered below.

The 'IT director' or 'chief information officer' (CIO) faces a continu-

Table 8.6   *Consequences of locating overall authority for IS/IT*

	Plusses	*Minuses*
IT directors	Technical expertise Accurate systems Sound technology Systems integration	IT not aligned Education omitted Information overload Technical solutions
Finance directors	Tight cost control Department coordination Training costs integrated Strict authorization	Not always best value for money Insufficient time to devote to IT Opportunities missed Short-term approach
Business-unit head	IT investments linked to the business direction Locally-focused systems Continuous development Shorter reporting structure	Systems not coordinated Incompatibility across business units Duplication of data Unnecessary costs incurred
Board of directors	Strategic direction Appreciation of broader impact of decisions Major problems tackled Funding allocated	Logistical details omitted IS/IT underexploited Infrastructure weak Slow to exploit technology

ally-changing job role. As applications development and operations are passed to the business areas to manage: (i) corporate IS functions will shift to a staff orientation, including coordinating strategy and planning for IS/IT across the whole business. Any line responsibilities will be either to serve the corporate body's IS needs or to manage 'interconnection issues', among systems, data and networks, and hence (ii) the CIO (in charge of such functions) will increasingly concentrate on setting strategy and policy in a similar way that the 'chief financial officer' (CFO) executes financial management responsibilities.[30]

Regarding the changing role and position of the CIO for the 21st century, *Harvard Business Review* invited a number of experts to comment on the question: *Are CIOs obsolete?*[31] The rationale that lies behind this question being that as IS/IT and business strategy are now so much an integral part of each other that all senior managers are—or should be—'information officers'. The central message from responses was that the role of the CIO will change in line with business development and that CIOs must assume a more central role in business strategy formulation (see Box 8.1).

Box 8.1   Are CIOs obsolete? Summary of responses from *Harvard Business Review*, March–April, 2000

Dawn Lepore, *CIO Charles Schwab*, argues that the CIO position has long been misaligned as most people don't understand its true potential. At Schwab, she is a peer to the various business heads and has a great deal of influence on the company's strategic direction, organizational structure and culture. She recommends that the CIO position should be broadly defined, well understood throughout the organization and that the incumbent be a strong contributor to strategy discussions as well as marketing and financial decisions. Critically, she argues that the position should report to the CEO. In identifying a potential CIO, she would advise companies to look for someone who has a background in technology, but who can also take a general management perspective.

Jack Rockart, *director of the Centre for Information Systems Research, Massachusetts Institute of Technology*, believes that it is a fundamental mistake to predict a CIO-less future. As in the past, the functions of the CIO will evolve as changes in the business environment dictate major changes in IS/IT roles, structure and processes. He believes that, while today's CIO should be a technology executive who provides direction and counsel to other senior managers, they are business executives first and technologists second. However, one of the shifts he is seeing is their role in ensuring an effective IT infrastructure.

Michael Earl, *London Business School*, similarly sees a change in the scope and depth of the CIO role, with both expanding. He cautions that, despite these changes, CIOs retain visible operational responsibilities, 'If the operational performance of IT is below standard, the CIO is dead.' He poses two questions: What competencies are required of a new CIO? Can one person do it all? Required competencies include technical competency, management know-how to lead specialists and integrate the function with the rest of the business, business acumen and leadership skills. He suggests that in the future this role may split into two with a CIO who is responsible for strategy, change and information resources working alongside a chief technology officer who is responsible for technology policy, IT infrastructure planning and operations (essentially someone responsible for *demand* management and someone responsible for the management of *supply*).

Tom Thomas, *chairman and CEO at Vantive*, sees the CIO position as inextricably linked to technology and the way in which different businesses use it. He argues that the positions of CEO and CIO are the only places in the company where there must be an integrated view of the business, and the two jobs should be considered as a partnership. In addition, the CIO should be knowledgeable about all the major functions of the business and understand the information drivers in the company.

Peter McAteer and **Jeffrey Elton**, *consultants at Giga Information Group* and *Integral*, respectively, note that today in many organizations the CIO position has devolved into a sort of heavyweight project manager, coordinating large IT projects and ERP deployments, with minimal input to corporate strategy. They define the position as 'manager or leader' first and 'technical specialist' second. In addition, they see the CEO as being at the centre of operations for strategy pertaining to technology and its implementation, noting that, if the role is going to be successful, it will usually require a change in the mindset of the company's top executives.

The role of the CIO in the organization has changed over the years, their titles often changing to reflect new focuses and emphases. Table 8.7 traces the evolution of the role of the CIO across the main technology shifts from mainframe to distributed (including advent of PCs) to the web-based and Internet era.

Part of the problem is not perhaps the need of the job, but the origins of the person filling it. Merely promoting, via a change in job title, a career IS/IT specialist seems to be unsuccessful since they generally remain 'outsiders' in the executive team. Some individuals may overcome the problem of background, but more success is likely if a high-flying non-IS/IT executive takes the role. This also upgrades the perceived importance of the task and should provide a business focus to its activities. However, research in the early 1990s by Earl and Feeny[32] tends to contradict this, in that successful CIOs, as judged by chief executives, are more likely to have a sound IT background.

There are five roles critical for the success of today's CIO.[33] They are:

- leadership;
- visionary;
- relationship builder;
- politician;
- deliverer.

Table 8.7 The changing role of the CIO (sources: based in part on D.F. Feeny and J.W. Ross, 'The evolving role of the CIO', in Research and Discussion Paper, Oxford Institute of Information Management, Templeton College, Oxford, 2000; and presentation by O. Le Gendre, Vice-President of Gartner at IT Governance Forum, Paris, 11 June 2001)

	Mainframe era	Distributed era	Web-based and Internet era
Applications portfolio	• Transaction processing—automation for efficiency	• Knowledge-worker support, interorganizational systems, ERP systems	• Electronic commerce, knowledge management, virtual organizations, supply chain re-engineering
Senior business executive attitudes to IS/IT	• IT for cost displacement and automation	• Increased involvement in IT issues and governance • Polarization of attitudes: IT as strategic asset or cost to be minimized	• IT, particularly the Internet, viewed as transformational • IT investments now more attractive in terms of costs and timescales • IS/IT now part of ongoing business conversation
Input to business	• Advisor on 'How to do', not 'What to do'	• Access to senior executives • Invited 'seat at table'	• Member of executive team having a 'seat at the table' • Helps define 'what to do'
Major tasks	• On-time delivery • Reliable IT operations	• Manage IS function • Provide infrastructure • Manage vendors	• Jointly develop business/IT model • Introduce management processes that leverage technologies, particularly the Internet
Role	• Functional head • Operational manager • Deliver on promises	• Strategic partner • Relationship builder • Technology advisor • Align IS/IT with business	• Visionary • Relationship builder • Technology opportunist • Drive and shape strategy

Table 8.8 *Profile of the CIO who adds value* (source: *after Earl and Feeny*)

---

1. *Behaviour*
   - Is loyal to the organization
   - Is open in management style
   - Is perceived to have integrity

2. *Motivation*
   - Is goal oriented
   - Comfortable as a change agent
   - Creative and encourages ideas

3. *Competencies*
   - Is a consultant/facilitator
   - Good communicator
   - Has IT knowledge
   - Able to achieve results through others

4. *Experience*
   - Sound experience in an IS development role (especially in systems analysis)

The leadership exhibited by the CIO is a key aspect in achieving success with IS. Two components of leadership of critical importance for the CIO are:[34]

- Ability to create a set of value expectations shared across all areas of the business—one sensitive to the realities of competency, competition and culture.
- Ability to deliver on those expectations measurably. CIOs must understand and express IT's value in a way that's meaningful to all executives.

Appointing a CIO alone is not a solution to all the management issues! Earl and Feeny define the attributes that a CIO must possess to ensure the appointment is, at least to some degree, successful (i.e. improves the value to the organization of IS/IT). They are shown in Table 8.8. The obvious conclusion is that people with all these attributes will be in short supply, which may explain the rapid turnover of people in such jobs.

In a bank or similar information-intense organization, having an IT director or CIO is the equivalent of an engineering director in a manufacturing company. IT is the technology of banking. However, he or she will not have jurisdiction over all applications. Equally, in less IT-dependent organizations, IT may well report via another executive, preferably one with a primarily commercial or business development role rather than a service role such as finance. IT will inevitably, for better or worse, be tarred with the brush of the department within which it sits. Within business units, 'IS manager' positioning faces similar problems and should depend on the criticality of the systems to the business: the more critical, the more senior and central should the role be to the running of the business. Again, indirect reporting should be through commercial rather than service activities to ensure that 'primary' activities (in value chain terms) obtain the appropriate emphasis relative to support activities.

One conclusion in all this vagueness is quite certain: that, as IS/IT becomes more critical to organizations, the more senior will become the executives with specific IS or IT responsibility, both in corporate and business unit terms. Equally certain is that the success of such a senior role in ensuring that strategies are developed and achieved will depend as much on the individual as his or her position on the organization chart. Both issues should be on the management agenda for regular review.

No doubt some companies will succeed without a coherent strategy for organizing, positioning and developing IS/IT resources, but most will need to address this aspect of strategy with considerable thought and insight. Whatever conclusion is reached, it will not be entirely satisfactory from every viewpoint and will need to be changed over time and probably supplemented or overlaid with some other IS/IT strategic management processes in the meantime.

COORDINATING MECHANISMS FOR THE STRATEGIC MANAGEMENT OF IS/IT

As mentioned earlier in the chapter, the majority of organizations in both public and private sectors have established some form of 'steering group' and other coordinating mechanisms for IS/IT. They are called many things, but usually have the words 'policy', 'strategy' or 'planning' in the title. According to Earl,[35] 'steering committees appear to be an obvious necessity in managing IT.'

Most writers agree that the reasons for establishing such committees are (one or more of):

- ensuring top management involvement in IS planning;
- ensuring the fit between IS and business strategy;
- improving communication with top and middle management;
- changing user attitudes to IT.

A study by Drury[36] showed that successful steering committees not only addressed each of them but also introduced a process of reaching decisions by consensus—something which can otherwise prove difficult with respect to IS and IT. Gupta and Raghunathan,[37] based on a large survey in US companies, concluded that steering committees were one of the most effective ways of improving organizations' IS planning, by assisting the integration of the IS function with the business and by coordinating planning activities.

From discussions earlier in the book, some other reasons for the establishment of such a grouping of senior managers focused on the management of IS/IT can be identified:

1. In Chapter 4, Kotter's organizational model was used to differentiate between formal and informal organizational arrangements. The formal organization structure reflects the way in which the business operates, whereas the 'dominant coalition' or informal structure essentially determines the future strategy of the organization. This implies that members of that coalition are scattered through the upper layers of the organizational structure, but are not necessarily the most senior and/or all from the senior management team. Using the jargon of Chapter 7, some senior executives may be 'caretakers' or 'controllers' by nature rather than the 'developers' and 'entrepreneurs' who drive things forward. It is important that the members of the 'dominant coalition' overtly include IS/IT on their agenda since:

    - they are, in practice, establishing business strategy and therefore will miss opportunities, etc. if they ignore IS/IT. They are in the best position to identify and evaluate the impact of IS/IT on the strategy;
    - they, by their attitude and behaviour towards IS/IT, are determining the role it plays in the business.

    It means that the dominant coalition, by intent or default, is setting IS/IT strategy and needs to be aware of that and the consequences of its interest or neglect! Any steering group, therefore, must include the main members of that coalition or power group.

2. In Chapter 3, the model of the evolving nature of IS/IT strategy showed how, in the most mature stage when the objective is to link IS/IT to business strategy, a coalition approach of users, senior management and IS/IT staff needed to be established. This sounds very similar to the argument above but extends the potential franchise to users and IS/IT staff as well as the strategy formulators. In essence, this may imply that a steering or policy group is not enough

to involve all necessary parties to the strategy process. This will be considered below.

3. A number of issues in portfolio management point to the need for strong coordination and a means of making decisions across the range of types of investment proposed and required. In particular, strategic applications, which are normally cross-functional, need executive management agreement and endorsement of the business benefits and commitment to the normally extensive change program needed to realize them.

4. Perhaps the most compelling reason is that the formal organization structures for IS/IT activities are never seen to be satisfactory by all the parties involved, and additional 'governing' processes become necessary, whether IT resources are centralized or decentralized. If IT resources are centralized, there is a need to assess and prioritize demand and set an appropriate resource level. If IT resources are decentralized there is a need to coordinate applications planning to ensure that incompatible, even disadvantageous, developments are not undertaken and that IT resources are employed where the greatest business benefit can be obtained.

These arguments perhaps explain the spread of steering groups during the past decade. Equally, some of the points made above may also explain why many of those groups fail to steer IS/IT in a beneficial or even consistent direction. Criticism of steering groups is often the only thing that users and IT can agree on, especially if they introduce delays, increase bureaucracy, fail to make decisions, etc. The list of comments is almost endless:

- 'wrong people/too many people attend; the right people don't attend';
- 'wrong terms of reference';
- 'discuss the wrong things';
- 'meet too infrequently/too often';
- 'make too many/not enough decisions';
- 'do not understand the real issues';
- 'are too remote from reality'.

The causes of these problems can probably be summarized into three major areas:

1. The wrong people are involved: the group does not include enough (if any) of the 'dominant coalition' to be willing or able to establish strategy. If the right people are involved, many of the other

problems disappear—the 'agenda' will contain items of strategic value only and the less important will be dropped. Decisions can and will be made. Obviously, the credibility of the steering group depends on the respect others have for its members, the evident importance of the matters they address and the results of decisions made. One important point is that executive managers, asked to 'serve' in such a group, must not be made to feel 'incompetent' by being asked to discuss and decide on subjects beyond their area of knowledge. This generally occurs if the agenda is dominated by technology as opposed to business matters.

2. The activities of the steering group and the decisions taken have to be integrated with the overall strategy processes in the business. This implies both interpretation of business objectives and key initiatives into IS/IT priorities and providing IS/IT input to the development of the strategy. Even in organizations with steering groups, many strategic initiatives are taken without thought for the implications on the existing IS/IT strategy, causing at least disruption and delay in delivering critical systems. Even worse, the initiatives may be counter to the current strategy and, in many cases, the initiative itself may need rethinking due to the detrimental effect it has on longer-term strategic development. 'Initiative overload' is a phrase commonly heard in recent years, and there appears to be real conflict between coherent strategic management and the plethora of initiatives, many of which—like bubbles—often 'fade and die'!

3. The group has no infrastructure to support it and carry out its actions, which, as agreed, become the strategy. The steering group needs to address two basic areas:

   • ensuring that the applications that are strategic in business terms are identified, developed and implemented successfully;
   • ensuring that policies for managing IS/IT as a key business resource are defined and adhered to.

This implies effective communication to and from the steering group among everyone who is involved in devising and implementing the strategy.

Using the strategic management model mentioned earlier in this chapter (see Figure 8.2), the role of the steering group becomes a key part of the formal strategy process: to establish the strategic direction, aligned to the business strategy. Two further stages exist, which no grouping of senior managers can expect to carry out personally:

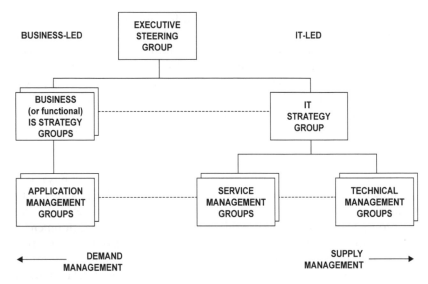

Figure 8.8   *Steering organization for IS/IT strategic management*

1. converting the strategy into viable plans for delivery of the applications and the allocation/procurement of the required resources;
2. implementing the plans by delivering the applications, through the actual deployment of the required resources.

Others will undertake these activities, but obviously there have to be strong links to and from the steering group, which cannot achieve much in a vacuum. It must both obtain relevant inputs from somewhere and have the means to ensure that its decisions are actioned. Most good ideas will originate lower down the organization. The steering group role is to evaluate opportunities resulting from those ideas in the context of the business, judge their worth, initiate appropriate action and then monitor whether success is achieved. Interpreting this in terms of the IS/IT strategic model defined earlier and shown in Figure 8.1, and considering the need to balance supply and demand effectively, a structure for a steering organization for IS/IT strategy is proposed in Figure 8.8. It reflects the need for continuity, overlap even, and feedback between developing and implementing the strategy, which should as far as possible be done by the same organizational groupings. It is very difficult in terms of knowledge and motivation to implement someone else's strategy. The main roles and responsibilities are outlined below and summarized in Table 8.9.

Table 8.9 *Responsibilities within the IS/IT coordination governance structure*

Executive steering group
- Interpreting business strategy and agreeing overall IS/IT policies
- Establishing priorities, agreeing resource and expense levels, authorizing major investments
- Ensuring that strategic applications (especially those that cross business areas) achieve their objectives
- Establishing the appropriate organizational responsibilities and relationships

Business (IS) strategy groups
- Identifying business needs, interpreting CSFs, assessing opportunities and threats and IS implications in that business area
- Prioritizing, planning and coordinating IS activities and expenditure in the area and ensuring planned benefits are delivered
- Ensuring appropriate user resources are allocated to projects and appoint application managers

IT strategy group
- Interpreting IT trends and developments in the context of the organization's business
- Ensuring resources are deployed to meet business priorities
- Developing IT resources and services in line with business IS plans and monitoring the performance of those resources
- Managing the supply of technology and specialist bought-in services
- Ensuring technical risks are minimized

Application management groups
- Identifying and specifying the needs, benefits, business resources and costs of applications to enable management to evaluate investments and set priorities
- Managing developments and ongoing use of systems to ensure benefits are maximized
- Ensuring business changes necessary to get the benefits carried out
- Ensuring that user resources are made available as needed and used effectively on projects

Service management groups
- Translating business needs into technical requirements and resource implications
- Selecting the optimum means of meeting the business needs
- Monitoring performance against budgets/service levels agreed with the business
- Ensuring technical solutions are tested and quality assured to avoid application failure
- Planning the development of services and resources to meet evolving demands

continued

Table 8.9   *(continued)*

Technology management groups
- Understanding technology development, formulating options and communicating the implications
- Assessing the capabilities of the technologies against known and potential needs
- Planning and managing infrastructure developments and migrations to minimize the risk to business applications
- Resolving technical issues/problems with suppliers and ensuring service groups are effectively supported

---

The Executive Steering Group

This group is as critical to the whole structure as the keystone is to an arch. Its membership should reflect the dominant coalition, which implies they are:

- able to recognize the potential of IS/IT in terms of the business strategy;
- keen to exploit IS/IT as a business weapon;
- able to influence the management of systems in the area of the business they represent;
- have the confidence of the executive to whom they report.

The steering group is a collection of people, not a collection of job roles. The individuals are what matter, not the role they currently fulfil, but it is important that all areas of the business are represented. That includes the IT group, although it is critical that an IT person does not chair the group. Leadership must come from the business, preferably from the chief executive or a highly respected nominee.

The group should meet regularly, if not frequently—probably four to six times per year. The lower levels in the structure should get together more frequently—maybe even weekly when a critical application is being developed. The main purposes of the steering group are:

- To ensure that the overall objectives of strategic management of IS/IT, listed in Table 8.2, are addressed effectively. Most of those objectives are impossible to measure, require careful judgement and consensus agreement among senior management as to whether any particular decision made is appropriate to the situation and capable of implementation.
- To direct the activities of the strategy groups and require responses in

due time, and to consider ideas and issues put forward by other groups.

- To address any issues that affect strategic applications and ensure their success is not jeopardized by organizational or resourcing problems. Equally, they need to ensure that the applications in the strategic segment (and related activity in the high potential and key operational segments) are all still relevant to the business as the business environment and strategy evolves. They must be willing to stop activity as well as initiate it.
- To act as the final judges to reconcile or settle the short-term contention for resources. Such urgent decisions must be made with an understanding of the long-term implications for the business and its IS/IT capability.
- To justify to the executives of the company that expenditures associated with strategic applications and on related R&D or infrastructure improvements are worthwhile and will be managed effectively.
- To ensure that experience is transferred across the organization, and that potential benefits of integration are not sacrificed merely for expediency in meeting local requirements.

It is not just what the steering group does that is important but also the way that it does it. Its process should be open, not secretive; its decisions should be communicated quickly and widely; it should demonstrate its willingness to consider ideas from the strategy groups that require such attention and it should be quick to redelegate trivial matters. They are all aspects of the IS/IT 'business culture' that must be established. Finally, it should ensure that successes are recognized as well as failures!

Business Unit (or Functional) IS Strategy Groups

Depending on the organization's structure, they may be established for each business unit or major function (or both if the organization consists of units and service functions). In a one-unit business, this role and the management steering group will clearly overlap.

Ideally, the representative of the business area on the executive steering group should chair the strategy process, although, equally ideally, business IS strategy should be part of the agenda for whatever business strategy process exists. Either way, the senior line managers involved in the business should be directly involved with the planning group.

While the obvious responsibilities include ensuring that business priorities and requirements are reflected in the planned application portfolio for the area, it is also this group's responsibility to ensure that the plans interrelate with plans in other areas and are understood by the IT strategy group. Where mismatches occur, problems should be resolved among the strategy groups, if at all possible, rather than be escalated to the executive steering group before alternatives can also be provided from which the best course of action can be chosen.

Having ensured that the application portfolio, priorities and plans reflect the business requirements, a number of other aspects must be addressed at this level:

- That appropriate approaches to development are adopted, given the classification of the application and the availability of central, local or external resources. Where the free market philosophy is appropriate, the business IS strategy group may make the decision without consulting the IT specialists.
- The group must ensure that project justifications include all relevant costs and benefits, and can be adequately resourced by the user areas concerned. Lack of availability of key user resources is often as much the cause of project delays as the availability of IT resources.
- The group must determine whether the portfolio is being developed to take maximum advantage of experience gained and investments already made in the area, and that the information resource is being managed effectively both locally and as part of the corporate resource.
- Implementation of systems will undoubtedly cause organizational change. Most major systems investments will need related organizational adjustments and even significant changes if benefits are to be realized, both within the business area impacted and at the boundaries with other functions. Understanding and suitable, coordinated and consistent, action needs to be established at this level as part of business planning. The group has the responsibility for ensuring that the expected benefits from the application plans are delivered.
- The group should establish appropriate application management groups for their own critical systems and developments, and ensure they are appropriately represented on such other groups on applications that affect the area. Those activities should be initiated, directed, responded to and in time even disbanded, by decisions at this level, unless the application is 'strategic' and cross-functional, when the decision belongs higher up!

It is clearly this group's responsibility to produce an IS strategy that converts business requirements into demand for applications, which are then managed to achieve the objectives identified. Establishing a coherent plan and associated resource and financial budgets are a key part of that process. Box 8.2 gives the terms of reference for such a group, established in one division of a global telecommunications provider.

Box 8.2: Terms of reference for the Systems Strategy Control Board in a division of a global telecommunications provider

1. Purpose
The primary purpose of the Systems Strategy Control Board (SSCB) is to ensure that the Division's business objectives are effectively supported by systems and processes. It also reviews the proposals and business cases of all projects requiring computing and systems development expenditure over €60,000, as defined in the Division's Business Case process. Project Managers and Financial Controllers are jointly responsible for ensuring that all business cases of projects requiring information systems-related expenditure over €60,000 have received SSCB concurrence. In addition the SSCB:

- sets the overall Systems Policy, where there needs to be a subset of the corporate Systems Policy as set by the Group Information Board* (of which the SSCB Chairperson is a member);
- determines the criteria for the prioritization of the Division's Systems Budgets, including recommending and allocating the budgets across the Divisional units in conjunction with the Finance Division;
- ensures that the computing operations and systems development requirements are fed into the five-year business planning process; and
- reviews internal trading agreements with our Group IS and systems suppliers and evaluates their performance.

2. Scope
- The SSCB has a Division-wide remit to address all aspects of information systems owned by or on behalf of the Division. This covers all computing systems charged to the Division by the central IS Group via Computing Operations Revenue Apportionment (CORA) and information systems development. The SSCB is complemented by the Service Development Forum, which should identify the impact on systems of the product and service portfolio and of marketing campaigns.

3. Responsibilities
The main responsibilities of the Board are as follows:

- to determine the strategic direction for systems and business processes;
- to ensure that the strategic direction is reflected in individual projects/initiatives;

- to ensure information is owned and managed as a corporate resource, to defined standards;
- to agree and implement corporate systems policy;
- to ensure that the Balanced Scorecard elements are assessed (particularly Information Assets);
- to help determine, in conjunction with Business Planning, the priorities for computing operations and development budget allocation;
- to validate major system project proposals, including the business cases;
- to identify links and dependences between projects and, so, recommend programme structures;
- to review continually the validity of the systems investments made (start, stop or amend); and
- to monitor and report on the performance of Group IS and [name of outsourcing vendor] computing systems and development suppliers on behalf of the Division.

Representation

The SSCB is chaired by the Division's Head of Systems, with representation from those within the Divisional units responsible for systems delivery and/or systems expenditure, including Business Planning. The individual responsibilities include:

- representing their specific unit;
- ensuring that Board decisions are implemented in the unit;
- representing the Board within the client units;
- participation in design approval;
- participation in priority setting and budget allocation; and
- supporting the Supplier Evaluation process.

5. Meetings

Frequency and Duration

- The SSCB meets every two months, unless otherwise agreed. The schedule of dates is published in advance for the calendar year.

Attendance

It is anticipated that attendance by the specified representatives will be given a high priority and that, wherever possible, the requirement to attend should be embodied within the representatives job descriptions. Where absence is unavoidable, a representative will send their nominated deputy, fully briefed, including the status of any action points outstanding. The deputy will be fully empowered to represent their Control Board member.

Decisions taken at the Board will be fully binding where absence results in no representation. The Control Board members will invite appropriate Project Managers to attend meetings to assist in decision making or to obtain a full progress report.

* Another coordinating mechanism, at Group level.

In most organizations, business plans have often been developed in a way that satisfies external requirements and suits the business culture or style of management. That process may have excluded or ignored IS planning. That cannot continue if the link is to be forged between the corporate steering and policy setting of IS/IT and the management of each application. In general, business planning itself is rarely a weak link in this overall structure, but the inclusion of IS in that planning is often done with reluctance and without great effect, if the earlier-mentioned surveys are to be believed.[38]

Application Management Groups

Every major project, group of related systems or major operational systems will demand significant user management and staff time to ensure that it 'works'. During development, it is critical that it is 'business project managed' and not seen only as an 'IT project'. The users will have to live with the application's consequences. One of the commonest reasons why systems fail in a business sense is that the project manager was not a heavily committed, knowledgeable and able user. Every organization has learned this lesson, the hard way, over the past 30 years! The key objective of application management is to deliver the required business benefits from the application. A process for ensuring that this can happen is described in Chapter 9.

Establishing system and service requirements and monitoring achievement is a critical aspect of application management. Most such problems should be able to be resolved at this 'implementation' level unless they affect overall plans or resourcing. Then, the strategy group must become involved.

Major existing systems, on which the area depends, and interrelated groups of systems, whether developed centrally or locally, require the same ongoing application management attention to ensure that they continue to fulfil requirements. Less time and effort should be devoted to support than to key operational or strategic applications unless the value of investment is significant.

It is becoming increasingly frequent for many applications to cross organizational and/or planning group boundaries, and some, such as enterprise systems, may involve most parts of the organization. 'Application management' is required irrespective of planning structures, and applications that cross organizational boundaries and/or have multiple users are notoriously difficult to manage coherently. There is not a strict hierarchical relationship; an application management group may report to many masters and, should conflict be unresolved, the 'application' may have to become an issue on the executive steering group agenda.

IT Strategy Group (and Service Management and Technical Management Groups)

The IT limb of the structure consists of three parts, all of which have been discussed earlier in the chapter. Overall resource and technology planning and development is the responsibility of the IT management team, but must also include or allow for resources not directly under its control. The head of the IS function should be a member of the management steering group, but in that role he or she is, first, a senior manager and, second, an IT professional.

An infrastructure is required to support the management team's planning and production of the 'IT strategy'. The IT strategy group should consist of the IT senior management team and, if appropriate, senior user managers who control significant resources or technologies. This split of responsibility is common in 'high-tech' companies, where technological use of IT is separated from commercial application. This group will bring together the resource implications of application plans as well as determine the main aspects of technology development and capacity. Its primary purpose is to produce the 'supply-side' strategy that best satisfies the demand resulting from the IS strategy process. It should direct the activities of the service and technical groups, which are probably departments rather than 'committees', and should be responsible for determining the appropriate sources of supply for technology and other resources. One responsibility it must undertake is to interpret the implications of IS/IT developments and trends for the executive steering committee in relation to the business. Some advantage will accrue by being technically advanced, provided it can be exploited in business terms.

The role of the subsidiary groups is summarized in Table 8.9. Other issues to be managed under these headings are considered in later chapters. What is important is to appreciate that close coordination along the implementation level, from business needs through service provision to technology acquisition, is just as vital to success as the effectiveness of the executive steering group. The quality of the relationship between user-biased application management and IT-biased service management groups will determine not only how well applications are managed during development but also whether the best application development approach is adopted in the first place. The ability of service and technical management groups to work together will determine whether technology is employed on the basis of what it does for the business, rather than just what it does! At the same time, the choice of the best technology within strategic and financial constraints will depend on the mutual understanding of these two groups. Technical specialists have a very important role in the organization, but they and business-orientated users often fail to communicate. The service groups are the interpreters in both directions, capable of understanding the languages of both business and technology. People working in such service groups will often have a split loyalty to the business and technology.

Summary

This structure or model brings together a number of facets of IS/IT strategic management:

- top management involvement where it is most useful (i.e. adds most value);
- business and IT balance in determining strategy;
- demand and supply management;
- strategy, planning and implementation requirements;
- exploitation of ideas generated from anywhere;
- command and control in effecting policy decisions;
- an organization-led approach to developing strategies and portfolio management;
- consistency over time in developing and implementing strategies;
- an ability to learn from and transfer experience.

From using the model in evaluating the management of IS/IT in many organizations, it is clear that, if one or more of the functions is missing, or is ineffective, or not linked properly to related functions, then either strategies are not being developed or they are not being implemented. Many organizations need variations of this model, depending on size, diversity or otherwise of the business, degree of corporate control exercised, the stage of IS/IT development and the variety and sophistication of technologies deployed.

Figure 8.9 represents the governance structure at a large European automobile manufacturer. It illustrates the activities that are both co-ordinated and managed by the central IS function (IS/IT strategy and planning, program control, program delivery and IT standards and policies) and the related governance bodies. It also highlights the major outputs of these coordinating mechanisms.

For example, the IT Policy Group is chaired by a board member and its membership is composed of senior business managers from the main business areas and the CIO. It focuses on:

- setting the level of company-wide and local IT spend;
- ensuring IS/IT investments support business priorities;
- approving proposed IT investments;
- agreeing balances between types of IT spend:

  —investment versus operational
  —application versus infrastructure
  —tactical versus strategic

- validating IS/IT direction and policies (e.g. outsourcing, IS function);
- monitoring performance against plans.

MANAGING THE IS FUNCTION AS A BUNDLE OF RESOURCES

In Chapter 2, the resource-based view of the firm was introduced. It was noted that this perspective has been gaining increasing prominence in the strategic management discipline over the last decade and, essentially, it takes the view that an organization is a 'bundle' of resources. With this perspective, the task for management is to integrate and coordinate these resources to create organization-specific competencies. Competitive advantage is seen as emerging from how this resulting set of competencies are deployed to achieve superior performance. Strategy formulation becomes a process of building and leveraging the necessary competencies—often referred to as core competencies—rather than merely identifying profitable positions in an industry. Competencies emerge out of the integration and coordination of resources. Resources can be both tangible and intangible. Tangible resources include land, buildings, computers and networks. Intangible resources include skills, knowledge, processes, customer relationships, brands, reputation and culture.

It is not unexpected that the logic and thinking behind the resource-based view has been applied to the management of IS, with the IS function portrayed as a bundle of resources. In the context of IS/IT

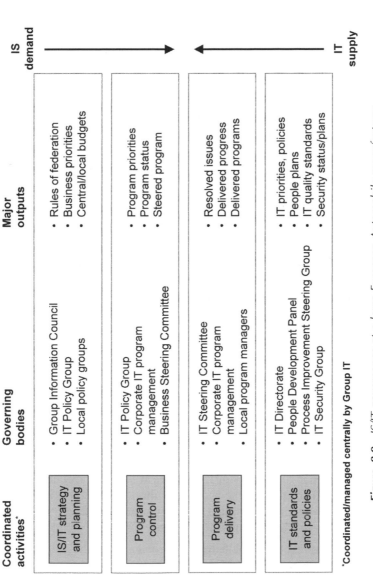

Coordinated activities*

IS/IT strategy and planning

Program control

Program delivery

IT standards and policies

Governing bodies

- Group Information Council
- IT Policy Group
- Local policy groups

- IT Policy Group
- Corporate IT program management
- Business Steering Committee

- IT Steering Committee
- Corporate IT program management
- Local program managers

- IT Directorate
- People Development Panel
- Process Improvement Steering Group
- IT Security Group

Major outputs

- Rules of federation
- Business priorities
- Central/local budgets

- Program priorities
- Program status
- Steered program

- Resolved issues
- Delivered progress
- Delivered programs

- IT priorities, policies
- People plans
- IT quality standards
- Security status/plans

IS demand →

← IT supply

*Coordinated/managed centrally by Group IT

Figure 8.9 IS/IT governance at a large European Automobile manufacturer

Table 8.10   *Feeny and Willcock's IS competencies*

IS/IT leadership	Integrating IS/IT effort with business purpose and activity
Business systems thinking	Envisioning the business processes that technology makes possible
Relationship building	Getting the business constructively engaged in IS/IT issues
Architecture planning	Creating a coherent blueprint for a technical platform that responds to current and future business
Making technology work	Rapidly achieving technical progress by one means or another
Informed buying	Managing the IS/IT sourcing strategy that meets the interests of the business
Contract facilitation	Ensuring the success of existing contracts for IS/IT services
Contract monitoring	Protecting the business's contractual position, current and future
Vendor development	Identifying the potential added value of IS/IT service suppliers

management, the primary resources are intangible—the skills and knowledge of staff as well as processes, structure and culture of the IS function. Tangible resources are less important, as these are available to all organizations in the open market—their purchase, configuration and management the result of the application of intangible resources. Feeny and Willcocks[39] have explored the competencies necessary to manage the IS function. In order to identify them, they highlighted three enduring challenges in the exploitation of IT that a company must successfully address over time:

- the challenge of business and IS/IT vision is to address the need for two-way alignment between business and technology;
- the challenge of delivery of IS services at low cost and high quality is being transformed by the evolving, vibrant service market;
- the challenge of IT design architecture—the choice of technical platform on which to mount IS services.

In order to address these challenges, they define what they refer to as nine 'core IS competences'[40]: IS/IT leadership, business system thinking, relationship building, architecture planning, making technology work, informed buying, contract facilitation, contract monitoring and vendor development. These competencies are briefly described in Table 8.10.

They assert that these competencies are required both to underpin the pursuit of high-value-added applications of IT and to capitalize on the

Figure 8.10   *A framework for IS competencies*

external market's ability to deliver cost-effective IS services. The challenge for the organization is to design, resource and structure an IS function to deliver these competencies.

An assumption underpinning this use of the resource-based view is that success with IS/IT depends on improving the management of the IS function and establishing the necessary competencies in this function to enable this to happen. This is not the complete story. Success with IS/IT must consider the actual exploitation and deployment of the technology, and the organization must also develop appropriate competencies for this to occur. No matter how good the IS strategy is and how successful the organization is in supplying IS services, if the technology does not support business changes and is not effectively used, benefits will not be realized. Marchand *et al.*[41] note that, to improve how businesses use information, managers must do more than excel at investing in and deploying IT. Organizations must combine those competencies with excellence in 'collecting, organising and maintaining information, and with getting their people to embrace the right behaviours and values for working with information.' These aspects lie outside the IS function, but are critical for success.

Building on these different views of IS competencies, a more comprehensive framework was developed during an extended research project undertaken with several major corporations.[42] Figure 8.10 illustrates a model that links strategy (both business, IS and IT) with IT supply and business exploitation. This is an extension of the model illustrating the business strategy–IS/IT strategy linkage introduced in Chapter 1.

Using this framework, the research identified six domains of IS competency: strategy, defining the IS contribution, defining the IT capability, exploitation, delivering solutions and supply. They provide a more complete picture and are defined as follows:

1. *Strategy:* the ability to identify and evaluate the implications of IT-based opportunities as an integral part of business strategy formulation and define the role of IS/IT in the organization.
2. *Define the IS contribution:* the ability to translate the business strategy into processes, information and systems investments and change plans that match the business priorities (i.e. the IS strategy).
3. *Define the IT capability:* the ability to translate the business strategy into long-term information architectures, technology infrastructure and resourcing plans that enable the implementation of the strategy (i.e. the IT strategy).
4. *Exploitation:* the ability to maximize the benefits realized from the implementation of IS/IT investments through effective use of information, applications and IT services.
5. *Deliver solutions:* the ability to deploy resources to develop, implement and operate IS/IT business solutions that exploit the capabilities of the technology.
6. *Supply:* the ability to create and maintain an appropriate and adaptable information, technology and application supply chain and resource capacity.

Each of these competency areas has a number of specific IS competencies—26 in total. They are listed and defined in Table 8.11.

This application of the resourced-based view is premised on the crucial importance to view IS competencies from an organizational rather than from a narrow IS functional perspective. IS competencies transcend traditional functional boundaries; critically, they are not located solely in the IS function, but spread right across the organization. For some competencies, particularly IT supply competencies, resource elements are primarily located within the IS function, but, for exploitation competencies, resource elements are primarily located outside the IS function. Figure 8.11 illustrates the balance between resources located in 'the business' and resources located in the IS function in delivering the competencies.

This logic explains why some IS functions can be very good at defining the technical infrastructure and developing systems, but the organization is not delivering benefits from this investment. Perhaps the 'wrong' systems are being developed? It serves to emphasize the importance of a strong business/IS partnership and that organizations must instil

Table 8.11 IS competency definitions

IS competency area	Competency	The ability to …
1. *Strategy*	1.1 Business strategy	Ensure that business strategy formulation identifies the most advantageous uses of information, systems and technology
	1.2 Technology innovation	Incorporate the potential of new and emerging technologies in long-term business development
	1.3 Investment criteria	Establish appropriate criteria for decision making on investments in information, systems and technology
	1.4 Information governance	Define information management policies for the organization and the roles and responsibilities of general management and the IS/IT function
2. *Define the IS contribution (IS strategy)*	2.1 Prioritization	Ensure that the portfolio of investments in applications and technology produce the maximum return from resources available
	2.2 IS strategy alignment	Ensure that IS development plans are integrated with organizational and functional strategic plans
	2.3 Business process design	Determine how IS can deliver 'best practice' in the operational processes of organizational activities
	2.4 Business performance improvement	Identify the knowledge and information needed to deliver strategic objectives through improved management processes
	2.5 Systems and process innovation	Carry out relevant R&D into how IS/IT can be used to create new ways of conducting business and new products and/or services
3. *Define the IT capability (IT strategy)*	3.1 Infrastructure development	Define and design information, application and technology architectures and organization structures and processes to manage the resources
	3.2 Technology analysis	Understand technology developments and make appropriate recommendations for organizational acquisition of technology and associated resources
	3.3 Sourcing strategies	Establish criteria and processes to evaluate supply options and contracts with suppliers

continued

Table 8.11 (continued)

Macro-competency	Competency	The ability to ...
4. *Exploitation*	4.1 Benefits planning	Explicitly identify and plan to realize the benefits from IS investments
	4.2 Benefits delivery	Monitor, measure and evaluate the (net) benefits derived from IS investment and use
	4.3 Managing change	Make the business and organizational changes required to maximize the benefits without detrimental impact on stakeholders
5. *Deliver solutions*	5.1 Applications development	Develop/acquire and implement information, systems and technology solutions that satisfy business needs
	5.2 Service management	Define service arrangements and performance criteria to match the business requirements (including project management)
	5.3 Information asset management	Establish and operate processes that ensure data, information and knowledge management activities meet organizational needs and satisfy corporate policies
	5.4 Implementation management	Ensure that new processes and ways of working are designed and implemented effectively in conjunction with new technology
	5.5 Apply technology	Deploy new/changed technology in the most cost-effective mode to deliver application benefits
	5.6 Business continuity and security	Provide effective recovery, contingency and security processes to prevent risk of business failure
6. *Supply*	6.1 Supplier relationships	Manage contracts and develop value-added relationships with suppliers
	6.2 Technology standards	Develop and maintain appropriate standards, methods, controls and procedures for the use of IT and associated resources
	6.3 Technology acquisition	Develop and apply procurement policies and procedures for the organizational acquisition of infrastructure components and specialist technologies/services
	6.4 Asset and cost management	Ensure technology, information and application assets are effectively maintained and costs of acquisition and ownership are understood and managed
	6.5 IS/IT staff development	Recruit, train and deploy appropriate staff and ensure technical, business and personal skills meet the needs of the organization

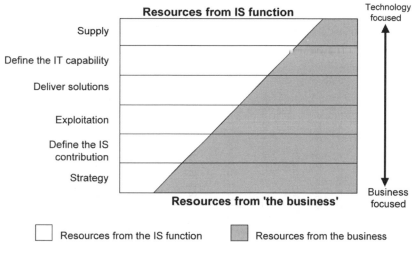

Figure 8.11   *Mapping location of resources against IS components*

appropriate behaviours and values regarding information and its use in the organization.[43]

The concept of IS/IT competencies can be used in a diagnostic mode to assess both the existence and level of current performance of each of the competencies. The current performance of each competency is assessed *relative* to required performance. This assessment is usually conducted in a workshop setting with both business and IT managers. Such a forum can serve to identify areas of weakness and thus requiring development. A 'spider diagram' from a series of workshops conducted in a global telecommunications equipment manufacturer shows the size of the gaps—especially in 'business-side' competencies—between the required level and the disappointing actual performance (see Figure 8.12). Needless to say, the IS function had previously been criticized for poor delivery of applications and technology, etc., but the analysis showed that the underlying causes of the problems were the business managers' and users' lack of knowledge, skills and poor understanding of what information and systems they required to meet business objectives.

IS/IT COMPETENCY: THE CRITICALITY OF THE HUMAN RESOURCE

The message from the previous discussion is that when IS/IT fulfils a strategic role in a business, the enterprise must develop and maintain a high level of competency in how it manages and uses IS/IT. As noted,

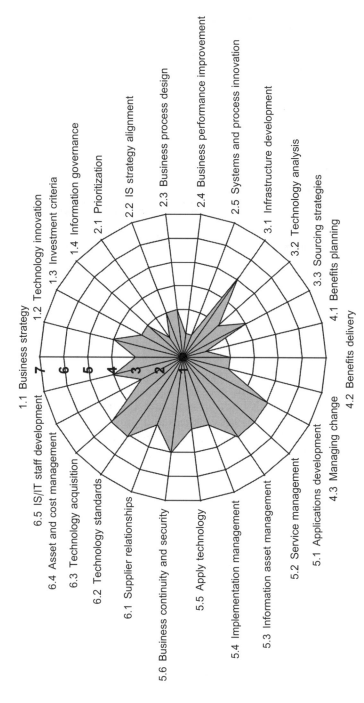

Figure 8.12 'Spider diagram' representation of performance of global telecommunications equipment manufacturer across IS competencies

competency can be considered as a combination of knowledge, skills, expertise and behaviours that reside in the people it deploys, and organizational processes that determine how to develop and exploit that expertise. Most of this chapter has focused on the latter component. It is worth considering a number of strategic issues concerning the people who deliver the other key component.

One aspect of the Manufacturers Trust Co. strategy, mentioned earlier in the chapter, that deserves more comment is the need to manage human resources as a corporate resource. Undoubtedly, one of the critical factors for any organization in achieving the best results from IS/IT is the quality of people involved in terms of knowledge, skills and experience. The ability to obtain and deploy highly-skilled IS/IT resources in adequate numbers will determine, in the long term, how well the business and IS/IT strategies are brought together. Whether these staff are located centrally or decentralized does not matter—the issues are similar. However, given the increasing choices of 'sourcing' options for resources, decisions on whether the people themselves need be employed by the organization, over the long term, are becoming more complex.

There are essentially four solutions to the development of the requisite skills, other than ensuring that the turnover of key staff is kept to a minimum by good 'hygiene factors' as well as career and personal development options. The four ways are:

1. Training new recruits from school or university, which is expensive. Also, people early in their careers are more likely to move on within three to five years.
2. Recruiting experienced staff from other organizations, which can be risky.
3. Training existing non-IS people, especially in application skills in user areas, which may require the development of new job roles.
4. Using external resources, either on a short-term basis to overcome peak loads, etc. or longer term to provide the organization with particular skills.

Consider the following scenario, which has become increasingly common, as an example of how the problems of selecting the best options manifest themselves.

The existing IS/IT resource is 'bogged down' in key-operational and support systems, mainly maintenance and rewrites. A new major strategic development is conceived, but cannot be resourced internally in the time required. A decision is taken to bring in external contract-based resources to develop the strategic application. What are the potential long-term consequences?

- An open-ended contract to meet an ever-changing requirement for strategic development?
- No one in the IS function is capable of understanding and supporting it in due course?
- What will the 'supplier' do with the knowledge?
- Demoralized staff who have to do the 'boring stuff', while others get the 'good' jobs? They leave—often to join the outsourcing vendor— and the situation worsens.

It can become a vicious circle. By referring to the rationale of the applications portfolio, it should be clear that the one area that must not be handed over to outside parties is that which provides the future business advantage! Equally, the one area that can be handed over with purely economic consequences is the 'support' quadrant, or much of what it contains. Outsourcing this work should be considered to release resources to use elsewhere. If the organization is to develop its competency and provide an attractive environment to retain its most skilled and effective people, then its own resources, IT and user, must be deployed on the challenging strategic or high potential systems, or the skills will become frozen in the past. It can even be more appropriate to use outside resources to deliver or maintain key operational systems to a clear contractual specification rather than use scarce internal resources. Quality control could be maintained by a strong quality assurance process applied to the supplier, in conjunction with explicit service-level agreements. Such a discipline can also discourage 'nice to have' enhancements being requested, since their delivery will require real external expense.

It may, of course, be necessary to buy in some special skills that the organization does not have to help develop even a strategic application. This resource should be bought with the objective of extracting that special knowledge for the benefit of the organization, by using it not just to deliver results but also to develop internal expertise.

The long-term aim of any strategy is to move resources out of the support quadrant by substituting less resource-intensive means, and, while ensuring that key operational systems are adequately resourced, develop the ability to carry out strategic and high-potential developments. Any alternative strategy will reduce the long-term capability of the organization, and increase the development and operational costs of applications in all parts of the portfolio. While many aspects of implementation and ongoing operation can be entrusted to external specialists, it is risky, even foolhardy, to allow external organizations to decide the strategic IS/IT direction. These ideas, in terms of the portfolio, are summarized in Figure 8.13.

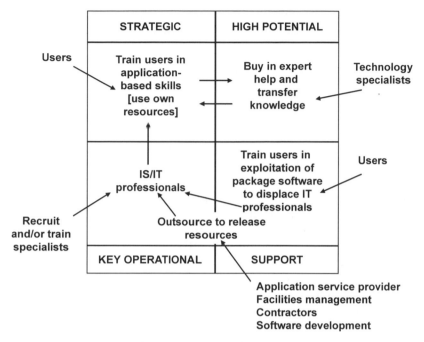

Figure 8.13   *Use of resources*

Peter Keen[44] discusses similar issues in more detail and considers not only the types of people required and their likely sources but also the job roles and skills, experience and career paths for each. He considers the spectrum of skills from business to specialist IT and defines four major role categories:

1. business services—requiring strong business, organizational and planning skills;
2. business support—business and organizational as well as some technical skills;
3. development support—strong technical and good business skills;
4. technical services—strong technical skills.

Many organizations are developing such new roles to link the traditional technical specialists via business-based dedicated people (e.g. business systems analysts) to the 'real' business management. These roles are required irrespective of where IS/IT reports in the organization. Many of these roles are critical to the determination of the applications and resulting business benefits (the IS strategy) as well as to deciding how best to deliver those applications successfully (the IT strategy).

MANAGING RELATIONSHIPS

Relationships play a key part in the management of IS/IT. On the one hand, both business and IS/IT specialists must work in harmony not only in developing the IS/IT strategy but also in the implementation of that strategy and delivering business benefits. On the other hand, as organizations look toward outsourcing, the strength of relationships with vendors becomes paramount in ensuring continued success with IS/IT. This is a critical risk factor associated with outsourcing and requires continual management attention.

Venkatraman and Loh[45] have examined the changing role of the IS function in terms of its relationships rather than its activities, especially given the wide range of sourcing options now available. They suggest that the IS function needs to define its 'locus of competency' clearly in terms of its value-adding capability, and then focus on managing three key relationships:

1. *With outside IT suppliers*, who will inevitably do increasingly more of the work through outsourcing arrangements. They also argue that a simplistic approach to outsourcing IT supply will leave a 'competency gap' in the organization, which could disable its ability to ensure that IS/IT fulfils its strategic role. And, as already noted, even where IT supply is fully outsourced, there are certain competencies that should never be outsourced.
2. *With the business managers and system users*, to enable the business to identify and realize the benefits from the application investments and to obtain maximum value from the services provided.
3. *With IT specialists in other companies*, especially trading partners, as increasingly more systems become interorganizational through extended and critical use of e-commerce and the Internet and even shared systems, as described earlier in the book.

They contrast this new role with the skills and values of a traditional organization, particularly cultural aspects, which are examined later in this chapter.

Internal Organizational Relationships

From Table 8.2, one of the requirements of the strategic management of IS/IT is 'to create a culture for the management of IS/IT that reflects the corporate culture.' This implies taking action to overcome the frequently-observed 'culture gap' that can exist between the IT specialists and the rest of the organization. Organizations are not culturally holistic—they contain subcultures often associated with functional specialism or geographical location. These subcultures can be dysfunctional. Information Technology as a functional specialism has been introduced to most organizations during the past 30 years and, as such, has introduced a new subculture, and one that is often difficult to reconcile with the dominant culture in the organization.[46]

The result—the so-called 'culture gap'—implies that, as with business strategy, the viability of the IS strategy will depend on the extent to which it is derived from the 'shared values' of those who have to implement the strategy. Simply put, do they *believe* in it as well as *agree* to it? In a study conducted by Grindley,[47] he found that the existence of the culture gap had serious strategic implications:

- 47% of IT directors stated that their main problem was the culture gap between IT and business professionals;
- 56% believe that the culture gap is inhibiting their organizations from gaining competitive advantage from IS/IT.

His survey concluded that, 'the culture gap is a deep-rooted problem, of a much more fundamental nature than the simple knowledge gap experienced when dealing with other specialists.'

The reasons why the IT specialism and its particular culture have proved difficult to integrate with the rest of the organization were described to an extent in Chapter 1. In particular, the work of Galliers and Sutherland[48] uses the well-known McKinsey '7S' model (strategy, structure, style, systems, shared values, . . .) to describe the evolving attributes of IT in relation to the increasingly strategic role of IS in organizations. Their analysis suggests a pattern of change in shared values and other attributes of the IS/business relationship as the organization increases in its dependence on IS/IT. But, they also have words of warning for those who would suggest radically-different approaches to IS/IT strategy and planning. They draw the following conclusions:

- each of the attributes needs to change as the organization becomes more dependent on its IT systems and the more mature in its planning of them;
- if any of the attributes is unsatisfactorily addressed in an early stage of the evolution, then the organization will be less able (or even unable) to achieve success in the latter, more demanding stages;

- positive attributes developed in the early stages should not be discarded later since the organization will have a legacy of products from the earlier stages to support;
- for an organization to succeed, without major hiatus or disruption of IT supply, it should address all of the 7S elements coherently at each stage before moving forward.

Table 8.12 summarizes the six stages as described by Galliers and Sutherland, focusing on the conclusions regarding the 'shared values' at each stage. In many organizations, it is the long-term effects of behaviour in Stages 2 and 3, as perceived by business managers, that make the relationship changes required in Stage 4 onward difficult to achieve. The table emphasizes perhaps the more negative aspect of the observed realities in Stages 4–6 in organizations than the desired, almost idyllic, relationships described by Galliers and Sutherland as prerequisites for success.

Crescenzi[49] used the same 7S view to describe why the majority of 'strategic systems' (25 out of 30 in a study) were unsuccessful. He concludes that the range of attributes and attitudes of IS functions and staff that are appropriate in a reactive, problem-solving, job-shop environment (i.e. 'support') are quite inappropriate when projects require a proactive, change-driven approach (i.e. 'strategic').

From a rational perspective, the approaches to organizational design and coordinating structures in this chapter are attempts to close or bridge the gap. Matching IT services to the different nature of IS requirements and use in the portfolio segments should reduce gaps at an operational level. The steering group structure attempts to allocate the decision making and planning processes to the most appropriate place and level in the organization, and provide the means for reconciling contention.

But, cultural issues are as much about beliefs and perceptions as about intellectual consensus. Before full 'congruence of shared values' can be achieved, the reasons for lack of congruence need to be understood. How this can be done using a cultural mapping technique ('the cultural web') is described by Ward and Peppard.[50] The purpose of the approach is to enable business and IT people to describe their perceptions of the relationship as a starting point for reconciliation, through changing either the way business people work with IT specialists or (more commonly!) vice versa. In most situations, change is required on both sides: business people understanding better the need for structure and discipline in IS/IT to avoid expensive failure; IT specialists appreciating the importance of responsiveness to external pressures and accepting the degrees of uncertainty and the often ambiguous nature of business decisions. Box 8.3

Table 8.12 Summary of the staged model of Galliers and Sutherland

Stage 1	Adhocracy	Very few, if any, shared values since the focus of IT is internal and they are unable or unwilling to seek a coherent relationship with the business. They relate more closely to IT suppliers
Stage 2	'Starting the foundations'	The 'priesthood' of IT begins to develop and IT staff perhaps cultivate a unique culture based on technology worship—often seriously at odds with the business
Stage 3	'Centralized dictatorship'	When IT management often reacts to business managers' concern over 'excessive spending' on IT and views of poor delivery performance by becoming defensive and exerting control over what it does to redress the balance
Stage 4	'Democratic dialectic and cooperation'	IT specialists recognize the need to work in cooperation with business managers toward achieving business goals, but still expect the business to cooperate with IT's set of values
Stage 5	'Entrepreneurial opportunity'	Recognition in the business that IT can deliver new, potentially strategic, benefits through innovative use often leaves the IT department looking after the legacy and struggling to provide any value to the newly 'liberated' users
Stage 6	'Integrated harmonious relationship'	Rarely achieved, due to the difficulties in reconciling differing values, overcoming historical precedents and prejudice, and requiring a new openness in all aspects of IT activity

describes the dimensions of the cultural web and illustrates how it was used by one pharmaceutical company.

Often, even when the relationship between IT specialists and the rest of the business is problematic, little effort is made to understand the causes of the problems. The remedy has normally involved 'reorganization', either of IT resources or the means by which they are controlled, resulting

Box 8.3 The cultural web and its application to exploring the culture gap

The culture web is a tool devised by Johnson* to assess the culture of an organization. While individuals may hold different sets of beliefs, there is at some level a core set of values, beliefs and assumptions commonly held throughout the organization. This has been referred to by Johnson as the *paradigm*. The paradigm governs and influences an organization's view of itself and its environment. Johnson argues that it is through this paradigm that an organization creates a relatively homogeneous approach to business. As it evolves through time and is reinforced by history, it sets out a repertoire of actions and responses that can be made in certain situations. The paradigm is protected by a 'web' of what Johnson refers to as *cultural artefacts*. They are described as follows:

- *Stories and myths*—In every organization, there are stories, some true, others either variations of the truth or simply myths. Examples are the big IT failures, the products that flopped, the legendary leaders and mavericks. In particular, new employees hear stories about those who broke the cultural norms and the consequences of their actions. Most have evolved over the years and have become part of the organization's folklore. What stories do is legitimize types of behaviour and are devices for telling people what's important in the organization. Like the fisherman's stories of ever larger fish, these stories can be rapidly distorted by the workings of the grapevine.
- *Symbols*—All organizations have their symbols, although they are often so ingrained that they may not be recognized. The dress code, the furniture, executive parking spaces are all symbols. At one particular insurance company, there were five different categories of restaurant and, as one progressed up the management hierarchy, the quality of both food and dining room décor improved considerably. Symbols also include company-specific language, which reinforces entrenched attitudes, like addressing managers as 'Mister'.
- *Rituals and routines*—Rituals are those aspects of organizational life that hold special significance and may include the monthly board meeting, the annual company barbecue and singing the company song. Routines refer to 'the way we do things here' and incorporate the core activities that the organization traditionally undertakes.

- *Control systems*—Organizations have particular control systems to monitor and encourage performance. Pay and reward systems, budgetary control systems and the management hierarchy are all examples of such systems. They serve to highlight what is valued by the organization.
- *Organizational structures*—Functions, departments, geographical-based business units, product-based business units, flat management hierarchies, large bureaucratic hierarchies are all examples of how the structure of an organization impact the paradigm.
- *Power structures*—Power lies with influence, particularly where such influence can reduce uncertainty. The power structures tend to reinforce the paradigm and, hence, they are often targets for change. This is particularly difficult given that those who may be required to change often hold the power.

In attempting to change their culture, many organizations manipulate the 'hard' elements of the web (i.e. the power structures, the control systems and the organizational structures), neglecting to address the more intangible elements. This is a mistake. All elements of the web must be examined and acted on if culture change is to take place and this change translated into tangible action and results.

The web, illustrated below, was derived from data collected from

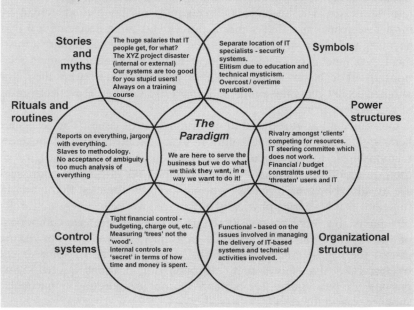

a global pharmaceutical organization that had sought to bring both IS staff and business staff closer together.** From the analysis, it was evident that the organization had worked hard at restructuring its IS function, improving the control of activities and getting line managers involved in decision making about IS. However, the symbols, stories and rituals, the 'softer' elements as perceived from 'the business' viewpoint, had changed little over this time. Senior management were unaware of this and the impact that it had on the ability of IS, and in particular the IS function, to work effectively in the organization.

*G. Johnson, 'Managing strategic change—strategy, culture and action', *Long Range Planning*, Vol. 25, No. 1, 1992, 28–36.
**Detailed coverage of cultural web analysis can be found in G. Johnson, 'Mapping and remapping organisational culture', in V. Ambrosini, G. Johnson and K. Scholes, eds, *Exploring Techniques of Analysis and Evaluation in Strategic Management*, Prentice-Hall, Hemel Hempstead, UK, 1998.

in either greater centralization or decentralization of either or both. In many large companies, these dramatic, and, it seems, increasingly more frequent, swings of the pendulum disrupt and even destroy any medium-term strategies. The arguments throughout this book (and agreed by most researchers) are that some resources and some decisions are best devolved and others are best centralized. The balance will require adjustment over time as problems will occur in the IS function/business relationship. It is better to resolve these problems than swap them for another set by reorganization, and probably damage the effectiveness of the strategy process.

Outsourcing has introduced an additional set of issues. The relevance here is that one alternative solution to an unsatisfactory IT/business relationship is to outsource the IS function in significant part, or in total, to an outside supplier. While a complex set of options and issues are trivialized by simple generalizations, it can be observed that many IS functions that have been physically outsourced were effectively 'culturally outsourced' (i.e. were not considered as an integral, strategic component of the organization) long before a convenient event, offer or excuse caused the real severance. This observation is verified to some extent by research[51] that shows that, although organizations quoted many reasons for outsourcing IT, a main reason for selecting a particular supplier was 'cultural fit'!

Beyond the Culture Gap

In research conducted in the late 1990s, an attempt was made to progress beyond merely using the label 'culture gap' as a variable in explaining the problems that can exist between the IS function and the rest of the business and explore in detail its nature and context. This research took the view that one of the problems with attaching the culture label is that it then becomes a *fait accompli*, and almost acceptance of the situation. The 'culture gap' becomes a convenient label to attach to a situation that is clearly causing a problem, but which organizations are either unable or unwilling to address. It was strongly suggested that the culture argument is often an excuse for, rather than the cause of, poor working relationships. In essence, culture is a symptom rather than a cause of an ineffective relationship between the IS function and the rest of the business and the consequential failure of organizations to exploit and leverage IS.

This research focused on identifying the organizational aspects to be managed in improving the relationship between the IS function and 'the business' and, consequently, the value derived from IS investments. Analysis of the empirical data from the three sites included in the study revealed five core dimensions. These dimensions are leadership, structures and processes, roles, relationships and behaviours (see Figure 8.14).

Research related to each of these dimensions can be found in the IS literature. However, the research reported in Peppard and Ward[52] indicated that each dimension on its own is not sufficient to address the organizational aspects of the relationship and that a more holistic perspective is required. For example, hiring a new CIO will not

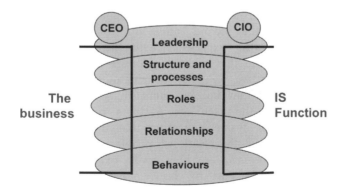

Figure 8.14   *Bridging the gap*

automatically solve problems regarding the inability of IS to deliver value; however, he or she may help in the creation of an environment for success. The other four dimensions must also be addressed. How the 'gap' can be bridged is addressed at the end of the chapter.

Managing Relationships with Vendors

It is a fact that outsourcing results in a dependence of the client organization on the vendor, yet there has been only limited research on building partnering relationships in outsourcing situations.[53] Outsourcing alliances are difficult, particularly as contracts are usually for between 3 and 10 years in an environment with rapid business and technological change. McFarlan and Nolan[54] note that customers who make an original decision based on efficiency will judge it differently if using effectiveness criteria later.

The importance of cultural fit in any outsourcing situation has already been noted, but, even then, a strong partnership is not guaranteed; building a strong partnership generally has to be worked on. Klepper used a sequential stage model of partnership development, developed by Dwyer *et al.*,[55] as a starting point for understanding the managerial interventions an organization might make to further the partnering process in outsourcing. This model consists of four stages: awareness, exploration, expansion and commitment. There are also subprocesses that work within the exploration, expansion and commitment phases that either move the parties closer to or further from the next stage. These are subprocesses of attraction, communication and bargaining, development and exercise of power, norm development and expectation development.

Awareness consists of recognition that the other party may be a suitable exchange partner, but with no exchange at this point. Exchange begins in the second stage of *exploration*. It is in the *exploration* phase, after experience with the vendor, that the two parties first appreciate that a deeper, longer-lasting relationship may be possible. In the *expansion* phase, benefits mount for both partners in the relationship and they become increasingly interdependent. In the *commitment* phase, the exchange partners receive such significant benefits from doing business together that they agree, explicitly or implicitly, to continue the relationship and partnership is cemented. Indicators of *commitment* are high levels of input to building and sustaining the relationship by both partners, consistency in the application of inputs and durability of a strong relationship over time.

BRIDGING THE GAP: IMPROVING THE CONTRIBUTION OF THE IS FUNCTION

In organizations where the relationship between the IS function and the rest of the business is poor, this severely impacts the ability of the IS function to make the sort of contribution that the business demands. Bridging this 'relationship' gap is not an easy task and can take many years to effect.

There has been some research that has explored how an organization can begin to improve the relationship between the IS function and the rest of the business. Earl and Sampler[56] have used the distinction between IS demand and IT supply in order to define a prescriptive model. They argue that supply and demand have to be managed, a process they refer to as 'market management' and have proposed a four-stage model that helps organizations balance supply and demand in managing IS/IT (see Box 8.4).

As a result of longitudinal research in three organizations, Peppard[57] constructed a model with six stages detailing the transformation process (see Box 8.5). Success in improving the contribution of IS/IT is initially premised on having strong IS leadership within the IS function and the importance of the IS Director/CIO having credibility within the business. As with the Earl and Sampler framework, the data from this research highlighted the importance of first getting the basics right—network uptime, availability and reliability of applications, help-desk response times, etc. It is fruitless engaging business management in dialogue if basic IT services are not being delivered. Key influencers within the organization then have to be enlisted before any realistic dialogue can be held with the business. A key element of transforming the value-added contribution of IS/IT is building the credibility of the IS function—it is important to remember that credibility must be earned and is derived from achievement and actual results. The overall conclusion from this research is that 'bridging the gap' between the IS function and the rest of the business is likely to take time and is primarily a people issue governed by the organizational legacy regarding IS/IT experiences. Box 8.5 describes the transforming stages and Box 8.6 illustrates the transformation program that a large UK bank put in place in order to improve the contribution of their IS function.

Box 8.4   Prescriptions for market management (*source:* M.J. Earl and J. Sampler, 'Market management to transform the IT organisation', *Sloan Management Review*, Summer, 1998, 9–17)

1. Recognize disequilibrium
At this opening stage, the organization first articulates, explores and analyses the crisis or loss of confidence in IT in general and the IS function in particular. Generally, there are both supply and demand issues causing problems. For example, IT may not be delivering or the business is not specifying and using the systems that it needs. Symptoms and prescriptions at this stage include:

- business needs not satisfied;
- technological problems;
- management assessment;
- start of new regime.

2. Emphasize supply management (supply first, demand second)
At this stage, the company seeks radical performance improvement of the supply side by setting delivery goals and beginning to rebuild the technology platform. The focus is on releasing and realizing value from the inherited IT situation. Prescriptions at this stage include:

- setting ambitious performance targets;
- beginning to rebuild technical platform;
- seeking early, visible results;
- setting application priorities.

3. Emphasizing demand management (demand first, supply second)
Stage 3 emphasizes demand management, shifting the focus from supply to demand, but not exclusively. The concern is with building IT capabilities and creating future value. Prescriptions at this stage include:

- work out the vision;
- define demand management processes;
- define value propositions;
- plan the infrastructure.

4. Maintain equilibrium
In this final stage, the company completes the transformation process by implementing final radical changes in both demand and supply sides. This stage is an ongoing state of equilibrium between

supply and demand. However, if business or technological discontinuities occur and the company does not deal with them, it can initiate a new transformation process by returning to Stage 1. Prescriptions include:

- recognizing that it is a continuous journey;
- rethinking governance;
- reskilling IT personnel;
- creating a partnership with business and vendors.

Box 8.5   A model for improving the value-added of the IS function (*source:* J.W. Peppard, 'Bridging the gap between the IS function and the rest of the business: Plotting a route', *Information Systems Journal*, Vol. 11, 2001, 249–270)

Stage 1: Get the basics right
The first stage involves focusing on the IS function itself, ensuring that it can deliver basic IT services. These are primarily technology focused and tactical, and include network uptime, availability and reliability of applications, and help-desk response times. This usually requires an examination of internal structures and processes, particularly in the areas of project management, quality of applications and quality of its customer service. The evidence from the research was clear in asserting that it is futile attempting to improve the relationship if the ability of the IS function to meet basic business expectations is either weak or non-existent. This usually entails establishing metrics to measure and assess performance. It is also important for the IS function to get business focused. However, obtaining the buy-in of all IS staff is crucial, if the IS capability is to develop further. A central ingredient is the leadership, credibility and vision of the IS director.

Stage 2: Enlist key influencers
Within any organization, there are particular individuals who are pivotal to what happens in it, the so-called opinion leaders or key influencers. If the transformation of the IS function is to progress, the evidence from research suggested that it is important to get these influencers on board before proceeding to the later stages; the visibility that these individuals bring is not only to add impetus to the process but can also decide the fate of the initiative. Enlisting key

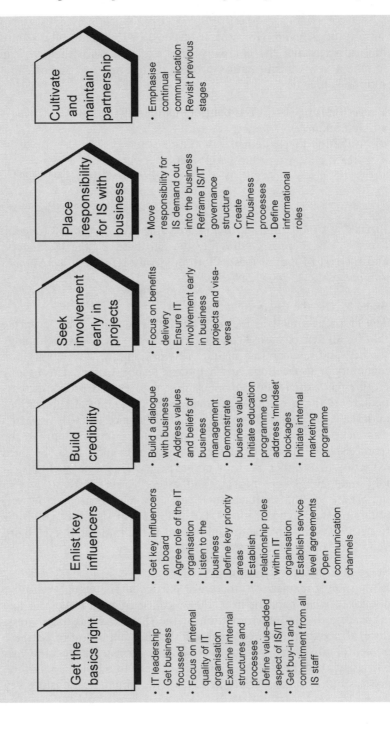

Get the basics right

- IT leadership
- Get business focussed
- Focus on internal quality of IT organisation
- Examine internal structures and processes
- Define value-added aspect of IS/IT
- Get buy-in and commitment from all IS staff

Enlist key influencers

- Get key influencers on board
- Agree role of the IT organisation
- Listen to the business
- Define key priority areas
- Establish relationship roles within IT organisation
- Establish service level agreements
- Open communication channels

Build credibility

- Build a dialogue with business
- Address values and beliefs of business management
- Demonstrate business value
- Initiate education programme to address 'mindset' blockages
- Initiate internal marketing programme

Seek involvement early in projects

- Focus on benefits delivery
- Ensure IT involvement early in business projects and visa-versa

Place responsibility for IS with business

- Move responsibility for IS demand out into the business
- Reframe IS/IT governance structure
- Create IT/business processes
- Define informational roles

Cultivate and maintain partnership

- Emphasise continual communication
- Revisit previous stages

influencers generally requires that there is some agreement reached as to the role and function of the IS organization. This is seen as not only giving clarity to the role and establishing expectations but also identifying areas of potential conflict that may have implications at later stages (e.g. centralizing some aspects of IS spend previously distributed across the organization or the imposition of technology standards).

Stage 3: Build credibility

While the previous stages focused on the key influencers, this stage focuses on incumbents at all levels in the rest of the organization. In establishing credibility, it is important to bear in mind that credibility is not something that is taken, but rather something that is given; in essence, it must be earned by the IS function and is derived from achievements and actual results. The research data suggested that building trust and mutual respect is a central aspect of the route toward true partnership; distrust on both sides can emerge over the years and is a legacy that can be difficult to discard. It is equally important to manage the expectations of the business and ensure that the IS function does not over-promise. Education plays a key role in this stage to impress upon business managers the process of value creation through IT and the key role that they play in this process.

Stage 4: Seek involvement early in projects

Having credibility is not an end in itself; rather, it establishes the launch pad for passing through the final stages. Without a credible IS function, business managers are unlikely to risk being involved or will be cautious in getting involved in IS-related matters, not to mention assuming responsibility for activities and decisions traditionally made by the IS function. The research suggested that the IS function should actively seek out the involvement of the business in IS projects. Equally, the IS function should get involved in projects when invited to by the business.

Stage 5: Place responsibility for IS with the business

The case data highlighted the importance of business managers taking responsibility for aspects of IS that traditionally may have been delegated to the IS function. This requires reframing the IS governance structure, as many 'IS decisions' taken by the IS function should often be the concern of business managers. The organization-wide nature of IS competencies and the distribution of component resources has already been noted, and resource elements from 'the business' are required for IS competencies to be enacted.

Stage 6: Cultivate and maintain partnership
Like any relationship, the relationship between the IS function and the rest of the business must be continuously worked on. Both technology and the business environments are continually changing requiring appropriate responses to be made. Yet, there is the danger of business management getting complacent and not recognizing their contribution to IS success—reiterating the fact that the resources underpinning IS competencies are enterprise-wide.

Box 8.6   Dulwich and Galway plc

The principal activity of Dulwich and Galway Financial Services Group (D&G)* and its subsidiaries is the provision of a comprehensive range of personal financial services. In addition, the Group's principal subsidiary, Postbank plc, provides a wide range of banking and financial services to business and local authority customers. The Group's objective is to provide for its personal and business customers a comprehensive range of mortgage, investment and personal banking facilities that are high in quality and competitive in price.

> *D&G recognises that the delivery of shareholder value depends upon our ability to create real value for our customers. This involves retaining and growing mutually beneficial relationships through the development of innovative products; speedy delivery through a wide range of accessible channels; excellent and flexible service; a strong brand; and anticipating and responding to changing customer needs* (Annual Report, 1997)

The Group, which employs nearly 7,500 employees, is divided into three strategic business units each responsible for a specific business area. The Retail Financial Services unit provides mortgage, investments and personal banking services. Postbank provides asset finance, money transmission and merchant services. Group Treasury are responsible for investments and management of corporate assets. The business units are supported by the group functions, which include Group Information Services (GIS) as well as Human Resources, Strategic Planning, Finance and Corporate Affairs.

GIS, employing approximately 650 staff at two sites, is responsible for the delivery and support of business initiatives by the exploitation of new and existing technology. Its immediate customers are all D&G business units. The ultimate customer is anyone who uses D&G Group services and products (e.g. High Street Customers, Corporate Customers, etc.). Core IT systems support over half a million mortgages and over 4 million investment accounts. These provide information for terminals operated by cashiers at over 350 branches and agents nationwide. Other systems provide support to over 1 million personal banking customers, and to a large number of blue-chip customers, as well as supporting the functions common to any financial services company (accounting, payroll, treasury, etc.).

GIS has traditionally had a rough time at D&G with a poor reputation; in the words of one senior IT executive, 'GIS was the whipping boy.' When projects did not go well, inevitably GIS got the lion's share of the blame. Given its weak position in the organization, it was also reactive to business needs resulting in the development of disparate systems and a real lack of systems integration, '... over the last five years we have been excluded from the business analysis side of things, we have been subservient to the business ...' To further reinforce its disillusionment, many of the business units simply bypassed GIS for IT services, going straight to third-party vendors.

The arrival of a new IT director in 1996 saw the beginnings of a programme to transform the performance of the function. Perhaps consolidating the need for change, the result of a mid-1997 GIS staff survey were quite a shock for the top team of GIS. This survey clearly indicated that morale was low, employees felt alienated, and turnover was on the rise. A survey of internal customer satisfaction, undertaken at the same time, highlighted that, at best, it was indifferent.

There had been pockets of activity to improve the performance of the IT function prior to the arrival of the new IT director. These included the service delivery transformation programme, improving the delivery of systems (time, cost, quality, etc.) and general productivity improvements. A balanced Business Scorecard was also introduced to track performance. However, the new IT director knew that a step change was required if any significant improvement in the value-added contribution of the IT function was to be made.

The World Class 2000 (WC2000) project was instigated during 1997. With this initiative, GIS set itself the task of becoming world class by the year 2000; that is, to achieve world-class performance in all elements of the Business Excellence Model (BEM). The BEM is based around a well-recognized framework originating for the European Foundation for Quality Management. The model's structure forces completeness of thought to not only understand the actions required to deliver objectives but also the actions required to support this delivery through considerations of all fundamental business drivers. The model is based around the following premise: Customer Satisfaction, People (employee) satisfaction and Impact on Society are achieved through Leadership driving Policy and Strategy, People Management, Resources and Processes, leading ultimately to excellence in Business Results.

These nine criteria encompass all the aspects necessary for an organization to operate successfully, and provides the underlying framework for assessing the performance of all or part of an organization. The model divides into two principle sections—business results and enablers. Results are what the organization achieves, and the enablers are how the organization is run. Each criterion has a different score, reflecting its relative importance.

The IT director's stated objective during 1998 was to 'create the environment in which we can develop our organisation towards World Class status.' He further noted that, '[S]uperior information systems capability is central to the achievement of D&G business objectives and will be critical to survival in an increasingly competitive environment ... The primary objective of Group IS is to deliver a World Class Service and thereby support Shareholder Value through the successful implementation of "Business Projects".'

Through WC2000, GIS had two central objectives. First, to be the first-choice supplier to the business units. One senior IT manager noted that, '... we want the business to come to us first, you know, and always give us the chance first of all, and we do that by, you know, demonstrating that we are as good or better than external suppliers.' Second, to be the first-choice employer for IS professionals; good people would come looking to A&L for employment and career.

The BEM provided the framework for constructing the transformation programme. To populate the BEM with actions took six months, and this process included workshops, interviews, and one-on-one sessions. The bulk of this work was done by the GIS execu-

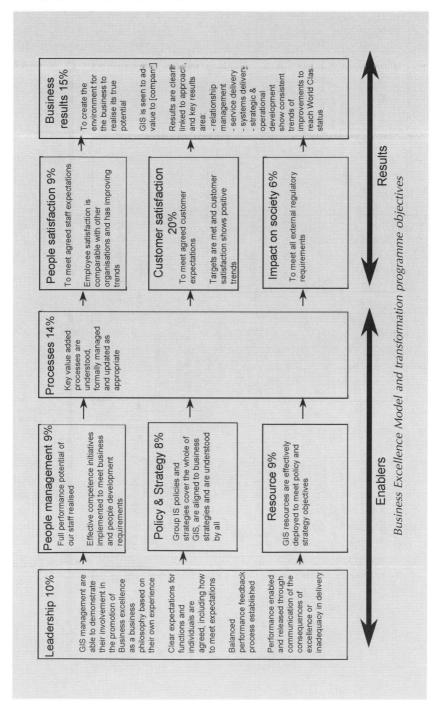

Business Excellence Model and transformation programme objectives

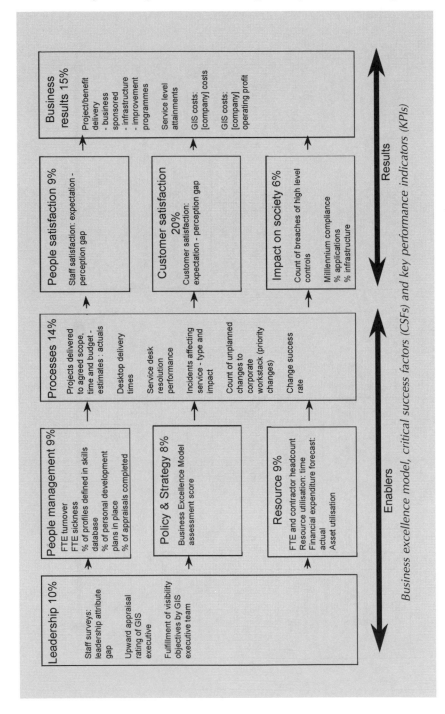

Business excellence model, critical success factors (CSFs) and key performance indicators (KPIs)

tive, with some support from its Organizational Development Unit. The performance of GIS in each of the nine elements of the BEM was assessed. This was done using the results of the customer and staff satisfaction surveys. Results for each element was analysed and an Organization Development process provided a diagnostic on the type and cause of the gaps between desired and actual performance of each element of the BEM.

Critical Success Factors were designed from these data by the top management team, which allowed subsequent development of Key Performance Indicators and the actions necessary to achieve them. These details were published in the 1998 GIS Operation Plan. According to a senior manager, 'the BEM gave us a complete framework rather than just focusing on a particular area ... not just knee-jerk decisions to some of the problems that we may have.' This plan is now updated twice per annum. GIS staff are kept updated on progress via regular briefings, monthly communications sessions, a newsletter and supporting documentation.

At the beginning of the initiative, GIS undertook a self-assessment exercise and scored 291 out of 1000. 'World class' is generally regarded as a score in excess of 500. To further illustrate the enormity of the task they faced, the Customer Satisfaction index maximum score is 200. In August 1997 D&G scored 63/200; by April 1998 it had improved to 67, still substantially lower than required. Employee Satisfaction in 1998 was 16 out of a maximum score of 90. By 2000 the company had achieved world-class status.

* Name has been changed.

SUMMARY

The previous chapter provided a framework of the applications portfolio and high-level management strategies for IS/IT. Subsequent chapters deal with aspects of strategy that, in many ways, are particular to IS/IT in terms of information, systems and technology. This chapter has attempted to consider the rationale for strategic management at the interface between the particulars of IS/IT and the general management of the organization. These strategies essentially address the matching and integration of the IS function to and within the business organization, and as such have to be defined by general management.

If these issues are not addressed both at the corporate level and for each of the main business units and functions, it is likely that, throughout the organization, behaviour will not be consistent with the strategy. The result will be failure to implement the strategy. It is obviously important to devise appropriate business-driven IS strategies and then appropriate IT-supply strategies. But, having a strategy is not going to lead to business success! Implementing and then updating that strategy as the business progresses is how success will occur. Mechanisms must be put in place to ensure that happens. A number of these mechanisms are considered in this chapter—primarily those concerning the organization of resources and their positioning in the business in relation to its other primary and support activities—and ways of ensuring that those resources are most appropriately deployed.

One conclusion, and hence an extension of the discussion into organizational overlays, is that, except perhaps in the simplest businesses, there is as yet no ideal organization structure for IS/IT within the business structure. This should perhaps not be surprising given the relatively recent arrival on the business scene of IS/IT and its rapidly-changing nature and importance. Many general managers perhaps wish the IS/IT management problem might 'go away' or become simple again—the 'IT manager' reports to Finance—but it will not, and will need to be addressed in every organization repeatedly over the coming decade.

Equally, other issues concerning IS/IT that management would perhaps prefer not to have to deal with are those resulting from the specialist people IS/IT involves. These people often have a career-versus-company conflict of loyalty and do not easily conform to the culture of the company. But, experienced, capable people with the requisite skills are becoming in even shorter supply, and without them business objectives may become unachievable. Strategies for ensuring that these critical resources are retained and developed are an essential part of the management strategy.

These organizational and resourcing issues of IS/IT strategy are those that become very critical during implementation and can lead to the failure to achieve what should have been a perfectly-feasible strategy, because they are ignored or dealt with ineffectively by the senior management of the enterprise.

ENDNOTES

1. M.J. Earl, 'Integrating IS and the organization: A framework of organizational fit', in M.J. Earl, ed., *Information Management: The Organizational Dimension*, Oxford University Press, Oxford, 1996, pp. 485–502.
2. R.E. Dvorak, E. Holen, D. Mark and W.F. Meehan, 'Six principles of high-performance IT', *The McKinsey Quarterly*, No. 3, 1997, 164–177; P.G.W. Keen, 'Information technology and the management difference: A fusion map', *IBM Systems Journal*, Vol. 32, No. 1, 1993, 17–39; T.C. Powell and A. Dent-Micallef, 'Information technology as competitive advan-

tage: the role of human, business and technology resources', *Strategic Management Journal*, Vol. 18, No. 5, 1997, 375–405; J.W. Ross, C. Mathis Beath and D. Goodhue, 'Develop long-term competitiveness through IT assets', *Sloan Management Review*, Fall, 1996, 31–42.

3. R.G. Hayward, 'Developing an information systems strategy', *Long Range Planning*, Vol. 20, No. 2, 1987, 100–113.

4. M.J. Earl, *Management Strategies for Information Technology*, Prentice-Hall, Hemel Hempstead, 1989.

5. It should be pointed out that other writers take a different perspective regarding information management. For example, while Marchand makes the distinction between IS, IT and IM, he views IM somewhat differently, relating it directly to the content, quality and use of information necessary for running an organization, such as operational controls, customer services and financial reporting. See D. Marchand, 'Creating business value with information', in D. Marchand, ed., *Competing with Information*, John Wiley & Sons, Chichester, UK, pp. 17–30.

6. Key research studies and papers include: A.C. Boynton, G.C. Jacobs and R.W. Zmud, 'Whose responsibility is IT management', *Sloan Management Review*, Summer, 1992, 32–38; C.V. Brown, 'Horizontal mechanisms under differing IS organization contexts', *MIS Quarterly*, Vol. 23, No. 3, 1999, 421–455; C.V. Brown and S.L. Magill, 'Alignment of the IS function with the enterprise: Towards a model of antecedents', *MIS Quarterly*, Vol. 18, 1994, 371–403; J. Dearden, 'The withering away of the IS organisation', *Sloan Management Review*, Summer, 1987, 87–91; G. DeSanctis and B.M. Jackson, 'Coordination of information technology management: Team-based structures and computer-based communication systems', *Journal of Management Information Systems*, Vol. 10, No. 4, 1994, 85–110; M.J. Earl, B. Edwards and D.F. Feeny, 'Configuring the IS function in complex organisations', in M.J. Earl, ed., *Information Management: The Organizational Dimension*, Oxford University Press, New York, 1996, pp. 201–230; J. George and J. King, 'Examining the computing and centralization debate', *Communications of the ACM*, Vol. 34, No. 7, 1991, 63–72; S.L. Hodgkinson, 'The role of the corporate IT function in the federal IT organization', in M.J. Earl, ed., *Information Management: The Organizational Dimension*, Oxford University Press, New York, 1996, pp. 247–269; J.L. King, 'Centralized versus decentralized computing: Organizational considerations and management options', *Computing Surveys*, Vol. 15, No. 4, pp. 319–340; R. Peterson, R. O'Callaghan and P. Ribbers, 'Information technology governance by design: Investing hybrid configurations and integration mechanisms', in *Proceeding of the 21st International Conference on Information Systems*, Brisbane, Australia, December 2000, pp. 435–542; V. Sambamurthy and R.W. Zmud, 'Arrangements for information technology governance: A theory of multiple contingencies', *MIS Quarterly*, Vol. 23, No. 2, 1999, 261–290.

7. From F. Keenan and T. Mullaney, 'Let's get back to basics, folks', *BusinessWeek, e.biz*, 29 October 2001.

8. 'Organising for the 1990s', *EDP Analyser*, Vol. 12, 1986.

9. A. La Belle, and H.E. Nyce, 'Whither the IT organisation?', *Sloan Management Review*, Summer, 1987, 75–85.

10. Merged with Chemical Banking Corporation on 31 December 1991.

11. M. Krumbholz, J. Galliers and N. Coulianos, 'Implementing enterprise resource planning packages in different corporate and national cultures', *Journal of Information Technology*, Vol. 15, 2000, 267–279; M.L. Markus, S. Axline, D. Petrie and C. Tanis, 'Learning from adopters' experiences with ERP: Problems encountered and success achieved', *Journal of Information Technology*, Vol. 15, 2000, 245–265; M.L. Markus, C. Tanis and P.C. van Fenema, 'Multisite ERP implementations', *Communications of the ACM*, Vol. 43, No. 4, 2000, 42–46; S.J. Simon, *ERP Software Configuration for Worldwide Markets: Issues of Strategic Fit*, Department of Decision Sciences and Information Systems, Florida International University, 1999; C. Stedman, 'Move to single global ERP system no easy task', *Computerworld*, 17 January 2000.

12. J.R. Buchanan and R.G. Linowes, 'Making distributed data processing work', *Harvard Business Review*, September–October 1980, 143–161; J. George and J. King, 'Examining the computing and centralization debate', *Communications of the ACM*, Vol. 34, No. 7, 1991, 63–72; S.L Hodgkinson, 'The role of the corporate IT function in the federal IT organisation', in M.J. Earl, ed., *Information Management: The Organizational Dimension*, Oxford University Press, Oxford, 1996, pp. 247–269; E.M. von Simson, 'The centrally decentralized IS organization', *Harvard Business Review*, July–August 1990, 158–162.

13. E.M. von Simson, 'The centrally decentralized IS organization', *Harvard Business Review*, July–August 1990, 158–162.

14. S.L. Hodgkinson, 'The role of the corporate IT function in the federal IT organization', in M.J. Earl, ed., *Information Management: The Organizational Dimension*, Oxford University Press, New York, 1996, pp. 247–269.

15. C.H. Sullivan, 'Systems planning in the information age', *Sloan Management Review*, Winter, 1985, 3–11.

16. J.F. Rockart, M.J. Earl and J.W. Ross, 'Eight imperatives for the new IT organisation', *Sloan Management Review*, Fall, 1996, 43–55.

17. N. Venkatraman, 'Beyond outsourcing: Managing IT resources as a value center', *Sloan Management Review*, Spring, 1997, 51–64.

18. *IS Lite: The Future*, Research Report, GartnerGroup, Egham, Surrey, 1999.

19. M.E. Earl and B. Khan, *How IT Departments Are Responding to the Challenges of E-Commerce*, Centre for the Networked Economy, London Business School, 2001, CNE WP04/2001.

20. *Evolving Competencies for IS Lite*, Research Report, GartnerGroup, Egham, Surrey, September 2000.

21. E.B. Swanson and C.M. Beath, 'Reconstructing the systems development organization', *MIS Quarterly*, Vol. 13, No. 3, 1989, 293–305.

22. M.J. Earl, B. Edwards and D.F. Feeny, 'Configuring the IS function in complex organizations', in M.J. Earl, ed., *Information Management: The Organisational Dimensions*, Oxford University Press, New York, 1996, 201–230.

23. *Managing the Devolution of Systems Responsibilities*, Butler Cox Foundation, Research Report 81, June 1991; M.J. Earl, B. Edwards and D. Feeny, 'Configuring the IS function in complex organizations', in M.J. Earl, ed., *Information Management: The Organizational Dimension*, Oxford University Press, Oxford, 1996, pp. 201–230.

24. Note that we use the term 'information management strategies' in a different way than Earl does. We use it to refer specifically to strategies regarding information.

25. T. Clark, R. Zmud and G. McCray, 'The outsourcing of information services: Transforming the nature of business in the information industry', in L.P. Willcocks and M.C. Lacity, eds, *Strategic Sourcing of Information Systems*, John Wiley & Sons, Chichester, UK, 1998, pp. 45–78.

26. L. Loh and N. Venkatraman, 'Diffusion of information technology outsourcing: Influence sources and the Kodak effect', *Information Systems Research*, Vol. 3, No. 4, 1992, 334–358.

27. M.C. Lacity, L.P. Willcocks and D.F. Feeny, 'The value of selective IT sourcing', *Sloan Management Review*, Spring, 1996, 13–25; M.C. Lacity, L.P. Willcocks and D.F. Feeny, 'IT outsourcing: Maximizing flexibility and control', *Harvard Business Review*, May–June 1995, 84–93.

28. L.P. Willcocks and M.C. Lacity, 'Introduction—the sourcing and outsourcing of IS: Shock of the new', in L.P. Willcocks and M.C. Lacity, eds, *Strategic Sourcing of Information Systems*, John Wiley & Sons, Chichester, UK, 1998, pp. 1–41.

29. C. Griffiths, 'Responsibility for IT: A gray area of management', in L. Willcocks, ed., *Information Management: The Evaluation of Information Systems Investments*, Chapman & Hall, London, 1994, pp. 223–250.

30. R.I. Benjamin, C. Dickinson, and J.F. Rockart, 'Changing role of the corporate information systems officer,' *MIS Quarterly*, Vol. 9, No. 3, 1985, 177–188.

31. 'Are CIOs obsolete?', *Harvard Business Review*, March–April, 2000, 55–63.

32. M.J. Earl and D. Feeny, 'Is your CIO adding value', *Sloan Management Review*, Spring, 1994, 11–20.

33. Conclusion from the authors' research as well as that of Earl. See M.J. Earl, 'Change isn't optional for today's CIO', in D. Marchand, T.H. Davenport and T. Dickson, eds, *Mastering Information Management*, Pearson Educational, London, 2000, pp. 69–72; and 'The chief information officer: Past, present and future', in M.J. Earl, ed., *Information Management: The Organizational Dimension*, Oxford University Press, Oxford, 1996, pp. 456–484; J.W. Peppard, 'Bridging the gap between the IS function and the rest of the business: Plotting a route', *Information Systems Journal*, Vol. 11, 2001, 249–270.

34. M.L. Pedersen and K. Rubenstrunk, 'The IT leadership vacuum', *CIO*, 15 September 1999.

35. M.J. Earl, *Management Strategies for Information Technology*, Prentice-Hall, Englewood Cliffs, New Jersey, 1989.

36. D.H. Drury, 'An evaluation of data processing steering committees', *MIS Quarterly*, Vol. 8, No. 4, 1984, 257–265.

37. Y.P. Gupta and T. S. Raghunathan, 'Impact of information systems steering committees on IS planning', *Decision Sciences*, Fall, 1988, Vol. 19, No. 4.

38. For example, R.D. Galliers, Y. Merali and L. Spearing, 'Coping with information technology? How British executives perceive the key information systems management issues in the mid 1990s', *Journal of Information Technology*, Vol. 9, No. 3, 1994.

39. D.F. Feeny and L.P. Willcocks, 'Redesigning the IS function around core capabilities', *Long Range Planning*, Vol. 31, No. 3, 1998, 354–367; D.F. Feeny and L.P. Willcocks, 'Core IS capabilities for exploiting information technology', *Sloan Management Review*, Spring, 1998, 9–21.

40. In their actual research, they used, the word 'capability', but the meaning is identical to how we have used the word competency.

41. D.A. Marchand, W. Kettinger and J.D. Rollins, 'Information orientation: People, technology and bottom line', *Sloan Management Review*, Summer, 2000, 69–80.

42. J.W. Peppard, R. Lambert and C.E. Edwards, 'Whose job is it anyway?: Organizational information competencies for value creation', *Information Systems Journal*, Vol. 10, No. 4, 2000, 291–323.

43. D.A Marchand, 'Why information is the responsibility of every manager', in D.A. Marchand, ed., *Competing with Information: A Manager's Guide to Creating Business Value with Information Content*, John Wiley and Sons, Chichester, UK, 2000, pp. 3–16; D.A. Marchand, W. Kettinger and J.D. Rollins, 'Information orientation: People, technology and bottom line', *Sloan Management Review*, Summer, 2000, 69–80.

44. P.G.W. Keen, 'Rebuilding the human resources of information systems', in M. Earl, ed., *Information Management: The Strategic Dimension*, Clarendon Press, Oxford, 1988.

45. N. Venkatraman and L. Loh, 'The shifting logic of the IS organization: From technical portfolio to relationship portfolio', *Information Strategy: The Executive's Journal*, Winter, 1994, 5–11.

46. E.H. Schein, *Organizational Culture and Leadership*, Jossey-Bass, San Francisco, 1992 (chapter 12, 'Management and information technology: Two subcultures in collision?', pp. 276–294).

47. K. Grindley, *Managing IT at Board Level: The Hidden Agenda Exposed*, Pitman Publishing, London, 1991.

48. R.D. Galliers and A.R. Sutherland, 'Information systems management and strategy formulation—the stages of growth model revisited', *Journal of Information Systems*, Vol. 1, No. 1, 1991, 89–114.

49. A.D. Crescenzi, 'The dark side of strategic IS implementation', *Information Strategy: The Executive's Journal*, Fall, 1988.

50. J.M. Ward and J.W. Peppard, 'Reconciling the IT/business relationship: A troubled marriage in need of guidance', *Journal of Strategic Information Systems*, Vol. 5, No. 1, 1996, 37–65.

51. G. Fitzgerald and V. Mitchell, 'The IT outsourcing marketplace: Vendors and their selection', paper presented at *The Management Challenges of IT Conference*, Cranfield School of Management, Cranfield, Bedford, UK, July 1994.

52. J.W. Peppard and J.M. Ward, 'Mind the gap: Diagnosing the relationship between the IT organization and the rest of the business', *Journal of Strategic Information Systems*, Vol. 8, 1999, 29–60.

53. Some research in this area includes B. Bensau and N. Venkatraman, 'Inter-organizational relationships and information technology: A conceptual synthesis and research framework', *European Journal of Information Systems*, Vol. 5, No. 2, 1996, 84–91; D. Lasher, B. Ives and S. Jarvenpaa, 'USAA-IBM partnerships in information technology: Managing the image project', *MIS Quarterly*, Vol. 15, No. 4, 1991, 551–565; W. McFarlan and R. Nolan, 'How to manage an IT outsourcing alliance', *Sloan Management Review*, Winter, 1995, 9–23; L.P. Willcocks and T. Kern, 'IT outsourcing as strategic partnering: The case of the UK Inland Revenue', in *Proceedings of the Fifth European Conference in Information Systems, Cork, Ireland, June, 1997*, pp. 1471–1489.

54. W. McFarlan and R. Nolan, 'How to manage an IT outsourcing alliance', *Sloan Management Review*, Winter, 1995, 9–23.

55. F. Dwyer, P. Schurr and S. Oh, 'Developing buyer–seller relationships', *Journal of Marketing*, Vol. 51, 1987, 11–27.

56. M.J. Earl and J. Sampler, 'Market management to transform the IT organisation', *Sloan Management Review*, Summer, 1998, 9–17.

57. J.W. Peppard, 'Bridging the gap between the IS function and the rest of the business: Plotting a route', *Information Systems Journal*, Vol. 11, 2001, 249–270.

9
Managing Investments in Information Systems and Technology

The applications portfolio will include a range of different IS/IT investments that have been identified as new developments or significant enhancements to existing systems. Before resources are assigned and development begins, several other steps need to be taken, including establishing the expected benefits of the investments, justifying the costs of the systems, technology and business changes involved and allocating priorities to individual developments across the portfolio. These decisions can all be aided by reference to application portfolio analysis, which provides a straightforward way of understanding the nature of the contributions expected from investments in relation to current and future business strategies. As was discussed in Chapter 8, organizational IS competencies in relation to establishing effective investment appraisal processes, setting priorities and delivering the benefits expected are key ingredients of successful IS/IT strategic management. Using the competency framework to assess organizations' overall IS capability often reveals major weaknesses in these areas. In particular, planning for and managing the benefits and the business changes essential to realizing them is cited as a continuing failing in many organizations.[1] Having a strategy is only a means to an end—delivering the business results required from the strategy is the main objective.

This chapter tackles some of the main issues relating to decision making and management of IS/IT investments:

- justifying investments in information systems and the associated technology, using various ways of assessing benefits;
- determining priorities, taking into account the range of economic

and other types of business benefit, resource constraints and logical factors of precedence;
- processes for managing the realization of the expected benefits;
- assessing the risks of the investments based on the characteristics of the application and the approach to its management.

INVESTMENT AND PRIORITY SETTING POLICIES

Investments in systems and technology compete with alternative investments such as buildings, plant, equipment, research and development (R&D) and advertising, for the organization's funds. IS/IT investments have traditionally been evaluated like capital projects such as plant and equipment assuming a fixed cost offset against net revenue over the life of the application. However, many modern applications are more like 'new business ventures' or business initiatives where the financial aspects of the outcome can only be guessed and the technology is only one component of a major change program. There is no simple answer to the question: on what basis should IS/IT investments be assessed against other investments? However, it is important that some general rules are established, within which applications and supporting technology requirements are evaluated. Otherwise, any strategy will be distorted over time by inconsistent, even arbitrary, decision making.

If the organization was able to develop, at any one time, all the applications demanded, inconsistent evaluation would not really matter. The overall return on IS/IT investment might be very poor, but at least the worthwhile would get done as well as the worthless! However, in most cases not all demand can be satisfied and priorities must be set. If no consistent justification approach is followed, the more beneficial applications may well be deferred, allowing those that make a lesser contribution to proceed. Assuming that does not mean an opportunity completely forgone, which may occur with delay, the resources and funds invested will have provided a poorer return than could have been achieved—hardly good management practice!

An obvious conclusion from the above is that the same principles and practice should govern the 'go–no go' decisions for individual applications and deciding priorities across applications competing for resources. The only additional factor, assuming that systems are not sequentially dependent, is the amount of resource consumed. The limiting factor is normally people, in quantity or quality (particular skills or knowledge), but the same logic applies whatever is the limiting resource (e.g. finance)—priority setting should enable maximum return from the use of that resource.

EVALUATING IS/IT INVESTMENTS

Much has been written about how investments in IS/IT should be assessed and justified. There is little, if any, consensus on how it should be done, but considerable consensus that the methods used are rarely appropriate! Several surveys have shown that there is still virtually no consistency in the practices used. Cooke and Parrish[2] discovered that 70% of organizations had no formal justification and post-implementation review process for IS/IT investments. Farbey et al.[3] found that only 50% of IS/IT projects were subject to formal preinvestment appraisal; in less than half the cases was a recognized financial analysis technique used, and in barely 30% was the outcome of the investment evaluated. They, like many others, suggest that given the wide variety of types of IS/IT investment and the wide range of benefit types, which can be quantified to greater or lesser degrees, a multiplicity of methods for justifying investments is needed. But, they recognize that selecting the right approach in any situation can itself be fraught with organizational and political problems.

Other analyses by Ballantine et al.[4] and Willcocks and Lester[5] suggest that traditional financial analysis techniques are still commonly in use, but that organizations are finding it increasingly difficult to use them as the types of benefit become more difficult to quantify adequately. Hochstrasser,[6] Peters[7] and Symons[8] all suggest ways in which different techniques can be used to evaluate different types of project. Interestingly, Lincoln and Shorrock[9] found that many successful 'strategic' IS/IT projects had bypassed the normal justification process used in the organization. Overall, organizations are far from satisfied with the techniques and processes they have for IS/IT investment appraisal—only 36% felt they were adequate in a survey[10] of major UK corporations.

Grindley[11] summed up the mistrust of conventional justification methods in two insights from his survey:

- 83% of IT directors admit that the cost–benefit analyses supporting IT investment proposals are a fiction;
- quote from a CEO: 'It's like there is a spontaneous conspiracy to exaggerate the benefits.' Many others would agree, no doubt!

A number of good papers on this subject are included in a book edited by Willcocks, entitled *Information Management: The Evaluation of Information Systems Investments.*[12] The approach described here is taken from one of the chapters of that book, but the authors recognize there is considerable merit in many of the other methods proposed. Farbey et al.'s book *IT Investments: A Study of Methods and Practice,*[13] for example, provides a detailed assessment of the issues involved and how different approaches to evaluation are needed to accommodate them.

A pure technology investment cannot strictly give a return on investment, unless it replaces an older technology and carries out the same functions more efficiently. Most technology investments are justified on the back of applications. Even if capacity and infrastructure components have to be purchased in advance of the need, the justification should be primarily based on their subsequent use in business applications and the resulting benefits. However, it is often difficult to associate all infrastructure investments with the subsequent benefits of using applications, even where sophisticated capital cost recovery accounting techniques are used. More comprehensive approaches to developing the case for investing in infrastructure are considered in Chapter 11.

Another point of evaluation logic, which is perhaps peculiar to IS/IT investments, is the way in which particular costs and benefits should be treated. Most accounting evaluation practices are conservative, expecting the worst and mistrusting the best. Raw IT costs have been reducing at 25% per annum for some 25 years, and this is difficult for accounting procedures to accept when evaluating systems with 5, 8 or 10-year lives. This changing reality of running costs of systems over time must be allowed for where shared resources are used. It is important to take a realistic (even marginal) view of the costs rather than a theoretical one. Equally frequently, the full costs of 'development' are not included. Normally, the IS function and procurement costs for hardware, software licences and purchased services are estimated in some detail, but costs incurred by business departments in specifying, testing and implementing the system are rarely included adequately.

On the other side of the coin, identifying and quantifying the benefits of any system can be a difficult, even impossible, task, as suggested above. In their book, Parker *et al.*[14] assess in detail the ways in which information and systems benefits accrue and how they can be quantified to help in justifying investments. They consider three main types of application:

1. *substitutive*—technology replacing people with economics being the main driving force, to improve efficiency.
2. *complementary*—improving organizational productivity and employee effectiveness by enabling work to be performed in new ways;
3. *innovative*—achieving a competitive edge by changing trading practice, creating new markets, etc.

They suggest ways in which each of the different types of application should be justified and define five basic techniques for evaluating benefits:

1. *Traditional cost–benefit analysis*, which allows for efficiency improvements in organizational processes resulting from automation (e.g. automating invoices and sending them electronically to customers via e-commerce, saving labour and data entry costs for all parties).
2. *Value linking*, which estimates the improvement in business performance, not just savings made, from improving the linkages between processes or activities (e.g. automatic reconciliation of orders, invoices and payments to enable accounts staff to spend more time resolving customer queries and issues, leading to fewer bad debts and less dissatisfied customers); or interactive component design with suppliers via a shared Computer-Aided Design (CAD) system, to reduce the number of iterations needed.
3. *Value acceleration*, which considers time dependence of benefits and costs in other departments of system improvements (e.g. giving sales data to buyers on a daily basis, improving their ability to respond to changes in demand and negotiate more effectively with suppliers). This implies that benefits can occur in other parts of the business, not just where the system is actually implemented.
4. *Value restructuring*, which considers the productivity resulting from process and organizational change and change of job roles (e.g. information-intensive tasks such as forecasting and planning can often only be improved by a combination of better systems and a change in organizational responsibilities).
5. *Innovation evaluation* attempts to estimate the value to the business of new business or new business practices levered from IS/IT (e.g. the launch of an online banking service may change the company image and attract new types of customers).

The above categories of benefit evaluation are suggested to be related to their application types and the portfolio classification, as shown in Figure 9.1. There are also obvious similarities with the benefits derived from different levels of IT-induced transformation described in Chapter 1.[15] By analysing costs and benefits using these techniques, the overall 'economics' of an application can be assessed. The ideas are certainly more creative in interpreting information's long-term value than traditional accounting views of systems investments.

Although it is important to quantify and express in financial terms as many of the costs and benefits as possible, it is simply not feasible to express all the benefits of 'systems' in financial terms, and it serves no useful purpose to develop spurious calculations to quantify the unquantifiable! If a new system will reduce staff frustration and stress by organizing policy and procedure information in an electronic library, accessible

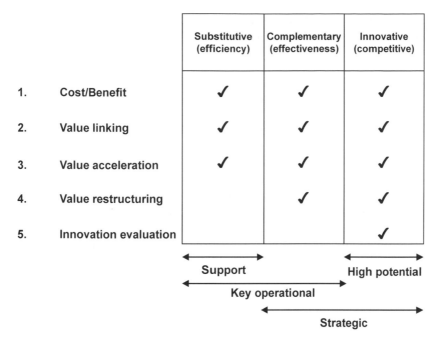

	Substitutive (efficiency)	Complementary (effectiveness)	Innovative (competitive)
1. Cost/Benefit	✓	✓	✓
2. Value linking	✓	✓	✓
3. Value acceleration	✓	✓	✓
4. Value restructuring		✓	✓
5. Innovation evaluation			✓

Figure 9.1   *Relationship between benefit types and the application portfolio*

from every desktop via an Intranet, it is difficult to calculate all the benefits financially even after the event, let alone before it has happened. However, as will be seen on page 442, it is important to determine in advance how any intended benefit will be measured. In this case, a staff survey could be an appropriate measuring instrument, along with measures of absenteeism or turnover to determine the overall effect.

What is more important is to base the assessment of application investments on the overall nature of the contribution they are expected to deliver to the business. The portfolio approach can offer help in making such judgements. The rationale for developing applications or investing funds and resources in each segment of the matrix is different, therefore the evaluation process should be different. The arguments used to justify a prototype system to model customer online buying behaviour are not the same as those used to justify a replacement of the general accounting system. Equally, response to a competitor's online service, which is causing customer attrition, and a decision to bring together data from disparate applications in a data warehouse require different approaches to evaluation. The risks and consequences of failure in the various segments are also different. This can be allowed for by requiring a higher predicted rate of return where the risk is higher, although this may in turn merely lead to creative accounting for the benefits! It is perhaps better to analyse the inherent nature of the risks and take appropriate action to deal with them, as far as possible, as will be outlined later.

The portfolio approach suggests that:

- Quantified, financial justification of applications is easier in the key operational and support quadrants, where most aspects of the application will be better known or can be determined, risks are lower and the rate of change is slower.
- A singular approach to investment justification will tend to produce one type of application to the exclusion of others. This argument is particularly strong where a scarce resource approach has been adopted and pure financial return on investment decides investment priorities—support applications will always be easier to justify financially.
- The way in which applications are planned and managed by the organization will also affect the way in which they are justified— whether they are customer-related applications integral to achieving business objectives or systems intended to save major costs in one part of the organization.

Figure 9.2 highlights some of the key points to be considered in the evaluation of applications in each segment.

Support Applications

The main argument for such systems is improving efficiency, which should be possible to quantify and convert into a financial argument for investment. Additional arguments may revolve around system and technology obsolescence and general staff productivity/time saving, and these may be difficult to identify accurately and therefore to quantify. In this segment, it is reasonable to expect potential benefits to be estimated before resources and costs are incurred to identify the most economic solution within the benefits achievable.

Again, if the application is competing with others for the limited resource, then a support application must show a good economic return for the allocation of a scarce resource. If, however, the project can be carried out within the user department's control, then it is reasonable that, since the budget or funding is under local control, the 'go–no go' decision is made by local user management. The IS/IT investment is an alternative use of funds to other investments locally and is not

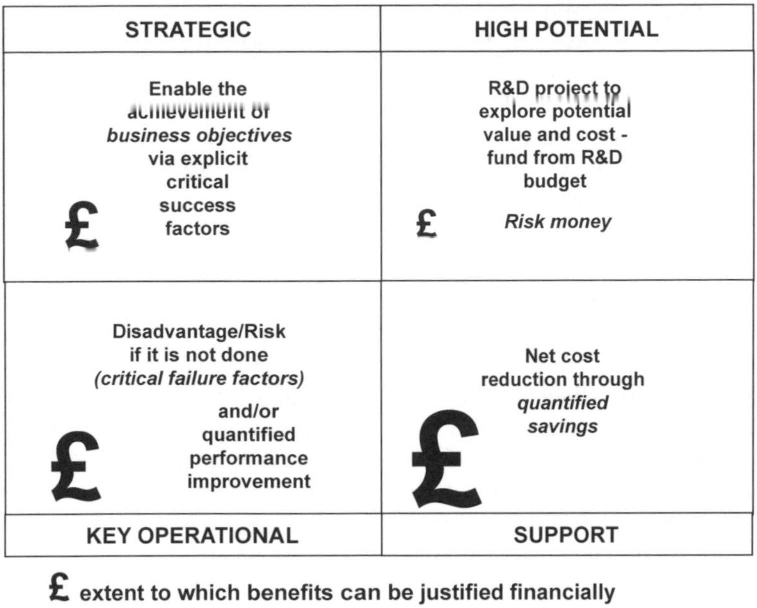

STRATEGIC	HIGH POTENTIAL
Enable the achievement of *business objectives* via explicit critical success factors £	R&D project to explore potential value and cost - fund from R&D budget £ *Risk money*
Disadvantage/Risk if it is not done *(critical failure factors)* and/or quantified performance improvement £	Net cost reduction through *quantified savings* £
KEY OPERATIONAL	SUPPORT

£ **extent to which benefits can be justified financially**

Figure 9.2 *Investment justification*

competing with alternative use of scarce IS/IT resources. It is to be hoped that user management will expect the case to be argued in predominantly financial terms, but if not that is their responsibility.

In summary, assuming a scarce resource strategy is being adopted centrally for most support applications, then any allocation of that resource should be argued on economic, return-on-investment grounds primarily. At the same time, some discretion can, without great risk, be left to local management via a free-market strategy.

Key Operational Applications

While, as far as possible, all costs and benefits of a new development, redevelopment or major enhancement to a key operational system should be converted to a financial evaluation, this may not allow for all the arguments involved.

For support systems, it was suggested that benefits should be estimated before any resource is allocated or costs determined. This is inappropriate for key operational applications, where financial benefits are not the only driving force. The most economic solution in the short term may not be the most effective over the long term given the role such applications play in the core business processes. This is the area for strict 'feasibility study' to find the best solution from a range of alternatives, each with differing costs, benefits and risks.

The business may suffer a serious disadvantage if a system fails or becomes less adequate in meeting the business needs as they evolve. It might be worth spending more to achieve a more adaptable or integrated solution that meets a range of needs more effectively and upon which new strategic applications can be built. Normally, this will increase the cost and make the overall benefits difficult to express financially. Some of those additional benefits will be able to be related to critical success factors (CSFs), which provide a clear link of the investment to the achievement of business objectives. An argument often used is 'what will happen to the business if we do not invest in improving this key-operational system?' and therefore 'can we afford the risk of not doing it?' Perhaps the term 'critical failure factor' is more appropriate when considering the possible disadvantages of not investing.

The implementation strategy that works best for key operational systems is monopoly, which implies a central control and vetting of all applications and enhancements. This enables a standard checklist of questions to be considered in the evaluation of any new project. Factors that are important (other than economic return) from either a business or IS/IT perspective can be allowed for and, if necessary, changed over time. The monopoly approach should also avoid implementing solutions based solely on economic expediency rather than business benefits, although it may mean that a particular application may cost more in the short term.

In conclusion, it should be stressed that, for key operational systems, the business unit management should be the final arbiter. It is their business that will suffer by lack of investment and they should (provided they can afford to pay) be allocated the necessary resource to meet such systems needs. It is clearly untenable to allow competitive disadvantages to develop due to lack of investment in IS/IT.

Strategic Applications

The fact that an application is deemed strategic implies that it is integral to achieving aspects of the future business strategy. Obviously, it is important to cost the investment and, where possible, put figures to the potential benefits, even if the latter are only ranges or orders of magnitude, not estimates suitable for a discounted cash-flow calculation. However, the main reasons for proceeding are likely to remain mainly non-financial—expressed as the business opportunity that is being created or the CSFs that the application specifically addresses.

The strategy most appropriate for this part of the matrix is central planning, whereby IS/IT opportunities and threats are being considered along with the business issues and strategies. Hence, an application will get the 'go–no go' decision based on how directly it relates to the business objectives and particular strategies. The benefits will derive from achieving those objectives by enabling the required business changes, not from the system alone. Whether this will actually happen is partly a question of luck (that the target does not move), partly of judgement (the quality of business acumen of senior managers) and partly good management of the application development and associated business changes.

A key issue is whether the management team, steering group or whoever makes such decisions is unified in endorsing the project and that the 'organization' deems the investment worthwhile. The critical factor is then resourcing the task sufficiently to achieve the objectives in the optimum timescale. This may need repeated senior management intervention to ensure that both user and IT resources are made available. The budget for such investments and financial control of actual expenditure should perhaps reside with the steering group to ensure that progress and resourcing are centrally monitored as well as planned.

High Potential Applications

The very essence of high potential projects is that the benefits are unknown and the objective is to identify the benefits potentially available and how they could be achieved. It should be justified on the same basis as any other type of R&D, and preferably from a general R&D budget rather than IS/IT funds. In practice, where the money comes from— R&D budget or IS/IT or user budgets—is important, but not critical. What does matter is not pouring money down the seemingly bottomless pit that R&D can become, if not properly monitored. It must be remembered that many high potential ideas tend to arise informally, based on individuals' creative thinking, rather than from formal planning, and it is important not to stifle creativity through excessive bureaucracy. However, many of the ideas simply will not work! and some control is essential to avoid significant waste of resources. It can be argued that many e-commerce/e-business investments in 2000–2001 could have benefited from better evaluation of their potential, before large sums were spent on IT implementations that were based on incorrect assumptions and little, if any, objective assessment of their potential value.

The idea of 'product champions' to be responsible for such projects, given a budget against agreed general terms of reference to deliver results or otherwise, is the most effective way of initiating and managing the high potential stage in application life cycles. No investment should stay in this segment for too long or have too much money spent on it. When initial allocations are used up, further sums have to be justified based on the evidence of the possible benefits, not just allocated in the vague hope of eventual success.

This approach fits the leading-edge and free-market strategies for the experimentation and assessment that high potential applications need. However, it should be obvious that those responsible for ensuring that central planning works for strategic applications must be aware of what is being evaluated in the high potential segment and by whom and over what timescale.

The above approaches to application justification in the various segments may lack the precision ideally required. But, this is no more than is true of other investments in research and development, advertising, reorganization, building new plant or facilities, or launching new products and services. IS/IT investments should be considered just as objectively and just as subjectively as other business investments. The portfolio approach allows the balance to vary according to the expected contribution required.

SETTING PRIORITIES FOR APPLICATIONS

As mentioned earlier, the mechanisms used to decide whether or not applications go ahead should also be used to set priorities across applications when they cannot all be done in parallel. Some priorities are logical—Project *B*, for analysing customer data, cannot proceed before Project *A* has built the data warehouse, for example—but many are largely independent of one another.

It is important to introduce a consistent, practical approach to priority setting if any strategy is to be implemented successfully. Short-term business pressures will change, projects will not proceed as planned, resources will not be available as expected, new opportunities and requirements will emerge. Each of these can cause changes to priorities and, unless a consistent rationale is employed, 'crisis management' will repeatedly override the strategy. Priorities need to be set in the short term to enable the best use of resources within the acquisition lead time for further resources, assuming these are actually obtainable. Priority setting is at the core of effective strategic management—selecting the best investments to pursue and, perhaps even more importantly, those to defer or abandon. Inadequate mechanisms for agreeing priorities are a significant cause of organizational failure to deploy IS/IT successfully.

Based on the earlier discussion of application evaluation, it should be seen that setting priorities across applications of a similar type (i.e. support, key operational, etc.) is not too difficult. After ranking them on similarly expressed benefits, the remaining parameter to optimize is the resource use. It is also prudent to modify the final ranking by consideration of the ability to succeed, to ensure that not just high-risk projects are tackled, resulting eventually in no achievement! Risk can either be allowed for as contingencies in cost and resources, or by reducing the expected benefits, or, in some cases, both. How risk can be assessed is considered later in this chapter.

Hence, three factors need to be included in the assessment of priorities:

- *What is most important to do*, based on the benefits identified.
- *What is capable of being done*, based on the resources available.
- *What is likely to succeed*, based on the risks of failure of each investment.

Hochstrasser[16] suggests a way of calculating a 'project priority value' that includes an assessment of 'potential barriers' to achievement of the benefits. He also classifies project types according to their strategic nature and whether the benefits can be aligned closely to the system itself or due to complementary improvements.

Within the *support* segment, setting priorities should not be too difficult. Those with the greatest economic benefit that use the least resources should get the highest priority. This will encourage users to express benefits financially and look for resource-efficient solutions, like software packages, to obtain a priority. Most organizations are experienced in delivering support applications and, consequently, they tend to be relatively low risk. The main consequence of failure is money wasted rather than major business problems, hence any more detailed priority assessment should be based on the relative financial risks of the investments.

Within the strategic segment, the basic rationale is to give priority to those applications that will contribute most to achieving business objectives, and use the least resources in the process. To assess this, some form of simple decision matrix, like that shown in Figure 9.3, can be useful in assessing the relative strategic contribution or weighting of the competing projects. Each application should be explained in terms of the degree to which (high, medium or low) it is relevant to achieving each of the critical success factors. It produces a 'score' or value for each potential investment based on the level of expected contribution to the current objectives.

	APPLICATION CONTRIBUTION		
	HIGH (3)	**MEDIUM (2)**	**LOW (1)**
<u>OBJECTIVE A:</u> CSF 1 CSF 2 CSF 3, etc.			
<u>OBJECTIVE B:</u> CSF 1 CSF 2, etc.			
<u>OBJECTIVE C:</u> CSF 1 CSF 2, etc.			
<u>OBJECTIVE D:</u> etc.			
TOTALS			

OVERALL TOTAL [   ]

Figure 9.3   *Strategic weighting via critical success factors*

It should be noted that, while CSFs cannot be weighted (by definition), the various business objectives can be ranked to indicate relative strategic priorities.

Like all decision-support tools, it should not be used mechanistically: a score of 25 is not necessarily better than 24, it means they are about equally important. Again, by dividing the 'score' by the quantity of limited resources required, the overall contribution from the options available can be maximized, especially in the short term.

Often, the benefits from strategic IS/IT investments are uncertain and depend on future events, making priority setting even more difficult. To address this issue, a number of researchers have proposed *real options analysis* as an alternative approach more appropriate to the nature of some IT investments, especially major infrastructure investments.[17] Essentially, an option is the right, but not the obligation, to act at some future date. The choice whether or not to act is dependent on specific situations occurring in the future, but it is usually uncertain as to which of the potential situations will actually happen. By taking an option (i.e. making an IT investment today), the possibility is provided to take some action(s) in the future when less uncertainty exists. While real options can be used to make investment decisions, the approach is more helpful in making choices among investment options available. In relation to the portfolio, the approach is best used for strategic and high potential applications where future uncertainty can be expressed in terms of different scenarios that can be subjected to 'what-if'-type assessments.

Working with a mid-sized Austrian auto parts manufacturer, Taudes *et al.*[18] applied real options to the problem of deciding whether to migrate from SAP ERP system R/2 to R/3. Even though the initial set of applications to be run under R/3 were the same as currently running under R/2, the real options analysis demonstrated that the future opportunities to introduce applications based on EDI, workflow management, document management and e-commerce justified the introduction of R/3. The higher implementation costs could be related to higher future benefits and the additional value provided by R/3 could be explained.

Setting priorities among key operational systems is more complex than support, but involves less uncertainty than strategic applications. The arguments for (i.e. benefits of) key operational investments will essentially comprise:

- financial;
- critical success factors (either directly or by enabling strategic developments);
- risk to current business (critical failure factors);
- infrastructure improvement.

Each of these benefit areas must be given some form of relative weighting based on the current business situation, to decide the preferred mix of benefits before looking at resource constraints. Then, the costs and/or resources used by the project should be compared against its relative importance in each of the four categories to establish overall priorities. Economic benefits are straightforward, and business objectives can be assessed via CSFs. The view of 'infrastructure' implies providing adequate technologies or improving the organizational capability to utilize its IS/IT, or enhancing specific competencies to improve the future business contribution from IS/IT. Risk to current business could be assessed by describing 'what risks are run if the project does not go ahead', which should be expressed in terms of the impact on the business, its probability of occurrence and an assessment of when the risk might arise. Applications scoring highly in all four categories are obviously higher in priority than those scoring highly in one, two or three categories, and those at each level in the ranking using fewer resources get priority. It is a subjective method, but it does allow for the strategic, financial, business and IS/IT perspectives to be included.

Buss[19] makes an important observation concerning, as he says, the 'misconception' that 'a steering committee can decide the priorities.' In general, he suggests, politics will interfere, representation in discussion will be unbalanced and the only common ground will end up as economics! He says the best way to set priorities is to make them the product of a formal planning process at corporate or business unit level. The mechanisms to be employed can be agreed by a steering group, but it should not be implemented as a meeting-based process.

Hochstrasser[20] argues that these mechanisms must be applied consistently across all projects, or the priority setting process will remain arbitrary and chaotic.

High potential applications are difficult to prioritize and will tend to be driven somewhat in the reverse of strategic applications: what resource is available to do it and then which application might best employ that resource? As discussed in Chapter 7, high potential applications are often 'individually' driven, a champion usually exists; it is the secondary resources that are the problem. While it sounds wrong to suggest that 'he who shouts the loudest' or 'has the most influence' will obtain priority, in this segment it may be the best way to allow priorities to be set because:

- the results will depend not just on the value of the idea, but also on the force with which it is pursued;
- setting objective priorities on scant evidence is not very reliable anyway.

If the idea potentially impacts many CSFs, it clearly stands out from others and should be elevated above the general scramble for R&D-type resources. In the discussion below, high potential applications are not considered as being in competition for IS/IT funds, but are funded from R&D general budgets. But, of course, they may well compete for key skills or resources.

The remaining task is to set priorities across the segments of the portfolio to decide how much resource to devote to the different types of application. This is not simple since the rationale for investment in each is different, as shown above. However, the approach recommended for key operational applications can be extended to cover the whole portfolio. Strategic applications will score heavily on CSFs, whereas

Table 9.1 *Examples of effect on weighting of various factors (High, Medium, Low)*

FACTOR	Objectives/ CSFs	Business risks	Infrastructure	Economics
1. All types of investment have to be cost-justified to meet strict ROI hurdles	L	L	L	H
2. Business is in weak position or in decline—short-term profitability	L	M	L	H
3. Business is in a high-growth market and satisfying the market demand is paramount	H	H	M	L
4. Environment is very competitive and business performance must be improved	H	H	L	M
5. Need for redevelopment of old systems. Systems and/or technology are out of date compared with competitors or peer organizations	L	H	H	M
6. New systems are required to support major business/organization change or rationalization	M	H	M	L
7. Technology cost performance enables lower costs for existing systems if redeveloped	L	L	H	H

support applications should deliver a good financial return. Management must decide the weighting they wish to attribute to each type of benefit and then rank the systems.

The relative weighting given to each will depend on a number of factors, a few of which are listed in Table 9.1. In general, the greater the confidence senior management have in their business strategy and collective judgement, without the need to be reassured by figures, and the trust they have in the competencies of business users and IT professionals in developing effective systems, the greater the weighting that will be given to CSFs, etc., relative to financial aspects. In a way, this is a sign of maturity of the organization regarding how it plans and manages IS/IT as described in Chapter 3. It also tends to reflect the relative strength of the enterprise within its industry: the stronger the position, the fewer IS/IT investments are expected (like other investments) to prove an economic case in advance.

If the overall plan is developed and maintained in a priority sequence, that reflects the ratio of benefits to be achieved (adjusted for risk) to the limiting resource consumed, then it helps both in short and long-term planning decisions because:

- resources can be reallocated where necessary from lower to higher-priority applications on a rational basis, with the agreement of line managers;

● appropriate resourcing levels for the future can be set, and action taken to obtain the right type of resources to meet the demands, based on a full understanding of the benefits achievable.

It is quite possible then to produce a 'planning system', that should keep the plans and resource utilization up to date. It is important to disseminate the current plan to all involved to aid understanding of the reasons for the relative ranking of any particular project. Mystery or uncertainty are far more destructive of strategies than the discussion and reconciliation of real problems.

Again, the above arguments may lack the precision ideally required for setting priorities. Much subjective judgement is inevitably involved, but 'rules' for inclusion of the relevant factors can be established, to avoid each priority decision being made on a different set of criteria.

BENEFITS MANAGEMENT

One of the factors that differentiates successful from less successful companies in their deployment of IS/IT, according to a number of surveys,[21] is the management resolve to evaluate IS/IT investments before *and after* they occurred. A survey of approaches to managing IS/IT benefits in 60 major organizations[22] revealed that only 26% of the companies always reviewed projects after completion to determine whether benefits were delivered—a finding in line with earlier surveys. However, as with previous surveys, most respondents believed that their organization's investment appraisal processes were not appropriate for the types of investment being undertaken, and 45% admitted overstating the benefits to gain approval, in the full and certain knowledge that no evaluation would be made after implementation! In the same survey, 76% of organizations believed there was significant scope for improvement in managing the benefits of IS/IT projects, but only 10% had any defined process as a basis for management action to deliver the benefits on which investments are justified.

There is limited value in any sophisticated system of investment evaluation and priority setting unless the 'system' is examined in terms of whether or not it delivers the business improvements required. Some form of post-implementation review must be carried out on a high percentage of projects to identify whether (i) they were carried out as well as possible and (ii) whether the benefits claimed (or possibly different benefits) were achieved or not. While preinvestment appraisal and post-implementation review are obviously important, they are essentially one-off 'snapshots' of the situation and, hence, insufficient in terms of

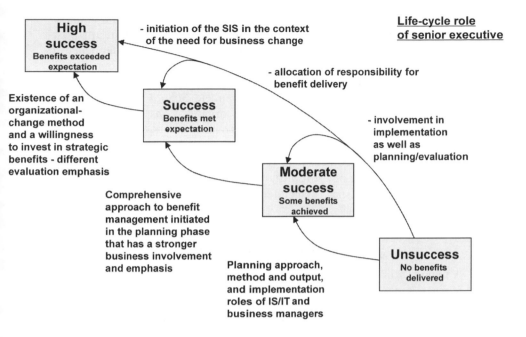

Figure 9.4   *Factors increasing the degrees of success in strategic information systems*

the actions needed to ensure that the maximum benefits available are delivered.

In a detailed study of 11 strategic IS/IT investments (varying in cost from £5m to £100m) across a range of industries,[23] a number of factors that differentiated success from failure were identified. While some were already well known (e.g. involvement of senior management throughout the project life cycle), the successful investments were characterized by a deliberate, comprehensive approach to managing the benefits and allocation of responsibilities to line managers for benefit delivery (see Figure 9.4). In addition, in highly-successful projects, management treated the IT investment as a component of organizational change and were able to use existing change management processes to ensure the business maximized the value of the IT investment through associated changes to business practices.

What is also clear from surveys and the study above is that it is becoming increasingly difficult, given the types of systems being implemented, to predict all the benefits that can be delivered. That increases the importance of having a process that actively addresses the management of benefits throughout the investment's life. In particular, any post-implementation review should focus not only on what has happened in terms of delivered benefits but should also consider what further benefits could now be gained. These issues prompted an extended research program at the IS Research Centre, Cranfield School of Management, in collaboration with major UK-based organizations, to develop new approaches to improving IS/IT benefit realization. Key aspects of the approach resulting from that work, and now in use in over 100 organizations, are described below. A Wentworth Research report[24] described the approach as one of the few that comprehensively addressed the range of management issues associated with maximizing actual benefits delivered.

The Context of Benefits Management

A major IS/IT development will consist of a large number of activities in business areas and the IS function. Any particular development will also rely upon an ongoing set of organizational competencies that enable new systems to be devised, implemented and operated successfully. These are not just technology competencies but also business competencies in defining its information and processing needs, managing the changes that are required to gain benefits from the technology and using the systems successfully. In essence, therefore, any major IS/IT development will consist of the mix of activities for which best practices and relevant methodologies have been developed over the last 30 years.

Systems development methodologies such as SSADM (Structured Systems Analysis and Design Methodology), DSDM (Dynamic Systems Development Methodology) and SSM (Soft Systems Methodology) are processes and methods designed to ensure that the right system is developed in the most appropriate way to agreed quality and performance requirements.

Project management methodologies like PRINCE (Project Management in a Controlled Environment) are essential for managing the activities and resources associated with a project to deliver the system and complete the other tasks to agreed times and costs. Most organizations now recognize that this is a shared responsibility between business and IT management. Ultimately, it is the business that suffers the real consequences of poor project management and business project managers are often appointed for major IS/IT investments, although their roles and responsibilities are not always clear.

As stated above, few organizations have a complementary process focusing on identifying and managing the business benefits required.

Often, this is seen merely as part of the investment appraisal approach to enable a valid business case to be developed. The results of the R&D program described above suggest that investment appraisal should be considered as one event (albeit an important one!) within an overall process that can be defined as:

> *Benefits Management: the process of organizing and managing such that potential benefits arising from the use of IT are actually realized.*

It would seem most appropriate that the business project manager should be responsible for this particular set of activities. The ability to achieve benefits from a particular investment will depend largely on the organization's experience and knowledge of what types of benefit IS/IT investments can or cannot deliver and how they can be obtained.

Based on the different objectives and rationale for the applications in each segment of the application portfolio, it can be seen that the mix of activities and their criticality to success will vary. Strategic applications imply that significant business changes will need to be made in association with the new system to create the desired advantage. Equally, understanding and defining the benefits required will need considerably more innovative thinking than, say, buying a new accounting package. Figure 9.5 summarizes the generic sources of benefit for the different segments in the matrix. These align closely with the 'information economics' concepts discussed earlier in this chapter.

While the Benefits Management process is applicable across the whole portfolio, its value increases as the issues associated with delivery of benefits become more complex. The inputs to the process provide a first understanding of the range of tasks involved. They essentially ask three questions:

- Why is the investment being made—what is causing the organization to change and how critical to its future is the successful management of the changes? (*the benefit drivers*)
- what *types of benefit* is the organization expecting from the investment overall—to reduce costs, improve operational performance, gain new customers, create a new capability, etc.? These need to be understood in general terms before detailed analysis of potential benefits in relation to the extent of change required is undertaken.
- How will other activities, strategic initiatives, business developments or organizational issues affect the particular investment either to facilitate or inhibit its progress and outcome? (*the organizational context*)

STRATEGIC	HIGH POTENTIAL
Business innovation and change **Business process restructuring**	**(R&D projects)**
Business effectiveness **Business rationalization and integration**	**Business efficiency** **Process elimination and cost reduction**
KEY OPERATIONAL	**SUPPORT**

Figure 9.5   *Generic sources of benefit for different applications*

An assessment of these inputs provides the background to setting objectives for the project and to identify the key stakeholders and their potential role in and influence on the project. The Benefits Management process then enables the relationship between the enabling technology and changes to processes, structures and working practices to be assessed, in combination, to identify the best way of realizing the maximum set of benefits from the investment.

Since the purpose of any IS/IT investment is to deliver improvements to business and/or organizational performance, it would seem logical that the main 'process' around which others should fit is benefits management, rather than the project management, investment appraisal or systems development approaches. These should be adapted to match the types of change involved in the investment and the range of benefits expected to be achieved. Figure 9.6 summarizes the context of the Benefits Management process described below.

THE BENEFITS MANAGEMENT PROCESS

In considering the activities required to manage the delivery of benefits, it has been assumed that the IT-based system is delivered to specification

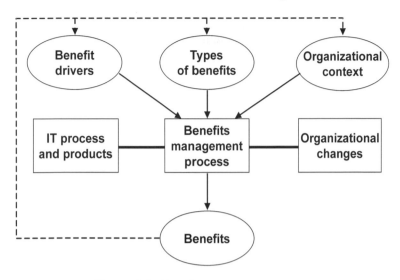

Figure 9.6   *Benefits management context*

(i.e. the technical part of the development is successful). However, as the benefits management process proceeds, it may cause revision to the specification, and it is assumed that effective change control processes can deal with this. The other related set of activities are organizational changes of many types that have to be made to deliver the benefits. The benefits management process should be the driving mechanism for these change activities. How to bring them about in detail is addressed in the wealth of change management and organizational development literature.

The model proposed here for a benefits management process draws heavily on total quality management philosophies and incorporates a number of tools and techniques from different sources to address particular aspects. The five steps in the iterative process are described in outline in the following subsections (see Figure 9.7). Each stage is considered in overview from the viewpoint of the business management roles and responsibilities, and key tools and techniques are briefly described. This description is a summary of the *Best Practice Guidelines*[25] developed for organizations to utilize the process.

Stage 1: Identification and Structuring of Benefits

Based on the outcome of the strategy processes, the overall business rationale for a new or improved system will have been identified: the nature of the types of target benefit and extent of change involved to

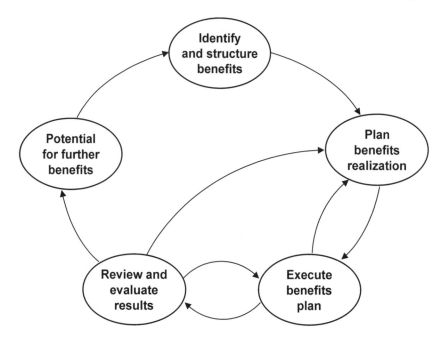

Figure 9.7 *A process model of benefits management*

obtain them will depend on their impact and criticality for the business strategy which in turn determines whether the system is strategic, key operational or support, as described in Chapter 7. If the nature of the benefits and/or how to obtain them is unclear, then the system should be put through the R&D stage implied by the high potential segment until they are better known. Hence, the whole benefit management process does not really apply to the high potential segment, but some of the techniques can be used to enable the benefits to be identified or assessed in terms of how best to achieve them.

Identifying the target benefits implies an iterative process of establishing the investment objectives and the possible business performance improvements that the system and associated changes should or could deliver. The achievement of each objective could well deliver a variety of different benefits across the organization and also to trading partners and customers: customer service improvements in one area could produce new marketing or selling opportunities; productivity gains in administration may release resources for 'front-office' activities. The process is inevitably iterative since objectives may be modified and new benefits identified as ideas and options are considered in the 'creative' stage of discussion, or perhaps rejected after more careful scrutiny. The benefits should also be tested against the 'benefit drivers' in the organization (i.e. the business strategy), to ensure they are relevant and that investment to achieve them will be endorsed by senior management.

All business performance improvements are measurable, and hence so are all the benefits delivered by information systems. Some can be measured directly in relation to the system (e.g. staff headcount reductions due to automation, decrease in product rejects due to quality control data, reduction in stock levels through a warehouse control system). Many of these can also be easily converted into financial values; where this can be done, it should be, to enable an economic appraisal to be made. In other cases, the measurement may be less direct. Better timing and control of deliveries should lead to more satisfied customers, which in turn may lead to increased sales or at least avoiding lost sales due to delivery problems. The level of customer satisfaction will need to be measured and some estimate made of the business benefits of improved delivery. These quantified benefits may not, however, be suitable to undergo rigorous discounted cash-flow calculations. In essence, every target benefit should be expressed in terms that can, in due course, be measured, even if the measure will be subjective (e.g. customer or staff opinion). These measurable improvements will be reviewed in Stage 4 of the process.

As an example, Frito-Lay,[26] the snack-food manufacturer, decided to equip its sales/delivery force with hand-held computers. The prototype system showed that this saved about three to four hours of administrative effort each week. The sales managers were asked to decide what that time saving could deliver as a benefit. It was agreed that each sales/delivery person should be able to increase their sales by between 3% and 10% per week, given the increased selling time available and their different customer mixes. This became one of the target benefits to be delivered by the system, and after implementation this was measured. An average of 6%, over and above general market growth, was achieved.

The final part of this stage is the determination of where in the business (or even in trading partners) each benefit should occur and, hence, who in the organization should be responsible for its delivery. This is a logic often overlooked in bringing in new systems, but 'ownership' of each of the benefits and clear allocation of responsibility for delivery is essential to success. This is easy to identify if the system is mainly within one function or area of the business, but it is more difficult when the system crosses functions, and especially when reorganization and rationalization of tasks across functions are integral to the delivery of benefits. Responsibility may have to be shared, but then this must be made explicit. Given that a manager is made accountable for the delivery of each of the intended benefits, any benefits lacking such ownership are removed from the list!

In most organizations, given that the investment could now be costed, etc., an investment proposal would be put forward at this point, but that should not happen until after Stage 2.

Stage 2: Planning Benefits Realization

Having identified and allocated responsibility for benefits to individuals (or perhaps teams), the next step is to determine the changes required for delivery of each benefit and how the IS/IT development will enable the changes and benefits to occur.

The output from this activity is described as a *benefit dependency network*, which relates the IS/IT functionality via the business and organizational changes to the benefits identified. Developing such a 'cause–effect' network is again an iterative process best conducted in a workshop mode, since, as changes required are identified, a network of interrelating changes and dependences will evolve, and the feasibility of achieving some of the benefits will be questioned. Equally, further benefits may well be identified. The overall structure of such a network is depicted in Figure 9.8, showing its two main components: the benefits and objectives that argue the case for investment and the change management plan required to achieve them. The changes are of two types— business changes and enabling changes—which can be defined as:

- *Business changes* are those changes to working practices, processes and/or relationships that will cause the benefits to be delivered (or begin to be delivered). They cannot normally be made until the new system is available for use and the necessary enabling changes have been made; for example, allocating more sales time to potentially high-value leads, identified by the new system, requires the system and perhaps other enablers to be in place.
- *Enabling changes* are those changes that are prerequisites for making the business changes and/or are essential to bring the new system into effective operation. These often involve defining and agreeing new working practices, redesigning processes, changes to job roles and responsibilities, new incentive or performance management schemes, training in new business skills, etc. (as well as the more obvious training and education in the new system). They can often be made, or have to be made, before the new system is introduced (e.g. agreeing a new sales account management and incentive scheme to ensure rewards reflect the attention to high-value customer needs).

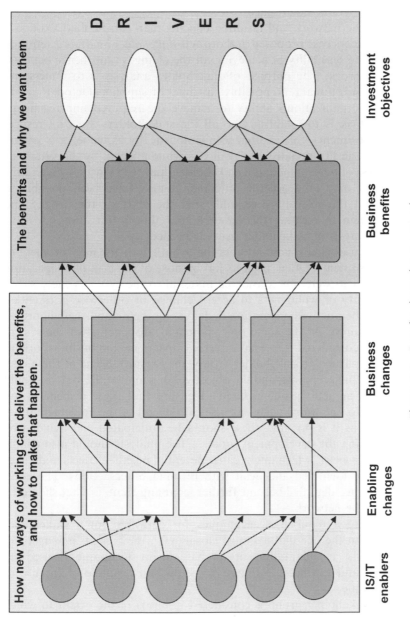

Figure 9.8 Benefits dependency network

As with the benefits, the ownership and responsibility for each change has to be identified and agreement reached on how successful achievement of the change will be determined.

Before the network and resulting benefits plan can be finalized and a sound business case proposed, a thorough *stakeholder analysis* is required to check the feasibility of achieving all the changes (and hence benefits) on the network. The purpose of stakeholder analysis is to understand those organizational (and possibly customer or supplier) factors that will affect the organization's ability to achieve the required improvements. The first task is to establish who all the stakeholders are with respect to the investment—this is often seen simplistically as whoever is paying for it and the IT specialists! In reality, anyone affected by the system or the process of development is a stakeholder, and the view they take of the investment may influence the outcome. It may have been possible to identify all the relevant stakeholders at the start of the project and involve them in creating the network, but this is not always feasible and an analysis of stakeholder issues is needed.

The main objective is to address the 'what's in it for me?' problem of IS/IT investments. Often, projects fail because of the lack of cooperation of parties who were not considered material to the system's success, but whose ability or willingness to accept change or otherwise is essential, requiring their active cooperation in delivering the real business improvements required. At the same time, potential 'disbenefits' of the system should be considered (i.e. what adverse impacts on the business, organization or particular stakeholder groups may result). Some of these may be deemed unacceptable, and the objectives or scope of the system should be revised or actions put in hand to ensure that these disbenefits are avoided. No one wants nasty surprises at the end of the implementation. So, as far as it is possible, these should be anticipated and avoided by action during the development process. The analysis should also enable stakeholder views, which might cause potential negative effects and hence risks, to be identified and dealt with through other actions. The additional actions identified become further 'enabling changes' that should be added to the network.

There are a number of techniques for carrying out a stakeholder analysis, but the one that fits most closely with the benefits management approach is an adaptation of an assessment technique devised by Benjamin and Levinson.[27] Figure 9.9 shows an example of the use of the technique.

Each stakeholder group is considered in terms of the extent to which they perceive the project produces benefits for them, relative to the amount of change they will have to undergo or endure before they see the benefits. Some form of resistance can be expected if they perceive the

Stakeholder group	Perceived benefits (disbenefits)	Changes needed	Perceived resistance	Commitment (Current and Required)				
				Anti	None	Allow it to happen	Help it happen	Make it happen
Customers	Configuration tailored exactly to needs - no testing / reject	None	None					
Sales and marketing managers	Improved customer service and product quality image	New incentives to get sales reps to use system with customers	Reluctance to change reps reward systems			C —	Action required?	→ R
Sales representatives	(Extra work in preparing requirements and quotes)	To use system and improve quality/accuracy of quotes	No time available to use/learn system. Loss of autonomy		C	Action required?	→ R	
Manufacturing/ Logistics	Removes need for configuration checking. Less returns/queries	Stop current checks to put onus on reps to get it right	Do not trust sales reps' accuracy in requirements/quote	C —	Action required?	→ R		
IT developers	New advanced system - remove old difficult to maintain system	Skills in expert system development	None					

Based on a project to implement an expert system for Product Configuration

Figure 9.9 Stakeholder analysis (source: after Benjamin and Levinson)

changes outweigh the benefits and if they have to endure significant change for no benefit. That resistance could cause major project risks. Based on the current positioning of each stakeholder and the required level of resources or support they are needed to provide, an action plan to move their perceptions or deal with their concerns can usually be devised. However, in some cases, the gap may be too great and the ambitions for the project reduced to enable at least some of the benefits to be realized. Whether substantial additional action is justified, or it is better to reduce the investment scope, depends on the number and value of the particular benefits that the stakeholder resistance may affect.

The other reason for the analysis of stakeholder interests is to consider aspects of business change outside the particular project and the possible implications on achieving the benefits. For instance, other business in-itiatives, reorganization and possible changes in key stakeholders may have a significant impact. The purpose of assessment is to obtain owner-ship and buy-in of relevant individuals and groups, and to identify organ-izational factors that will enable or disable the achievement of the benefits, or otherwise significantly affect the outcome. Figure 9.10 shows an example of part of an actual benefit dependency network for a successful CRM project.

The essence of the first two stages of the process can be summed up as a series of questions that have to be answered in order to develop a robust business case for the investment and a viable change management plan to deliver the benefits. These questions and their relationships are shown in Figure 9.11. Only when this assessment has been completed and the feasibility of achieving the target benefits thoroughly tested should a business case requesting funding for the IS/IT investment be developed.

Presenting the Business Case

How the case for investment has to be described to senior management will depend on the processes and procedures in the organization. However, based on the research, a format for presenting business cases was developed that has proved to be more appropriate than many others—based on its adoption in many organizations. Figure 9.12 outlines the basic format and logic of the argument for investment. The case should start with the context within which the need for invest-ment in change has arisen—the drivers. The objectives for the invest-ment—the situation that should exist on a successful completion—linked to the specific business drivers causing investment should follow. The benefits should be expressed in tabular rather than list form showing (a) how they arise (the columns) and (b) how explicitly they can be stated in advance (the rows).

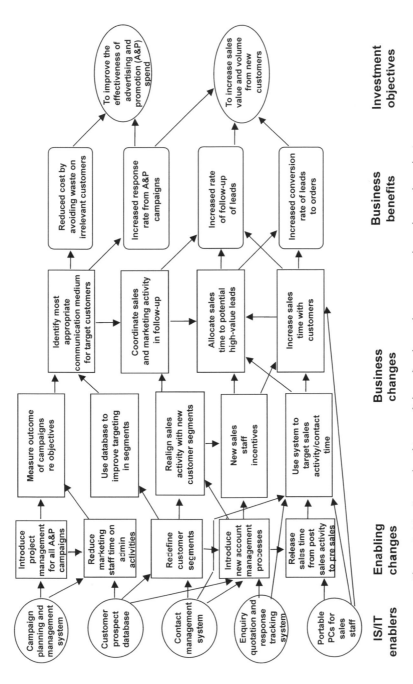

Figure 9.10 *Example of (part of) benefits dependency network—sales and marketing system*

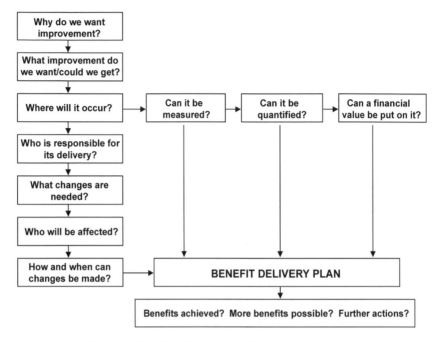

Figure 9.11   *The dimensions of benefit management*

The structuring of the benefits into columns based on whether they result from innovation (doing new things), performance improvements (doing things better) or reducing or eliminating unnecessary activities (stop doing things) may appear simplistic, but it increases the understanding of the nature of the changes that create the benefits.

The structure of the rows needs some further explanation. In constructing the network and benefits plan, every benefit needs to be attributed with a measure or measures to define how its delivery will be assessed. These may be specific, objective measures (i.e. it is *measurable*) or informed, subjective assessments (i.e. it is *observable*). Both imply sufficient is known about the current situation that it will be feasible to assess how much the situation has improved following the changes. This is, however, insufficient to justify spending large sums of money!

Quantifiable benefits are those for which sufficient evidence or data exists to forecast how much improvement should result from the changes. For example, eliminating a cause of delivery failure to customers will reduce customer complaints (due to that cause) to zero. To quantify

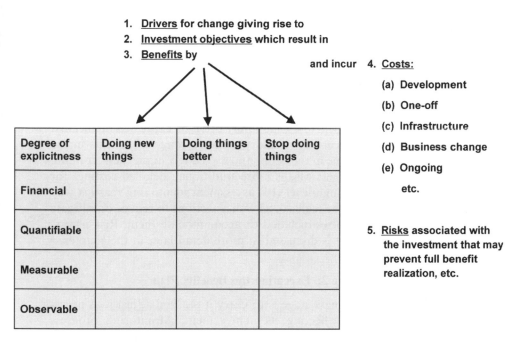

1. <u>Drivers</u> for change giving rise to
2. <u>Investment objectives</u> which result in
3. <u>Benefits</u> by

and incur 4. <u>Costs:</u>

   (a) Development

   (b) One-off

   (c) Infrastructure

   (d) Business change

   (e) Ongoing

   etc.

5. <u>Risks</u> associated with the investment that may prevent full benefit realization, etc.

Degree of explicitness	Doing new things	Doing things better	Stop doing things
Financial			
Quantifiable			
Measurable			
Observable			

Figure 9.12   *The investment proposal—making the case*

many of the benefits may require further work; for example, detailed study of particular activities, introducing new measures of current performance, transfer of experience from similar projects, external benchmarking or modelling of achievable performance improvements or even running pilots or prototypes to test estimates or assumptions about the effects of new ways of working. This is worth the effort if the potential benefit is significant, both to produce a rigorous, arguable business case and to reinforce the importance of the business change activities in the benefits plan. Once the levels of improvement can be calculated or estimated, some of those benefits should be able to be expressed *financially* by multiplying by a unit cost or value. Using the above example: delivery failures may have led to customer attrition and the value of lost business can be calculated, plus the additional cost saving associated with dealing with returns and redelivery.

This reflects normal approaches to evaluating benefits, but gives a more explicit structure for their expression and forces more rigour across the range of benefits. If there are no quantifiable or financial benefits that can be explicitly described, then either the investment is not viable or the project is still high potential at this stage and further R&D work is needed.

Support applications would be expected to produce financial benefits in the 'do better' and 'stop' columns, since they address well-known tasks and activities. At the opposite end, strategic investments should produce new ways of doing business, the benefits of which are more difficult to quantify and express financially in advance as discussed earlier, as well as a range of 'do better' benefits, which may often be expressed financially. Key operational applications should produce a range of benefits in the 'do better' column, some in the 'stop' and even a few in the 'new' column.

The rest of the business case is more traditional: detailed costings for the investment and a high-level risk assessment identifying reasons why the benefits might not be realized, as well as actions to reduce or mitigate the risks, or contingencies included to accommodate them. Risk assessment and management is discussed in more detail later in the chapter.

Stage 3: Executing the Benefits Plan

As with any plan, the next stage is to carry it out and adjust it as necessary, as issues arise affecting its achievement. Monitoring progress against the activities and deliverables of the benefits plan is just as important as for the IS/IT development plan, and the two plans are components of the overall project plan. It may be necessary to establish interim targets and measures to evaluate progress toward key milestones or the final implementation. It is the business project manager's responsibility to decide what action to take in terms of reviewing the scope and specification of the system or its business justification. During this stage, further benefits may also be identified, and again the business project manager should decide on appropriate action to plan for the benefit or defer it until Stage 5. Equally, it may become apparent that intended benefits are no longer feasible or relevant and the benefits plan should be modified accordingly, along with any consequent reduction in the IS/IT functionality. Factors outside the benefits plan itself such as changes in the organization or problems in meeting the requirements at the intended cost will, of course, initiate reviews of the project deliverables and plan and, in turn, cause a reassessment of the benefits plan and even the business case.

Stage 4: Reviewing and Evaluating Results

Once the new system, business changes and the benefits plan have been implemented, there must be a formal review of what was and was not achieved. This evaluation has two purposes:

- to maximize the benefits of the particular investment;
- to learn how to improve benefits delivery from future investments.

All comprehensive project management, systems development and change management methodologies include a review process following implementation, and they should be carried out prior to the benefit review. The results of those assessments may provide explanations for the non-delivery of intended benefits, as well as knowledge to improve the management of future projects or systems design. Such post-implementation reviews are often in place in organizations, but tend to be held behind the closed doors of the IS function and are reviews of the implementation process rather than the investment outcome. This review is a business review aimed at maximizing the benefits gained from the particular system and increasing the benefits from future IS/IT investments.

The evaluation should involve all the key stakeholders and focus on what has been achieved, what has not (or not yet) been achieved and why, and identify further action needed to deliver outstanding benefits, if possible. The reasons for lack of benefit delivery may be due to problems in any of the earlier stages, hence they may have to be revisited to correct the situation. Another aspect of this review is to identify any unexpected benefits that have arisen and understand how they came about. This again may prove valuable input to the first stage of the process in future projects.

It is worth stating that any post-implementation review should not become a 'witch-hunt'; it must be an objective process with future improvements in mind, not a way of allocating blame for past failures. If it is seen as a negative process, honest appraisal and a constructive critique of what has happened become impossible and the whole process falls into disrepute or is not carried out.

Stage 5: Potential for Further Benefits

Much of the research referred to earlier has shown that it is often impossible to identify all the benefits of a system in advance.[28] Further benefits often become apparent only when the system has been running for some time and the associated business changes have been made. If, as has been suggested, more benefits are actually identifiable after the event than before it, where there is no review process these will probably never be identified.

Therefore, having reviewed what has happened, it is equally important to consider what further improvement could now be possible as a result of implementing the system and associated changes. This should be a creative process similar to Stage 1, involving the original stakeholders and any others who may be able to contribute, based on the knowledge now available for new opportunities to be identified and fed into the first stage of a new iteration of the process. If this is not done, many available benefits may be overlooked. If maximum value is to be gained from the overall investment in IT, benefit identification should be a continuing process, from which IS/IT projects are defined. Often, in the past, the project was defined first then benefits were 'created' in order to justify the cost. IS/IT planning should be driven by the delivery of a benefit stream that improves business performance at the optimum manageable rate.

Benefits Management: Summary

In the 1970s, it became clear that the activities involved in the IT aspects of IS development could be brought together into a coherent approach or methodology to improve the reliability and quality and reduce the costs of the process. Most surveys show that two-thirds of IS/IT investments fail to deliver the expected benefits, and one of the reasons for this is that little attention is paid to actually delivering the benefits! Most organizations now recognize that, to get 'value for money from IT', they must actively manage the value component as well as the costs. Understanding the full range of issues involved in achieving the benefits through IT-enabled change is still incomplete. No framework is yet available that will fit the needs of all types of application, the wide variety of benefits they can deliver or the different circumstances within which they must be achieved.

The process described here, including further tools and techniques involved in each stage, was developed by studying what actually happened on a number of major projects in large companies. Some of these were trying actively to manage the benefits, others were not. Using the benefits management approach, it was possible to understand why some projects were more successful than others in delivering benefits. By applying the approach to new projects, it was possible to both avoid the 'loss' of benefits that were clearly achievable and, in most cases, to identify and realize more extensive benefits than had been identified in previous, similar projects.

A secondary outcome of applying the approach is that IT costs can actually be reduced for some investments. In the extreme case, the project is cancelled because no benefits can be delivered! But, more commonly, the essential IT functionality required can be identified more explicitly in relation to the benefits the functionality actually produces, thus eliminating costs that deliver nothing of benefit. It is also possible to reduce the amount of IT functionality deployed by making more changes in business practices to utilize package software 'off the shelf' or to reduce procedural complexity rather than automate it!

Many organizations have realized that this approach to managing benefits is not peculiar to IS/IT projects and can be used to improve the success of other change programs, business developments and strategic initiatives. Of course, in more and more of these, IT is one of the enablers of change, and many organizations have taken the stance that, apart from infrastructure projects, there are now really no IS/IT projects *per se*—there are only change projects that have significant IS/IT components. As one IT director explained, 'introduction of benefits management improved the business–IT relationship more than any previous initiative, resulting in IT being seen as integral to the business and a major contributor to business performance.'

ASSESSING AND MANAGING INVESTMENT RISKS

As part of the appraisal of investment viability, it is essential to assess the potential risks: both the risks of failing to deliver anything at all and, more commonly, of failing to deliver some or all the benefits. Extensive research into the reasons for information systems investment failure by Lyytinen and Hirschheim[29] suggested that failure can occur in four domains:

1. *Technical failure*—this is clearly the domain of IT, who are responsible for the technical quality of the system and the technology it uses. Technical failure is increasingly less common and is often the cheapest to overcome.
2. *Data failure*—this is a shared responsibility between IS/IT professionals and the users who input the data. Obviously, good design, processing integrity and sound data management practice are the responsibility of IS, but not everything can be legislated for and the effectiveness of business processes and procedures and data quality control fall clearly in the user domain.
3. *User failure*—while some blame for the users misunderstanding the system may accrue to the IS/IT professionals, the primary responsibility for ensuring users are trained to use the system appropriately and to its maximum capability must rest with the business management. A major weakness in many implementations is inadequate training, and many systems become less effectively used over time as staff change and ongoing training investment is insufficient, even non-existent.

The risks that cause failure in these three domains are largely *process* or *content* risks (i.e. risks due to poor understanding or definition of requirements or how they can be satisfied, or inadequacies in the process of development and implementation). Most good software engineering, systems development and project management methodologies have risk assessment and management techniques that, if applied rigorously, can deal with the majority of these causes of project failure.[30]

4. *Organizational failure*—systems may be satisfactory in meeting particular functional needs, but may fail because they do not satisfy the organization overall, due to inadequate understanding of how the system relates to other processes and activities. For example, a budgetary control system specified for and by accountants at the centre may fail to meet the needs of line managers to plan and control different types of business expenditure. Responsibility here clearly lies outside the IS/IT domain and must be shared by line and senior management for not aligning systems with organizational needs.

The Lyytinen and Hirschheim analysis considered only these four domains, but a fifth and increasingly more serious area of failure exists:

5. *Failure in the business environment*—the systems are or become inappropriate to external or internal business requirements due to changing business practices instigated by others, or by not supporting the business strategy adequately, or simply by not coping with the volume and speed of business process needs effectively or economically. The responsibility for this is essentially senior management's, although, without active user and IT input, they cannot be expected to identify or understand the problems, or be able to take action to correct them.

In a study of 'abandoned projects', Ewusi-Mensah and Przasnyski[31] conclude that economic and technical factors were not major factors in contributing to management decisions to abandon projects before completion. Most were abandoned due to organizational factors such as loss of management commitment and political and interpersonal conflicts (i.e. these are serious areas of potential risk in a project). Interestingly, for the majority of projects they studied, of which 40% were considered 'strategic' and 60% were 'urgent', 85% were not seen as high risk at the start and 64% were expected to deliver considerable benefits. As with abandonment, major investment failure in Categories 4 and 5 above is due to lack of understanding of the *contextual* factors that produce project risks, or the inability to identify or address emergent issues that introduce risks of not achieving the required outcome. It is these types of factor, inherent in the nature of the objectives of investment or in the organization's ability to manage change, that conventional risk analysis techniques do not adequately address.

The riskiness of IS/IT was brought into sharp focus in the 1990s, with the much-publicized and well-analysed failure of a number of large projects[32] such as those in the London Stock Exchange (TAURUS), the London Ambulance Service, the Performing Rights Society, Prudential Europe's Unite project (which aimed to allow near real-time processing of orders for new policies and pensions via the Internet), and a joint Benefits Agency and Post Office project.[33] Despite all that can be done to bring structure and certainty to the process of information systems developments, they are often still inherently risky adventures at times, as all the evidence of poor success rates confirms. The more strategic IS/IT investments become, the greater the consequence of failure and the more difficult it is to foresee and deal with the range of risks involved. The approach described here is the flip side of the benefits management coin—factors affecting the organization's ability to deliver benefits from a system that technically, at least, works! The purpose in assessing risks is to understand them, such that the investment scope can be amended to avoid them or effective action can be taken before or during the process to deal with them.

The risks of each development need to be assessed in order to improve the chances of success, but management need to understand the relative risks of all the developments in the portfolio in order to set sensible priorities, as mentioned on page 431. This means comparing the risks of strategic, key operational and support applications in a consistent way. (High potential systems are inherently very risky and the R&D approach is used to minimize the consequences of the risk in business and financial terms.)

As described in Figure 9.5, the 'generic' causes of benefit in each of the other segments of the portfolio relate to the degree of business change required in addition to the increasing uniqueness of the system from support to strategic. The assessment approach described here is intended to address the risk factors that are due to the nature and degree of change involved, as well as the organization's ability to achieve those changes. It is additional and complementary to the risk analysis and management techniques, embodied in existing formal methodologies, that should also be used to address more traditional content and process risk factors.

Clearly, from the above, the outcome of change in strategic projects is less certain than in key operational or support, and the organization's experience in managing the types of change involved in a strategic project is likely to be less than for the other two. It is therefore almost certain that strategic investments will 'score' more highly in any risk assessment relative to, in turn, key operational or support. This 'riskiness' should, of course, be offset by the scale of the benefits that will result if the investment succeeds. How to interpret the risks of projects in different portfolio segments is described later.

The approach builds directly on the creation of a benefits dependency network, which is in essence a cause–effect network of relationships, linking IS/IT functionality via enabling changes to business changes, which, when implemented with that, will deliver measurable benefits in line with investment objectives.

Following the development of the benefit management research, two further research programs were undertaken at Cranfield, to study a number of major IT-enabled change projects. A new framework was developed that identified success factors in each stage of the overall process,[34] and a further program of action research followed to test the effectiveness of the framework on large, complex, live projects.[35] One aspect of this study was to incorporate risk assessment of the change aspects in the framework and evaluate its effectiveness in identifying and addressing those risk factors. Potential factors were identified from both IT and business change literature[36] and classified within four major headings, posed as questions:

A. What kind of change will be involved?
B. How ready is the organization to accommodate the change?
C. How will the organization react to the change?
D. How dynamic is the context within which the change is to be effected?

Under each heading, a number of factors (total 25) provide the basis for assessing probable overall success and identifying particular areas for management attention and action. Box 9.1 describes the factors and the five-point scale used to assess the potential impact of each factor, as well as the degree of overall risk in relation to each of the questions A to D above.

The analysis should be undertaken by the project management team, probably in a workshop mode to gain a consensus view. Having agreed a score on each factor, a summary average score for each category can be calculated. Any individual factor scoring 4 or 5 should cause relevant aspects of the project to be reviewed in order to:

•   identify the possibility of changing its scope or the development approach to reduce the risk; or

Box 9.1   IT-enabled change—risk-factor analysis

Factor	Range

A.1 Business impact — Marginal ←————→ Core (1 2 3 4 5)

A.2 Degree (scale, scope, size) of change — Low ←————→ High (1 2 3 4 5)

A.3 Pace of change — Gradual ←————→ Rapid (1 2 3 4 5)

A.4 Technology innovation — Familiar ←————→ Novel (1 2 3 4 5)

A.5 Novelty of business solution — Familiar ←————→ Novel (1 2 3 4 5)

A.6 Clarity of vision of intended outcome — Sharp ←————→ Vague (1 2 3 4 5)

Category A: Kind of change — Incremental change ←————→ Radical change (1 2 3 4 5)

B.1 Level of dissatisfaction with the status quo — High ←————→ Low (1 2 3 4 5)

B.2 Strength of drivers and constraints—balance — Positive ←————→ Negative (1 2 3 4 5)

B.3 Business sense of ownership — Strong ←————→ Weak (1 2 3 4 5)

B.4 Agreement on project objectives by key stakeholders — Agreed ←————→ Controversial (1 2 3 4 5)

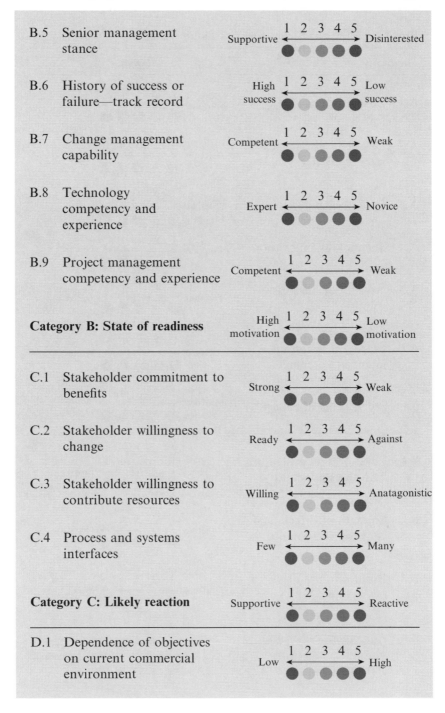

B.5　Senior management stance

Supportive 1 2 3 4 5 Disinterested

B.6　History of success or failure—track record

High success 1 2 3 4 5 Low success

B.7　Change management capability

Competent 1 2 3 4 5 Weak

B.8　Technology competency and experience

Expert 1 2 3 4 5 Novice

B.9　Project management competency and experience

Competent 1 2 3 4 5 Weak

Category B: State of readiness

High motivation 1 2 3 4 5 Low motivation

C.1　Stakeholder commitment to benefits

Strong 1 2 3 4 5 Weak

C.2　Stakeholder willingness to change

Ready 1 2 3 4 5 Against

C.3　Stakeholder willingness to contribute resources

Willing 1 2 3 4 5 Anatagonistic

C.4　Process and systems interfaces

Few 1 2 3 4 5 Many

Category C: Likely reaction

Supportive 1 2 3 4 5 Reactive

D.1　Dependence of objectives on current commercial environment

Low 1 2 3 4 5 High

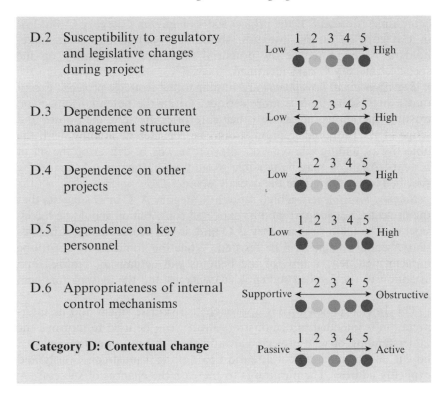

D.2 Susceptibility to regulatory and legislative changes during project

Low 1 2 3 4 5 High

D.3 Dependence on current management structure

Low 1 2 3 4 5 High

D.4 Dependence on other projects

Low 1 2 3 4 5 High

D.5 Dependence on key personnel

Low 1 2 3 4 5 High

D.6 Appropriateness of internal control mechanisms

Supportive 1 2 3 4 5 Obstructive

Category D: Contextual change

Passive 1 2 3 4 5 Active

- agree actions that can address the underlying cause(s) of the weakness; or
- establish appropriate contingencies to accommodate problems; or
- perhaps all three, in the case of a 5!

If the average for any category is 4 *or* 5 or 50% or more of the category factors are 4 or 5, there is cause for considering whether the investment as intended will succeed. However, the interpretation and alternative courses of action vary according to the portfolio positioning.

Strategic investments are likely to score highly in Categories A and D. Provided this is offset by low scores in Categories B and C and action can be identified per high-risk factor, as above, the project should still be viable. However, if this is not the case, actions should focus on reducing risk factors in B and C by reviewing the change components of the benefit dependence network to reduce the scale, severity or speed of change to make it more manageable. Alternatively, some benefits may have to be forgone or postponed by accepting that not all the changes are achievable at present. If the project scores highly in Category C, but low in Category B, careful attention should be paid to particular stake-holders' issues to reduce the potential resistance, by focusing on the specific Category C risks identified.

Key operational investments are similar to the strategic projects, except that a high score in A is more serious. Given the potential impact on existing operations, unless all other categories are low, the nature and scope of the proposed solution should be considered carefully, with the objective of finding a lower-risk, alternative way of delivering the set of benefits. Again, it may be possible to address particular risk factors by specified action to reduce the overall 'score'.

Support investments—a high score in Category A, C or D suggests that the project is not support! and its expected contribution should be recon-sidered. The main risk category is C and, if this scores highly, it implies that essential changes will be resisted. While the application can still be implemented, few, if any, of the benefits will actually be realized and attention to the detailed stakeholder concerns and the reasons for them is needed.

This brief overview of this approach to risk assessment and its inter-pretation is intended to demonstrate how it can be used to improve the understanding of why projects can and do fail, but, more importantly, how it directs management attention to aspects it must consciously and explicitly address. The purpose is to increase the chances of success!

This approach is relevant to most IS/IT projects, although some, because of their uniqueness or sheer size, incur additional risks. Griffiths and Willcocks[37] have reviewed such projects and compared relative success and failure in terms of the risks involved.

SUMMARY

The purpose of all investments in IS/IT is to deliver improvements in aspects of organizations' activities. Some may be in response to legislative or regulatory requirements and must be done to avoid breaching laws or regulations. Most, however, are discretionary—the money could always be spent on other things—and IS/IT investments compete for the funds available and, perhaps more significantly, the time and priorities of people in the organization. If the benefits are to be delivered, the commit-ment of resources and skills over an extended period is required.

Most of the literature in the field focuses on 'appraisal', not 'manage-ment'. IS/IT investments are inherently risky, many fail to deliver the intended benefits—some because the benefits were never achievable, others because the risks were not identified or understood and many because the development was inadequately managed. This chapter has attempted to describe an overall, balanced approach that can increase the chances of success in both identifying and delivering the available benefits.

IS/IT investments are becoming increasingly complex in terms of the way in which they impact an organization's performance. Gaining the benefits from IS/IT is increasingly dependent on changes in business practices, and even in organizational roles and structures. This chapter has dealt with application investments, rather than infrastructure investments, which are considered in Chapter 11. Applications are the primary channel through which infrastructure investments deliver business benefits, other than lower IT costs. Applications, therefore, must explicitly or implicitly justify most of the costs of infrastructure through the benefits they deliver.

Since the applications make different contributions to a business, as described by the applications portfolio, they need to be appraised in different ways. This is well understood, but, as yet, methods of investment appraisal do not adequately reflect this complexity and the subtleties involved. The approach described here offers some practical guidance to the most appropriate ways of assessing the different types of investment.

Priority setting, while allowing for logical precedence of development and key resource availability, should be based on the same principles as investment appraisal to maximize the benefit stream from the plan. Obviously, the delivery of the ideal benefit stream will be affected by the risks of the individual projects. Therefore, the risk assessment process should be driven by the effect of the risks on delivering benefits, based on the nature of the benefits. Most of this is well known, if not always practised successfully. However, what is far from common practice is the proactive management of the benefit delivery itself. A process and related techniques, which have helped address this weakness in many organizations, have been described.

The importance of post-implementation reviews is also emphasized as the means by which organizations can learn from experience, both good and bad, and become more successful with their IS/IT investments. The value of strategic planning is mainly in selecting the right things to do, but poor implementation, which fails to deliver the benefits of these 'right things', can easily negate the value of planning.

ENDNOTES

1. *Benefits Realisation ... Many Happy Returns*, Wentworth Research, IT Management Solutions Report, Egham, Surrey, UK, 1998.
2. D.P. Cooke and E.B. Parrish, 'Not measuring up', *CIO*, 15 June 1992.
3. B. Farbey, F. Land and D. Targett, 'Evaluating investments in IT', *Journal of Information Technology*, Vol. 7, No. 2, 1992.
4. J.A. Ballantine, R.D. Galliers and S.J. Stray, 'Information systems/technology investment decisions: The use of capital investment appraisal techniques in organisations', in *Proceedings of the 1st European Conference on IT Investment Evaluation*, Henley, UK, September, 1994.
5. L. Willcocks and S. Lester, 'Evaluating the feasibility of information systems investments: Recent UK evidence and new approaches', in L. Willcocks, ed., *Information Management: The Evaluation of Information Systems Investments*, Chapman & Hall, London, 1994.
6. B. Hochstrasser, 'Evaluating IT investments: Matching techniques to projects', *Journal of Information Technology*, Vol. 5, No. 4, 1990.
7. G. Peters, 'Beyond strategy-benefits identification and management of specific IT investments', *Journal of Information Technology*, Vol. 5, No. 4, 1990.
8. V. Symons, 'Evaluation of information systems: Towards multiple perspectives', in L. Willcocks, ed., *Information Management: The Evaluation of Information Systems Investments*, Chapman & Hall, London, 1994.
9. T. Lincoln, and D. Shorrock, 'Cost justifying current use of information technology', in T. Lincoln, ed., *Managing Information Systems for Profit*, Wiley, Chichester, UK, 1990.
10. J.M. Ward, P. Taylor and P. Bond, 'Identification, realisation and measurement of IS/IT benefits—an empirical study of current practice', *European Journal of Information Systems*, Vol. 4, 1996, 214–225.
11. K. Grindley, *Managing IT at Board Level*, Pitman Publishing, London, 1993.
12. L. Willcocks, ed., *Information Management: The Evaluation of Information Systems Investments*, Chapman & Hall, London, 1994.
13. B. Farbey, F. Land and D. Targett, *IT Investment: A Study of Methods and Practice*, Butterworth-Heinemann, Oxford, 1993.
14. M.M. Parker and R.J. Benson, with H.E. Trainor, *Information Economics*, Prentice-Hall, Englewood Cliffs, New Jersey, 1992.
15. N. Venkatraman, 'IT induced business re-configuration', in M.S. Scott Morton, ed., *The Corporation of the 1990's: Information Technology and Organisational Transformation*, Oxford University Press, New York, 1991, pp 122–158.; and 'IT enabled business transformation: From automation to business scope redefinition', *Sloan Management Review*, Winter, 1994, 73–87.
16. B. Hochstrasser, 'Evaluating IT investments matching techniques to projects', *Journal of Information Technology*, Vol. 5, No. 4, 1990.
17. A. Taudes, 'Software growth options', *Journal of Management Information Systems*, Vol. 15, No. 1, 1998, 165–185; M. Benaroch and R.J. Kauffman, 'A case for using option pricing analysis to evaluate information technology project investments', *Information Systems Research*, Vol. 10, No. 1, 1999, 70–86; A. Kambil, J.C. Henderson and H. Mohsenzadeh, 'Strategic management of information technology: An options perspective', in R.D. Banker, R.J. Kauffman and M.A. Mahmood, eds, *Strategic Information Technology Management: Perspectives of Organizational Growth and Competitive Advantage*, Idea Group Publishing, Middletown, Pennsylvania, 1993.
18. A. Taudes, M. Feurstein and A. Mild, 'Options analysis of software platform decisions: A case study', *MIS Quarterly*, Vol. 24, No. 2, 2000, 227–243.
19. M.D.J. Buss, 'How to rank computer projects', *Harvard Business Review*, January–February 1983, 118–125.
20. B. Hochstrasser, 'Evaluating IT investments matching techniques to projects', *Journal of Information Technology*, Vol. 5, No. 4, 1990.
21. See, for example: *The Strategic Use of IT Systems: A Survey*, Brunel University/Kobler Unit, Imperial College, London, 1990; K. Kumar, 'Post-Implementation evaluation of computer-based information systems: Current practices', *Communications of the ACM*, Vol. 33, No. 2, 1987, 204–212.
22. J.M. Ward, P. Taylor and P. Bond, 'Identification, realisation and measurement of IS/IT benefits: An empirical study of current practice', *European Journal of Information Systems*, Vol. 4, 1996, 214–225.
23. P. McGolpin and J.M. Ward, 'Factors affecting the success of strategic information

systems', in J. Mingers and F. Stowell, eds, *Information Systems: An Emerging Discipline?*, McGraw-Hill, London, 1997, pp. 287–327.

24. *Benefits Realisation ... Many Happy Returns*, Wentworth Research IT Management Solutions Report, Egham, Surrey, UK, 1998.

25. J. M. Ward and P. Murray, *Best Practice Guidelines for Benefits Management*, ISRC-BM-2001, Information Systems Research Centre, Cranfield School of Management, Cranfield, Bedford, UK, 2001.

26. L.M. Applegate, *Frito-Lay Inc, Strategic Transition (A)*, Harvard Business School Case Study, Boston, 1993.

27. R.I. Benjamin and E. Levinson, 'A framework for managing IT-enabled change', *Sloan Management Review*, Summer, 1993, 23–33.

28. E. Brynjolfsson, 'The productivity paradox of information technology: Review and assessment', *Communications of the ACM*, Vol. 36, No. 12, 1993, 67–77; and E. Brynjolfsson and S. Yang, 'The intangible benefits and costs of investments: Evidence from financial markets', in K. Kumar and J. DeGross, eds., *Proceedings of the Eighteenth International Conference on Information Systems*, Atlanta, Georgia, 1997, pp. 147–166.

29. K. Lyytinen and R. Hirschheim, 'Information systems failures: A survey and classification of the empirical literature', *Oxford Surveys in Information Technology*, Vol. 4, 1987, 257–309.

30. H. Barki, S. Rivard and S. Talbot, 'Toward an assessment of software development risk', *Journal of Management Information Systems*, Vol. 2, No. 10, 1993, 203–225; and M. Keil, 'Pulling the plug: Software project management and the problem of project escalation', *MIS Quarterly*, Vol. 19, No. 4, 1995, 421–447.

31. K. Ewusi-Mensah and Z.H. Przasnyski, 'Factors contributing to the abandonment of information systems development projects', *Journal of Information Technology*, Vol. 9, 1994.

32. C. Griffiths and L. Willcocks, 'Are major technology projects worth the risk?', in *Proceedings of the 2nd European Conference on IT Evaluation*, Henley, UK, July, 1994. See also C. Sauer, *Why Information Systems Fail*, Alfred Waller, Henley, UK, 1993.

33. Most of these examples are of projects in the public sector. The failures of large private and commercial sector IT projects are often not made public.

34. J.M. Ward and R. Elvin, 'A new framework for managing IT-enabled business change', *Information Systems Journal*, Vol. 9, 1999, 197–221.

35. The results of this research have not yet been published in a journal, but are included in two reports: R. Elvin, A. Davies and J. M. Ward, *The IT and Change Framework Version 2*, Report ISRC-ITC-2001, Information Systems Research Centre, Cranfield School of Management, Cranfield, Bedford, UK, 2001; and J. M. Ward and G. Dhillon, *IT and Change Research Project Report*, ISRC-ITC-97017, Information Systems Research Centre, Cranfield School of Management, Cranfield, Bedford, UK, 1997.

36. Sources of risk factors included (in addition to literature already cited): D. Boddy and D. Buchanan, *Take the Lead: Interpersonal Skills for Project Managers*, Prentice-Hall, Hemel Hempstead, UK, 1992; D. Buchanan and D. Boddy, *The Expertise of the Change Agent*, Prentice-Hall, Hemel Hempstead, UK, 1994; J. Balogun and V. Hope-Hailey, *Exploring Strategic Change*, Prentice-Hall, Hemel Hempstead, UK, 1999.

37. C. Griffiths and L. Willcocks, 'Are major technology projects worth the risk?', in *Proceedings of the 2nd European Conference on IT Evaluation*, Henley, UK, July 1994.

10
Strategies for Information Management: Towards Knowledge Management

The information management strategy is one of the areas of strategy that lies behind the management of the application portfolio. Its aim is to ensure that the organization obtains the greatest possible value from its information resource and to enable its cost-effective management and protection. While the IS strategy addresses *how* the organization is going to use information and for what purpose, it is critical to ensure that the information that underpins the applications is managed effectively.

The nature of business information that requires managing has changed in the last several years from primarily numbers and text to now include images, pictures, graphics and multimedia. This shift from 'lean' to 'richer' information presents new challenges for the traditional role of information management. Information management has also become the basis for many new Internet-based business models—ebay.com, Amazon.com, Betdaq.com and Covisint are obvious examples here—highlighting just how strategic it has become.

Data are the raw material of information—the raw facts or observations—with information usually portrayed as 'data in context' or data that have been given some meaning. Yet, a key challenge for all organizations is to transform information into knowledge that can subsequently be utilized to effect action and business results. Both information and knowledge are, at the same time, related yet quite distinct. Innovation, for example, demands not only information but also the application of knowledge from a variety of sources. Information can be considered as explicit knowledge, but much knowledge is tacit and personal, rendering it particularly difficult to identify, capture, store and deploy. The increased recognition of the importance of knowledge for competitiveness and the espoused relationship between information and knowledge has seen many chief information officers (CIOs) and IT directors being asked to either support or drive knowledge initiatives within their organizations, particularly as technologies emerge that support and enhance the management of knowledge. Yet, the nature of knowledge means that a different mindset is required in its management compared with managing information—there is an argument that knowledge *per se* cannot be managed, and that only its context can.

Information management embodies policies, organizational provisions and a comprehensive set of activities associated with developing and managing the information resource. Its effectiveness relies on implementing coherent policies that aim to provide relevant information of sufficient quality, accuracy and timeliness at an appropriate cost, together with access facilities suited to the needs of authorized users. At the same time, it must be recognized that much of the information used by employees in a business is not automated, and that while some information can be tightly managed, users will gather information from informal as well as formal sources. This informal information cannot be managed in the same regulated way. An additional necessity is for an environment within the organization that is conducive to promoting appropriate behaviours among employees regarding information.

This chapter explores information, knowledge and their management. It begins by outlining the management agenda regarding the treatment of information as an asset. It considers the acquisition, protection, utilization, accessibility and dissemination of information, as well as the promotion and management of initiatives to derive maximum benefit from the resource. It also examines the development, management and marketing of an enterprise-wide information model, and the application of the principles of Information Asset Management (IAM). The second part of this chapter is concerned with knowledge, its use and management, particularly in exploring the relationship between information and knowledge. The challenges that the nature of knowledge poses for its management are highlighted. The chapter also examines the role of technology in the management of knowledge.

INFORMATION AS AN ASSET: THE SENIOR MANAGEMENT AGENDA

The importance of information[1] as a key asset continues to grow, following a period where its production, complexity, volume and demand have rocketed, but where satisfaction of the real information needs of the organization has been limited due to many obstacles. Often, this can be due to a lack of clarity in identifying business-driven requirements. However, the IS/IT strategy process should point to major opportunities from exploiting information. The challenge is to ensure that this information is of the highest quality possible, particularly in terms of timeliness, accuracy, completeness, confidence in source, reliability and appropriateness.

Many organizations are plagued by poor quality information. From his work with telecommunications operator AT&T, Redman[2] found that:

- Many managers are unaware of the quality of information they use and often mistakenly assume that because it is 'on the computer' that it is accurate.
- At an operational level, poor information leads directly to customer dissatisfaction and increased cost. Costs are increased as time and other resources are spent detecting and correcting errors.
- Poor information quality can result in subtle and indirect effects. For example, significant mistrust can ensue when the information from one part of the business, say order entry, that is used by another, perhaps customer billing, is unreliable.
- Inaccurate information makes just-in-time manufacturing and self-managed work teams infeasible. The right information needs to be at the right place at the right time. To illustrate the severity of this problem, one manufacturer was still allowing customers to purchase particular products that it was no longer making via its website.
- Poor information in financial and other management systems mean that managers cannot effectively implement business strategies. Decisions are no better than the information on which they are based.

In addition, a consequence of the Internet has been an explosion in the volume of information that is available to employees. This information is of varying quality, and one of the challenges that organizations face today is assessing this quality. Information from the Net is not subject to any review standards, policies or quality control procedures.

There is also a growing requirement for integration of information flows at individual and departmental/functional levels, and across processes and organizational boundaries, which poses a variety of complex challenges. Communications capability is expanding all the time, as local and wide area networks flourish and the number of external sources of information swell. There is also a stimulus from technology 'push', influenced by the growing availability and improvement in tools such as middleware, advanced data dictionaries, web design tools, database technologies, and computer assisted software engineering (CASE) tools.

In most instances, effective information management is far from straightforward, and there are many obstacles to navigate:

- Information resides in multiple electronic 'libraries' and proprietary databases and on multiple technical platforms, which are not well integrated or easily accessible. These are the legacy of many years of uncoordinated, evolutionary development, and may result in poor quality and inconsistent presentation.
- Some information is computer-based and well structured, stored in centrally managed databases and applications; some is less structured, and stored in many independent and dispersed PCs or on corporate Intranets; and there is still a huge volume of unstructured and non-automated or unrecorded information.
- Information is created for different purposes by different people at different times and based on differing definitions, resulting in many conflicts and inconsistencies.
- There is both a backlog in meeting information requirements and legacy systems, requiring integration with newly developed and packaged applications.
- Complex information exchanges exist across organizational boundaries, comprising a mixture of electronic, paper-based and verbal communication.

These varying contexts create an 'information ecology'[3] that, if not managed coherently, can seriously undermine organizational performance. Addressing issues relating to information and its management is not a task that can be abdicated outside managerial ranks or delegated to the IS function.

In the UK, the Hawley Committee[4] explored the role of the Board of Directors in managing information. As its starting point, it took the view that information is a significant issue for Boards in fulfilling their responsibilities and is the heart of supervising what an organization does. Members of this Committee highlighted the difficulties they were continuing to experience at Board level in the direction and control of information and information systems. They also highlighted the fact that misuse of information and damage to the systems that hold critical information can seriously harm performance and reputations, and that the Board itself may be hampered in carrying out its duties by poor availability or poor presentation of information.

The Committee developed an agenda for Boards regarding information and its management. While the report says little that is not said elsewhere, what is new is *who* is saying it. An outline of this agenda is presented in Box 10.1. Tools were also developed by the Committee to support Board members in managing their organization's information resources and a number of these are drawn upon in the chapter.

AN INFORMATION CULTURE

Essential for the success of any information management strategy is the existence of an appropriate 'information culture'.[5] An information culture can be defined as the values, attitudes and behaviours that influence the way employees at all levels in the organization sense, collect, organize, process, communicate and use information. Marchand[6] has identified four common information cultures that exist in organizations today. They are:

- *functional culture*—managers use information as a means of exercising influence or power over others;
- *sharing culture*—managers and employees trust each other to use information (especially about problems and failures) to improve their performance;
- *enquiring culture*—managers and employees search for better information to understand the future and ways of changing what they do to align themselves with future trends/directions;
- *discovery culture*—managers and employees are open to new insights about crisis and radical changes and seek ways to create competitive opportunities.

Each type of culture influences the way employees use information—their information behaviour—and reflects the importance that senior management attribute to the use of information in achieving success or avoiding failure. However, establishing an effective information culture can be a challenge. Davenport captured this point succinctly when he noted that 'effective information management must begin by thinking about how people use information—not with how people use machines'.[7] Changing a company's information culture requires altering the basic behaviours, attitudes, values, management expectations and incentives that relate to information. 'Changing the technology only reinforces the behaviours that already exist.'

Strassmann[8] uses the word 'politics' when considering information management, as he believes that this term, perhaps more aptly than any other, captures what it is really about. He sees information management seeking to answer the same questions as those raised in politics. He

Box 10.1 Information as an asset: the Board Agenda

The Hawley Committee proposed that all significant information in an organization, regardless of its purpose, should be properly identified, even if not in an accounting sense, for consideration as an asset of the business. It asserted that the Board of Directors should address its responsibilities for information assets in the same way as for other assets (e.g. property or plant). This implies a new approach to how information should be treated and requires a Board to make clear to management what actions it wishes to be taken and who is responsible for action and compliance.

The Board should satisfy itself that its own business is conducted so that:
1. the information it uses is necessary and sufficient for its purpose;
2. it is aware of and properly advised on the information aspects of all the subjects on its agenda;
3. its use of information, collectively and individually, complies with applicable laws, regulations and recognized ethical standards.

The Board should determine the organization's policy for information assets and identify how compliance with that policy will be measured and reviewed, including:
4. the identification of information assets and the classification into those of value and importance that merit special attention and those that do not;
5. the quality and quantity of information for effective operation, ensuring that, at every level, the information provided is necessary and sufficient, timely, reliable and consistent;
6. the proper use of information in accordance with applicable legal, regulatory, operational and ethical standards, and the roles and responsibilities for the creation, safekeeping, access, change and destruction of information;
7. the capability, suitability and training of people to safeguard and enhance information assets;
8. the protection of information from theft, loss, unauthorized access, abuse and misuse, including information that is the property of others;
9. the harnessing of information assets and their proper use for the maximum benefits of the organization, including legally protect-

ing, licensing, reusing, combining, re-presenting, publishing and destroying;
10. the strategy for information systems, including those using computers and electronic communications, and the implication of that strategy with particular reference to the costs, benefits and risks arising.

notes that information management is the process by which those who set policy guide those who follow policy. 'Where control over information changes the alignment of power, information politics appears. Whether that turns out to be constructive is something that must be resolved through information management. Who gets what data and who converts data into information? Who balances the competing interests of leaders and followers? Who benefits from the ownership of information?'[9]

Marchand *et al.*[10] have developed the concept of *information orientation* to represent a measure of how effectively a company manages and uses information. Their research indicates that IT practices, information management practices and information behaviours *all* must be strong and working together, if superior business performance is to be achieved. The researchers have developed a methodology to assess information orientation, an overview of which is provided in Box 10.2.

IMPLEMENTING BUSINESS-WIDE INFORMATION MANAGEMENT

A well-managed information resource is arguably as essential as an effective IT infrastructure. Back in the late 1980s, Drucker,[11] in an article titled 'The coming of the new organisation', predicted that the typical organisation of the 21st century would be information based. He claimed it would be flatter, having drastically slimmed down its management size and levels, and would be populated mainly by knowledge specialists, working in fluid interdisciplinary teams. Everyone would be responsible for meeting their own information needs, and the organization as a whole would be required to have a unified vision and an information architecture, and to have abandoned former parochial views on information and its role. His predictions can now be seen to be happening.

However, promoting the management of information as a corporate resource does not imply building an all-embracing corporate database,

Box 10.2   Information orientation

In their research, Marchand and colleagues* identified 15 specific competencies associated with effective information management and use. They were categorized under three headings:

- *information technology practices*—a company's capability effectively to manage information technology (IT) applications and infrastructure to support operations, business processes, innovation and managerial decision making (four competencies);
- *information management practices*—a company's capability to manage information effectively over the life cycle of information use, including sensing, collecting, organizing, processing and maintaining information (five competencies);
- *information behaviours and values*—a company's capability to instil and promote behaviours and values in its people for effective use of information (six competencies).

The information orientation (IO) of a company measures its effectiveness in managing and using information. IO is calculated by measuring performance across these three categories.

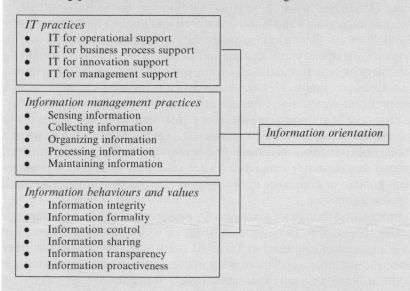

*D.A. Marchand, W. Kettinger, and J.D. Rollins, 'Information orientation: People, technology and bottom line', *Sloan Management Review*, Summer, 2000, 69–80.

Table 10.1 *Establishing the scope and purpose of information management: sample set of questions*

- What is the extent of information that the business is interested in?
- Why does it need the information, and what beneficial impact can be ensured?
- How much of it resides in centrally managed computer systems, dispersed departmental or individual PCs, in paper-based forms or in people's heads?
- How much of it is new or external information, currently not collected?
- Which information is used by a broad cross-section of the business and needs consistent, coherent policies to avoid ambiguity and conflict?
- What information is strategic and linked to strategic applications?
- What high potential information is likely to become strategic?
- When and how can it be delivered, or made accessible, where it will be most useful?
- How can it be verified, and what other information is required to turn it into useful knowledge?
- Which information needs to be integrated across applications, and what technical challenges does this pose?

---

but does support information independence. True information independence is achieved when there is no relationship between *how* or *where* information is stored and *how* it is accessed and applied by different users. It should be possible to vary requirements without impacting the storage structure or efficiency of information access. Conversely, it should be possible to restructure databases from time to time, without interfering with access demands. This can occur when a business embarks upon a comprehensive migration from one applications environment to another. It may take years and comprise many intermediate stages. It can also occur when organization-wide information needs change, such as when a public utility becomes privatized and is required to focus on commercial dictates and customer demands; or when corporate information management policies or even basic information architectures change in line with business evolution.

From an information management perspective, there are numerous factors that need to be considered, some of which can be deduced from a list of questions outlined in Table 10.1. By answering these and other pertinent questions, a framework for implementing information management can be established. This framework will define:

- a set of objectives and policies for effective information management;
- a program for introducing information management to meet the objectives;

- the creation and maintenance of the information architecture and business or enterprise model;
- what information services should be provided, and how to organize to offer them in the most effective way;
- what implementation issues exist, and how to tackle them.

Objectives of Information Management

The main objective of information management is to satisfy the demand for information, and thus deliver value to the business. This demand is expressed in the information requirements of applications, and the information access and delivery services required by users. Value is delivered through:

- enabling the business to make the right decisions;
- improving the effectiveness of processes and their outcomes;
- providing timely and focused performance information;
- the preservation of organizational memory;
- improving the productivity and effectiveness of managers and staff.

Behind the main objective should be further objectives relating to the quality, cost, accessibility, safety and stability of the information, and others relating to the benefits that can be delivered through shared information, common definitions, an enterprise model covering information and processes, and a modelling capability. These objectives are explored in some detail in the following subsections.

Delivering Value to the Business

Delivering value to the business is the key rationale behind an information management strategy—to add value by exploiting information as a core business resource. In meeting that objective, the potential value of information, especially in the core competitive processes (the primary activities in the value chain), will be harnessed to its fullest extent. While Chapter 5 considered opportunities for gaining strategic advantage through IS/IT, in setting out to manage information, it is presumed that such opportunities have been examined and the information requirements confirmed. This will have been documented clearly in the business IS strategy, along with any other information requirements.

The Hawley Committee developed a framework to help in structuring the value of different types of information asset. Illustrated in Figure 10.1, it can be very useful in reaching agreement among senior business

Types of information asset	Value/Importance defined by		
	Price paid or potentially paid (IPR) less costs	Impact of theft, damage or loss, major errors	Potential to increase revenue or reduce costs
Market and customer information			
Product information			
Specialist knowledge			
Business process information			
Management information and plans			
Human resource information			
Supplier information			
Accountable information			

Figure 10.1 *Mapping the value of information assets* (source: Information as an Asset: The Board Agenda, *KPMG/IMPACT, London, 1994)*

managers as to its impact on business value as well as to the consequences of theft or damage.

Since information needs to be managed in line with its value to the business, it is helpful to 'weight' areas within the total information set, according to their required contribution. A similar portfolio model to that used to categorize applications can be used to rank the information portfolio (Figure 10.2).

Strategic

Information, both internal and external, that is crucial to strategic and competitive business initiatives and principally associated with business drivers, objectives or measures of success, represents the greatest potential value. Some but not all this information may exist within the available information environment in the business. Typical requirements are shown in Table 10.2. These are all business-driven needs, demanding flexible and often high-performance response.

A number of different types of response may be needed to meet strategic information requirements:

- Implementation of newly developed or purchased applications to satisfy new information requirements that cannot be met from existing applications, which provides flexible systems that can be

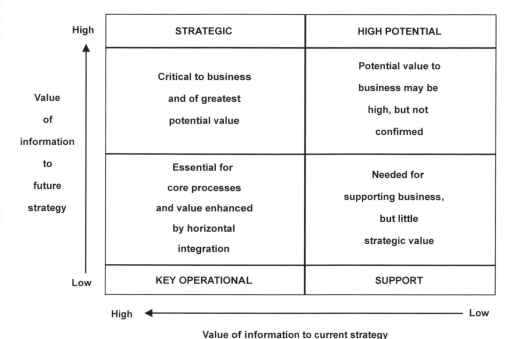

Figure 10.2 *Value of information to the business*

Table 10.2 *Typical strategic information requirements*

- Access to new information about markets, customers, competitors, suppliers or other external bodies to improve competitiveness
- Establishment of electronic links with external bodies, to speed up and improve communications and, in some cases, to lock in trading partners
- Access to external information such as market research databases or database marketing facilities to gain external intelligence
- Restructured existing information in order to meet the critical success factors of the business or its external partners
- Capability to integrate and utilize multimedia data
- Very fast access to integrated information so that visibility is provided from end to end of the key processes and information-based services can be delivered effectively throughout the processes
- Access and filtering mechanisms for unstructured information to satisfy executive information needs relating to critical business issues
- Performance measures to monitor progress on strategic factors
- Modelling data to perform 'what if' analysis on crucial business issues
- Better information about staff to enable more effective use of the human resource

adapted as business needs evolve and assists in gaining sustainable competitive advantage.

- Substantial initiatives to enable information to be shared in a controlled manner across existing, newly developed and packaged applications, and to be able to 'switch in' and 'switch out' applications with minimum disruption and risk. Examples of this are described later in the chapter.
- Short-term interim solutions, depending on providing access to 'locked-in' information. This may be through either direct or intermediate bases of easily accessible information. Appropriate tools are required to deliver information to business users, or enable them to extract it themselves. The aim is to obtain value from information in existing, but inappropriate, data structures.
- Development of an enterprise model to facilitate decision making such as:
  —top-level business decisions consistent with the 'declared' IS strategy;
  —process redesign proposals or new development proposals resulting from the IS strategy;
  —as a basis for mapping various architectures (information, application portfolio, technology, product), as described in Chapter 4 as a tool for planning IT supply, evaluation and decision making.

These responses reflect the nature of resulting initiatives' combining application, information and technology developments. For example, associated initiatives may be needed to expand the IT infrastructure, to extend communications capabilities or to deal with multimedia information.

High Potential

High potential information is generally new information, with unproven value to the business. Its sources, structures and relationships may not be fully understood, but, as potentially valuable systems are being clarified, their information requirements must be confirmed in terms of defining the best way of satisfying business needs, so that they can be included in the information management umbrella at the appropriate time. The essence of operating in this quadrant is in rapid evaluation of a prototype application or information acquisition, processing or dissemination technology:

- Single-user systems need not necessarily be subject to corporate information administration, as long as the reliance placed on their information is not greater than its integrity warrants.

- In some cases, it may be the possibility of exploiting latent information that is the driving force in exploring a high-potential opportunity; for example, historical transaction information about customers that could lead to more effective targeting of marketing activity. In others, it is the desire to improve business performance that prompts the extension of information content and usage; for example, collecting customer-specific requirements, so that customer satisfaction is based on a more personal service in meeting these requirements.
- Other high potential activity could be the trial of some new technology that relates to information management like desktop videoconferencing. This could be driven by IT 'push' from the IS function, or could reflect free market experimentation in a user area, as described in Chapter 7.

Key Operational

The largest volume of information is probably associated with the key operational systems, integral to core operational processes and essential for their effective day-to-day running. Requirements here are likely to be driven by avoidance of disadvantage and may focus on greatly enhancing value through integration across applications and processes, enabling rapid and consistent communication, especially to the external interfaces, where strategic requirements take over (e.g. production status information relating to a customer order).

There could also be opportunities to improve business productivity, and remove duplication and risk of misinformation. These opportunities must nevertheless be assessed in terms of the benefit they could deliver against the probable high cost of implementation and the likely restrictions to developing related strategic applications in the short term.

Support

Information contained only in support systems, though necessary, is not likely to contain much latent value. In some cases, it may even be a burden on the organization when it is constrained by legislation or bound by corporate instructions to supply or store information, without any business benefit being recognized. Effort expended on information management or integration should be kept to a minimum, consistent only with efficiency and necessity.

There is no assumption that, to deliver value, information must be stored and transmitted via computer and communications technology. It may be transmitted verbally as with face-to-face conversations, or in hard-copy paper form in books, journals, directories, instruction leaflets and so on. On the other hand, emerging electronic information transfer media such as videoconferencing, groupware, Intranet and Internet may be introduced to improve the richness of the interchange.

Making the Most of Current Systems

Even if the long-term plan is to replace existing systems and databases, it is very likely that they will continue to be used for some time as they contain much of the necessary information and processing functionality. It is therefore important to consider how to obtain the maximum contribution from the information in current systems and those still under development. This must be achieved by managing the existing information contained within existing systems, which is frequently 'imprisoned' in multiple corporate files and databases, with considerable duplication, obsolescence, inconsistencies, inefficient linkages and poor exploitation. They may have been poorly designed in the first place. In addition, employees are not very well trained generally to use information. These factors can all lead to competitive disadvantage and must be rectified, if the business case warrants this. If progress is to be made toward implementing effective information management, it is essential to provide efficient access to information in these existing databases. However, if multiple versions of key subject databases such as 'customer', 'product' or 'order' exist, then it is no easy task to rationalize the various versions and harder still to integrate them with any newly defined databases, or object databases, based on the corporate information architecture. Until unique versions of subject databases, or identically maintained versions, are available, managing information globally implies managing the differences between actual database versions and consistent data dictionary definitions.

Typically, there is a huge investment in systems, and in most sizeable organizations the cost of maintaining these can be as much as 70–80% of the annual expenditure on systems and technology. Very rarely can the investment be written off—and even if it could be justified, replacements could not be found or implemented quickly. Nor can support and maintenance be abandoned. So, in planning the migration to a new system, it is important to obtain maximum value from current systems. Meanwhile, the provision of critical business information with the necessary quality attributes in an appropriate set of target databases should be the objective of any migration and must still be justified against the business need. This is likely to be a long, multi-step process of progression toward an elusive goal.

It is essential to evaluate the contribution of information in existing systems, with reference to business information needs. Sometimes, systems will already have associated information and process models and some will be recorded in dictionary systems. Frequently, however, this is not the case, and the structure and contents of individual systems need to be identified if their value is to be assessed. The evaluation process serves several purposes:

- Documentation of the information structure and processes, and system linkages, which helps in plotting the migration path to the desired systems and information architecture, and also in any initiative that may be put in place to enable information sharing and systems integration.
- Recognition of whether current systems are able to provide information to satisfy business needs, either directly or after enhancement.
- Identification of information that can be usefully transferred to an intermediate base of consolidated information for subsequent accessing, perhaps to satisfy composite needs or unstructured enquiries.

Few tools are available for unscrambling the conceptual framework in existing systems, but some CASE tools can provide reverse engineering facilities that can backward-track and document components of existing systems, capturing data definitions, data flows and data and process models.

Provision of a Stable Integrated Information Framework

In aiming to provide a stable information base, there are strong arguments for it being integrated, at least throughout the core business processes. Prompted by many factors in the business environment, it is expected that there will continue to be a steady increase in the number of knowledge workers, and growth in the volume and complexity of internal and external information needed to meet a variety of demands. This means more people wanting more access to more information that is distributed more widely. These increased demands call for improved gathering and dissemination across a wide area such as:

- exchange of information with trading partners;
- support within decision-making processes;
- *ad hoc* end-user enquiries;
- boardroom strategy and planning systems;
- creating new knowledge by combining specialist information;
- obtaining business intelligence through the Internet and external databases.

Widespread sharing of information from a variety of sources requires considerable integration, based on a representative global information model. All users can then look at the same or consistently related models, with the same meanings and definitions and, by and large, the same or copied occurrences of information. Assuming the model is correct, some of the benefits of a well-structured, stable, integrated information resource, which can be easily and quickly adapted, are listed in Box 10.3.

For example, an organization may want to link information about the services a particular customer has used in order to contain risk (e.g. a bad debt in one area would constitute a bad risk in another), or to maximize opportunities by being able to offer the customer a complete range of services. It is for this purpose that many financial service institutions have attempted to implement channel integration strategies to provide a coherent view of the customer across all channels and products.

Opportunities exist in many other fields, including government departments. For example, the UK's Department of Social Security may wish to provide a potentially valid claimant with information and advice on a range of benefit entitlements, or alternatively to provide the authorities with a better chance of detecting false claimants. In these and most cases, the total view is needed at the business–customer interface, more so than at the centre, since the contact takes place in distributed branches.

Rapid Response to Dynamic Business Needs

Rapidly responding to changing business needs is closely related to the previous aim. Not only should the information framework be stable and integrated but it should also facilitate a swift response to an unexpected business need. The 'window' may only be open for a brief period. A completely healthy systems and information architecture that can enable a virtually instant response is a rare occurrence, but there is much that can be done.

The business models derived from top-down analysis and based on aligning business and information reflect the information-sharing requirements of the business throughout its internal value chain, and into adjacent organizations. During analysis of the value chain, and in particular in examining the information logistics of primary activities, opportunities for deriving competitive advantage by improving information flows will have been examined and built into the required architecture. The ability to satisfy unexpected needs can best be provided if consideration is given to them during the processes of information planning. Applying informed second-guessing, potential information

Box 10.3 Benefits delivered by a stable integrated information framework

- *Businesses better equipped with information to respond as necessary:* to change direction, monitor market and customer needs, competitor activity, build relationships with business partners, and so on.
- *Direct savings achieved in the long run:* even though introducing information management is costly, fragmentation is even more costly when taking into account multiple duplication of information capture, confusion caused by information inconsistencies, and the frustration and chaos in reconciling differences. It can be the cause of lost opportunities through lack of cohesive information.
- *Intraorganizational and interorganizational cooperation improved by making information available across boundaries to a broad community of authorized users:* some of these may be external users, having their own requirements for accessing information; for example, customers placing orders, suppliers enquiring into the status of manufacturing schedules to meet just-in-time delivery requirements, financial analysts collecting global economic figures. In these cases, both user and (information) supplier are beneficiaries.
- *Support for managing businesses in a more integrated way:* traditionally, many businesses have been functionally orientated and IT has supported individual business functions quite effectively. There is now a requirement toward integration along business processes in order to be more customer and market orientated, and thus more competitive. This demands taking a horizontal view across the business; for example, linking all activities relating to a customer and reorganizing information in such a way that the whole of the customer's relationship with a business is logically brought together and presented at the point of contact with the customer—face to face, on the telephone, in concurrent processing, when a written order, query or complaint arrives, or when electronic channels are used.

needs and their sources, relationships and flows can be built into the initial information architecture.

The most appropriate structure for an organization's information and systems is usually that which mirrors the organization itself. Thus, if the organization is divisionalized and highly decentralized, then the information resources—both applications and information—are probably also best disposed in that form. Determining how best to implement the conceptual architecture is part of the IS/IT strategy process. Clearly, it is also part of the process to look toward future business needs before embarking on what could be very extensive development or redevelopment of systems and information structures. The benefits that can then be delivered are swift responses to:

- identify and exploit an opportunity;
- identify and counter an unexpected competitive action;
- build pre-emptive defence against possible competitive threats;
- supply information to assess a business risk or the probability of its occurrence.

Improved Efficiency and Effectiveness of Information Processes

Improving information processes is an aim of many organizations, and good information planning and management should play a substantial role in meeting this aim. There are a number of factors that contribute to improving efficiency:

- Initially, increased investment is required to create an appropriate integrated infrastructure of 'managed' information. Thereafter, while initial project development costs may be higher, benefits are reaped over a long period in reduced maintenance costs and greatly extended effective life and reliability of applications.
- Critical information is consistent across the business and not plagued by incompatibility problems.
- If a well-constructed data dictionary is employed, fewer information-related program errors are incurred.
- High-level languages, associated with advanced and reliable database management systems (DBMSs), reduce programming effort considerably (e.g. in generating enquiries and reports).

In defining the information architecture along with new applications, many problems can be avoided. But, in considering the current portfolio, it could be worthwhile seeking out long-standing culprits in the form of obsolete information or unmatched needs and supply:

- Archived information held longer than needed.

- Information disseminated when it is no longer needed. Where this used to apply to hard-copy reports, it may now apply to files of information distributed electronically, but never accessed by users.
- Useful information available, but not used.
- Inefficient methods of capture, manipulation, storage or distribution.
- Duplication in several activities—capture, storage, transmission.

Duplication in one or another of these forms is very common. It is usually a consequence of independent developments, and is often perpetuated out of lack of trust between system 'owners'. It is clearly a source of potential errors when information is input more than once. It is not uncommon to find ten or even more different customer databases, some held only on PCs or personal digital assistants (PDAs), in an organization where an extensive portfolio of systems has been built over a number of years. Few, if any, of these will be identical in definition or content. Overlapping is often extensive, even where the products or customers of the enterprise differ widely from division to division and thus from database to database. The degree of overlap varies from case to case. For example, publishers of journals and magazines will have one set of customers who are subscribers and another who are advertisers. In this circumstance, there may be little overlap, nor much potential for generating business from combining the two. Where multiple copies of information exist, whether the physical information needs to be centralized or distributed more widely is an implementation and operational issue.

Multiple databases, which have grown out of independent developments, can demonstrate a number of differences. They can contain entirely different coding structures and they may also incorporate different definitions of entities, ambiguous or conflicting meanings, and different logical relationships. In the worst cases, they imply polarization, mistrust and a widespread lack of confidence in combining and sharing information. In these cases, the task is more than one of *information management*; it requires major cultural change as outlined earlier in the chapter. One of the objectives for introducing information management practices involves gaining the confidence of disaffected business users and sometimes colleagues in the IS function.

The risks associated with duplication of information input and storage can be greatly reduced by seeking to enter, update and store information once only. Duplication risks thereafter will be linked to the number of databases into which information is transferred and their distribution around the organization. In systems integration, multiple updating becomes part of the functionality of the integration.

Other factors affect the effectiveness of information processes and of the users who depend on them, but most of these are tackled within the identification of business IS demand and the resultant information architecture. Characteristics that then determine effectiveness include the availability of required information, ease of access by end-users, timeliness, quality, integrity and consistency. These all fall within information management policies and 'service' criteria.

THE PRACTICE OF MANAGING THE
INFORMATION ASSET

The practice of managing and marshalling the information asset is often called *information asset management* (IAM), although there is no universal agreement about its precise definition or constituents, its component activities, scope, organizational focus, policies and tools. It is additionally called by other names, 'information resource management' and 'corporate data management' being two favourite alternatives. It is significantly different from data administration or data management applied at system or business-function level, having a much wider significance and value. In asset-management terms, IAM seeks to build up the information assets of an organization at an acceptable cost, so that they can be employed to deliver value to the business. A definition of IAM and its constituents is given in Table 10.3.[12]

Table 10.3 *IAM and its constituents*

- *IAM* is a holistic approach to the management of the information assets of an organization. The emphasis is on integral, efficient and economic management of all the organization's information. It means getting the right information to the right people at the right time
- *Data (information) administration* is the identification and classification of business information and associated requirements, development of a corporate architecture, development of procedures and guidelines for identifying and defining business data (information)
- *Data dictionary administration* entails describing and cataloguing the information available
- *Database administration* involves design and development of a database environment for recording and maintaining data (especially machine-readable data), development of procedures and controls to ensure correct usage and privacy of data, operational timing, monitoring and housekeeping
- *Information-access services* ensure provision of support services and hardware and software to enable end-users to locate, access, correctly interpret and, where appropriate, manipulate the information available

Table 10.4   *Provisions of IAM*

- *Principles and guidelines*, which form the charter for defining IAM scope and provisions
- *Policies and procedures* for definition, management and usage of information, including its acquisition, protection, dissemination and disposal
- *A business encyclopaedia* of information definitions and usage
- *An enterprise model* and other business models referencing all types of information
- *Multimedia information* in files, databases and in an information 'warehouse'
- *Services, methods and tools* to enable IAM activities like information administration, appropriate for the level of information management required
- *Services* to deliver information to users, and tools for users to access information directly
- *Mechanisms* for enabling information sharing
- *Skills, competencies and knowledge* in information management disciplines and the information pertinent to the business

---

In this book, IAM is assumed to include those activities and a number of further components. It contributes a major element of the information-related requirements, in pursuit of business targets. It supplies or facilitates the business in providing a range of standards, guidelines, deliverables and services, as indicated in Table 10.4.

Principles and guidelines for IAM

Principles and guidelines for IAM should be given careful consideration, both when IAM is first introduced and when it is reassessed and updated to meet changing business needs. Aspects to consider include criteria for:

- determining the cost versus value of providing information;
- defining standards of information quality, accuracy, security and timeliness;
- responsibilities and allocation of ownership;
- satisfying the individual's need for information;
- sources and types of information to be catered for;
- what levels and forms of information should be provided (e.g. raw, unit, summary, etc.);
- how to determine the scope and methods for key practices (e.g. enterprise modelling, information sharing);
- principles relating to making the user community aware of the scope of IAM, and how to optimize their use of information;

- what constitutes an issue that needs to be resolved, and the means to do so.

Determining the Right Scope and Structure of Information to be Managed and Modelled

A key issue in IAM is deciding what is the right scope for the 'managed' information environment and how it should be structured. The total information environment does not stop at an organization's boundaries; it extends into the external environment, inhabited by customers, buyers, competitors and other organizations and influences. This external environment is very volatile and can never be modelled completely, nor can its contents be captured easily and made accessible. Internally, information is often fragmented and growing ever more so, as users of personal computing have built up their own caches of information. Systems designed to meet specific business needs are unable to communicate directly with one another, and are often unable to share, exchange or combine information effectively, because of inbuilt differences in definition or usage. Figure 10.3 illustrates the various information environments associated with a typical business. A significant portion of the information may be automated, but usually only a small proportion is managed.

The target scope of the managed environment is determined by business needs and priorities. Typically, it will contain information that must be accurate and reliable such as customer order information or billing information. It is information used by a broad section of the business and often by its external partners. Everyone uses a common definition and, while there may be more than one copy of the information, it is managed by procedures that ensure consistency and integrity. Primarily, this is the information used by key operational applications.

For any business, IAM has its foundation in its business IS strategy, where information needs are defined and the information architecture for each business unit is constructed. When several business units have developed their own IS strategies, either independently or collaboratively, they may decide to compare and rationalize, and possibly combine all or part of their information architectures or application portfolios. As long as due consideration is given to likely long-term needs as well as to immediate requirements, it may make very good business, resource and economic sense to collaborate in this way. Where two businesses have entirely different technology strategies, then the collaboration can extend no further than the conceptual architecture level. More frequently, a single business unit opts to introduce IAM within its own boundaries and sometimes in even smaller subdivisions of the business.

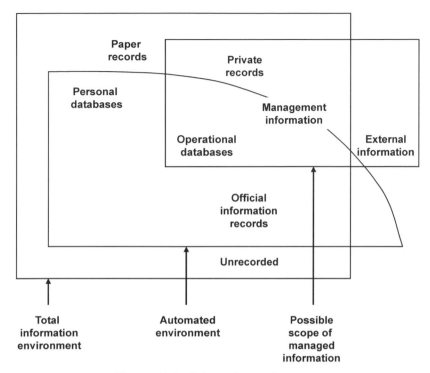

Figure 10.3 *Information environments*

Questions of centralization and decentralization of decision making, steering mechanisms, location of applications and resources, which were discussed at some length in Chapter 8, can be applied in much the same way in consideration of the ownership, location and management of information, and the location of the supporting IAM resources.

Whatever the business scope in terms of business units, the information architecture becomes the long-term implementation blueprint for IAM in that business, although it is extremely unlikely that the whole set of business information would be managed. At first, only certain parts of the architecture may be analysed beyond a global level, but piece by piece the information relevant to the business's key processes will be added until an information blueprint is complete to an appropriate level. This is likely to be a continuous process, and it will never be static, as new information is taken into the managed resource and perhaps other information is excluded as not having current significance and not warranting being managed under the IAM umbrella. Care needs to be taken to prevent this becoming a case of permanent analysis, without any value being delivered.

Remember, there is no suggestion that the information in the business environment should be stored in a single comprehensive database. Far from it—it is almost certain that there will be a number of separate databases in use. However, every attempt should be made to retain consistency of definitions across all databases and to confine the entry of information so that it is only input once. It is quite possible for there to be several copies of the same database, depending on the systems integration approach taken for linking legacy systems, new applications and packages.

Information Sharing

The ability to share information is a usual requirement when introducing IAM. Sharing can encompass interfaces within one business unit, several units, divisions or companies within the same group, and with external organizations. In its simplest form, information sharing means that only one copy of a piece of information is held and that all authorized users have access to it. In practice, this is very difficult to accomplish, because the same information is often used by several legacy applications, each with their own databases, and by installed packaged applications. Complexity increases if multiple vendors, hardware platforms, operating systems, DBMSs and network protocols are involved. In this case, it is very difficult to achieve a single source of information, and the complexity and risk increase if the situation is volatile and frequent changes to the environment and application portfolio are expected. Then a solution that incorporates consistent copies of information must be found, which enables information sharing and information management to be accomplished. This can be a very complex technical problem, well outside the scope of this book. A 'flavour' of the possibilities are considered in the next few subsections.

Single Vendor Solutions

Here a large proportion of the application portfolio is covered by one enterprise system supplied by one vendor, who also supplies the required integration. This approach has the great advantage that all functionality comes already integrated, but it is a feasible solution only if the organization is willing to lock into a single vendor, for one and possibly multiple sites, and is also willing to sacrifice the existing applications, covering this area.

This may be successful when requirements are relatively uniform and it meets information management and information-sharing requirements internally, if not externally. But it tends to have a number of drawbacks from other points of view:

- For most, except the simplest, businesses, no single vendor solution will meet all requirements, and the shortfalls have to be procured from other vendors and then integrated with the main applications. Many organizations pursue a 'best-of-breed' strategy, actively sourcing solutions from multiple vendors.
- Having to replace existing applications may produce a poor return on investment for those applications, plus the high cost of new software and training costs.
- The chosen solution may not be a good fit for all strategic business units (SBUs) if it is implemented across the whole organization.
- There is a higher risk in depending on a single vendor, who may also charge higher-than-average rates for support and development of the applications.

Point-to-Point Integration

Here tight connections are built between applications that need to share data in an integrated environment. The approach is evolutionary, and is relatively easy and low cost if only a small number of connections need to be made. However, if the numbers of applications, operating systems, DBMSs or interfaces are significant, and changes happen frequently, then it is both costly and high risk, as each interface is unique. Changing, upgrading or adding an application, or making changes to the application and network configuration, can produce risks of failure at any point in the business or technology environment.

Data Access

Data access means providing data access to users across the business regardless of the location of the users or the source of the information. This solution gives desktop tools to users for data manipulation, decision support, *ad hoc* enquiry and report generation. Its main focus is the provision of an information library or warehouse, refreshed with operational data on a regular basis, from operational systems, to perform limited integration and analysis functions. A data warehouse requires powerful servers to deliver high performance to all users.

Integration Using Middleware

Middleware is software implemented in a distributed environment that enables applications to 'talk' to one another and exchange information. In support of IAM, it enables information sharing in a distributed multivendor environment. Independent, but consistent, information is held in each application, and the middleware controls the synchronization and transmission of information between applications. There are various types of middleware that support different information integration requirements. The concept of *enterprise architecture integration* (EAI) is often encountered in relation to application integration, but is essentially similar to middleware, differing only in that it provides more sophisticated functionality.

Preparation for information sharing entails:

- determining the business needs and benefits—defined in the business IS strategy;
- defining the technical requirements and the practicalities of the provision (access mechanisms, security, risk, communications capability, centralization or decentralization, single or multiple copies of data sets);
- describing the information to be shared and the community of authorized users;
- defining the interworking requirements across the applications;
- deciding how to overcome barriers brought about by differences in management style and local values and culture within an organization;
- resolving issues of interdepartmental or company rivalry.

It is less likely that cultural factors will pose problems if the information-sharing requirement is largely restricted to a single SBU and its commercial partners in its value chain, than if the issues of shared information straddle business units in a larger corporate organization, or international boundaries, as in multinational companies. Logical arguments for sharing have to be weighed carefully against potential conflicts.

ACTIVITIES OF IAM

If IAM is being established at corporate level, then the main decisions will be made by the executive steering group, and those affecting the SBU by the business steering group (as described in Chapter 8); if it is being established at SBU level, then the business steering group for the SBU is the decision-making body. The activities and tasks involved are described in Box 10.4.

Developing the Enterprise Model

The enterprise or business model is the highest level model that is produced during the IS strategy process or within IAM. A business model is illustrated in Figure 4.3. It may have several components, which are described in more detail in Chapter 4:

- *A global hierarchical process and activity model* that mirrors the current structure of the business. It is used to identify business activities, by decomposition from the highest level functions of the business. It can be used to confirm the content and boundaries of the primary and support business processes.
- *A global process model* that shows the primary and supporting business processes, their relationship and the principal information and material flows. It is usually possible to map this onto the value chain model.
- *A global entity model* that includes all the high-level business entities that are of crucial interest to the business.
- *The activities and entities* linked together in a matrix, which represents a conceptual information architecture, indicating the relationships between the constituents and possible application areas.

The purpose of the enterprise model is as a basis for:

- Providing a coherent picture of the business, independent of physical structures, as a communications and planning tool.
- Identifying essential changes to the business to meet business objectives.
- Identifying major streamlining opportunities to the processes, without having to consider organizational factors.
- Seeking innovative opportunities, like those described in Chapter 5, around the value chain.
- Defining the most suitable applications and information architecture that would meet the business needs and would move the business in the direction of an integrated and flexible environment.
- Defining the information entities that should be managed on behalf of the whole business.
- As a benchmarking tool in the evaluation and selection of large business software packages such as for enterprise resource planning (ERP) or customer relationship management (CRM) in terms of

Box 10.4   Tasks performed within IAM

Section 1: Data (Information) Administration Tasks

- *Information planning*, which is a top-down task started in the strategic planning process and continued at a tactical level in IAM, in association with prioritized business initiatives.
- *Identifying business information requirements*, also undertaken in IS strategy process and business analysis.
- *Setting information definition standards and procedures*, including naming and abbreviation conventions. This also entails:
  - —selecting the medium and methods for recording the definitions, usually on a data dictionary, encyclopaedia or repository;
  - —defining procedures and communicating them to business and IS/IT users;
  - —introducing monitoring procedures for compliance with standards;
  - —measuring their effectiveness;
  - —assessing the impact of changes in information definition or relationships, resulting from changes in the business.

  Information administration and data dictionary administration work closely together in this area.
- *Managing the corporate information models*, determining their most appropriate form and their total scope, levels of decomposition, where separate models are relevant, and how they interface or overlap.
- *Coordinating the solving of information-related problems*. These may range from promotion and implementation of a policy to achieve a single source of information entry to internal disputes over information sharing and access rights.
- *Communicating with the business*, which includes promoting awareness of the role of information, and informing the business what information it possesses, where it is located, what its precise definition is in business terms, how it relates to other information and so on. Some of this is in conjunction with data dictionary administration.
- *Establishing and implementing process, activity and information analysis at a higher level than system level*. The task involves selecting methods, techniques and tools, and developing standards and procedures for their use throughout the information life cycle. They must integrate comfortably with systems

development methods and end-user computing. Part of the responsibility is to promote their use and to provide advice, training and assistance where necessary. There is also a quality role, to ensure conformance and consistency of analysis deliverables.

The deliverables are information models, process and information flow diagrams, activity decomposition diagrams and architecture matrices, as described in Chapter 3. The level of detail in the deliverables is determined by the type of analysis being performed, which may be strategic (enterprise level), overview (business process) and detailed analysis (application area) levels. The top level is strategic analysis, and its aim is to produce a global structured plan of the business information and processes. Models at this level are necessarily lacking in detail.

In practice, information administration takes responsibility for the enterprise models, and where contention occurs—when, for example, the scope of two overview areas overlap—then this must be resolved by data administration.

- *Establishing controls and procedures for information security and recovery, privacy (ensuring compliance under the Data Protection Act) and integrity.*

Section 2: Data Dictionary Administration Tasks

- *Providing an authoritative source of information to users and IS/IT groups on information.* It has the unique opportunity of putting information in context for the business at large, but the data dictionary must be clearly seen as a general management communication tool and not as the preserve of IT. In effect, it is the glossary and dictionary of the business.
- *Evaluating, selecting and implementing data dictionary management software.*
- *Setting up and coordinating the data dictionary contents,* the meta-models of data and functions.
- *Establishing standards and procedures* for use of the data dictionary and monitoring conformance.
- *Working with information administration* on information definition and impact analysis, and *with development and database administration* on application and database integration, development and maintenance.

Section 3: Database Administration Tasks

- *Undertaking design, development, implementation and operational tasks* associated with the business's logical and physical data-bases.
- *Setting technical standards, procedures and guidelines* for database activities, data input, update and access.
- *Evaluating and selecting database management software* to suit the technical infrastructure specified to support the business, implementing and maintaining the software, and implementing change control procedures.
- *Monitoring and controlling* the environment and database services to the business.
- *Protecting the integrity of the environment and investigating security problems.*
- *Undertaking periodic reorganization and restructuring, performance monitoring and tuning.*
- *Performing any necessary housekeeping tasks* such as back-up, archiving, recovery and restart.
- *Working closely with data administration and data dictionary administration* to ensure policies are followed and the impact of implementation issues is assessed.
- *Keeping abreast of database technology*, either new to the industry or as yet unused by the business.
- *Working with systems development* in ensuring that database usage is planned effectively for new applications and existing systems to give optimal user benefit, while complying with database standards and policies.
- *Working in package selection teams* to evaluate database designs to ensure that they meet defined standards of performance, structure and integration requirements.

Section 4: Information Access Tasks

- *Formulating, implementing and monitoring policies and procedures* relating to ownership, responsibility, security and access rights.
- *Promoting benefits of information management*, shared information and appreciation of the value of information.
- *Ensuring that high-quality information is available and accessible*, whether in operational databases, extracted information databases or external information.

- *Providing tools and techniques* that enable users to access information. This entails the provision of:
  - —software mechanisms that integrate the environment and enable information sharing, as described earlier in this chapter;
  - —delivery of information to users 'ready for use' or for further local manipulation;
  - —tools and access to an information 'warehouse' of information extracted from operational files;
  - —tools in the local PC, workstation or desktop environment to access local or widespread information.

their conformance to the architecture. Further investigation is needed to assess their conformance to other aspects of the principles, policies and procedures of IAM.

The enterprise model must be owned by the business, particularly at executive and business steering group levels. There are some problems and risks associated with it. It may be difficult to gain management commitment to the modelling process and to its use thereafter. This becomes a distinct possibility if the management group has had unsatisfactory experiences at some stage. Another problem is in ensuring that the level of analysis is contained at a high level, so as not to get overwhelmed by detail or to lose sight of essentials.

POLICIES AND IMPLEMENTATION ISSUES

Information planning at a strategic level demands top management involvement, without which there could be an unhealthy IT orientation to the plans. It is necessary for issues to be resolved at this level and the outcome specified in policies. The types of policy that are established at this level affect the organization as a whole. A few relate to physical issues, others to matters of central coordination, authority and responsibility, enabling access and the scope of managed information. There may also be a continuing need for marketing into the business community, to raise the level of commitment for treating information as a core business resource, and to educate the business about the inherent cost and value characteristics of information. There will be other issues that reflect the particular requirements of individual organizations.

Extent of the 'Managed' Information

As indicated earlier in this chapter, the extent of the information resource to be 'managed' must be broadly determined. Although it is unlikely that a policy will lay down the precise boundaries of managed data, guidelines are needed for information administration. However, hard-and-fast rules would be inappropriate, since the status of information changes from time to time.

At any one time, some user information will be corporate, mainly in strategic and key operational applications, some will be personal, mainly high potential and support, and thus excluded from formal information management. Over time, the personal information may move into a managed status (e.g. as it becomes more widely applicable, or as its value grows and the application moves or is redeveloped for the strategic or key operational segments). Sometimes, managed information becomes 'unmanaged' after it is extracted from the managed environment into a local environment, as when applications move from key operational to support segments, where information may be manipulated in non-standard ways. There needs to be a method for identifying what information is held by users that may have a wider usefulness. This can happen frequently in a free market environment, where user areas are innovative, and users develop their own applications and manipulate information skilfully to meet their own requirements. The challenge is clarifying the definition of each information element, ensuring that it fits consistently in the relevant models and recording the details in the data dictionary. Once the criteria for setting boundaries have been determined, the task of bringing information into a managed environment is relatively slow and needs careful coordination and control.

Clearly, there is a cost associated with managing information and this needs to be justified and then committed to, because the controls and procedures must not be irksome or inhibit business flexibility and creativity, but should be seen to be of value in themselves.

Organizational Responsibility for IAM

Responsibility for coordinating IAM activities in most instances needs to be centralized, but certain elements may be delegated to one or more business areas, responsible for client–server computing and access matters, or to local IAM units in each SBU in a decentralized business. In certain instances (e.g. where several SBUs have almost complete autonomy), a central IAM function may not be desirable, and each SBU may set up its own. However, if the corporate body has a significant say in SBU IS/IT policy, and if any attempt is made to standardize systems and information architectures across the company, then central coordination is probably desirable.

A number of other organizational factors should be considered:

- Skilled specialists may be needed to set up and implement IAM and to train the in-house staff in the skills required.
- Other specialists may be needed to create the distributed and integrated environment.
- Because it may be a continuous process, sufficient resources must be allocated.
- There is no one organizational structure that is universally appropriate. It is possible to have a structure with all IAM activities encompassed within the IS function, and managed at the same level as IS/IT development, etc. This could represent either a corporate or SBU structure. An alternative is for information management residing outside the IS function, which retains only database administration. In this case, the structure contains corporate information management as well as information management at SBU level. This would be repeated for each SBU.

Authority and Responsibility for Information

Criteria for determining ownership and the responsibilities associated with this for acquiring, storing, maintaining and disposing must be decided. Standards for maintaining quality, privacy, consistency and integrity, and for providing the required levels of security, must also be determined, and responsibilities assigned appropriately. In addition, access rules should be laid down.

These criteria, standards and responsibilities have to be set by user management with advice from the IAM group and communicated to all users of information, along with details of what information is available and who has the responsibilities throughout the various stages of the information life cycle.

It is, of course, vital to explain the benefits of managed information to the user community and to deliver them, otherwise a natural disinclination to part with 'my' information may turn into outright lack of co-operation or even hostility. This is where top management commitment combined with well-thought-out and implemented policies are needed. Two-way trust is involved; users having faith in the integrity of the data and data administrators trusting the users not to corrupt or misuse it.

Information Security

It is necessary to protect critical information from accidental or deliberate destruction, corruption or loss. This is an issue that is growing in importance since organizations are so dependent upon their information, and its exposure to risk is so great. Computer hackers are a growing breed of criminal.

Shared databases are prevalent and the number of terminals that can gain access to information continues to expand, as does the awareness of users. The risk of damage through physical failure or human intervention is also growing and must be analysed and contained as far as possible. The Data Protection Act in the UK and similar legislation in other countries puts an onus on organizations to protect private data.

Figure 10.4 presents a template describing major categories and levels of risk against critical information assets developed by the Hawley Committee. They argued that it should be reviewed by the Board from time to time along with the method of protection.

Measures to protect information should be implemented where they are necessary and can be shown to be effective. Barriers can be designed and built into hardware and software, as can recovery procedures. These can be supplemented by audit and other security monitoring procedures.

Implementation Issues

For the introduction or extension of IAM to succeed, it must be linked to specific business goals and tied to the achievement of desired business benefits, which could be stock reduction, new product development, accelerated availability of information, staff productivity, reduction in errors or improved decision making. Effective information management targeted at a few critical items of information, especially those that straddle internal or external boundaries, will repay the effort and serve as a good example for extending the 'managed' environment. Total information management is neither practical nor cost-effective.

Naturally, there are problems associated with implementing IAM. One of the most difficult is in bridging the gap between 'top-down'-defined databases and existing databases, and the resulting need to 'manage' or reconcile the differences. There may also be difficulties in managing expectations. Some may view the process as a means of identifying application opportunities, others a systems and information architecture, others creating database designs. These expectations may all be relevant, but they need to be pulled together under the business expectations of im-

Areas of risk	Level of risk defined by:			Comments on protection
	Impact on organizational performance	Likelihood to happen	Context: who, where, when, how	
Accidental damage/ loss (e.g. corruption/ deletion from computer)				Technical procedures Back-up Education
Deliberate acts of theft, or abuse/misuse				Security procedures Infringement penalties
Loss of people				Contractual terms Registration
Inaccurate and untimely information				Validation procedures Education
External relations (e.g. customer/ supplier)				Trading security Contractual terms
IPR protection, sale and acquisition				Contractual terms Registration
Destruction of facilities				Physical security Contingency planning
Legal and accountability				Education Protection of assets

Figure 10.4 *Information assets: common areas of risk and protection* (source: Information as an Asset: The Board Agenda, *KPMG/IMPACT, London, 1994)*

proving business performance over a long period through optimal exploitation of IS/IT.

Other issues that were noted by Goodhue *et al.*[13] in 1988 and are still relevant today are:

- Time and cost. If broadly-based IAM is being implemented, key people have to commit themselves. This level of commitment is difficult to obtain and to keep. Total implementation is very expensive and is a lengthy process. This level of expenditure will often be resisted if current systems are performing effectively and IAM is not being implemented on the basis of developing new strategic systems to support business objectives.
- Changes to business requirements may impact plans while information planning and implementation is under way. This must be expected and allowed for.
- Systems developed while IAM is being implemented take longer and cost more, due to the inevitable learning curve and to increased upfront analysis effort. This is a problem for line managers who want quick results and good return on investment. It is also difficult for IS managers who are resistant to allocating the extra effort.
- Removal of local autonomy when information is allocated 'managed' status. Application packages can be difficult to absorb within IAM policies, and the integration of legacy and new applications and databases is a complex issue.
- New skills are needed that are sometimes not easily acquired by existing staff.

MANAGING KNOWLEDGE RESOURCES

The investments that organizations are making in IT are generating huge volumes of information. For example, CRM systems generate vast amounts of transactional information about customers. A challenge faced is creating knowledge and insight from this information to inform business decisions. Even with effective information management strategies, most organizations are not succeeding in turning information into knowledge and results. Even those that do are doing so only temporarily or in a limited area of the business.[14]

One fact is without contention: knowledge is crucial for the competitive success of all commercial organizations, and, like information, if they desire to harness it to create business value, they must develop strategies to manage it effectively.[15] Managing knowledge embraces not just its exploitation but the acquisition, creating, storing and sharing of this resource—all with a deep understanding of the business and strategic context. No organization, of whatever size, is immune to the requirement for knowledge and the need to manage it effectively. Even the smallest enterprise needs to know about customers, competitors, pricing, new products, etc. Consequently, the concept of knowledge management (KM) has attracted much attention over the last decade, particularly as IT is seen as enabling the management of knowledge resources.

Davenport and Marchand[16] pose the question, 'Is KM just good information management?' They argue that there is a large component of information management in KM and that much of what passes for the latter is actually the former. Nonaka *et al.*[17] contend that the 'knowledge management' that academics and business people talk about often means just 'information management', although Teece[18] notes that the latter can certainly assist the former. However, true KM goes well beyond information management.

The recurring questions about knowledge management are, 'How do I do it?' and 'How do I ensure that my organization exploits its knowledge?' While the concept of managing knowledge is appealing, the meaning of the term knowledge is elusive.[19] Organizations are therefore faced with the task of managing something that they recognize as being vital, but yet have great difficulty in describing, particularly in a way that assists them in creating business value.

What Is Knowledge?

The concept of knowledge has been the subject of study and debate since the dawn of civilization. The creation of meaning, the role of language and symbols and the process of creating knowledge—learning—have occupied the minds of philosophers, educationalists, economics, neurologists, linguists and psychologists, to mention just a few disciplines.[20] What is widely accepted is that knowledge is the result of human evolution, the intelligent brain, and is a particularly human characteristic in that knowledge is inseparable from the human being. While data and information can arguably exist independently, knowledge cannot. It only exists in humans. Consequently, a distinction is often made between the object— the *known*—and the subject—the *knower*—of knowledge.

Although the terms 'information' and 'knowledge' are often used interchangeably, they are quite different.[21] While knowledge and information can be difficult to distinguish, they both involve more human participation than the raw data on which they are partly based. Information is data that has been given structure and knowledge is information that has been given meaning.[22] In essence, knowledge is information that has been interpreted by individuals and given a context. Thus, knowledge is the result of a dynamic human process, in which humans justify personal information produced or sustain beliefs as part of an aspiration for the 'truth'[23] and can be portrayed as information combined with experience, context, interpretation and reflection.[24]

The interpretation of information a person receives is relative to what he or she already knows.[25] It is suggested that man cannot grasp the meaning of information about his environment without some frame-of-value judgement. So, for knowledge to be created from information, a belief system is necessary, as is a process of converting and interpreting information to produce knowledge.

Furthermore, knowledge is not a static object, it is in constant flux and, from an individual's perspective, this is where the concept of *knowing* rather than knowledge is perhaps more relevant. Blacker,[26] in a review of the organization theory literature, contends that, '... rather than talking of knowledge, within its connotation of abstraction, progress, permanency and mentalism, it is more helpful to talk about the process of knowing ... [which] is situated, distributed and material.' In distinguishing between *knowledge* and *knowing*, Cook and Seely Brown[27] assert that 'knowledge is a tool of knowing, that knowing is an aspect of our interaction with the social and physical world, and that the interplay of knowledge and knowing can generate new knowledge and new ways of knowing.'[28] 'If only our organisation knew what knowledge it has ...' is another, more pragmatic expression of the problem!

The Concept of Knowledge Management

It is now regarded as axiomatic that the knowledge contained within an organization is one of its most precious resources.[29] Arguments, eloquently expressed elsewhere, and a basic tenet of resource-based theory, assert that managing an organization's knowledge may be the sole factor that keeps it competitive because all other resources are to a large extent imitable.[30] It therefore follows that the management of such a resource is crucial, especially creating the conditions for its beneficial deployment. Furthermore, the changing nature of the marketplace has placed even greater emphasis on knowing how to operate competitively. Being competitive in marketplaces that are increasingly global and de-regulated requires that companies be innovative (a knowledge activity itself), not just in their products and services but also how they compete in their chosen market. They therefore need to know in considerable depth what their customers and competitors are doing or are likely to do, and, furthermore, they must know how to leverage this knowledge.[31] As more and more products and services become commoditized, the more 'know-how' about customers' needs, preferences, etc.

becomes the added-value an organization has to have in order to be a chosen supplier, rather than straightforward 'product excellence'.

There is an argument that KM is actually a contradiction in terms, being a hangover from an industrial era when control modes of thinking were dominant.[32] If knowledge is information combined with experience, context, interpretation and reflection, the use of the term KM, suggesting that knowledge can be managed, is to misunderstand the nature of knowledge. There is a suggestion that only the 'context' and conditions surrounding knowledge can be managed. Some practitioners suggest that knowledge sharing is a better description, while others prefer 'learning', as a key challenge in implementing KM is sense-making and interpretation.

Notwithstanding these arguments, knowledge is key both to creating competencies—including IS competencies as discussed in Chapter 8—and in integrating them into an organizational capability.[33] Knowledge of what specific resources exist in a business is essential for the competent management of its operation. A competitive capability requires a further class of knowledge—knowledge of the market and the players in it, and knowledge of how to exploit the competencies within the organization so as to address the needs of the marketplace in a way that will distinguish it from the competition.

Consider, for instance, a team of managers and specialists meeting and working together to formulate a bid for a major international engineering contract. The bid is a complex one involving not just product specialists but also expertise in contractual law, international taxation, exporting, global supply chains, complex sourcing, costing and finance. Furthermore, the bidding activity will not be the straightforward sequential application of one expertise after another, but is more likely to be the iterative exploitation of these expertises, since a change in one expert's input could have consequences elsewhere. In a gathering of such experts, each will bring their functional competency to bear on the bid-making activity set. However, to make a successful bid will need more than the sum of the parts—what is needed is the managerial know-how necessary to integrate these into a successful bid process. An organization that develops such a competency is likely to win more business. Without institutionalizing such a competency, the organization is likely to respond to potential new business opportunities with a flurry of activity rather than deploying a coherent business process.

In these two contrasting approaches, it is worth noting the use of knowledge. In the bid-as-an-activity-set approach, knowledge belongs to each of the experts and exists as discrete packages within that expert domain (e.g. tax law). In the bidding-is-a-business-process approach, formal attempts are made to retain the knowledge that is diffused within the working team of how to integrate the contributions of several experts in order to make a successful bid.

The DIKAR Model

A model that helps locate *packaged* knowledge[34] and *diffuse* knowledge within a business-related context is the DIKAR (Data, Information, Knowledge, Action, Results) model (see Figure 10.5). Introduced in Chapter 4, it illustrates the relationship between data, information, knowledge, action and results. This model has also proved useful in understanding and framing KM issues, and in helping to compare and assess the different perspectives that are being exercised by those pursuing KM.

The conventional way of interpreting and using the model is to view it from left to right as a value spectrum (i.e. to begin with basic data and progress through a series of stages, each containing more business value than the previous, culminating with the 'right' business results). As we progress from left to right, the business value that the stages yield potentially increases. The linkages between each of the stages are just as important as the stages themselves. They represent the activities by which the value is increased, typically including procedures, systems, processes, organizational structures, administration, skills, etc. These linkages characterize some of the organization's competencies and will vary even between very similar organizations—due to history, culture, various constraints and, most importantly, management's world view on how business is done. Within any company, the nature of the linkages between any two stages will also differ. Basically the further to the left

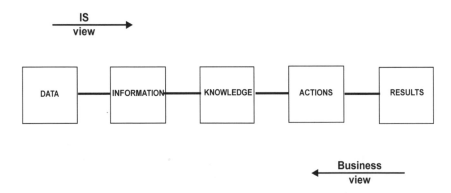

Figure 10.5 *The DIKAR model (source: after Venkatraman)*

(the data end) the more we can expect to see defined procedures and the extensive application of technology; while to the right (the results end) what occurs will depend much more on people—as individuals, as groups and as directed by management.

Using the DIKAR model in left-to-right mode is very useful in understanding (in a knowledge and information sense) how business is actually done. For an organization's core processes, senior managers should have a firm and detailed grasp on how DIKAR applies to those processes (i.e. it is in essence their business model). The application of experience, knowledge, technology and business acumen to the linkages is likely to improve the overall core process in a targeted incremental fashion. This has been the traditional approach in applying IT to business processes.

However, when the organization steps outside its day-to-day processes and instead sets itself new goals or new results targets, the left-to-right use of the model cannot explain how to achieve them. Examples of this would be how to launch a new competitive offensive, how to break into a new market, how to innovate or, indeed, to effect any radical change in the organization. In such circumstances, the data–information–knowledge–action chain does not exist. The DIKAR model, however, can still be helpful if we reverse its usage to right to left. In its RAKID direction, a number of fundamental questions are posed: Given desired results what actions are needed to achieve them? Given a set of actions what do we need to know to perform the actions? What information and data are required in order that we are in a knowledgeable position to design and affect action? Answering these questions all demand knowledge.

The linkages in the RAKID mode of the model are essentially integrative—given an end point, what resources does an organization have to bring together to get there and how does it bring them together? The necessary resources will consist not just of the obvious such as money, manpower, equipment and skills, but are likely to include processes, structures, roles and knowledge—so-called intangible resources. It is perhaps the knowledge of how to integrate such a range of resources in a new way to achieve new results that is the most potent form of KM.

Traditionally, businesses have focused more management attention on physical resources and those resources that can be measured, which usually means the intangible resources such as process, roles and knowledge might never enter return-on-investment evaluations. But, in a competitive environment, these are perhaps the most valuable since they are difficult to imitate and are also the vehicle for innovative approaches to new challenges. The effects of globalization, liberalization and deregulation on markets has been generally to make those markets harder to

survive and prosper in—there are potentially more competitors and substitute products and services competing for customers' interests. The
appropriate response to this is unlikely to be to 'turn up the wick' on
the existing traditional resources and their deployment. Instead, companies have to find ways of making the marketplace aware of the new
capabilities that will distinguish them from existing or potential competitors. These capabilities will arise only if the management is competent
in ways of integrating resources in new added-value ways. Hence, when
designing processes that include the sharing and transfer of knowledge
either explicitly or implicitly, the configuration of roles in the process
should guide the strategy for information provision.

The role of KM in this 'new results' scenario is to marshal knowledge
and experience not just of all the necessary specialisms but also of how to
integrate them into a new capability that the market will place value on,
such as for the complex bid example as outlined above. Once achieved, a
capability should be retained and actively supported, including
technology support. In practice, however, bids like that described
above tend to be treated as a 'one-off' and as a task outside the
experts' 'normal' day-to-day job. The experience accumulated in
winning or losing bids is not retained as corporate learning—so the
wheel is reinvented many times and no one is apparently alarmed by
this. Losing a bid tends to be attributed to more straightforward causes
such as price, lead time or what the value proposition was, rather than
examining how the organization went about creating and presenting the
value proposition.

The knowledge of each expert can in a sense be thought of as a knowledge 'package'—some of it even being capable of being codified. The
knowledge of acting together so as to create a new capability will be
much more diffuse and will reside within the bid team and will be
much harder to document let alone codify. However, the outcomes of
the team's activities will be capable of being documented and these can
form the basis of learning. How to manage specialized 'packaged knowledge' and how to integrate it with and manage 'diffuse knowledge' such
as exists in teams is one of the key goals of KM.

The Location of Knowledge and the Issues in
Managing Knowledge

The past few years has seen a number of organizations introduce chief
knowledge officers (CKOs) and knowledge managers as a formal step to
managing their knowledge assets.[35] Referring to the DIKAR diagram,
such a manager, who would be naturally located in the centre 'knowledge

stage', can view the organization's knowledge assets and their attendant management issues from two perspectives: 'downstream' toward data and 'upstream' toward results.

Starting from the knowledge box in the DIKAR model and looking toward data and information, the knowledge manager has a certain set of issues to contend with that are different from the 'upstream' view. Knowledge in this circumstance can be thought of as a body of information, formally written down and capable of being readily assimilated into the company's systems. The issues of KM here are identifying the knowledge, its location, validating it and verifying its value, obtaining it in a useful form, determining where it is most useful in the business and making it available there in an appropriate form, using suitable technology, and finally ensuring that the knowledge is used beneficially.

Looking 'upstream', the knowledge manager is now operating with a set of issues around the kind of knowledge that determines actions, and actions that need certain knowledge—the domain of know-how. This kind of knowledge is more diffuse and tacit, and invariably resides in peoples' heads. An example could be an organization that seeks to move into a new overseas market—it will require somebody who knows how to set up supply chains into that market quickly, knows the business scene there, the relevant legal and tax factors, the culture, etc. This is primarily experiential knowledge, although some of it can be made explicit to a certain degree (e.g. customs regulations). Someone who knows the working relationship between businesses and a country's civil servants has knowledge that is hard to codify. The knowledge manager has to operate in a much more personal domain—the motivation to share hard-won knowledge of the experiential kind is not usually high, the individual is 'giving away' their value and may be very reluctant to lose a position of influence and respect by making it available 'to everyone'. This situation and the inherent nature of knowledge can make it difficult to capture.

There is nevertheless a strong desire, almost a belief, that as technology platforms get 'more intelligent' that this know-how can be captured (e.g. with expert systems) and suppliers of 'knowledge systems' are keen to advance the point. The assumptions underpinning this view are likely to be too simplistic. While at one level it is clear that rules that have evolved over time can be encoded, some behaviours owe more to 'chaotic' factors than logical left-brain activity. The organic nature of knowledge highlights how 'mind-maps' and other such mapping techniques are more appropriate than information architecture diagrams.[36]

A more complex variation on know-how is the 'team'. Here knowledge is distributed among a group of people, each contributing in different ways to this overall know-how. Furthermore, the team itself can create knowledge by its own activities. Teams also represent an effective way of generating learning, of marshalling knowledge and disseminating it. Here the knowledge manager has to contend with facilitation of team activities, providing frameworks for more formal knowledge handling, and ensuring its recording so that learning can occur. Typically, companies see the gradual build-up of knowledge repositories that, if carefully constructed and subsequently used intelligently, can help in moving up learning curves, and remove duplication and reinvention.

These three ways of considering knowledge in organizations are summarized in Table 10.5. This table contrasts the nature of knowledge within each category as well as identifying both specific management issues as well as those management concerns that transcend all categories.

Communities of Practice

A central lesson emerging from research is that if KM is going to be successful, then organizations must concentrate on people. The importance of people as creators and carriers of knowledge is forcing organizations to realize that knowledge lies less in its databases than in its people.[37] Davenport and Prusak[38] note that when Ford wanted to build on the success of the Taurus, the company found that the essence of that success had been lost with the loss of the people who created it. The knowledge required was not stored in databases, nor could it be.

Research shows that people most freely share experiences in informal, self-organizing networks. Consequently, it becomes necessary for organizations to create and promote those environments. Often labelled *communities of practice* (COP), these are groups of people informally bound together by shared expertise and passion for a joint enterprise.[39] COPs exist to build and exchange knowledge, and, in the process, develop the capabilities of members. They differ from project teams, who are composed of employees assigned by management, in that they select themselves. The 'glue' that holds the community together is the passion, commitment and identity with the group's expertise, while for a team it's the goals and project milestones.

In a study of a COP conducted by Breu and Hemmingway[40] at a commercial utility in the UK, they found that in being prepared to accept the informal activities of its employees, the organization gained significant benefits. Their findings support motivational theories that advocate the human desire to make social contribution in the case of the COP they studied, sharing knowledge and experience with other members of this organizational community.

Table 10.5 Types of knowledge and associated KM issues

	Knowledge as body of information	Knowledge as know-how: The Individual	Knowledge as know-how: The Team
Nature of knowledge	• Explicit • Codifiable • IS/IT can play a part • Packaged	• Tacit • Personal • Diffuse	• Tacit • Fluid • Dependent on team dynamics • Diffuse
KM issues	• Finding it • Validation • Value assessment • Obtaining it at reasonable cost • Integration with own system • Making available to the right population in the right form • Sensible use of technology • Ensuring subsequent beneficial use	• Establishing suitable processes for extraction • Tight ownership • Reluctant to impart • Motivation and reward • Experiential, thus hard to encode • Trust • Finding suitable way of passing on learning • Limited role for technology	• Formal management of essentially free-form activity • Establishing suitable frameworks and processes • Members' own perception of their role • Mutual trust—need 100% buy-in • Formal learning mechanisms • Dissemination • Creating and using knowledge repositories • Technology has a background role
Common KM issues	Knowledge about knowledge (knowing it exists and where: its context and hence its importance) Understanding the relevant business context Ownership and buy-in to KM processes Updating and reuse of knowledge Demonstrating causal link between KM activity and business benefit		

The Role of IT in KM

There are two dominant and contrasting views of knowledge management that can be gleaned from the above discussion: the engineering perspective and the social process perspective (see Figure 10.6). The engineering perspective views knowledge management as a technology process. Many organizations have taken this approach in managing knowledge, believing that it is concerned with managing 'pieces of intellectual capital'. Driving this view is the view that knowledge can be codified and stored; in essence that knowledge is explicit knowledge and therefore is little more than information.

The alternative view is that knowledge is a social process. As such, it asserts that knowledge resides in people's heads and that it is tacit. As such, it cannot be easily codified and only revealed through its application. As tacit knowledge cannot be directly transferred from person to person, its acquisition occurs only through practice. Consequently, its transfer between people is slow, costly and uncertain. Technology, within this perspective, can only support the context of knowledge work. Indeed, Walsham argues that IT-based systems used to support KM can only be of benefit if used to support the development and communication of human meaning.[41] One reason for the failure of IT in knowledge management initiatives is that the designers of the knowledge systems fail to understand the situation and work practices of the users and the complex 'human' processes involved in work.[42]

While technology can be used with knowledge management initiatives, it should *never* be the first step.[43] KM is primarily a human and process issue. Once these two aspects have been addressed, then the created

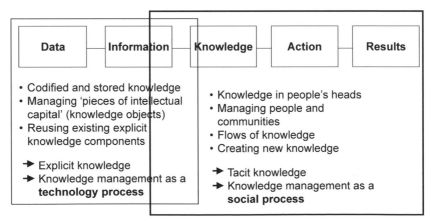

Figure 10.6 *Mapping knowledge perspectives on DIKAR model (source: draws on the work of K. Breu at Cranfield School of Management)*

processes are usually very amenable to being supported and enhanced by the use of technology. This is certainly the case in global companies where geographical barriers to knowledge movement and sharing are large. The degree to which information technology can directly contribute to business activity attenuates according to left-to-right progression across the DIKAR model. Around the knowledge point in the model, the nature of the IT contribution alters. To the left, IT can actually work directly on the data/information, even creating additional data/information. In significant knowledge exchange this is not the case.

Zack[44] sees IT providing a seamless 'pipeline' for the flow of *explicit* knowledge enabling:

- capturing knowledge;
- defining, storing, categorizing, indexing and linking digital objects;
- searching for ('pulling') and subscribing to ('pushing') relevant content;
- presenting content with sufficient flexibility to render meaningful and applicable across multiple contexts of use.

As indicated earlier, knowledge sharing can be complex, personal and has an organic aspect to it. The most effective way of achieving sharing is the face-to-face conversation where much more happens than the mere exchange of words. However, this can be uneconomic especially for geographically dispersed companies. The role of technology alters to being a facilitator of connectivity, and its success lies in how well it can emulate the richness of the conversation channel. Desktop videoconferencing currently comes closest to being such a channel. This is not the mere provision of a facial image on a PC screen, but extends to include its own procedural rules and is backed up by a high-bandwidth infrastructure carrying shared and concurrent access to data, images, video clips, searchable documents, etc. BP Exploration has invested heavily and successfully in this technology and claims significant cost savings in new drillings through shared learning around the globe.[45]

Other technologies that are making a contribution 'on the right of DIKAR' are 'interactive' Intranets and the combination of document management and workflow management systems. The latter is especially useful in situations where large complex multi-part documents such as contracts, regulatory submissions, etc. need concurrent attention from several experts with these experts possibly residing in different countries. Seely Brown[46] argues, based on his work in Xerox, that organizations should be seen as 'communities of communities', and that new technologies such as Intranets are suited to provide support to the development of effective communication.

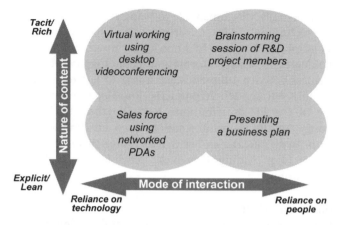

Figure 10.7 *Content and interaction in knowledge management* (source: K. Breu, Cranfield School of Management)

Figure 10.7 positions a number of technologies on a schematic, mapping the nature of the content against the mode of interaction. Content can be considered along a continuum from lean to rich. Mode of interaction refers to whether there is a reliance on technology or people. Some technologies like videoconferencing are suitable for exchange of rich content. Sales Force Automation (SFA) tools are suitable for communicating 'lean' content such as customer details and contact history.

Knowledge Has to Be Managed

There is little return in merely collecting knowledge, making it accessible and then waiting for business activities to improve purely because of the sheer abundance of knowledge. Management must intervene to leverage the benefits, and the appointments of CKOs often reflect this.

There are structural, cultural and managerial barriers to KM as well as the usual issues of lack of time and money to mount such initiatives. People are both the path and barrier to successful KM. While they are the key to success, they also have the potential to frustrate KM plans and programs. The root of this dilemma resides in the fact that knowledge sharing is not natural—there is a reluctance to divulge years of hard-won experience, especially if the divulgence is also associated with possible redundancy or reduction of status. Furthermore, experienced 'business-winners' such as senior consultants in a management consultancy or senior partners in a law firm, while acknowledging the value of onward transmission of their know-how to less experienced staff, will generally still rate one hour of fee-earning work well above one hour of knowledge-sharing activity. Changing that belief is a 'hearts and minds' issue and not a training issue.

In such circumstances, value has to be demonstrably placed upon knowledge sharing and corporate knowledge creation and stewardship. In most organizations, this will mean leadership by example from the top. Reward structures need to be visibly in place—and these may not necessarily be financial rewards—as do formal learning loops and best-practice sharing mechanisms like communities of practice.

Additionally, there is a need to have a senior executive overview or policy on what KM is and what it means for the business and how it is linked to business drivers and plans. Unfortunately, in many organizations, KM still resides outside mainstream management activity. And, while it does, it will struggle to deliver any demonstrable tangible benefits. Mere assertions, however strongly delivered, that knowledge is a vital resource and needs to be handled as such have little chance of inducing the necessary changes for knowledge-leveraged benefits to appear.

Obstacles for Effective KM

Research conducted at the Cranfield School of Management has identified culture as top of the list of concerns among organizations regarding knowledge management.[47] Turning a 'we don't do it like that' attitude into 'who knows how to do it better?' demands a sea change in working practices and relationships. People and cultural issues dominate as both the necessary means and the key inhibitor to sharing and exploiting knowledge. The obstacles are summarized in Table 10.6.

People are either reluctant to change or to change quickly. Working styles are often ingrained into organizations, and, in many cases, the production and sharing of knowledge—as opposed to a more tangible product—is still regarded as distracting or even career-threatening. Schutze and Boland[48] report the problems encountered in implementing a new competitor intelligence system in a large US organization where the democratization of information access and the open sharing of information that the new systems facilitated was at odds with the competitive intelligence analysts view of themselves as 'anointed' gatekeepers of this information. An organization's internal structures can act as inhibitors; they are often inflexible, fragmented and separated into functional silos. In addition, the evidence suggests that there is even greater reluctance to share knowledge outside the company, among partners, suppliers and customers—a reason why strategic alliances often flounder.

Table 10.6   *Barriers to successful knowledge management*

People	Management	Structure	Knowledge
Inertia to change	The fear of giving	Inflexible company	Extracting knowledge
Too busy—no time	up power	structures	Categorizing knowledge
to learn	The difficulties of	Fragmented	Rewarding knowledge
No discipline to act	passing on power	organizations	Understanding
Lack of motivation	Challenging	Functional silos	knowledge
Constant staff	traditional	Failure to invest	management
turnover	company style	in past systems	Sharing between key
Transferring	Imposed constraints		knowledge groups
knowledge to	Lack of understanding		Making knowledge
new people	about formal		widely available
Teaching older	approaches		
employees new			
ideas			

KM is an expensive undertaking and ironically, if a business is in highly competitive markets, expensive not to do. Regarding the DIKAR model, companies who have disparate infrastructure platforms, who have not invested in information management and whose executives have never seriously debated the role of information in their business activities are unlikely to make headway in KM unless these issues are addressed. There are some basic first steps such as issues of codification of knowledge (most organizations report that this takes far longer than estimated), education and sometimes changing the organization to value knowledge sharing before any return on the investment can begin to be realized. These basic requirements absorb time, money and, crucially, senior management attention.

This means that KM initiatives must have leadership—knowledge sharing must be demonstrated and rewarded by senior managers, otherwise organizational fiefdoms will continue to prevail. Depending on how territorial and how early in the KM process an organization is, the aggregation of these costs may seem a price too high—but the evidence suggests that there are no short cuts. Conversely, many global companies who perceive their marketplace to be a highly competitive environment have concluded that it is expensive not to do KM.

SUMMARY

The introduction or extension of information management must be linked to specific business goals and tied to the achievement of business benefits. Benefits such as stock reduction or improvements in staff productivity can be quantified easily; others are more qualitative such as accelerated information availability and improved decision making due to having pertinent information.

Effective information management targeted at a few critical items of information, especially those that straddle internal or external boundaries, will repay the effort and serve as a good example for extending the managed environment. Total information management is neither practical nor cost-effective. A sensible balance between short-term pay-offs and long-term achievement of a target information architecture is needed.

Some cultural issues must be tackled with sensitivity:

- line management preference for short-term results and positive return on investment, over building up value in the information assets;
- removal of local autonomy when information is allocated the 'managed' status;
- possible opposition from the IS function itself to IAM becoming the 'IT' focus of business attention.

Successful implementation of an information management strategy means achieving maximum contribution to the business over an extended period, at an acceptable cost and risk, and with the commitment of the business community at large. IAM is one of the principal mechanisms put in place to aim continuously for optimizing this value. This chapter has attempted to highlight the criteria that affect obtaining the right balance, and to address some practical issues associated with introducing new activities into the business, both inside and outside the IS function.

The whole of the information environment throughout an organization cannot be treated in the same way, and it is useful to categorize it in an information portfolio, related to business needs and potential. The starting point for implementing IAM may be having identified high-level information portfolios for each business unit, aligned to their respective application portfolios and their business needs. The aim then is to bring information into the managed environment according to needs and priorities, and the risks associated with not managing it. This entails:

- focusing on strategic information that must be managed;
- evaluating the key operational information in the current portfolio and determining how best to exploit its potential, at acceptable cost and risk;
- maintaining a watchful eye on high potential information that may

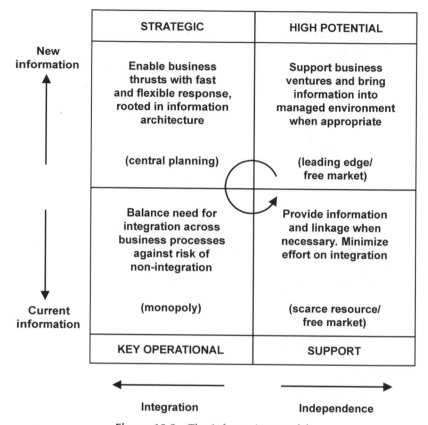

Figure 10.8 *The information portfolio*

become strategic, but where structures and relationships are as yet hazy;

- perhaps choosing to ignore low-potential, support information that does not warrant a high priority for being managed.

Figure 10.8 illustrates the differing aims around the information portfolio. In managing the information portfolio over time, there is naturally an increase in the ability to integrate more information and thus to build up the information assets of the business. A sensible balance must be struck between the cost of integration, especially where old systems are retained, and the overall cost to the business of not integrating them, as well as between the freedom given to end-users to create and use information innovatively and the disciplines imposed within the managed environment.

Knowledge management is more diffuse and organic in its nature and execution than information management. This is because knowledge resides primarily within people, or groups of people, and thus has complexities not found in straightforward procedural activities. Typically, knowledge sharing has aspects of trust and politics associated with it, and requires an appropriate culture, reward system and managerial approach to be developed.

The personal nature of knowledge ownership has to be understood and accommodated before it can be managed. Where communities of practice have been constructed, success is only achieved when mutual respect for everyone's actual, rather than possible, contribution occurs; anything less and they begin to degrade as employees feel their effort is not being matched by others causing a retreat to more selfish, old behaviours. Leadership by example appears to be key in achieving a truly open knowledge environment. As an emerging topic of study within the field of IS, we have much to learn about how knowledge can be effectively 'managed' before we can understand how best to deploy IT to improve the processes involved.

ENDNOTES

1. In this chapter, the concepts of 'information' and 'data' are used interchangeably. In reality, a distinction can be made between them, but this is superfluous to the discussions in this chapter. For an elaboration of the distinction, see P. Checkland and S. Holwell, *Information, Systems and Information Systems: Making Sense of the Field*, John Wiley & Sons, Chichester, UK, 1998.

2. T.C. Redman, 'The impact of poor data quality on the typical enterprise', *Communications of the ACM*, Vol. 41, No. 2, 1998, 79–82; T.C. Redman, 'Improve data quality for competitive advantage', *Sloan Management Review*, Winter, 1995, 99–107.

3. T.H. Davenport, *Information Ecology: Mastering the Information and Knowledge Environments*, Oxford University Press, New York, 1997.

4. *Information as an Asset: The Board Agenda*, KPMG IMPACT, London, 1994. The terms of reference of this Committee were, 'To develop guidelines for Boards of Directors with regard to the information assets for which an organisation is legally and ethically responsible. In particular, to propose mechanisms which promote within an organisation: shared understanding of information assets; definitions of importance and value; protection against risks of accident, misuse and lost opportunity; proper authorised use; optimum use for stakeholder benefit.'

5. T.H. Davenport, *Information Ecology: Mastering the Information and Knowledge Environments*, Oxford University Press, New York, 1997.

6. D.A. Marchand, 'What is your company's information culture?', *Mastering Management, Financial Times*, 8 December 1995, pp. 10–11.

7. T.H. Davenport, 'Saving IT's soul: Human-centred information management', *Harvard Business Review*, March–April 1994, 119–131.

8. P.A. Strassmann, *The Politics of Information Management*, The Information Economics Press, New Canaan, Connecticut, 1994. See also T.H. Davenport, E.C. Eccles and L. Prusak, 'Information politics', *Sloan Management Review*, Fall, 1992, 53–65.

9. P.A. Strassmann, *Governance and Information Management: Principles and Concepts*, The Information Economics Press, New Canaan, Connecticut, 2000.

10. D.A. Marchand, W. Kettinger and J.D. Rollins, 'Information orientation: People, technology and bottom line', *Sloan Management Review*, Summer, 2000, 69–80.

11. P.F. Drucker, 'The coming of the new organisation', *Harvard Business Review*, January–February 1988, 45–53.
12. Based on the work of B.G. Watson, *Information Management in Competitive Success*, Pergamon Infotech, Maidenhead, UK, 1987.
13. D.L. Goodhue, J.A. Quillard and J.F. Rockart, 'Managing the data resource: A contingency perspective', *MIS Quarterly*, Vol. 12, No. 3, 1988, 373–392.
14. T.H. Davenport, J.G. Harris, D.W. DeLong and A.L. Jacobson, 'Data to knowledge to results: Building an analytic capability', *California Management Review*, Winter, 2001, 117–138.
15. G. von Krogh, J. Roos and K. Slocum, 'An essay on corporate epistemology', *Strategic Management Journal*, Special Issue, Summer, 1994, 55–71; S. Wikström and R. Normann, *Knowledge and Value: A New Perspective on Corporate Transformation*, Routledge, London, 1994; S.G. Winter, 'Knowledge and competence as strategic assets', in D. Teece, ed., *The Competitive Challenge*, Ballinger, Cambridge, MA, 1987, pp. 159–184; I. Nonaka and H. Takeuchi, *The Knowledge-Creating Company: How Japanese Companies Create the Dynamics of Innovation*, Oxford University Press, New York, 1995.
16. T.H. Davenport and D.A. Marchand, 'Is KM just good information management?', in D.A. Marchand, T.H. Davenport and T. Dickson, *Mastering Information Management*, Financial Times/Prentice-Hall, London, 2000, pp. 165–169.
17. I. Nonaka, R. Toyama and N. Konno, 'SECI, *Ba*, and leadership: A unified model of dynamic knowledge creation', *Long Range Planning*, Vol. 33, No. 1, 2000, 5–34.
18. D.J. Teece, 'Strategies for managing knowledge assets: The role of firm structure and industrial context', *Long Range Planning*, Vol. 33, 2000, 35–54.
19. In this chapter, we are not seeking to enter into either a philosophical or epistemological debate regarding the concept of knowledge; this has been more eloquently addressed elsewhere. For example, see M. Foucault, *The Archaeology of Knowledge and The Discourse on Language*, Pantheon, New York, 1972; M. Polanyi, *Personal Knowledge*, University of Chicago Press, Chicago, Illinois, 1958; G. von Krogh and J. Roos, *Organisational Epistemology*, Macmillian, Basingstoke, UK, 1995.
20. For example, K. Boulding, 'The economics of knowledge and the knowledge of economics', *American Economic Review*, Vol. 58, 1966, 1–13; F. Hayek, 'The use of knowledge in society', *American Economic Review*, September 1945; M. Polanyi, *The Tacit Dimension*, Routledge and Kegan Paul, London, 1966; A. Reber, *Implicit Learning and Tacit Knowledge: An Essay on the Cognitive Unconscious*, Oxford University Press, New York, 1993; J.-P. Sartre, *Being and Nothingness: An Essay on Phenomenological Ontology*, translated by H.E. Barnes, Methuen, London, 1957.
21. I. Nonaka, R. Toyama and N. Konno, 'SECI, *Ba*, and leadership: A unified model of dynamic knowledge creation', *Long Range Planning*, Vol. 33, No. 1, 2000, 5–34; P. Checkland and S. Holwell, *Information, Systems and Information Systems: Making Sense of the Field*, John Wiley & Sons, Chichester, UK, 1998.
22. See R. Glazer, 'Measuring the knower: Towards a theory of knowledge equity', *California Management Review*, Vol. 40, 1998, 175–194; and P. Checkland and S. Holwell, *Information, Systems and Information Systems: Making Sense of the Field*, John Wiley & Sons, Chichester, UK, 1998. In addition, information theory holds information to be independent of meaning. See C.E. Shannon and W. Weaver, *The Mathematical Theory of Communication*, University of Illinois Press, Urbana, Illinois.
23. See I. Nonaka, 'A dynamic theory of organizational knowledge creation', *Organization Science*, Vol. 5, 1994, 14–37; and J. Seely Brown and P. Duguid, *The Social Life of Information*, Harvard Business School Press, Boston, 2000.
24. T.H. Davenport, D. DeLong and M. Beers, 'Successful knowledge management projects', *Sloan Management Review*, Winter, 1998, 43–57.
25. I. Nonaka, 'A dynamic theory of organizational knowledge creation', *Organization Science*, Vol. 5, 1994, 14–37.
26. F. Blacker, 'Knowledge, knowledge work and organizations: An overview and interpretation', *Organization Studies*, Vol. 16, No. 6, 1995, 1021–1046.
27. S.D.N. Cook and J. Seely Brown, 'Bridging epistemologies: The generative dance between organizational knowledge and organizational knowing', *Organization Science*, Vol. 10, No. 4, 1999, 381–400.
28. Spender envisages an organization as a system of 'knowing activity' rather than as a system of applied abstract knowledge. See J.C. Spender, 'Making knowledge the basis of a dynamic theory of the firm', *Strategic Management Journal*, Vol. 17, Winter Special Issue, 1996, 42–62. Five claims on knowing have been suggested by Roos and von Krogh: 'knowing is distinction-making, knowing is caring, knowing is languaging, knowing is shaping the future, competence is not an asset, it is an event.' See J. Roos and G. von Krogh, 'The

epistemological challenge: Managing knowledge and intellectual capital', *European Management Journal*, Vol. 14, No. 4, 1996, 333–337.

29. R.M. Grant, 'Towards a knowledge-based theory of the firm', *Strategic Management Journal*, Winter Special Issue, 1996, 109–122; J.P. Liebeskind, 'Knowledge, strategy, and the theory of the firm', *Strategic Management Journal*, Winter Special Issue, 1996, 93–107; D. Leonard-Barton, *Wellsprings of Knowledge: Building and Sustaining the Sources of Knowledge*, Harvard Business School Press, Boston, 1996; I. Nonaka and H. Takeuchi, *The Knowledge Creating Company*, Oxford University Press, New York, 1995.

30. R.M. Grant, 'Towards a knowledge-based theory of the firm', *Strategic Management Journal*, Winter Special Issue, 1996, 109–122; S.G. Winter, 'Knowledge and competence as strategic assets', in D. Teece, ed., *The Competitive Challenge*, Ballinger, Cambridge, Massachusetts, 1987, pp. 159–184.

31. J. Pfeffer and R.I. Sutton, 'Knowing "what" to do is not enough: Turning knowledge into action', *California Management Review*, Fall, 1999, 83–108.

32. S. Denning, *The Springboard: How Storytelling Ignites Action in Knowledge-Era Organizations*, Butterworth-Heinemann, Boston, 2000.

33. R.M. Grant, 'Prospering in dynamically-competitive environments: Organizational capability as knowledge integration', *Organization Science*, Vol. 7, 1996, 375–387; R.M. Grant, 'Towards a knowledge-based theory of the firm', *Strategic Management Journal*, Winter Special Issue, 1996, 109–122; U. Zander and B. Kogut, 'Knowledge and the speed of the transfer an imitation of organizational capabilities: An empirical test', *Organisational Science*, Vol. 6, No. 1, 1995, 76–92.

34. Often referred to as 'stocks' of knowledge as per Machlup. See F. Machlup, *Knowledge, Its Creation, Distribution and Economic Significance, Volume 1: Knowledge and Knowledge Production*, Princeton University Press, Princeton, New Jersey, 1980.

35. M.J. Earl and I.A. Scott, 'What is a chief knowledge officer?', *Sloan Management Review*, Winter, 1999, 29–38.

36. See C. Despres and D. Chauvel, 'How to map knowledge management', in D.A. Marchand, T.H. Davenport and T. Dickson, eds, *Mastering Information Management, Financial Times/ Prentice Hall*, London, 2000, pp. 170–176.

37. J. Seely Brown and P. Duguid, *The Social Life of Information*, Harvard Business School Press, Boston, 2000.

38. T.H. Davenport and L. Prusak, *Working Knowledge: How Organizations Manage What They Know*, Harvard Business School Press, Boston, 1998.

39. E.C. Wenger and W.M. Snyder, 'Communities of practice: The organizational frontier', *Harvard Business Review*, January–February, 2000, 139–145. See also J. Lave and E.C. Wenger, *Situated Learning: Legitimate Peripheral Participation*, Cambridge University Press, Cambridge, 1991 where the concept of 'community of practice' was first introduced.

40. K. Breu and C. Hemingway, 'Collaboration in communities-of-practice: Motivation, resources and benefits', paper presented at *2nd Annual Conference of the European Academy of Management* (EURAM), Stockholm, Sweden, May, 2002.

41. G. Walsham, 'Knowledge management: The benefits and limitations of computer systems', *European Management Journal*, Vol. 19, No. 6, 599–608.

42. L. Suchman, 'Making work visible', *Communications of the ACM*, Vol. 38, No. 9, 1995, 56–64.

43. T.H. Davenport and L. Prusak, *Working Knowledge: How Organizations Manage What They Know*, Harvard Business School Press, Boston, 1998; *The Cranfield and Information Strategy Knowledge Survey: Europe's State of the Art in Knowledge Management*, The Economist Group, London, 1998; R. McDermott, 'Why information technology inspired but cannot deliver knowledge management', *California Management Review*, Summer, 1999, 103–117.

44. M.H. Zack, 'Managing codified knowledge', *Sloan Management Review*, Summer, 1999, 45–57.

45. S.E. Prokesh, 'Unleashing the power of learning: An interview with British Petroleum's John Browne', *Harvard Business Review*, September–October, 1997, 146–168.

46. J. Seely Brown, 'Internet technology in support of the concept of "communities-of-practice": The case of Xerox', *Accounting, Management and Information Technology*, Vol. 8, No. 4, 1998, 227–236.

47. *The Cranfield and Information Strategy Knowledge Survey: Europe's State of the Art in Knowledge Management*, The Economist Group, London, 1998.

48. U. Schutze and R.J. Boland, 'Knowledge management technology and the reproduction of knowledge work processes', *Journal of Strategic Information Systems*, Vol. 9, 2000, 193–212.

11
Managing the Supply of IT Services, Applications and Infrastructure

This chapter considers a number of strategic aspects of organizational IS/IT competencies that have not been covered in preceding chapters. The focus is on competencies in the 'Define the IT Capability', 'Supply' and 'Deliver Solutions' components of the model described in Chapter 8—see Figure 8.10. In particular, to complement the discussion of the management of demand-side IS strategies, this chapter discusses the equivalents on the supply side, but from a managerial not technical perspective. Overall, the supply side or IT strategies can be considered as a number of IT 'services' that the organization uses to enable deployment and exploitation of IS/IT. Those services can be provided by an in-house organization or an external supplier or, most commonly today, by a combination of the two. The nature of those services is first explored and then considered in terms of the different types of service management strategy that can be adopted.

Within the range of IT services, application development, or perhaps application *provision* given the move to buying or renting rather than building systems, is discussed in more detail since it is the 'service' that has the greatest impact on business development through IS/IT. Chapter 9 discussed the management of IS/IT investment and risk, with the assumption that the application development and implementation itself is successful, enabling the organization to realize the expected benefits. This chapter considers some of the issues to be addressed to ensure the development or provisioning process works effectively.

Planning for, justifying and managing investments in IT infrastructure has always been problematic, due to the large 'gap' between infrastructure provision and investment and the visible return for the cost involved. Some important considerations in managing infrastructure development are discussed in this chapter. Finally, an ever-increasing percentage of organizations' IT services are being provided by external parties—outsourcers—in order to both improve IT economics and obtain skills, competencies and resources that cannot easily be provided in-house.

As discussed in Chapter 8, outsourcing has been a major IT strategy topic over the last 10–15 years, yet it has existed since organizational computing began in the 1960s. Many companies started using IT via bureau services provided by computer manufacturers, often supplemented by network and time-sharing services. Using package software is a form of outsourcing, not only of the development of that software but also of the design of the process models for the business activities covered. Subcontracting of both commodity programming and specialist design and implementation skills has been a common practice since the 1970s and many organizations have also employed IT consultants in a range of roles. 'Facilities Management' companies took over the running of many organizations' data centres in the 1980s. Outsourcing is therefore not new, but now almost any aspect of IT supply can be outsourced, including the provision of services traditionally delivered by applications, and the marketplace for such services is both considerable and influential. Outsource service providers like EDS and Internet Service Providers (ISPs) like AOL are now the largest buyers of IT equipment from the manufacturers. Strategic aspects of outsourcing, both decision making and management are considered toward the end of this chapter.

The scope implied by the chapter title is enormous, and there is no intention to provide full and comprehensive coverage of all possible areas. Instead, important strategic management aspects are covered in overview and the reader is referred to other texts that cover the subjects in much greater depth.

IT SERVICE STRATEGIES

In the late 1980s, it was observed that the role of the IS function in many organizations had changed from a production mode to mainly a service mode of operation.[1] Production (or construction) implied designing and developing application software and delivering operational systems—combinations of hardware and software to the business users. Adopting a service orientation, while including the delivery and support for applications, implies a wider range of approaches to enabling the business users to obtain and utilize information, systems and technology to meet their needs, as and when requirements arise. In the 1980s, organizations established 'Information Centres' that supported 'end-user computing' on PCs and provided access to centrally held information and also external sources. It is estimated that 70–80% of IT costs in most organizations are now spent on services, rather than the development or purchase of application software or IT hardware.

That the IS function was providing a range of services has been recognized in Service Level Agreements (SLAs) for aspects of IT such as network uptime, response times and help-desk support for many years. However, two issues have driven the need to be more explicit about service management. First, many businesses now deliver some aspects of their product or service to customers via IS/IT, or via service centres that are totally dependent on IS/IT, implying that the quality and performance of IT services are visible not only internally but externally and affect the business performance and customer relationships directly. Second, as more and more aspects of service have been outsourced, contracts with suppliers defining service availability, performance and cost have become integral to IS management. If outsourcing decisions are to be based on objective, comparative data, then applying the same rationale for measuring service performance delivered by in-house resources is essential. While there is considerable literature on establishing service-level agreements and measuring service performance, there is very little concerning developing 'IT service strategies'—strategies that are linked closely to delivering and enhancing overall business performance. This is due in part to the difficulty in understanding and measuring the organizational benefits delivered from services. It is easier to measure service deficiencies and costs.

However, there is a considerable body of literature, based on studies of service businesses, that can be used to understand and classify types of IT service, help select appropriate service strategies and address issues in the development and delivery of such services. Using that literature on customer services, a more strategic and business-driven approach to IT service management can be defined. An overview of how that can be done is described below. Once the nature and business contribution of IT services can be understood more clearly, decisions on sourcing can be made more objectively. The need to integrate the development of IT service strategies with application management strategies to produce a distinctive 'IS capability' for the business is considered further in the last chapter.

TYPES OF IT SERVICE

The activities to be managed with regard to IT service provision in an organization were introduced in Chapter 8 (see Table 8.4). These can be classified in a number of ways according to the nature of the service provided (as in Table 8.4) and how customers or clients utilize the service. Most classifications of IT services take a supply-side view, but, by using models from operations management and customer service, a user or demand-side view can be developed. First, however, some of the characteristics and nature of services in general and IT services in particular need to be considered:

- The service user is, to some extent at least, involved in the delivery process and influences the performance of the service. Different users have different expectations of the service and varying knowledge of how to use it. However, based on their general experience, service users now expect a high quality of service (availability, responsiveness, first-time problem resolution, etc), as they perceive it, whenever they avail of any service, whether it be internal or external. Measuring service performance is primarily about measuring user perceptions of the service delivered against their expectations.

- Services are, to a large extent, produced and consumed simultaneously based on a user request to be served. This implies that it is difficult to build an inventory of work and schedule activity and resources due to the uncertainty of demand. Equally, idle service capacity cannot be reused unless resources are flexible and can be deployed across a range of services or the work profile can be balanced across demand-driven and 'off-line' or developmental activities.

- However 'technical' the service, people and the role they play are critical to the perceptions of the service received—the 'service experience'. Proficiency and efficiency in satisfying the need are essential, but service quality will equally be judged on the nature of the personal interaction between the user and provider, at the point of delivery.

- The more the user understands what is involved in the service delivery process, its complexity or otherwise, the more their expectations of performance will match what can actually be achieved. Equally, if users can see the 'queue' for the service they require, the more 'reasonable' they become in their expectations. Often, the queue for IT services is not visible to the users, unlike in a physical environment such as a fast-food outlet or a sophisticated call centre, which informs callers of their queue position.

- There is often a difference between the user of the IT service and who pays for it, implying different perceptions of service value. This is similar to business-class or first-class travel, where the traveller may enjoy the convenience and quality of treatment, but the company may not see the very significantly higher cost as justified. The IS budget holder may not be a significant user of IT services, and those who do use the service may be unaware of the costs of its provision.

As discussed in Chapter 8, one way of classifying IT services is based on their relationship to the supply and delivery of IT components such as hardware and application software to the business. In essence, this approach describes the service in terms of the IT-based activities involved, rather than the nature of value derived by the business or the service process required to meet users' needs. It is the latter view that creates an understanding of the range of service attributes needed, enabling the service to be designed and then operated to meet business requirements.

Classifying services according to the technical similarities of activities (e.g. technology delivery and maintenance services, application development services, strategy and planning services) is helpful from an IT resourcing and sourcing perspective. However, it tends to reinforce any user perceptions that, to obtain an effective service, the user has to know how and where to find the solution as well as how to define the problem! It is a view that considers the efficiency and organization of the IS function first and the effectiveness of service provision and the needs of the user second. Even within the broad categories described in Table 8.4, different components will need quite different service delivery processes to meet the users' needs (e.g. capacity planning versus business analysis).

A Service Process-based Classification

From the literature on service management, a matrix based on two key dimensions of the customer view of services can be developed (see Figure 11.1) that is relevant to the majority of IT services. The dimensions are:

- the nature and extent of user–provider contact involved; and
- the degree to which the service is customized to each user or user interaction.

This enables the development of four broad categories of service processes: 'Service Factory', 'Job Shop', 'Mass Service' and 'Professional Service'.[2] Both the *perceived* and *actual* value delivered by the service is different in each of the four quadrants, highlighting that different management issues must be addressed in each category. Service processes with

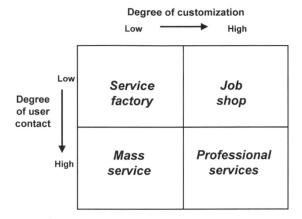

Figure 11.1   *Generic service models*

a high degree of customer contact are more difficult to control and standardize than those with a low degree of customer contact. In a high-contact system, the customer availability and priorities affect the timing of demand, the efficiency of resources used in delivering the service and the quality, or perceived quality, of service since the customer is involved in the process.

Service Factory: relatively low user contact and a low degree of customization. Obvious examples are many of the 'back-office' services such as security, capacity and network maintenance, software release/upgrades and installation of basic desktop facilities. Changes to applications to deal with statutory or compliance requirements (e.g. the Euro) would also be included in this category. Performance measurement can be relatively objective, based on supply-side delivery to agreed service levels, rather than the perceptions of particular service recipients. Key management issues in providing the service are: defining service-level agreements, scheduling service delivery and forecasting demand to avoid overload and promote 'off-peak' usage. Clearly, these types of service are the most amenable to outsourcing.

Job Shop: low user contact, but high customization, where much of the work is again done in the back office, but in response to particular, and possibly one-off, user needs. Software development, technical product evaluation and vendor assessment would be typical of this segment. While the service requests will vary in nature, some consistency in the approach or methodology is needed in order to estimate the time and resources needed and evaluate performance and quality of service across the range of customized tasks performed. User perceptions of their satisfaction with the outcome of each request will be in relation to the 'contract' agreed for the particular request. Accurate estimating of the work involved and ensuring schedules, as well as output quality, are met are essential to achieving customer service expectations. Many of these aspects of services can also be outsourced, but only after the task and service requirements are clearly defined for the eventual supplier. Management issues include: task prioritization and resource scheduling, flexible resourcing (internal and external), quality and consistency of 'back-office' service processes and methods, and defining meaningful performance measures.

Mass Service: considerable user contact and interaction, but low customization. Typically, help desks and essential IS/IT skills training would be in this quadrant, given the 'one-size fits all' rationale to deliver consistent quality of service economically, either from internal or external resources. The attributes of the service staff are critical to the user perception of the performance, hence the development of appropriate interpersonal and communication skills will be as important as their 'technical' knowledge. Given the high degree of user interaction, it has to be clear to both recipient and provider how much of the service is prescriptive and how much discretion is allowed to customize (to a degree) the delivery to the needs and circumstances of the recipient. In many organizations, 'expert users' are established, and it is important that the individual providing the service understands whether they are dealing with the expert or a relative 'novice'. While some flexibility is essential to accommodate the varying levels of user knowledge, a lack of clear service boundaries can produce a drift toward the professional services box. Equally, a lack of interpersonal skills and an overly-prescriptive approach will make the service 'feel' more like the service factory described above.

Measurement of service performance has to be a balanced view between actual performance against the 'contract' plus the recipients' perceptions of the service received. While, once more, these can be outsourced, softer, cultural issues, rather than just economic and technical, need to be considered in choosing the service supplier. The management issues include those for the service factory, but, in addition, involve establishing service parameters and boundaries (degrees of discretion versus prescription), developing staff with the necessary combinations of personal and technical competencies and matching resource levels to the cycles in demand.

Professional Services: while these are highly customized and involve considerable user contact, they are also typified by relatively few, but complex, 'transactions' with any particular user. Considerable judgement and discretion is implied in the provider, to understand and respond to the user requirement and identify the best way to satisfy the needs, or not, if the requirement does not justify this type of service. To a large extent, how the 'transaction' evolves will rely on either the service user being able to articulate the needs or facilitation to enable the articulation. Equally, the availability of user resources and the knowledge they have about how to use the service effectively will have a significant effect on the service provision. Strategy development, consultancy, business analysis and systems, and process design are services that are normally in this category. Measurement of service performance is essentially subjective, based on how well the perceived need was met, the effectiveness of the process and the nature of the interaction with the service provider. It is not really feasible to set Service Level Agreements in this area, but each 'transaction' will need agreement on schedules, deliverables, costs, etc. if perceptions of performance are to be satisfactorily reconciled with expectations.

The management issues in this quadrant include those of the job shop, but, in addition, the knowledge, personal skills and resourcefulness of the individual staff involved will be crucial to satisfying the users. Obviously, discretion, rather than prescription, will generally be required, implying staff with the understanding and experience of accurately eliciting and then translating requirements through planning to delivery, probably using a range of resources, are essential.

The management issues are summarized in Figure 11.2. Although it is tempting to allocate each of the IT service activities to a 'box', the organization has choices about the way it wishes the services to be

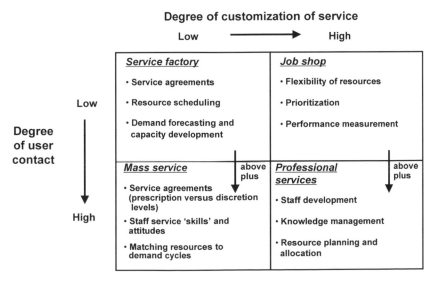

Figure 11.2 *Service models: some key management issues*

operationalized. Many of the service archetypes can be provided to different people through different processes. Training, for example, can be bespoke and tailored to an audience, and thus considered a professional service, or provided as a standard training course, in essence a mass service. If the course is delivered over the Web, it is more correctly positioned as a service factory. In a large pharmaceutical company, for economic reasons, it was decided to centralize application support within the large technical help desk. 'Traffic' volumes were low, very few application users phoned or emailed the help desk, preferring still to consult a local IT person on site, who then could contact the help desk if necessary. The reason was that the real value to the users were the 'workarounds' that the local IT person, with in-depth application knowledge, could suggest while the problem was being fixed. It is important to understand how users derive value from the service before deciding how to provide it.

Examples of types of service that would frequently sit in each quadrant are given in Figure 11.3. Application development or provisioning, which is discussed in the next section, might use a number of the services, located in different quadrants, during the project.

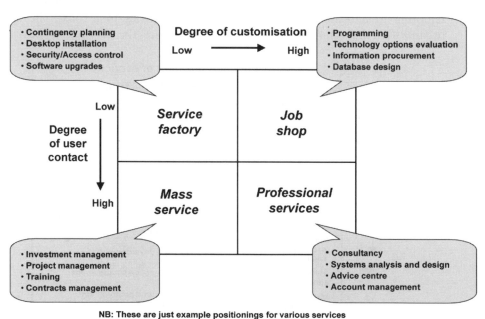

NB: These are just example positionings for various services

Figure 11.3   *Service models and IT services—examples*

IS/IT Service Quality

Considerable research has been done to develop approaches to defining service quality and measuring both the technical and 'emotional' (i.e. how the user experiences the service) quality.[3] That literature is too extensive to describe in detail here, but an overall framework for structuring and developing an IT service is shown in Figure 11.4. It also forms the basis for measuring the service components in terms of performance to specification and perceived performance by the users. It does rely on the service consumers being able to define the value they expect to obtain from the service—a difficult concept. Often, this has to be in terms of the negative consequences of service unavailability or underperformance, to justify the cost against failure of the business to operate 'normally'. Establishing more effective and relevant ways of describing and then measuring the value derived by both individual users and the organization in total is a major challenge for future IS strategy development, as discussed in the final chapter.

Many IS functions carry out customer service satisfaction surveys, but, if not well constructed, the results can be misleading. Before asking a user to evaluate a service, or its more detailed attributes such as availability or responsiveness, the importance or otherwise of the service or service

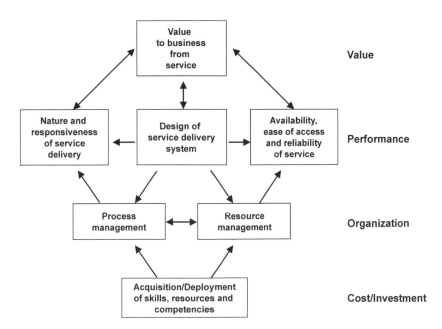

Figure 11.4 An overall service framework

attribute to the user needs to be understood. 'Importance' is a surrogate for service value in terms of how dependent the user is in carrying out his or her role and tasks on the quality of service received. Evaluating services, in achieving the required performance for those who depend on it, is more important than satisfying those for whom it is of no great consequence. Therefore, any satisfaction survey must first determine the context within which the user is judging performance.[4]

However services are assessed or measured, users will continually expect improvement, for it to be 'perfect' on every occasion. Of course, there will always be ways, at a cost, of improving any aspect of the service. However, it may not be worthwhile to expend more resources to deliver the ultimate expectations, and an assessment of whether 'gaps' in service delivery are worth overcoming or whether actions to change user expectations are more valid. Work by a number of researchers[5] studying the nature of gaps that can occur in IT service delivery, based on general service management, is very helpful in understanding why the gaps exist and to select the best options for closing them. Figure 11.5 shows the basic model for assessment.

The causes of the gaps (1–5) are as follows:

1. Not understanding what users expect or value due to:
    —a lack of user needs analysis;
    —ineffective communication by either or both parties;
    —excessive bureaucracy in the IS function.
2. Setting the wrong IT Service Standards due to:
    —lack of commitment to IT services by IS management;
    —perceptions of infeasibility in meeting user demands;
    —inadequate task definition and standardization or inadequate resourcing to standards set;
    —absence of objectives for the service to achieve and/or inappropriate performance measurements.
3. Underperformance of the service due to:
    —role ambiguity, including the user's role in service delivery;
    —lack of resource availability;
    —lack of actual or perceived controls;
    —lack of teamwork and inappropriate resource use, or inappropriate use of the service.
4. Poor communication of what the service is and can deliver due to:
    —a propensity to overpromise and/or overreact to 'complaints';
    —inconsistent communication across the user communities;
    —lack of visibility of the service process.
5. Expectation versus perception gap due to:
    —not understanding user requirements and reasons for them;

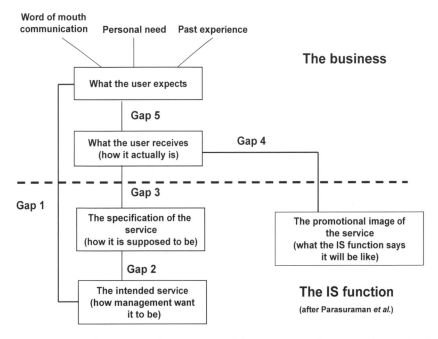

Figure 11.5   *The gaps in the IS service delivery (*source: *based on the work of Parasuraman, Berry and Zeithaml)*

—users not understanding the service process and the implications of
   their demands;
—user expectations actually being impossible to satisfy!

Regular and balanced assessment of service performance is required to
detect emerging problems and issues, the causes and consequences, in
order to adjust the appropriate components of the service framework.
Failure to do so will directly or indirectly impact business performance,
resulting in a poor perception of the role and value of IS/IT in the organization, and difficulties for the IS function to obtain resources and
investment to deliver the IT strategy. While most assessment of performance is carried out to enable pertinent improvements to be made, the
assessment may well reveal areas of apparent overperformance! If the
perceived performance is judged by users to be high but, in reality,
compared with similar organizations, actual performance is poor, the
business is suffering a degree of 'delusion' if it believes it is using IS/IT
successfully!

In the context of outsourcing decision making for IT services, Lacity and Hirschheim[6] provide a simple yet effective matrix for summarizing perceptions of the inevitable trade-off between the service delivered and the cost to the organization of the service provision (see Figure 11.6). Senior management will pay attention to the costs of IT, but are probably minimal users of services, whereas users themselves are very aware of the quality of services, but probably unaware of costs. Ideally, to satisfy both, providing a premium service at minimal cost is the objective, but rarely achievable in every aspect of service.

Choices have to have been made on objectives for each of the other segments—whether the strategy should be to maintain the services at existing levels and find more cost-effective means of meeting them or whether to improve the services by justifiable investment. This must be made explicit to both business users and senior management or once more expectations will not be aligned. If users perceive a service as poor and management deem it expensive—the Black Hole—it may be too late for IS management to retrieve the situation and alternative service suppliers may be considered without reference to the IS management! Outsourcing strategies and the associated issues are considered later in this chapter.

APPLICATION DEVELOPMENT AND PROVISIONING STRATEGIES

As stated earlier, application development might be better labelled application 'provision', in the sense that many applications are now bought in rather than custom-built in-house. The proportion of application software custom-built versus purchased packages varies across industries. In financial services, 80% of all applications were custom-developed even in 2001, whereas the figure for manufacturing industries is much lower.[7]

The emergence of Application Service Providers (ASPs), providing rented software via the Internet, is the latest development in this area; the role and potential of ASPs is considered later in the chapter, under outsourcing. Although less application software is produced in-house, custom-built software is often developed by third parties, and most large software packages require extensive configuration and even some customization before they are implemented. The trend for more and more of an organization's applications to be designed and developed by major software houses or 'business solutions' companies is likely to continue. It is not the purpose of this section to consider all aspects of application development and implementation. There are many good texts covering systems design and development methods and their applicability,

	Minimal cost	Premium cost
Premium service	**Superstar** *Meets senior management and users' ideal expectations*	**Differentiator** *Meets user expectations but needs to find more cost-effective ways of sustaining performance*
Minimal service	**Commodity/ Low-cost producer** *Meets senior management expectations but users may go elsewhere ...*	**Black hole** *Failure to meet either group's expectations!*

Figure 11.6 *IT cost/service trade-off (source: M.C. Lacity and R. Hirschheim, Beyond the Information Systems Outsourcing Bandwagon: The Insourcing Response, John Wiley & Sons, Chichester, UK, 1995)*

software engineering, database design and project management.[8] The intention here is to consider a number of strategic issues that have to be addressed in the context of enabling the desired application portfolio to be realized successfully, leading to the delivery of the desired benefits.

The challenges for application development or provisioning have become more demanding as IS/IT has become integral to business performance. At the same time, the business environment has been changing more quickly and dramatically, producing increased uncertainty and the need for flexibility and adaptability of processes and systems. The main issues for application development can be summarized as:

- providing new applications more quickly in response to changing business demands;
- more cost-effective production or acquisition of more types of application and reduce ongoing maintenance costs;
- increasing the quality and reliability of the software as it becomes integral to the business processes;
- developing more customer-focused applications that can be used easily by untrained people;
- devising more flexible or adaptable applications than can be enhanced or modified quickly at low incremental cost;
- providing efficient, seamless integration of business activities across different applications from the desktop;

- ensuring maximum value can be gained from the information assets of the organization.

In other words—faster, cheaper, better, more flexible and easier to use! Few of these are new demands, except perhaps customer-centric designed systems, but the history of IS/IT has been one of increasing expectations of what can be done 'relatively easily', promoted largely by the IT industry, counterbalanced by the inherent difficulties of designing and implementing complex computer-based systems in complex and evolving businesses.

ALIGNING THE DEVELOPMENT APPROACH TO THE APPLICATIONS PORTFOLIO

The use of the applications portfolio as a guide to the overall approach to key issues in applications management was discussed to some degree in Chapter 7. Within the principles described there, this section considers in more detail the approaches to development or providing the applications, especially the differences across the portfolio.

Strategic Applications

For strategic systems, speed of development and flexibility of design are essential, and cost is less important especially when the goal is gaining and sustaining competitive advantage. The 'window of opportunity' may be short-lived or uncertain. They are best achieved through a close partnership between business users (preferably senior managers who understand the emerging business needs) and very experienced IS/IT business analysts, to ensure that the business needs are analysed and met in the most effective way. This is especially important when the system has external linkages to customers or suppliers and is delivering benefits to both parties. There is often a need for incremental development, since new options and needs will be discovered as implementation proceeds. Typically, the system is not automating an existing business process, but changing or creating one.

Few organizations have developed successful strategic systems without first having established coherent business application and information architectures for key operational systems. Strategic systems frequently use information from a number of different existing systems. The information in the strategic application will often need to be vertically integrated with these underlying systems and may also import information from outside sources. An example of this comes from some financial institutions, which are now able to offer integrated current, savings and loans (like mortgages) netting off the interest accrued in each and minimizing the amount held in the current account. This required taking data from the underlying different product systems, which are account-orientated, linking all the accounts together by individual customer, then managing the customers' accounts accordingly. Where the underlying product systems have evolved in a piecemeal fashion with relatively little thought toward the total view of the relationship with the customer, this has proved difficult, but new 'online' banks have been able to design the systems from a customer viewpoint.

To create effective new applications, easy access to relevant information is very important and often best served by advanced database technology—relational or object-oriented—associated with a sophisticated data dictionary. Another approach may be to apply a component-based development to produce a set of key objects, stored as reusable modules in a repository. Some objects may be created by 'shrink-wrapping' software modules taken from key operational systems. Both relational and object databases containing the principal elements of the corporate model give the necessary flexibility in terms of viewing, manipulating and accessing information.

Strategic systems are likely to be complex or will become complex as functions are added incrementally. They are also required to be developed quickly, and the application may have to be 'generated' many times as it is changed. A Dynamic Systems Development Methodology (DSDM) incorporating prototyping is most effective here in clarifying needs and options, and building components and applications. Speed, flexibility and complexity all lead to problems of controlling the development, and a DSDM combines time boxing and deliverables/version management to avoid subsequent expensive rework or maintenance. Continuity in terms of the development team, both business and IT members, will be critical to managing the evolving knowledge in an environment that will not encourage accurate documentation, adherence to standards or the best in quality-control processes. Those standards should not be ignored, but business expediency will have to overrule technical idealism in many cases, especially if adherence could extend the development time and perhaps miss the business opportunities.

This need would also argue for the use of integrated development environments employing Rapid Application Development (RAD) tools. The initial analysis and design can be performed using automated tools that would then produce code, which, though not particularly efficient, will at least be very quickly developed and enable changes to be identified and implemented rapidly.

The speed of development of the application is on balance more important than its cost of operation, but high performance, especially if the system is used by customers, could be a critical success factor. Eventually, these applications will probably become key operational, when they may need to be reimplemented in order to make them more efficient and less costly in their operation. Interconnectability, often via middleware rather than full integration, may be the initial goal, in order to assess the value of the strategic system while protecting the installed base of key operational systems. Many front-end consumer Web applications were initially interfaced with core processing systems to 'test the market', but the most successful were those that were quickly integrated with those core processes to deliver end-to-end responsiveness to the customer. The Internet flight-booking systems of easyJet, Ryanair and Southwest Airlines, compared with more traditional airlines, are good examples.

As these systems are taking the enterprise into new areas, there will often be a need for new business processes, competencies or operational skills as well as technical knowledge. For example, in the use of data warehouses and data mining, knowledge of advanced statistical analysis techniques would be required. A customer relationship management system may require customer service staff to develop selling skills. User management must ensure that these essential business skills are developed or the application will fail to be exploited to advantage.

It is unlikely that available software packages will provide all the requirements for this type of application. Significant advantage cannot accrue from generally available software, unless the business adds value to the package (e.g. by considerable enhancement, finding a new use of the package or changing business practices in an innovative way). In these cases, the package becomes a unique application and, as such, it must be supported as if it were tailor-made. Alternatively, a short-lived advantage could accrue from being the first user of a new package—but success could be very quickly and easily copied. It is also high risk to be the first user of an externally supplied package that would normally be tried out in the high potential segment. Fundamentally, sustained advantage comes from the uniqueness of the application, which others cannot easily replicate or improve upon.

Key Operational Applications

These are generally the 'workhorse' systems, carrying out the main operational processes of the business (e.g. customer order entry and fulfilment should be well designed both in business process and technical terms). Key operational systems need to be efficient and robust, to deliver cost-effective and problem-free use over an extended period. Since they often have to be integrated with other primary business process systems, they benefit from adhering to information management standards and from complying with the evolving long-term systems and information architecture. They can often be met by application packages or third-party-developed software, but further development may be needed to provide effective integration, resource sharing and information management. By selecting a comprehensive package (e.g. ERP), the additional work can be avoided, but some user needs may have to be compromised. When developed in-house, they are usually produced using traditional project management (e.g. PRINCE) and formal structured methods (e.g. SSADM), automated with software and information engineering tools. In most cases, key operational 'developments' are replacements for old systems and design and construction, or configuration in the case of a package, must be comprehensive and precise if business operations are not to be adversely affected on implementation. There is always a trade-off to be made between the system functionality provided and the extent of the business change that can be made to reduce process complexity, especially with large software packages. Therefore, it is important to understand which core process is most critical to success.

Often, bringing in a package is the best way of achieving integration of application requirements among the various departments or functions, who would otherwise attempt to satisfy their own needs without regard to the effects on others. 'Making the package work' can often override localized objectives, although, if badly managed, it could become a target for every department to engineer its failure! Unlike support-type packages, however, a key operational package will probably need considerable IS professional support to ensure that integration and effective operation are achieved.

Key operational applications will tend to be functionally complex, have integrated interfaces and dependencies and should satisfy requirements with minimum compromise of the user's main needs. Even where a package is selected, it may have to be customized, despite the risks involved—and this will require a thorough technical understanding of how the package works as well as what it does. Whether a system is developed or a package modified, an accurate specification of *what it has to do* and *how it has to do it* will have to be established. A structured logical model of the system must be developed to enable the application to be engineered accurately. That model, documented or simulated via software engineering tools, and supporting data dictionaries, etc. must be maintained and updated whenever the system changes. Strict change-control procedures must be in place to prevent errors being introduced, when amendments and upgrades are implemented. These errors may not be easy to predict since they may only manifest themselves in downstream systems.

Because this type of system will require ongoing modification in order to avoid falling behind the business requirements, there should be a high level of technical support skills available for both emergency action and changes. If a package is used, it can present difficulties to the organization when new releases of the underlying application package need to be implemented (i.e. changes may have to be made even if the business does not require them). Worse still, if the package has been heavily customized, valuable new functionality that becomes available may not be able to be adopted. For many of these systems, a dedicated support team is required after implementation, consisting of both users and IS professionals. It is important to develop skills related to the specific system, not just employ generalists to correct and amend the system when available. Releases of new versions of the system software must be carefully tested, updated user training carried out and reviewed in terms of the effective use of the new functionality.

Support Applications

If new support applications are required or existing ones are to be replaced, the most appropriate solution is to buy in sound standard proprietary packages that meet the business requirements as closely as possible. The package should not be customized: business processes and procedures should be amended to fit the package. Very rarely can an organization justify the allocation of valuable skills and resources to developing support systems for themselves or the future costs of modifying every new package release to satisfy their business idiosyncrasies.

The resources required to implement a package for both key operational or support environments are frequently underestimated. Requirements still need to be carefully analysed and documented, and the evaluation process undertaken must be linked to the justification, prioritization and benefit management processes. Even if no tailoring of the package is necessary, there are often interfaces to be built to existing systems and databases, and there may be considerable work needed to configure package parameters, undertake user training programs, develop adequate testing material, convert existing data and implement the system. An allowance of resources may also be needed for the work involved in vendor management relating to supply and service activities.

Even if the 'databases' in the packages are not ideally suited to the organization's information architecture, integration of information is often less critical in support applications than the ability to transfer information. Meeting the task requirement in the overall most efficient way is essential to success, therefore packages should not be ruled out just because they cannot be integrated. User needs are paramount in the final choice, but the IS function's veto of certain options must be allowed if they cannot provide support for the required technical environment, otherwise overhead cost build-up will offset the direct efficiency benefits. Equally, it is best to adopt a low risk or conservative approach, only selecting packages with a well-established base of customers, rather than be the first user of a new package, however good its apparent features. A package selection checklist can easily be drawn up to help users to define requirements and decide on options.

Support systems, because they are not critical to success, are prime candidates for outsourcing to a third party, especially if the system is using up resources that are needed on more important applications and, in addition, the organization needs to develop different skills.

High Potential 'Applications'

As discussed in Chapter 7, the term 'applications' is perhaps inappropriate in the high potential segment, since it is the research and development (R&D) activity enabling new technology to be tried out to ascertain its potential applications for the organization, or to explore the potential of technology in relation to an innovative business idea. The need is for independent, rapid, low-cost development of prototypes and even pilot implementations that, if they fail, can be abandoned without wasting significant resources. Since risk is high and success is far from certain, effective cost control is essential.

As has been said before, these R&D-type activities should be separated from mainstream systems, to enable them to be evaluated on their merits. The main objective is to evaluate the business potential of applying any technology, but in some cases the potential may not only be where the initial use of a new technology is tried. This may mean splitting the prototyping objectives into those that are application-specific and those that are for more general learning. Equally, the potential of the technology should not be explored in abstract without some application in mind. This is a recipe for pouring money down the drain. Clear terms of reference or objectives should be established at the start, but they may need to be consciously (and overtly) modified as knowledge is acquired.

The most obvious danger is that users and even senior management become so enthusiastic about a successful prototype that it becomes a fully operational system, even though it is made of 'string and glue' and has not been designed for use on a large scale. Many good ideas, especially for Internet applications, have proved less than successful when implemented, since the required performance or reliability could not be achieved in operation. An example is boo.com's clothing website, which was far too slow in loading complex graphics. This frustrated potential customers and probably contributed to the company's demise.

Often, the organization will have to acquire or develop new technological skills to develop the applications and support the process of evaluation. Some skills may have to be acquired through the vendor or outside experts, but it is important that effective knowledge transfer occurs during the evaluation phase, to avoid future dependence on technical skills only available outside.

While high-potential applications should be evaluated in association with a particular technology, it may be that more than one option exists for evaluation. It can be advisable to carry out parallel, competing R&D projects focused on one business application, especially if the potential benefits appear very high, if speed is of the essence and/or competitors are carrying out similar evaluations. However, in this case the eventual decision criteria must be clearly spelled out or the process will only leave more uncertainty at the end than there was at the start!

Figure 11.7 summarizes some of the key issues in managing application developments in each of the segments of the portfolio.

THE SPECIAL CASE OF 'ENTERPRISE SYSTEMS'

The 1990s saw the extensive implementation of Enterprise (or Enterprise-wide) Systems (ES) across many industries. The best known are probably the Enterprise Resource Planning (ERP) packages provided by a range of vendors, initially for the manufacturing sector. Since then, versions of ERP have been developed for other industries such as logistics, utilities, health care, retail and even education. ES systems, either package based or custom built, have been developed across most industrial and commercial sectors, ranging from Customer Relationship Management (CRM), Call Centre Management, Supply Chain Management (SCM), Policy Administration (in insurance) to Electronic Patient Records in health care. Their chief characteristic is that they affect a large number of organizational processes and functions, standardizing and integrating information and activities. Few are truly enterprise-wide in the sense that they deal with all the business information needs, but all have a significant influence on the overall IS strategy of the organization. ES do not normally fit into any one of the four portfolio segments, given the activities covered and the range of potential benefits available. Therefore, they often involve a combination of all the portfolio issues, the mixture being dependent on both the intent of the investment and the current situation across the activities.

STRATEGIC	HIGH POTENTIAL
• Application generators • Dynamic Systems Development Methodologies (DSDM) • Joint Application Development teams (JAD) - share knowledge • Iterative development via prototypes/pilots • Create new processes and databases • Effective links to key operational systems - but protect core systems • Packages unlikely to meet needs unless modified to unique version • Design for adaptability to meet changing needs	• Prototyping and business pilots of applications to test performance, scaling, acceptance • Evaluation of benefits and how to achieve them • Rapid, low-cost, iterative development • Business champion • Fixed time/cost allowance • New skills/skills transfer from external expertise • Independent - low integration
• Structured Systems Development Methodologies (SSDM) • Software engineering • Industry-specific packages - integrate/interface across packages but minimal customization • Corporate data management controls • Combined systems and business knowledge in development team • Process re-engineering • Strict specification and change control processes • Design for performance	• Standard functional packages - compromise business needs to package capabilities. No customization • Low-risk, proven solutions • Outsource operation and maintenance - if cost-effective • Interface, not integrate • Use package databases and data standards • Design procedures and processes to use the software efficiently • Buy, not build
KEY OPERATIONAL	SUPPORT

Figure 11.7 Development approaches and characteristics

While part of the reason for the growth in their use has been the development of comprehensive packages by the software suppliers, five other issues have accelerated their adoption:

- replacement of existing systems to satisfy the Y2K requirements, more cost-effectively than amending all the existing applications;
- replacement of non-integrated legacy systems by integrated applications and data bases to reduce long-term costs and provide higher-quality systems that incorporate industry 'best practice';
- increasing legislation and regulation in many industries has made

'compliance' a major issue, and buying comprehensive 'compliant' software can help avoid the serious consequences of failure to satisfy the regulators;

• provision of application architectures and business processes, to enable quick and effective moves into electronic commerce and internal adoption of e-business practices;

• in multinational or global organizations, the need to expand the business by rapid replication of existing business models, to use resources and knowledge flexibly across products, services and markets as well as to deal consistently and effectively with large global customers.

Overall, whatever the particular type of ES, the main differences from more traditional IS developments are the ambitious intentions, the application complexity and cross-functional scope, the range of different stakeholders involved, and extent of business and organization changes needed to accommodate the new business models inherent in the ES. Oh! and the possibility of bringing the business to a grinding halt if it fails!

In the late 1990s many papers and books were written to provide understanding of these issues, their interrelationships and how to address them.[9] Most writings to date have been based on the now extensive experience available from ERP implementations, but the lessons are equally valid for other ES developments. The main ones are summarized here.

While ES implementations are, based on their scope and potential impact, major organizational change initiatives, many default to become 'software projects'. In a survey of the success criteria[10] for ERP projects, 89% were judged successful—the software worked and the project was delivered close to time and cost forecasts. But only 25% had achieved the intended business benefits. The example in Table 11.1 perhaps summarizes the main reasons for this. The company concerned implemented an ERP package twice! The first time was unsuccessful, but they realised why and had the courage to try again and this time succeeded.

This company's experience is not unusual—many organizations are reimplementing such systems to gain the benefits that were not achieved the first time. A major pharmaceutical company implemented an ERP system worldwide in the 1990s across all its manufacturing units, but allowed considerable degrees of freedom to each unit in how it 'customized' and utilized the package. As a result, the major supply-chain benefits that were expected did not accrue. The reimplementation is more standardized and requires the units to change their practices to

Table 11.1 *Implementing 'Enterprise Resource Planning' systems—one company's experience* (source: Achieving the Benefits from Software Package Enabled Business Improvement Programmes, *Best Practice Guidelines*, IMPACT, London, 1998)

First attempt—failure	Second attempt—success
IS led, with insufficient knowledge of the business function concerned	Business Function led, by a newly recruited manager, experienced in the function, supported by IS
Belief that the requirements were simple and already known—just use the package to automate the current processes	Site visits and reviews of other companies procedures to establish best practice and system requirements
Belief that this was a low-risk and straightforward implementation	Knowledge that this would require some major changes
Lack of business buy-in led to both the new and old (mainly manual) system remaining in place, and little move by the business to adopt the new system	New procedures completely replaced the previous system and all staff were required to use them; facilities for the old system withdrawn
Little business change	Organizational and business process changes
Bespoke amendment of package. Longer and more complex system build, and difficulty applying upgrades	Minimal changes to the package, and innovative use of built-in facilities. Shorter delivery timescale and easy future upgrade paths
Costs, no benefits	Benefits have exceeded expectations

improve the performance and agility of the supply chains for all the main products.

One general theme from research[11] into ES implementations that has emerged reflects this recurring two-phase approach. Phase I involves creating a coherent link between the future business vision and how the ES either creates that vision or enables it to happen. Unfortunately, that vision often ignores or minimizes the current problems and constraints that limit the organization's ability to implement the ES successfully. A more appropriate approach to the first phase is to establish an overall vision for how the business will operate once the full benefits of the ES can be realized, but set an initial intent that delivers a 'new baseline' where the problems and constraints have been removed. Phase I implementation should deliver this new baseline, often via a basic, even limited, standard (or 'vanilla') implementation of the software with associated

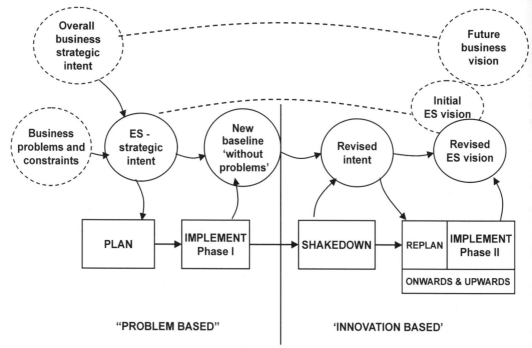

Figure 11.8 *Enterprise systems—the two-stage view of implementation*

essential business practice changes. Studies[12] show that business performance often deteriorates immediately after implementation, and contingencies to allow for this are needed—increased inventories, more
resources and informing trading partners of expectations. A 'shakedown'
phase normally follows in which an understanding of:

(a) how to optimize performance through further changes to business
practices and software reconfiguration; and
(b) how further benefits can now be achieved by using more capabilities
of the software and by more radical or extensive business and organizational changes.

A new vision (hopefully not much reduced from the original!) is then
needed to develop new objectives and plans to achieve innovations in
business processes and practices based on the ES capability now available
to the business. A model, based on the results of a number of studies but
using much of the terminology of Markus *et al.*,[13] is shown in Figure 11.8.
The two stages can be summarized as 'problem based' to achieve a new
starting point from which 'innovation-based' development can be

launched. At the start of such a large, ambitious project, it is difficult to get sufficient consensus on what the future will look like and how to get there, when a wide variety of current issues and problems are the focus of day-to-day management attention across the organization. Removing those problems releases the organizational ability to envisage and agree how new ways of conducting business can be created.

As was said earlier, the implementation of an ES is a business transformation program, not an IS/IT project. Very few fail because of the inadequacies of the technology. When they do fail, the reasons are organizational and, in many cases, due to different perceptions of the intent and benefits and extent of changes required between senior executives and operational line management and among the line managers in different functions or units. Evidence from one study[14] is that successful implementations have been carefully, even slowly, planned to gain the understanding and commitment of the majority, if not all, the stakeholders to the benefits and establish how best to implement the changes in each area, followed by rapid implementation. Often, two-thirds of the project duration was effectively 'planning' and one-third was implementation. Many failures resulted from a short planning phase, during which few of the differences in perceptions were addressed or reconciled, followed by an interminable implementation phase!

As was also said earlier, there has been considerable literature published in the last 5 years on this topic; Table 11.2 contains a summary of some of the particular key issues that need to be addressed in relation to the 'special case' of ES. There are, of course, further specific issues associated with the type of ES involved (e.g. ERP and CRM systems). Details can be found in some of the publications referenced in the endnotes.[15]

STRATEGIES FOR MANAGING THE IT INFRASTRUCTURE

This section is concerned with the management of the technology infrastructure from a strategic perspective and, in particular, the issues affecting investment in its development and its contribution and alignment to the business strategy.

Defining IT infrastructure and its components is becoming more difficult as technology evolves and becomes increasingly a business utility. Perhaps the best definition is 'the enabling base of shared IT capabilities which provide the foundation for other business systems.'[16] This definition by McKay and Brockway includes the managerial expertise to provide IT services as well as the technology itself. Many authors[17] include 'services' in the IT infrastructure, since it is difficult to separate

Table 11.2   *Key issues in Enterprise Systems implementation*

- To succeed, business models will have to change and so will business and organizational structures and relationships. The drivers and need for change must be understood throughout the organization.
- Corporate IS/IT initiatives are often distrusted by the business units or functions due to increasing control and loss of autonomy.
- There must be explicitly identified benefits both to the corporation and to most, if not all, the units/functions involved, to enable the business changes to be made: *but* implementing an ES will rarely deliver sufficient immediate benefits to justify the cost and effort. Exploiting the new capability will deliver further benefits, which need to be identified at the start and actioned once the basic implementation is completed.
- It is the business changes enabled by the Enterprise Systems (ES), not the software, that produces the major and lasting business benefits.
- The technology is rarely the cause of failure, it is normally the result of organizational or cultural issues being unresolved or a poor implementation process.
- A strong, empowered, multidisciplinary, business-led team using sound project management principles is essential to success.
- Changing the performance measures (and even reward systems) to reflect the interdependencies resulting from the new business model are essential, if behaviours are to change.
- Poorly defined or ineffectively communicated business vision and strategy will reduce the ES to a technology project only, owned by the IS function!
- Most organizations realize (after the event) that more resources and expertise should have been devoted to change management!

the issues of infrastructure management associated with its procurement from those affecting its use in services and applications. IT infrastructure is therefore considered to comprise:

- Physical infrastructure, which consists of a range of network, hardware and base software products and services, deployed to enable applications and the general purpose use of technology to function successfully. A component is considered as being part of the infrastructure if it is used by more than one application (e.g. middleware) or by a wide range of people. Hence, software such as groupware to enable knowledge sharing and collaborative working is part of the infrastructure, since it has many applications. It can be argued that Enterprise Systems software packages, once installed, are essentially part of the infrastructure, given the range of activities they support and the influence they have over the business and IT architecture.

- Architectures, which describe the physical infrastructure and show the current and, where possible, future configurations. As well as models of the physical infrastructure and where it is located, etc., these also include models of information, processes and organizational structure. The technology architecture is a representation of a set of hardware and software components, described in terms of how they support the applications and information requirements of the business.
- Policies and standards, which cover technology aspects to determine how the infrastructure, its acquisition, deployment and support are managed. These address matters such as sourcing, contracts, service levels, back-up and recovery, contingency plans and, increasingly importantly, security and access controls.
- Management processes to ensure investments in infrastructure are coherently planned and justified, and relationships with technology suppliers and outsourcing providers are appropriate for their role in enabling the business strategy.

The nature of IT services and the related strategic issues were discussed earlier in this chapter, and the management of outsourcing is covered in the last section of this chapter. The purpose of this section is to deal with infrastructure strategy from a general management, not a technical perspective—references to more comprehensive texts on particular aspects are provided.

LINKING THE IT INFRASTRUCTURE WITH THE BUSINESS STRATEGY

Business Objectives of Technology Management

The purpose behind the overall management of the technology infrastructure is to provide an appropriate set of technology, resources, processes and services to meet the evolving needs of the business and the organizational ability to apply them effectively. Specifically, this means underpinning the application portfolio and general-purpose use of IT tools in the short and medium term, and undertaking investments to make justified improvements to the infrastructure to meet longer-term, but uncertain organizational and business needs. This implies a continuous migration plan to move from the current technology infrastructure to the most appropriate set of components to match systems and information architectures, probably passing through multiple stages over a number of years.

In response to business drivers pulling the IT supply strategy, such as cost-effectiveness, flexibility and responsiveness, remote working, global-

Table 11.3 *Examples of objectives for developing the IT infrastructure*

- Provide an appropriate infrastructure to sustain the performance of current applications and development or enhancement of business applications deemed to be critical to meeting business needs.
- Maximize the use of current information and facilities available in the existing applications and technology.
- Provide sufficient integration and consistency across the infrastructure, to minimize cost, maintain quality, and to enable internal and external inter-connectivity.
- Facilitate an increase in the productivity of users and their business processes, by equipping them with desktop tools and office software, accessibility to the information they require, and the networking capability to communicate internally and externally as needed (e.g. via Intranets and the Internet, groupware, email, videoconferencing and desktop applications).
- Facilitate rapid application development by providing a modern tool set, and training for users and IS developers.
- Reduce complexity and non-standardization so as to ensure flexibility and responsiveness to change at all organizational levels and locations, and enable staff mobility and consistency of user knowledge required across the organization.
- To build and manage an infrastructure, to serve the whole group, that can handle high-volume multimedia communications within the group and enable communications with customers and suppliers in a consistent and economic way.
- To provide the ability to change business and organization structures without major delay, cost or disruption due to IT constraints. This might also include the ability to minimize the costs and complexity of mergers, acquisitions and divestments.
- To have an infrastructure that is compatible and comparable with other organizations in the industry to gain full benefits from industry IS/IT developments.

ization and employee productivity, there will be a number of specific IT objectives to be met, as illustrated in Table 11.3. However, it may not be possible, for financial, technical or human reasons, to be able to provide an ideal infrastructure at any given time. At best, the technology infrastructure can evolve at the rate demanded by the business and IS plans, but, if necessary, these plans may have to be modified to a rate determined by the evolution of technology or the economics of acquiring and using it.

Business Basis for Managing Technology

Most of the issues that have to be addressed by business managers with responsibility for technology are business issues. In order to manage technology effectively, it is not necessary to get deeply involved in technical details. This chapter does not attempt to do so either, except in so far as it is necessary to explain the concepts or address the issues raised by technology. Technology changes so quickly; it is beyond even most technical people to keep up to date, and even more difficult and less valuable for business managers to attempt to do so. However, more business managers are required to have enough understanding of the strategic issues to improve their decisions concerning technology: a set of principles by which they can assess the various issues, to ensure a well-rounded decision-making basis and increased likelihood that the long-term best interests of the business are upheld.

Managers responsible for planning, developing and managing the infrastructure are expected to provide a continually improving and expanding service to the business, in response to the demands of the business strategy and any organizational evolution. Additionally, they need to keep abreast of new and emerging technology and current competitive usage of IT, and put forward suggestions as to how technology might be deployed to gain advantage or create new business options. Two particularly enduring problems of IT infrastructure management, in combination, create a number of difficulties for organizations:

- it must be developed as a base for future, uncertain use of applications rather than merely matching current business functionality[18] (i.e. keeping ahead of the needs);
- it is difficult to define the value derived from IT infrastructure[19] (i.e. it is seen as a cost).

The prime difficulty, therefore, is making investments to meet uncertain needs in something that has no explicit value! Therefore, it is important to link infrastructure development to relevant parts of the business strategy. Most organizations could identify current business problems that would result from inadequate infrastructure, but it is more difficult to foresee the future problems that would result from failure to invest in its development. So, some of the issues to be faced are:

- *Linking technology investments to business needs*—how to relate the specific requirements for investment in technology to the business needs, and to determine the implications of gaining or not gaining approval, and how to make sure that the proposed development is the best way of obtaining the indirect benefits. While per unit costs of technology are going down, spending on IT is still increasing, with investments in new applications both for business systems and individual or group working, and in the automation of more activities, like workflow management. This seems to be acceptable because of the growing belief and some evidence that an effective IT infrastructure enables organizational responsiveness and employee flexibility[20]—all critical characteristics in most of today's businesses—and facilitates coping with growing complexity. This is endorsed by individuals, who, by and large, enjoy the increased power they can obtain from IT. However, all the evidence does not point at realized productivity gains in all uses of IT. Reports suggest[21] that white-collar productivity has not actually improved during the 'desktop' era and there is some evidence that misuse or inadequate skills have caused negative effects on productivity. Justification of infrastructure investments is considered briefly below, within the overall rationale for IS/IT investment covered in detail in Chapter 9.

- *Identifying technical opportunities*—although business managers do not need an in-depth understanding of technology, they do need sufficient understanding of its capability to achieve the business requirements, in terms of its ability to: (i) improve or radically change the products and services of the business, and develop electronic trading capabilities, (ii) improve the productivity and effectiveness of business processes and people and (iii) impact the economics of the business.

- *IT investments by others*—how existing and potential competitors, customers and suppliers are using or could use technology to improve their competitive positions and the likely consequences in terms of (i) impact on the market and customers, (ii) changing relationships and cost structures within the value chain and (iii) threats or opportunities created by new IT-based entrants in the industry. Business managers need the knowledge to assess the situation, understand the options available, assess their implications and be able to respond accordingly in terms of commissioning the investments or provisioning by outside parties.

- *Technical implications and 'hype'*—most business managers are required to make important business decisions, or required to recommend strategies to the overall management team. They are unlikely to have an in-depth understanding of how the multitude of technologies work, but must know enough to be able to ask sensible questions and not to be confused by the advice of potential suppliers or 'in-flight' magazine articles and even TV adverts! However, they will need to rely on technical management and specialists to explain and interpret the essentials for them. Technical management also need to be sufficiently business aware to extract the relevant, factual information from the supplier pressure and hype, so that they do not fall into line with the technology vendors themselves in promoting the 'solutions looking for problems', based on technically irresistible offerings, rather than business need and sound assessments of performance, cost and risk.

- *Business and technical awareness*—the CIO or IT director not only has a responsibility to instil business judgement and awareness in his technology experts but also to implant a sound, albeit high-level, understanding of technology and technical issues in general management.
- *How to make decisions about IT resources*—this includes the sourcing and, where appropriate, outsourcing of infrastructure products and services.

One major issue for senior management to address is the determination of the degree to which they wish the organization to function as an integrated whole or as separate entities. This decision will have a significant influence on the type of infrastructure that is developed and its overall cost, especially in multi-unit organizations. A model developed by Keen[22] and shown in Figure 11.9 can help management form an opinion on the need for commonality and connectivity across the IT infrastructure. Keen describes two dimensions:

- *reach*—the extent to which the infrastructure must enable connections across systems and platforms among internal and external users;
- *range*—the breadth of services, and variety and volume of different types of information, documents, images, etc. that will be shared among internal and external parties.

In considering how to meet integration requirements, a business needs to define an architecture that delivers the essential levels of capability, *reach* and *range*, and plan to migrate to it gradually. It should determine key parameters; for example, the required responsiveness, speed and efficiency in terms of connectivity and access across the community, and the current and future processing and communication capacity it expects to need.

A study of 26 major international firms by Broadbent *et al.*[23] confirmed that those seeking and achieving inter-unit business synergies had invested in infrastructures that produced high levels of reach *and* range. This also tended to include common application packages using common databases. The study also found that the firms who had integrated business, IS and IT planning processes had more extensive IT infrastructure capabilities in both of Keen's dimensions. Interestingly, the study confirmed, as perhaps expected, that generally the firms

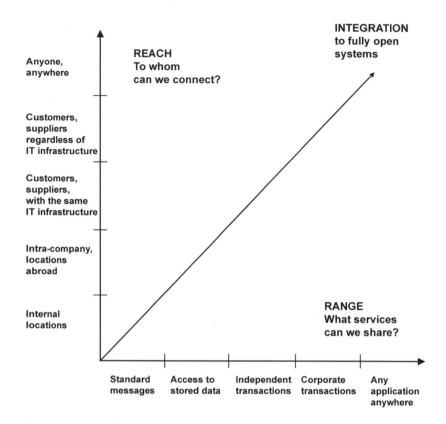

Figure 11.9   *Reach and range (*source: *from P.G.W. Keen,* Shaping the Future, *Harvard Business School Press, Boston, 1991)*

where information was a major component of the product or critical to the value-adding processes, such as oil exploration or research, had invested most in infrastructure as a 'capability' (i.e. centrally planned, coordinated investments with strong controls on IT expenditure).

JUSTIFICATION OF INFRASTRUCTURE INVESTMENTS

Infrastructure contributes to the delivery of business benefits in a number of different ways, and the justification of expenditure, either for procurement of capital items or purchasing software licenses or network or hardware capacity from third-party suppliers, needs to be presented on the basis of the particular contributions being made. These can be described under five headings as depicted in Figure 11.10.

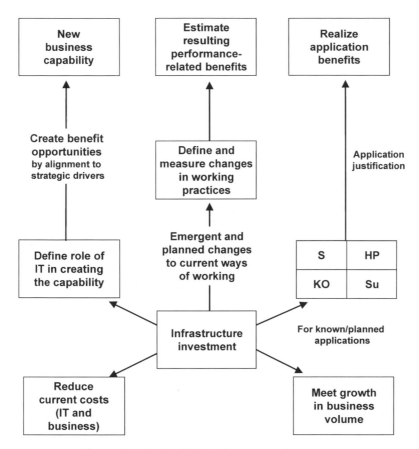

Figure 11.10 *Justifying infrastructure investments*

1. *Application-specific*—infrastructure costs can be justified in part on the basis of the benefits delivered by applications that will use the infrastructure, and the relevant costs should form part of the business justification for those applications. This implies a link between the planned applications portfolio developments and the infrastructure required to enable them. This can be done via a composite Benefits Dependency Network, a technique described in Chapter 9, showing infrastructure components as the enablers of the applications, business changes and benefits.

2. *To reduce costs of running and supporting existing applications, by using more cost-effective technology*—this is most likely to arise in relation to support or some key operational applications as well as

personal productivity and communications usage. The justification will depend on cost savings, mainly in the IT budget, but there may be business cost savings, especially by providing easier-to-use desktop tools or lower-cost means of communication. Included in this category is the 'forced' need to replace a technology that is or is becoming obsolete (i.e. it will no longer be supported or is no longer available because the vendor has ceased to supply the technology or even gone out of business!). As with any technology investments that involve supporting existing applications, it is prudent to question whether each application is still necessary to the business. If it is, there may be several options:

- transferring the application to other existing technology already in use in the business, which may be a less efficient solution, or through replacement with new technology more in keeping with IT policies relating to nominated platforms and standardization across the business;
- modifying or redeveloping the application to take advantage of more cost-effective technology, either existing or new;
- cutting down the functionality of the application to the essentials and delivering them by one or other of the above means.

3. *To enable growth in the volume of business transactions*, both internal and external, or to accommodate the changing mix of transactions, (e.g. customers switching to Internet ordering from the call centre). The growth in transaction volume may be due to changing business practices rather than genuine business volume increases. Customers are tending to move to just-in-time satisfaction of requirements and more single-line ordering rather than consolidating purchases, causing further increases in internal transactions, but still expect rapid response and high service levels. In combination, these create increasingly high-peak loads as well as overall increases in transaction volumes. At the same time, more information is being transferred in many of the transactions (e.g. in the form of multiple large attachments to emails, complex images and video), requiring further network, processing and storage capacity increases. In terms of benefits, it is important to consider three different types of argument for increased capacity:

- that required to deal with increased business activity (i.e. real growth), which leads to increased revenue;
- that needed to accommodate the changing mix of transaction types, which should be offset by savings to be made elsewhere. The increasing move to electronic as opposed to paper transac-

tions should produce cost savings associated with printing and paper handling; and

- that required to deal with increasing use of capacity for purely internal reasons. Whether this is of net benefit to the organization needs to be determined in terms of the changes in business practices that are emerging, rather than being planned. For example, centralizing corporate information on an Intranet can produce reduced costs and benefits due to accuracy and consistency, provided its content is managed effectively. If every user is extracting and storing the information they require, along with other pages of information downloaded from the Internet, demands for increased network and server capacity are not justified costs. Equally poor user practices in dealing with accumulations of emails may lead to significant, unjustified capacity increases.

4. *Changes in working practices*—this means deliberate changes as opposed to emergent changes as in Item 3 above, although improved practices developed informally should be extended and built on, based on the benefits that have resulted. Such changes may be associated with specific applications, in which case the benefits should be related via the application to the associated infrastructure. However, increasingly, changes in processes and practices can be made via the use of the infrastructure without major application investment. For example, a bank, having set up its 'product catalogue' on an internal website, stopped sending product update information on paper to its several hundred branches. Two benefits resulted: a large paper cost saving and fast, consistent, up-to-date information to customers in the branches. 'Filing' the mass of paper received in the branches was a problem, often leading to delays in staff having the latest information at the counter.

Another significant area of potential benefit, which was discussed in the previous chapter, is associated with knowledge sharing within and across organizations. While research[24] has shown that knowledge sharing is driven by people not technology, communities of interest and/or practice—the main conduit of sharing—work best when the management encourages and facilitates their development *and* provides the necessary resources, including technology. Again, where extended infrastructure to support content-rich media (e.g. desktop videoconferencing), is put in place to enable organizational knowledge management, the intended and resulting benefits can and should be specifically identified and measured. Equally, findings from other research[25] suggest that 'workforce agility' or organizational flexibility, to respond quickly and effectively to changes in the market place, is increased by the provision of a consistent, high-quality, integrated IT infrastructure supporting all users and all applications.

5. *To create a new business capability* that is required for the future business strategy, an explicit strategic intent or a particular strategic initiative. While the details of how the intent will best be met may as yet be unclear, a demonstrated connection between the IT infrastructure implicit in achieving the strategy can often be made. For example, an energy company stated that one of its strategic intentions was 'to become location independent', enabling its technical and professional staff to perform their jobs wherever in the world they happened to be. This was the main justification for a major investment in network capacity and portable workstations, although benefits in other categories were also delivered.

   In the UK, the concerted move to e-government—the electronic access and delivery of government services to the public and others—has led many local authorities to justify the major infrastructure investments required as an integral part of their future strategies. The argument is that the IT infrastructure is, over the long term, a replacement for the traditional infrastructure of local government—based on an extensive 'office coverage' of the authorities' geography. As the infrastructure to enable 'online' access and mobile working by professional staff is implemented, savings in the capital and operating cost of existing office and depot sites are used to offset the IT costs. The reduction in these traditional 'delivery channels' is then planned and implemented, to realize the savings as early as possible, and the net cost reduction achieved is continuously monitored by both management and the elected council.

Overall, any infrastructure investment should be assessed against all of these five criteria to identify the contribution, if any, it is expected to make in each and the direct or indirect benefits that should be realized. It has been argued that firms need to consider their IT infrastructure more as a 'capability' than merely a 'utility', or cost of doing business, in order to align the use of technology with the business strategy.[26] As mentioned in Chapter 9, some authors have proposed the use of real options analysis to address the inherent uncertainties in investments in IT infrastructure, especially in the last of the categories above. Bulasubramarian and colleagues[27] have developed a formal methodology based on real options to evaluate and compare different IT infrastructure investments along with other alternative investments. Their experience in using the approach is that it not only influences the outcome of the decision but also improves understanding of how to align business drivers with the business capabilities that can be developed from an appropriate IT infrastructure. This is likely to be increasingly important as more aspects of IS/IT will become part of the 'infrastructure', either purchased as an 'integrated set' or provided by outsourcing vendors of one form or another. Many organizations are seeking to obtain their infrastructure from outsourcers, to reduce their need for scarce technical expertise in-house and to be able to buy what they need incrementally rather than as higher risk, expensive capital purchases. Outsourcing strategies are considered at the end of this chapter, but outsourcing of IT infrastructure and service provision does not absolve management of the responsibility for defining its role in the strategy or justifying the investment involved.

TECHNOLOGY STRATEGIES IN A MULTI-BUSINESS UNIT ORGANIZATION

Throughout this book, there has been a focus on achieving a coherent IS/IT strategy for a business unit, because each business unit should seek to maximize the benefits from its information, systems and technology, and it is most feasible to achieve that coherence at business unit level. However, most corporations consist of a number of businesses and there is a need to consider the strategic management of technology supply and services across the businesses to obtain the maximum corporate and business unit benefits.

This corporate dimension has been considered in previous chapters in terms of the factors that drive the degree of beneficial central coordination and control over and above the business units. The main factors affecting the technology strategy can be summarized as business-driven factors, including the following:

- degree of intercompany trading;
- similarity of products and business processes;
- coherence of markets served, channels of distribution used and main suppliers;
- similarity in scale of operation;
- industry maturity and competitive situation of units;
- geography, especially in international companies;
- how corporate management exercises its control over the units' business strategies and activities;
- the rate of business and organizational change.

They can also be summarized as IS/IT supply-driven factors, which include:

- the economics of processing and procurement;
- availability of skills and human resources;
- availability of technologies and vendor services in different countries and areas;
- the existing IS/IT investments in the different units.

Often, however, these 'logical' factors can become obscured by organizational and political factors due to the way the business units have been developed or acquired and/or the degree of real trust that exists between the corporate centre and the units. This desire for conformity or independence often manifests itself more emotionally over the control of IT than many other business issues, especially in companies that grow by acquisition, where IT environments often pre-date the organizational relationships. Based on the above factors, there appears to be a structured way of addressing these issues, which is consistent with the earlier discussion of achieving application, information and organizational coherence and synergy to the degree required by the business relationships. It is important that the degree of IT conformity or divergence reflects the business, organizational and cultural characteristics of the organization, not the preference of IT specialists, or it will fail in the long term to deliver corporate benefits.

The extent to which the corporation should direct the technology architecture and the selection process cannot be prescribed, but there is perhaps an escalating scale of corporate intervention that can be considered. At the lowest level, this can provide benefit even if the organization is a conglomerate, buying and selling businesses and operating in many industries with companies of varying sizes and differing business situations. At the highest level, the benefits will be far greater in a corporation that has a number of companies in the same overall industry. The three levels are described in Box 11.1.

This three-level approach is obviously somewhat simplistic, but it is an attempt to reflect in technology management terms the likely business and corporate cultures that will prevail across the spectrum from a 'financial conglomerate' to a highly-focused and organically-developing corporation. Essentially, it suggests an increasing need for central coordination across business units as the intention to gain economic *and* application or process *and* information and knowledge benefits becomes more important. The progression follows a rationale from the support, via the key operational to the strategic/high potential quadrants of the portfolio, in terms of increasing potential gain from central coordination of technology strategy in order to gain the business benefits both corporately and in each part of the business. It also reflects the need to transfer technology knowledge across the organization to gain the

Box 11.1 Managing technology in a multi-business-unit organization

Level 1: Lowest level of control by the corporation over the SBUs—Technology Economics

Centralization of technology control will be mainly an economic issue to exploit corporate buying power with suppliers and ensure that resources are not unnecessarily duplicated. This will have most effect at the 'commodity' end of technology—in data communications, processing power and basic operational software as well as related technical skills to support IT operations. Even if the companies have different application requirements, establishing a target environment based on supply economics can enable selection decisions in each unit to consider a preferred set of options. These will not be mandatory, but will be expected to be adopted, unless the local economics are poor, perhaps due to the unit's size or because its application needs cannot be adequately satisfied. Some centralized resources and skills will then be available to support the companies' implementation and operation of the main hardware, operating systems and networks, and even application packages. This can make the preferred solutions more attractive to the units, provided the charge-out of costs from the centre is equitable. The central resource can also act as the main point of contact with suppliers to ensure that the corporation obtains the best value from group purchasing, and monitor centrally the vendor performance against agreed service levels as and when problems arise anywhere in the organization.

In most, even diverse, organizations, telecommunications management is usually centralized to provide the necessary skills, manage the capacity, deal with major vendors and ensure costs are not unnecessarily incurred.

Level 2: Moderate level of control by the corporation over the SBUs—Application Benefits

If the corporation has a number of businesses operating in different industries, but of a limited number of types (e.g. several manufacturing businesses as well as some distribution and/or service companies), there may be opportunities for further benefits at the corporate level or at a subgroup level, over and above those mentioned at Level 1. For instance, manufacturing companies may all need some form of Enterprise Resource Planning (ERP) system or each SBU may operate in similar supply chains or trade in similar ways. There is probably some similarity in the type of applications required for comparable internal and external processes, therefore benefits will exist if application software knowledge and even resources are shared among the units. This will add weight to the need for consistency of basic operating environments, otherwise the benefit of application knowledge will be reduced by the need to support diverse implementations on different hardware and operating systems, and deal with a large variety of suppliers. The benefits are not purely economic, although obviously the ability to replicate business benefits is a financial gain. The benefits also accrue by enabling companies of perhaps different sizes and in different stages of maturity to develop applications ahead of their own local ability to develop the necessary skills. Similarly, applications may even be run centrally and hence be able to be upgraded as the hardware and software base changes with less cost and disruption to the units.

The potential downside is that the units do not develop their own business application and technical expertise, to move beyond using IT for essentially support and key operational applications. Too much centralization of IT control can lead to reduced innovation at a unit level, and, if there is no unit or group level management or IS/IT business steering mechanism, merely satisfying the 'lowest common denominator' of needs can stifle overall and local progress.

Level 3: Highest level of control by the corporation over the SBUs—Information Asset Management

Where companies are in the same industry and/or trade with one another and/or deal with a similar customer or supplier base, there is probably business advantage to be gained from strong coordination of technology management at corporate level. Not only are there economic and application supply-side benefits but also significant benefits from sharing information and knowledge as well as its proficient and consistent processing throughout the company and in systems linking the company to its trading partners. For example, they may use a common Customer Relationship Management (CRM) system *and* share a common customer database. Here, it is worth ensuring that the technology environments are consistent to the level of data management software, communications standards and some application software, even if to any one unit company the 'overhead' may appear uneconomic. The benefits of strong central direction and hence support in terms of skills and resources may again be negated if innovation is stifled. A corporate mechanism to deal with strategic and high potential areas of development must be in place. Equally, the corporation may need to fund part of the cost of technology in the units to encourage commonality. This implies that the units may have to compromise some requirements, and the consequences of such compromise must be understood. The compromise may not always be worthwhile— meaning that the corporate architecture must evolve and develop with the needs and not become a force for business stagnation due to the limited options it allows.

greatest and earliest return from IS/IT competencies possessed by the organization, wherever they exist.

OUTSOURCING STRATEGIES

A *selective* or *smart* sourcing approach using multiple vendors is an increasingly popular strategy to minimize risks, maximize benefits and reduce costs[28] and is likely to be the preferable choice of the future. Willcocks and Sauer[29] report that selective and in-house sourcing had success rates of 77% and 76%, respectively, but only 38% of total outsourcing deals (80% or more of IT activities outsourced) were successful, 35% failed and 27% had mixed results.

Many organizations have chosen a 'best of breed' approach to their outsourcing strategy, contracting with a variety of vendors for the delivery of IT services. For example, British Petroleum (now BP) contracted with three suppliers under an umbrella contract obliging the suppliers to work together. According to BP's IT director at that time, John Cross, '[w]e decided against receiving all our IT needs from a single supplier as some companies have done, because we believed such an approach could make us vulnerable to escalating fees and inflexible services. Instead, we sought a solution that would allow us both to buy IT services from multiple suppliers and to have pieces delivered as if they came from a single supplier.'[30] BP reported that this sourcing strategy reduced IT staff by 80% and reduced IT operating costs from $360 million in 1989 to $132 million in 1994.[31]

While the risks of using a single vendor are mitigated with a multi-sourcing strategy, they are replaced by the additional time and resources required to manage multiple suppliers. The key to a successful multi-sourcing arrangement is vendor coordination and management.[32] To achieve this requirement for seamless service delivery, BP appointed one of its three vendors as the primary contractor at each of its eight business sites. The role of the lead vendor was to coordinate the services provided by all three suppliers to the businesses supported by that site.

We have also seen joint ventures between vendors and clients being established where risks and rewards are established. These include vendors buying client's shares or vice versa, or both parties taking a stake in a new entity,[33] illustrating that their fortunes are bound up together. General Motors took an equity stake in EDS, with EDS effectively operating as a subsidiary of the car manufacturing giant, although since 1996 it has been free to pursue its own strategies. The Swiss Bank–Perot Systems $6.25 billion deal saw both partners agree to sell solutions to the banking industry, with the bank having an option to buy up to 25% of equity in Perot Systems.

One of the largest outsourcing vendors EDS introduced the concept of 'co-sourcing' to refer to contracts where there is a strong element of 'win–win' between the parties. Payment to the vendor is based in part on the performance achieved by the customer. These performance-based contracts (as opposed to fee-based) are proving popular, particularly as experience with outsourcing has been mixed. For example, in 1998, US truck manufacturer Freightliner Corporation outsourced to Debis for IT services in a $70 million, five-year deal. This amount was based on what Freightliner estimated it would have spent over that period on the IT operations that it outsourced. However, Freightliner pays Debis only a baseline amount to cover the vendor's costs. Any profit depends solely on Debis generating savings. When Debis saves Freightliner money by performing IT services at less cost than Freightliner's original IS function estimate, the two companies split the savings based on an agreed percentage.[34]

Risks Associated with Outsourcing

Many companies are disappointed with their results from having outsourced IT activity, and research consistently demonstrates that, despite the growing maturity of vendors and their clients, the practice of outsourcing continues to be a high-risk process. A survey conducted by UK magazine *Computing* revealed that just one-quarter of IT directors would use their main outsourcing vendor again.[35] Research[36] has identified the following risk factors:

- *Treating IT as an undifferentiated commodity to be outsourced.* This risk is more a reflection of management's view of IS/IT than anything else, failing to see the contribution or potential contribution that IS/IT could make regarding competitive applications. Proponents often see outsourcing as an opportunity to offload headcount. Yet, IT is different from other areas of the business: it evolves rapidly, the economics of supply continually change, IS penetrates all areas of the business and switching costs are high.

- *Incomplete contracting.* This risk is a reflection of the environment within which IT outsourcing takes place, particularly the difficulties in constructing and agreeing long-term contracts in the face of rapid business and technical change. Who, for example, in the early 1990s, could have foreseen the impact the Internet would have on commerce and the opportunities it would provide?

- *Lack of active management of the supplier on (a) contract and (b) relationship dimensions.* Vendor performance must be continually monitored; it has not been unknown for the vendor to devote their attention to winning new business once the contract has been signed. Relationships with vendors require continual development if they are to add value—this requires considerable management time. Later in this chapter, the process of building relationships with vendors is explored.

- *Power asymmetries developing in favour of the vendor.* This is one of the big risks, particularly for long-term contracts. Vendors may attempt to reinterpret the contract, particularly as they often look to recoup investments in the later years of the contract and seek opportunities to make higher charges for services not covered in the original contract. Vendors may themselves subcontract work and may not manage the relationship any better than the client could, but at a significantly higher cost.

- *Inexperienced staff.* Even the biggest vendors experience the same problems as an internal IS function in recruiting experienced staff. And, the reality of many outsourcing deals is that the original staff of the IS function, outsourced to a vendor, often end up back working for the client! In addition, it is important to ensure that vendor staff skills and knowledge are continually updated rather than be allowed to remain relevant to the 'legacy' that (most often) has been outsourced.

- *Outsourcing for short-term financial restructuring or cash injection rather than to leverage IT assets for business advantage.* Managers often engage in outsourcing because they do not perceive any value from their IT expenditures and consequently wish to minimize the costs. While outsourcing to cut costs has an appeal, the longer-term downside can be serious. As Nigel Morris, president of US credit-card group Capital One, succinctly noted, 'If you have a business that churns out products, then outsourcing makes sense. But ... IT is our central nervous system ... if I outsourced tomorrow I might save a dollar or two on each account, but I would lose flexibility, and value and service levels.'[37]

- *Hidden costs.* Proponents of outsourcing argue that IT costs are more clearly defined with outsourcing. However, there can be many hidden costs. The severance package for terminated or transferred employees may be a hidden cost of outsourcing. In a survey of 76 organizations that had a total of 223 contracts, Willcocks and Fitzgerald[38] found that hidden costs were the biggest outsourcing problem. One recommendation is to establish *if* and *where* the vendor makes a profit.[39]
- *Managing multiple vendors.* It is difficult enough managing a single vendor, but the management of multiple vendors adds additional complexity, particularly regarding coordination. One tends to find that each has their own agenda and intention to increase their business with the client. A number of strategies adopted by companies to minimize any risk were highlighted earlier.
- *Loss of innovative capacity.* Once a significant part of IT has been outsourced, there is a danger that the organization can lose the competency to identify innovation-based opportunities from IS/IT. Chapter 5 has highlighted the importance of actively seeking IS/IT opportunities in developing a competitive strategy. Earl[40] notes that much learning about the capability of IT is experiential, a key point particularly when exploring competitive impact opportunities.
- *Cultural incompatibility.* It is important to ensure that the organizational culture and work practices are compatible with those of the vendor.[41]

Willcocks and Sauer[42] recommend a prudent approach to such issues as IT outsourcing contracts, supplier claims, the risk behind disguised multi-supplier contracts, supplier capabilities and resources, single-supplier and long-term deals. From their research, they have developed a risk analysis framework highlighting the various risks that can arise over time. Illustrated in Figure 11.11, it highlights the contextual risk factors, risks associated with contract construction and post-contractual risks. Organizations must ensure that they consider all these factors in making the outsourcing decision in constructing any subsequent contracts and managing the contract during its lifetime. Generally, selective sourcing to multiple suppliers—on relatively short-term, detailed and regularly revisited contracts—has been the effective approach to mitigating the risks of IT outsourcing.

GUIDELINES FOR OUTSOURCING DECISIONS

Although there are no simple rules in making outsourcing decisions, a number of lessons can be deduced from general experiences to date. Such

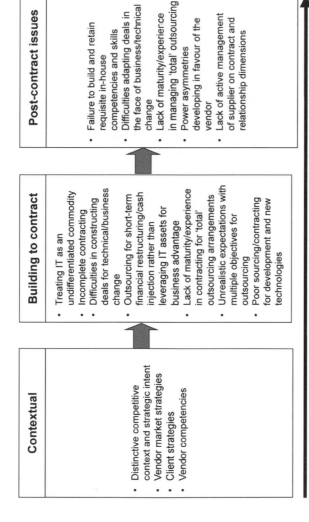

Contextual	Building to contract	Post-contract issues
• Distinctive competitive context and strategic intent • Vendor market strategies • Client strategies • Vendor competencies	• Treating IT as an undifferentiated commodity • Incomplete contracting • Difficulties in constructing deals for technical/business change • Outsourcing for short-term financial restructuring/cash injection rather than leveraging IT assets for business advantage • Lack of maturity/experience in contracting for 'total' outsourcing arrangements • Unrealistic expectations with multiple objectives for outsourcing • Poor sourcing/contracting for development and new technologies	• Failure to build and retain requisite in-house competencies and skills • Difficulties adapting deals in the face of business/technical change • Lack of maturity/experience in managing 'total' outsourcing • Power asymmetries developing in favour of the vendor • Lack of active management of supplier on contract and relationship dimensions

Time and change

Figure 11.11 *Outsourcing risk-analysis framework* (source: L. Willcocks and C. Sauer, 'High risks and hidden costs in IT outsourcing', Financial Times Mastering Risk, May 2000)

guidelines will help the decision makers on various issues such as whether to outsource or not, whether to employ one or more vendors or how to cluster the services under contracts.

Managers should not make a one-time decision whether to outsource or not. Instead, they should create an environment in which potential suppliers, external vendors as well as the internal IS function, are constantly competing to provide IS/IT services. Organizations should choose to outsource carefully selected, non-core activities that can be accomplished quicker, cheaper and better by vendors. Earl[43] argues that companies should first ask why they should not *insource* IT services. Indeed, actual outsourcing or, at the very least, the threat of outsourcing is often the symptom of the problem of demonstrating the value of IS.[44]

DiRomualdo and Gurbaxani's[45] research indicates the importance of understanding the different types of strategic intent for IT and the role that outsourcing can play before making any decision. They highlight three strategic intents driving outsourcing:

- IS improvement—'Do IS better';
- business impact—'Use IT to achieve better business results';
- commercial exploitation—'Exploit IT assets externally'.

Each type of strategic intent for IT outsourcing requires different approaches and tactics to be successful. The nature of the strategic intent also drives the type of contract, payments and incentives, pricing provisions and performance measures. Deciding on a sourcing strategy should be based on a combined assessment of business, economic and technical factors,[46] the relative importance of each being determined by the strategic intent.

Business Factors

In assessing the business factors relating to the outsourcing decision, two separate dimensions of business contribution should be considered: *competitive positioning* and *business operations*. The competitive positioning view considers the type of contribution made by an IT activity, whether it is a 'commodity' or a 'differentiator'. An IT activity will be a commodity if it is not expected to distinguish the business from its key competitors, whereas differentiators are IT activities that are expected to provide the capability for the business to achieve competitive advantage. The business operations dimensions can be assessed as either 'useful' or 'critical':

- *Critical differentiators*. IT activities that are not only critical to business operations but also help to distinguish the business from its competitors. Organizations should look to insource such activities, although they may avail themselves of third-party expertise. These activities would normally be ones that are directly related to creating and sustaining strategic applications, plus the related R&D activity required to identify and prove that differentiation can be achieved.

- *Critical commodities.* IT activities that are critical to business operations, but fail to distinguish the business from competitors (key operational application areas). Here, organizations should 'best-source', but, because of the risks, assessment should be based on clear evidence that the vendor can meet stringent operational requirements.

- *Useful commodities.* The myriad, mainly support, IT activities that provide incremental benefits to the business, but fail to distinguish it from competitors. The strategy here is generally to outsource, as third-party vendors are likely to have achieved low cost through economies of scale and standardization.

Technical Factors

Technical factors guide the choice of supply source and the form of supply arrangements. Two issues need assessment: the degree of technology maturity (i.e. level of maturity in use of technology), and degree of technology integration (i.e. whether IT services require a high or low degree of integration). The latter often limits the options for multiple sourcing if highly integrated services are essential and if the organization is mature or advanced in its technologies—there may be fewer vendors capable of providing services to match the in-house alternatives, even where costs are high. It may not be possible to achieve cost reductions without reductions in the technical quality obtained.

Economic Factors

From their research, Lacity and Hirschheim[47] concluded that the cost efficiency of vendors largely depends on adoption of efficient management practices and, to a lesser extent, economies of scale. In addition, they also found that the internal IS function often possesses equivalent or superior economies of scale to vendors for many activities. Table 11.4 compares costs between the internal IS function and outsourcing vendors across a number of cost drivers.

In a longitudinal study of evaluation practices in 26 organizations in the lead-up to making IT sourcing decisions, Willcocks and colleagues[48] found that existing internal IT evaluation processes often made it difficult

Table 11.4   *Theoretical economies of scale* (source: *from M.C. Lacity and R. Hirschheim,* Beyond the Information Systems Outsourcing Bandwagon: The Insourcing Response, *John Wiley & Sons, Chichester, UK, 1995)*

Source of IS costs	Internal IS function	Outsourcing vendors
Data centre operating costs	Comparable to a vendor for 150–200 MIP range	Comparable to large IS function. Inherent advantage over small IS functions
Hardware purchase costs	Large companies: volume discounts comparable to a vendor	Volume discounts comparable to large IS function. Inherent advantage over small companies
Software licensing costs	Comparable due to group licenses	Comparable
Cost of business expertise	Inherent advantage	
Cost of technical expertise		Inherent advantage
Cost to shareholders (the need to generate a profit)	Inherent advantage	
Research and development costs		Inherent advantage
Marketing costs	Inherent advantage	
Opportunity costs		Inherent advantage
Transaction costs	Inherent advantage	

to make objective economic comparisons with outsourcing vendor bids. Difficulties in evaluating and then comparing in-house performance include evaluating total IT contribution, identifying full costs, benchmarking and external comparisons, the role of charging systems and the adoption of service-level agreements by the in-house operation. While it is important to make the most beneficial economic choice, it is even more important to ensure the outsourcing decision is in alignment with the overall IS/IT strategy.

In making sourcing decisions, a company's primary objective should be to maximize flexibility and control so that, in the provision of IS/IT services, the organization can pursue different options as it learns more or its circumstances change.[49]

Contractual Issues

Any decision to outsource will generally result in a contract been drawn up between the organization and the vendor. One of the biggest mistakes companies make is signing suppliers' standard contracts. Such contracts usually contain details that not even a company's legal staff can always understand, especially if the company is outsourcing a technology with which it is not familiar. Interestingly, research indicates that, when companies decided to outsource, detailed contracts were more likely to be successful than relational contracts.[50] Should it ever come to a dispute, only three things matter: the contract, the contract and the contract!

Another way to maintain control over outsourcing arrangements is to split an IT operation between two or more suppliers, thus establishing a threat of competition. According to Lacity and Hirschheim,[51] most of the companies that outsourced emerging technologies experienced disastrous results because they lacked the expertise to negotiate sound contracts and evaluate suppliers' performances. The different contractual issues can be categorized further:

- *Length of contract.* An organization should try whenever possible to sign short-term contracts. Short-term contracts are desirable because they ensure that the prices stipulated will not become out of step with market prices. For economic reasons, companies often look to contract for 10 years or more and to establish a strategic relationship with the supplier. However, contracting for IT services for such a length of time is very risky. As John Cross, IT Director at BP Amoco, pointed out in 1999, 'in the course of five years we experienced two generations of technology.'
- *Service definition.* Services should be defined in a relevant manner according to their purpose and critical business factors. The definition should include the aim and scope of the service and, if applicable, any elements specific to the client's organization. The contract should include regular reviews of service definitions according to changing business needs and technical imperatives.
- *Service-level requirements specifications.* Service-level requirements and the performance metrics must be developed and expressed in both business and technical terms wherever possible, to ensure their relationship to business success factors is clear to both parties. Targets or target ranges for each metric should also be specified.
- *Service-level measurement and verification.* In short-term transactions, the client or a third party should carry out measurement, verification and reporting of the service-levels delivered. In long-

term contracts, the vendor should also report the achievement of service level targets. In either case, the client must also institutionalize periodic or contingent review and verification procedures.

- *Incentives for service-level attainment.* The purpose here is to set up the necessary positive and negative incentive systems that ensure that performance targets are met. Long-term relationships between client and vendor are characterized by stronger reputation effects, which is in itself an effective incentive mechanism for the vendor. Positive, reward-based incentives can be employed when the target is volatile (indeterminate in advance) or when it is hard to achieve. Deterrent incentives and penalties can be employed when the service is critical to the business or when the target is easy to achieve. The conditions for extreme situations such as termination and/or change of vendor should also be clearly specified.

- *Coordination and communication mechanisms.* A steering committee and/or review board should be set up. This should comprise membership from both parties for top-level direction and corrective adjustments to the relationship and the contract. The information collected through monitoring and measurement must be fed to the decision-making bodies for continuous review of performance and to set relevant targets for improvement. It may be advisable to involve an independent third party in the review board to advise or even arbitrate where problems arise, or, perhaps more importantly, to pre-empt disputes.

In negotiating any contract, a negotiating team should be formed, headed by the top IT executive, and include a variety of specialists. The negotiating team should include in-house technical experts, an IT outsourcing consultant and a contract lawyer specializing in IT who can detect hidden costs and clauses in contracts. Further, in negotiating contracts, there are a number of lessons listed in Table 11.5 that have been gleaned from the practical experience of organizations.

Post-contract Management

During the lifetime of the contract, the following are important principles to remember:

- *Collect fines for non-compliance.* Some companies see a vendor performance shortfall as an opportunity to extract non-monetary payback, extracting some free service on the side in lieu of penalty charges. While such a compromise may be expedient, it sends the wrong message to vendors and undermines the company's position.

Table 11.5 *Lessons gleaned from practical experience of organizations*

- Discard the vendor's standard contract
- Do not sign incomplete contracts
- Measure everything during the baseline period
- Specify escalation procedures
- Beware of 'change of character' clauses
- Include cash penalties for non-performance
- Include a termination clause
- Take care of your people post-contract

- *Don't be afraid to confront the vendor.* Many companies fight hard to win penalty provisions from vendors only to find themselves averse to levying charges or forcing a dispute of any kind. Indeed, conflict avoidance is one of the most common scourges of outsourcing relationships. Ultimately, the company itself is responsible for user satisfaction; so, when a vendor doesn't deliver, it's a client's responsibility to let them know. And go to the top when necessary: involving the senior management of the vendor is often the easiest way to resolve disputes that can otherwise become bogged down in 'technical' arguments.

APPLICATIONS SERVICE PROVIDERS

The convergence of software and IT infrastructure to an Internet-centric environment has enabled the application service provider (ASP) concept to emerge. In its simplest form, an ASP is a third-party service firm that deploys, manages and remotely hosts a pre-packaged software application through centrally-located servers in a 'rental' or lease arrangement. In exchange for accessing the application, the client renders rental-like payments (see Figure 11.12). An early example of an ASP is Hotmail (www.hotmail.com), which provides an email address, with storage and access from any web browser. Individuals with a Hotmail account can access their email and send email from any location as long as they are connected to the Internet. Software is evolving from custom-coded, proprietary applications to pre-packaged or off-the-shelf applications and now to the development of net-centric applications.

No matter how the ASP is structured, the ultimate objective is a 'seamless' service, in which the client interacts only with the ASP. The most significant elements of a 'seamless' integration of services include providing the hardware and software, integration and testing, a secure

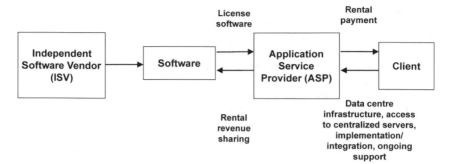

Figure 11.12   *Schematic of application service provider*

network infrastructure, reliable mission-critical data centre facilities and a highly qualified team of IT experts managing the entire solution. The primary categories of services ASPs are providing to date are:

- *Applications provisioning*—essentially providing an information-handling capability, either through proprietary applications such as property management, specialized health-care patient record keeping or analytical/mathematical services or widely-used software packages from the leading ERP and CRM vendors.
- *Infrastructure operations* can include provisioning the customer's desktop environment, as well as operating data centres to host the applications. Data centre operations include the full range of hardware/systems software management, security and disaster recovery as well as the necessary back-office systems such as service usage, monitoring, accounting and billing.
- *Network connectivity*—providing connections to the Internet for end-customers or the application provider (essentially acting like an ISP). Reliability, performance and security of network communications are potentially weak links in the chain.
- *Supporting services*—providing hardware installation and mainten-ance services at customer sites or end-to-end management services for all aspects of implementation and operations across the entire ASP delivery chain for the duration of the ASP contract.

Currently, ASPs are primarily targeted at small or medium-sized enter-prises (SMEs) that cannot afford their own IS functions or computing infrastructures. They provide a fully functioning, 'big-time application' (e.g. such as enterprise resource planning software), accessed via the Internet or a private network without having to pay for the installation, the hardware or the software. Price per user per month (PUPM) has emerged as the standard pricing method for ASP services. The roots of this model stem directly from user-based license pricing for applications. As with user-based applications pricing, the PUPM model allows ASPs to manage pricing based on number of users as well as by categories of users. User categories include designations such as 'power user' or 'inquiry or casual user', which refer to access privileges and functionality. In the future, we are likely to see transaction-based pricing such as billing (price per invoice), e-commerce (price per purchase) and e-marketplaces (price per item bought or sold). The future benefits of the ASP model are seen as:

- Reducing 'costs of ownership'. Although costs and service levels vary widely according to the types of application service provided, studies have indicated that, by renting an application from an ASP, a company can save between 30% and 60% over purchasing and managing the hardware and software for the application themselves.
- Providing more predictable costs with less financial risk. Pay-as-you-go pricing takes the economic burden of buying software and attendant hardware and transfers it to the ASP.
- Flexibility to exit or radically change operating scale. ASP contacts are typically one year with minimal or no exit fees. Many ASPs represent multiple software package vendors, and clients are generally free to add or change services as needed.
- Quicker deployment of new applications and IT capabilities. There can be a significant reduction in the overall cycle time to put a new information system into productive operation.
- Significant reduction in technology complexity. Buying software has always meant having to buy at once all the technology necessary to support it—networks, hardware, support software. ASP's remove that complexity from the equation—theoretically, at least—by providing all the supporting technology themselves. The organization buys a business service rather than a software application and all that goes with it.[52]

The ASP model is relatively new and unproven, and the initial forecasts of its impact as with e-business and e-marketplaces have proven over-optimistic, mainly because the economics of the model are dependent on customer volumes. At this stage, customers seem wary of making use of ASPs either due to the, as yet, few proven advantages as well as a lack of clarity as to the value-added of ASPs and their differing service offers. In selecting an ASP, the checklist in Table 11.6 should be used to clarify what is or is not offered.[53]

Table 11.6 *Checklist for selecting ASP*

- Failsafe back-up servers to ensure $24 \times 7 \times 365$ application uptime
- Automatic load balancing to ensure accessibility
- Functional access limited by highly configurable application-level security
- Automatic off-line data back-up scheduling
- Service level agreements (SLAs) to ensure performance levels are maintained
- Secure Internet access to application servers, via VPN (virtual private network), etc.
- Support for non-public electronic transaction transmissions like EDI
- System set-up function templates to speed implementation
- Simple sign-up to make adding new users easy
- User statistics logs showing user activity by application
- Automatic data upload/download from applications
- Email delivery of user alerts, application reports, etc.
- Online FAQs (frequently asked questions), manuals, training courses
- Online support via email, self-service helpdesks, real-time Internet chat

---

Scott McNealy, CEO of Sun Microsystems, is typical of the enthusiasts in the industry who are promoting the ASP service model: 'Five years from now, if you're a CIO with a head for business, you won't be buying computers anymore. You won't buy software either. You'll rent all your resources from a service provider.'[54] In 2002, the customers remain to be convinced, but much can happen in five years in the IT world.

SUMMARY

This chapter has attempted to describe strategies for managing technology in line with previous strategic approaches to resourcing, information and applications. As such, it has dealt with the strategic issues that need to be managed, issues associated with acquisition, sourcing and application of technology and related services rather than by the specific problems of deploying certain types of technology. The key issues tend to be similar across technologies and have to be considered as part of the overall strategic IS/IT management process and understood by those who are not intimately familiar with any particular technology. Technology strategy should never become the exclusive domain of technologists, although obviously their input to the general management process is very valuable and must be able to be incorporated effectively. Four points are worth reiterating in summary:

1. The theme of the technology strategy should always reflect how it can be deployed to add value to the business. Future business success will occur because today's technology is well used and managed. No sensible organization will assume that future technology will resolve current problems in due course—it is more likely to exacerbate them.

2. The organization must be aware of how technology is being deployed and for what purpose by others in the industry, and even in other industries. The influence of what others—customers, suppliers and competitors—are doing and the technology they are using will become a significant factor in determining strategic technology options in the future, especially for firms that cannot easily adopt a leading role in their environment. A responsive 'following' strategy can be very successful, but it requires accurate monitoring of developments elsewhere. Even then, there is a considerable organizational learning process to manage.

3. It is in the technology that an organization is vulnerable to undue outside pressure from IT suppliers, whose interests will not always coincide with those of the business. That is only to be expected, but it means that the organization must adopt a coherent procurement approach, as it would with any set of critical suppliers. As such, it should also exploit the knowledge and resources of those vendors who are also supplying many other organizations, even some in the same industry. Almost every IT vendor will claim to be providing 'business solutions'. It is important to find out how effective those 'solutions' are elsewhere and, in particular, how they are affecting the industry. The organization would be unwise to rely exclusively on its own judgement of particular technologies without a broader understanding of the business context in which they are being deployed. Many companies ignore this and are led up many blind alleys. Establishing mutually-beneficial business partnerships with a number of key IT suppliers can be very important, provided the management of the business remains in the driving seat!

4. The approach, role and skills of the IT specialist need to change, as the role of technology becomes increasingly ubiquitous and its control becomes ever more decentralized, for example, to:

   - demonstrate business acumen and think creatively about how technology could add new dimensions to the competitive success of the business as well as deliver performance improvements across many business and organizational activities;
   - make sure the infrastructure supports responsiveness and flexibility, and investment in its development not only delivers best

value from the sourcing options available but is aligned with the long-term strategic intentions of the business;

● evolve the infrastructure so that it supports a wider range of e-business based activities, both internal (e.g. knowledge management) and external (e.g. e-commerce);

● obtain understanding and commitment from business managers to the increasingly critical role that IT infrastructure fulfils in the organization and develop a coherent investment plan with a clear rationale that is understood and supported by business managers.

ENDNOTES

1. 'Organising for the 1990s', *EDP Analyser*, Vol. 12, 1986.
2. See R.W. Schmenner, 'How can service businesses survive and prosper', *Sloan Management Review*, Spring, 1986, 21–32.
3. K. Albrecht, *At America's Service*, Dow-JonesIrwin, Homewood, Illinois, 1988; C. Gronroos, 'From scientific management to service management: A management perspective for the age of service competition', *International Journal of Service Industry Management*, Vol. 5, No. 1, 1986, 5–20; A. Parasuraman, V.A. Zeithaml and L.L. Berry, 'SERVQUAL: A multiple item scale for measuring consumer perceptions of service quality', *Journal of Retailing*, Vol. 64, No. 1, 1988, 12–40; V. Zeithaml, A. Parasuraman and L.L. Berry, *Delivering Quality Service: Balancing Customer Perceptions and Expectations*, The Free Press, New York, 1990.
4. G. Whyte, A. Bytheway and C. Edwards, 'Understanding user perceptions of information systems success', *Journal of Strategic Information Systems*, Vol. 6, 1997, 35–68; T.P. van Dyke, L.A. Kappelman and V.R. Prybutok, 'Measuring information systems service quality: concerns on the use of SERVQUAL questionnaire', *MIS Quarterly*, Vol. 21, No. 2, 1997, 195–208.
5. J.M. Kohlemeyer III and J. Ellis Blanton, 'Improving service quality', *Journal of Information Technology Theory & Application*, Vol. 2, No. 1, Spring, 2000; L.F. Pitt, R.T. Watson and C.B. Kavan, 'Service quality: A measure of information systems effectiveness', *MIS Quarterly*, Vol. 19, No. 2, 1995, 173–185; L. Pitt, P. Berthon and N. Lane, 'Gaps within the IS department: barriers to service quality', *Journal of Information Technology*, Vol. 13, 1998, 191–200.
6. M.C. Lacity and R. Hirschheim, *Beyond the Information Systems Outsourcing Bandwagon: The Insourcing Response*, John Wiley & Sons, Chichester, UK, 1995.
7. In financial services, approximately 80–90% of software is developed in-house. Data taken from presentation by C. Kaiser and S. Pollard, Financial Services Software, Lehman Brothers, November 2001, London.
8. D.E. Avison and G. Fitzgerald, *Information Systems Development: Methodologies, Techniques, and Tools*, McGraw-Hill, London, 1998; W.S. Humphrey, *A Discipline for Software Engineering*, Addison-Wesley, New Jersey, 1995; J.M. Nicholas, *Project Management for Business and Technology: Principles and Practices*, second edition, Prentice-Hall, New Jersey, 2001; K. Schwalbe, *Information Technology Project Management*, Prentice-Hall, New Jersey, 2001.
9. N.H Bancroft, H. Seip and A. Sprengal, *Implementing SAPR/3: How to Introduce a Large System into a Large Organization*, second edition, Manning Publications, Greenwich, Connecticut, 1998; T.H. Davenport, *Mission Critical: Realising the Promise of Enterprise Systems*, Harvard Business School Press, Boston, 2000.
10. *Achieving the Benefits from Software Package Enabled Business Improvement Programmes: Best Practice Guidelines*, The IMPACT Programme, London, 1998.
11. *ERP's Second Wave: Maximising the Value of ERP Processes*, Deloitte Consulting, New York, 1998; M.L. Markus, S. Axline, D. Petrie and C. Tanis, 'Learning from adopters' experiences with ERP: Problems encountered and successes achieved', *Journal of Information Technology*, Vol. 15, 2000, 245–265; *Achieving the Benefits from Software Package*

Enabled Business Improvement Programmes: Best Practice Guidelines, The IMPACT Programme, London, 1998.

12. *Achieving the Benefits from Software Package Enabled Business Improvement Programmes: Best Practice Guidelines*, The IMPACT Programme, London, 1998.

13. M.L. Markus, S. Axline, D. Petrie and C. Tanis, 'Learning from adopters' experiences with ERP: Problems encountered and successes achieved', *Journal of Information Technology*, Vol. 15, 2000, 245–265.

14. *Achieving the Benefits from Software Package Enabled Business Improvement Programmes: Best Practice Guidelines*, The IMPACT Programme, London, 1998.

15. N.H. Bancroft, H. Seip and A. Sprengal, *Implementing SAPR/3: How to Introduce a Large System into a Large Organization*, second edition, Manning Publications, Greenwich, Conneticut, 1998; T.H. Davenport, *Mission Critical: Realising the Promise of Enterprise Systems*, Harvard Business School Press, Boston, 2000; S. Knox, S. Maklan, A. Payne, J. Peppard and L. Ryles, *Customer Relationship Management: Marketplace Perspectives*, Butterworth-Heinneman, 2002.

16. D.T. McKay and D.W. Brockway, 'Building IT infrastructure for the 1990s', *Stage by Stage*, Vol. 9, No. 3, 1989, 1–11.

17. M. Broadbent, P. Weill and B.S. Neo, 'Strategic context and patterns of IT infrastructure capability', *Journal of Strategic Information Systems*, Vol. 8, 1999, 157–187.

18. R.B. Grossman and M.B. Parker, 'Betting the business: Strategic programs to rebuild core information systems', *Office Technology & People*, Vol. 5, No. 4, 1989, 235–243.

19. N.B. Duncan, 'Capturing flexibility of information technology infrastructure: A study of resource characteristics and their measure', *Journal of Management Information Systems*, Vol. 12, No. 2, 1995, 37–57.

20. K. Breu, C. Hemmingway, D. Bridger and M. Strathern, 'Workforce agility: The new employee strategy for the knowledge economy', *Journal of Information Technology*, forthcoming 2002.

21. P.A. Strassman, *The Squandered Computer: Evaluating the Business Alignment of Information Technology*, The Economics Press, New Canaan, Connecticut, 1997 and *Information Productivity: Accessing the Information Management Costs of US Industrial Companies*, The Economics Press, Conn, 1997; *Productivity in the United States, 1995–2000*, McKinsey Global Institute, October, 2001.

22. P. Keen, *Shaping the Future*, Harvard Business School Press, Boston, 1991.

23. M. Broadbent, P. Weill and B.S. Ned, 'Strategic context and patterns of IT infrastructure capability', *Journal of Strategic Information Systems*, Vol. 8, 1999, 157–187.

24. *Releasing The Value of Knowledge: A Cranfield School of Management and Microsoft Survey of UK Industry*, Cranfield School of Management, Bedford, UK, 2000.

25. *Creating the Agile Workforce: An Executive Summary*, Cranfield School of Management, Bedford and Microsoft, Reading, UK; K. Breu, C. Hemmingway, D. Bridger and M. Strathern, 'Workforce agility: The new employee strategy for the knowledge economy', *Journal of Information Technology*, forthcoming 2002.

26. M. Broadbent, P. Weill and B.S. Neo, 'Strategic context and patterns of IT infrastructure capability', *Journal of Strategic Information Systems*, Vol. 8, 1999, 157–187.

27. P. Bulasubramarian, N. Kulatilaka and J. Storck, 'Managing information technology investments using a real options approach', *Journal of Strategic Information Systems*, Vol. 9, 2000, 39–62.

28. W.L. Currie, 'Outsourcing in the private and public sectors: An unpredictable IT strategy', *European Journal of Information Systems*, Vol. 4, 226–236; W.L. Currie, 'Using multiple suppliers to mitigate the risks of IT outsourcing at ICI and Wessex Water', *Journal of Information Technology*, Vol. 13, No. 3, 1998, 169–180; M.C. Lacity, L.P. Willcocks and D.F. Feeny, 'The value of selective IT sourcing', *Sloan Management Review*, Spring, 1996, 13–25; M.C. Lacity, L.P. Willcocks and D.F. Feeny, 'IT outsourcing: Maximizing flexibility and control', *Harvard Business Review*, May–June 1995, 84–93; A. Kakabadse and N. Kakabadse, *Smart Sourcing*, Palgrave, Basingstoke, UK, 2002.

29. L. Willcocks and C. Sauer, 'High risks and hidden costs in IT outsourcing', in *Financial Times Mastering Risk*, May 2000.

30. J. Cross, 'IT outsourcing: BP's competitive approach', *Harvard Business Review*, May–June 1995, 94–104.

31. J. Cross, M.J. Earl and J.L. Sampler, 'Transforming the IT function at British Petroleum', *MIS Quarterly*, Vol. 21, No. 4, 1997, 401–423.

32. L.P. Willcocks and M.C. Lacity, 'Introduction—the sourcing and outsourcing of IS: Shock of the new', in L.P. Willcocks and M.C. Lacity, eds, *Strategic Sourcing of Information Systems*, John Wiley & Sons, Chichester, UK, 1998, 1–41.

33. M. Lacity and R. Hirschheim, 'What problems are organizations solving with IT outsour-

cing?', in W. Currie and R. Galliers, eds, *Rethinking MIS*, Oxford University Press, Oxford, 1997, pp. 316–360.
34.   H. Baukney, 'Can we share?', *CIO Magazine*, 15 June 2000.
35.   *Computing*, 20 September 2001.
36.   M.J. Earl, 'The risks of outsourcing IT', *Sloan Management Review*, Spring, 1996, 26–32; M.C. Lacity and L.P. Willcocks, 'An empirical investigation of IT outsourcing practices: Lessons from experiences', *MIS Quarterly*, Vol. 22, No. 3, 1998, 363–408; M.C. Lacity and R. Hirschheim, *Beyond the Information Systems Outsourcing Bandwagon: The Insourcing Response*, John Wiley & Sons, Chichester, UK, 1995; F.W. McFarlan and R.L. Nolan, 'How to manage an IT outsourcing alliance', *Sloan Management Review*, Winter, 1995, 9–23; L.P. Willcocks, M.C. Lacity and T. Kern, 'Risk mitigation in IT outsourcing strategy revisited: Longitudinal case research at LISA', *Journal of Strategic Information Systems*, Vol. 8, 1999, 285–314; L.P. Willcocks and M.C. Lacity, 'IT outsourcing in insurance services: Risk, creative contracting and business advantage', *Information Systems Journal*, Vol. 9, 1999, 163–180.
37.   L. Willcocks and C. Sauer, 'High risks and hidden costs in IT outsourcing', in *Financial Times Mastering Risk*, May 2000.
38.   L.P. Willcocks and G. Fitzgerald, *A Business Guide to IT Outsourcing*, Business Intelligence, London, 1994.
39.   L.P. Willcocks, G. Fitzgerald and M. Lacity, 'To outsource IT or not?: Recent research on economics and evaluation practice', *European Journal of Information Systems*, Vol. 5, 1996, 143–160.
40.   M.J. Earl, 'The risks of outsourcing IT', *Sloan Management Review*, Spring, 1996, 26–32.
41.   A. DiRomualdo and V. Gurbaxani, 'Strategic intent for IT outsourcing', *Sloan Management Review*, Summer, 1998, 67–80; G. Fitzgerald and V. Michell, 'The IT outsourcing market-place: Vendors and their selection', paper presented at *The Management Challenges of IT Conference*, Cranfield School of Management, Bedford, UK, July 1994.
42.   L.P. Willcocks and C. Sauer, 'High risks and hidden costs in IT outsourcing', *Financial Times: Mastering Risk*, 23 May, 2000.
43.   M.J. Earl, 'The risks of outsourcing IT', *Sloan Management Review*, Spring, 1996, 26–32.
44.   M.C. Lacity and R. Hirschheim, *Beyond the Information Systems Outsourcing Bandwagon: The Insourcing Response*, John Wiley & Sons, Chichester, UK, 1995.
45.   A. DiRomualdo and V. Gurbaxani, 'Strategic intent for IT outsourcing', *Sloan Management Review*, Summer, 1998, 67–80.
46.   See M.C. Lacity, L.P. Willcocks and D.F. Feeny, 'Sourcing information technology capability: A framework for decision-making', in M.J. Earl, ed., *Information Management: The Organizational Dimensional*, Oxford University Press, New York, 1996, pp. 399–425. The discussion that follows draws on this paper.
47.   M. Lacity and R. Hirschheim, 'What problems are organizations solving with IT outsourcing?', in W. Currie and R. Galliers, eds., *Rethinking MIS*, Oxford University Press, Oxford, 1997, pp. 326–360.
48.   L. Willcocks, G. Fitzgerald and M. Lacity, 'To outsource IT or not?: Recent research on economics and evaluation practice', *European Journal of Information Systems*, Vol. 5, 1996, 143–160.
49.   M.C. Lacity, L.P. Willcocks and D.F. Feeny, 'IT outsourcing: Maximizing flexibility and control', *Harvard Business Review*, May–June 1995, 84–93.
50.   M. Lacity and R. Hirschheim, 'What problems are organizations solving with IT outsourcing?', in W. Currie and R. Galliers, eds, *Rethinking MIS*, Oxford University Press, Oxford, 1997, pp. 326–360.
51.   M.C. Lacity and R. Hirschheim, 'Information systems outsourcing bandwagon', *Sloan Management Review*, Fall, 1993, 73–86.
52.   For an informed discussion on this and other aspects of ASPs, see J. Hagel III and J. Seely Brown, 'Your next IT strategy', *Harvard Business Review*, October 2001, 105–113.
53.   From 'The value of opting for an ASP', Sponsored Supplement, *CIO Magazine*, 2000.
54.   Quoted in M. Raisinghani and M. Kwiatkowski, 'The future of application service providers', *Information Strategy: The Executive's Journal*, Summer, 2001, 16–23.

12
Strategic Planning for Information Systems: *Quo Vadis?*

By now, it should be clear that information technology (IT) has today assumed great prominence in most organizations. Thanks primarily to the hype that has accompanied the Internet, particularly that surrounding e-commerce and the dot.com phenomenon, IT has become an important item on the agenda of senior business management. Following the run-up to the millennium, which was dominated by investment to deal with the 'Y2K' problem, a combination of latent demand and Internet-based opportunism resulted in a very significant increase in spending on IT as management bought into anything with the 'e' label. However, for many organizations, the economic returns from this spending have not been forthcoming. The recent McKinsey[1] study of IT and productivity noted that 'contrary to conventional wisdom, widespread application of IT was not the most important cause of the post-1995 productivity acceleration.' The report went on to note that 'where IT did play a role, it was often a necessary but not sufficient enabler of productivity gains. Business process changes were also necessary to reap the full productivity benefits ...' Clearly, technology on its own, no matter how leading edge, is not enough, which may seem an obvious statement to make, but this lesson has yet to filter through to many management teams. There is now a danger in some organizations that IT may lose its position on the management agenda as it is seen, yet again, as having failed to deliver on its promise.

Rangan and Adner[2] diagnosed this prevailing situation when they noted, 'while the powerful technology of the Internet opens the way to new opportunities (new markets, new customers, new products and new ways of doing business), it carries in its wake the threat that the pursuit of opportunity will be driven by what is technologically feasible, rather than what is strategically desirable.' This, unfortunately, is often what has been occurring and lies behind many of the problems that organizations have been experiencing regarding their IS/IT investments. Buying technology solves no problems; in fact, it tends to create more. It does enable new opportunities; but those opportunities can only be realized from its business application within a strategic context.

The high-profile failure of online sports and fashion retailer boo.com is illustrative of the 'irrational exuberance' that surrounded IT investment in the late 1990s. As *The Economist* observed at that time, 'boo.com went bust not because it was a dot.com, but because it was a badly run business. Its management was inexperienced, over ambitious, guilty of serial execution errors and uninterested in controlling costs. On-line or off-line, that is a rap list long enough to sink most firms.'[3] So, despite using some very sophisticated technology, boo.com failed for fundamental business and management reasons.

While business imperatives must dominate most decisions regarding IS/IT, there is one constant that ensures that organizations will never remain static: that is change. No matter whether the economy is shrinking or growing, and regardless of industry sector, organizations will always be under pressure to change. For many years, it was enough for IS/IT investment to keep up with business change and for the IS function to provide effective support services to the business. In the mid-1980s, the strategic information systems era arrived with the emergence of the use of IT for competitive advantage. Yet, nearly 20 years later, competitive advantage from the use of IT has proved elusive for most organizations. The majority, however, through lack of IS/IT investment, are at a competitive disadvantage. As we have illustrated throughout this book, the roles of IS/IT, the IS function and the CIO have also changed significantly during this time. The IS function and the CIO must not only keep up with business strategy but are increasingly expected to inform, and even drive, strategic thinking.

In this book, we have shown that the conventional view that business strategy drives IS strategy, which in turn drives IT strategy, is not sufficient for this expanding role of IS/IT. Such a perspective effectively ensures that IS/IT investment will always lag behind business strategy. It can also limit strategic options by denying senior managers insight into either the opportunities offered by new technology or the reality of what IS/IT can actually deliver. If IS/IT is to make a genuine contribution to business strategy, a different model and logic is required that allows the capabilities of IS/IT to be an intrinsic component of strategy rather than one of its consequences. While we have presented an approach and tool kit for IS strategy development and emphasized that it is a continuous process, there is still a danger that it is seen as a once-off activity and that, once completed, senior managers can get on with their 'real' jobs. In addition, the approach presented also shows how organizations can seek out opportunities for IS/IT—a strategic information systems era perspective. Even with well-thought-out IS/IT strategies, we have seen organizations fail to deliver business benefits. The strategic management of IS/IT must therefore be expanded. Our research is pointing us toward the emergence of a fourth era in the evolution of IS/IT in organizations. But, before elaborating on this emerging new era, a resume of some of the key ideas from the earlier chapters follow—to summarize the situation today. It also considers what has happened in the past six years, since the second edition of the book, and how these developments have affected the IS/IT strategy field.

A BRIEF RESUME OF SOME KEY IDEAS

As a significant organizational activity, strategic planning for IS/IT is now 20 years old. Whatever processes are being successfully developed and adopted today have to be considered against the backdrop of an erratic evolution of IS/IT in most organizations, the increasing business pressures faced by organizations, and the opportunities and constraints presented by the technology and our understanding of how to use it.[4] All these are changing faster than ever before, hence the IS strategy process and management approaches need to evolve and respond to a more challenging environment and organizations need to learn from experience how best to develop an IS/IT strategy and execute the plans. Carrying out IS/IT strategic studies can help reorientate the IS/IT strategy process in many organizations, but, as has been said already, IS/IT strategy formulation and planning is an ongoing process, not an event, and repeated studies do not offer a smooth path to success.

Comparing the development of IS strategies to the development of business strategies offers some insight. Tools and techniques of business strategy are continuing to develop and processes are changing—especially in devolving to and involving more of the business expertise and knowledge that is spread throughout the organization. At the current stage of IS/IT development, organizations still have to think explicitly and overtly about IS strategy, and, for all the understanding of the need for integration with the business strategy, it seems it may still be some time before it becomes intuitively included in day-to-day strategic thinking. The IS/IT strategy process must continue to evolve to become a natural part of business strategic management both in concept and in practice. This needs to happen soon, given that, in most industrial, commercial and public sector environments, IS/IT is steadily but surely changing the products and services, trading structures and relationships of firms in many industries, and the nature of business activities, organizational structures and how people work.

During the 1990s, theories of business strategy and competitive advantage also evolved. As described earlier in the book, resource-based theory, when compared with previous theories, perhaps offers a better explanation of why some organizations achieve and sustain advantage over an extended period. This is of particular relevance to the role of IS/IT, given that it is an increasingly significant business resource, available to more and more organizations as technology economics improve. Throughout this edition, the basic tenets of resource-based theory (as well as research findings from others who have explored its relevance to the subject) have been referred to in order to explain, where possible, why the strategic management of IS/IT is more successful in some organizations than others. The latter part of the chapter returns to this theme when the future of IS/IT strategies is considered.

It is unrealistic to attempt to summarize all the contents of the 11 preceding chapters. However, there are some basic ideas or models that are core concepts in any approach to IS/IT strategy formulation and planning. Foremost is its relationship with the business environment and business strategic management. As Figure 12.1 shows, there are five key relationships, as described in Chapter 1, and can be summarized as follows:

a.   technology can support the strategy of an organization (alignment of business and IS/IT strategies);
b.   technology can also define the business, shaping the business strategy (competitive impact of technology);
c.   competitor moves influence and affect the organization and the markets in which it competes;
d.   strategic plays made by the organization influence the market and competitor moves;
e.   technological innovations can have a disruptive impact on industries, often redefining the boundaries of traditional industries.

Understanding the implications and achieving the appropriate impact is obviously a complex and difficult process due to the need to react quickly to a range of changing circumstances, and to plan ahead to actually obtain and implement the applications and supporting infrastructures. Organizations have limited resources and the key to effective strategy is deploying them on the activities that deliver most value to the organization.

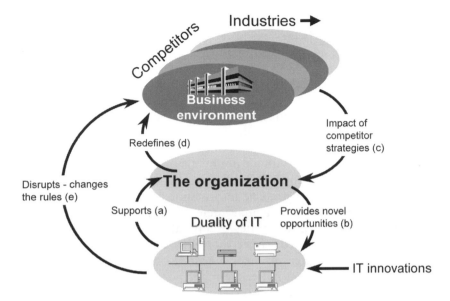

Figure 12.1   *The influence and impact*

In order to enable an ongoing IS/IT strategy process that allows for evolving circumstances, the main inputs—the external and internal business and external and internal IS/IT environments—have to be reviewed continually. The importance and implications of each have been discussed in Chapter 3. The eventual result of the assessment and analysis of these is the application portfolio required or possessed at any point in time by the business. That portfolio of business applications and its supporting information and IT infrastructure will be contributing more or less successfully to the business in relation to its environment and its strategy. This implies that applications should be managed according to their value or contribution to the business. One important feature of the portfolio approach is that it allows for the products of both 'top-down', formal strategic analysis and creative, informal strategic thinking. By managing the whole portfolio in relation to the way the contributions of applications can change (a life-cycle view), the best aspects of formal and informal planning are blended together. In practice, this reconciles the views of those who argue the merits of strategy 'formulation' (by analysis) or strategy 'formation' (by emerging synthesis).

Any IS/IT strategy process must be capable of rapid and partial reuse to interpret changes in any of the inputs and adapt the strategy appropriately. This implies a framework for quick and accurate interpretation, in IS application terms, of changes in the environment. The framework is effectively the 'logical' steps in the strategy process whereby techniques can be adopted and applied in a coherent yet focused way. Following discussion in Chapters 4 and 5 of the various techniques—derived from IS/IT and business strategy formulation and planning approaches—such a framework is described in Chapter 6.

The portfolio merely represents a target for the business, how it can be delivered needs to be expressed in more detail, in terms of the development and beneficial operation of applications, and the provision of resources and technology. Without doubt, the most important and hence challenging area of the portfolio for business management is the strategic quadrant. The nature of strategic information systems was described in Chapter 1, where the new management challenges involved in these applications were outlined. Strategic applications involve changing the way business is conducted, either externally or internally, and consequently require a degree of involvement by senior management not traditionally expected and not easily made possible. How the organization chooses to organize and govern the IS activities and how roles and responsibilities are allocated will have a significant effect on whether or not it can devise and achieve the optimum set of applications, as discussed in Chapter 8.

The other major components of IS/IT strategies, each of which has to be managed effectively within the overall strategy, were considered in more detail in the latter part of the book. These components, the *3i's*—investment, information and infrastructure—were each considered within the overall concepts of the portfolio. High-level, 'generic', IS/IT application management strategies were described in Chapter 7; they provide the guiding principles that lead to consistent decision making and relevant ways of managing each of the 3i's above, once more regarding the existing or intended contribution to the business. These implementation 'strategies' can be related sensibly to the different approaches to planning that are likely to define the need for applications (see Figure 7.6). This suggests a natural alignment between the means by which decisions are made on *what* is required and *how* best to satisfy the requirement.

Any IS/IT strategy will be the result of many compromises. The issues that affect where and how those compromises should be made will change due to external, as well as internal, factors and the processes of IS/IT strategic management must ensure that the net effect of these compromises is not detrimental to the business strategy. As organizations become more dependent on IS/IT for business success and development, the compromises will be made less and less due to supply-side issues, although the problem of compromising the long-term plans to satisfy short-term business issues will remain. The decisions are business decisions and the strategy should provide at least the basis of understanding the implications and guidance as to the best trade-off.

IS STRATEGY FORMULATION AND PLANNING IN THE 1990s

If the 1980s were characterized by the emergence of desktop computing and the acceptance that IS/IT could deliver competitive advantage, the 1990s could be characterized by:

- An emphasis on alignment between IS/IT and business management across a number of dimensions, as described by Venkatraman and others, in order to balance the influence of IS/IT on business development with the need to deploy IS/IT to improve performance. The influential Venkatraman and Henderson alignment model, described in Chapter 1 (Figure 1.8), is reproduced again as Figure 12.2.
- The rapid increases in connectivity available through IT at all levels—global, industry, interorganization and within organizations and between people—has made providing, accessing and exchanging information easier or cheaper than ever before, opening up new options for every organization and creating opportunities for completely new organizations to enter industries and provide new information-based products and services. Although many had flawed business models or little competency outside building web applications, the dot.coms created an enormous awareness of the potential

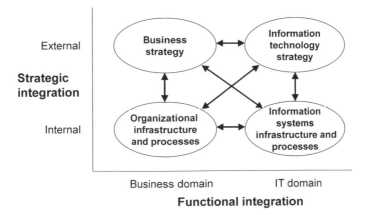

Figure 12.2   The strategic alignment model

of IT (or 'e') among business managers. As we write, business-to-business (B2B) e-marketplaces or e-hubs are having less actual impact than pundits predicted in 2000, mainly because the forecasts were quite ridiculous, but also because the potential improvements to industry performance take time to be understood, in addition to the not insignificant time required to implement new processes and systems among trading partners and assimilate the changes.

• Equally, rapid developments in the IT 'supply chain' are enabling more and more of an organization's requirements for IS/IT to be sourced from external suppliers. Increasing the options available is only an advantage if the organization knows *what* it is trying to achieve and *why*, otherwise *how* it does it will be a constraint to its strategy, whether its IS/IT requirements are sourced internally or externally. *Smart sourcing* is easy to prescribe, but not that easy to achieve successfully, as discussed in the previous chapter.

• The widespread implementation of business re-engineering initiatives in organizations recognized that, potentially, more benefits from IS/IT investment would emerge through the redesign of processes to make use of the capabilities provided by technology, compared with simply deploying IT to improve existing processes.

During the 1990s, some writers expressed scepticism about the value or even the feasibility of producing strategic IS plans in the increasingly dynamic IT and business environment. Much of that scepticism was based on the apparent lack of success in many organizations of implementing the strategies they had developed. However, the reasons for this 'failure' could be due to three factors:

1. the appropriateness of the IS/IT strategy formulation and planning process given the particular circumstances of the organization;
2. the feasibility of achieving the objectives of the IS/IT strategy process;
3. the relevance of the output from the process to the business situation.

It is the last of these that can be observed and described in terms of success and failure, but it is wholly dependent on the other two factors, which is where the problems usually lie. The quality of the output will only improve if expectations are based on achieving a realistic IS strategy from an appropriate process. The real need is to manage IS/IT strategically over an extended period, ensuring that IS/IT delivers the maximum possible benefit to the business. IS/IT strategy formulation and planning is only one component of strategic management. It would seem unwise to suggest that IS/IT strategy formulation and planning is not valuable, based on the often overambitious objectives set and the inappropriate processes that many of the organizations have employed. Earl's work, in particular, demonstrates the need for an 'organizational' approach to IS strategy formulation and planning in the complex environment of today. The research evidence available shows that only a minority of organizations appear to have adopted an adequately 'organizational' approach to IS strategy.

It has also been argued that the IS strategy process has not kept pace with the impact, complexity or expectations of information systems and technology. Some have likened the early 'formulative' IS planning methods to 'structured methods' for IS development and they suffer from similar limitations. Fink,[5] Ciborra,[6] Checkland[7] and others suggest that, just as 'soft systems' methods offer a more 'organization-friendly' counterbalance to structured methods, an equivalent 'softer', iterative organization-wide ability to think and learn about the impact of IS/IT is needed to complement more technique-based planning processes. The issues of IS strategy development, as discussed earlier, can be separated into impact and alignment aspects. Since many of the impact issues will need more dispersed, organic and iterative processes for assessment, this also has implications for improving the alignment of IS/IT strategies, both in their development and their implementation.

When the second edition of the book was published in 1996, the final chapter attempted to predict how IS/IT strategic planning might develop in the coming years. In particular, two emerging themes were explored:

- organizational development based on IS/IT;
- industry development based on IS/IT.

While these have proved to be important to many organizations, the detailed evolution has not perhaps followed the predicted path. Some further implications of these still-evolving aspects of the role and impact of IS/IT are considered below.

ORGANIZATION DEVELOPMENT BASED ON IS/IT

Perhaps the predictions of Drucker,[8] embodied in a quotation from his thought-provoking article, are, to some degree, occurring in almost every organization. He wrote: *'we are entering a period of change—a shift from the command and control organisation, to the information-based organisation—the organisation of knowledge specialists ... it is the management challenge of the future.'*

The downsizing and delayering that has occurred during the past decade has changed the nature of organizational structures, with an emphasis on matrix or 'team-based' structures in the deliberate intent of both achieving 'more with less' and changing the way the business is operated and managed. Whether this can be said to be based around the 'organization of knowledge specialists' is less clear; however, these changes have in turn produced significant effects on the way IS/IT is used and managed.

In parallel with these changes to structure, brought about primarily by economic and competitive pressures, many of the forecast implications of the changes in the economics and capabilities of IT put forward by Zuboff[9] and others have also occurred. Zuboff talked about 'informating' the workforce, whereby job scope is extended due to the information available to the clerical and professional staff, 'empowering' them to make more decisions without the need for functional separation and control of activities. This again leads to team-based structures rather than hierarchical ones. The combination of an infrastructure of powerful workstations on every desk, now also in most briefcases and homes, and mobile personal digital assistants (PDAs), linked through web-based networks—both fixed and wireless—in addition to advances in software functionality and ease of use, have made new ways of working possible. They are not, however, always to the benefit of the individual who is now able to stay connected to his or her work 24 hours a day, leading inevitably to organizational expectations of staff working longer hours.

Handy[10] considered the whole subject of how future organizations will be 'structured', if at all! Like others, he suggested that 'intellectual capital' is the critical strategic resource of many organizations in achieving advantages.[11] The technology employed in systems of information and knowledge management will be the key enablers to release this new 'capital'. He correctly predicted that IT would change what people do, where and how they do it and the organizations they do it for or in! IT, combined with social changes, changing demographics and the economic consequences, will mean that organizations will have to use information systems and organizational knowledge better, not only to remain competitive but also to be able to obtain and keep highly skilled staff.

Both Handy and Drucker suggested how organizational structures will continue to change, becoming flatter, more federal and more flexible, comprising a management or professional critical core of people, a largely subcontracted set of specialist skilled resources and a flexible, part-time distributed low-skilled workforce, all linked through IT-based systems to plan, allocate and control the work to be done.

All this implies that businesses and organizations may be built around information structures rather than IS being used to make a business or organization structure work more effectively. It could therefore be argued that 'organizational design' rather than 'organizational fit' should be a key consideration in IS/IT strategy.[12] Strategies for dealing with the organizational relationships, job and people issues will become more important. In current IS/IT strategies, the potentially far-reaching implications on organization structuring and job roles are only really just being considered. However, many reorganizations of structures, activities and the roles of individuals have destroyed information and knowledge structures, and have meant that IS/IT investments are prematurely obsolete and have to be replaced or simply decay into uselessness.

Others suggest that reorganization is less feasible because of constraints imposed by systems (or even technology), which is at least a realization that IS/IT and the organization are interrelated. Obviously, IS/IT use can be made more responsive to organizational and personnel changes by better design. However, in the future, management should consider how it can develop the organization to exploit IS/IT before making the changes. This will require a far better understanding of the impact of IS/IT on organizational relationships, job roles, use of knowledge, etc., which in time will provide new techniques of analysis to add to the strategic tool kit. While organizations seem willing to invest large sums in technology, they seem less willing to invest in educating and training their staff to use it effectively.

While rapid advances in IT have enabled more and more types of information (documents, images, voice, video, etc.) to be captured, stored and processed and exchanged more efficiently and usefully, the plethora of ways in which IT is employed could either reduce the overall benefit or even create significant future business problems. A word of warning was sounded in the conclusions of the Massachusetts Institute of Technology's 'The Corporation of the 1990s' research program.[13] Two of the conclusions were:

1. integration, both internally and with external partners, provides the main opportunities for improving business effectiveness through IS;
2. information (asset) management will remain a major problem and limit the rate at which business changes can be made.

This implies that major challenges remain for IS/IT strategy if maximum organizational and business benefit is to be obtained from IS/IT. Managing the 'information (and knowledge) assets' of an organization has emerged as an area of significant concern, as discussed in Chapter 10.

Industry Development Based on IS/IT

As early as 1987, Robinson and Stanton[14] proposed a developmental model of the increasing opportunities presented by what has become known as e-commerce. They identified four main types of potential benefit:

1. *process automation* (e.g. exchange of orders, invoices, etc.);
2. *boundary extension*—integrating processes carried out among trading partners and probably changing the way these processes are carried out internally in each partner;
3. *service enhancement*—sharing more or different types of information with trading partners to improve the performance of the value chain;
4. *product innovation*—providing products and services that customers require based on information.

We have, of course, seen all these opportunities extend to business-to-consumer (B2C) relationships with the commercialization of the Internet.

The consequence of this is that organizations are now focused on developing new relationships with both customers and suppliers; implementing customer relationship management (CRM) systems being one example of this trend. Rockart and Short[15] suggested that five forces are causing organizations to enter mutually-dependent relationships that—without effective support from IS/IT—will not always be successful. The forces are:

- *globalization*—in terms of both markets and sources of supply;
- *time to market*—the ability to develop and deliver new products quickly requires cooperation with suppliers and channels of distribution;
- *risk management*—in order to understand and share risks across trading partners by sharing information about changing market demand;
- *service*—being able to provide service excellence by bringing together resources and knowledge to meet more demanding customer expectations;
- *cost*—carrying out essential value-adding processes at the lowest cost, based on where in the industry the tasks can be carried out most economically.

They argued that IT provides the essential 'wiring together', or connectivity, of individuals and organizations to meet these demands. This becomes ever more important as organizations focus on 'core competencies' and rely on others to provide the complementary resources and services required. They also recognize that this 'value chain integration' of external information-based relationships requires internal changes and a realignment to external-facing processes from functional structures This in turn requires a reorientation of internal systems and (from yet another direction!) the need for systems to support team working—both internal and in collaborative teams with people in other organizations. All of this implies that a key role for the IS function is to establish the infrastructure to make this possible, by working closely with their counterparts in partner organizations.

Many of the predictions of Malone and colleagues[16] regarding electronic marketplaces are turning into reality, albeit more slowly than predicted. They argued that electronic markets will make fundamental changes to how some firms conduct their business. They predicted that firms would move away from vertical integration within the value chain and toward specialization in one process within the value chain. Trading exchanges between consumers and the firms in the chain, as well as among those firms, have become more widespread and more efficient, reducing the potential economic advantages of the firm carrying out a number of processes in the chain. The focus on organizational 'core competencies' as a source of advantage also suggests a similar evolution for perhaps different reasons.

An obvious conclusion that can be drawn is that a key input to many organizations' business strategies should be the potential changes in business relationships and market and industry structures that IS/IT investments are creating. This increases the importance of including IS/IT in the earliest stages of business strategic thinking, to understand the potential impact. Given the relatively unpredictable way electronic markets and electronic commerce have evolved to date, it becomes even more important to have a process that enables new strategies to emerge and be blended together with existing strategic intentions, as described in Figure 3.2.

THE ORGANIZATIONAL COMPETENCIES TO MANAGE IS/IT STRATEGICALLY

In previous editions of this book, a structural model of the relationships among business, IS and IT strategies was at the core of the alignment concerning *what* had to be done and *how* it could be done. That model (see Figure 1.6) is still important, given that many organizations fail to realize that the IS strategy is the essential link between business strategy and the use of IT. However, it does not really represent the continuous

Figure 12.3   *Information systems competencies*

nature of strategy formation and its implementation. As has been said earlier, having strategies is not enough—the organization must be able to deliver the benefits those strategies predict, to all relevant stakeholders and be able to adapt the strategies quickly and effectively as circumstances change. This implies the existence of organizational competencies that enable continuous interaction among the key components of strategic management—establishing the strategic vision and direction, planning and implementation. These are no longer sequential steps but, particularly in the case of IS/IT, need to interact and be changed as options or constraints emerge.

Based on our research, which, as described in Chapter 8, built on the work of others who have studied information, systems and technology-related competencies, a more appropriate model that represents the world of IS/IT strategy was described. That model is reproduced in Figure 12.3.

This model illustrates the organizational competencies required for IS/IT to make a sustained contribution toward strategic objectives and continuously deliver value to the organization. The *strategy* competency is the ability to identify and evaluate the implications of IT-based opportunities as integral parts of business strategy. *Defining the IS contribution* refers to the ability to translate business strategy into an IS strategy. This includes the ability to plan process and systems changes in such a way that they match business priorities. *Defining the IT capability* involves translating strategy into information architectures and IT infrastructures that will serve business needs effectively over the long term. *Exploitation* is the competency to maximize the business benefits realized from IS/IT investments through the effective utilization of business information, software applications and IT services. *Delivering solutions* is the organization's capacity to develop, implement and operate IS/IT solutions for the business that exploit the capabilities of available technologies. Finally, the *supply* competency involves creating a resource capacity and supply chain for maintaining business information, applications and IT infrastructure.

The main purpose of the model as a strategic management tool is to enable an organization to identify the reasons why it is more or less successful in managing IS/IT. Those reasons are based on its ability or otherwise to carry out, consistently well, each and all of the 26 IS competencies described in Chapter 8. The view presented in this model balances the need to have resources from both the IS function and the rest of the business deployed in a way to both identify the best IS/IT investments and gain the full benefits from them. In today's environment, and we believe even more critically in the future, any organization that does not possess the full range of competencies, in-house or provided by proficient external suppliers, will be seriously inhibited from gaining many of the benefits available from IS/IT.

While there has been much criticism of the 'competencies' of IS functions and IS/IT professionals by many writers, other studies show that merely improving the quality and calibre of IS/IT resources achieves little if the organization is not capable of utilizing them effectively. The example quoted in Chapter 8 and depicted in Figure 8.12 is typical of the situation found in many organizations.

In a recent survey,[17] a cross-section of IT directors/CIOs and business managers, from a range of industries, were asked to assess their organizations' actual level of performance of each area of IS/IT competency, in relation to the level essential to achieve long-term sustained success. While not generalizable, the results were unerringly consistent across all the organizations in the survey. Only those competencies that 50% or more respondents deemed inadequate are included in the list below, with the top three being deemed inadequate by over 80%. Figure 12.4 shows the positioning of the areas of weakness on the competency model:

1. *business strategy*—an *inability* to ensure that business strategy formulation identifies the most advantageous uses of information, systems and technology;
2. *benefits delivery*—an *inability* to monitor, measure and evaluate the benefits delivered from IS/IT investment and use;

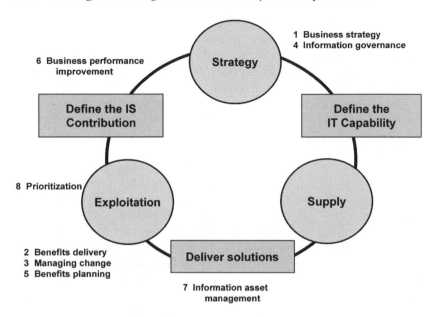

Figure 12.4 *Information systems 'in competencies'*

3. *managing change*—an *inability* to make the business and organizational changes required to maximize the benefits without detrimental impact on stakeholders.

4. *information governance*—an *inability* to define information management policies for the organization and the roles and responsibilities of general management and the IS function;

5. *benefits planning*—an inability explicitly to identify and plan to realize the benefits from IS investments;

6. *business performance improvement*—an *inability* to identify the knowledge and information needed to deliver strategic objectives through improved management processes;

7. *information asset management*—an *inability* to establish and operate processes that ensure data, information and knowledge-management activities meet organizational needs and satisfy corporate policies;

8. *prioritization*—an *inability* to ensure that the portfolio of investments in applications and technology produces the maximum return from the resources available.

It could be argued that these are the 'eight imperatives' for strategic IS management in the same way that others have proposed 'eight imperatives for the IS function'! It is not a coincidence that, in this book, large sections of many chapters are devoted to approaches and techniques of direct relevance to these particular eight competencies. Interestingly, *all* the competencies in the framework under the heading 'exploitation' were deemed to be inadequate (i.e. Benefits Planning, Change Management and Benefits Delivery).

The respondents to this survey were predominately from the IS function, thus giving an unbalanced view. However, having carried out IS competency assessments in many organizations when business and IS managers evaluated their situation together, the same eight areas of relative 'incompetency' are consistently in the top ten.

Of course, there are interrelationships among both competencies and incompetency. A lack of ability in one competency can produce inabilities elsewhere, and it is important to identify these relationships. For example, in a large bank, it was concluded from the analysis that the inability to set and sustain priorities was the root cause of many apparent inabilities elsewhere. No processes or mechanisms existed for agreeing and setting priorities and the almost continuous reprioritization, and the organizational conflict that resulted, undermined the overall strategy and disrupted many major investment programs. In a travel company that had ventured into selling on the Web via an almost in-dependent Internet channel, it was concluded that serious problems in the Information Asset Management competency, resulting in higher costs across all retail channels, were preventing any net benefits from the new channel. Eventually, a reorganization was deemed the only way to reintegrate information management both across all channels to market and with core operational systems. In a telecommunications company, it was agreed among business and IS/IT executives that incoherent Information Governance was creating serious ambiguities in roles and responsibilities across the business and IS function. In particular, respon-sibility and accountability for benefit delivery was seen by business managers as the responsibility of the IS function—clearly something they could not achieve. New governance mechanisms combined with new investment management, benefits planning and delivery processes were introduced to achieve more appropriate, clearly-defined roles and responsibilities.

These are just a few examples of how an analysis of the level of IS/IT competency or incompetency can identify key problem areas and be used to instigate corrective action. Our conclusion is that organizational in-ability to make effective use of IS/IT and the associated resources is as much a result of inadequate competencies in the business functions as the calibre of the IS/IT resources it has available. Greater understanding of the organizational causes of these inabilities, and how they can be remedied, is an aspect of IS/IT strategic management that has only just begun to be explored.

A BUSINESS CHANGE PERSPECTIVE OF IS/IT

A core observation from this discussion is that one way of thinking about the strategic potential of IS/IT is to view it as requiring IS competencies that can be leveraged to deliver strategic business initiatives. From this perspective, the strategic contribution of IS/IT will emerge from senior management's awareness of how different IS competencies in the organization can be exploited to satisfy market needs and how the IS competencies themselves contribute to enabling new strategic initiatives. Creating business awareness and understanding of IS competencies is something that the IS function itself must learn to do. Recent research conducted at the Information Systems Research Centre at Cranfield School of Management suggests that this understanding is best achieved by viewing IS/IT in the context of integrated change projects, where IS competencies are deployed alongside the other essential ingredients of organizational change. This requirement to shift emphasis from 'IT projects' to 'change projects' and programs, if business benefits are to be forthcoming, is a recurring finding from our research.

The extent and calibre of an organization's IS competencies will either increase or limit its options for change from the use of IT. From this perspective, the IS competencies define the organization's ability to identify and deliver successfully IS/IT-related changes, in relation to the demand-side drivers that cause the changes the organization has to make or wants to make (see Figure 12.5). 'Incompetency' in any aspect of IS/IT management can severely impact an organization's ability to determine, make and assimilate IS/IT-enabled change. Developing a realistic strategy involves managing supply and demand so that change initiatives work toward a common direction and competencies are developed according to business requirements.

The first part of this book addressed the issue of engagement in the strategic 'conversations', and the latter part considers the development of the competencies required to enable the results of those discussions to bear fruit.

Matching the development and availability of IS competencies with the business's demands for change requires understanding of the underlying philosophies of strategic decision making. Although the nature of strategic decision making varies among organizations, there are some broad similarities. In the Anglo-American business culture, strategic change has tended to be target driven. Typically, this begins with a definition of

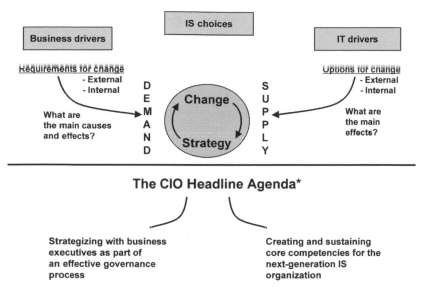

The CIO Headline Agenda*

Strategizing with business
executives as part of
an effective governance
process

Creating and sustaining
core competencies for the
next-generation IS
organization

Figure 12.5 *Strategy as the management of change* (*Shaping CIO Agendas in
an 'E' World, GartnerGroup, Stamfort, Connecticut, 2002))

desired outcomes—the *ends*—and then works backward to find ways of
achieving them and to determine the competencies and resources required
(see Figure 12.6). This approach assumes that, regardless of the demands
made by strategic change projects, the business will be able to find the
necessary ways and means to achieve them. When this proves impossible,
a change project will, at best, be only partially successful. The strong
focus on measures in relation to strategic objectives can also create
problems in the Anglo-American model. In particular, if the links
between objectives and measures are not entirely clear, people will
tend to focus on what is being measured, sometimes to the exclusion of
equally critical but hard-to-measure elements of the change project or
program.

The Japanese model of strategic change has traditionally been the
reverse of the Anglo-American version. Rather than working top-
down from a strategic plan or vision, strategy has been driven bottom-
up by identifying opportunities to exploit existing competencies and
resources—the *means*. Consensus is reached as to what is possible from
the existing resource base—Japanese manufacturing techniques are good
examples here. While this has proven effective in outmanoeuvring competitors over the short to medium term, the lack of long-term vision and
objectives created its own problems, as the stagnation of the Japanese
economy during the 1990s and into the 2000s demonstrates. Evolving

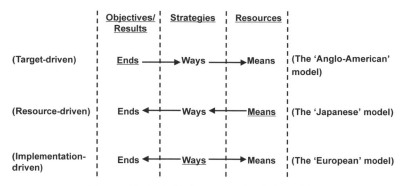

Figure 12.6   *Different strategic philosophies*

competencies and resources on a tactical basis, without some form of long-term direction, can prevent organizations from developing new competencies required in a changing environment.

The European model differs again. It is driven primarily by implementation—the *ways*—rather than objectives or available resources. The focus on implementation as a way of reconciling means and ends probably makes this model better suited to today's environment of rapid and unpredictable change related to either ends or means. As business conditions change and new enablers of change emerge, the implementation emphasis of the strategy process provides continual balancing of change capabilities and demands for change, while remaining responsive to short-term opportunities.

IT is a key resource of today's organizations—a key enabler of change—as are the skills and competencies it has to use the technology. The *ways* an organization chooses to deploy technology and the associated resources (the *means*) are the strategies, which in turn will determine the results (or *ends*) the organization can achieve. It is suggested that the focus of IS/IT strategic management should first be on the ways the organization can conduct its business using IS/IT and the ways IS/IT can enable it to change—rather than business objectives or the capabilities of IT. For example, customer relationship management (CRM) software is a resource; how an organization decides to deploy the software and change the ways it manages customer relationships will determine what it can actually achieve.

IS Competencies and Organizational Dimensions

The differences between the three strategy philosophies show that effective and workable strategy arises from a balanced understanding of ends,

Figure 12.7 *Information systems competencies and the organizational ingredients*

ways and means. The traditional Anglo-American model, however, places most of its emphasis on the ends (i.e. business objectives). Far less attention is paid to understanding the resources and competencies available and the level of change that can be used to either effect or achieve. Understanding IS competencies and their potential contribution to defining and implementing strategic change can help, provided the organizational reasons for the relative levels of competency can be understood.

In addition to the six areas of competency described earlier, this model shows five organizational dimensions that, from our research, affect either the development of a competency or its deployment. As illustrated by the five 'organizational ingredients' in Figure 12.7, problems with any of the competencies may be associated with leadership, structures and processes, roles, relationships and behaviours—these aspects were introduced in Chapter 8. An analysis of the inadequate IS competencies in relation to these five factors can reveal causes of the lack of competency in an organization and, consequently, what action can be taken to overcome those weaknesses and improve the ability of the organization to deliver a visible and significant business contribution from IT-enabled change programs. Again, from our experience in applying the assessment technique in many organizations, inappropriate *structures and processes* and *roles* are most commonly the root cause of weaknesses, although ineffective *leadership* is often not far behind. The other two dimensions—issues in *relationships* and *behaviours*—are rarely the cause of problems, but are often the visible effects of problems elsewhere.

The IS/IT Contribution: Creating Business Value

Any organization ultimately makes investments in IS/IT to create value for its stakeholders, whether they are shareholders, customers, employees or others with a vested interest in sharing in its success. In the late 1980s and early 1990s, studies reported a 'productivity paradox'[18] and fueled a quest for economic analysis to determine whether links existed between IT investment and productivity and IT investment and profitability. A significant body of research has explored the relationship between IS/IT investment and business performance—between the means and ends— and the results have been diverse. At an industry level, results have been inconclusive. At an organizational level, where the findings are more meaningful for management, the results have illustrated the obvious: some organizations have achieved benefits from their investments, while others failed to achieve much from their spend! Conducting this type of research is fraught with difficulty, as it is a complex task to isolate the IT variable and determine whether or not it actually contributed directly to the outcome.

Even if a positive relationship between IT investment and performance improvement can be demonstrated to provide the case for making an investment, it gives little guidance regarding the value-creation process. Indeed, it does caution against placing too much emphasis on investment proposals that only define the expected return on investment. Whether benefits that justified the investment actually occur is less certain; an issue that the Benefits Management process introduced in Chapter 9 seeks to resolve. Moreover, IT value does not occur at a point in time, but rather unfolds over time through the effective use of the applications and the infrastructure.

Economic studies, although valuable in illustrating the apparent pay-off or otherwise of IT, provide inadequate explanations of how IT value is actually created—the ways. One thing is certain: business value is derived from business change, whether through better processes, improved products or services, access to markets, enhanced decision making, greater efficiency or better resource utilization. More recent research[19] has suggested that investments in complementary assets (e.g. management skills and user knowledge) are critical to delivering the return on IT investment. Investments in other areas such as training, process redesign and change management programs enable the benefits from IS/IT to be obtained.

The most helpful theoretical model to date explaining the steps involved in IS/IT value creation (i.e. linking IS/IT investment to business performance) has been proposed by Soh and Markus.[20] Illustrated in Figure 12.8, the model captures the major ingredients of the recipe for transforming IS/IT investments into improved organizational performance. The recipe suggests the necessary processes and the sequence that leads to success: organizations spend on IS/IT and, subject to varying degrees of effectiveness during the management of IS/IT, obtain IS/IT assets. 'Quality IS/IT assets, if combined with the process of appropriate use, then yield favourable impacts. Favourable IS/IT impacts, if not adversely affected during the competitive process, lead to improved business performance.'

Most previous IS/IT strategy research has focused on the first and last parts of the model, essentially the means and ends. The middle process of Figure 12.8, connecting IT assets to their impacts—the ways—is the least well understood, particularly in areas such as defining what constitutes appropriate use, how use differs depending on the type of IT investment and the organizational competencies in using IT. These are essentially implementation issues.

Establishing the value derived from IS/IT spend remains an enduring question and one that has yet to be satisfactorily resolved. 'Value for money' from IT has traditionally focused on the money spent, which is relatively easy to calculate, rather than the value derived. There has been considerable study of the 'total cost of ownership' of IT, but only recently has the emphasis shifted to 'total benefits of ownership'. We have already noted that organizations are spending an increasing percentage of their IT budgets on IT services, rather than on traditional hardware and software. However, calculating the business value derived from these services still proves elusive. Further research is needed in this area if we are to be able to understand and assess the 'total benefits of ownership'.

A FOURTH ERA: THE IS CAPABILITY

We believe that, as IS/IT assumes even greater significance in every organization's day-to-day operations and its future strategy, the strategic information systems era introduced in Chapter 1 is being superseded by the requirement for a distinct IS capability. An IS capability was defined in Chapter 1 as the ability of an organization to deliver business value from investments in IS/IT continuously and suggested that this is now heralding the emergence of a new fourth era—what we call the IS

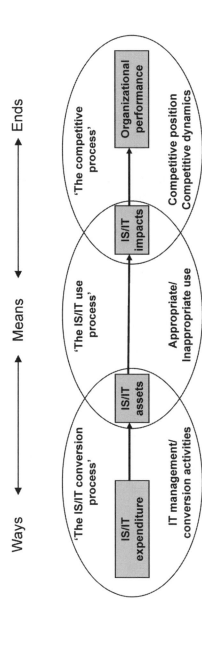

Figure 12.8 *How IT creates business value (source: adapted from C. Soh and M.L. Markus, 'How IT creates business value: A process theory synthesis', in Proceedings of the 16th Annual International Conference on Information Systems, Amsterdam, The Netherlands, December 1995, pp. 29–41.*

capability era. It is not necessary for all investments made in IS/IT to deliver business advantage—some may, others may just yield a good return from the level of investment being made, improving the performance of 'key operational' and 'support' processes.

This IS capability goes beyond seeking alignment or searching out for competitive opportunities from IS/IT. It is something that is built into the very fabric of the organization to enable it continuously to identify, obtain and sustain the benefits available from astute IS/IT investment. The closest analogy is perhaps the focus on quality that has become ingrained in the activities of many manufacturing and service organizations; it is just not questioned and occurs automatically and is part of the ethos of the company.

We saw in Chapter 1 that, while some organizations have managed to gain advantage from IS/IT, very few have achieved it on a continuous and ongoing basis. Technology is no longer proprietary and is 'freely' available in the open market to all firms competing against each other. Competitors will soon catch up through imitation or even overtake the organization either through a more innovative application or by deploying newer and cheaper technology for a similar purpose. There is now a perpetual requirement to innovate with IS/IT to effect change *and* to adapt business processes and practices to respond to change created by others.

By combining four views of how IS/IT contributes or otherwise to organizational performance, we suggest that the concept of an IS capability can become more than just a conceptual concept. The characteristics of an 'excellent capability' can be distinguished with a view to understanding and assessing the IS capability in an organization and finally, but not perhaps yet, defining strategic development routes to creating and improving this capability. The four views that we suggest can be synthesized are:

- the process theory of how IT can be used to create business value;
- the IS competencies required to enable a distinctive capability;
- the 'European' strategic philosophy that the ways in which we choose to manage and utilize IS/IT define what we can achieve and the resources required;
- the resource-based theory of the firm (which was described earlier in Chapters 1 and 2).

From our research, we see this capability as having three central dimensions: fusing business knowledge with IS knowledge, a flexible and reusable IT platform, and an effective use process (see Figure 12.9). These three dimensions must be working in harmony. The capability in

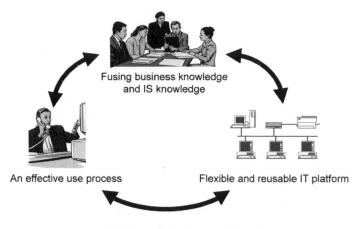

Figure 12.9   IS capability

turn is underpinned by the IS competencies. These three dimensions are discussed in more detail before examining the links between IS competencies and the IS capability.

Fusing IS knowledge and business knowledge to ensure the conception of strategies to utilize technological innovation, to seize opportunities quickly and to implement these strategies successfully, including managing change and making appropriate technology-sourcing decisions. It also involves knowing the extent of change that the business is capable of absorbing.

Managing IS/IT and delivering business benefits is essentially a knowledge-based activity. The management of IS is not one activity but a complex and multidimensional set of tasks and processes, incorporating many different but interdependent aspects. It involves integrating and coordinating knowledge from many different individuals coming from different disciplines and backgrounds, with different experiences and expectations, located in different parts of the organization. This obviously demands a close partnership between IS staff and business staff, each bringing their own knowledge and experiences to bear.

Of course, the wider the knowledge base being integrated, the more complex are the problems of creating and managing underpinning competences. Grant[21] believes that this integration is not possible without a structure for organizational competencies. This structure does not correspond with the organizational structure or hierarchy. Grant points out that the uniqueness of an organization's knowledge base makes it impossible to offer a specific form of organization for exploiting knowledge. However, organizations of differing knowledge bases and different structures can compete equally well.

In their research on outsourcing, Lacity *et al.*[22] found that 'numerous companies consider outsourcing partly for the access to greater IT knowledge it would bring.' But the challenge such organizations face is in integrating this knowledge with other internal resources, and perhaps it is the inability to exploit this combined knowledge base that explains why many organizations have experienced disappointing results from their outsourcing decisions. Indeed, Scarbrough[23] argues that outsourcing decisions could be usefully viewed in terms of the organization of knowledge. As noted earlier in the book, Earl[24] suggests caution regarding outsourcing when he noted that much learning about the capability of IT is experiential, and that organizations tend to learn to manage IS by doing, not appreciating the challenges until they have experienced them.

A flexible and reusable IT infrastructure provides the technical platform and resources needed to have the ability to respond quickly to competitor moves as well as the capacity to launch innovative IS applications supporting new process designs or business initiatives. This infrastructure is the technical 'supply side' component of the IS capability. Through the deployment of knowledge and skill, some of which may be bought in, the organization 'creates' an IT infrastructure that influences future options and speed of response and has a degree of permanency attached to it. So, if the senior IT management team of an organization changes for example, the infrastructure that they may have been responsible for shaping remains behind.

We have seen in Chapter 11 that the IT infrastructure provides the shared foundation of the organization's ability for building business applications. While many software applications are built to serve one specific business purpose, other applications and most hardware, networks, operating systems and databases are designed to be shared and to serve many business purposes. Yet, a major problem with IT infrastructure is that it is usually not adequately planned for. The IS function has generally been 'obliged to grow its IT infrastructure clandestinely, by small increments hung on the shirt-tales of particular applications for which a direct benefit can be demonstrated.'[25] It is generally accumulated rather than built to serve the business in times of change; consequently, it is often fragmented and technically incompatible.

As also discussed in Chapter 11, the IT infrastructure only defines the technological capability required to support the business and its strategy, if it adequately addresses the need for flexibility to deal with changing business priorities. Indeed, one of the reasons organizations often choose outsourcing is the belief that the vendor will provide them with this flexibility; research findings show that this may not always be the case.[26]

An effective use process to link IS/IT assets with value realization, through the application of the technology as well as creating an environment conducive to collecting, organizing and maintaining information, together with embracing the right behaviours for working with information.[27] The use process has two aspects: using the technology and working with information.[28]

Technology by itself has no inherent value; this value must be unlocked, a task that can only be achieved by people. While it might seem somewhat superficial to state, technology must be actually used for benefits to be delivered! This use takes place within business and management processes. Exploitation of the technology by deploying it to deliver business benefits requires knowledge and skills. Some threshold level of IS use must be achieved, before an impact can be observed, but, beyond that level, more use does not necessarily lead to more or better impacts.[29]

The use process is also concerned with information itself. We saw in Chapter 10 that Davenport[30] recommends organizations to place more emphasis on 'human-centred information management' or 'people-centred management activities' aimed at improving behaviours and values for more effective information use and at improving the way people behave with information. This line of reasoning softens the temptation of organizations to focus solely on technology implementation.

A MODEL LINKING THE IS CAPABILITY WITH IS COMPETENCIES AND RESOURCES

From our work with a number of organizations, we have constructed a model to represent the components of the IS capability. Illustrated in Figure 12.10, the model has three levels: the resource level, the organizing level and the business level. The *resource* level denotes the resource components that are the key ingredients of the IS competencies. In managing IS, resources are essentially people and their skills, knowledge and behavioural attributes. The *organizing* level is concerned with how these resources are mobilized and marshalled via structures, processes and roles to create IS competencies. It is, however, only at the *business* level that the capability actually manifests itself and is ultimately recognized in superior organizational performance. All organizations have an IS capability. For some, however, it is weak and severely affects that organization's ability to affect or assimilate IS/IT-related strategic change. Those with a strong IS capability can both leverage IS/IT-enabled change for business advantage and also absorb change.

In order to illustrate the link between resources and the IS

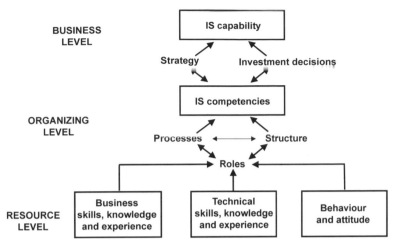

Figure 12.10   *From resource to capability*

capability, we first develop the relationship between resources and the IS competencies.

From Resources to IS Competencies

In an organizational context, competencies are embedded in organizational processes[31] and 'business routines'[32] and are bounded by the structure of the organization.[33] The expression of a particular competency in an organization depends on people applying their knowledge, integrating their knowledge, interacting with others and coordinating their actions—this they do by performing roles in processes. Consequently, people, as the receptacles of knowledge, are central to a particular IS competency manifesting itself, assuming that a conducive environment exists in the organization. Figure 12.11 illustrates that collective performance of IS/IT competencies contributes to the expression of the IS capability, highlighting that people, as resources, can contribute to a number of the IS/IT competencies.

Processes

The perspective of a process presented in this book suggested that viewing a process as 'a set of activities' has emerged out of manufacturing industry and is a fairly rigid viewpoint of the concept and may not be either appropriate or indeed applicable in all situations, particularly in knowledge-oriented environments. In such contexts, we have argued that it is more appropriate to view the concept of process in terms of roles, as

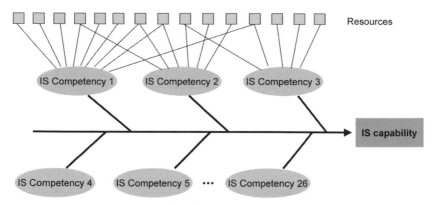

Figure 12.11   *Resources and competencies*

well as activities, with a process portrayed as 'a collection of roles colla-borating and interacting to achieve a particular goal.' Such a view is of particular relevance in complex tasks or processes, where bringing together specific knowledge and skills is critical to the ability of the or-ganization to perform the task.

Roles

The concept of roles and role theory is useful in understanding the be-haviour of individuals in both groups and organizations. The history of role theory dates to the 1930s, when sociologists and anthropologists studied roles as a key to explaining the origins of social behaviour.[34] Since then, role theory has emerged as a recognized discipline. Building on the sociological roots of role theory, Graen[35] developed a 'role systems model' in which behaviour in a particular role is the result of organizational demands, social demands and personal demands. Katz and Kahn[36] applied similar ideas to their organizational role theory, which emphasizes organizational factors, interpersonal factors and attri-butes of the person.

In an organization, an employee's primary role is indicated by a position title and specified by a 'job description'. However, employees are likely to have to perform different roles at different times. In order that the organization can achieve its goals and objectives, the work of individual members must be linked into a coherent pattern of activities and relationships and this is achieved through the 'role structure' of the organization.[37] While roles can be tightly or loosely defined and have different degrees of discretion associated with them, they do encompass the expected behaviours attached to a position or job. Individuals may perform many roles, operate within a number of processes and consequently contribute to many IS competencies.

Human resource management theorists describe a range of factors that distinguish the ability[38] of an individual to perform a particular role.[39] These are:

- Skills—*know how* of the job, which implies the physical ability to produce some action. This might be the ability to program in Java or draw data flow diagrams.
- Knowledge—*know what* of the job, the ability to understand what the role demands of the person. For example, knowledge of what is involved in constructing an IS strategy or in building relationships with vendors.
- Behaviours and attitudes—*know why* of the job, the personal attributes or aptitudes that make knowledge useful and enable skills to be acquired in the first place. Personal characteristics are important and indeed may be crucial in service-oriented roles; for example, IS staff having empathy with users in delivering many IS services, particularly those with a high degree of user contact.

Structures

Both processes and roles are framed by the organization structures. Structure is traditionally seen as being concerned with the systematic arrangement of people, departments and other subsystems in the organization. The structure of the organization can affect the performance of processes, particularly those that cross departmental or functional boundaries. The concept of business process re-engineering emerged as a consequence of the problems of functional organizations and called for a greater focus on process in designing organizations. We have already argued in Chapter 8 that resource elements of IS competencies are not located solely in the IS function, but are spread throughout the organization.

From IS Competencies to IS Capability

It is only at the business level that the IS capability actually manifests itself, reflecting the organization's ability to achieve sustained superior performance through IS/IT. As has been argued above, this requires fusing IS knowledge and business knowledge, establishing a robust and flexible technical platform and instituting an effective use process.

The extent to which IS competencies contribute toward the IS capability is dependent on two aspects: the strategy and investment decisions. Both define whether the IS capability is a source of competitive advantage, a mere necessity for competitive parity or, indeed, whether it is placing the organization at a competitive disadvantage. Although having an IS capability is a business imperative today, different organizations may choose to resource it in different ways, but almost all rely on a combination of internal and external resources and even some externally provided competencies.

Barney[40] refers to competencies as organizational characteristics that 'enable an organization to conceive, choose and implement strategies.' A firm could potentially identify an advantage by conceiving an innovative strategy that depends on IT, but successfully implementing such a strategy will be dependent on the current status of the IT infrastructure, the organization's ability to successfully deploy appropriate resources as well as to implement and operate new processes and systems.

Similarly, succeeding with Enterprise Systems (ES) is not as dependent on the technology and applications as much as it is on the organization's capacity to implement and manage change.[41] As discussed in Chapter 11, the first implementation of an ES normally involves recognizing current problems and constraints to progress that more integrated processes and systems will eliminate. This will undoubtedly cause many existing IS competencies to be reassessed and improved to enable the organization to be operated and managed as an integrated whole, using information and systems in new and quite different ways. As the end of the stage, if successful, the organization will have an improved business and IS capability that, through further changes in business practices in addition to innovative extensions of its systems, can produce new strategic opportunities. As outlined in Chapter 11, the evidence from research suggests that, while the problems and constraints exist, it is very difficult for organizations to envisage the potential that an ES-based capability provides.

From Capability to Improved Business Performance

An IS capability only delivers actual value through implementation, in terms of the way it is used in improving business performance. Both the intended improvement in performance and the way IS/IT delivers or creates that improvement should be explicitly stated in the business and IS strategies. Figure 12.12 illustrates how we see IS competencies fitting within an overall model of the organization and its performance. It illustrates the relationship between business strategy, IS/IT strategy, IT operations and services, business operations and performance. This model emphasizes that business performance ultimately derives from business operations—the configuration of people, processes, structure, manufacturing, etc.—not directly from IT, even though technology may be a core

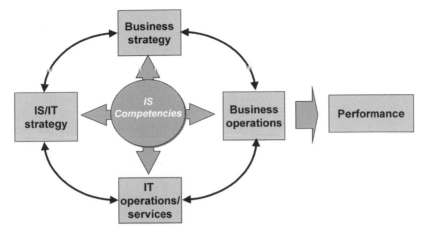

Figure 12.12 *The relationship between IS competencies and business performance*

component without which business operations could not be performed successfully.

Direction and purpose for business operations is given by the business strategy, which, while shaping the IS/IT strategy in terms of defining requirements, is itself impacted by opportunities provided via IS/IT. As we outlined in Chapter 1, the IS/IT strategy determines the *what* and *how* of IS/IT, and provides the blueprint for IT operations and services.

The IS competencies impact all four areas of the model. They determine the extent to which IT opportunities are incorporated in business strategy, the effectiveness of business operations, how well the IT infrastructure is designed and resourced, and the level of performance achieved by IT operations and the quality of IT services.

A weakness in any area of IS competency affects the overall IS capability and directly or indirectly impacts the business operations and ultimately affects business performance. We believe that the new IS alignment is concerned with how well the organization develops and utilizes its IS competencies in each of the four areas of the model. This implementation-based view contrasts with the traditional view that just considers the alignment of the business and IS/IT strategies or the structures and processes of the IS function and activities in relation to the business organization.

In a global reinsurance brokerage where we undertook research, the effectiveness of this new alignment was clearly evident. From our analysis, all the company's IS competencies were extremely strong relative to what was required given its business strategy, even though many of the resources and IT supply competencies were sourced externally. The company has recognized the value of information and its effective management to its competitive success. The IT director is a member of the Board of Directors and has a very strong partnership with the group CEO. They regularly attend IT conferences together. He is a key player in the business strategy decision-making process; one colleague noted, 'I think that he is forward-thinking enough to be looking at new technologies and that he is brave enough to take the decision to go with things,' and this often means driving the business strategy. A quote from its IS/IT strategy document best illustrates how IS/IT is deployed in the company: 'Information systems cannot afford to wait for a clear and detailed specification of *"strategy"* from the business and customers it is trying to serve. It is more a question of applying IS/IT foresight to the situation, in order to make reasoned assumptions to an appropriate course of action.'

There is also a close partnership between the IS function and the rest of the business. Indeed, this is probably helped as the IT director is responsible for both IT operations and most of the business operations (the exceptions being marketing and risk management). Roles are clearly specified, particularly in the delivery of IT services. The philosophy of the IS function was described by one IT manager as 'we help you to help yourself', in reference to the fact that they work closely with the business. The company has not set out to develop and nurture the 26 IS competencies explicitly, but they are present and they do provide an explanation of why the company has probably been the most successful player in its industry over the last 20 years and recognized by its peers as being innovative regarding the deployment of IT.

CONCLUSION

The discussion of a proposed 'fourth era', where an organization's performance will be significantly dependent on its IS capability, recognizes that IS/IT now plays an integral role in the majority of business operations. In previous eras, the focus of IS strategy was on selecting the most beneficial set of IS/IT investments to make and managing them successfully through to implementation. This in itself became more challenging as applications became both more complex and more strategic, demanding innovative thinking about IS/IT use and the ability to make increasing degrees of business change to deliver the benefits. However, there was an implication that any organization could achieve this by excellence in developing its strategy—excellence in the sense of astute assessment of the impact of IS/IT and accurate alignment of IS/IT strategies with business strategies.

The concept of an IS capability suggests that an organization will not be able continually to achieve both of them unless it has a track record of successful implementation, through which it develops a full set of IS competencies. This in turn implies a focus on *the ways it decides on* and deploys IS/IT, learning from success and failure, rather than concentrate on what technology can do (*the means*), or try to align IS/IT use to business objectives (*the ends*) that often arbitrarily, set the investment and change agenda.

Perhaps fueled by the hype that continually surrounds IT, management seem to be still hoping for the 'silver bullet'—that merely possessing a technology will deliver untold benefits. The recent relabeling of IS/IT as 'e' seemed to reignite that dream. The stock market boom in technology stocks and unsubstantiated claims for the 'new economy' increased that misplaced confidence for a time. However, to requote the Microsoft chairman, Bill Gates: 'I have a simple but strong belief. The most meaningful way to differentiate your company from your competition, the best way to put distance between you and the crowd, is to do an outstanding job with information. *How you gather, manage and use information will determine whether you win or lose.*'[42]

Taking advantage of all that technology offers requires an enduring ability within an organization to understand how systems and information use can improve its performance and create new options. This requires sustained investment in developing IS competencies that, once in place, enable the organization to exploit the technology, systems and information it has and with the knowledge acquired make further investments, each of which delivers explicit, measurable value. Balancing the need to innovate in IS/IT use with the need to exploit fully the organization's IS/IT resources and assets is one of the main reasons for having an IS/IT strategy. Strategic management is about making informed choices based on an understanding of the relative benefits of different options *and* having the ability to deliver those benefits.

Perhaps this book would be better entitled *The Strategic Management of Information Systems* since much of the content is not solely about devising a strategy but also about making it work. What is certain is that, although 'IT fads' will come and go, the use of IT will pervade more and more aspects of organizational activity and people's working and personal lives. It is here to stay. Therefore, if organizations are to enjoy the benefits that can be realized from its adept application and avoid the problems its inept use can produce, they will need to develop IS/IT strategies that are fully integrated into the business strategy and capable of being implemented successfully. There is still much to learn, and we have already commenced this quest as we prepare for the fourth edition!

ENDNOTES

1. *Productivity in the United States, 1995–2000*, McKinsey Global Institute, October 2001.
2. S. Rangan and R. Adner, *Profitable Growth in Internet-Related Business: Strategy Tales and Truths*, Working Paper 2001/11/SM. INSEAD, Fontainebleau, France, February 2001.
3. 'From dot.com to dot.bom', *The Economist*, 1 July 2000.
4. Swanson and Ramiller have addressed the issue of social cognition that drives innovations in new information systems. They introduced the concept of an *organizing vision* and explain how a collective, cognitive view of new technologies enables success in IS innovation. Martin and Kambil have examined how managers' experiences with a specific strategic information technology in their industry influences cognitive managerial tasks associated with new information technologies. See E.B. Swanson and N.C. Ramiller, 'The organizing vision in information systems innovation', *Organization Science*, Vol. 8, No. 5, 1997, 458–474; and L.L. Martins and A. Kambil, 'Learning from experience: Managerial interpretations of past and future information technologies', in *Proceedings of the 16th Annual International Conference on Information Systems*, Amsterdam, The Netherlands, December 1995, 43–54.
5. D. Fink, 'Information systems planning in a volatile environment', *Long Range Planning*, Vol. 27, No. 6, 1994, 108–114.
6. C. Ciborra, 'The grassroots of IT and strategy', in C. Ciborra and T. Jelessi, eds, *Strategic Information Systems: A European Perspective*, John Wiley & Sons, Chichester, UK, 1994, pp. 3–24.
7. P. Checkland, *Systems Thinking Systems Practice*, John Wiley & Sons, Chichester, UK, 1981.
8. P.F. Drucker, 'The coming of the new organisation', *Harvard Business Review*, January–February 1988, 45–53.
9. S. Zuboff, *In the Age of the Smart Machine*, Basic Books, New York, 1988.
10. C. Handy, *The Age of Unreason*, Business Books, New York, 1989; and *The Empty Raincoat*, Hutchinson, London, 1994.
11. For more on the *intellectual capital* perspective, see B. Arthur, 'Increasing returns and the new world of business', *Harvard Business Review*, July–August 1996, 100–109; T.A. Stewart, *Intellectual Capital*, Doubleday, New York, 1997; K.E. Sveiby, *The New Organizational Wealth*, Berett-Koehler, San Francisco, 1997; J. Peppard and A. Rylander, 'Using an intellectual capital perspective to design and implement a growth strategy: The case of APiON', *European Management Journal*, Vol. 19, No. 5, 2001, 510–525.
12. R. Lambert and J. Peppard, 'IT and new organisational forms: Destination but no road map', *Journal of Strategic Information Systems*, Vol. 2, No. 3, 1993, 180–205.
13. M.S. Scott Morton, ed., *The Corporation of the 1990s: Information Technology and Organizational Transformation*, Oxford University Press, New York, 1991.
14. D.G. Robinson and S.A. Stanton, 'Exploit EDI before EDI exploits you', *Information Strategy: The Executive's Journal*, Spring, 1987.
15. J.F. Rockart and J.E. Short, 'IT in the 1990s: Managing organisational interdependence', *Sloan Management Review*, Winter, 1989.
16. T.W. Malone, J. Yates and R.I. Benjamin, 'Electronic markets and electronic hierarchies', *Communications of the ACM*, Vol. 30, No. 6, 1987, 484–497.
17. Conducted by authors at *IT Directors Forum at Cranfield School of Management*, October 2001.
18. The productivity paradox referred to the fact that, despite the vast sums of money invested in IT each year, the productivity pay-offs were either unclear or did not manifest themselves in studies, particularly in macroeconomic analysis. Economist Robert Salow noted at the time, 'we see the computer age everywhere except in the productivity statistics' (*New York Times Book Review*, 12 July 1987).
19. E. Brynjolfsson and S. Yang, 'The intangible benefits and costs of investments: Evidence from financial markets', in K. Kumar and J. DeGross, eds, *Proceedings of the 18th Annual International Conference on Information Systems*, Atlanta, Georgia, 1997, pp. 147–166.
20. C. Soh and M.L. Markus, 'How IT creates business value: A process theory synthesis', in *Proceedings of the 16th Annual International Conference on Information Systems*, Amsterdam, The Netherlands, December 1995, pp. 29–41.
21. R.M. Grant, 'Prospering in dynamically competitive environments: Organisational capability as knowledge integration', *Organization Science*, Vol. 7, 1996, 375–387.
22. M.C. Lacity, R. Hirschheim and L.P. Willcocks, 'Realising outsourcing expectations: Incredible promises, credible outcomes', *Journal of Information Systems Management*, Vol. 11, No. 4, 1994, 7–18.
23. H. Scarbrough, 'The external acquisition of information systems knowledge', in L.P

Willcocks and M.C. Lacity, eds, *Strategic Sourcing of Information Systems*, John Wiley & Sons, Chichester, UK, 1998, pp. 137–161.

24. M.J. Earl, 'The risks of outsourcing IT', *Sloan Management Review*, Spring, 1996, 26–32.

25. Index Foundation, *Building the New Information Infrastructure*, Index Foundation Final Report 91, CSC Index, London, 1993.

26. T. Clark, R. Zmud and G. McCray, 'The outsourcing of information services. Transforming the nature of business in the information industry', in L.P. Willcocks and M.C. Lacity, eds, *Strategic Sourcing of Information Systems*, John Wiley & Sons, Chichester, UK, 1998, pp. 45–78.

27. D.A. Marchand, W. Kettinger and J.D. Rollins, 'Information orientation: People, technology and bottom line', *Sloan Management Review*, Summer, 2000, 69–80.

28. T.H. Davenport, 'Saving IT's soul: Human-centred information management', *Harvard Business Review*, March–April 1994, 119–131; T.H. Davenport, *Information Ecology: Mastering the Information and Knowledge Environments*, Oxford University Press, New York, 1997; D.A. Marchand, W. Kettinger and J.D. Rollins, 'Information orientation: People, technology and bottom line', *Sloan Management Review*, Summer, 2000, 69–80; S.M. McKinnon and W.J. Bruns, *The Information Mosaic*, Harvard Business School Press, Boston, 1992.

29. C. Soh and M.L. Markus, 'How IT creates business value: A process theory synthesis', in *Proceedings of the 16th Annual International Conference on Information Systems*, Amsterdam, The Netherlands, December 1995, pp. 29–41.

30. T.H. Davenport, 'Saving IT's soul: Human-centred information management', *Harvard Business Review*, March–April 1994, 119–131.

31. G. Stalk, P. Evans and L.E. Shulman, 'Competing on capabilities: The new rules of corporate strategy', *Harvard Business Review*, March–April 1992, 57–69; D.J. Teece, 'Strategies for managing knowledge assets: The role of firm structure and industrial context', *Long Range Planning*, Vol. 33, 2000, 35–54. To further confuse an already confusing area, Mascarenhas *et al.* suggest that competencies can be 'reliable processes'. See B. Mascarenhas, A. Baveja and M. Jamil, 'Dynamics of core competencies in leading multinational companies', *California Management Review*, Vol. 40, No. 4, 1998, 117–132.

32. K.E. Marino, 'Developing consensus on firm competencies and capabilities', *Academy of Management Executives*, Vol. 10, 1996, 40–51.

33. R.M. Grant, 'Prospering in dynamically competitive environments: Organisational capability as knowledge integration', *Organization Science*, Vol. 7, 1996, 375–387.

34. R. Linton, *The Study of Man*, Appleton-Century, New York, 1936; G.H. Mead, *Mind, Self and Society*, University of Chicago Press, Chicago, 1934; B.J. Biddle and E.J. Thomas, *Role Theory: Concepts and Research*, John Wiley & Sons, New York, 1966.

35. G. Graen, 'Role-making processes within complex organisations', in M.D. Dunnette, ed., *Handbook of Industrial and Organisational Psychology*, Rand McNally, College Publishing Company, Chicago, 1976, 1201–1245.

36. D. Katz, and R.L. Kahn, *The Social Psychology of Organizations*, second edition, John Wiley & Sons, New York, 1978.

37. L. Mullins, *Management and Organisational Behaviour*, third edition, Pitman Publishing, London, 1993.

38. The concept of *ability* is widely used in the organizational behaviour literature.

39. P.L. Ackerman and L.G. Humphreys, 'Individual differences theory in industrial and organizational psychology', in M.D. Dunnette and L.M. Hough, eds, *Handbook of Industrial and Organizational Psychology*, second edition, Vol. 1, Consulting Psychologists Press, Palo Alto, California, 1990, 223–283; R.M. Belbin, *Team Roles at Work*, Butterworth-Heinemann, Oxford, UK, 1993; D. Katz and R.L. Kahn, *The Social Psychology of Organizations*, second edition, John Wiley & Sons, New York, 1978; B.M. Staw, 'Dressing up like an organization: When psychological theories can explain organization action', *Journal of Management*, Vol. 17, No. 4, 1991, 805–819; K.E. Weick, *The Social Psychology of Organizing*, second edition, Addison-Wesley, Reading, Massachusetts, 1979.

40. J.B. Barney, *Gaining and Sustaining Competitive Advantage*, Addison-Wesley, Reading, Massachusetts, 1997.

41. Davenport makes this point regarding the implementation of ERP systems from similar vendors in industries where they have become the *de facto* standard and in themselves yield no advantage. See T.H. Davenport, 'Putting the enterprise back into enterprise systems', *Harvard Business Review*, July–August 1998, 121–131.

42. B. Gates, *Business @ the Speed of Thought: Using a Digital Nervous System*, Penguin Books, London, 1999.

Index

Aalsmeer Flower Auction 17–18, 33
accounting issues 13–14, 169–70, 292, 345, 351
actions 204–9, 276–7, 288–96, 354–9, 506–16
activities 153–62, 187–8, 192–7, 219–22, 244–73, 280–96,
   306–8, 354–9, 438–9, 482–4, 492–502, 524–6, 606–14
alignment issues 44–7, 179, 182–3, 239–44, 342–5, 584–9,
   613–14
alliances 84, 261–2, 362–3, 404–5, 564, 591
American Hospital Supplies 25, 27–8, 32, 132
analytical techniques 70–85, 160–2, 179–239, 277–98,
   305–9, 480–1, 506–16, 585–7, 596–8
annual plans 185–6
Anthony model 11, 14
application portfolios, 8–17, 38–58, 118–22, 136–55,
   160–7, 193–203, 231–44, 277–96, 381–4, 420–2, 585–7;
   classifications 300, 305–38, 355–9, 424–5, 542;
   disintegration dangers 341–5; enterprise systems 542–7,
   561–3, 574, 612; information management 476–502,
   518–19, 560–3; investment evaluations 420–65, 554–9;
   management issues 299–345, 364–84, 476–502, 518–19,
   536–43, 560–3, 585–7; matrices 87–95, 299–338;
   multiple SBUs 263, 295–6, 334–7, 344–54, 364, 559–63;
   priorities 421–2, 430–6, 558–9, 596–8; services 536–43
application service providers (ASPs) 534, 573–6
applications: concepts 4–5, 17, 41–4, 277–98, 300–45,
   355–9, 374, 381–4, 534–43, 585–7; provisions 522–80;
   types 4–5, 300, 305–38, 355–9, 524–34
architecture models 192–200, 205, 348–9, 353–4, 386–96,
   484–6, 549, 594–8
ARIS tools 196
ASPs see application service providers
automated teller machines (ATMs) 43

B2B see business-to-business
B2E see business-to-consumer
back-office systems 24
backbone environments 301–38
balanced scorecards 159, 192, 204–8, 211, 213–16, 237,
   285–7, 292
batch processes 8–9
benchmarks 9–11, 214, 225–6
benefits: dependence networks 444–9; investments 4–5,
   35–6, 68–9, 293–6, 324–5, 388–91, 420–65, 484–6,
   554–9, 581–3, 602–14; management issues 436–55, 458
boards of directors 364–84, 469–72, 500, 595–8, 614

bottom-up approaches 122–5, 161–2, 288–96, 321–3, 374,
   599–600
BPR see business process re-engineering
brainstorming sessions 159, 238–9, 514
brands 7, 68, 95, 384–5
budgets 9, 65–70, 143, 151–2, 169–70, 185–6, 200–1, 228,
   326–7, 430–6
bulletin boards 337
business: area plans 191; cases 201, 448–55, 480; drivers
   189, 192, 213–16, 310–11, 549–51, 598–600; growth
   dimensions 93–5; information systems strategy 279–98;
   models 105–6, 157, 160, 185–6, 273, 482–4, 493, 587–8;
   needs 159; process analysis 213–16, 226–34, 280–5
business process re-engineering (BPR) 23–7, 111, 180–3,
   201–6, 216–26, 233–4, 239, 270–3, 329–31, 588–9
business strategies 38–119, 123–33, 144–6, 154–66,
   179–244, 276–98, 341–8, 365–71, 386–96, 568–9,
   582–93; concepts 187–92, 239–44, 347–8, 365–7, 374–84,
   549–63, 582–9, 593, 605–8, 612–14; core constituents
   187–92, 593; infrastructure considerations 549–63,
   585–9, 594–8
business-to-business (B2B) 6–8, 588
business-to-consumer (B2E) 6–7

call centres 33, 94
capabilities 52–8, 70, 83–4, 288–96, 386–96, 508–16, 558–9,
   582–3, 594–614
caretaker managers 333–4, 371
CASE see computer aided software engineering
'cash cows' 89–95, 325–31
centralization issues 48–50, 300–23, 333–7, 342–59, 372,
   399–402, 428–9, 472, 483–502, 560–3
centrally planned strategies 312–23, 333–7, 342–59, 429
change xiv, 141–50, 163–8, 182–3, 220–2, 231–4, 272–7,
   369, 514–16, 581–617; benefits management 444–55,
   458; concepts 444–9, 581–7, 596–617; risk assessments
   455–62; stakeholder analyses 446–55
checkpoints 155–8, 162–3
chief information officers (CIOs) 364–84, 576, 582–3, 595,
   598–9, 614
clean-sheet approaches 220–2
client servers 322
commitment benefits 171, 212, 231, 238, 404
communication needs 155–7, 171–5, 187–8, 192, 227–34,

334–7, 369–84, 404, 468–9, 477–8, 494–5, 513–16, 531–4, 571–3, 587–9, 609–14
communities of practice (COP) 510, 513–14
comparative judgements 139–41
competencies *see* core competencies; competitive advantages 17–35, 65–70, 95–122, 134–44, 152, 165–7, 182–3, 291–302, 568–9, 584–7, 604–14; investment evaluations 424–6, 611–14; sustainability needs 52–8, 67, 111–16, 134, 242, 325–38, 384–96, 584, 605
competitive forces 95–111, 132–4, 165–7, 179–80, 239–44, 261–2, 283–5
competitors 51–8, 65–70, 71–116, 132–4, 165–7, 203–4, 239–73, 283–5, 384–617
complementary benefits, investments 423–30
complex environments 301–38, 353–4, 467–9
composite matrix 300–5
computer aided software engineering (CASE) 123, 469, 481
computer systems 76–85, 162–3, 322, 368, 384, 469, 474, 480–1; *see also* information technology; historical background 8–63, 146, 270–3, 368, 454, 480–1, 523–4; infrastructure considerations 547–63, 574–6
consumers 6–8, 240–73, 592–3; *see also* customers
context needs: benefits management 438–55; knowledge 503–4; strategy 34, 48–52, 64–85, 139–44, 153–9, 187–99, 203–4, 227–34, 240–96, 340–5, 456–7, 585–98
continuous improvements 111–12, 133, 135–6, 141–2, 220–2, 304–5, 325, 327–38
contributions 387–96, 581–3, 594–603
contrived value chains 271–2
control systems 9–25, 49–50, 198–202, 291–2, 318–58, 371–84, 401–2, 564–73, 589–90
convergence issues 20
core competencies 46, 71–85, 111–16, 164–6, 187, 233–4, 241–4, 280–5, 291–2, 363–9, 384–96, 420, 522–615; concepts 384–96, 592–615; definitions 386–96; gaps 396–405, 531–4; knowledge management 505–21; spider diagrams 391–2
corporations 147–8, 163, 168, 196–7, 209, 239–40, 334–7, 344–5, 559–63
costs 64, 96–116, 142–6, 151–8, 169–70, 240–73, 292–6, 310, 325–38, 475, 554–9, 592–3; ASPs 574–6; centres 350–4; information exchanges 253–5, 587–8; investment evaluations 421–65, 500–2, 554–9; IS/IT evolution 9–12, 18, 22, 35, 40, 68, 423–6, 480–1, 498–502, 592–3, 603; outsourcing 360–4, 530–6, 563–76; services 360–4, 530–6, 592–3, 603
creative thinking 7, 66–70, 82, 114–16, 159–62, 180, 237, 242–85, 293–6, 340–5, 585–7
critical success factors (CSFs) 46, 128–9, 137–41, 159, 162, 165, 184–94, 204–16, 237–9, 279–302, 375–84, 426–36, 477–8, 571–3
CRM *see* customer relationship management
CSFs *see* critical success factors
culture issues 83–4, 144, 164–6, 180–9, 197, 226–34, 343–5, 384–415, 470–2, 560–3, 598–9, 605; concepts 384–415, 470–2, 605, 609–14; gaps 384–415, 566; information management 384–415, 470–521, 560–6, 609–14
current situations 41–4, 65–70, 82–5, 143–4, 154–66, 182–236, 280–96, 341–5, 480–1, 587–95
customer relationship management (CRM) 32, 52, 109,

147, 219, 234, 250–62, 273, 308–9, 326, 384–96, 493–7, 502, 542–7, 562–3, 592–3
customers 26–58, 71–94, 100–16, 138, 167, 171, 194–7, 207–19, 240–73, 288–96, 345, 384–96, 446–55, 502, 542–7, 562–3, 592–3
customized services 526–34

data: *see also* information … ; administration needs 484–502; analytical techniques 160–2, 179–236, 280–7, 480–1, 506–16; concepts 466–72, 481, 503–4; dictionaries 175–6, 469, 484–502; DIKAR model 204–7, 506–16; fact-finding tasks 184–236; failures 455–62; flow diagrams 195–7, 205, 280–91, 293–4, 481, 506–16; modelling 38, 156, 175–6, 193–7, 205, 280–5, 481, 488–502; warehouses 308–9, 426, 491–2
data processing (DP) 8–25, 38–44, 50, 120–1
Data Protection Acts 74–5, 500
databases 10, 18–22, 149, 198–200, 233, 308–9, 469, 472–4, 480–516, 531, 535, 540–1
decentralization issues 48–50, 300–23, 333–7, 342–59, 372, 399–402, 428–9, 472, 483–502, 560–3
decisions 1–2, 15–35, 65–70, 156–7, 173–5, 203, 207, 227–34, 277, 289, 301–38, 340–59, 363–4, 598–600; *see also* priorities; concepts 356–9, 598–600, 614; information management 475–521; investments 420–65, 598–600, 608–14; location considerations 356–9; outsourcing considerations 566–73, 607, 612; steering groups 370–85, 429, 434–6, 492–502, 572–3; support systems 18, 202, 432–3
delivery issues 13–14, 153–77, 179, 192–207, 387–96, 448–50, 531–80, 594–8, 601–14
demand-side issues 20, 36, 44–58, 87–95, 136, 144–8, 160–4, 183–7, 233–4, 245–8, 269–79, 308–23, 349–54, 363–4, 374–84, 405–7, 586–7, 598–600
deregulations 67, 78, 81
developer managers 332–4, 371
diagramming tools 155–62, 173–6, 195–7, 205
differentiation issues 98–100, 106–7, 109–12, 115–16, 138, 240, 261–2, 564–6, 568–9, 615
diffusion issues 48–50, 125, 300–1, 303–5, 350–4
DIKAR model 204–7, 506–16
distribution channels 94–5, 100–11, 245–73, 296
diversification considerations 95, 127
documentation needs 156–7, 160–6, 173–6, 184–6, 200–1, 289, 481, 513–14, 537–8
'dogs' 89–95, 325–31
dominant coalitions 226–34, 371–7
dot.coms 6–7, 29–31, 36, 51, 58, 68, 78, 99, 101, 242, 466, 542, 573, 582, 587–8
DP *see* data processing
DSDM 438, 537, 543
duplication problems 47, 200, 220, 310, 334–7, 351–4, 485

e-commerce 1–8, 29–33, 68–77, 94–111, 132, 142, 238–62, 270–1, 302–9, 345–6, 360, 368, 429–30, 466–8, 541–2, 573–6, 581–8, 615; concepts 5–8, 248, 260, 558, 587–8, 592–3
e-procurement 32, 33
ecological factors 70, 74–85
economic factors 70–85, 280–5, 351, 361, 560–3, 569–70, 581–3, 590, 602–3
EDI *see* electronic data interchange

EDS 523, 564
effective processes 118–78
effectiveness forces 2, 22–3, 34–8, 69, 121–2, 137–44,
    151–3, 292, 343–5, 423–30, 475, 484–6, 506–16, 591–2
efficiencies 21–2, 34–5, 38–40, 49–50, 100–11, 121–2,
    132–3, 140–1, 151–3, 245–73, 292, 310, 325–38, 350–4;
    information management 484–6, 506–16; investment
    evaluations 423–30
EIS *see* executive information systems
electronic data interchange (EDI) 5, 29, 35, 252, 270, 433
electronic point of sale (EPOS) 18, 43, 105
enabling policies 358–9, 444–55, 600, 608–9
end-user computing (EUC) 15–19, 49–50, 151, 173–5,
    198–203, 346–71, 383, 498, 524–80
ends 598–604, 615
enquiry systems 15, 18
enrichment concepts 140–1
enterprise models 490–502, 542–8, 561–3, 574, 612
enterprise resource planning (ERP) 4–5, 32, 43, 109, 147,
    250, 273, 308, 344, 357, 433, 493–7, 539–48, 561–3, 574,
    612
entities 38, 192–200, 205, 287, 293–4, 484–502, 506–16
entrepreneurs 332–4, 371
environmental effects 48–52, 65–85, 111–16, 129–35,
    141–4, 153–60, 179–279, 301–62, 487–521, 583–91
EPOS *see* electronic point of sale
ERP *see* enterprise resource planning
EU *see* European Union
EUC *see* end-user computing
evolutionary developments 1–70, 86–7, 120–2, 146, 152,
    192–3, 322–3, 423–6, 491, 506–16, 583–9, 592–3
exception reports 15
executive information systems (EIS) 34–5
executive summaries 163–4, 166
expectations 144, 150–2, 500–2, 531–4, 589–90
experiences 1–2, 16–22, 87–95, 135–6, 383–4, 503–4,
    507–16, 583
expert systems 202, 219
explicit knowledge 466–7, 508–16
exploitations 387–96, 468–70, 475–6, 502–3, 522–3, 594–8,
    601–8
external context, strategy 34, 48–52, 64–85, 139–44, 153–9,
    187–99, 203–4, 227–34, 240–96, 340–5, 456– 7, 585–98
external systems 26–58, 197, 240–4, 488–502
external value chains 244–73, 280–96, 482–4

fact-finding tasks 184–236
failures 455–62, 544–5, 582, 588–9, 615
federal structures 349–54, 385, 590–1
filtering mechanisms 231–2
finance departments 13–14
finance directors 364–84
Financial EDI 5
financial institutions 71, 80, 267
first movers 7
flexibility needs 102–3, 108–9, 134, 200, 310, 575, 605–8
forecasts 9, 13–15, 65–70, 185–6, 589–91
formal formulations 153, 168–9, 340–5, 371–7, 467, 585–7
formulation methods 81–5, 119–22, 134–55, 168–73,
    182–3, 226, 277–98, 307–23, 365–7, 384–5, 585–98
free-market strategies 312–13, 315–23, 331, 333–4, 498
functional decomposition diagrams 205

functional structures 81–2, 145–9, 217–19, 239–40, 263,
    377–84, 587–91, 611
future prospects 16–17, 41–4, 65–70, 83–4, 144, 154–66,
    185–6, 197–8, 237–96, 305–45, 575–6, 587–614
fuzzy models 195

gap analysis 197–200, 232–4, 396–405, 531–4, 566
general applications 4–5
generic strategies 98–9, 106–7, 112, 240, 311–38, 586–7
goal-oriented judgements 139–41, 144, 286, 598–600
governance issues 46–7, 166, 171–5, 201, 339–45, 351–4,
    372–92, 596–600, 614
groups 146–7, 151
hardware 3–5, 8–63, 76–7, 151, 368, 523–4, 548–9, 603
Harvard Business School 65, 206, 365–7
Hawley Committee 469–72, 475–6, 500–1
high-potential applications 43, 277–88, 300–38, 343–5,
    393–6, 541–3, 560–3; information management
    477–502, 518–19, 560–3; investment evaluations 424–36,
    439–55, 457–62
historical developments 1–63, 65–70, 146, 200–1, 270–3,
    368, 454, 480–1, 523–4
human resources 53–8, 71–85, 98–9, 127–9, 137, 155–8,
    162–71, 185–6, 190, 201–2, 224–5, 263–73, 343–5,
    446–55; concepts 384–405, 557–9, 590–1, 609–14;
    critical aspects 391–6; information management
    468–502, 590–1, 608–14; intangible resources 384–96,
    468–72, 590–1; knowledge 503–21, 557–9, 590–1,
    609–14; organizational modelling 226–34, 280–5; roles
    610–11, 614

IAM *see* information asset management
ICT *see* information and communication technologies
impact analysis 39–41, 179–80, 197, 238, 281–5, 290–6,
    584–5, 589, 603–4
implementation issues 85–6, 120, 130–9, 155–62, 188–97,
    277, 308–45, 355, 374–84, 390–2, 436–55, 497– 502,
    586–600, 615
inbound logistics 264–73
industry developments 592–3
industry requirements planning (IRP) 250
informal formulations 153, 168–9, 280–5, 303–4, 340–5,
    371–7, 467, 585–7
information 253–5, 472, 476–502, 586, 587–8; *see also* data
    ... ; analysis 38–41, 159–63, 173,
    204–36, 480–1, 506–16; centres 11, 19–20, 121, 355,
    374–84, 523–4; concepts 466–502, 503, 586–91, 605–15;
    culture issues 384–415, 470–521, 560–6, 609–14;
    DIKAR model 204–7, 506–16; dynamic needs 481–4;
    efficiency/effectiveness improvements 484–6; enterprise
    models 490–502, 542–8, 561–3, 574, 612; environmental
    effects 487–521; integration considerations 468–9,
    481–4, 507–16, 587–9, 606–8; knowledge contrasts
    503–4; management issues 466–521, 549–51, 560–3,
    590–1, 596–8, 605–15; orientation concepts 472–3;
    qualities 468–72, 486; responsibilities 494–7, 499–502;
    security needs 74–5, 494–502, 527, 531, 576; sharing
    needs 466–521
information asset management (IAM) 467, 486–521
information and communication btechnologies (ICT) 3
information systems (IS) 2–5, 37–41, 44–58, 119–236,
    276–98, 339–419, 581–617; concepts 2–5, 37–41, 44–58,

144–5, 231–4, 354–9, 587–9, 612–14; culture gaps
　384–415, 566; demand-side issues 20, 36, 44–58, 87–95,
　136, 144–8, 160–4, 183–7, 233–4, 245–8, 269–79,
　308– 23, 349–54, 363–4, 374–84, 405–7, 586–7, 598–600;
　evolutionary developments 1–70, 86–7, 120–2, 146, 152,
　192–3, 322–3, 423–6, 491, 506–16, 583–9, 592–3;
　historical background 8–63, 146, 200–1, 270–3, 368,
　454, 480–1, 523–4; investment evaluations 420–65,
　554–9, 581–3, 602–14; IS/IT strategy 44–58, 64–117,
　118–298, 349–54, 365–7, 374–84, 583–617; IT contrasts
　2–5, 40–1; organizational management 339–419; value
　chains 245–73, 280–96, 405–10, 482–4
information technology assessment and adoption (ITAA)
　301–2
information technology (IT) 1–63, 76–85, 119–78,
　180–236, 311–23, 339–419, 472–3, 522–617; concepts
　2–5, 37–41, 44–58, 76–85, 144–5, 311–23, 472–3,
　522–83; evolutionary developments 1–70, 86–7, 120–2,
　146, 152, 192–3, 322–3, 423–6, 491, 506–16, 583–9,
　592–3; historical background 8–63, 146, 200–1, 270–3,
　368, 454, 480–1, 523–4; infrastructure considerations
　547–63, 574–6, 585–9, 594–8, 606–8; investment
　evaluations 420–65, 554–9, 581–3, 602–14; IS contrasts
　2–5, 40–1; IS/IT strategy 44–58, 64–117, 118–78, 180,
　182–275, 299–338, 349–54, 365–7, 374–84, 583–617;
　knowledge 512–16, 557–9, 560–3, 605–8; organizational
　management 339–419; productivity myths 581–3, 602–3;
　reporting issues 364–84; services 374–84, 522–80;
　strategy groups 374, 382–4; supply-side issues 20, 36–58,
　87–95, 144–8, 160–7, 278–9, 299–338, 349–54, 374–96,
　405–7, 522– 87, 594–608; value chains 245–73, 280–96,
　405–10
infrastructure considerations 45–54, 105, 151–3, 267–8,
　340–419, 547–63, 574–6, 585–98, 606–8
infusion issues 48–50, 300–1, 303–5, 350–4
initiation processes 136–7, 155–9
innovations 7, 36–7, 50–116, 122, 142–3, 161–2, 180,
　207–8, 213–16, 239, 261–2, 283–96, 302–45, 389– 96,
　584–7; components 466–7, 566; evaluations 424–62,
　500–2, 554–9, 581–3, 602–14; research and development
　83, 99, 265, 318–38, 377, 389, 421–42, 452, 541–3
inputs 153–5, 217–19, 279–98, 339, 439–55, 585–7
insourcing 359–64, 386, 390–2, 402, 524, 534, 612
intangible resources, concepts 384–96, 466–521, 590–1
Integral 367
integration considerations 10–19, 47–8, 132–3, 151–3, 164,
　203, 251–3, 325–59, 397–405, 468–9, 481– 4, 507–16,
　574, 587–91, 606–8
interactive digital television (iDTV) 8, 77
internal competitors 245–7
internal context, strategy 34, 48–52, 64–85, 139–44, 153–9,
　187–99, 203–4, 227–34, 240–96, 340–5, 456– 7, 585–98
internal systems 26, 32–58, 187–8, 207–8, 213–16, 244,
　262–73, 277–96, 396–405, 585–7, 593–8, 612
internal value chains 244, 262–73, 280–96, 482–4, 593
Internet 1–8, 24–36, 55–78, 94–111, 132, 142, 238, 242–67,
　270–1, 302–9, 322, 345–6, 360, 368, 429–30, 466–8,
　541–2, 558, 581–3, 592–3, 615; ASPs 573–6; dot.coms
　viii, 6–7, 29–31, 36, 51, 58, 68, 78, 99, 101, 242, 466, 542,
　573, 582, 587–8
interpretation techniques 204–6, 285–6, 307–8
interviews 158–9, 175–6, 185–6, 209

Intranets 308, 331, 425, 469, 513–14
investment centres 353–4
investments 4–5, 16–22, 44–58, 64–73, 98–9, 119–25,
　130–1, 158–69, 185–6, 239–44, 280–338, 581–3, 602–14;
　benefits 4–5, 35–6, 68–9, 293–6, 324–5, 388–91, 420–65,
　484–6, 554–9, 581–3, 602–14; decisions 420 65,
　598–600, 608–14; evaluations 422–65, 500–2, 554–9,
　581–3, 602–14; infrastructure considerations 547–63;
　management issues 420–65; post-implementation
　reviews 436–55; priorities 421–2, 430–6, 558–9; research
　and development 83, 99, 265, 318–38, 377, 389, 421–42,
　452, 541–3; risks 130–1, 172–3, 344, 355, 357–9, 420,
　426, 455–65
IRP *see* industry requirements planning
IS *see* information systems
IS Lite 353–4, 363–4
IT *see* information technology
ITAA *see* information technology assessment and
　adoption

job-shop models 526–34

key influencers 407–9
key performance indicators (KPIs) 185–6, 208
know-how 504–5, 509–16, 611
knowing concepts 504
knowledge 1–2, 34–5, 53–77, 85–6, 153, 161, 187–8,
　204–19, 324–37, 368, 583–608; *see also* information ... ;
　concepts 384–96, 466–7, 472, 475–6, 502–21, 541–2,
　583–4, 589–91, 602–14; DIKAR model 204–7, 506–16;
　information contrasts 503–4; IT role 512–16, 557–9,
　605–8; management considerations 466–7, 502–21, 530,
　541–2, 560–3, 589–91, 605–15; obstacles 514–16
KPIs *see* key performance indicators

lateral thinkers 161
leaders 364–84, 403–9, 407–9, 516, 601–2
leading-edge strategies 312–13, 315–23, 430
learning processes 2, 17–22, 135–6, 207–8, 213–16, 383–4,
　508–16, 572–3, 583, 615
legacy systems 1–2, 16, 18–19, 143, 151–3, 405, 469, 474,
　480–1, 490
legal factors 70, 74–85
lessons learned 2, 17–22, 135–6, 383–4, 572–3, 583, 615
life cycles 13, 16–19, 43, 66–7, 83–95, 100–1, 255–62,
　280–5, 324–6, 332, 585–7
logistics 245–73
London Business School 366
loyalty cards 37, 105

M&As *see* mergers and acquisitions
m-commerce 6
McFarlan Strategic Grid 42–3, 299–300
McKinsey 7Ss model 397
mainframe computers 8–9, 14, 16, 322, 368
management by objectives (MBO) 285–6
management information systems (MIS) 15–25, 38–44, 50,
　198–9, 202–3, 231
management issues 9–26, 38–44, 53–87, 115–16, 120–9,
　137–44, 152–8, 164–78, 198–216, 226–34, 274–98,
　593–8; application portfolios 299–345, 364–84, 476–502,
　518–19, 536–43, 560–3, 585–7; benefits management
　436–55, 458; boards of directors 364–84, 469–72, 500,

management issues; boards of directors (*cont.*) 595–8, 614; CIOs 364–84, 576, 595, 598–9, 614; coordination mechanisms 166, 171–5, 345, 370–84; generic strategies 311–38, 586–7; governance needs 46–7, 166, 171–5, 201, 339–45, 351–4, 372–92, 596–600, 614; human resources 393–405; IAM 467, 486–521; information management 466–521, 549–51, 560–3, 590–1, 596–8, 605–15; infrastructure considerations 547–63, 574–6, 585–9, 594–8, 606–8; investments 420–65; knowledge management 466–7, 502–21, 530, 541–2, 560–3, 589–91, 605–15; multiple SBUs 263, 295–6, 334–7, 344–54, 364, 559–63; objectives 285–6, 343–54, 364–84, 549–50; organizations 339–419, 585–602; post-implementation reviews 436–55; relationships 32, 52, 109, 147, 219, 234, 250–62, 273, 308–9, 326, 384–405; resources 339–419, 430–6, 467–521, 596–602; risks 420, 426, 455–62, 500–1, 564–73, 592–3; services 374–84, 522–80; steering groups 166, 171–5, 345, 370–85, 429, 434–6, 492–502, 572–3; styles 332–4, 364–84; supply perspectives 522–80

market management 405–7
marketing issues 170–2, 256–73
markets 8, 83, 87–116, 142–4, 239–73, 283–5, 476–8, 584–5, 592–3
marketspace concepts 8
mass-service models 526–34
Massachusetts Institute of Technology (MIT) 44–5, 181, 366, 591
matrix structures 590–1
maturity levels 47, 144, 155–7, 371–7
MBO *see* management by objectives
means 598–604, 615
measurable benefits 450–2
media pressures 71, 80
mergers and acquisitions (M&As) 362
methodologies 17–22, 279–85, 322
middleware 469, 492, 548–9
minicomputers, historical background 8–9, 14, 16
MIS *see* management information systems
mission statements 82, 128, 144, 189–92, 205, 211, 280–6, 342–5
MIT *see* Massachusetts Institute of Technology
monopoly strategies 312–13, 315–23, 333–7, 346, 428
motivation issues 162–3, 170, 229, 369
multiple SBUs 263, 295–6, 334–7, 344–54, 364, 559–63

natural value chains 271–2
networks 24–7, 51, 76–7, 266–8, 355–65, 384, 398–402, 444–9, 548–9, 574–6, 590
new entrants 95–111, 261–2
niche markets 110–11, 240
Nolan model 9–12, 14
normative judgements 139–41

objectives 82, 111–59, 164, 185–92, 205–16, 280–96, 342–5, 549–50, 588–602; application priorities 430–6, 549–50; information management 474–86, 549–50; levels 285–6, 549–50; MBO 285–6
office automation 15–17, 19–20, 76, 175–6
online banking 33, 55–7
open standards 5–6
operational systems 4–25, 38–44, 69, 112–22, 146–8, 196–203, 213–14, 239–86, 300–54, 381–2, 393–6, 560–3,

612–14; information management 477–502, 560–3; investment evaluations 424–8, 430–6, 439–55, 457–62; services 538–43
opportunities 1–11, 27, 38–52, 69–107, 122–49, 159, 165, 180–7, 204–11, 241, 261–2, 276–345, 584–617
organizations 1, 45–58, 85–99, 123–5, 133–4, 143–8, 155–9, 187–8, 197, 201–16, 226–34, 269–96, 311–34, 483–4, 585–614; culture issues 384–415, 470–521, 560–6, 605; development considerations 589–91; failures 456–62, 588–9; IAM 498–502; management issues 339–419, 585–602; modelling techniques 226–34, 280–96, 371–7; multiple SBUs 263, 295–6, 334–7, 344–54, 364, 559–63
outbound logistics 264–73
outputs 153–77, 179, 192–207, 217–19, 588–9
outsourcing 329–64, 386, 390–6, 402–5, 523–80, 588, 607–8; concepts 390–6, 402–5, 523–43, 549, 563–76, 588, 607, 612; contracts 566, 571–3, 576; guidelines 566–73; risks 564–73, 607; stages 404

PCs *see* personal computers
PDAs *see* personal digital assistants
performance issues 2, 13–40, 53, 78–81, 131–44, 185–6, 204–26, 243–8, 269–79, 475, 581–3, 596–615; benefits management 436–55; process importance–performance assessments 225–6; services 530–43
personal computers (PCs) 15–22, 76–7, 146, 469, 474, 485, 513–14
personal digital assistants (PDAs) 6, 485, 514, 590
PEST analysis 70–85, 280–5
physical tools 176
planning systems 9–14, 64–178, 276–96, 321–3, 342–55, 435–6, 452–5, 581–617
policies 91–5, 357–9, 402, 549–63
political factors 70–85, 127–9, 280–5, 367–70, 401–2, 434–6, 470–2, 515–16, 558, 559–63
portfolio matrices 87–95, 299–338
post-implementation reviews 436–55
power structures 401–2, 470–2, 515–16, 565
preferred customers 261
preferred suppliers 362–4
pressure groups 71, 77–85
primary activities 263, 289–96, 354–9, 482–4
priorities 13, 47–8, 123–33, 152, 168–9, 191, 205, 240–4, 277, 285–96, 344–5, 357–75, 385, 390–2, 530; *see also* decisions applications 421–2, 430–6, 558–9; concepts 430–6, 558–9, 596–8, 607; investments 421–2, 430–6, 558–9
privatizations 67, 78, 81
'problem children' 89–95, 324–32
processes xiii, 18–27, 44–7, 69–70, 81–5, 102–11, 118–88, 192–7, 201, 213–26, 277–98, 588–614; benefits management 439–55; BPR 23–7, 111, 180–3, 201–6, 216–26, 233–4, 239, 270–3, 329–31, 588–9; concepts 217–22, 292–6, 384–96, 605–14; DIKAR model 204–7, 506–16; identification methods 219–24, 292–6; importance–performance assessments 225–6; maps 222, 282–5; perspectives 217–19; service classifications 526–34; value chains 244–73, 280–96, 482–4
productivity myths, IT 581–3, 602–3
products 7, 36–7, 50–3, 65–70, 83, 87–116, 240–73, 283–5, 323–32, 476–9
professional service models 526–34

profits 87–95, 130–1, 169–70, 207–16, 241–8, 264–79, 353–4

project management 39, 47–8, 170–1, 201–2, 438–40, 458–62, 528, 531

prototypes 37, 242, 310, 326, 425–6, 541–2

provisions, applications 522–80

public pressures 71, 79–85

quality assurance 142, 202, 261, 302, 325–38, 394–5, 475, 530–43, 605, 613

quantifiable benefits 450–2

R&D *see* research and development

range concepts, infrastructure considerations 553–4

rapid application development (RAD) 202, 537–8

reach concepts, infrastructure considerations 553–4

real options 432–6, 558

real-time systems 18

recruitment issues 393–6

redundant processes 194, 272, 484–5

relationships 591–602: customers 32, 52, 109, 147, 219, 234, 250, 255–62, 273, 308–9, 326, 384–96; management issues 32, 52, 109, 147, 219, 234, 250–62, 273, 308–9, 326, 384–405; users 9–13; vendors 404–5

reorganization issues 13–14, 18–19

reorientation issues 13–14

reputations 384–5, 469

research and development (R&D) 83, 99, 265, 318–38, 377, 389, 421–42, 452, 541–3

resource life-cycle (RLC) 255–62, 280–5, 287–9

resource management 339–419, 430–6, 467–521, 596–614

resource-based views, strategy 66, 111–16, 127, 137, 140–8, 164–5, 201, 240–4, 271–2, 312–13, 325–9, 384–419, 584–614

responsibilities 357–9, 494–7, 499–502, 516

restraining policies 358–9

results 204–7, 209–16, 506–16

risks: assessments 455–62, 500–1, 544–5, 564–73; concepts 455–62; investments 130–1, 172–3, 344, 355, 357–9, 420, 426, 455–65; management issues 420, 426, 455–62, 500–1, 564–73, 592–3; outsourcing 564–73, 607

rituals 400–2

RLC *see* resource life-cycle

roles 610–14

routines 400–2, 609

SAM *see* strategic alignment model

SAP 4, 52, 344, 433

SBUs *see* strategic business units

scarce resource strategies 312–13, 333–4, 336, 426–7

SCM *see* supply chain management

scope: information management 488–90, 497–8; planning activities 144–9, 151–5, 157–8, 168

security needs 74–5, 494–502, 527, 531, 576

segmentation benefits 37, 106, 234, 261–2

service level agreements (SLAs) 524–34, 569–76

service-factory models 526–34

services: application portfolios 536–43; centres 350–5, 374–84, 523–4; concepts 386–96, 522–80, 592–3, 612–14; core competencies 386–96, 522–80; costs 360–4, 530–6, 592–3, 603; ERP 542–7, 561–3, 574, 612; generic models 526–34; information management 484–502; management issues 374–84, 522–80; process-based

classifications 526–30; quality considerations 530–43; strategy 523–80; types 354–9, 524–34; value chains 264–73, 526–34

shared values 397–415; *see also* culture . . .

shareholders 6, 68, 71, 77–85, 90, 130–1, 207–8, 602–3

short-term views 1, 126, 277–91, 430–1, 565–6, 586–7

SIS *see* strategic information systems

situation analysis 66, 82–4, 240–1

skills 2, 16, 46–58, 83, 98–9, 127–9, 144, 150–9, 162–6, 175, 187–8, 197, 201–2, 225–9, 324–5, 600–14; concepts 384–96, 602–3, 607–14; outsourcing 360–4, 386, 393–6, 523, 565–73, 607

SLAs *see* service level agreements

social factors 3, 70–85, 190, 197, 226–34, 280–5, 371–7, 512–16, 610–11

soft issues 127, 155, 162–3, 164–6, 169–70, 589, 608

software 3–5, 15–19, 76–7, 109, 149–51, 175–6, 250, 344, 355, 523–49, 603; ASPs 534, 573–6; historical background 8–63, 368, 523–4

specialization centres 353–4, 397

specific applications 4–5

spider diagrams, core competencies 391–2

sponsors 158, 164–5, 171–2

spreadsheets 15, 19

SSADM 438, 539, 543

SSM 438

stakeholders 6, 68, 71, 77–85, 90, 113, 223–9, 245–73, 446–62, 602–3

standardization considerations 102–3, 202, 549–63

'stars' 89–95, 324–31

steering groups 166, 171–5, 345, 370–85, 429, 434–6, 492–502, 572–3

stories 400–2

strategic alignment model (SAM) 44–7, 179, 239–44, 587–9, 613–14

strategic applications 4–5, 42–4, 277–88, 300–38, 343–5, 381–2, 393–6, 560–3; information management 476–502, 518–19, 560–3; investment evaluations 424–36, 439–55, 457–62; services 536–43

strategic business units (SBUs) 81–2, 145–70, 196–7, 209–16, 229, 239–73, 283–5, 295–6, 334–59, 375–84, 491–502, 559–63

strategic frameworks 66, 70–85, 134, 151–78, 276–98, 386–96, 585–7

strategic information systems (SIS) 16, 22–58, 240–1, 437–8

strategic management 65–87, 115–16, 277–98, 339–419, 581–617

strategic planning 9–14, 64–178, 276–96, 321–3, 342–55, 435–6, 452–5, 581–617

strategic thinking 66, 69–70, 86, 111–12

strategy 7, 44–58, 65–117, 190–1, 276–98, 311–38, 365–7, 581–617; barriers 1, 125–9; competitive strategies 95–111; concepts 7, 44–58, 65–117, 190–1, 276–7, 311–38, 365–7, 386–96, 581–617; context needs 34, 48–52, 64–85, 139–44, 153–9, 187–99, 203–4, 227–34, 240–96, 340–5, 456–7, 585–98; cycle initiation 136–7, 155–9; development methods 81–6, 118–78, 188–92, 208–16, 226–34, 291–6, 320–3, 332, 340–5, 355, 374–84, 583–7, 594–8; environmental effects 48–52, 65–85, 111–16, 129–35, 141–4, 153–60, 179–279, 301–62, 487–521, 583–91; evolution 13–14, 65–70, 86–7,

strategy; evolution (*cont.*) 120–2, 146, 152, 192–3, 322–3,
    583–4, 587–9; evolving nature 65–70; formulation
    methods 81–5, 119–22, 134–55, 168–73, 182–3, 226,
    277–98, 307–23, 365–7, 384–5, 585–98; generic strategies
    98–9, 106–7, 112, 240, 311–38, 586–7; implementation
    issues 85–6, 120, 130–9, 155–62, 188–97, 277, 308–45,
    355, 374–84, 390–2, 436–55, 497–502, 586–600, 615;
    information management 466–521, 560–3, 590–1,
    605–15; infrastructure considerations 547–63, 574–6,
    585–9, 594–8, 606–8; IS/IT strategy 44–58, 64–117,
    118–338, 349–54, 365–7, 374–84, 583–617; objectives 82,
    111–59, 164, 185–92, 205–16, 280–96, 342–5, 549–50,
    588–602; outsourcing 390–6, 402–5, 523–43, 549,
    563–76, 588, 612; planning contrasts 69–70; problems 1,
    125–9, 158, 165, 200; resource-based views 66, 111–16,
    127, 137, 140–8, 164–5, 201, 240–4, 271–2, 312–13,
    325–9, 384– 419, 584–614; services 523–80, 612;
    techniques 86–117, 149, 151–62, 175–6, 180–239,
    277–98, 583–4; tools 86–117, 149, 151–62, 173–6,
    180–239, 277–98, 583–4
strengths 71–85, 165, 185–6, 204–6, 211, 280–96, 305–9
structure 9, 46–54, 81–5, 105, 144, 151–61, 180–8, 192–7,
    217–19, 239–40, 263, 277–96, 340–419, 586, 601–14;
    centralization issues 48–50, 300–23, 333–7, 342–59, 372,
    399–402, 428–9, 472, 483–502, 560–3; deliverables
    163–6; federal structures 349–54, 385, 590–1;
    information management 472, 483–90, 515–16, 560–3,
    590–1, 606–8; IS 8–11, 162–6; matrix structures 590–1;
    organizational modelling 226–34, 280–5, 371–7; types
    349–54, 377–85, 401, 472, 483–4, 590–1, 611
subprocesses 224–5, 404
substitute factors 95–111, 261, 423–30
success factors 26, 35–46, 128–41, 159, 162–5, 184–94,
    204–16, 237, 241–4, 279–302, 375–87, 426–36, 477–8,
    571–3, 584–9, 612–15
Sullivan's matrix 48–50, 300–1, 303–5, 350
suppliers 27–58, 71–85, 95–111, 171, 240–73, 288–96,
    362–4, 387–96, 592–3
supply chain management (SCM) 542–7, 588
supply-side issues 20, 36–58, 87–95, 144–8, 160–7, 278–9,
    299–338, 349–54, 374–96, 405–7, 522–87,
    594–608
support applications 4–5, 42–4, 120–2, 175–6, 200–3, 239,
    263–5, 277–85, 291–6, 300–45, 355, 381–2, 393–6;
    information management 477–502, 518–19, 560–3;
    investment evaluations 424–7, 430–6, 439–55, 457–62;
    services 540–3
sustainability needs, competitive advantages 52–8, 67,
    111–16, 134, 242, 325–38, 384–96, 584, 605
SWOT analysis 83–4, 165, 185–6, 204–6, 211, 280–96,
    305–9
symbols 400–2
synergies 263, 295–6, 334–7, 344–9, 351–4
systematic approaches, redesign methods 220–2
systems analysis and design 39–41, 139, 193–202, 306–7,
    355, 438–9, 480–1, 506–16, 529–35

t-commerce 6
tacit knowledge 466–7, 474, 508–16
tactical decisions 1–2, 135–6, 141–2, 286

tangible resources, concepts 384–5
teams 153–9, 170–5, 225, 314–15, 332, 368, 472, 509–16,
    590–1
technical failures 455–62, 588–9
technical management groups 374–84
technical services 259–60, 355–9, 395–6
technological factors 70–85, 120–5, 142–57, 167, 180–6,
    203–7, 226–34, 267, 280–5, 311–23, 344–54, 366–7,
    581–617; *see also* information technology; Internet;
    infrastructure considerations 547–63, 574–6, 594–8,
    606–8; organizational modelling 226–34, 280–5, 371–7;
    outsourcing 361–2, 386, 523–80, 588
terms of reference (TOR) 136–9, 158, 172, 378–81, 541–2
threats 66–85, 98–107, 141–4, 165, 180–7, 204–6, 211, 241,
    280–96, 305–9, 375
three-era model 22–5
top-down approaches 13–14, 121–5, 156, 161–2, 191, 195,
    274, 288–96, 482–4, 500–2, 585, 598–600
TOR *see* terms of reference
total quality management (TQM) 142
training requirements 158–9, 201–2, 355, 393–6, 528–9,
    531, 602–3
transformation programmes 405–15
trends 1, 5–8, 184, 204, 375

UK Academy of Information Systems (UKAIS) 3
unions 71, 78–85, 228
United Nations (UN), EDIFACT 5
users 9–19, 32–58, 123–9, 136, 151, 173–5, 198–203,
    346–59, 370–1, 382–3, 396–405, 498, 524–80, 602–8;
    failures 455–62; services 524–80

value: centres 350–4; chains 180–8, 194–5, 200, 205, 209,
    229, 244–73, 280–96, 405–10, 482–4, 526–34, 585–614;
    configuration models 265–8; networks 266–8; shops
    266–8
value-added issues 22–6, 35, 53–8, 100–1, 110, 131–41,
    151–9, 165, 180–8, 203–8, 220–9, 241–73, 292–302,
    325–38, 350–4, 386–410, 585–7, 602–14; CIOs 367–70,
    576, 595, 614; core competencies 386–96, 522–80,
    592–615; information management 475–86, 605–8;
    investment evaluations 424–55, 581–3, 602–14
value-added network suppliers (VANS) 5–6
vendors 169, 171, 353–4, 360–4, 386, 396, 404–5, 490–1,
    563–76, 607
videoconferences 513–14
virtual teams 51, 368, 514
vision 24, 36–44, 82, 144, 162–9, 189–92, 208, 302, 310,
    351–4, 367–70, 386–7, 472, 594–600

WAP *see* wireless application protocol
ways 598–604, 615
weaknesses 71–85, 165, 185–6, 191–2, 204–6, 211, 280–96,
    305–9
'wildcats' 89–95, 324–32
wireless application protocol (WAP) 6
workshops 159, 173, 391–2, 444
World Trade Organization 75–6

XML 250